Eccentric America

THE BRADT TRAVEL GUIDE

Lowell Thomas Award, Best Guidebook 2002
Society of American Travel Writers

Best Travel Book of 2001
North American Travel Journalists Association

PUBLISHER'S FOREWORD

The first Bradt travel guide was written in 1974 by George and Hilary Bradt on a river barge floating down a tributary of the Amazon. In the 1980s and '90s the focus shifted away from hiking to broader-based guides to new destinations – usually the first to be published on these places. In the 21st century Bradt continues to publish these ground-breaking guides, along with others to established holiday destinations, incorporating in-depth information on culture and natural history alongside the nuts and bolts of where to stay and what to see.

* * *

I first met Jan Friedman at the Book Passage Travel Writers' Conference in California in 1998. She was there extending her knowledge of travel writing and I was part of the faculty teaching prospective guidebook writers. I knew immediately that I wanted Jan to write a Bradt guide, but it took a couple of years to decide what. *Eccentric America* was an inspired choice. The first edition has been our best-selling guide in the US since the moment it was published (ironically it was overtaken only once – by *Iraq*). Jan's enthusiasm and knowledge of eccentricities in her home country are boundless – and infectious. It's a pleasure to be her publisher!

Hilary Bradt

19 High Street, Chalfont St Peter, Bucks SL9 9QE, England
Tel: 01753 893444 Fax: 01753 892333
Email: info@bradtguides.com
Web: www.bradtguides.com

Eccentric America

THE BRADT GUIDE TO
ALL THAT'S WEIRD AND WACKY IN THE USA

Jan Friedman

Bradt Travel Guides Ltd, UK
The Globe Pequot Press Inc, USA

Second edition published in 2004

First published in 2001 by Bradt Travel Guides Ltd,
19 High Street, Chalfont St Peter, Bucks SL9 9QE, England
www.bradt-travelguides.com
Published in the USA by The Globe Pequot Press Inc, 246 Goose Lane,
PO Box 480, Guilford, Connecticut 06437-0480

Reprinted with amendments 2002
Reprinted with amendments 2003

British Library Cataloguing in Publication Data
A catalogue record for this book is available from the British Library
ISBN 1 84162 090 4

Photographs
Front cover: Pylon Men, Peter Maxfield, www.pmaxfield.com
Back cover: Hamburger Harley by Harry Sperl, photo © Harrod Blank,
www.harrodblank.com
Text: Harrod Blank (HB), Les Blank (LBl), Lisa Browning (LB), Chad Copess
Photo/South Dakota Tourism (CC), Noreen Crimmins (NC), Duane Flatmo,
www.duaneflatmo.com (DF), Randall Frost (RF), Larry Harris (LH), High Poiny CVB
(HP), Tom Joynt (TJ), Tim Klein (TK), Holly Kreuter, www.desertdrama.com (HK),
Ohio Division of Travel & Tourism (OH), Ann Parker (AP)

Illustrations Dave Colton, www.cartoonist.net
Maps Alan Whitaker
Typeset from the author's disc by Wakewing, High Wycombe
Printed and bound in the USA by Versa

Author

Jan Friedman has spent most of her life in the San Francisco Bay Area where, she says, ' they take their eccentricity very seriously'. A travel writer, photographer and former tour guide, she explored 56 countries before discovering that her very own could offer as much adventure as the most exotic foreign locale. Her previous edition of *Eccentric America* won two book awards.

DEDICATION

This book is dedicated to delightful deviates everywhere who make the world a saner and more interesting place.

Contents

Acknowledgements		**x**
Preface		**XI**
Introduction		**XIII**
Guide to the Guide		**XV**

Chapter 1   **Northwestern Region**   **1**
Washington 1, Idaho 10, Oregon 13, Montana 17, Wyoming 19

Chapter 2   **Western Region**   **21**
San Francisco 21, Northern California 31, Southern California 38, Nevada 53, Las Vegas: the ultimate quirkyville 53, Nevada: everywhere *but* Vegas 62, Arizona 66, Utah 75

Chapter 3   **North Central Region**   **79**
Wisconsin 79, Minnesota 92, Iowa 99, Illinois 102, Michigan 108, Indiana 114, Ohio 119, North Dakota 123, South Dakota 124, Nebraska 127

Chapter 4   **South Central Region**   **129**
Texas 129, New Mexico 144, Colorado 150, Kansas 158, Oklahoma 162, Missouri 166, Arkansas 171, Louisiana 175

Chapter 5   **Northeastern Region**   **179**
New York State 179, New York City 185, Vermont 194, New Hampshire 197, Maine 198, Massachusetts 202, Rhode Island 206, Connecticut 207, New Jersey 210, Pennsylvania 213, Maryland 221, Delaware 224

Chapter 6   **Southeastern Region**   **227**
Washington, DC 227, Virginia 230, West Virginia 233, Kentucky 235, Tennessee 238, North Carolina 245, Mississippi 250, Alabama 254, Georgia 256, South Carolina 259, Florida 260, Florida: the rest of the state 265

Chapter 7   **Cross-Country Quirks**   **277**
A car-crazed culture 277, It's a guy thing 277, Art cars 278, Peculiar pursuits 280, Pet pursuits 284, Curious collections 285, Keep an eye out... 285, Corporate kudos 285

Appendix 1   **Further Reading**   **287**
State Index   **293**
Alphabetical Index   **303**

LIST OF MAPS

Eccentric America	VIII–IX	Missouri	167
The Heights of		Montana	XX
Eccentricity	XVIII–XIX	Nebraska	122
United States of		Nevada	22–3
America	inside cover	New Hampshire	195
		New Jersey	211
Alabama	251	New Mexico	145
Arizona	67	New York State	182
Arkansas	167	North Carolina	226
California	22–3	North Dakota	122
Colorado	145	Ohio	110
Connecticut	195	Oklahoma	159
Delaware	211	Oregon	XX
Florida	262	Pennsylvania	211
Georgia	251	Rhode Island	195
Idaho	XX	South Carolina	251
Illinois	78	South Dakota	122
Indiana	110	Tennessee	226
Iowa	78	Texas	132
Kansas	159	Utah	67
Kentucky	226	Vermont	195
Louisiana	167	Virginia	226
Maine	195	Washington	XX
Maryland	211	Washington, DC	226
Massachusetts	195	West Virginia	226
Michigan	110	Wisconsin	78
Minnesota	78	Wyoming	XX
Mississippi	251		

CANADA

Seattle
WASHINGTON
(41)

Portland

OREGON
(16)

Helena
MONTANA
(9)

NORTH DAKOTA
(4)

Bismarck

IDAHO
(8)
Boise

WYOMING
(6)

SOUTH DAKOTA
(14)
Pierre

Northern
California
(79)

NEVADA
(46)

Salt Lake
City
UTAH
(7)

Cheyenne

NEBRASKA
(8)
Omaha

San Francisco

CALIFORNIA

Las Vegas

Denver
(23)
COLORADO

KANSAS
(11)
Topeka

(55)
Southern
California

Los Angeles

San Diego

(27)
ARIZONA

Tucson

Albuquerque

NEW MEXICO
(24)

OKLAHOMA
Oklahoma
City
(21)

Lubbock

El Paso

Fort Worth   Dallas

TEXAS
(42)

MEXICO

Houston

San Antonio

Corpus
Christi

P A C I F I C   O C E A N

**KEY TO SYMBOLS USED
ON STATE MAPS**
🛡 Festivals & events
❀ Eccentric environments
⚱ Museums & collections
🕴 Activity
🕴 Monument
? Curiosity
🎭 Theme experience
🏘 Quirkyville (cities & towns)
🏛 Grandiose schemes
✗ Quirky cuisine
! Just plain weird
$ Shopping
🚐 Tours
♨ Rooms with a skew
☆ Locations with more than
   one of the above

KEY TO STATE MAPS

State name	**TEXAS**
State capitals	● AUSTIN
	○ SACRAMENTO
Large cities	● Dallas
Other cities	○ Galveston
Major roads	═══════
Other main roads	───────
International boundary	▪-▪-▪-▪-▪
State boundary	▪▪▪▪▪▪▪

ECCENTRIC AMERICA

0 ━━━━ **200km**
0 ━━━━ **200 miles**

N

Bradt

CANADA

ATLANTIC

OCEAN

GULF OF MEXICO

MINNESOTA `29`
Duluth
Minneapolis/ St Paul
WISCONSIN `33`
Sault Ste Marie
Milwaukee
Madison
IOWA `13`
Des Moines
Chicago
MICHIGAN `16`
Lansing
Detroit
Toledo
ILLINOIS `30`
INDIANA `18`
Indianapolis
OHIO `9`
Columbus
Buffalo
Kansas City
MISSOURI `10`
St Louis
Lexington
KENTUCKY `15`
WEST VIRGINIA `8`
ARKANSAS `12`
Little Rock
Memphis
TENNESSEE `24`
Nashville
Chatanooga
NORTH CAROLINA `20`
Raleigh
S CAROLINA `5`
Columbia
MISSISSIPPI `16`
Jackson
ALABAMA `10`
Montgomery
GEORGIA `9`
Atlanta
`6`
Savannah
LOUISIANA
New Orleans
Mobile
Jacksonville
FLORIDA `55`
St Petersburg
Miami

VERMONT `7`
MAINE `15`
Montpelier
Portland
NEW HAMPSHIRE `4`
`55`
Albany
NEW YORK
MASSACHUSETTS `11`
RHODE ISLAND `6`
Hartford
New York
CONNECTICUT `11`
PENNSYLVANIA `26`
Philadelphia
NEW JERSEY `8`
DELAWARE `4`
MARYLAND `11`
WASHINGTON DISTRICT OF COLUMBIA (DC) `5`
VIRGINIA `11`
Richmond

KEY TO THIS MAP

State name — **TEXAS**
Number of mapped sites — `14`
Capital city — ■
Other city — ○
International boundary — ▬ ▪ ▬ ▪
State boundary — ▬ ▬ ▬ ▬

States covered in chapter 1
States covered in chapter 2
States covered in chapter 3
States covered in chapter 4
States covered in chapter 5
States covered in chapter 6

Acknowledgements

A book like this nature could never happen without the hundreds of people who, after they stopped laughing at the nature of my request, threw themselves into the task of tracking down American weirdness. First and foremost there's Katherine Meusey, my researcher, who put in months of work chasing down new eccentricities for this edition and fact-checking all the entries. It certainly helps that she's a great fan of weirdness and can sniff out a potential entry anywhere in the country. Richard Baguley, Katherine's husband, produced an amazing spreadsheet so I can keep everyone in the eccentric loop.

Initially, more than 800 tourism bureaux were involved in this project, suggesting sites, confirming details, obtaining photos, marking maps and providing travel assistance during research trips. The Travel Industry Association of America (TIA) and Travel Publicity Leads also helped by emailing their subscribers with my media request and I couldn't have gotten along without The Entertainment Book and Enterprise Rental Car's discounts. Once word got out, however, it was an ever-evolving network of informants, many alerted to my quest by the *Eccentric America* website, that provided the leads that resulted in so many of this edition's new entries. I'm so grateful for their interest and participation.

Naturally, there are many others I'd like to thank: Amy Rennert, my agent; Hilary Bradt, Tricia Hayne, Adrian Phillips, Debbie Everson and the rest of the staff at Bradt Travel Guides in the UK; Jane Reilly and the staff at Globe Pequot in Connecticut; Peter Handel, publicist extraordinaire; Gerald Cohen and Alan Whitaker for their help with the *Heights of Eccentricity* map; Elaine Petrocelli and all the mentors at the Book Passage Travel Writers Conference who so willingly share their skills and encouraging words with aspiring writers; Bill Bryson, Dave Barry, Jill Conner Browne, Carl Hiaasen, P J O'Rourke, Doug Lansky, Tim Cahill and David Sedaris, famous writers who, unbeknownst to them, inspire me to ever quirkier heights; and, finally, to my dear friends and family who by now are used to my breathless request 'Ya gotta read this, you won't believe it!'

Preface

I used to think I had to leave the United States in order to have an adventure. Off I would go, ticking off country after country in search of ever-more-exciting experiences. Then, after visiting 56 of them, I started having a bit more adventure than I'd bargained for. A hostage-like experience in South America, brought about by a sudden government collapse, caused my daughter to inquire if I'd written a will, while a somewhat harrowing, month-long drive across South Africa had my parents ruing the day I'd ever learned to read a map. Even though I prefer traveling alone, I began to question whether I had an obsession that might require some analysis (too expensive) or, at the least, some redirecting (too boring). Just about that time I was offered the opportunity to write *Eccentric America*.

To this day I don't know if I was chosen for the job because the publisher thought I was a 'nutter', as they say in England, or because I live in San Francisco and she figured 'it takes one to know one'. Whatever the reason, I set off on what I imagined would be a fairly dull assignment in light of the kind of traveling I was accustomed to. I'd been practically everywhere in the United States and, while I enjoyed regional foods and geographic variety, I pretty much thought our melting pot had morphed into a lightly seasoned stew. Plus there's precious little adventure to be had in homogenized motel chains and fast-food stops; corporations bought up our highways long ago. I thought I'd be looking at roadside with a twist. Little did I realize how many real people, with the oddest of obsessions and the most peculiar of pursuits, were out there just waiting to be seen and heard.

Once I started looking – really looking – beyond the surface of my mistaken stereotypes, I found not a stew, but a cornucopia of distinct dishes cooked up by people likely to change the recipe on a whim. I found a country full of individualistic people, states and regions with quirky characters lurking all over the fringes of their tourism landscapes. I saw what it really means to be adventuresome – to be free to express one's individuality and to have the courage to do so. The people who ended up in this book exemplify the American dream, perhaps not in terms of money or power or prestige, but certainly in terms of freedom.

As a whole, as a society, we Americans are fiercely proud of our independent heritage and of our trailblazing qualities. We're a culture based on unprecedented opportunity to achieve individual potential and the freedom to behave in a manner that both delights and shocks foreign visitors. But the truth is, as individuals most of us are conformists. Within our little bubbles of society, however eccentric they may be, we go along with the crowd, with the 'norm'. We may think of ourselves as rugged individualists by our activities or political views, but, as singular individuals, most of us are pretty predictable. What we once thought unconventional has become commonplace, just average.

I met so many truly unique people in the course of writing this book, people willing and eager to share their unconventional passions and visions; people able to burst out of society's bubble. I've gained a whole new appreciation for those who see our world through slightly skewed glasses. I feel so vanilla compared to these chocolates, rocky roads, and almond-caramel-raspberry-fudge swirls. I've been enriched, as I hope you will be, by their stories, activities and achievements, as well as by their unwavering determination to stay their own personal courses.

When I started my research, I worried that people might be offended at the title. It turned out that only a handful of the many thousands of people I spoke with took offence at the suggestion they – or their attraction – might be eccentric. In fact, dozens of folks went out of their way to convince me of their eccentricity so they might be included in the book. It turns out that eccentricity is perceived as an honor, a validation of our uniqueness that usually goes unacknowledged.

The scope of this book is staggering even to me and yet I uncover more eccentrics every day. (There are about 900 entries in this edition.) I'm so captivated by their courage and achievements that I can't stop looking, which probably means that I'm becoming eccentric myself in this obsessive quest for weirdness. I hope this is a good thing, because I think we need to be reminded of the value of nonconformity. I like to think that sharing their stories will make a difference, not only in their lives, but also in yours. It surely has in mine.

Jan Friedman
San Francisco, California
April 2004

Introduction

Defining eccentricity is like defining beauty – it all depends on who's doing the judging. According to Webster, an eccentric can be defined as someone whose behavior varies wildly from the norm, which, if the circumstances were right, could even mean you! The beauty of this definition is that it allows society to change its mind – as it often does – as to whom it labels deviant, delightful or otherwise. California and Florida, for example, consider most any behavior normal, but put the average San Franciscan in Iowa and they'll be wearing an 'E' on their forehead soon enough.

Behaving eccentrically, however, is not the same as being crazy, even if appearances would sometimes seem to indicate otherwise. Just because someone opens an umbrella-cover museum, or applies 18,000 coats of paint to a baseball, or lives in an underground art warren, it doesn't mean they're suffering from mental illness. In fact, they're doing quite the opposite, namely following their bliss. Their unique peculiarities allow them the freedom to behave in ways that most of us find odd or scary. They're lucky – they don't care what others think. They only need to live up to their own expectations to be happy.

But who gets to decide who's eccentric and who gets dismissed as a crazy old coot? That's not an easy question to answer. To some extent it has to do with money. If a poor person acts strangely, they could be labeled crazy, but if someone is rich and/or functional enough to open a tourist attraction, their behavior is more likely to be elevated to the status of eccentric. As long as eccentrics don't actually do any harm, society will usually let them go on about their business, however bizarre that business may be. Outspoken and out of step, eccentrics are tolerated with good humor, while those considered crazy are whisked out of sight.

According to a clinical study of eccentrics by Dr David Weeks, whose book, *Eccentrics: A Study of Sanity and Strangeness*, covered both British and American subjects, eccentrics are happier than the population as a whole. By choosing to behave unconventionally, and by not needing reinforcement from others, they enjoy a freedom that eludes most of us. Happily indulging their obsessions, they'll persist at whatever makes them happy regardless of what society may think. For the most part, they don't suffer from the kinds of stress and anxiety that plague so many of us. They're also healthier, making far fewer visits to doctors than the norm. The term itself – mental illness – implies the need of a cure and it's hard to make a case for treating health and happiness.

As non-conformists, eccentrics usually revel in being different. (This is not to say that their path to self-acceptance came easily. As children they were out of step with their peers and had to come to terms with being different.) They're highly creative, motivated by curiosity, and often idealistic, just wanting to make the world a better place through their contributions. And who's to say we're not all enriched, or inspired, by a man who can spend 20 years building a three-story mountain in God's honor out of hay, adobe, window putty and old paint?

True eccentrics have absolute faith that their way is the right one and if you can't see the light, well … it's your loss. This is especially true of eccentrics who passionately pursue a strange idea or concept. Elizabeth Tashjian, the Nut Lady of Connecticut, worshipped nuts and her home was a sanctuary to them, a place where she could keep them safe from nutcrackers. Nancy Townsend, also known as Mother Goose, invented duck diapers so people can keep birds as house pets. Opinionated and outspoken, eccentrics like these think that if you'd just come around to their way of thinking, you'll be as happy as they are. They'll bend your ear for hours if you'll let them, going on and on about the virtues of their passion, be it collecting frogs or planning to shoot themselves into space in a homemade copper egg. By filtering out what is inconsequential to them, they're free to focus, usually obsessively, on their peculiar pursuit. For them, happiness is the light at the end of a funnel.

Many eccentrics function perfectly well in society even if they do measure success with a crooked yardstick. Brother Joseph, a cleric in Alabama, spent decades building a concrete Holy Land out of cold-cream jars, all the while performing his usual duties. John Davis of Kansas built himself a gigantic grave memorial featuring almost a dozen life-size statues depicting all the phases of his life. Passionate collectors, such as Ken Bannister, the Banana Man, and Mildred O'Neil, the Shoe Lady, lead mostly balanced lives despite their obsessions with acquiring particular objects. There's a loopy logic to their thinking; a strange sanity that lets them express themselves more freely than the rest of us without being carted off to the loony bin.

Able to live in unconventional settings, or in unconventional ways, eccentrics don't need other people to affirm their identities. Richard Zimmerman of Idaho, dubbed 'Dugout Dick', likes caves so much that he's spent a good chunk of his life digging them and living in them. Marta Beckett opened an opera house in Death Valley, painting an audience on the walls so she didn't have to dance by herself. Michael Kahn and Leda Livant live in an undulating warren of art forms in the Arizona desert. It's not that these people are loners. They just use solitude to fuel their creative juices and they're usually delighted to share the results with you.

In order for eccentricity to flourish, people need the right set of circumstances, most importantly freedom of speech and a culture that encourages individual expression without fear of negative consequence. A healthy society thrives on a variety of ideas, including the far-fetched and extreme, whereas one that demands complete conformity is doomed to eventual failure. Thus, it should come as no surprise that America, Great Britain and other Western societies are at the top of the pecking order, eccentrically speaking. It also explains why you're never going to see an eccentric guide to Saudi Arabia or China. In the right place, at the right time, eccentrics become assets to a community, proof of their success as free and capitalistic societies.

Unfortunately, modern society sometimes tries to treat behavior that 'varies widely from the norm' with drugs, doing a great disservice to those who live on its fringes. Eccentrics often display brilliant creativity and genius along with their quirks. Imagine the loss to society if Newton or Einstein had been given Prozac to modify their thinking. Most eccentrics just want to live out their own realities and to leave the world a better place. They want to infect you with their enthusiasm so you, too, can be as happy as they are. *Eccentric America* takes you into their world, giving you the opportunity to come away enriched by the experience.

Guide to the Guide

Discovering *Eccentric America* means getting in your car and tracking down some of America's most delightful deviates. But it won't always be easy. Eccentrics and their creations can be unpredictable – or difficult to find. Hours can change abruptly. The weather can affect their attractions – or their moods. Or, they just up and vanish, their quirky legacies left to languish from inattention. That said, it's worth putting up with some uncertainty to experience the unique and entertaining qualities these oddballs have to offer.

You'll probably need supplemental road maps for the areas you're visiting. Since the guide covers such a vast country, the maps in this book won't always give you the detail you need. When you get near your destination, especially to those way off the beaten path, ask a local to direct you the rest of the way. Most of these attractions are well known to those who live in the area although, occasionally, you may need to ask several people along the way.

Unless an attraction is noted as 'Free', you can expect an admission charge that varies by age and season.

If the contact information given in this book becomes out of date, it doesn't mean that the activity or attraction no longer exists. It may have moved, changed contact numbers or websites, been renamed, or been taken over by someone new. Try searching online for current information or for the location's chamber of commerce or tourist bureau. Locals will usually be able to track down what you need. Also, log on to **www.eccentricamerica.com**; the website will post updated travel information as it comes in. It may take a bit of sleuthing on your part to search out these wayward entries but you'll usually be rewarded for your efforts. Along the way you might even meet some budding eccentrics.

FESTIVALS AND EVENTS

Most of America's festivals, celebrations and events are unique in that they're based on pop culture, on relatively recent events, or on themes created simply as a reason to have fun. With the exception of Native American traditions, American history doesn't go back more than a few hundred years and our cultural newness explains how we come to celebrate weird festivals like Mike the Headless Chicken Days or the Redneck Games. But with almost 200 events nationwide, there's hardly a dull moment in America, eccentrically speaking. In this category you'll discover where (and, perhaps, why!) folks wrestle in mashed potatoes, hurl cow patties and pumpkins, carve SPAM™, race furniture downhill on skis, and swing at each other in a pillow fight. You'll also find wacky events like Frozen Dead Guy Day, the Roadkill Cookoff and a Rotten Sneaker Contest.

ECCENTRIC ENVIRONMENTS

'Outsider artists', sometimes referred to as self-taught or visionary artists, are responsible for the 34 eccentric environments described in this book. An outsider is someone with no formal art training who becomes obsessed with creating one specific kind of art. In this category are castles, Holy Lands, futuristic visions, dinosaur parks, bizarre sculptures, and houses made from unconventional materials like paper, bottles or printing plates. Often these creations are the result of a syndrome called concretia dementia, an excessive compulsion to build using whatever materials are readily available, usually concrete, bottles, cans, scrap metal and other industrial and household junk. (This dementia most often strikes people in their later years.) The majority of eccentric environments you can visit were built in the early and mid-1900s, before the advent of drugs to control compulsive behavior. Today, if one of your relatives started building a concrete and scrap-iron tower in your backyard, you'd have them on Prozac – and in a Lazy-Boy – in no time, squelching their propensity to turn your home into a tourist attraction.

MUSEUMS AND COLLECTIONS

Americans are among the world's most skilled and prolific collectors, sometimes creating objects just for the sheer joy of collecting them. In fact, if more than three of something exists, someone's probably organizing it on eBay. Throughout the country you'll find quirky museums and halls of fame proudly displaying the odd and curious results of years spent amassing these strange and bewildering collections that have usually been the focus of their founder's lives. Collections like these generally begin by accident or as an occupational sideline, with their owners becoming more and more avid over time in the pursuit of their desired objects. The range of experiences awaiting you is quite astounding and includes outhouses, mustards, presidents, SPAM™, vacuum cleaners, drain tiles, bananas, celebrity lingerie, and bad art.

ATTRACTIONS

Kitschy, kitschy koo. Here you'll find the offbeat and the wacky, attractions like weird buildings, goofy gardens, wax museums, dinosaur parks, and the kind of kitsch roadside for which America is famous. An occasional activity, like indoor skydiving, is also included here. Most of these attractions are commercial, for-profit enterprises, which doesn't mean they're not eccentric. While some are professionally designed and managed, others are homemade and quite funky. Varying widely in quality and character, they're unique to America.

QUIRKYVILLE

Quirkyvilles are towns with a twist, places with some strange claim to fame that sets them apart from the mundane. Whether it's a mayor who insists on putting concrete hippos on street corners, one with a leash law for cats, or a town that speaks its own language, these hotbeds of quirk are worth a detour, if only to find out what on earth their citizens are thinking.

TOURS

New York City, Los Angeles, San Francisco, Las Vegas and New Orleans all have their own sections and the distinctive character of these big cities can often be best appreciated by taking tours, especially of – and by – the offbeat. Listed are dozens of tours led by knowledgeable guides who are themselves interesting characters or are leading a tour that fits our eccentric theme.

JUST PLAIN WEIRD

This catch-all category describes about a hundred people or places that defy labeling, although it could be said that most of the 900 entries in this book could fit in this category. You'll find entries here for the toilet paper tree, a building with furniture hung on the outside, funeral home miniature golf, eccentric grave memorials, a woman known as Mother Goose who invented duck diapers, and a pizza-store employee with his own memorial restroom. So, if a listing didn't fit naturally into one of the other categories, or if it has a multiple personality, you'll find it here.

ODD SHOPPING

Americans are no slouches when it comes to shopping and our gift shops are famous for catering to a tourist's every whim. Among the bizarre offerings you'll find here is Skeletons in the Closet, the Los Angeles Coroner's Office gift shop; a botanica selling powdered iguana foot and good luck sprays; and shops selling costumed cockroaches and moose-poop earrings.

QUIRKY CUISINE

Memorable for their quirky character, these restaurants are indeed curious places. They're reviewed not for the quality or price of their food, but rather because they provide an entertaining eating experience. They also give you an alternative to the utter predictability of America's chain restaurants. Most of these establishments are run by highly individualistic people or by corporations who know how to make eccentricity pay.

ROOMS WITH A SKEW

Entries for these quirky quarters include an underwater scuba-diving hotel, an Indian hogan, a primitive cave, several former jails, some teepee villages, a sod-house bed and breakfast, a few islands and lighthouses and a drive-in movie motel where you watch the movie from bed through 'picture' windows. Like the eating establishments above, you can expect to find some very out-of-the-ordinary individuals behind those front desks.

QUIRK ALERTS

These are entries worthy of extra attention, either because the story is just too weirdly wonderful to be missed or because it's a not-to-be-forgotten eccentricity that no longer exists.

CROSS-COUNTRY QUIRKS

Some weirdness knows no bounds, spreading across state lines with abandon. The cornucopia of peculiar pursuits, bizarre behaviors and eccentric experiences portrayed in this chapter could be taking place right in your own hometown. Here's where you find out about competitive eaters, historical reenactors and where take part in a murder mystery. Maybe you want to sleep with ghosts, learn how to make brain-tanned buffalo hide shelters, live as if it were the Middle Ages, or visit folks practicing for an exploration of Mars. Eccentric activities like these spring up in the most unexpected places and you just never know … a new group could be forming as we speak.

All Americans are weird

You've probably heard the expression, 'All Americans are weird'.
Now you can see just how weird they really are!

America varies considerably when it comes to the eccentric landscape and not all weirdness is created equal. Based on the number of entries per state, you can see the heights to which some rise on the quirkiness scale and the depths to which some states sink when it comes to providing a culture that encourages colorful behavior.

Sure, you'd expect to see California and Florida at the top of any eccentric pyramid, but you may be surprised to see Washington and Wisconsin ranking right up there among the oddest. Size, population, and regional differences alone can't explain the wide variations, eccentrically speaking, among the 48 states. What do Illinois and Pennsylvania offer that the surrounding states don't? Why is Oregon so mundane, nestled as it is between two such extreme neighbors? What is it about Florida that spawns so many eccentricities compared to the states around it?

THE HEIGHTS OF ECCENTRICITY

What stands for quintessentially quirky in Nebraska might not even register on the eccentric scale in California, a quality this map can't measure. It also can't measure the relative expressiveness of a region's quirkiness quotient. In San Francisco, for example, they take their eccentricity very seriously, unlike Los Angeles, which behaves more like a wriggling puppy dog, anxious for you to rub its touristic tummy.

If you thought you could just drive across America, hopping from state to state in search of eccentric sites, you might prefer an airplane instead of a car. Jumping from California to Texas to Florida in search of the quirkiest spots in America means driving across some states where there's barely an eccentric blip on the plains of conformity. On the other hand, quantity doesn't always mean quality, as a read through *Eccentric America* will clearly show. When it comes to weirdness, some American somewhere will always measure up.

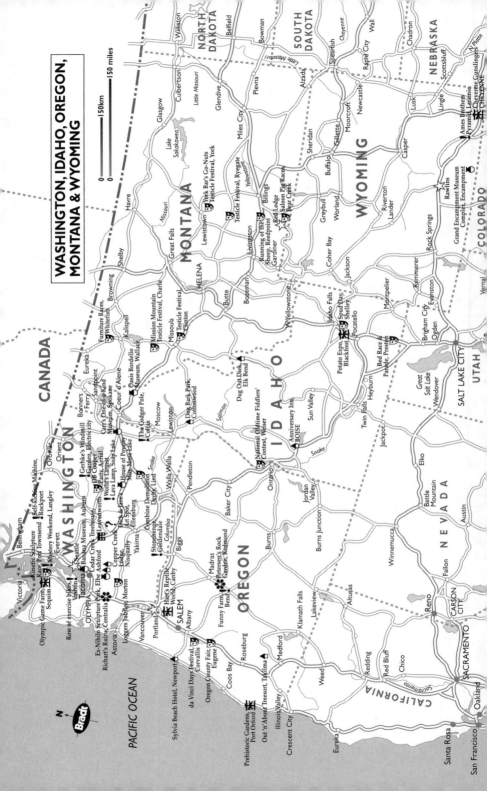

Northwestern Region

WASHINGTON
Festivals and events

Before being consigned to the scrap heap, aging farm combines belching their last are brought to the **Combine Demolition Derby** in the small farming community of Lind. Wheat threshers that are all threshed-out get patched together with baling wire and duct tape, then decorated for the beauty pageant that kicks off the event. The machines, which must be at least 25 years old and certified inoperable for harvest, are then paraded before the crowd with the owner of the 'most beautiful' combine getting a cash prize. Combat takes place in a dirt arena, the lumbering machines bashing feebly at one another until all but one are disabled and towed off the field in disgrace.

> **Combine Demolition Derby**, held annually in June. Contact the Lind Lion's Club, 108 E 1st St, Lind, WA 99341; ↘ 509 677 3501; web: www.lindwa.com/lind'sweekend.html

Children and families race against corporations and the military in the **Milk Carton Derby**, a colorful, if not exactly seaworthy flotilla of crafts made from at least 50 half-gallon milk cartons each. The object is to get the human-powered contraption across 1,200 feet of water to the finish line, an objective not always achieved. Each milk carton supports only about 4lb of weight so folks start collecting milk cartons months in advance of the event. Awards are given in many categories including one for the most impressively designed and decorated craft. The derby has been kicking off Seattle's Seafair activities for 33 years.

> **Milk Carton Derby**, held annually in July. Contact Seafair, 2200 6th Ave, Ste 400, Seattle, WA 98121; ↘ 206 728 0123; web: www.seafair.com

Let's set the stage. D B Cooper is famous for one single act – he hijacked a jet in 1971 and parachuted into the Washington night with $200,000 of ransom money tied to his waist. He disappeared forever, leaving behind a legacy as the country's only unsolved hijacking. On the edge of Lake Merwin is the tiny (pop 700) town of Ariel that became, for a time, headquarters for the search team. Since 1974 the town has held a **D B Cooper Party** at the Aerial Store to honor their only claim to fame. Two hundred and fifty fans show up each year, with one once coming from as far away as Australia. In the five-year milestone years, the number of fans is nearer 500. Always the Saturday after Thanksgiving, the party lasts only a day, starting around 1pm and ending, usually, by midnight. If the guests are feeling creative, they'll start a storytelling contest, giving a prize for the best story of what might have happened to old D B. They always have a look-alike contest, with fans showing up dressed as

ECCENTRIC CALENDAR
WASHINGTON

February	**Mystery Weekend**, Langley (page 2)
June	**Combine Demolition Derby**, Lind (page 1)
June 21 (Summer solstice)	**Summer Solstice Parade**, Fremont District of Seattle (page 6)
July	**Milk Carton Derby**, Seattle (page 1)
August	**Loggers Jubilee**, Morton. Held the second weekend of August (page 2)
September	**Bug Blast**, Seattle (page 3)
October	**Port Townsend Kinetic Sculpture Race**, Port Townsend. Held the first weekend of October (page 3)
November	**D B Cooper Party**, Aerial. Held the Saturday after Thanksgiving (page 1)

IDAHO

June	**National Oldtime Fiddlers' Contest**, Weiser (page 10)
September	**Spud Day**, Shelley. Held on the third Saturday in September (page 10)
November/ December	**Bed Race and Parade**, Preston. Held the weekend after Thanksgiving (page 10)

the hijacker was – in a suit with a backpack, a parachute, goggles and no shoes. Otherwise they just hang around, listening to music and keeping the story alive.

D B Cooper Party, held every November, always the Saturday after Thanksgiving. Aerial Store, 288 Merwin Village Rd, Aerial, WA 98603; ↘ 360 225 7126. 10 miles east of Woodland off Hwy 503. Look for the Merwin Dam sign.

The town of Langley really knows how to plan a party. On the last weekend in February, it involves the entire population, plus guests, in a quirky Mystery Weekend. The town, an art colony just three blocks long by two blocks wide, boasts around 1,000 residents. The **Mystery Weekend** is a two-day interactive play that takes place all over town. Written by local authors, it involves local actors, shopkeepers, the mayor, and everyone else who wants to play. The entry packet includes a newspaper that has stories about the mystery, a map with the location of the crime, and where to find clues. Participants go around town collecting the clues and interviewing folks in the streets, shops and cafés. Not everyone is truthful, which adds to the fun. When you think you know who done it, you submit your entry at the visitor center. On Sunday evening the 'detectives' gather the 'suspects' on stage, solving the mystery in a little playlet. Drawings are held for various prizes among those who guessed correctly.

Mystery Weekend held annually in February in Langley, WA. Contact Langley Chamber of Commerce, PO Box 403, Langley, WA 98260; ↘ 360 221 5676; web: www.whidbeynet.net/langleychamb/

The **Loggers Jubilee** is known as the grandaddy of all logging shows but in addition to logging events, the show is also famous for its lawnmower and bed

OREGON

July   **da Vinci Days Festival,**
Corvallis (page 13)
Oregon Country Fair,
Eugene (page 13)

MONTANA

March   **Cardboard Classic**, Red Lodge.
Part of the Red Lodge Winter
Carnival (page 18)

April   **Furniture Races**, Whitefish (page 18)

May   **York Bar's Go-Nuts Testicle
Festival**, York (page 18)

June   **Mission Mountain Testicle Festival**, Charlo (page 18)
Ryegate Testicle Festival, Ryegate (page 18)

July   **Iron Horse Rodeo**, Red Lodge (page 17)

**August/
September**   **Running of the Sheep**, Reed Point. Held on Labor
Day weekend (page 18)

September   **Clinton Testicle Festival**, Clinton (page 18)

and keep in mind...   **Bear Creek Saloon & Steakhouse Pig Races**, Bear
Creek. Pig races run Sunday–Thursday from Memorial
Day to Labor Day (page 19)

races. They're sticklers for making sure the lawnmowers are the real thing; no souped-up modifications are allowed. The bed races on Main Street involve four girls pushing a wheeled bed carrying a male rider who has to weigh at least 100lb.

> **Loggers Jubilee**, held annually the second weekend in August in Morton, WA; web: www.loggersjubilee.com

The annual **Bug Blast** at the Burke Museum is your chance to get intimate with the critters that make up over 90% of the Earth's creatures. You can paw through a pile of toasty compost, make bug crafts, get your face bug-painted and, if you dare, eat bugs too. The museum promises a '100% creepy, crawly good time, touching large, live bugs and eating little, fried ones'.

> **Bug Blast**, held annually in September. Contact the Burke Museum of Natural History & Culture, Box 353010, University of Washington, Seattle, WA 98195; ☏ 206 616 3962; web:
> www.washington.edu/burkemuseum/

The Greater **Port Townsend Kinetic Sculpture Race** is one of a handful of colorful competitions involving human-powered art sculptures. What started out as a few artistic improvements to a tricycle in the late 60s has led to a crop of contraptions competing on terrain that varies from pavement to mud and hills to rivers. The machines can be any size, decorated in any theme and made of anything – machine parts, gears, wheels, etc – as long as they move by human power alone. Kinetinauts, as their creators are called, compete for the most coveted award of all, the Mediocre Award, that of finishing right in the middle. The next-to-last award is the next best thing.

Port Townsend Kinetic Sculpture Race, held annually the first weekend in October. Contact the Kinetic Sculpture Race, PO Box 451, Port Townsend, WA 98368; ↘ 360 379 4972

Eccentric environments

Richard 'Richart' Tracy considers himself rich-in-art, an understatement considering he lives among hundreds of bizarre art objects that have taken him 15 years to create. The house behind **Richart's Ruins** (aka The Art Yard) is surrounded by posts topped with all sorts of weird stuff while the yard itself is an endless maze of trails through junk sculptures and assemblages. He's known to hide out among the junk, listening to visitor comments and popping out to talk with you only if he likes what he hears.

Richart's Ruins, 203 M St, Centralia, WA 98531; ↘ 360 736 7990

Big Red, a bright pink 'woman' with road-reflector breasts, welcomes you to **Dick and Jane's Art Spot** in Ellensburg, a private home with a yard straight out of fantasyland. Dick Elliott and Jane Orleman have filled their home and property with a mad mixture of oddball sculpture that started out as junk and ended up with personality. They've been working at this for 12 years, creating such assemblages as Eric Etch-a-Sketch, a Polaroid camera man, an 'art lives' fence and a bicycle tire tree. Dick and Jane run a janitorial service called Spot and have a dog named Spot, too.

Dick and Jane's Art Spot, 101 N Pearl St, Ellensburg, WA 98926. Located across from the police station.

Museums and collections

Artist Dan Klennert prefers an open field to an art gallery, populating his four-acre **Ex-Nihilo Sculpture Park** with dozens of life-size scrap-iron people and animals. Welded from machinery scrap, pure junk and wood, his work reflects his passion for scrounging, an activity he's been doing since childhood. From 12-foot cowboys to people on Harleys, from dinosaurs to horses, Dan displays his work outdoors so 'my metal offspring can run free and my creative spirit can hang out long after I'm gone.'

Ex-Nihilo Sculpture Park, located near the west entrance to Mount Rainier National Park about 3 miles east of the town of Elbe, WA on State Route 706; web: www.danielklennert.com. *Park open year-round; gallery open mainly weekends May–Oct.*

Carr's One-of-a-Kind Museum really is just that, a privately owned collection of unusual stuff like celebrity limousines, a Chinese junk made of matchsticks and a navy destroyer. Marvin Carr, a retired World War II vet, has a penchant for collecting weird things such as a 13-foot snake that electrocuted itself by chewing through a stereo cord, a full case of President George Bush's inaugural champagne, a model ship made of 27,500 matchsticks, and a 99-year-old wheelchair. His car collection includes Elvis Presley's Lincoln, Jackie Gleason's limo and JFK's personal Lincoln, which, they say, played a part in the affair he allegedly had with Marilyn Monroe.

Carr's One-of-a-Kind Museum, 5225 N Freya St, Spokane, WA 99217; ❧ 509 489 8859; fax: 509 489 8859. *Open Sat–Sun 1.00–4.00pm.*

Monte Holm is a wealthy man who came from a very dysfunctional family, so dysfunctional that he had to leave at age 13 in the middle of the Great Depression. He rode the rails for six years, begging for food and standing in bread lines. (One of his favorites was the soup kitchen run by Al Capone.) Life was miserable and Monte vowed that if he ever had money, he'd be good to people. He also vowed that no-one would ever kick him off a train again. Monte arrived in Washington with one thin dime in his pocket. He parlayed that over the next 40 years into a successful junkyard business in Moses Lake. Next door to the junkyard he built a warehouse, stocking it with antique cars, old steam engines and enough interesting old stuff to keep you entertained for hours. And behind the warehouse, which he called the **House of Poverty Museum**, sits the **Mon-Road Railroad** where you can see a real train, including the 1915 presidential passenger car that once carried presidents Wilson and Truman. No one pays a dime at the museum; in fact, you leave richer for the experience.

Mon-Road Railroad and House of Poverty Museum, 258 Commerce Way, Moses Lake, WA 98837; ❧ 509 765 6342. *Just go to the junkyard and ask to see the museum. Usually open Mon–Fri 8.00am–3.00pm.*

You'd never guess that Ann Lovell, the mild-mannered Auburn librarian, is bonkers over bananas. Also known as Anna Banana, she's curator of the **Washington Banana Museum** she's set up in her home. Her collection, amassed over 20 years, numbers an astounding 4,000 banana-related items: magnets, jewelry, cookie jars, cookbooks, cartoons, pillows, inflatables, crates, shipping labels, fabrics, aprons and boxer shorts. She talks on a banana phone, writes with banana pens, reads by a banana floor lamp, even has a banana Christmas tree. You never know when an event is going to trigger such a collecting frenzy. For Ann it was a trip to Hawaii and an Anna's Bananas T-shirt. Without being consciously aware of it, she just started buying things with bananas, any size, any material and for any purpose. Today, she's a leading expert on banana crates, labels, and invoices, and hopes the Smithsonian may someday be willing to take her collection. For now she just enjoys sharing her passion and playing her tape of 40 banana songs while she shows you around. Her most prized banana? A Chiquita fiberglass banana cello.

Washington Banana Museum, Auburn, WA; ❧ 253 833 8043; web: www.bananamuseum.com. *Call Ann for an appointment.*

Attractions

Kitschy, kitschy, coo … the animals at the **Olympic Game Farm**'s drive-through zoo range from the unbearably cute (performing mommy and baby bears) to the disgusting (a pushy, slobbering buffalo who sticks his snout through your open car window). The farm is home to a variety of species, many of which are veterans of the movie business. They roam free while you stay caged in your car. They'll perform all kinds of antics to entice you to toss them bread, for sale at the entrance; fail to feed them and your car may get a few bumps and dings. The dangerous animals stay behind electric fences so the experience is pretty safe as long as you use some common sense.

Olympic Game Farm, 1423 Ward Rd, Sequim, WA 98382; ❧ 800 778 4295 or 360 683 4295; web: www.olygamefarm.com

Famous for its Frank Gehry architecture, the **Experience Music Project** is a spectacularly eccentric building complex that is best appreciated when seen from the observation tower of the nearby Space Needle. The building, with its swooping lines, metallic roofs, undulating walls and vibrant colors, has been compared to a melted down electric guitar. In the Sky Church entry hall, the world's largest video screen plays videos produced just for the museum: videos with throbbing motion, pulsating light and swirling colors. The floor is translucent with glowing time capsules filled with objects donated by various bands. Your museum guide is a hand-held computer that lets you hear narration, interviews and music. In glass-walled studios you can follow electronic prompts that show you how to play the drums or an electric guitar. The main exhibit hall has tens of thousands of items, including Ray Charles' debut recording, a 1960s' FBI file investigating the lyrics of 'Louie, Louie', and Janis Joplin's floral bell-bottoms, c1970.

Experience Music Project, Seattle Center Campus, 325 5th Ave N, Seattle, WA 98109; ☎ 877 EMPLIVE or 206 EMPLIVE; fax: 206 770 2727; web: www.emplive.com

Quirkyvilles

Seattle's **Fremont Neighborhood**, formally known as 'The Center of the Universe', has an official motto – De Libertas Quirkas (Freedom to be Peculiar). Residents take this responsibility very seriously, as evidenced by an abundance of street art, particularly the **Fremont Troll**. This ugly but much-loved two-ton, 18-foot high scary monster was sculpted by artists who won a design competition. Lurking under the Aurora Bridge, it clutches a real VW bug. In October, bathed in orange light and sporting a bicycle rim nose ring, the troll hosts Trolloween, a strange celebration involving costumed playlets, chanting, drumming and dancing. The troll reflects the neighborhood's feelings, often being adorned with various expressions and costumes. **Waiting for the Interurban** is a crowd of stone commuter figures patiently waiting for a trolley that never comes. They're usually dressed up by the residents in all manner of costume and political sentiment. This interactive statue has played host to endless displays of affection: engagements, weddings, and memorials of all kinds. Anyone can decorate the figures as long as the message is not commercial and as long as they clean up afterward.

An infamous bronze statue of **Lenin** sternly keeps an eye on the goings-on in the district. A teacher found the toppled figure while living in Slovakia and mortgaged his home in order to it ship it to Fremont. It's for sale and the proceeds will go to support art causes. Fremont is known for its Saturday night **outdoor cinema**. Flocks of people lounge outside on funky furniture and rubber boats, dressed in costume and watching their favorite cult and classic B movies in the only walk-in outdoor theater in the West. An Applause-O-Meter determines the best urban campsite, the most creative seating and the best costume. The **Fremont Rocket,** with its neon laser pods, hovers on a nearby building, an actual defunct rocket rigged to emit clouds of vapor at regular intervals throughout the day. The diverse, European-style **Sunday Market** takes place rain or shine and serves as a community gathering spot.

Practically everyone in the neighborhood turns up at – and in – the annual summer **Solstice Parade**. A wild throng of naked, painted bodies, bizarre floats, and costumed marchers gather for a raucous celebration of the longest day of the year. Controversial subject matter and outrageous behavior is encouraged.

Fremont Neighborhood, located in North Seattle, WA. Contact Fremont Chamber of Commerce, PO Box 31139, Seattle, WA 98103; ☎ 206 632 1500; web: www.fremontfair.com

'Oyez, oyez, oyez'. Loosely translated that means 'hark' or 'listen', both of which you're supposed to do when a town crier comes your way. The tourist town of **Leavenworth** actually has such a position, a **town crier** who announces the news at the town's many Bavarian-themed festivals and events. Last time they advertised for applicants, though, no-one showed up for an interview. The national media got wind of the story (by word of mouth?) and by the following week they had dozens of applicants. Would a town crier in Brooklyn preface the news with 'Oy vey, oy vey, oy vey'?

> **Leavenworth**, Washington. Contact the Leavenworth Chamber of
> Commerce, PO Box 327, Leavenworth, WA 98826; ✆ 509 548 5807;
> web: www.leavenworth.org

Tours
Windsor Olson is a real private eye who takes visitors to the locations of some of Seattle's most grisly crimes. **Private Eye on Seattle** investigates a mass murder, the Tong wars, a million-dollar burglary, bordellos, arsonists and the soy sauce murder mystery.

> **Private Eye on Seattle**, Seattle, WA; ✆ 206 365 3739; web:
> www.privateeyetours.com

A number of companies provide amusing glimpses of Pioneer Square's abandoned subterranean world, among them Bill Speidel's *Underground Tour*. Accompanied by a wise-cracking guide, you'll wind through the long abandoned storefronts under Seattle's streets, hearing about the exploding-toilet debacle that forced the city to raise the streets 14 feet up as well as the scandals that gave rise to the expression 'skid row'.

> **Underground Tour**, 608 First Ave, Seattle, WA 98104; ✆ 206 682 4646;
> web: www.undergroundtour.com

Just plain weird
Spinning playfully in their field, the one hundred windmills made from junk such as coffee pots, cookie tins, machinery parts, jello molds, hubcaps and chandeliers are all that's left of the almost 500 that Emil and Eva Gehrke created before their deaths in the late 1970s. Community volunteers keep the whirligigs maintained at **Gerhke's Windmill Garden**.

> **Gerhke's Windmill Garden**, located along Hwy 155, one mile
> southwest of Coulee Dam near Electric City, WA.

Talking about holding a grudge! Back in 1938 the Colfax High football team lost to arch-rival St John. Fast-forward half a century and you have a bunch of geezers in their late sixties playing a rematch, only now they're playing tag style rather than tackle. To commemorate the event they hired a woodcarver, famous for his whimsical style, to carve a totem pole with the likenesses of all 50 of them wearing leather football helmets. The **Codger Pole**, as it is known, is topped off with a 15-foot-tall carving of a codger.

> The **Codger Pole**, located on John Crawford Blvd just off Main Street in
> Colfax, Washington.

The **Self-Kicking Machine** in front of the Rockport Country Store was built by Myra Benton in the 1950s. To use the contraption, you stand (appropriately bent)

Quirk Alert

There's a new quirkyville in the offing. The tiny town of Soap Lake (pop 1,700) is trying to build the **World's Largest Lava Lamp** (web: www.giantlavalamp.com) to revitalize its sagging tourism business. The region, known for its geological bed of lava, is a natural place for such a lamp. 'After 14 million years, lava will be returned to Soap Lake,' says Brent Blake, one of the lamp's most devoted boosters. The town is in the midst of feasibility and budget studies, but in the meantime you can see a giant banner of the proposed lamp on Main Street. If all goes well, the 65-foot-high lamp will be 18 feet in diameter with an observation deck around its middle offering views of Soap Lake. It will also light up, just like the real thing.

in the designated spot, turn the crank, and a chain of four revolving boots will do their job.

Self-Kicking Machine, Rockport Country Store, 53071 State Route 20 (between Marblemount and Annacortes), Rockport, WA 98283; ☎ 360 853 8800

It looks like **Stonehenge** – same size and shape – but it's the last thing you'd expect to see sitting in the Klickitat Hills. Commissioned by lumber magnate Sam Hill in the 1930s, the replica of the famous English ruin was meant to honor the country's World War I losses. Seems that Sam was under the mistaken impression that the real Stonehenge was a burial ground and would thus be a fitting memorial.

Stonehenge, located at the intersection of State Hwy 14 in Goldendale, WA, 4 miles from the Maryhill Museum of Art; web: www.maryhillmuseum.org/about.htm. *Free*.

On the land bridge between Vashon and Maury islands sits a **row of exercise bikes** – along with an occasional rowing machine – that faces the sea, available for anyone with a yen to pedal or row. People have been adding to the array ever since a guy named Jim Smith discarded the first two bikes there years ago so folks could enjoy the view while exercising. Lots of people stop to have their pictures taken, including a gang of biker dudes in leather and chains. Jim estimates that 40 bikes have probably perched seaside on their way to exercise equipment heaven.

Row of exercise bikes, located in Vashon Island, WA. Contact the Vashon-Maury Island Chamber of Commerce, PO Box 98070, Vashon, WA 98070; ☎ 206 463 6217; web: www.vashonchamber.com

Cal Poly's famous Bubble Gum Alley finally has a competitor. On the wall outside the Market Theater is Seattle's **gum wall**, a fine example of community 'gum art'. Theater guests waiting in line for weekend improv performances artfully stick their gum to the wall. It now reaches up to 15 feet high in an ever-spreading mass. People stick pennies into it, sculpt images and words and leave wads of happy faces. Fortunately there are several gum vendors nearby so you can leave your contribution too.

Gum wall, located outside the Market Theatre at 1428 Post Alley, Seattle, WA 98101; ✆ 206 587 2414

Odd shopping

At Pike Place Market you'll find a stall that gives new meaning to the phrase 'catching a fish'. At **Pike Place Fish** they literally fly through the air, tossed about by fish-flinging fishmongers as they go about their work. World famous for this entertaining way of getting the job done, there's never a missed photo-op here – the employees will mug and pose for, and with, anything. Owner John Yokoyama, who bought the place in 1965, simply set out to become world famous without advertising, taking his cue from Muhammad Ali who, he points out, didn't say 'I *believe* I'm the greatest!'

Pike Place Fish, 86 Pike Place, Seattle, WA 98101; ✆ 800 542 7732 or 206 682 7181; web: www.pikeplacefish.com

Joe Standley had a life-long passion for nature's curiosities, collecting oddities like a preserved prospector, the Lord's Prayer engraved on a grain of rice, fleas in dresses, a three-tusk walrus and the smallest ivory elephants in the world. He began this Seattle collection during the Civil War, eventually calling it **Ye Olde Curiosity Shop**. There've been many imitators since, but he was one of the first to recognize the drawing power of weird.

Ye Olde Curiosity Shop, 1001 Alaskan Way, Pier 54, Seattle, WA 98104; ✆ 206 682 5844; web: www.yeoldecuriosityshop.com

Quirky cuisine

Order a dessert known as 'The Bulge' at **The 5 Spot** restaurant and you'll have to sign a liability waiver guaranteeing you won't sue the establishment if you gain weight. A concoction of sugar-coated dried bananas, macadamia nuts and ice cream topped with whipped cream and syrups, the dessert is served only after you sign a release form promising not to impose any kind of obesity-related lawsuit should you develop love handles or saddle bags as a result of devouring it. The restaurant's owner devised the release to draw attention to the absurdity of holding restaurants responsible for the American epidemic of obesity.

The 5 Spot, 1502 Queen Anne Ave N, Seattle, WA 98109; ✆ 209 285 7768; web: www.chowfoods.com/5-spot.asp

Rooms with a Skew

You can spend the night in a tipi at **TipiTrek** or you can sign up for their three-night Indian living experience. Owners David and Christine Pitkin supply you with horses for riding and rafts for the river, your only transportation options. Fortunately they'll also supply teachers and guides who show you how to ride the horse and raft the river. They'll also tell you stories, put on shows and demonstrate native crafts, skills, and games. You can eat the meals prepared by the hosts or cook for yourself over a campfire.

TipiTrek, 14517 37th Ave NE, Lake Forest Park, WA 98155; ☎ 206 695 9446 or 206 310 0742; web: www.tipitrek.com. *Season runs May 1–Oct 1.*

Captain John Jones delivers the mail by jet boat in the rugged reaches of Hells Canyon and you can go along with him on his weekly, overnight run. You'll visit the isolated ranches on his route, spending the night at the **Copper Creek Lodge** deep in the heart of the canyon. The mail run goes through come hell or high water.

Copper Creek Lodge, located 2 miles west of the Nisqually entrance to Mt Rainier National Park. Contact Great Getaways, 35707 SR 706 E, PO Box 159, Ashford, WA 98304; ☎ 877 325 5881 or 360 569 2799; web: www.greatgetaways.com

Nestled 50 feet up in the trees is the **Cedar Creek Treehouse**, a forest retreat with a view of Mount Rainier from your bed. Reached by a suspension footbridge threaded through a cedar rainforest, the 16-foot-square structure, wrapped around a huge cedar, seems to float in the treetops. It's equipped with solar power, water, a gas stove, an icebox and sink in the kitchen, and a toilet and washbasin in the bathroom. Nearby is The Observatory, an octagonal treehouse 100 feet above the ground, reached only by climbing harness and ladder. The owners, Bill Compher and his wife Leslie, are musicians; they'll take requests for special occasion serenades.

Cedar Creek Treehouse, PO Box 204, Ashford, WA 98304; ☎ 360 569 2991; web: www.cedarcreektreehouse.com

IDAHO
Festivals and events

In Preston folks get together with up to ten of their friends or co-workers, make a bed out of anything that a person might conceivably sleep on, strap on helmets, don pajamas, and then race down Main Street, content to make fools of themselves for all to see. Prizes are awarded for the fastest bed, the prettiest, and for best costumes. Halfway through the course, participants have to stop, switch bedclothes, and make their bed. The **Bed Race and Parade** is part of Preston's Festival of Lights.

Bed Race and Parade, takes place annually the weekend after Thanksgiving. Contact the Preston Chamber of Commerce, 49 N State St, Ste A, Preston, ID 83263; ☎ 208 852 2703; web: www.prestonidaho.org

The little town of Shelly, population 3,500, swells to 10,000 or more during their annual **Spud Day** festival. The highlight of the celebration is the Spud Tug, a tug-of-war over a gigantic pit of mashed potatoes mixed up by a cement truck and then poured into a foam-lined pit. Anyone who wants to participate can sign up to be on a team and is weighed before each tug to make sure the teams are evenly matched. Each tug ends with one team climbing out of the pit, good and yucky.

Spud Day, held annually the third Saturday in September. Contact the City of Shelley, 101 S Emerson St, Shelley, ID 83274; ☎ 208 357 3390; web: www.governet.net/ID/CI/SHE/home.cfm

It takes six days of fiddling around to win the **National Old Time Fiddlers' Contest** in Weiser, long considered the fiddling capital of the world. Hundreds of

Quirk Alert

RECORDING MARATHON

For 24 years the Reverend Robert Shields recorded every detail of his life in what is now known as the **world's longest diary**. He rarely left his house so he wouldn't get behind in logging everything he ate, every move he made, all the junk mail he received, every dream he remembered and most all of his bodily functions. Until suffering a stroke in 1996, he spent four hours a day on his obsession. The 35-million-word diary, consisting of 90 carefully labelled boxes of typewritten, bound, legal-size ledgers, is being preserved by Washington State University which is in the process of putting the diary on to acid-free materials for protection over time.

entrants from every state, many of them winners of local and regional championships, gather for a week of jamming and friendly competition. Each fiddler has four minutes to play a hoe down, a waltz and one other tune of their choice to qualify. Going over the time limit by even a second can cost them the title. If you've never been to a fiddling event, you'll be surprised at how much musical variety you'll hear. Each state, and even each region within a state, has its own unique sound and experienced fiddlers can tell where a person is from just by listening to his or her music. Folks of all ages – even children – participate in the competition.

National Old Time Fiddlers' Contest, held annually in June in Weiser, ID; ☎ 800 437 1280; web: www.fiddlecontest.com

Museums and collections

The girls left in a hurry, such a hurry that their clothes, make-up and personal possessions were all left behind. During your tour of the **Oasis Bordello Museum** you'll find out why the girls had to leave in such haste as well as how the brothel managed to operate without hindrance until well into the 1970s. Proprietress Michelle Mayfield shares information gleaned from the ladies' hairdressers, local policemen, the establishment's former bouncers and maids, and even from the ladies themselves. It's a glimpse into the past, with details that range from poignant to hilarious.

Oasis Bordello Museum, 605 Cedar St, Wallace, ID 83873; ☎ 208 753 0801; web: www.imbris.net/~mrmayfield/oasis%20museum%20main.htm

Attractions

Blackfoot, known as the potato capital of the world, is home to Idaho's **World Potato Exposition**. Besides learning everything you'll ever want to know about potato farming, you'll see the world's largest potato chip – a two-foot Pringle – and get a chance to buy potato fudge, potato ice-cream and potato hand-cream at the gift shop.

World Potato Exposition, PO Box 366, Blackfoot, ID 83221; ☎ 800 785 2517 or 208 785 2517; web: www.ida.net/users/potatoexpo. *Open Mon–Sat 10.00am–7.00pm May–Sept.*

Rooms with a Skew

The world's biggest beagle B&B welcomes you to **Dog Bark Park** in Cottonwood, home of chain-saw artists Dennis Sullivan and his wife, Francis Conklin. You can't miss the place – Toby, the 12-foot-tall pup, sits under the chin of Sweet Willy Colton, a creature that soars to an astounding 30 feet. Sweet Willy sleeps four in his two-story unit: you enter through his belly. The loft is in the pup's head; the plumbing is at the rear, naturally. The park got its name from Dennis, who claims he can hear hundreds of dogs barking when he puts his ear up to a dead tree. He carves all sizes of dog, as well as bears, wolves, moose, fish and raccoons, out of Ponderosa pine using a chain-saw.

> **Dog Bark Park & Inn**, Route 1, Box 199L, Cottonwood, ID 83522;
> ↘ 208 962 3647; web: www.dogbarkparkinn.com; email:
> dogbarkpark@camasnet.com. *Open daily 11.00am–4.00pm; Sweet Willy open April 1–Oct 1 by reservation.*

For 55 years Richard Zimmerman, aka **Dugout Dick**, has been digging caves using only a pick, a shovel, and a pry bar, all the while looking for precious metals. He hasn't had much success at finding any but he has managed to eke out a living renting out the caves for $5 a night or $25 a month to campers or wannabe hermits. Some of his tourist caves are heated with homemade stoves vented with a milk-can stovepipe. Built-in beds hang from the rock walls, and kerosene lamps supply the illumination. Don't expect room service. Richard himself lives in a four-room, warren-like cave that has no electricity, heating, or plumbing, at least not of the modern kind. An ice cave provides refrigeration, wood-burning stoves provide heat and car windshields set into the rubble walls serve as windows to keep out the weather and let in light. Now 88, Zimmerman emerges from his cave to attend church as well as visit the tavern where he's famous for quoting the Bible chapter and verse. He likes to write songs about his Salmon River home and used to entertain himself, before he became too frail, by simultaneously playing the guitar and harmonica while dancing. He's been profiled in a book called *Idaho Loners* by Cort Conley, which is devoted to the state's many hermits, solitaries and individualists.

> **Richard 'Dugout Dick' Zimmerman**, Hwy 93, Elk Bend, ID. Located above the banks of the Salmon River and visible from Hwy 93. Look for the 'Ice Caves', 'Dugouts', and 'Cave Man' signs.

The Anniversary Inn in Boise is a theme hotel with rooms like Sleeping Beauty's Suite, a medieval setting that features a drawbridge leading to your room and breakfast in the turret. The Oregon Trail suite has a bed in a covered wagon; Mammoth Ice Cave, complete with stalactites, boasts a hot tub. The Hay Loft is two stories with a windmill waterfall shower.

> **Anniversary Inn**, 1575 Lusk Ave, Boise, ID 83706; ↘ 877 386 4900;
> web: www.anniversaryinn.com

OREGON
Festivals and events

It's not quite the spectacle that Burning Man has become, but neither is it just a bunch of aging hippies desperately clinging to the past. The **Oregon Country Fair** is a modern, somewhat sanitized version of a 1960s' be-in. Still idealistic, yet realistic at the same time, the fair has evolved in 30-something years into an event now drawing mainstream families and corporate types along with the requisite hippies. Somehow the fair manages to please a very diverse crowd with an eclectic mix of crafts, food, entertainment and environmental guilt. There are 350 booths in all, peddling everything from portable yurt homes to log tables, brooms, masks, puppets and herbs. The food ranges from burritos to blintzes and from deep-fried bananas to organic juices. There's a full spectrum of entertainment, with musicians, magicians, jugglers, puppets, belly-dancers and storytellers. Cozy performance spaces on the fringes offer eco-folk music, a poetry circus and a variety of alternative acts while a bevy of wandering performers do their thing as well. When you get tired, dozens of masseurs and bodywork therapists are there to rejuvenate you. To make learning more entertaining, the staff provides performances by creative thinkers to get their messages across.

Of the 150,000 or so people who attend the three-day event, around 7,000 will camp at the site, using solar-heated showers, eating organic food, recycling, composting and joining feel-good 'om-m-m' circles. At issue for fairgoers past is whether the country's premier 'alternative' festival has sold out to the 'destructive, consumerist death culture' believed to be contrary to 'communitarian thinking'. If you ask the folks at the Community Village, they'll tell you they're working to expand their consciousness beyond the fair and out into the world at large. It doesn't sound like the message – or the medium – has changed all that much since the 1960s.

> **Oregon Country Fair**, held annually in July in Eugene, OR. Contact Oregon Country Fair, 442 Lawrence St, Eugene, OR 97401; ↘ 541 343 4298; web: www.oregoncountryfair.org. *Open 11.00am to 7.00pm daily during the fair.*

The **da Vinci Days Festival** in Corvallis celebrates art, science and technology with kinetic sculpture races, street performers, storytellers and participatory art projects. Teams of people who have designed and built a human-powered, all-terrain sculpture try to ride their vehicle through a 100-foot mud bog, down two miles of river, across 3,000 feet of pasture, and over a 100-foot sand trap. Besides speed and terrain worthiness, teams are also scored on the artistry of their sculpture and on the overall show they put on for the spectators. They make fools of themselves for your viewing pleasure, so cheer them on encouragingly. Besides the kinetics, the festival offers skateboard and roller-blade contests, a sidewalk chalk art competition, a canine Frisbee championship, and enough fair food to keep you going a long time.

> **da Vinci Days Festival**, held annually in July in Corvallis, OR. Contact da Vinci Days Festival, 760 SW Madison Ave, Suite 200, Corvallis, OR 97333; ↘ 541 757 6363; web: www.davinci-days.org

Eccentric environments

Like most gardens filled with rock, stone and concrete sculptures, **Petersen's Rock Garden** is a fairyland of castles, bridges, moats, ponds, towers and churches, studded with patriotic touches like the Statue of Liberty. Representing the last 17 years of his life, Danish immigrant Rasmus Petersen preferred laboring in his garden to farming, using stones and minerals he collected within an 85-mile radius of the garden. The grounds are lovingly landscaped and maintained by his stepdaughter. The museum also has a fluorescent rock display that glows under black light.

> **Petersen's Rock Garden**, 7930 SW 77th St, Redmond, OR 97556;
> ☎ 541 382 5574; web: www.narrowlarry.com/nlpete.html

Museums and collections

Some people just never outgrow their need to play with toys. Frank Kidd's passion for vehicular toys, mechanical banks, police badges, railroad locks and character toys eventually led him to open **Kidd's Toy Museum** so he could share his toys with others. His wife, Joyce, contributes her collection of teddy bears, dolls and holiday collectibles.

> **Kidd's Toy Museum**, 1301 SE Grand Ave, Portland, OR 97214; ☎ 503
> 233 7807; web: www.ourworld.compuserve.com/homepages/JulieKidd/
> antique.htm. *Open Mon–Fri 8.00am–5.30pm; Sat 8.00am–1.00pm.*
> *Admission free.*

If you want to share the story of your visit to Saturn, Lawrence Johns is willing to listen. Director of the new (2003) **Portland Alien Museum**, that's his job – to collect evidence and research to display in the converted home that houses his long-term obsession. The only UFO museum west of Roswell, NM, the museum features newspaper stories reporting close encounters with aliens, video monitors showing crop circles and evidence from the Roswell incident itself. With a doctorate in theology and a passion for art, he hopes his museum will provide a valuable public service as well as entertainment. Considering that he offers a 3D alien roller-coaster film, entertainment might top the list.

> **Portland Alien Museum**, 1716 NE 42nd Ave, Portland, OR 97213;
> ☎ 503 287 UFOS; web: www.alienmuseum.com. *Open*
> *Sat–Sun 11.00am–6.00pm, weekdays by appointment.*

It may not be very glamorous, but the lowly vacuum cleaner played a big role in freeing us from drudgery. Spanning a 100-year history, **Stark's Vacuum Cleaner Museum** in Portland displays models ranging from the old hand-pumped versions to today's super suckers. We can thank a night janitor named James Spangler for inventing the future Kirbys, Royals, Hoovers and Eurekas we all appreciate.

> **Stark's Vacuum Cleaner Museum**,
> 107 NE Grand Ave, Portland, OR; ☎ 800
> 230 4101 or 503 232 4101; web:
> www.starks.com. *Open Mon–Fri*
> *8.00am–7.00pm; Sat 9.00am–5.00pm.*

As the world's leading consumer nation, America's had a lot of help from advertisers on how to shop and what to buy. The **American Advertising Museum** in Portland spans almost 300 years of social history, telling the story of

America's spending habits from colonial days to modern times. It's a fascinating look at one of the quirkier aspects of American culture, showcasing such groundbreaking events as registered trademarks, celebrity endorsements and silly slogans as signs of the times. Why is it that folks who swear they never watch TV still seem to know the commercials?

American Advertising Museum, 211 NW 5th Ave and Davis St, Portland, OR 97209; ℄ 503 226 0000; web: www.admuseum.org. *Open Mon–Fri by appointment, Sat noon–5.00pm.*

Attractions
Feeding chickens to the alligators is one of the highlights at **Hart's Reptile World** in Canby. So is snake petting, although the kids seem more enthusiastic than the adults. Live mice and rabbits are kept on hand for snake food on weekends; the Easter Bunny Feed is an annual, if macabre, event. Owner Mary Esther Hart lovingly cares for the animals, mostly discarded pets or reptiles confiscated during drug raids. If an alligator or large snake is on the loose somewhere, chances are she'll be called to the rescue. Mary Esther says she prefers reptiles to cats and dogs because they're quiet and because she's genuinely fond of all things reptilian. Godzilla the Alligator is one of the park's stars; 11 feet long, he's the largest alligator in captivity outside of zoos; Mary Esther rescued him from a field in California. Binky is a tame, 17-foot python.

Hart's Reptile World, 11264 S Macksburg Rd, Canby, OR 97013; ℄ 503 266 7236; web: www.hartsreptileworld.com. *Open daily 11.00am–5.00pm.*

Prehistoric Gardens is filled with concrete replicas of dinosaurs and amphibians peering amusingly above dense foliage. It's the setting of this park, in a landscape similar to our fantasies of dinosaur environments, which make this 'lost world' so much fun. You can't help but be entertained by the two-dozen 'authentic' species in this forest menagerie created by Sculptor E V Nelson who spent 40 years crafting his creatures.

Prehistoric Gardens, 36848 S Hwy 101, Port Orford, OR 97465; ℄ 541 332 4463. Located halfway between Port Orford and Gold Beach, OR. *Open daylight hours from 9.00am; hours vary seasonally. Call for information.*

Tours
They're dark, musty and have to be explored by flashlight. **The Portland Underground Tour** takes you into the vast network of underground tunnels and cells that held the unfortunate captives who had been 'shanghaied'; that is snatched from the bars and brothels above and sold into unwilling slavery. Long known as the most dangerous port in America, working men who couldn't resist the allure of Portland's sinful pursuits risked being drugged and then dropped through trapdoors into the catacombs below. Held captive until sea captains purchased them, they then faced at least six years of unpaid labor aboard a trading ship before they could make the return voyage from the Orient.

Portland Underground Tour. ℄ 503 622 4798; web: www.members.tripod.com/cgs-mthood/shanghai_tunnels.htm

Just plain weird
Leprechauns are rumored to live in the **world's smallest park**. Certified by Guinness as, indeed, the world's smallest, this two-foot diameter circle, all 452.16

square inches of it, was officially dedicated to the city on St Patrick's Day in 1948. **Mill End's Park**, as it's formally known, was journalist Dick Fagen's answer to an ugly, gaping hole left in the median strip near his office. Tired of seeing the eyesore from his second-story window, Dick planted flowers there one day and, eventually, the city took over maintenance of the plot. From time to time citizens make their own tiny contributions: flying saucers, Ferris wheels, statues and a swimming pool for the leprechauns.

    Mill End's Park, located at SW Front & Taylor Sts in Portland, OR.

Most people can think up weird things to do, but rarely get around to acting on their impulses. At the **Funny Farm** in Buffet Flat, Gene Carsey gives himself permission to do whatever pops into his head. For example, a bowling ball garden – the largest of its kind in the world; he even sells packets of bowling ball seeds. The farm's collection of bowling balls, now 300 strong, keeps growing because folks donate their no-longer-used balls. There's a wall covered with brightly colored washing machine agitators, in front of which he's thoughtfully supplied political picket signs just in case you're gripped by a sudden need to agitate. After all, he says, 'without agitators, nothing in the world would come clean'. A *Wizard of Oz* theme sort of meanders through the place, sometimes featured, sometimes forgotten. At the heart-shaped Love Pond he offers a Free Wedding Day each June. Gene and his partner Mike take in unwanted animals so goats, llamas, sheep, pigs, chickens, cats, duck, dogs, donkeys and turkeys wander the farm.

    Funny Farm, 64990 Deschutes Market Rd, Bend, OR 97701; ↘ 541 389 6391; web: www.funfarm.com

Quirky cuisine

Serving only coffee, tea and dessert, the eclectic **Rimsky-Korsakoffee House** is tucked away in the living-room of an old, possibly haunted, Portland residence. Artist and musician Goody Cable thinks of the café as her canvas with the décor and menu designed in such a way that people play starring roles. Each table memorializes someone famous, particularly classical composers and artists. Classical music plays softly in the dimly lit background. Weird stuff happens like tables moving as you eat and toilet paper coming by way of a mermaid in the 'under-the-sea' bathroom. Nothing matches, and Goody likes her guests as eclectic as the décor. The place has a cult-like fan following which is a good thing because there's no sign out front. You have to locate it by the address alone.

    Rimsky-Korsakoffee House, 707 SE 12th Ave, Portland, OR 97214; ↘ 503 232 2640

Rooms with a Skew

Finally – you can sleep and drink beer at school. The **Kennedy School Hotel** turned the classrooms into guestrooms, the cafeteria into a pub and the auditorium into a movie theater. Artwork spans the hallways, illustrating the school's history. The gymnasium still has a basketball court for guest use and the guestrooms still have blackboards and cloakrooms. The Kennedy School is a delightful example of successful historical-building preservation.

    Kennedy School Hotel, 5736 NE 33rd Ave, Portland OR 97211; ↘ 503 249 3983; web: www.mcmenamins.com

For Michael Garnier, taking the path less traveled led him to the treetops. A counter-culture, 60s' hippie, Michael saw an oak tree that just begged for a treehouse to grace its branches. Having failed in a previous attempt to open a conventional B&B, he built the treehouse and started renting it out, drawing the attention of county building officials who ordered him to tear it down. Not to be deterred, he proved that it was structurally sound by stuffing it with 66 people, two dogs, and a cat. Then, ignoring county officials completely, he started building more treehouses, dubbing his handiwork the **Out 'n' About Treesort**.

Guests loved the charming and comfortable, if quirky, quarters. But the county came back, this time ordering him to stop charging for the unique accommodations. Michael responded by letting guests stay for free as long as they bought a 'treeshirt' for $75–125. Officials weren't at all amused and a contentious eight-year legal battle ensued. Eventually Michael prevailed and the Treesort finally became 'legal' in 2001. Today it boasts a dozen different treehouses, each with a distinct personality and each easily, if unconventionally, accessible.

The Swiss Family Complex features a parent's unit with the separate children's unit connected by a swinging bridge. Then there's a two-story treehouse, another one reached by a spiral stairway in one tree connected by a platform to another stairway in yet another tree, and one reachable by ladder and suspension bridge. The communal bathrooms are ground level but you can always use the chamber pot if you don't feel like climbing down during the night. Pack light!

Out 'n' About Treesort, 300 Page Creek Rd, Takilma, OR 97523; ↘ 541 592 2208; web: www.treehouses.com

At the **Sylvia Beach Hotel** in Nye Beach, all the rooms are decorated in a literary theme. The Edgar Allen Poe room has a pendulum over the bed as well as a stuffed raven. Dr Seuss has a trundle bed, a drafting table, hats, fish, colorful murals and Seuss memorabilia. The Mark Twain room is full of quotes and woodsy ambiance; The Hemingway has a twig bed set in a fishing and hunting theme. The Inn is designed so guests can easily congregate and converse. Even the dining-room follows that premise, serving all meals family-style at a communal table.

Sylvia Beach Hotel, 267 NW Cliff, Newport, OR 97365; ↘ 541 265 5428; web: www.sylviabeachhotel.com

MONTANA
Festivals and events
The annual **Iron Horse Rodeo** in Red Lodge brings motorcyclists together for a weekend of competition. In the slow race, contestants have to go as slow as possible and are disqualified if their feet touch the ground; the last one to the finish line wins. Next, the front tire of the cycle has to push a keg as fast as possible to the finish. Finally, riders are tested by throwing a water balloon over a bar ahead of themselves, then catching it, unbroken, on the other side. They also have to gather unbroken eggs while riding the bike; ride over a teeter-totter and return with their feet still on the pegs; and run the course again, this time backwards, replacing the unbroken eggs. Points and time determine the winner.

Iron Horse Rodeo, held annually in July. Contact Red Lodge Area Chamber of Commerce, 601 North Broadway, Red Lodge, MT 59068; ↘ 888 281 0625 or 406 446 1718; web: www.redlodge.com/beartoothrally/

Sofas, chairs and bathtubs take to the slopes at Big Mountain Resort's annual **Furniture Races** in Whitefish. All manner of furniture (very loosely defined) is firmly attached to skis, towed to the top of the slope, and then raced full-throttle down to the bottom. Competitors are judged on speed, ability to stop reasonably close to the finish line and on style. Winner gets a new piece of furniture.

> **Furniture Races**, held annually in April in Whitefish, MT. Contact Big Mountain Ski and Summer Resort, PO Box 1400, Whitefish, MT 59937; ↘ 800 858 3930 or 406 862 2900; web: www.bigmtn.com

At the Red Lodge Winter Carnival, the highlight of the weekend is the **Cardboard Classic** when costumed racers slip and slide down the hill in their corrugated craft made only from cardboard, glue and duct tape. The same festival features firemen in full gear racing down the hill with a 50-foot section of fire hose.

> **Cardboard Classic**, held annually in March at the Red Lodge Winter Carnival. Contact Red Lodge Area Chamber of Commerce, 601 North Broadway, Red Lodge, MT 59068; ↘ 888 281 0625 or 406 446 2610; web: www.redlodge.com/carnival/

You need to know only one word to describe Montana's favorite festivals: balls. As in testicles. As in **Testicle Festivals**. Half a dozen communities pay tribute to the business parts of the bull by marinating them in beer, breading them, then frying them in hot oil. The result resembles breaded tenderloin even though technically they're breaded 'tendergroin'. Many places in the world consider testicles a delicacy, so consuming them with copious amounts of beer isn't all that strange. It's only when some partygoers start painting their own with fluorescent paints that it gets weird.

> **Clinton Testicle Festival**, held annually in September. Contact Rock Creek Lodge, Clinton, MT 59825; ↘ 406 825 4868; web: www.testyfesty.com

> **Mission Mountain Testicle Festival**, held annually in June. Located 50 miles from Missoula, MT. Contact Branding Iron Bar and Grill, Charlo, MT 59824; ↘ 406 644 9493

> **Ryegate Testicle Festival**, held annually in June in Ryegate, MT; ↘ 406 568 2330

> **York Bar's Go-Nuts Testicle Festival**, held annually in May in York, MT; ↘ 406 475 9949

Reed Point's only paved road is the site for the annual **Running of the Sheep**. This don't-blink-or-you'll-miss-it burg is outnumbered ten-to-one when hundreds of sheep are herded through the six-block town. The event brings in thousands of visitors to watch the parade and the 'Smelliest Sheepherder' and 'Miss Sheep Drive' competitions. There's no danger of being gored by a sheep. They don't even run; in fact, if you try to join them, the whole flock will probably stop dead in their tracks.

Running of the Sheep, held annually on Labor Day weekend (early September). Contact Reed Point Community Club, PO Box 402, Reed Point, MT 59069; ↘ 406 326 2325. Main St in Reed Point, Exit 392 from I-90.

Several hundred race enthusiasts cheer for their porker to bring home the bacon at the **pig races**, sponsored by Bear Creek Saloon, the only bar left in Bear Creek since the other one closed in 1980. The pigs, enthusiastic participants, race around an oval track every Thursday–Sunday, Memorial Day (end of May) through Labor Day (beginning of September). The races begin at 7pm and continue for several hours, with two dozen highly competitive piggies racing in about a dozen heats. All betting proceeds go to fund local scholarships.

Bear Creek Saloon & Steakhouse Pig Races. Contact Bear Creek Saloon, 108 Main St, Bear Creek, MT; ↘ 406 446 3481; web: www.redlodge.com/bearcreek

WYOMING
Museums and collections
There's a place behind bars for you at the **Wyoming Frontier Prison Old West Museum** in Rawlins where the tour guides demonstrate quite a sense of humor. For example, during pitch-black night tours, one guide tells of prison suicides while another drops a surprise into your group. You can try out the gas chamber, going so far as to be strapped in and having the door shut. This is reality tourism at its best. They also sponsor a Cowboy Poets' Gathering in July, special Halloween Night tours in October and Christmas in the Big House in December.

Wyoming Frontier Prison Old West Museum, 500 Walnut St, Rawlins, WY 82301; ↘ 307 778 7290 or 307 324 4422

At the **Grand Encampment Museum Complex** in Encampment, you'll come to understand the practicality of having a two-story outhouse; that is, one for summer (below) and one for winter (above). Before the advent of indoor plumbing, folks had to use outhouses and keeping the path to the potty cleared of snow in the winter was an added aggravation. Two-story outhouses solved the problem. The museum also has a folding bathtub from 1895 and a square grand piano.

Grand Encampment Museum Complex, 807 Barnett Ave, Encampment, WY 82325; ↘ 307 327 5308 or ↘ 307 327 5558; web: www.encampment.1wyo.net/GEMuseum.html

The **Carbon County Museum** in Rawlins certainly has one of this country's most grotesque items of memorabilia: a pair of shoes made from the skin of an executed killer. This bizarre artifact was the product of an inept train robber in the 1880s by the name of Big Nose George. George's nose was so big that there wasn't any point in wearing a mask; he was easily identified and subsequently captured, mask or no mask. After several failed attempts at escaping from jail, he was finally

Quirk Alert

Cosimo Cavallaro (web: www.cosimocavallaro.com) is an artist fixated on cheese. In 2001 he put the tiny town of **Powell, WY** (pop 5,500) on the map by covering a vacant, soon-to-be-demolished house – inside and out – with melted pepperjack cheese. The artist first melted down 10,000lb of cheese that had been softened in barrels of heated water, then pumped the warmed cheese through a hose, spurting into the house. He covered the entire interior, including the furniture and drapes, finishing up by cheesing the entire exterior. The chamber of commerce thought the whole event quite entertaining and threw a parade in the artist's honor. The neighbors weren't nearly so enamoured of the event. In the past Cosima had 'cheesed' a NYC hotel room as well as covering the model Twiggy with canned cheese substitute.

hanged and pronounced dead by a Dr John Osborn. Inexplicably, the doctor then cut off the top of the bandit's skull, made a death mask of his face from plaster of Paris, and removed skin from George's thigh and chest before sealing his remains in a whiskey barrel. (The deceased's nose was too big to allow the lid of a coffin to close.) Osborn then made a pair of shoes from the dead man's skin that he wore quite proudly in public. The good doctor went on to be elected Governor of Wyoming and served as Secretary of State under President Wilson. It's hard to decide which is freakier: the shoes themselves or the obvious lack of judgement on the part of the voters. You can see the gruesome tale unfold at the museum.

Carbon County Museum, 904 West Walnut St, Rawlins, WY 82301;
✆ 307 328 2740; web: www.wyshs.org/mus-carboncty.htm

Attractions

Businessmen by day, cowboys by night, the **Cheyenne Gunslingers** are the goodwill ambassadors of Cheyenne. Neither reenactment nor stunt group, this band of volunteers perform their mock gunfights and Western skits during the summer months in Gunslinger Square as well as putting on shows throughout the year for charity and non-profit groups. Their skits are funny, corny and usually involve an attempted hanging of someone for the crime of wearing 'non-Cheyenne' clothes. Try not to show up in shorts with black socks.

Cheyenne Gunslingers, PO Box 1916, Cheyenne, WY 82003; web: www.cheyennegunslingers.org. *Season runs from the first Saturday in June through July.*

Just plain weird

Standing lonely and forlorn on an 8,000-foot-high plateau near Laramie, the **Ames Brothers Pyramid** is a seven-story monument to two men's egos. Built in 1882 on the highest point along the route of the Union Pacific Railroad, the pyramid looked down on the tracks and the town that the Ames brothers had bribed Congress to finance. When the tracks and the town were abandoned, so were the brothers, whose giant-size portraits, carved into the stone, are admired by no-one and look out upon nothing.

Ames Brothers Pyramid, Laramie, WY. Located east of Laramie on I-80.

Western Region

SAN FRANCISCO
Festivals and events

It's the wildest, largest, and one of the oldest footraces in the world. The **Bay to Breakers Race** draws 75,000 to 110,000 participants ranging from casual joggers and costumed partygoers to elite runners and centipedes (groups of 13 people tethered together). While the world-class runners compete for cash prizes, the world-class party joggers vie for costume recognition. One group, calling themselves the Spawning Salmon, runs upstream against the dense waves of rushing humanity. Live bands entertain the runners and fans along the seven-and-a-half-mile route. The elite runners lead the pack followed by serious, then not-so-serious joggers. The Back of the Pack is a special section for walkers and baby strollers. You'll see a lot of political statements among the costumed runners, as well as a few expressing themselves by wearing nothing at all. From there the party moves to the **Footstock Festival** at the Polo Field in Golden Gate Park. Don't even think about driving in the city on Bay to Breakers Sunday. Special public transportation is scheduled to handle the hoards.

> **San Francisco Bay to Breakers Race**, held annually in May in San Francisco, CA. Contact Bay to Breakers at ↘ 415 808 5000; web: www.baytobreakers.com

> **Footstock Festival**, immediately follows the Bay to Breakers Race at the Polo Field in Golden Gate Park in San Francisco, CA. web: www.baytobreakers.com

The largest benefit treasure hunt in the country, the **Chinese New Year's Treasure Hunt** sends a sell-out crowd (1,800 strong) through the streets of San Francisco pursuing clues that often take them right through the tumult of the New Year's festivities. The parade and hunt, while not affiliated events, take place around the same time and place, adding to the drama of this rigorous game of urban exploration. Teams of up to nine players get a map with clues; it takes about four hours to complete the adventure. You don't need to know San Francisco geography to play since most of the clues relate to popular culture, current events, and the kind of general knowledge you haven't dredged up since college.

> **Chinese New Year's Treasure Hunt** takes place late January/early February. ↘ 415 564 9400; web: www.Sftreasurehunts.com

Howard Street becomes 'How Weird Street' during the **How Weird Street Faire**. This annual gathering of self-expressionists turns the district into a carnival of quirkiness featuring performance art, music, dancing, shopping (the Bizarre

21

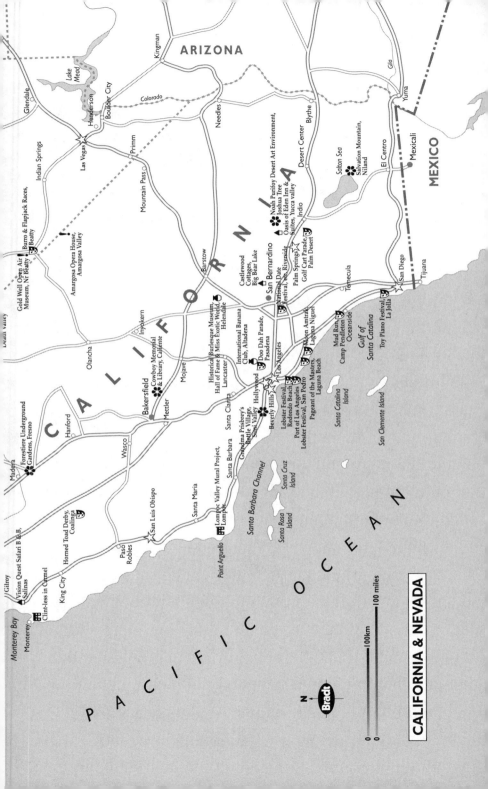

ECCENTRIC CALENDAR
NORTHERN CALIFORNIA

January/February	**Chinese New Year's Treasure Hunt**, San Francisco (page 21)
April	**How Weird Street Faire**, San Francisco (page 21)
April 1	**St Stupid's Day Parade**, San Francisco. Always held at noon (page 26)
May	**Calaveras County Fair and Jumping Frog Jubilee**, Calaveras County. Held on the third weekend of the month (page 32)
	Horned Toad Derby, Coalinga (page 32)
	Footstock Festival, San Francisco. Event follows the San Francisco Bay to Breakers Race (page 21)
	Kinetic Sculpture Race, Ferndale. Normally held on Memorial Day weekend (page 31)
	San Francisco Bay to Breakers Race, San Francisco (page 21)
June	**Haight-Ashbury Street Fair**, San Francisco (page 26)
July 4	**Kenwood World Pillow Fighting Championship**, Kenwood (page 31)
September	**How Berkeley Can You Be? Parade and Festival**, Berkeley (page 32)
	Poison Oak Show, Columbia (page 33)
October	**Exotic Erotic Halloween Ball**, San Francisco (page 24)

SOUTHERN CALIFORNIA

February	**National Date Festival and The Blessing of the Dates**, Riverside County (page 40)
June	**Mud Run**, Camp Pendleton (page 39)
July	**Moon Amtrak**, Laguna Niguel. Mooning takes place annually the second Saturday in July (page 38)
July/August	**Pageant of Masters**, Laguna Beach (page 38)
August	**Toy Piano Festival**, La Jolla (page 39)
September	**Lobster Festival**, Redondo Beach (page 40)
	Port of Los Angeles Lobster Festival, San Pedro (page 40)
October	**Underwater Pumpkin Carving Contest**, San Diego (page 41)
November	**Doo Dah Parade**, Pasadena (page 39)
	Palm Desert Golf Cart Parade, Palm Desert (page 39)

Bazaar), and a peculiar assortment of costumes, some limited to just full body make-up.

How Weird Street Faire usually held in April; web: www.howweird.org

Halloween is an especially revered time in San Francisco when the city moves from weird, which is the norm, to the positively insane. People of all persuasions descend on the Castro, dressed in unimaginably creative and outlandish costumes.

NEVADA

January	**Elvis Impersonator Contest and Fan Convention**, Las Vegas (page 54)
	National Cowboy Poetry Gathering, Elko (page 63)
June	**Black Rock Desert Self-Invitational Golf Tournament**, Black Rock Desert. Normally held around the Summer Solstice (June 21) (page 62)
August	**Festival in the Pit**, Battle Mountain (page 64)
August/September	**Burning Man Festival**, Black Rock Desert. Held on Labor Day weekend (page 62)
September	**Camel Races**, Virginia City (page 63)
October	**Beatty Burro and Flapjack Races**, Beatty (page 63)
	Fetish & Fantasy Ball, Las Vegas (page 54)
	Kit Carson Trail Ghost Walk, Carson City (page 63)

ARIZONA

January	**Bed Races**, Oatman. Held the second Sunday in January (page 66)
February/March	**Renaissance Fair**, Apache Junction. Held every weekend in February and March (page 72)
March	**Chandler Ostrich Festival**, Chandler (page 68)
April	**Great Cardboard Boat Regatta**, Tempe (page 68)
July 4	**Egg Fry**, Oatman. Part of annual July Fourth celebration (page 66)
September/ October	**Cow Pasture Golf**, held at Bar Flying V Ranch east of Springerville (page 68)

UTAH

April	**Festival Royale of Himmeisk**, Cedar City (page 75)

An average of 300,000 people turn out for this major San Francisco holiday. Originally the predominantly gay Castro district was the hub of activities, but the celebration became too large to fit into the district. With the crowds now spread out between the Castro and the Mission district, it's easier to see and appreciate the artistry that's gone into the costumes. Food booths line the streets alongside face painting and henna tattooing stations for those who show up sans costume. The city has come a long way from the time in 1961 when a person could be arrested for impersonating the opposite sex. Halloween is October 31.

It's famous, it's wild and it's wicked – it's the **Exotic Erotic Halloween Ball**, one of the most uninhibited celebrations of erotica on the planet. Originally an underground, bizarre-erotica gathering, the ball has gone more mainstream, if you can call the world's largest and sexiest masquerade party mainstream. Fifteen thousand people attend and many spend all year planning their costumes – or lack of them. As sexy as burlesque, as loud as a rave, the ball is every bit as carnal as carnival. Celebrities like Nicholas Cage, Joe Montana, Madonna and Dennis Rodman lend their panache, although the event hardly needs celebrities to achieve notoriety. With $10,000 in prizes for the winners of the Mr and Miss Exotic Erotic and other costume contests, there's no shortage of shocking, electrifying creativity. Adults only!

> **Exotic Erotic Halloween Ball**, held annually in October in San Francisco, CA. Contact the Exotic Erotic Ball ❱ 888 EXOTIC 6 or 415 THE BALL; web: www.exoticeroticball.com

One hundred thousand folks descend on Haight Street during the annual **Haight-Ashbury Street Fair**. The fair aims to relive the district's famed 1960s' heydays with a laidback, do-your-own-thing kind of feel. For a tour of the Haight at other times, see the Flower Power tour listing below.

> **Haight-Ashbury Street Fair**, held annually in June on Haight St between Stanyan St and Masonic Ave. Contact the Haight Ashbury Street Fair, 1621 Haight St, PMB #134, San Francisco, CA 94117; ❱ 415 863 3489; web: www.haightstreetfair.org

Dress in costume and bring noise makers, confetti and socks to be part of the April Fool's Day **St Stupid's Day Parade**, put on by the First Church of the Last Laugh. The parade, pure political satire that also mocks the religion of business, has been marching through San Francisco's financial district since 1979, stopping to stage mini-events in front of public and corporate buildings. (For example, the Pacific Stock Exchange is the setting for the sock exchange.) Workers lean out their windows to watch as marchers pass by chanting 'No more chanting!', and covering up the private parts of statues along the way.

> **St Stupid's Day Parade**, always held at noon on April Fool's Day (April 1) in San Francisco, CA. Contact First Church of the Last Laugh; web: www.saintstupid.com/parade.htm

Museums and collections

Charles Schultz of *Peanuts* fame helped found the **Cartoon Art Museum** that explores how comics influence politics and pop culture. Displays going back to the 1730s celebrate the history and art of satirical cartooning.

> **Cartoon Art Museum**, 655 Mission St, San Francisco, CA 94103; ❱ 415 CARTOON; web: www.cartoonart.org. *Open Tue–Sun 11.00am–5.00pm.*

Attractions

The **Wax Museum at Fisherman's Wharf** is a dynamic, state-of-the-art facility with 280 figures in settings so realistic you almost feel like you're intruding. Murals, music and sound effects add to the eerie reality, as does the drama of the settings themselves. Dictators stand together amid rubble; Hitler shares a war room with Mussolini and Tojo; and Eisenhower and MacArthur stand among sand bags and a World War II jeep in front of an elaborate mural. Bill Gates looks suitably nerdy next to distinguished scientists Freud and Newton. The Last Supper scene is fully narrated, while a Van Gogh painting is rendered in a 3D wax display.

> **Wax Museum** at Fisherman's Wharf, 145 Jefferson St, San Francisco, CA 94133; ☎ 800 439 4305 or 415 202 0400; web: www.waxmuseum.com. *Open daily 10.00am–9.00pm.*

Tours

It would be difficult to find a tour of San Francisco that didn't touch on the weird or wacky. The corner of Castro and Market streets is known as the gayest four corners on Earth. That's where you meet Trevor Hailey for her **Cruisin' the Castro Tour**, a walking tour of the Castro from a highly entertaining and historical point of view. Trevor radiates with personality as she puts the gay and lesbian experience – and the city itself – in sociological and psychological perspective. By the time your tour is over, you'll have a much better understanding of the chain of events that allowed California, San Francisco and the Castro district to become such Meccas of tolerance. The tour includes a lovely lunch so you have plenty of time to ask questions and discuss current issues.

> **Cruisin' the Castro Tour**, leaves from Harvey Milk Plaza, Castro & Market Sts; ☎ 415 550 8110; web: www.webcastro.com/castrotour. *Tours available Tue–Sat.*

Meet the ghosts who call San Francisco home with Jim Fassbinder, a genuine member of the International Ghost Hunters' Society and the Institute for Paranormal Research. Jim leads quite a convincing tour around elegant Pacific Heights on his **San Francisco Ghost Hunt Walking Tour**. Dressed in a black cape and top hat, his passion for his subject is obvious. 'The spirits tell us if they're willing to have visitors today,' he says. He does his part by building a profile of each ghost and setting the mood. You do yours by getting into the spirit of the hunt. By the time you've heard the stories and seen the haunts of half a dozen ghosts, you may become a believer yourself, especially when you see the spot where a key jumps mysteriously in the palm of your hand.

> **San Francisco Ghost Hunt Walking Tour** departs every Mon, Wed, Fri, Sat and Sun at 8.00pm, year round, rain or starshine from Queen Anne Hotel, 1590 Sutter, San Francisco, CA; ☎ 415 922 5590; web: www.sfghosthunt.com

City Guides Neighborhood Walks offers dozens of free walking tours given by individuals with a specific expertise and a passion to share it with visitors. Cityscapes and Public Places is a good one if you want to understand political correctness. Other offerings include the Earthquake and Fire Walk, Literary North Beach, and Sacred Places, Brothels, Boardinghouses and Bawds, a two-block stroll that looks at the 'shady' profession and the contribution it made to the city's growth.

City Guides Neighborhood Walks, depart daily from various locations around San Francisco. Contact City Guides, c/o San Francisco Public Library, Main Library, 100 Larkin St, San Francisco, CA 94102; ☎ 415 557 4266; web: www.sfcityguides.org

Walking tours of the Mission District Murals are offered by **Precita Eyes Mural Arts Center.** With urban graffiti a problem in all big cities, this is a unique way to decriminalize it while at the same time preserving the Mission's culture.

Precita Eyes Mural Arts Center, 348 Precita Ave, San Francisco, CA 94110; ☎ 415 285 7311; web: www.precitaeyes.org

Explore the tie-dyed cradle of hippie culture with a guide who was part of it all at the **Flower Power Haight-Ashbury Walking Tour.** The Haight was at the heart of the 1960s' counter-culture movement, the center of the Summer of Love and Be-Ins, and home to music greats like Jimi Hendrix, Janis Joplin and Jerry Garcia. One resident, Manny the Hippie, used to appear regularly on David Letterman's late-night talk show, teaching America how to talk hippie. You'll see the Grateful Dead house and the stairs where they posed for the famous poster, call in at the house where kidnapped Patty Hearst was held hostage and learn how a dense mass of confused humanity managed to get along sleeping in vans and sharing way too few bathrooms.

Flower Power Haight-Ashbury Walking Tour, PO Box 170106, San Francisco, CA 94177; ☎ 415 863 1621; web: www.hippygourmet.com/haighttour.html

It's a big, red, shiny Mack fire engine and you get to ride on it, bells clanging, from the waterfront, across the Golden Gate Bridge to Sausalito and back again on a campy tour called **San Francisco Fire Engine Tours and Adventures.** Owners Robert and Marilyn Katzman dress you in fireman coats, pile on the blankets and charge off to dramatic vista points around the bridge as well as on it. The tour in their 1955 open-air truck is hardly low key as Marilyn quickly has you singing silly ditties while people on the streets gawk in amazement. As you pass under the south tower of the bridge Marilyn explains how she managed to tap dance on *top* of it. She regales you with stories and little-known fire-fighting facts. Did you know, for instance, that in the old days, before city fire departments, volunteer brigades were paid by the fire and there was lots of competition among them to get to a fire first and claim the rewards? When more than one unit arrived at the scene, there was considerable fighting – not of the fire, but between units. The fire engine also tours North Beach, Chinatown and Pacific Heights. The Katzmans live in a real, restored firehouse bought from the city when modern fire trucks became too large to fit through the doors. They even have a Dalmatian and a real pole to slide down from the upper floors.

San Francisco Fire Engine Tours and Adventures. Tours depart from The Cannery at Fisherman's Wharf; ☎ 415 333 7077; daily except Tuesdays; web: www.fireenginetours.com

It's all about romance and lust, animal style, at the **San Francisco Zoo Valentine's Day Sex Tours**. The tram tour, hosted by a zoo guide who explains novel ways to love your lover, takes you from the birds and the bees to animals that may – or may not – cooperate by demonstrating their amorous techniques. The tour ends with truffles and champagne.

> **San Francisco Zoo Valentine's Day Sex Tours** held annually in February in San Francisco, CA. Contact San Francisco Zoo, 1 Zoo Rd, San Francisco, CA 94132; ☎ 415 753 7080; web: www.sfzoo.org

'Where's the F'ing Beach in North Beach' is just one of ten comedy tours of San Francisco led by the accomplished comedians of **Foot! Tours**, working professionals who delight in making you laugh while you learn. One tour, 'Nude, Lewd, and Crude' covers the rise of strippers, comics, and beats in North Beach; another, 'Instant City – Just Add Gold', deals with the glitter, greed, and growth of San Francisco. Founder Robert Mac describes his company as a combination 'comedian-guided, game-show, historical walking tour'. You'll hear all kinds of offbeat stories while playing along in a walking game-show that involves misfortune cookies and valuable imaginary prizes. It's a highly entertaining way to learn about this most eccentric of cities from some of its more eccentric inhabitants.

> **Foot! Tours**, ☎ 415-793-JEST; web: www.foottours.com

Sister Carmen Barsody and Reverend Kay Jorgensen lead a most unusual 'tour', scheduling day-long retreats on the streets of San Francisco's homeless neighborhoods. Part of the Faithful Fools Ministry, these **Street Retreats** challenge you to face your fears and shatter your notions about those living in poverty.

> **Street Retreats**, ☎ 415 474 0508; web: www.faithfulfools.org/projretreat.htm

Just plain weird

You expect to find furniture *in* a building, not *on* it. But at an abandoned tenement at Sixth and Howard streets, artist Brian Groggin launched a project he called **Defenestration**, defined as the act of throwing a person or thing out of a window. Twenty-three pieces of seemingly animate furniture hang out the windows and run down the sides of the four-story building, looking, perhaps, for freedom or maybe a chance to dance with the appliances for sale across the street. Tables, chairs, lamps, grandfather clocks, a refrigerator and couches hug the walls, their legs seeming to grasp the surface. The furniture, like the

Quirk Alert

EMPEROR OF SAN FRANCISCO

San Francisco is a fertile breeding ground for eccentrics. One of its most famous was **Emperor Norton**, a flamboyant businessman who proclaimed himself Emperor of the United States in 1859 after he lost all his money. Immensely popular, people greeted him with a bow or a curtsy and saw to it that the penniless eccentric had a decent place to live and never went hungry. He ate free of charge wherever he pleased and the city made him a new uniform when his became too tattered. Three seats were reserved for him at public performances: one for the emperor and two for his well-behaved canine companions. Dressed in naval regalia, he attended every public function and made daily rounds of his domain, making sure that order and harmony were maintained. He would anoint do-gooders with titles like 'Queen for a day', resulting in people following him around and hoping for a chance to help an old lady across the street while in his presence. Norton even printed his own currency which was accepted everywhere in the city without question. If he needed money, he'd levy a 'tax' for a dollar or two. When he died in 1880, tens of thousands attended his funeral. He's buried at Woodlawn Cemetery in Colma, San Francisco's adjacent cemetery town.

neighborhood, is cast off and appreciation deprived. Brian rescued the pieces, 're-animating' them for their new role. For the installation itself, Brian held an Urban Circus with artists, performers and musicians, many dressed as clowns, putting on freak shows and vaudeville-style acts. Participants included members of the Church of the Subgenius, the Cacophony Society, Circus Redickuless, First Church of the Last laugh and the Sisters of Perpetual Indulgence. The property was donated by the owners who have the building up for sale – with or without the furniture.

> **Defenestration**, 214 Sixth St at Howard, San Francisco, CA; web: www.defenestration.org and www.metaphorm.org

If you're going to take in just one show while in San Francisco, make sure it's **Beach Blanket Babylon**. This fast-paced, satirical musical review, famous for its ludicrous headdresses and zany characters, has been playing to sell-out crowds for 24 years. It's the quintessential San Francisco experience: irreverent, topical, and joyously funny. The review follows Snow White around the world as she looks for love in all the wrong places. Animate and inanimate objects cavort in the most riotous ways and pop culture, religion, sex and politics are all targets for sarcastic songs. The costumes are extraordinary and the foot-stomping finale always brings down the house.

> **Beach Blanket Babylon**, Babylon Blvd, Green St, San Francisco, CA; ☎ 415 421 4222; web: www.beachblanketbabylon.com

Rooms with a Skew

'Peace Through Tourism' is the motto at the **Red Vic Bed and Breakfast & Art** where you can live like a hippie if you wish. Originally a 'country resort', San

Francisco's Red Vic still reflects California quirkiness. Located in the heart of the Haight district, famous as the hippie capital of the 1960s, this hotel has seen it all, from the peace movement to the ecology movement to the movement for social justice. True to its heritage, it has a meditation room, motivational videos, meditative art and visual poetry. Its theme rooms have names like Summer of Love and Flower Child; one of the bathrooms has an aquarium – the fish swim in the pull-chain toilet's tank. Owner Sami Sunchild likes to think of the place as an alternative to corporate tourism (which it certainly is!), pointing out the conversations that take place around the breakfast table and the international friendships in the making.

Red Vic Bed and Breakfast, 1665 Haight St, San Francisco, CA 94117; ➘ 415 864 1978; web: www.redvic.com

NORTHERN CALIFORNIA
Festivals and events

The **World Championship Kinetic Sculpture Race** covers a 38-mile course stretching from Ferndale to Arcata, drawing the winning participants from various other kinetic sculpture races held around the country. A kinetic sculpture is an imaginative, often wacky – but always ludicrous – contraption designed to travel along an obstacle course on land, through mud, and over deep harbor waters. These machines can be simple crafts piloted by a single person, or they can be quite complex, well-engineered vehicles powered by a team of pilots. Used bicycles, gears and machine scraps usually play a big role in their construction, as do a lunatic sense of humor and a wildly inventive brain. The 36-year-old race has in the past been nominated for a Nobel Peace Prize for recognizing unsung genius, promoting non-polluting transport and lifting the spirit of the communities that hold the race. Past entries have included a six-man dinosaur, an eight-man iguana, a family of ducks and a flying saucer. The **Ferndale Kinetic Sculpture Museum** showcases sculptures from previous races.

There are a number of quirky race rules. The personal security rule requires that each sculpture carry a comforting item of psychological luxury, namely a homemade sock creature made from a not-too-recently washed sock. Another stipulates that each vehicle must be human powered, with no pulling, pushing or paddling allowed, although the natural power of water, wind, sun and gravity can be used. The sculptures must also fit on public roads and follow the rules of the open road. Mom's high-anxiety clause dictates a quick-exit strategy. The honk-and-pass politeness rule requires yielding the right of way to another sculpture that wants to pass. A one-finger salute is encouraged. Time penalties are incurred for rule infractions, while time bonuses are given for carrying a passenger, called a barnacle, along the entire course. The Mediocre Award is given for finishing exactly in the middle. The Next to Last Award is highly coveted, making the end of the race particularly exciting. Awards are also given for best costume, the most memorable breakdown and the most interesting water entry. The winner of the Speed Award gets to be addressed as 'Most Visionary Professor'.

Kinetic Sculpture Race, held annually in May, usually Memorial Day weekend. Contact Ferndale Arts and Cultural Center (also the Ferndale Kinetic Sculpture Museum), 580 Main Street, Ferndale, CA 95536; ➘ 707 834 0529 web: www.kineticsculpturerace.org

Remember those pillow fights you had as a kid? And how much fun it was to play in the mud? Well, you can do both at the same time at the annual **World Pillow**

Fighting Championships, now in its 35th year. Anyone over the age of 14 can enter as long as they leave their maturity outside the arena. Competition begins by straddling a slippery wet pole suspended over a pit of mud. Holding a wet feather pillow in one hand, you slither along the pole to the starting position, an achievement in itself. During combat your hands can't touch the pole and you can't use your feet to unseat your opponent. Your only weapon is the pillow that can be swung using one or both hands. The first contestant to topple his opponent into the mud wins the fall; two out of three falls wins the bout. You have to swing at least every 30 seconds. If a minute passes without anyone falling, the bout continues with one hand behind your back. After yet another minute without a fall, fighting continues holding the pillow with both hands. As long as you're prepared to fall down, get muddy and be laughed at, you're qualified to enter. Sign in to play no later than 9.00am.

> **Kenwood World Pillow Fighting Championship**, held annually on July 4 in Sonoma County between Santa Rosa and Sonoma, 60 miles north of the Golden Gate Bridge, off Hwy 12, 14 miles from Santa Rosa. The fair is in Plaza Park on Warm Springs Rd, two blocks from the highway; ↘ 707 833 2440; web: www.kenwoodpillowfights.com.

Two thousand frogs get involved in the **Calaveras County Fair and Jumping Frog Jubilee**. There's a lot at stake here as frog jockeys compete for some serious money: $5,000 if the frog breaks a world record, $1,000 if it equals the record and $500 if it just wins without setting any record. The winning jumper in 1928, the first year the Jubilee was held, bounded just three-and-a-half feet. The world record holder today is Rosie the Ribiter who went 21 feet, 5.75 inches. That's the equivalent of a human jumping the length of a football field.

> **Calaveras County Fair and Jumping Frog Jubilee**, held annually the third weekend in May in Calaveras County, CA. Contact Frogtown, PO Box 489, Angels Camp, CA 95222; ↘ 209 736 2580; web: www.frogtown.org

If you didn't get enough in Calaveras, the annual **Horned Toad Derby** in Coalinga pits 'Toadtanic' and 'Toadquila' against their challengers while firemen compete in human water-fights. The toads are captured in the Coalinga Hills with permits since they're a protected species. Very PC, very California.

> **Horned Toad Derby** held annually in May in Coalinga, CA. Contact Coalinga Chamber, 380 Coalinga Plaza, Coalinga, CA 93210; ↘ 800 854 3885 or 559 935 2948; web: www.coalingachamber.com

Berkeley, often referred to as Berserkly, holds its own spoof version of the already irreverent Pasadena Doo-Dah Parade during the city's **How Berkeley Can You Be?** festival. The vibrant diversity of cultural, political, and ethnic groups that make up the town, home to the University of California, is a perfect breeding ground for this most eccentric of events. Seventy-five organizations show up to make fun of themselves or others. Past entrants included a café that catapulted giant meatballs on to a huge plate of spaghetti, pregnant mothers from Birthaways marching with synchronized contractions, a group called the Fashion Police and around 80 of the country's most delightfully daft art cars.

> **How Berkeley Can You Be?** Parade and Festival held annually in September in Berkeley, CA. Contact John at Café Venezia, ↘ 510 849 4688; web: www.howberkeleycanyoube.com

Ever so carefully is how the contestants in the annual **Poison Oak Show** compete for prizes in categories such as best arrangement, most potent-looking leaves, and best poison oak accessory or jewelry item. There's also a prize for the most original poison oak dish (recipe included) and for the best photo of a poison oak victim.

Poison Oak Show, held annually in September. For information send an SASE to PO Box 1897, Columbia, CA 95310; ↘ 209 533 4656; web: www.columbiagazette.com/poison.html

Eccentric environments

Baldasare Forestiere found an unconventional way to beat the central valley's heat. He moved underground, eventually living in the subterranean paradise he'd created. Using only hand tools on the native hardpan rock, he spent 40 years sculpting a network of tunnels, alcoves, caverns, grottos, and patios well below ground. Strategically placed skylights and airshafts provided the ideal conditions for growing the plants and trees that make **Forestiere Underground Gardens** such an accomplishment. The aquarium had a glass bottom through which to observe the tropical fish – from below. Today his daughter keeps her father's spirit alive as well as his gardens.

Forestiere Underground Gardens, 5021 W Shaw Ave, Fresno, CA 93722; ↘ 559 271 0734; web: www.undergroundgardens.com. *Open Sat–Sun with tours at noon and 2.00pm Sept–mid-May (closed Thanksgiving–Jan 1), Wed–Sun with tours at 10.00am, noon, and 2.00pm mid-May–Sept. Some evening tours available during this time.*

The evil spirits of those killed by her husband's famous Winchester rifle, dubbed the 'Gun that Won the West', tormented Sarah Winchester. When both her baby and her husband met untimely deaths, she consulted a medium who convinced her that continuous building would appease the evil spirits set on revenge. Fortunately she had the money, $20 million worth, to hire carpenters to build 24 hours a day, 365 days a year, until her death 38 years later. The **Winchester Mystery House** in San Jose is the bizarre result, with 160 rooms, staircases that lead nowhere, chimneys that end below the ceiling, doors that open into walls and a window built into the floor. The house 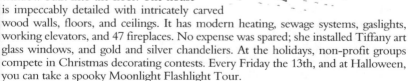 is impeccably detailed with intricately carved wood walls, floors, and ceilings. It has modern heating, sewage systems, gaslights, working elevators, and 47 fireplaces. No expense was spared; she installed Tiffany art glass windows, and gold and silver chandeliers. At the holidays, non-profit groups compete in Christmas decorating contests. Every Friday the 13th, and at Halloween, you can take a spooky Moonlight Flashlight Tour.

Winchester Mystery House, 525 South Winchester Blvd, San Jose, CA 95128; ↘ 408 247 2000; web: www.winchestermysteryhouse.com. *Open daily 9.00am–5.00pm Jan 1–Apr 24 and Oct 18–Dec 31, daily 9.00am–5.00pm (7pm weekends) Apr 25–Jun 12 and Sep 2–Oct 17, 9.00am–7.00pm Jun 13–Sep 1.*

Litto, the Pope Valley Hubcap King, collected more than 2,000 hubcaps over a 30-year period. He arranged them, decorated with bottles and pull tops, into various constructions at **Litto's Hubcap Ranch** in Pope Valley.

> **Litto's Hubcap Ranch**, 6654 Pope Valley Rd, 2.1 miles NW of Pope Valley, CA; web: www.janesaddictions.com/damonte01.htm or www.napavalley.org

Museums and collections

It's a small museum, but then you don't need a lot of space to display almost every Pez candy dispenser ever made, 550 in all. The **Burlingame Museum of Pez Memorabilia** represents more than a decade of collecting by Gary and Nancy Doss who readily admit their strange fixation has taken over their lives. Pez, the quirky plastic statues that spit candy from their necks, are beloved by young and old alike. The museum, along with their website, draws collectors from all over the world. A Make a Face model from the 1970s can fetch $4,500 if it's still in the box; a 1960 model with a working slide rule can cost $800. An interactive display tells you everything you'd ever want to know about Pez. Gary needs only half a dozen more containers to make his collection complete; unfortunately, those last six will set him back around $18,000.

> **Burlingame Museum of Pez Memorabilia**, 214 California Dr, Burlingame, CA 94010; ☎ 650 347 2301; web: www.spectrumnet.com/pez. *Open Tue–Sat 10.00am–6.00pm; Sat 10.00am–5.00pm. Closed major holidays. Free.*

Every year the best yo-yo players in the country end up at the **National Yo-Yo Museum** in Chico to compete for two national titles: the yo-yo single and the yo-yo double championships. New tricks are introduced every year to keep players on top of their game. The museum is home to the Duncan family collection as well as to the world's largest wooden yo-yo that was yo-yo-ed half a dozen times by a crane over San Francisco Bay. During the **annual championships** held the first Saturday in October, you'll likely meet Steve Brown whose claim to fame is being the most tattooed yo-yo spinmeister in the world.

> **National Yo-Yo Museum**, 320 Broadway, Chico, CA 95928; ☎ 530 893 0545; web: www.nationalyoyo.org
>
> **National Yo-Yo Championships**, held the first Saturday in October

A red car dangles from a tree; a cluster of arms reaches up from the grass; and a stack of filing cabinets 60-feet high pierces the meadow. These are all part of an non-intimidating-by-design art experience, the **di Rosa Preserve**, a 250-acre complex of almost 2,000 modern art pieces displayed in both indoor and outdoor settings. The collection is the passion of one man, Rene di Rosa, 84, who has been collecting art from emerging California artists for 40 years. Almost 750 artists are represented, their work chosen for no other reason than because di Rosa fell in love with it. Expressing an intense dislike for stuffy, pretentious art galleries, the work is displayed in a manner simply meant to be experienced and without explanatory signs of any kind. The preserve is di Rosa's legacy, a gift of art you needn't understand, just enjoy.

> **di Rosa Preserve**, 5200 Carneros Hwy, Napa, CA 94559; ☎ 707 226 5991; web: www.dirosapreserve.org

Attractions

Bonfante Gardens, a horticulturally-based theme park, is famous for its **circus trees**, often featured in the mid-1900s by Ripley's Believe It Or Not! The trees were created by Axel Erlandson who, motivated by divine inspiration, spent 40 years of his life shaping and grafting the bodies and arms of trees into complex coils and spirals. He formed them into fantastical shapes like arches, hearts, lightening bolts, basket weaves, and rings. After Axel's death in 1964, many of the trees – sycamores, ash, cork and box elders – died before preservation efforts could take hold. Eventually, 19 of them were bought by park owner Michael Bonfante, and then carefully transported 50 miles to the park. Bonfante, with its gentle rides and lush plant life, is geared towards families with young children as well as garden lovers.

> **Bonfante Gardens Family Theme Park**, 3050 Hecker Pass Hwy,
> Gilroy, CA 95020; ☎ 408 840 7100; web: www.bonfantegardens.com.
> *Hours vary seasonally.*

Quirkyville

The verbal equivalent of a secret handshake, Boontling is the language once spoken exclusively in **Boonville**, a tiny, isolated, gritty little town with a population of around 700. The 1,200-word language was widely spoken from the mid-1800s to the mid-1900s, but has slowly died out along with the 'codgy kimmies' (old men) who kept it alive. Fortunately, you can read about it when you stop for 'gorms' (food) or 'zeese' (coffee) in town.

> **Boonville**, California. Contact the Anderson Valley Chamber of
> Commerce, PO Box 275, Boonville, CA 95415; ☎ 707 895 2379; web:
> www.boont.com/chamber. Learn more about harpin' boontling, the local
> lingo of the Anderson Valley, at web: www.avbc.com/visit/boontling.html

Oh-so-environmentally-correct **Davis** takes its frogs very seriously, so seriously that it spent $14,000 to build a **Toad Tunnel** so the little darlings wouldn't get squished by traffic when their seasonal migration path was disrupted by a new roadway. The mayor, backed by legions of pro-frog advocates, prevailed upon the city to spend the money to install a 12-inch diameter metal tube under the new roadway so the creatures could continue to find the way to their promised land. Unfortunately the toads ignored their new tunnel because there's no longer any habitat awaiting them on the other side. Despite local efforts to entice them back with their own 'hotel' on the other side, they seem to have abandoned their old stompin' grounds, perhaps moving on to a community with less time on their hands.

> **Davis Toad Tunnel**. Directions: from I-80, exit Richards Blvd going east.
> From Richards/Cowell, turn left onto PoleLine/Lillard. Turn right onto
> Fifth St, then immediate right into the Post Office parking lot, where you
> can park when visiting the Tunnel.

You might think they take their fashion way too seriously in **Mill Valley** when you see the **Fashion Police** handing out tickets at parades and civic events for infractions such as 'failure to yield to good taste'. Patrolling on roller blades in chic bike shorts, the clothes cops are actually employees of a local clothing store. The bright yellow citations include fashion faux pas like 'did not listen to significant other', 'Inappropriate dress for body type', and 'bad banana khaki karma'. If you've been cited you can bring in your ticket for a discount. Most men consider it an honor to attract their attention, dressing even more appallingly than normal.

> **Fashion Police of Mill Valley**. Contact Famous for Our Look, 96 Throckmorton St, Mill Valley, CA 94941; ☎ 415 388 2550

Carmel is an incredibly picturesque village, famous for its past mayor, Clint Eastwood, and for its ordinance banning high-heeled shoes. The reason for the law is simple: the streets are cobblestone or brick, the many ancient trees have roots protruding in the walkways, and the city got tired of trip-and-fall lawsuits. Anyone spotted wearing the offending shoes will be reminded of the ordinance, but their credit card will still be accepted in the shops even if they are scofflaws. Clint Eastwood ran on a platform that he would allow ice-cream to be sold on the streets again.

> **Carmel**, CA. Contact Carmel California Visitor and Information Center, San Carlos between 5th and 6th, Carmel-by-the-Sea, CA 93921; ☎ 800 550 4333 or 831 624 2522; web: www.carmelcalifornia.org

Odd shopping

The **Lucky Mojo Curio Company** is one of the country's premier 'spiritual merchants', expert in the kind of products needed for hoodoo and voodoo rituals. They make spells, amulets and potions, things like 'court case bath and floor wash', body-part ritual candles, and penis-bone charms (mostly made from raccoons) for those wanting to influence their luck. The company's retail store is located at the rear of their manufacturing facility, nestled under a redwood tree. As odd a shop as you'll ever find, this is a fascinating place to see herbs, roots, oils, minerals, zoological curios and tools for magical spell-craft.

> **Lucky Mojo Curio Company**, 6632 Covey Rd, Forestville, CA 95436; ☎ 707 887 1521; web: www.luckymojo.com

Bones, books, and bugs clutter **The Bone Room**, an eccentric shop that draws skeleton lovers from all over the West to shop amid this huge collection of human and animal skulls, embalmed insects and, when available, accessories like antique caskets and insect jewelry. Mainly of interest to scientists, museums, artists, designers, doctors and photographers, the just plain curious are also welcome, often purchasing earrings made from mink penis bones or beetle wings as well as lucite bracelets with spiders and scorpions inside.

> **The Bone Room**, 1569 Solano, Berkeley, CA 94707; ☎ 510 526 5252; web: www.boneroom.com

Quirky cuisine

You could wear your gaudiest outfit and most frightening wig to **Ciao Bella!** and you'd blend right into the décor. This place is wild in both spirit and ambiance, which explains why people drive for hours just to hang out here. The wait staff, including Tad, the owner, takes dance breaks between courses, performing crazy numbers on a stage near the tables. Weird stuff, like cartoon and movie star cutouts, old 78 records, road signs and cross-dressed Barbie dolls, hangs from everywhere – the ceilings, the walls, the trees, even the shingles. It's a riot of color and a riotous experience.

> **Ciao Bella!** 9217 Hwy 9, Ben Lomond, CA 95005; ☎ 408 336 9921

Quirk Alert

Emily Duffy is creator of the **BraBall** (web: www.braball.com), almost 2,000lb worth of bras measuring five foot four inches in diameter, the height of the average woman. After hooking and rolling together 18,000 bras, she's hoping the resulting ball will draw attention to the fact that women are way too hung up on body image. She feels, given the choice, that most women would just as soon dispense with the things entirely. By holding a series of charity 'Roll-Ons' in support of breast cancer awareness, she was able to finish the ball in just three years with bras donated from all over the country. Emily drives around in her art car, the Vain Van, a vehicle covered with beauty products and messages about vanity and self-image. Often dressed to match her car, she drives her gentle, humorous message across the country, participating in various art car parades.

Rooms with a Skew

Three hundred exotic, endangered, and extinct-in-the-wild African mammals and birds are among the guests at **Safari West Wildlife Preserve and Tent Camp** near Santa Rosa. The tents are charming, African-style canvas with hardwood floors and en-suite bath located close – but not too close – to the animals. You can learn how to track animals, take a wildlife tour in a safari vehicle, or visit the walk-through aviary. The preserve is open to day visitors by reservation as well as to overnight guests.

Safari West Wildlife Preserve and Tent Camp, 3115 Porter Creek Rd, Santa Rosa, CA; ↘ 800 616 2695 or 707 579 2551; web: www.safariwest.com

Walk with the animals. Talk with the animals. Sleep (practically) with the animals at **Vision Quest Safari B&B.** Your accommodation is an African-style tent bungalow surrounded by big cats, elephants, ostriches, zebras, and monkeys. All these animals are superbly trained creatures, stars of television and movies working for Wild Things Animal Rentals. In the morning your breakfast might be delivered by an elephant or baboon (accompanied by a trainer, of course). This close encounter of the wild kind also offers several experiences to enhance your visit. The Pachyderm Package gives you two hours with the elephants – you bathe, walk, ride, socialize, and pose for pictures sitting on their trunks. Walk with the Animals is a four-hour, also hands-on adventure. If you can't stay the night they offer daily, drop-in public tours.

Vision Quest Safari B&B, 400 River Ranch Rd, Salinas, CA 93908; ↘ 800 228 7382 or 831 455 1901; web: www.wildthingsinc.com/html/b_b.html. *Expensive*.

The **Railroad Park Resort,** 50 miles north of Redding, has the Caboose Motel and a restaurant /lounge built inside antique railroad cars.

Railroad Park Resort, 100 Railroad Park Rd, Dunsmuir, CA 96025; ↘ 530 235 0420; web: www.rrpark.com

Castlewood Cottages in Big Bear Lake features cabins decorated in themes like King Arthur, Anthony and Cleopatra, *Gone with the Wind*, and Enchanted Forest.

The Castle Garden cabin has a waterfall, a moat, a spiral staircase to the tower bedroom and a mural of the English countryside that goes all around the room.

> **Castlewood Cottages**, 547 Main St, PO Box 1746, Big Bear Lake, CA 92315; ↘ 909 866 2720; web: www.castlewoodcottages.com. *Reservations recommended 3–4 months in advance.*

In Clear Lake, the **Lake Haven Motel and Resort** is a funky fisherman's motel with cabins decorated inside and out, including the roof, with Old West theme props and memorabilia.

> **Lake Haven Motel and Resort**, 100 Short St, Clearlake Oaks, CA 95423; ↘ 707 998 3908

SOUTHERN CALIFORNIA
Festivals and events

This has to rank among the wackiest event to ever have originated in a bar. **Moon Amtrak** draws hundreds of people to a chain-link fence between the Mugs Away Saloon and the railroad tracks on the second Saturday in July. Otherwise respectable people then do something they normally wouldn't dream of doing – they drop their drawers and 'moon' the two-dozen passenger trains that pass by that day. When it gets dark they moon by flashlight and by lanterns hung on the fence, hundreds of bare buns glowing in the flickering light. The mooning, which has been going on since a bar challenge started it all 25 years ago, draws crowds to both sides of the fence. The trains are booked solid months in advance for moon day. No one actually sponsors or organizes this event; it just has a life of its own.

> **Moon Amtrak** takes place annually the second Saturday in July across from Mugs Amway Saloon in Laguna Niguel, CA; web: www.moonamtrak.org. *Directions: Northbound on Interstate-5: exit 'AVERY PKWY'. Turn west at the end of the off-ramp. Short block street ends at 'T' intersection, Turn north (right) on Camino Capistrano. The train tracks will be on your left. It's 1.2 miles to Mugs Away Saloon, Please don't park next to the chain-link fence by train tracks; that's where the 'mooning' happens.* Free.

The ultimate example of life imitating art occurs every summer at the **Pageant of Masters** in Laguna Beach. Part of the Festival of Arts, the pageant is a living re-creation of classical art masterpieces, portrayed by real people posing to look exactly like their counterparts in original works of art. Volunteers are required to hold their poses for 90 seconds without moving. The audience sits out under the

stars in an outdoor amphitheater and watches scene after scene unfold as the giant reproductions of famous works of art are exposed. Several times during each performance the lights are turned on as the backdrops and foregrounds are rolled into place and you see the costumed, made-up volunteer 'actors' take their various spots. As the music begins, the actors freeze and the three-dimensional tableau takes form as an art masterpiece. Occasionally a pigeon perches on one of the living statues. The evening always closes with a living representation of Leonardo Da Vinci's *The Last Supper*.

> **Pageant of Masters** held annually in July and August in Laguna Beach, CA. Contact Pageant of the Masters, 650 Laguna Canyon Rd, Laguna Beach, CA; ↘ 949 494 1145; web: www.foapom.org

The **Mud Run** at Camp Pendleton is so popular that registration is cut off after the first 3,500 racers sign up. A family affair, the course is 10km worth of slippery mud walls, straw obstacles, slimy mud pits, and knee- to waist-deep water. Competitors race individually or in teams over the rugged terrain, many of them doing so in costume. Make no mistake – while entertaining, this rugged race is no walk in the park.

> **Mud Run**, held annually in June. Contact Race Office, Box 555020, Camp Pendleton, CA 92055-5020; ↘ 760 725 6836; web: www.camppendletonraces.com

Practically everybody in town seems to enter the **Palm Desert Golf Cart Parade**. The ubiquitous carts, street-legal year-round in Palm Desert, abandon the town's 100 golf courses for the day and gather for an event that's been going on for 40 years. Each year's parade has a different theme, such as 'Salute to America' or 'It's Showtime', and the carts dress appropriately, transforming into all manner of floats and objects.

> **Palm Desert Golf Cart Parade**, held annually in November. Contact the Palm Desert Chamber of Commerce, 73-710 Fred Waring Dr, Ste. 114, Palm Desert, CA 92260; ↘ 760 346 6111; web: www.golfcartparade.com

Some people are so fond of toy pianos that they dedicate an entire festival to them. At the **Toy Piano Festival**, held at the UCSD Music Library, they hold the instrument in high esteem, composing music for it and treating the toy as if it were seriously capable of playing actual music. Prior to the events, the Geisel Library hosts a toy piano-themed mail art show, inviting anyone to send in a handmade postcard, poem, or photo paying tribute to a toy piano. The museum itself has quite a collection of the tinkley instruments.

> **Toy Piano Festival**, held annually in August. Contact the UCSD Music Library, 9500 Gilman Dr 0175Q, La Jolla, CA 92093; ↘ 858 534-8074; web: orpheus.ucsd.edu/music/

Fifteen hundred madcap marchers make up the outrageously satirical **Doo-Dah Parade**. Unlike the structured Tournament of Roses Parade that it spoofs, anyone with an appreciation of irony can march in the Doo Dah, organized by the Unorganizers Unofficial Committee. Each year they anoint a Queen; in 1997 it was the deceased Lily Hodge, whose ashes were carried in an urn along the parade route by her husband who claimed Lily had always loved the parade. The Doo Dah has spawned such legends as the Briefcase Marching Drill Team, the Hibachi Marching Grill Team, and the Invisible Man Marching Band. With marchers like Jerking Man, Confused Dogs in Drag, the Flying Toilet and the Graveyard Farmers, it's no wonder 40,000 people cram the streets to see the spectacle. Want to see the spoof of the spoof? Check out Berkeley's Doo Dah Parade in the northern California section.

> **Doo Dah Parade**, held annually in November. Contact Pasadena Convention and Visitors Bureau, 171 South Los Robles Ave, Pasadena, CA 91101; ↘ 800 307 7977 or 626 795 9311; web: www.pasadenavisitor.org or www.pasadenadoodahparade.com

How do you call a lobster? Hint: it doesn't involve a cell phone. At the **Port of Los Angeles Lobster Festival**, you gather at the shore, face the ocean, flail your arms about and shout, chant, rant and rave. This is a lot easier for the 12 and under set that compete for a prize computer, but there's nothing to stop you from making a fool of yourself if you wish, unless, of course, you consider your pride. In the old days, grown fishermen opened the lobster season by performing this ritual; whether this improved the catch is anyone's guess. If you'd rather not do the hootin' and hollerin' bit, you can opt to dress up your pet as a lobster – or as any seafood item – and enter the Lobster Dog Pet Parade. If your pet can't, or won't, wear the costume, then build a float with a kid's wagon, put your stubborn pet in it, and drag it along the parade route. If all else fails, dress yourself as a lobster and carry your pet. The parade is based on the legendary exploits of Bob the Lobster Dog who hung out on the docks and supposedly guided in the fleet by barking.

> **Port of Los Angeles Lobster Festival**, held annually in September in Ports O'Call Village, San Pedro, CA; ↘ 310 366 6472; web: www.lobsterfest.com

Redondo Beach has its annual **Lobster Festival**, too, a zany three-day feast and fest with attendees wearing lobster costumes, grass skirts, Hawaiian shirts and bikinis. They're never short of high-school athletes to compete in the Clam Linguini Eating Contest.

> **Lobster Festival**, held annually in September in Redondo Beach, CA. Contact Redondo Beach Visitors Bureau, 200 N Pacific Coast Hwy, Redondo Beach, CA; ↘ 310 376 6911 or 310 374 7373; web: www.lobsterfestival.com

If you wear a turban or dress like an Arabian knight you get into the **National Date Festival** in Riverside County for free. Otherwise, pay the admission, join 250,000 others, and watch jockeys decked out like Ali Baba ride in little chariots hitched to some really big birds during the Ostrich Races. Root for your favorite dromedary during the camel races; cringe during the live alligator wrestling; cheer at the Bull-o-rama Rodeo, and enjoy a Monster Truck making mincemeat out of a car. What does all this have to do with dates? Nothing really, except to celebrate that the region produces 95% of all the dates grown in the United States, and to offer a prayer for date fertility at the **Blessing of the Dates**.

> **National Date Festival** and the **Blessing of the Dates** held annually in February in Riverside County, CA; ↘ 800 811 FAIR or 760 863 8247; web: www.datefest.org

San Diego Diver's Supply sponsors an **Underwater Pumpkin Carving Contest** on the Saturday nearest Halloween. Scuba divers bring their own pumpkin and dive-knife, and then carve underwater. Judging is done later on the beach.

Underwater Pumpkin Carving Contest, held annually at the end of October at Kellog Park/LaJolla Shores, San Diego. Contact San Diego Diver's Supply, ☏ 619 224 3439 or Ocean Enterprises, ☏ 858 565 6054; web: www.oceanenterprises.com

Eccentric environment

'Whatever come up, comes out'. That's Noah Purifoy's explanation for the art he produces from found objects. **The Noah Purifoy Desert Art Environment**, near the windswept town of Joshua Tree, is two acres of sculpture created by the elderly artist since he moved to the desert in 1989. Always drawn to discarded objects, Noah made a conscious decision as a young man never to buy new materials for his art, finding junk to be evocative and feeling that each piece carries with it the history of its former owners. Dozens of large sculptures, freestanding and suspended, surround his mobile home. An educated man with three university degrees, Noah prefers being alone so he can work on his assemblages. Many are whimsical: towering stacks of twisted cafeteria trays; crosses challenging voodoo fetishes; a train made of bicycle wheels, old vacuum cleaners and beer kegs. Others are more philosophical, inviting contemplation: The White House, open to the sky but with sealed-up windows and The Cathedral, a wooden building with no doors or windows.

Noah Purifoy Desert Art Environment, located in Joshua Tree, CA; ☏ 213 382 7516; web: www.noahpurifoy.com. Call and leave your fax number to receive a map and directions. There are no fences and you can park anywhere you like. The site covers 7¹/₂ acres so wear comfortable shoes. It's open all day and there are no fees. At the entrance you'll find a self-guided tour map.

Sixteen years ago, Leonard Knight's hot-air balloon, carrying the message 'God is Love', failed him on an impossibly bleak and barren patch of desert near the Salton Sea. It was here, in this inhospitable place, that Leonard had a vision: God wanted him to paint his message on the side of a mountain. There was only one problem. He would have to build the mountain first. Today, **Salvation Mountain** and its message of love and redemption is three stories high and about a hundred feet wide, a brilliant patch of incongruity rising up out of the desolate landscape. Molded entirely by hand, Leonard, who is in his seventies, made the mountain out of hay bales, adobe, old paint, window putty and truly astounding tenacity. For all these years, he's lived at the foot of his handmade mountain in a ramshackle truck with no electricity, plumbing or water. Besides the mountain itself, Leonard is working on a 'balloon', again building it out of hay bales, adobe, and paint, as well as a 'hogan', a multi-room structure supported by trees made from old tractor and car tires, tree branches, telephone poles and yet more adobe and paint.

To say that Leonard is happy is an understatement. He's a genuinely warm, intelligent, dedicated man, fully aware of his eccentricity. He won't accept any money, asking only for old paint with which he constantly touches up his mountain so it'll stay shiny. He welcomes visitors and delights in telling you about his passion, pressing postcards of his creation into your hands so you can help him spread the word of God's love. A colossal achievement, Leonard's mountain is a monument devoted to peaceful coexistence. Unfortunately, the government didn't always see it quite that way, declaring the place a toxic nightmare a few years back. They were ready to bulldoze it when a legion of Leonard's fans successfully petitioned the legislature to declare it a work of religious art and therefore immune from destruction. He and his mountain are now famous all over the world thanks to occasional busloads of international tourists and a host of print and broadcast media stories. If you can, bring old paint when you come to visit. But even if you arrive empty handed, you'll come away with postcards and a memory that won't soon depart.

Salvation Mountain, Niland, CA located south of I-10, 5 miles east of Hwy 111 at Niland. Contact Leonard Knight, PO Box 298, Niland, CA 92257. *Visit anytime.*

Love of garbage motivated a 60-year-old woman to spend the last 25 years of her life transforming her third-of-an-acre lot into **Grandma Prisbrey's Bottle Village** in Simi Valley. Using hundreds of thousands of bottles and objects scavenged from the dump, she built 13 now-decaying structures to house her varied collections along with sculptures, shrines, wishing wells and walkways. Television tubes form a fence; walkways glisten with broken shards of glass and pottery. A spooky doll-head shrine has discarded heads perched on top of tall poles, while a birdbath is imbedded with car headlights. The pencil house held her collection of 17,000 pencils; there's also a house made of shells and a shrine made of horseshoes. The Leaning Tower of Bottle Village and an Intravenous Feeding Tube Fire Screen give you some idea of the lengths to which Grandma would go to express her quirky sense of humor. While alive she delighted in giving you the 25-cent tour, peppering her commentary with anecdotes, then playing the piano and singing risqué songs to you in the meditation room. She died in 1988 after living a tragic life that probably led to her strange obsession. She married her first husband when she was just 15 – and he was 52 – and had seven children by him, six of whom died during her lifetime. She also lost another husband, a fiancé, and all but one of her siblings.

Grandma Prisbrey's Bottle Village, PBVC, PO Box 1412, Simi Valley, CA 93062; ☎ 805 583 1627; fax: 805 527 5002; web: www.echomatic.home.mindspring.com/bv/. *Visits are by appointment only.*

Death Valley is a pretty good description of the middle of nowhere. It's the last place you'd expect to find an opera house; the last place you'd expect to find a dancer in her late seventies performing for royalty and nobility, bullfighters and gypsies, monks, nuns and cats. The **Amargosa Opera House** in Death Valley Junction is the unlikely place where Marta Becket, an elderly artist and dancer, has spent a good chunk of her reclusive life. Up until the time she and her husband Tom had a flat tire at the Junction en route to a concert tour, her life was fairly normal, at least as normal as life can be for an artist with a tortured soul. While the tire was being repaired, Marta came upon the ruins of the Pacific Coast Borax Company, an abandoned hotel and outbuildings rotting in the sun. But Marta had eyes for just one thing: a crumbling theater building formerly used for company events. Marta had found a place for her soul. 'I had to have that theater,' she said, believing she would find new life in it and, in doing so, 'perhaps be giving it life. Here,' she continued, 'I would commission myself to do work that no-one else would ever ask me to do.' Renting, then finally buying, the property, she scheduled performances and danced, regardless of whether she had an audience of a few, one, or none.

Mostly, there were none and after a while she imagined a Renaissance audience completely surrounding her. So, acting on her vision, she spent four years painting her audience on the walls of the theater. The king and queen have the center box, accompanied by nobility. Two of her cats watch from red velvet cushions. Musicians play, ladies dance. Characters from her imagination spilled out on the walls: revelers, ladies of the night, gypsies, children, courting couples and Indians performing for the entertainment of the king and queen. Now she would never have to dance alone. Word of her accomplishment spread and before long, there were real people sitting in real chairs. Today, after more than 40 years in Death Valley, Marta enjoys packed audiences for most of her cool-season performances.

> **Amargosa Opera House**, PO Box 8, Death Valley Junction, CA.
> Contact ☎ 760 852 4441; web: www.amargosa-opera-house.com.
> Located on Hwy 160 north to Bell Vista, turn left, 30 miles to Death
> Valley Junction. *Performances run Oct–May.*

Smack dab in the middle of the Watts district, scene of the explosive civil rights riots of 1965, rises Simon Rodia's **Watts Towers**, a monumental work of folk art that took the Italian immigrant 33 years to construct. Intended as a tribute to his adopted country, the enormous structure includes three towers (the tallest of which is 99 feet high), a gazebo, patios, birdbaths, spires and a structure he called the Ship of Marco Polo. The steel sculptures are covered with mortar and imbedded with tens of thousands of pieces of tile, pottery, cooking utensils, linoleum, seashells and glass, and Seven-up and Milk of Magnesia bottles (Simon especially liked the green and deep blue bottle colors). Working from 1921 to 1954, Simon labored alone, using only simple tile-setter's tools and a window washer's belt and buckle to scale the heights. The giant towers dwarfed his tiny house. When he decided he was finished, he sold the place for a pittance and simply walked away. While his efforts weren't always appreciated by his neighbors, or by the city, today Watts Towers is renowned worldwide. The newly opened Watts Towers Art Center displays folk art exhibits and gives tours of the towers.

> **Watts Towers**, 1727 E 1765 East 107th St, Los Angeles, CA 90002;
> Towers and Art Center, ☎ 213 847 4646; web: www.trywatts.com. *Open
> Tue–Sat 10.00am–4.00pm, Sun noon–4.00pm. Group tours approximately every
> half-hour. Individual tours given Sat–Sun only;
> please call for appointment.*

Paul de Fonville and his wife Virginia are obsessed with keeping the memory of the cowboy alive. At their remote property in Walker Basin they've established the **Cowboy Memorial and Library**, housing their extensive collection of saddles, branding irons (possibly the largest in the country), spurs, ropes, whips and other cowboy gear in giant tractor-trailer vans until they can afford to build a proper museum. Outside they've set up a corral, chuck wagon and other tools and trappings of the cowboy trade, hoping to create a permanent memorial to a lifestyle long replaced by freeways and housing tracts. They love to show people around and, if you ask nicely, Paul will let his horse kiss him on the lips, a stunt that got him onto the pages of the *National Enquirer*.

> **Cowboy Memorial and Library**, 40371 Cowboy Ln, Caliente, CA 93518; ↘ 661 867 2410; web: www.tehachapi.com/cowboy. *Open Tue–Sun 10.00am–5.00pm. Free.*

Museums and collections

You won't know quite what to make of the **Museum of Jurassic Technology** in Culver City, which seems to be precisely what the museum is all about. As you wander through the labyrinth of impeccably displayed exhibits, you won't be alone as you stare quizzically and ponder the sanity of what you're observing. This is a very, very strange place where, according to curator David Wilson, confusion can lead to a very creative state of mind; so creative, in fact, that you could end up believing that eating a mouse on toast can cure bedwetting. It's a place where literature, dreams, and science collide, a place to be fascinated by the inexplicable. The museum's exhibits aren't necessarily what they seem to be and they ask questions that don't necessarily beg to be answered. The more you see, the less you understand. It's not that you have to suspend belief, just that you have to give up the notion of certainty and just go with the enigma flow. You'll see spore-inhaling ants, incredibly detailed peach-pit carvings, inventive theories on the nature of oblivion and bats that can seemingly fly through solid objects. You can't quite be sure exactly what is fact and what is fiction, which is the fun of it all.

> **Museum of Jurassic Technology**, 9341 Venice Blvd, Culver City, CA 90232; ↘ 310 836 6131; fax: 310 287 2267; web: www.mjt.org. *Open Thu 2.00–8.00pm; Fri–Sun noon–6.00pm. Closed Thanksgiving, Christmas, Easter, 1st Thu in May. Admission free, donation suggested.*

People keep sending Ken Bannister things with bananas on them or things shaped like bananas. This is because Ken, who seems to be a perfectly normal man in other ways, has been collecting all things banana for 30 years. Known as the Banana Man, his collection has been certified by the *Guinness Book of Records* as the 'largest collection of individual fruit items amassed by an individual in the world'. He and his bananas have been on the *Tonite Show* and he even appeared on a revival of *What's My Line*. His obsession began in 1972 when he started handing out 'smiley' banana stickers at conventions to promote his (non-banana) business. Banana Man took off from there and now that he's retired, he's grown so accustomed to the attention that he devotes himself full time to his persona. At his Banana Museum in Altadena, Ken arranges his 17,000-item collection in sections: hard items, food and drug items, clothing, sofa items, and wall items. He's the

Top Banana of the **International Banana Club** with 8,500 members in 17 countries. When you send him a banana item you get a banana merit; collect enough merits and you'll earn a Banana Degree. Bananas are good for you, he says, with no fat, no cholesterol and lots of potassium, calcium, and vitamins. The record for fast banana eating stands at 12 bananas in two minutes.

International Banana Club, Altadena, CA; ℡ 626 798 2272; web: www.bananaclub.com. *Visits by appointment only.*

The world of burlesque is still alive at the **Historical Burlesque Museum and Hall of Fame** in Helendale. Lovingly run by 70-something Dixie Evans, formerly known as the Marilyn Monroe of Burlesque, the museum is crammed to the gills with gowns, feather boas, panties, lingerie and other memorabilia from the golden age of strippers. Located on an isolated, ramshackle ranch in the desert, roughly halfway between Los Angeles and Phoenix, the retired burlesque queen delights in taking you back into her past, smiling coquettishly, chattering enthusiastically and happily posing for pictures amid the stuff dreams 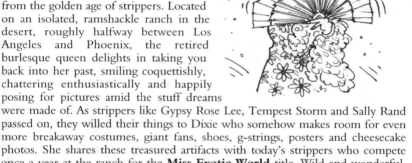 were made of. As strippers like Gypsy Rose Lee, Tempest Storm and Sally Rand passed on, they willed their things to Dixie who somehow makes room for even more breakaway costumes, giant fans, shoes, g-strings, posters and cheesecake photos. She shares these treasured artifacts with today's strippers who compete once a year at the ranch for the **Miss Exotic World** title. Wild and wonderful, gaudy and glamorous, Dixie's museum is a memorial to the gone, but not forgotten, days of burlesque. Be aware: there's no air conditioning, so you may want to visit during the cooler months.

Historical Burlesque Museum, Hall of Fame and **Miss Exotic World**, 29053 Wild Rd, Helendale, CA 92342; ℡ 760 243 5261; web: www.exoticworld.com. *Open Tue–Sun 10.00am–4.00pm.*

Most every baby boomer can remember sneaking illicit peeks into the shop windows of Frederick's lingerie stores. At the **Frederick's of Hollywood Lingerie Museum and Celebrity Lingerie Hall of Fame** you'll see the 'software' that made Mr Frederick famous and the underwear of the famous that wore his sexy creations. His motto was 'Don't dream it … live it', and he not only gave folks plenty to dream about, he made it easy to buy the paraphernalia of which fantasies are made. Above the retail store is the museum with undies of the rich and famous: Ethel Merman's girdle, Mae West's marabou negligee, Tom Hanks' boxer shorts, Susan Sarandon's garter belt, and one of Madonna's infamous bustiers. It isn't difficult to imagine Cher, Loni Anderson, Joan Collins and Robert Redford in their unmentionables on display, either. Phyllis Diller left instructions: her bra is embroidered with the words 'this side up'. From mementos of Hollywood's golden girls to underwear from every cast member of *Beverly Hills 90210*, the museum reinforces the image of Hollywood as a romantic and glamorous place.

Frederick's of Hollywood Lingerie Museum and Celebrity Lingerie Hall of Fame, 6608 Hollywood Blvd, Hollywood, CA; ✆ 323 466 8506; web: www.seeing-stars.com/Museums/Fredericks.shtml. *Open daily 10.00am–10.00pm.*

It's an odd, odd world inside the **Hollywood History Museum**, home of Jayne Mansfield's white picket fence, Russell Crowe's *Gladiator* costume, and Hannibal Lecter's entire jail cell set from *Silence of the Lambs*, complete with straitjacket and head muzzle. Just opened in 2003 in the historic Art Deco Max Factor building, the eclectic, 2,800-item collection belongs to Donelle Dadigan, a Los Angeles real estate developer who spent ten years relentlessly pursuing her vision of a museum that would let people see the real Hollywood. The non-profit museum also has Tommy Lee Jones' *Men in Black* suit, Rudy Vallee's megaphone, Elvis Presley's bathrobe, and fake eyelashes belonging to Joan Crawford.

Hollywood History Museum, 1660 N Highland Ave, Hollywood, CA; ✆ 323 464 7776. *Open Thu–Sun 10.00am–5.00pm.*

Some eccentrics, infused with the unshakable belief that their way is the right way, manage to attract huge followings. Logically located in the Hollywood land of make-believe, the **L Ron Hubbard Life Exhibition** canonizes the guru who started the 'religion' of Scientology. You can't just browse the 30 or so displays honoring the man who supposedly was proficient in several dozen fields, though. You have to take a tour of the high-tech exhibition that dramatizes not only his stories and accomplishments but also the pearls of wisdom he uttered on his way to riches. If you can believe it, Mr Hubbard was – among other things – a master mariner, a police officer, a photographer, an artist, a naval intelligence officer, a daredevil pilot, an explorer, a horticulturist, and a science fiction writer. By the time you finish the highly dramatized, two-hour tour, the only thing you'll be certain of is his marketing skill.

L Ron Hubbard Life Exhibition, 6331 Hollywood Blvd, Los Angeles, CA; ✆ 323 960 3511; web: www.lronhubbardprofile.org/exhib.htm. Located in the Hollywood Guaranty Building at the corner of Ivar and Hollywood Blvd. *Open Fri–Sat 10.00am–11.30pm.*

The **Ripley's Believe It or Not! Museum** in Hollywood features a human-hair bikini; a replica of a half-ton man who weighed 1,069lb when he died at the age of 32; art made from dryer lint; a fur-covered trout used in a hoax; and hand-painted potato chips.

Ripley's Believe It or Not Museum, 6780 Hollywood Blvd, Hollywood, CA 90028; ✆ 323 466 6335; web: www.ripleys.com. *Open Sun–Thu 10.00am–10.00pm; Fri–Sat 10.00am–11.30pm.*

The **Guinness World Records Museum** tells the story of a man who, in 1900, walked on his hands from Vienna to Paris, a distance of 871 miles. He averaged 1.58mph and completed the journey in 55 ten-hour 'walking' sessions. It also tells of a woman with 20-inch fingernails, a VW Bug with 18 students crammed inside, and a frozen cricket spitting record of 32½ feet. Thousands of world records are brought to life here in vivid displays that help you really experience the bizarre lengths to which people will go to become a Guinness record holder.

Quirk Alert

Angelyne (web: www.angelyne.com) is representative of those 'only in LA' stories. Back in 1984 she was promoting her rock band by putting up posters along the Sunset Strip. On a whim, she put up a billboard of herself that showed only her buxom blonde bombshell image along with her first name. The billboard became the talk of the town and, almost overnight, she became famous – not for anything she did, but for simply being on billboards. Hundreds of billboards, bus stop panels, and murals later, she's become a quirky icon of Hollywood. The Angelyne phenomenon resulted in television and magazine interviews, radio shows, personal appearances and film cameos all over the world. The billboards ran not just in LA, but also in New York, Washington, DC, England, and Europe. Her persona is famous: an aging bombshell, extra big on top with an extra tiny waist, and driving a pink Corvette. Picture Barbie at 50 and counting. Her fan club has 20,000 members, her logo merchandise is sold all over the world, and spotting Angelyne (in person or in her car) is an obsession with many. There's even a website for addicted Angelyne spotters. On her own website she'll 'escort' you around the city, showing you the secrets of Hollywood and some of her own very special secret places as well. Her fame is quite an achievement considering it started out as a figment of her own imagination. She ran (and lost) for mayor of Hollywood.

Guinness World Records Museum, 6764 Hollywood Blvd, Hollywood, CA; ☎ 323 463 6433

Perfectly capturing one of America's greatest obsessions, the **Petersen Automotive Museum** in Los Angeles is dedicated to the influence of the automobile on American life. You'll see hundreds of classic cars, trucks, sports cars and motorcycles displayed in theme settings that showcase Americans' love affair with their cars. The museum offers special theme shows such as Hollywood Star Cars, Art Cars, Monster Trucks, and an exhibit showcasing the Low Rider Tradition.

Petersen Automotive Museum, 6060 Wilshire (at Fairfax), Los Angeles, CA; ☎ 323 830 CARS; web: www.petersen.org. *Open Tue–Sun 10.00am–6.00pm. Admission charge.*

Attractions

If you're going through Death Valley, a visit to **Scotty's Castle** is a must. Sitting virtually in the middle of nowhere and appearing like a mirage in the desert, the castle was built in the 1920s by a wealthy Chicago couple, the Johnsons, who traveled west to check on an investment they'd made with a man named Walter Scott. A rowdy, fast-talking con artist, Scott had been bilking investors by claiming that he was building a castle from the profits from a nearby gold mine. When the Johnsons discovered they'd been defrauded, they befriended 'Scotty' and went along with his scam in the hopes they could recover their money. It was the Johnsons who actually built the castle. During the tour, the guides dress as characters from 1939 and bring the castle's heyday back to life.

Scotty's Castle, located in Death Valley National Park, Death Valley, CA; ➘ 760 786 2392; web: www.nps.gov/deva/scottys1.htm. Directions: I-15 north to US-95, north to SR-267 west (left at Scotty's Junction) to Death Valley National Park and on to Scotty's Castle. *Open daily 9.00am–5.00pm. Admission charge.*

Some of the most stunning showgirls in Palm Springs collect Social Security retirement income. The long-legged lovelies of the **Fabulous Palm Springs Follies** are all between 55 and 87 years old, performing vaudeville-type variety acts during the November through May season. This is no geriatric lounge act. The show is a vibrant extravaganza with Ziegfeld-era production numbers, animal acts, and time-warp comedy shtick. More than a million people have watched these performers shatter stereotypes about old age with their astounding vitality and skill.

Fabulous Palm Springs Follies, 128 South Palm Canyon Dr, Palm Springs, CA 92262; ➘ 760 327 0225; web: www.palmspringsfollies.com. *Follies season is Nov–May annually.*

Quirkyville

With 61 murals, Lompoc is one of America's premier mural cities. Devised as a way to enhance the local economy, the **Lompoc Valley Mural Project** uses art to attract tourism. The huge murals are painted on the sides of buildings, each a different style and theme. Some trick the eye as in the trompe l'oeil depiction of a three-story mansion. Others illustrate Lompoc's claim to fame as the Flower Seed Capital of the World while still others pay tribute to the town's historic events and people.

Lompoc Valley Mural Project. Pick up a free map for a self-guided tour or arrange for guided group tours at the Chamber of Commerce, 111 S I St, Lompoc, CA 93436; ➘ 800 240 0999 or 805 736 4567; web: www.store.yahoo.com/lompoc

Tours

Tour guide Anne Block will pick you up in her gold Caddy and show you around the 'real' LA, demystifying a city that many people find alien and intimidating. She takes you beyond the standard tour-bus dreams-come-true rap, concentrating on the eclectic, offbeat and outrageous cultural aspects that real people who live here experience. Specializing in the 'gloriously unusual', she calls her business **'Take My Mother★ Please'** since so many of her clients hire her to take their relatives around so they don't have to. Anne delights in finding the madcap, offbeat soul of the place she truly loves, exploring the ever-changing pop culture that makes Los Angeles so fluid and fascinating. After a day with this vivacious, hip, 50-something woman, you'll see the city in a whole new light and perhaps even understand the quirky essence of one of the most eccentric places on Earth. She began her tour business after escorting the famous comedienne Lily Tomlin to a film festival in Berlin. Anne's tours are totally customized depending upon your interests. Some of her clients' favorites include a beauty day on the Sunset Strip and the Pretty Woman tour, based on the famous movie.

Take My Mother* Please Tours (* or any other VIP) Tours, PO Box 35219, Los Angeles, CA 90034; ➘ 323 737 2200; fax: 323 737 2229; web: www.takemymotherplease.com

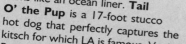

Quirk Alert

Southern California is known for its bizarre buildings. The Los Angeles area is home to two donut-shaped stores: **The Donut Hole** and **Randy's Donuts** – along with a Coca-Cola building that looks like an ocean liner. **Tail O' the Pup** is a 17-foot stucco hot dog that perfectly captures the kitsch for which LA is famous. Venice sports the **BinocularBuilding** while Beverly Hills has the **Witch's House**. In central California there's a building shaped like a **bulldozer**, the office of the United Equipment company in Turlock. It even has dirt and rocks piled in front of the 'blade'. The president of the company sits where the engine should be.

Bulldozer Building, visible just off Highway 99, 70 miles north of Fresno in Turlock

The Donut Hole, 15300 E Amar, La Puente, CA; ✆ 626 968 2912

Randy's Donuts, 805 W Machester, Inglewood, CA; ✆ 310 645 4707

Tail O' The Pup, 329 N San Vicente Blvd, West Hollywood, CA 90048; ✆ 310 652 4517; web: www.tail-o-the-pup.com

Binocular Building, located on Main Street, Venice Beach, CA

The Witch's House, 515 N Walden Dr, Beverly Hills, CA; ✆ 310 271 8174

Just plain weird

The college town of San Luis Obispo has a truly unique claim to fame: an alleyway whose walls are covered on both sides by tens of thousands of pieces of gum, mostly of the bubble variety. **Bubble Gum Alley** got its first blob sometime in the 1950s and it became a tradition for students to leave a lasting impression on the town by leaving their wads behind. The city tried several times to clean the alley, but finally gave up the effort in the 1960s.

> **Bubble Gum Alley**, located in downtown San Luis Obispo, CA. Contact San Luis Obispo Chamber of Commerce, 1039 Chorro St, San Luis Obispo, CA 93401; ✆ 805 781 2777; web: www.visitslo.com

Venice Beach is an example of quintessential California weirdness, a happy confluence of individual expression, sparkling energy and joie de vivre that amazes visitors. You never know what you'll find, only that you'll always find something that confuses or amuses. The district features **Abbot's Habit**, a café that holds naked poetry readings; **Audrey's Good Vibrations**, where they sell remedies for whatever ails you emotionally – stuff like flower essences for 'letting go of the past' or for 'protection from psychic attack'. There are enough fortune-tellers on the beach to predict that tourists will always keep coming back for more. Even the street performers are ultra-quirky: The World's Greatest Wino proffers jokes, songs and sexual counseling, and there's a guy who balances a chair on his chin – while someone's sitting in it. The Sandman makes large-scale sculptures, worthy of a museum, that vanish with the tide. At **Perry's Beach Café** you can take a roller-blade tour, gliding among the walkers, bikers, and skaters while gawking at the muscle-building jocks and colorful characters behaving bizarrely, expecting to be noticed.

> **Abbot's Habit**, 1401 Abbot Kinney Blvd, at California Ave, Venice; ☎ 310 399 1171
>
> **Audrey's Good Vibrations**,1204 Abbot Kinney Blvd, Venice; ☎ 310 838 0832
>
> **Perry's Beach Café & Rentals**, various locations along the beach walk, Venice & Santa Monica; ☎ 310 372 3138

Odd shopping

It's one thing to sell vintage clothes, but what about selling just vintage shoes, just from the 1920s–1970s, and never worn to boot? The **Re-Mix Shoe Company** sells such shoes for both men and women in their vintage department, shoes like genuine white bucks, saddle shoes and wing tips as well as swing dance and wedgie styles. They also sell a line of reproductions. The experience is almost like shopping in a museum.

> **The Re-Mix Shoe Company**, 7605 Beverly Bvd, Los Angeles, CA 9003; ☎ 888 254 1813; web: www.remixvintageshoes.com

If you can't find your favorite beverage from the past (and present) at **Galco's Old World Grocery**, then it probably no longer exists. This one-stop shop for pop has the country's largest selection of specialty sodas under one roof, including microbrews, imported, and original old-time sodas. The store looks unimposing from the outside but inside, with its 1970s' décor, you'll find 450 different varieties of sodas from rare old-timers like Nehi and Moxie to hot new brands hoping to hit the big time. They also sell dozens of old-fashioned 'school-store' candies, bottled waters and hundreds of brands of beer.

> **Galco's Old World Grocery**, 5702 York Bvd, Los Angeles, CA 90042; ☎ 323 255 7115; web: www.sodapopstop.com

Only in LA could you shop where the witch doctors do – at **Farmacia Million Dollar Botanicas** at the corner of Third and Broadway in downtown LA. This place is, hands down, the most bizarre shopping experience you can have and still be legal. The merchandise is based on various beliefs that herbs, candles, love potions, amulets, spells, powders, saints and rosaries can influence health and happiness. A bewildering array of air-fresheners, liquids and oils claim to offer peace and protection, health and wealth, love and luck and spiritual cleansing. Take Dr Buzzard's Court Case Bath and Floor Wash, for example, a liquid to be used when mercy is needed and when you want the scales of justice to tip in your favor. If you're going to court, pour it in your bath; if it's your business that's being judged, pour it in the water used to wash your firm's floors. The Black Destroyer is a powerful oil that 'destroys curses, hatred, resentment, envy and any evil intention towards you or your home'. Powdered iguana foot offers protection while burning candles in the shape of certain male and female body parts will inflame the passions of your intended. A mysterious powder called Tied Up and Nailed pictures an unfortunate man bound in ropes and nailed to the floor. It's meant to ensure that a business deal you really want will, indeed, happen. They're working on a website so you can see the bizarre inventory for yourself. It's no wonder they do such a booming repeat business. For every purchase there's someone out there who's going to have to shop for an antidote. It's unlikely you'll ever see a sale on at a spell-breakers.

Farmacia Million Dollar Botanicas, 301 S Broadway (corner of 3rd and Broadway), Los Angeles, CA 90013; ↘ 213 687 3688

Wacko is an outlandish place that sells strange, weird and outrageously fun things like inflatable palm trees, white-trash refrigerator magnets (for your front porch refrigerator), head bobbers, lava lamps, a voice changer and books like *101 Uses for Tampon Applicators*. The store is crammed with whimsical cookie jars, lunchboxes, greeting cards and teapots; there's enough kitsch to keep you busy for several hours. Owner Billy Shire just buys anything that appeals to him, commenting that 'bad taste is timeless'.

Wacko, 4633 Hollywood Blvd, Hollywood, CA; ↘ 323 663 0122; web: www.soapplant.com. *Open Mon–Sun, hours vary.*

'Part of you thinks it's in poor taste, part of you wants an X-Large.' That's the slogan at **Skeletons in the Closet**, an improbable gift shop in the Los Angeles Coroner's Office. The shop, squeezed into a second-floor office, sells hats, mugs, clothing, toe tags, beach towels, mouse pads, key chains, magnets and more, all carrying the Coroner's name along with a cute body-outline logo. The 'body bag' garment bag is especially apropos. The idea for the shop came about quite by accident. Employees often had souvenir items made for company events like picnics and sporting competitions. Friends and relatives clamored for a chance to buy these unique items so a tiny 'shop' was set up in a janitor's closet. The rest is history. The shop is so popular they're getting ready to take over yet another office. The funds raised at the shop support the Youthful Drunk Driver Visitation Program. They're dying for your business.

Skeletons in the Closet, Los Angeles County Coroner's Office, 1104 N Mission Rd, 2nd Floor, Los Angeles, CA 90033; ↘ 323 343 0760; web: www.lacoroner.com. *Open Mon–Fri 8.00am–4.30pm.*

Quirky cuisine

Talk about starving artists! You never know who will be on hand to entertain you during your meal – and thus earn theirs – at **Cafe Tu Tu Tango**. This theme restaurant is designed like an artist's loft in Barcelona, only here fine art and performance artists work and create while you dine on selections from the appetizers-only menu. The décor is upscale artist-garret and all the artwork is for sale. You may see salsa-dancing stilt walkers, tarot card readers, belly-dancers, strolling musicians, singers and, of course, artists working at their easels. Their service motto is: 'You don't have to cut off your ear to get attention here'. One of half a dozen in this unique chain, each restaurant has its own local artists and entertainers working for their supper.

> **Cafe Tu Tu Tango**, 20 City Blvd, Orange, CA 92868; ↘ 714 769 2222 and 1000 Universal City Drive #H-101, Universal Clty, CA 91608; ↘ 818 769 2222; web: www.cafetututango.com

Typhoon Restaurant serves a variety of insect dishes along with their traditional Asian cuisine. On the dinner menu you'll find deep-fried waterbugs stuffed with chicken, stir-fried crickets, Manchurian ants sprinkled on potato strings and white sea worms (crispy style, of course) served on a spinach leaf.

> **Typhoon Restaurant**, Santa Monica Airport, 3221 Donald Douglas Loop S, Santa Monica, CA 90405; ↘ 310 390 6565; web: www.typhoon-restaurant.com

Hotel Bel Air offers dining with a behind-the-scenes spin. Table One is a private dining-room with windows and mirrors that look into the adjoining kitchen so you and seven friends can watch the preparation of your lunch or dinner. Custom menus satisfy your every whim.

> **Hotel Bel Air**, 701 Stone Canyon Blvd, Los Angeles, CA 90077; ↘ 800 648 4097 or 310 472 1211; fax: 310 476 5890; web: www.hotelbelair.com

Rooms with a Skew

After Bill Kornbluth retired in 1991, he bought a run-down motel and transformed the place into a highly personalized theme property. The **Oasis of Eden Inn & Suites** features 14 theme suites, all created and built by Bill and his friends, one of whom is an ex-Hollywood prop man. The Cave Room and the Jungle Room are among his wildest creations although the Rockin' 50s Suite, with its bed in a faux Cadillac, also deserves a wild rating. The New York, New York comes with furniture designed as buildings – they even light up. Others, such as the Esther Williams Suite with its wall mural of synchronized swimmers and ceiling of clouds, are more sedate but no less kitschy. Designed as a relaxing getaway, each suite has its own hot tub.

> **Oasis of Eden Inn & Suites**, 56377 29 Palms Hwy, Yucca Valley, CA 92284; ↘ 800 606 6686 or ↘ 760 365 6321; web: www.oasisofeden.com

Grandmother of kitsch, the **Madonna Inn** in San Luis Obispo has been famous for its décor since opening with just a dozen rooms in 1958. Today the inn has 109 theme rooms, all of them so gaudy and over-the-top that choosing the most outrageous would be quite a challenge. The Caveman Room is certainly a contender with its rock walls, rock ceilings and furniture covered in animal skins. So is the Madonna, a riot of red, pink, rock and crystal. Plumbing often does weird things at this inn, with water flowing in places you'd never expect. Plus there's enough fake fur and plastic to make Martha Stewart weep. Stop in even if you're not staying there to gawk at the public rooms and watch people walking around with their mouths hanging open. The men's bathroom in the lobby usually has as many women as men in there, all snapping pictures of the rock waterfall activated by you-know-what. Be sure to bring your camera.

Madonna Inn, 100 Madonna Rd, San Luis Obispo, CA 93405; ↘ 800 543 9666 or 805 543 3000; fax: 805 543 1800; web: www.madonnainn.com

Ballantines Hotel in Palm Springs has 1950s-style plastic-and-chrome theme rooms and suites with furniture by the likes of Eames, Miller and Knoll. The place is upscale, fun, and artsy, and they stock classic and B movies that you can watch in rooms dedicated to movie and musical stars. The sun deck is covered with green Astroturf, 50s' music is playing, and breakfast is served in your room on 50s-style Melmac.

Ballantines Hotel, 1420 North Indian Canyon Dr, Palm Springs, CA 92262; ↘ 800 780 3464; fax: 760 320 5308; web: www.ballantineshotels.com

At the **Standard Hotel Hollywood**, the sign is hung upside down and there's a glass enclosure behind the reception desk that serves as a space for human performance art. During the evening hours, models and actors are hired to 'live' in the glass box for the night and do whatever they want. Always clad in white underwear, some sleep, read, write, do their nails, knit, or watch TV. Some wear additional clothing; others may not. In the daytime the enclosure is filled with an odd assortment of stuff. The on-site barber shop gives you the latest do – or tattoo – so you'll be appropriately styled to join the 20- and 30-something crowd in the bar or on the pool deck. The property used to be a nursing home and has been redone in an over-the-top, retro 50s-meets-Y2K theme. The lobby ceiling is carpeted and the rooms have silver beanbag chairs. The **Standard Hotel Downtown** features a rooftop sundeck with a heated pool, pool toys and private cabanas with heated vibrating waterbeds. Waitresses are dressed as cheerleaders with an 'S' appliquéd on their panties.

Standard Hotel Hollywood, 8300 Sunset Blvd, Hollywood, CA 90069; ↘ 323 650 9090; fax: 323 650 2820; web: www.standardhotel.com

Standard Hotel Downtown, 550 South Flower at 6th St, Los Angeles, CA 9007; ↘ 213 892 8080; web: www.standardhotel.com

NEVADA

In Nevada, practically everything is 'in the middle of nowhere' but the state goes one step farther, calling US 50 the **Loneliest Road in America**. Running east to west across the state from Lake Tahoe to the Utah border, the highway is almost totally empty. (The AAA warns its members to stay off the road unless they're sure of their survival skills.) The only sights to break the monotony include a pile of windblown sand near Fallon that's popular with off-roaders, a fort near Dayton, the railroad museum in Ely, a Pony Express station at Cold Spring and water at the Lahonton Reservoir. You can pick up a **Route 50 Survival Kit** at Chambers of Commerce, museums, restaurants, motels and gas stations in any of the five towns along the route. Stop in all five and you'll get a survival certificate signed by the governor himself. You may find a shoe tree about a hundred miles east of Reno on US 50.

LAS VEGAS: THE ULTIMATE QUIRKYVILLE

Las Vegas is the world's finest example of corporate eccentricity. It is eccentricity by design and eccentricity for profit; eccentricity on a scale difficult to grasp even after you've been there. The weirdness is so pervasive, so all-encompassing, that it becomes commonplace, so much so that people living there become immune to it all. The mega resorts and casinos along the strip embody American pop culture in their architecture with buildings that are witty, absurd, bizarre, ludicrous, inventive and totally original. Experience the strip at night and you'll be part of something so bright that astronauts could see it from space. Each new resort raises the bar on outrageousness in a place already so over the top that it doesn't seem possible to go any higher.

Flipping through the *Yellow Pages* gives you a taste of how strange the city really is. There are pages and pages of bail bondsmen, badge-making companies, convention entertainers, wedding chapels, Elvis impersonators, costume rentals, tattoo parlors and, ahem, 'entertainers'. There are more weird places to explore than you'll have time or energy for. The myriad of unique businesses here have unprecedented freedom to flourish in a virtually uninhibited environment. While there is normal life outside the tourist areas, this guide concentrates on the places you're most likely to visit: downtown and the strip. Entries are divided into casino/resort weirdness and weirdness of the non-casino, even individual, kind. Keep in mind that eccentricity Mid-West style wouldn't even register a blip on the Vegas scale. You've got to be really, really weird, or way, way, way over the top to get noticed in this Mecca of madness.

Festivals and events

If your inner hound dog gets all excited at the prospect of a hundred Elvis impersonators swarming around you, then join the world's largest Elvis Presley fan club (it's free) so you can get tickets to the **Elvis Impersonator Contest and Fan Convention**. Usually held each January, the event is the culmination of a year-long, cross-country search for the best 'King' in the land.

> **Elvis Impersonator Contest and Fan Convention**, held annually in January at the Westward Ho Casino. Contact the Elvis Fan Club, PO Box 272014, Columbus, OH 43227; ✆ 614 239 9688; web: www.elviscontest.com

Considered one of the world's naughtiest bashes, Vegas's annual **Fetish & Fantasy Ball** is one of the country's ultimate adult Halloween festivities. Attracting 6,000 revelers, the bash features fire shows, an exhibitionist stage, a haunted house and graveyard, erotic entertainment and skits, and outrageous vendors. An After Hours party follows the ball just in case you haven't seen enough for one night. Remember, you're the show, so dress to thrill.

> **Fetish & Fantasy Ball**, held annually in October in Las Vegas; web: www.halloweenball.com. *Must be over 21 to attend.*

Non-casino eccentricities
Museums

By any standards, Liberace was strange. The flamboyant pianist, known as 'Mr Showmanship', opened the **Liberace Museum** himself in 1979 to make sure everything shone and glittered to his satisfaction. One building houses his cars, pianos and awards; the other features his costumes, his jewelry and some furnishings from his Palm Springs estate. The King of Kitsch had twin beds, one for himself and one for his 26 dogs. He wore the world's largest rhinestone, an 115,000-karat number weighing 50lb. It went nicely with his grand piano – that was covered in etched mirror-tiles and had a plexi-glass lid. His famous Purple

Costume took six months to create by six, sunglass-wearing seamstresses who wore the dark glasses to protect their eyes from the glare of the beads and rhinestones. The volunteer guides enjoy sharing Liberace stories, and the gift shop is truly high camp. The newly expanded museum now features over-the-top décor that would have made Liberace proud: lots of glass and glitz, neon, fuchsia (his favorite color), and his portrait gracing an exterior wall.

Liberace Museum, 1775 E Tropicana, Las Vegas, NV 89119; ☏ 702 798 5595; web: www.liberace.org. *Open Mon–Sat 10.00am–5.00pm; Sun noon–4.00pm.*

Some of the ghosts of Vegas' past have been rescued from the bone yard and burn brightly once again thanks to the efforts of the **Neon Museum**, an organization that rehabilitates the giant neon signs that made the 'old' Las Vegas so visually memorable. Dating from the 1940s, the glittering, animated signs that lured you to the casinos, bars and hotels have since been replaced by electronic signage. Half a dozen of the neon signs now proudly light up downtown's Fremont Street and the Neon Museum hopes to display several dozen more such signs now awaiting rescue in a nearby bone yard.

Neon Museum, 731 S 4th St, Las Vegas, NV 89101; ☏ 702 229 5366; web: www.neonmuseum.org. *Two outdoor 'galleries' can currently be seen at the 'bone yard' which is open by appointment only.*

Elvis is all over the city, eating at restaurants, taking the bus and using the men's room just like everyone else. He's also well represented at the **Elvis-O-Rama Museum**, the number one museum in Vegas. Liberace, who's honored at the *other* number one museum in Vegas, inspired Elvis at the beginning of his career. (A little-known fact is that both were twins at birth.) Liberace lent Elvis a jacket for his first appearance in Vegas and Elvis gave Liberace a ceramic hound dog. Elvis-O-Rama's owner, Chris Davidson, has been collecting King memorabilia since childhood and has created an impeccable, entertainingly displayed tribute. It's the largest collection of Elvis memorabilia outside of Graceland.

Elvis-O-Rama Museum, 3401 Industrial Rd, Las Vegas, NV; ☏ 702 309 7200. *Open daily 10.00am–7.00pm*

The **Guinness World of Records Museum** is unusually graphic, with exhibits that elicit gasps and laughs. The world's largest barf bag collection is there, along with an 'Eeuuw – gross' display of eating records. Compare yourself with the world's tallest, smallest, oldest, most tattooed and heaviest humans as well as see the world's largest collection of refrigerator magnets.

Guinness World of Records Museum, 2780 S Las Vegas Blvd, Las Vegas, NV; ☏ 702 792 0640. *Open daily 9.00am–6.00pm.*

Gaming memorabilia fills the **Casino Legends Hall of Fame**, a surprisingly interesting museum with lots of video to supplement the artifacts gathered from casinos now defunct. You can trace the whole history of gambling, see exotic chip collections now worth millions and experience the cultural implosions Vegas is famous for. Vintage audio and videotapes play constantly in the background. Sections are devoted to showgirls, entertainers, gamblers, builders and visionaries, and to the bad guys (Mafia) who ran 'da joint' until Howard Hughes cleaned up the place in the 1960s.

Casino Legends Hall of Fame, located at the Tropicana, 3801 S Las Vegas Blvd, Las Vegas, NV; ✆ 888 826 TROP; web: www.tropicanalv.com. *Open daily 9.00am–9.00pm.*

Attractions

Talk about off the wall – you'll be literally bouncing off padded ones at **Flyaway Indoor Skydiving**. Flapping around like a bird stuck in a silo, you'll 'fly' in a vertical wind tunnel with updraft speeds up to 115mph. But first you need to attend flight school. Here you learn how to position your body for maximum uplift; practice the 'tuck and roll', which is how you exit the updraft safely; and learn the communication hand-signals. Then you'll watch a lawyerly video explaining all the ways you could be hurt or killed (no-one ever has been); and sign your life away on the liability release form.

After that, it's into your flight suit, knee and elbow pads, helmet, ear plugs and goggles. Then it's into the wind tunnel with up to four of your soon-to-be-best friends. Since your body isn't likely to agree with your decision to leap into a void, your flight suit has handles so your trainer can pull you into and out of the maelstrom. The tunnel itself is a giant, padded, cylindrical tube with a turbine engine mounted in the floor. The first person to fly flings themselves off the side and on to the air current. Or at least that's the idea; your mind is willing, but somehow your feet stay firmly planted along the outer rim. That's where the handles come in and, before you know it, you really are flying. Exiting the air current isn't quite as scary as entering it, and once you get the hang of it, you're ready to go again and again. For an extra charge they'll record a video of your flight.

Flyaway Indoor Skydiving, 200 Convention Center Dr, Las Vegas, NV 89109; ✆ 702 731 4768 or 877 545 8093; web: www.flyawayindoorskydiving.com. *Open seven days a week. Hours are seasonal; phone for current times.*

As the number of strip mega-resorts grew, traffic at downtown casinos fell and the business owners there knew they had to come up with something spectacular to lure folks off the strip. The **Fremont Street Experience** was their solution – a $70 million canopy covering four blocks of downtown Vegas. Called a 'space frame', it's the world's largest electronic 'sign', filled with 2.1 million light bulbs, strobe lights and robotic mirrors. Several times nightly the casino lights dim and the canopy explodes with sound and color in a throbbing animated display that leaves the thousands of viewers below gaping in astonishment.

Fremont Street Experience, Las Vegas, NV; ✆ 800 249 3559 or 702 678 5600; web: www.vegasexperience.com

Steven Spielberg is responsible for **Gameworks Showcase**, an industrial-looking, underground environment combining a bar, restaurant, interactive games and the world's tallest indoor rock-climbing structure. Surge Rock has more than a dozen different routes, varying in difficulty, that end 40 feet in the air or extend all the way to the top, 75 feet up. One couple even got married on the rock, complete with wedding gown, tuxedo and minister. The minister and the bride, who was wearing a white helmet with a 35-foot train, rode a hoist to the 40-foot ledge; the groom had to climb. When the vows were complete and the minister said, 'You may now kiss the bride,' she glided to the top in the hoist while the poor groom had to claw his way up another 35 feet to collect his kiss.

Gameworks Showcase, 3785 Las Vegas Blvd, Suite 10, Las Vegas, NV 89109; ☎ 702 432 4263; web: www,gameworks.com. *Open Sun–Thu 10.00am–midnight, Sat–Sun 10.00am–2.00am.*

You'd expect Nevada, a place of extremes, to be home to a company like **Thrillseekers Unlimited**. Rich Hopkins, an extreme-sports coordinator, offers the ultimate in extreme sporting experiences. His five-day 'Ultimate Extreme' vacation includes paragliding, bungee jumping, rock climbing/rappelling, MotoSk8 racing, 'indoor' and tandem skydiving, street luge, base-jumping and a glider flight. If that's not enough excitement for you, then try his five-day 'Stunt Experience'. This vacation involves, among other things, learning to fall from high places, transferring out of speeding cars and taking fake bullet hits. They're insured. Are you?

Thrillseekers Unlimited. Contact Thrillseekers Unlimited, 3172 N Rainbow Blvd, Ste 321, Las Vegas, NV 89108; ☎ 866 4X-STUNTS or 702 669 5500; web: www.thrillseekersunlimited.com

Odd shopping

How can you pass up a chance to visit the largest wig store in the country? After all, Vegas is all about illusion; you might as well indulge in some of your own at **Serge's Showgirl Wigs**. It's not likely you'd experiment like this if you weren't on vacation and you may even decide to bring a new persona or two back home with you.

Serge's Showgirl Wigs, 3350 East Sahara Ave, Las Vegas, NV 89103; ☎ 800 947 9447 or 702 732 1015; web: www.showgirlwigs.com

Even if you're not into gambling, you'll be amazed at what you can buy at the **Gambler's General Store**. Besides aisle after aisle of every gambling item available in the world, there are hundreds of videos and computer games, and thousands of gambling books, including: *Chip Wrecked in Vegas*; *Play Poker, Quit Work, and Sleep till Noon*; and *How to Become a Casino Cocktail Waitress*. There's an acrylic toilet seat filled with coins (so you can sit on your assets) and an astounding array of collectibles from brothels and casinos, including chips, cards, ashtrays and glasses. Marked cards and loaded dice make fun souvenirs.

Gambler's General Store, 800 South Main St, Las Vegas, NV 89101; ☎ 800 322 2447 or 702 382 9903; fax: 702 366 0329; web: www.gamblersgeneralstore.com. *Open daily 9.00am–5.00pm.*

This store brings a smile of recognition to your face the minute you walk in the door. 'Hey,' you exclaim, 'I had one of those!' Depending on your age, you're either looking at your past or shopping for cool retro to impress your friends. **The Attic** is filled with 1950s', 1960s', and 1970s' clothing and furnishings from boots to saddle shoes, *Teen* to *Vogue*, and plastic dinettes to lava lamps. Its two floors are crammed, brimming and overflowing with merchandise you won't believe is fetching that much money. Owner Victor Politis didn't start out envisioning a store as wild and wacky as this. He was in the used-textile recycling business; the retro stuff was just the icing on the cake. Eventually he had so much stuff in his yard that the neighbors complained and he was forced to open the Attic. Today he and his wife design outrageous furniture and clothes to add to their displays. They burn incense, serve pastries and drinks, and have a website as offbeat as their merchandise.

The Attic, 1018 S Main St, Las Vegas, NV 89101; ↘ 702 388 4088; web: www.atticvintage.com. *Open Mon–Sat 9.00am–5.00pm.*

At **Bonanza Gifts**, the world's largest gift shop, you'll see virtually every wacky and tacky souvenir available on the planet. If Bonanza doesn't have it, no-one's thought to make it yet. Their collection of Elvis clocks is amazing, as are the Elvis sunglasses with sideburns, a spinning mirrored ball (how romantic!) and the bubble butt boy. The place goes on and on, with every trinket, novelty and gag you've ever seen in a catalog. You'd have to have a sense of humor to work at a place like this, listening to 'Honey, you won't believe this but…' all day long. But they get even when you stand before a man-size, stuffed King Kong, sitting on a park bench next to his well-stuffed girlfriend. All of a sudden you hear a sound – that sound – and people start looking nervously around, sniffing the air. You gotta' love that remote-controlled whoopee cushion.

Bonanza Gifts, 2440 Las Vegas Blvd S, Las Vegas, NV 89104; ↘ 702 385 7359

Smack dab on the strip, between Sahara and the Stratosphere, sits **Ray's Beaver Bag**. Inside sits Ray and his cronies looking for all the world like they stepped out of the 18th and 19th centuries. The store sells supplies for mountain men and reenactors, things like antique muzzle-loading firearms, genuine cooking equipment, jackets sewn with porcupine quill needles, and patterns for making authentic clothing and equipment. Mountain Men Rendezvous are big business and the participants are sticklers for totally authentic trappings and behavior. Some go so far as to adopt the personality of a specific mountain man, a personality gleaned from reading old letters. Others portray a specific decade or era such as trappers working for the East India Company. Ray and his buddies couldn't be a greater contrast to the modern environment raging outside their door.

Ray's Beaver Bag, 727 Las Vegas Blvd S, Las Vegas, NV; ↘ 702 386 8746

Quirky cuisine

You can see, touch, play and experience all things Harley at the **Harley-Davidson Café**. While eating all-American road food amid the memorabilia, you're immersed in a 3D world of past, present and future Harley culture. A conveyor belt runs throughout the restaurant, showcasing the newest bikes. There's an enormous chain-link electric flag covering one whole wall, custom one-of-a-kind and celebrity bikes, and a 28-foot-high 15,000lb Harley replica bursting through the façade to the street. On Valentine's Day they sponsor Harley weddings.

Harley-Davidson Café, 3725 Las Vegas Blvd S, Las Vegas, NV 89109; ↘ 702 740 4555; web: harley-davidsoncafe.com

Rooms with a Skew

Kitsch done Vegas style means really over-the-top and **Viva Las Vegas Wedding Chapel and Hotel** offers some of the kitschiest quarters anywhere. The themed suites are so rich in detail that you won't have any trouble playing along once you stop giggling and gasping at the décor. Most famous is the Elvis and Priscilla suite with its pink Cadillac bed backed by a headboard replicating the gates of Graceland, in turn backed by walls 'fauxed' to look like the mansion and its grounds. The Gangsta' Room features a dead body outline stitched right

Quirk Alert

WEDDINGS VEGAS STYLE

Once famous for quickie weddings, Vegas today is also famous for theme weddings. Settings from the sublime to the ridiculous beckon the love-struck who have variously chosen to get hitched in a red, white and blue helicopter; on the star-ship *Enterprise*; in an Egyptian tomb; in a hot-air balloon with 12 witnesses; in a car at a drive-through chapel; and in the S & M room of a sex-theme chapel. The character doing the marrying might be a John Travolta character, a gangster, the Godfather, the grim reaper, or more variations of Elvis than you can shake your hips at. You can even get married in the buff, wearing just a veil and a bow tie. Disco, sports, rock, horseback, and skydiving – you name it, and someone in Vegas will do it while getting hitched.

into the bedspread; the Gothic Room has a coffin version. Straight out of the 50s, you might expect a bar hop on roller skates to be bringing room service in the Diner Room. Many of their rooms match their theme weddings. The Intergalactic Wedding, complete with theatrical lighting, fog and an 'illusion' entrance, comes with the starship chapel, space character cardboard cutouts and a ceremony by Captain Quirk. The Egyptian wedding involves male slaves carrying the bride, a goddess dancing for the groom, and King Tut as the minister. A night in the matching suites naturally follows.

Viva Las Vegas, 1205 Las Vegas Blvd, Las Vegas, NV 89104; ✆ 800 574 4450 or 702 384 0771; web: www.vivalasvegasweddings.com

Casino-related eccentricities

Even within the casinos you can find engrossing, offbeat diversions that let you escape the clanging madness for an hour to two.

At the Rio you can put on a costume and be part of the **Rio Suite Hotel and Casino's Masquerade in the Sky**. Floating in Mardi Gras-style contraptions suspended from a ceiling track, you'll ride along with the showgirls, throwing beads down to the crowd below. While your costume is designed to cover you completely, theirs most certainly is not.

Rio Suite Hotel and Casino's Masquerade in the Sky, 3700 W Flamingo Rd, Las Vegas, NV 89103; ✆ 800 746 7153 or 702 252 7777; web: www.playrio.com

The **Lion Habitat** at the MGM Grand displays five real live lions at any one time. A glass tunnel lets you circulate beside, around, and under lions being entertained by a trainer tossing big doggie bones. The lions would probably prefer to have a good chew on the swarms of video-camera toting tourists below, all craning their necks and exclaiming 'Wow!' in ten languages. You can opt to get your picture taken with adorable baby cubs. The **Rain Forest Café** probably has the largest concentration of fake leaves on the planet. Amazon tourist music accompanies the waterfalls, birds, butterflies, monkeys and simulated tropical rainstorms. All that's missing are the mosquito bites.

Lion Habitat and Rain Forest Café, MGM Grand, 3799 Las Vegas Blvd S, Las Vegas, NV 89109; ☎ 800 929 1111 or 702 891 1111; web: www.mgmgrand.com

The **Las Vegas Hilton's** *Star Trek* **Experience** beams you up to a *Star Trek* action sequence via a motion simulator ride that thrusts you into, and back from, a 20-minute encounter with Captain Kirk and his crew. You're given a briefing on the bridge and taken to the shuttle bay, dodging Klingon warships along the way. Costumes, make-up, weapons, special effects and props from the movies and TV series keep you entertained at the History of the Future Museum while you're waiting in line. At Quarks Bar and Restaurant you can order the Wrap of Kahn, a Romulan Warbird, and Glop on a Stick. The Molecular Imaging Chamber transports you into a *Star Trek* scene to get your picture taken. You can even get married on the bridge of the USS *Enterprise*.

Las Vegas Hilton's *Star Trek* **Experience**, 3000 Paradise Rd, Las Vegas, NV 89109; ☎ 888 GO BOLDLY or 702 732 5111; web: www.startrekexp.com

A 250lb head from a decapitated Lenin statue is encased in plexiglass in the vodka freezer at the **Red Square Restaurant** at Mandalay Bay. The surface of the bar is made of ice. Also at Mandalay Bay is the **Aureole**, a restaurant with a four-story wine tower holding 10,000 bottles of wine. The tower is surrounded by catwalks and encased in glass. 'Flying' wine angels wearing form-fitting black outfits ascend to retrieve your selection. (The management took umbrage at the suggestion that this upscale dining experience could be considered the least bit strange.) The Travel Channel calls the bathroom at the **China Grill Restaurant** the 'World's Best Unisex Bathroom'. It's a centrally located unisex restroom with opaque glass wall stalls that offer shadowy glimpses of your next-stall neighbor. The whole structure is separated from the dining-room by only a metal beaded curtain. Best for use by extroverts.

Red Square Restaurant, Mandalay Bay Resort and Casino, Las Vegas, NV; ☎ 877 632 7800; web: www.mandalaybay.com

Aureole Restaurant, Mandalay Bay Resort and Casino, Las Vegas, NV; ☎ 877 632 7800; web: www.mandalaybay.com/dining/restaurants.jsp

Mandalay Bay Resort & Casino, Las Vegas, NV; ☎ 702 632 7777 or 877 632 5300; web: www.mandalaybay.com

Twenty million dollars buys a lot of reality at **Madame Tussaud's Celebrity Encounter** at the Venetian Resort. Five themed environments showcase a hundred wax figures that are so realistic you'd swear they were real. Each figure

Quirk Alert

CHANNELING AN ALIEN

'I am Knut. I bring you love' intoned George Van Tassel, addressing one of his interplanetary spacecraft conventions in the 1950s. Knut, it turns out, was an entity supposedly stationed on an alien supply ship not far from the Great Rock Mojave Desert site where the UFO's contactees were gathering. Van Tassel, who was channeling his alien along with the many others who believed they had survived physical encounters in spaceships from planets other than Earth, also believed he had received instruction from Knut to build a device that would restore physical youth to humans. Raising money from the sale of his books, I Rode a Flying Saucer, and Into This World and Out Again, he built a structure in 1959 that he called the Integriton. It didn't restore much youth to Van Tassel; he died despite spending considerable time rocking in a chair inside his fantasy. His 'eccentrocity' has since fallen into ruin.

takes up to six months to craft and costs $30,000–45,000. Unlike most wax museums, you can wander among the displays here, copping a feel here and there and pretending you belong among the rich and famous. You could easily go through a whole roll of film snapping Kodak moments sure to liven up your computer screen.

Madame Tussaud's Celebrity Encounter Wax Museum, Venetian Casino Resort, 3355 Las Vegas Blvd S, Las Vegas, NV; ↘ 702 367 1847; web: www.madame-tussauds.com. *Open daily 10.00am–11.00pm.*

Treasure Island's trademark event is its outdoor Buccaneer Bay Show that plays late afternoons and evenings. Swashbuckling pirates defend their ships at 90-minute intervals with cannons, munitions and much bravado. Smoke billows, waves crash, seagulls chatter and a ship goes down in flames only to rise again for the next battle. The show has run more than 13,000 times and been seen by 23 million people. The high diver has fallen 80 miles, the captain has swung 150 miles, the ship has sunk 50 miles and the cast has used more than half a million towels since the show opened.

Treasure Island Buccaneer Bay Sea Battle, 3300 Las Vegas Blvd S, Las Vegas, NV 89109; ↘ 800 288 7206 or 702 894 7111; web: www.treasureisland.com. *Shows nightly. Free.*

Main Street Station Casino, Brewery and Hotel offers men a once-in-a-lifetime opportunity to express themselves in a way they never dreamed possible – by peeing on a piece of the Berlin Wall. The bathroom, the most photographed men's room in Vegas, has a steady stream of guys standing outside whispering, 'Go on in, honey … it's clear' to their female companions. German affidavits authenticate the rubble as being a genuine piece of the rock. The slab is big enough for three guys to express themselves at once. The casino has been used in movies like *Con Air*, *Casino* and *The Hustler*. For a corporation, Main Street Station is eccentric in that they refuse to use voice mail because it's too impersonal.

Main Street Station Casino, Brewery and Hotel, 200 N Main St, Las Vegas, NV 89101; ↘ 800 713 8933 or 702 397 1896; web: www.mainstreetcasino.com

NEVADA: EVERYWHERE *BUT* VEGAS
Festivals and events

If any event in America defines 'bizarre', it would have to be **Burning Man**. Thousands of people spend up to seven days in the bleakest stretch of nowhere in the whole country, creating the fifth largest city in Nevada for that week. Yet when it's over, there's no sign it ever took place. Impossible to easily describe, one participant said that trying to explain Burning Man to someone who has never been there is like describing sex to someone who has never had it.

Try imagining an outdoor gallery big enough to hold 30,000 performance artists and you get an idea of the scope of this event. Everything and everybody there is a work of art, creating, celebrating, and entertaining in a free-spirited social experience with no boundaries beyond courtesy. You survive through barter and exchange and through trust that your needs will be met, since money and commerce are banned. You cook pancakes, your neighbor supplies watermelon. Forethought is optional, as are inhibitions. Some choose to experience the event sans clothing; others wear body paint or elaborate costumes. Many arrive with huge art and architectural installations; others with participatory entertainment. Everything is done anonymously and no-one takes – or is given – credit for anything. It's an outpouring of lunatic creativity; an eccentric mix of art, music and wilderness camping. Burning Man itself is one giant act of performance art, with everyone attending becoming part of the show. This instant town attracts the young, the old, the right, the left, the straight, the stoned, the introvert, the extrovert and the just plain curious.

The Burning Man website is astoundingly complete, giving detailed instructions for collective survival. You're expected to arrive prepared to handle the extreme weather conditions (110° during the day to near-freezing at night) and to be totally self-reliant. Theme camps and villages have to be registered in advance so on-site maps can be reasonably accurate. There's an FAC page, a first-timer's guide, a volunteer board, a survival guide and even a Burning Man glossary. The packing list includes common sense, an open mind and a positive attitude. The site makes it clear the event can stretch your physical, mental, emotional and spiritual boundaries. Death does not entitle you to a refund.

At Burning Man, you give the gift of yourself, unencumbered by cell phones, money and your rank in the outside world's pecking order. It's a chance to try on new personas, shed the shackles of your preconceptions and burst loose of your own bonds – simply because you give yourself permission to. And when you leave, joining one of the world's biggest traffic jams, you take every trace of the world you built with you and the desert returns to its splendid isolation.

Burning Man Festival, held annually on Labor Day weekend in Black Rock Desert, NV; located 120 miles north of Reno, NV. Contact Burning Man, PO Box 884688, San Francisco, CA 94188; ↘ 415 TO FLAME; web: www.burningman.org

You have to be really motivated to play the **Lucifer's Anvil** golf course, mainly because you have to drive hours into the barren Nevada desert to find it. But the participants in the **Black Rock Desert Self-Invitational Golf Tournament** are more than happy to make the trek considering the tournament is one of the highlights of their golfing addiction. This bizarre game began 16 years ago when Doug Keister and a few of his buddies dragged some old golf clubs and some coffee cans out into the remote desert to celebrate Doug's 40th birthday in a novel way. Making up rules as they 'played', they discovered the unfettered joy of hitting a ball on a 'course' with no boundaries. That first experience was so much fun that they came back the next year to play again, this time bringing along a few more friends. Now dozens of teams participate in the tournament, playing a nine-hole course on which all the holes have to be painted so you can see them on the rock-hard playa ground. The graphic designs are wild, often involving optical illusions and props. Considering that the course is located in the middle of 600 square miles of nothingness, the fact that the tournament exists at all is quite a feat.

Black Rock Desert Self-Invitational Golf Tournament, held annually at the Summer Solstice around June 21. Visit web: www.keisterphoto.com for details.

Filling those long, lonely nights by the campfire was (and still is) a challenge for cowboys and they passed the time by composing poetry, narrative verse with meter and rhyme, about their life on the range. Today these poets compete in poetry competitions and the **National Cowboy Poetry Gathering** is the grandaddy of such events. More than 8,000 appreciative enthusiasts from around the country show up each year to hear and be heard, keeping the oral traditions of the craft alive.

National Cowboy Poetry Gathering, held annually at the end of January. Contact the Western Folklife Center, 501 Railroad St, Elko, NV 89801; ↘ 775 738 7508; web: www.westfolk.org

Virginia City is an old mining town, sister city to Alice Springs, Australia. Since 1987 these two towns have alternated hosting the annual **Camel Races**. Several dozen jockeys attempt to coerce their stubborn mounts across the finish line in a race with as much control as you'd have over a toddler at a birthday party. The slapstick event also involves ostrich races, so you can imagine the melee.

Camel Races, held annually in Virginia City, NV. Contact International Camel Races, Virginia City Chamber of Commerce, PO Box 464, Virginia City, NV 89440; ↘ 702 847 0311; web: www.allcamels.com

The ghosts are waiting for you at Carson City's annual **Ghost Walk**. The self-guided event has you following a blue line through the city's historic district, stopping at historic houses where professional actors portray various ghosts from the past who lived in Carson City.

Kit Carson Trail Ghost Walk, held annually in October in Carson City, NV. Contact Carson City Convention and Visitors Bureau; ↘ 775 687 7410; web: www.carson-city.org

If you're wondering what burros and pancakes have to do with each other, take a look at the **Beatty Burro and Flapjack Races**. Following an Old West ritual, each contestant has to load up their burro the way the prospectors did, with pick, shovel and other prospecting accouterments. Then the race begins, each participant trying valiantly to lead his charge around the track. There's much foot-dragging and ass-sitting (some of it human), but eventually the burros are prodded or carried to the end of the track where the prospector has to unload the gear, build a small fire without using any tinder, cook a pancake and feed it to the burro. The first burro to swallow a cooked flapjack wins. Since burros are quite fond of flapjacks, they often try to eat it before it's cooked and another battle between man and beast ensues, much to the delight of the spectators.

> **Beatty Burro and Flapjack Races**, held annually in October in Beatty, NV. Contact Beatty Chamber of Commerce, 119 Main St, PO Box 956, Beatty, NV 89003; ↘ 866 736 3716 or 775 553 2424; web: www.beattynevada.org

Eccentric environments
Dooby Lane is a mile-long stretch of inscribed rocks and funky sculpture in the desert outside of Gerlach. Named after Guru 'Dooby' Williams, the eccentric who created the work, Dooby Lane is a quirky diary of his philosophy. Inscribed with sayings like 'Believe Only What Can Be Proved' and 'The Best Things In Life Are Not Things', the path makes for an entertaining walk and inspired a book titled *Dooby Lane: A Testament Inscribed In Stone Tablets*.

> **Dooby Lane**, located on the edge of the Black Rock Desert just outside of Gerlach, NV. Directions: From Gerlach, follow NV-447 northwest approximately 1 mile to the junction of NV-447 and Washoe-County-34. Stay to the right on WC-34. The entrance to Dooby Lane is about two miles from the Texaco station.

A remarkable conglomeration of old car bodies, bottles, machinery, bones, wheels, tree branches and railroad ties, **Thunder Mountain** was the work of a Creek Indian named Frank Van Zandt, aka Rolling Mountain Thunder, who created it as a haven for Native American consciousness. Mixed with concrete and molded into sculpture, his flotsam creations attracted a community of spiritually minded people who contributed to the shrine in the 70s and 80s. Today the property is protected by his children who welcome visitors for self-guided tours.

> **Thunder Mountain**, located on I-80 outside of Imlay, NV. Imlay is between Winnemucca and Lovelock, about 120 miles east of Reno.

Quirkyville
Being dubbed the '**Armpit of America**' would have to be a city's worst nightmare and the touristically challenged town of Battle Mountain, population 3,000, wasn't thrilled by their dubious distinction. Writer Gene Weingarten bestowed the title upon them in the *Washington Post Sunday Magazine* in December 2001, citing its 'lack of character and charm, its pathetic assemblage of ghastly buildings and nasty people' and its location 'in the midst of harsh and uninviting wilderness'. The townsfolk have gamely accepted their fate, however, and managed to convince the Old Spice deodorant company to sponsor an annual **Festival In the Pit**. They toss deodorant instead of eggs, hold a 'quick-draw' antiperspirant contest and sponsor an armpit beauty pageant. The story of Battle Mountain's rise to armpit fame is a fascinating one; you'll find a link to it on the town website.

> **Festival in the Pit**, held annually in August. Contact the Battle Mountain Chamber of Commerce, 625 S Broad St, Battle Mt, NV 89820; ↘ 775 635 8245; web: www.battlemountain.org

Just plain weird
Probably the biggest and oldest shoe tree in America – as in a tree hung with hundreds of pairs of shoes – stands alongside Nevada's 'Loneliest Road in

Quirk Alert

A FUTURE ECCENTROSITY?

A corporate 'eccentrosity' in the making, New Millennium Holy Land is a whopper of a grandiose plan. Jesus will rise over the freeway 33 stories high, welcoming you to a $1.5 billion venture near Mesquite, Nevada. If it ever gets built, the theme park will have computer animation and holography to bring the Bible alive, a pavilion of world religions, and a re-creation of Hell … (insert your own wisecrack here). Oh, and you'll be able to ascend to the top of Jesus' head for a view of the surrounding desert. The Holy Land folks also thought it might be a nifty idea to build a Noah's Ark as long as they're in the neighborhood. If it ever comes to pass, the ark, precisely 465 feet long, 105 feet wide and 48 feet tall, will be built on a high mesa, illuminated at night and made to appear to be floating on water.

Let's face it – if Noah had gotten his message from God while living in America, we'd have had a Noah's Ark Theme Park and Petting Zoo before you could say 'thunder and lightning'. Want to bet there'll also be a heavenly light show and gift shop? According to the developers, they chose this desert area because it resembles Israeli terrain. Might they also hope to snag some of the 30 million motorists on their way into or out of nearby Sin City, aka Las Vegas?

America'. No one really knows how this one got started but the most credible story involves a couple on their way to the altar. Apparently the bride began to get cold feet so the would-be groom threw her shoes up into the tree so she couldn't run away. Regardless of its origin, the first pair spawned another, and another, then another. Today an amazing array of footwear adorns the tree and thousands more shoes lie in a nearby gully.

Nevada Shoe Tree, located on the north side of Hwy 50 near Middlegate, NV. The tree is located on US Hwy 50 between Fallon and Austin, NV, about three miles east of the junction with state Rte 361.

The decayed ghost town of Rhyolite is a particularly appropriate setting for a non-traditional art installation called the **Gold Well Open Air Museum**. Ghostlike figures, looking like humans draped with sheets, appear to float in the vast, empty landscape. One of the figures, the Ghost Rider, stands beside his rusty bicycle, a fitting portrayal of the decaying setting. A soaring nude woman, perched high atop a telephone pole, is worshiping the sky with outstretched arms. The ghost town itself is unusually interesting because it was built to be permanent. Rhyolites thought they'd have an endless supply of gold, but the town was deserted in 1916 after just 15 years. The Bureau of Land Management provides caretakers for the town – interesting, eccentric characters who hang out as volunteer G-hosts, willing and anxious to share their stories with you.

> **Gold Well Open Air Museum**, located near Rhyolite and Beatty, NV, approximately 2.5 miles west of Beatty off State Hwy 374. Contact Gold Well Open Air Museum, c/o 3008 Mason Ave, Las Vegas, NV 89102; ↘ 702 870 9946; web: www.fundraiserx.com/goldwell.html

UFO watchers have been gathering for years at the **Little A 'Le' Inn** south of Rachel in the hope of seeing the same flying saucers that Bob Lazar claimed to have seen in 1988. Back then, there were supposedly nine of the saucers holed up in a hillside hangar; Bob claims he even worked with the aliens to repair one of their craft. Wednesday nights seemed to be a good time for the aliens to take their saucers out for a spin, so Bob started bringing friends out to the desert to watch. When a Las Vegas TV station broadcast Bob's story, folks began flocking to the site on Wednesday nights. Inn owners Pat and Joe Travis weren't all that convinced that aliens regularly hung out in their neck of the scrub, but what the heck, it was good for business. They changed the name of their bar from the Rachel Bar and Grill to the Little A 'Le' Inn and stocked up on logo hats, mugs and souvenirs.

Meanwhile, the highway, Route 375, that runs past the Inn has been designated the **Extraterrestrial Highway** and the Inn itself sits just ten miles from the entrance to **Area 51**, a well-known, top-secret government installation where some sort of alien exchange program is supposedly taking place. Rumors of recent spacecraft sightings around Area 51 are always circulating and the highway itself is marked with road signs featuring images of spaceships.

> **Little A 'Le' Inn & Motel**, HC 61, Box 45, Rachel, NV 89001; ↘ 775 729 251; web: www.aleinn.com

> **The Extraterrestrial Highway** runs north–south, north of Area 51, Nellis AFB Bombing and Gunnery Range and Tonopah Test Range, from Warm Springs to Ash Springs, NV. Contact Tonopah Convention and Visitors Authority, ↘ 775 482 3558.

> **Area 51** located near Rachel, NV. Contact Tonopah Convention and Visitors Authority, ↘ 775 482 3558; web: www.tonopahnevada.com

ARIZONA
Festivals and events

Oatman is a real Old West mining ghost town. Fewer than 200 folks live there now, but 50,000 visit annually. It's genuinely quirky and full of eccentric characters. In January, during the height of the tourist season, they hold bed races. Five people make up each team – one in the bed and four pushing. Halfway through the figure-eight course they have to stop, change the bedclothes and then exchange pajamas with another team member before racing to the finish line. Also in Oatman you can answer the age-old question, 'How hot does it get in the desert in July?' You get ten minutes to find out at the July Fourth High Noon Sidewalk Egg Fry. Hundreds

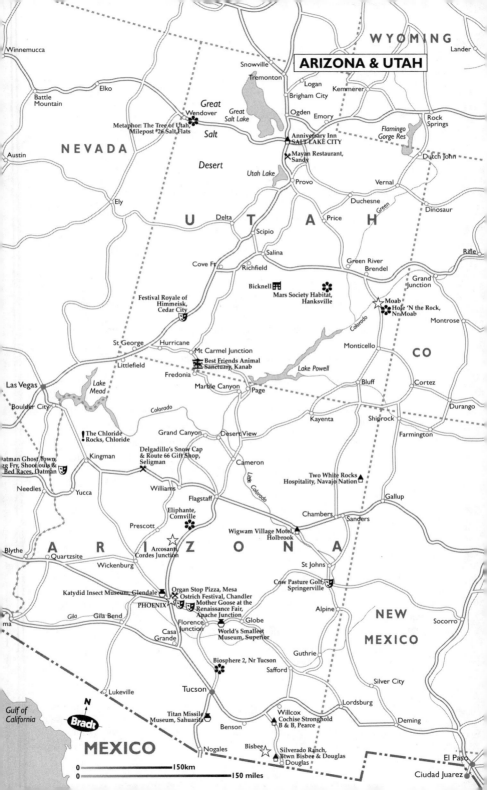

WYOMING

ARIZONA & UTAH

Lander

Winnemucca

Snowville

Tremonton

Logan

Kemmerer

Rock Springs

Battle Mountain

Elko

Great Salt Lake

Brigham City

Ogden

Emory

Flamingo Gorge Res

Austin

NEVADA

Wendover

Metaphor: The Tree of Utah
Milepost #26 Salt Flats

Great Salt Lake

Salt

Anniversary Inn
SALT LAKE CITY

Mayan Restaurant, Sandy

Dutch John

Ely

Desert

Utah Lake

Provo

Duchesne

Vernal

Dinosaur

UTAH

Delta

Price

Green

Scipio

Salina

Green River

Rifle

Cove Ft

Richfield

Brendel

Grand Junction

Bicknell

Mars Society Habitat, Hanksville

Festival Royale of Himmeisk, Cedar City

Colorado

Moab

Hole 'N the Rock, Nr Moab

Montrose

CO

St George

Hurricane

Mt Carmel Junction

Monticello

Littlefield

Best Friends Animal Sanctuary, Kanab

Lake Powell

Bluff

Cortez

Las Vegas

Fredonia

Marble Canyon

Page

Durango

Boulder City

Lake Mead

Colorado

Kayenta

Shiprock

Farmington

The Chloride Rocks, Chloride

Grand Canyon

Desert View

Kingman

Delgadillo's Snow Cap & Route 66 Gift Shop, Seligman

Cameron

Little Colorado

Two White Rocks Hospitality, Navajo Nation

atman Ghost Town,
g Fry, Shoot outs &
Bed Races, Datman

Needles

Yucca

Williams

Flagstaff

Chambers

Sanders

Gallup

Eliphante, Cornville

Blythe

Quartzsite

Prescott

ARIZONA

Wigwam Village Motel, Holbrook

Wickenburg

Arcosanti
Cordes Junction

St Johns

Cow Pasture Golf, Springerville

NEW MEXICO

Katydid Insect Museum, Glendale

Organ Stop Pizza, Mesa
Ostrich Festival, Chandler

Mother Goose at the
Renaissance Fair,
Apache Junction

Alpine

Socorro

ma

Gila Bend

Gila

PHOENIX

Globe

Casa Grande

Florence Junction

World's Smallest Museum, Superior

Guthrie

Silver City

Biosphere 2, Nr Tucson

Safford

Lukeville

Tucson

Lordsburg

Deming

Gulf of California

N

Bradt

Titan Missile Museum, Sahuarita

Benson

Willcox

Cochise Stronghold B & B, Pearce

MEXICO

Nogales

Bisbee

Silverado Ranch, Btwn Bisbee & Douglas

Douglas

El Paso

Ciudad Juarez

0 ———— 150km

0 ———— 150 miles

of folks compete for prizes, trying to fry the best-looking, best-cooked egg using whatever they think will speed the sizzle along – tin foil, magnifying glasses, mirrors and a variety of strange contraptions. Since the temperature hovers between 105° and 115°, generating heat isn't too big a problem. That same day, Oatman is witness to dozens of 'gunfights' as groups of staged gunfighters from other Western towns converge for a day of competitive shoot-outs. The town is famous for its wandering burros, a legacy of the old mining days. The day ends with a burro-biscuit toss. A burro biscuit is hay that's already made one trip through the burro. They're painted gold, then folks let 'em fly. The record is Oatman to San Diego. It seems one of the biscuits hit the bumper of a moving car and wasn't discovered for 700 miles. The nearby Gold Road Mine hosts an occasional murder mystery event.

> **Oatman Ghost Town**, Egg Fry, Shoot-outs and Bed Races located centrally on Historical Route 66 between Kingman, AZ, Bullhead City, AZ, Laughlin, NV, and Needles, CA, approximately 30 miles from each.

> **Egg Fry**, part of annual July Fourth celebration.

> **Bed Races**, held annually second Sunday in January. Contact Oatman-Gold Road Chamber of Commerce, PO Box 423, Oatman, AZ 86433; ↘ 928 768 6222; fax: 928 768 4274; web: www.oatmangoldroad.com

Cow Pasture Golf is one wacky game on the range and it's played each year as a charitable benefit at the Cowboy Golf Tournament. Horses serve as caddies, carrying three clubs in a pouch made from the leg of a pair of jeans. The course is full of sagebrush, coarse grass, rocks, boulders and cows. To compensate, the holes are coffee-can size and marked with tree branches. At one hole, you have to hit right off a high cliff; with luck, your ball lands in the wading-pool 500 feet below.

> **Cow Pasture Golf**, held each September or October at Bar Flying V Ranch east of Springerville. Contact the Cowboy Cow Pasture Golf Association, ↘ 520 333 2123; web: http://events.cowboy.com/ event_details.cgi?ID=878; or Round Valley Chamber of Commerce, PO Box 31, Springerville, AZ 85938; ↘ 520 333-2123; web: www.springerville-eagar.com

Tempe hosts the **Great Cardboard Boat Regatta** every spring on Tempe Town Lake. Competition is fierce as more than 50 companies and organizations vie to create the most creative, lake-worthy craft. Participants work on their boats for months, often attending clinics to learn how to make one sturdy enough to hold up to ten people. They're restricted to nothing but cardboard, paper tape, paint, and glue. Past entries included the zoo's huge giraffe, with the crew dressed to match; a giant burrito; a 50s' pink Cadillac crewed by the 'Pink Ladies', and the *Crouching Tiger, Sinking Dragon*, a 40-foot-long dragon boat.

> **Great Cardboard Boat Regatta**, held annually in April. Contact the Rotary River Rally hotline at ↘ 480 682 9065; web: www.rotaryriverrally.com

It's not all that easy to ride an ostrich. Just ask any of the bird jockeys who race these creatures at the **Chandler Ostrich Festival**. Now in its 16th year, the races are the highlight of the festival, drawing 300,000 folks to watch the daily shows. Ostriches are more than a few plumes short of a boa. With a brain the size of your thumbnail, they don't train easily, if at all. In addition to the races, they have an ostrich parade, ostrich alley where you can find all kinds of ostrich products, extreme stunt activities, and plenty of music and rides. The region was once renowned for raising the exotic birds for their valuable plumes.

Chandler Ostrich Festival, held annually in March. Contact the Chandler Chamber of Commerce, 25 S Arizona Pl, Ste 201, Chandler, AZ 85225; ➤ 480 963 4571; web: www.ostrichfestival.com

Eccentric environments

Mary Lou Gulley hardly knew the father who built her a castle, yet she's spent the last 53 years living there and leading tours of his off-kilter creation. The **Mystery Castle** began in the late 1920s when Boyce Gulley had to leave his family and coastal home and head to the desert for health reasons. Remembering how his precious little daughter became dismayed when the waves washed away her sandcastles, he vowed to build her a real one that could never be swept away. He found the perfect place in the Arizona Desert. For 18 years he toiled building the castle, enduring ridicule, poverty and hardship. The result, an odd pueblo-style structure, has belltowers, shrines, 18 rooms and 13 fireplaces, all built of bottles, throwaway bricks, railroad ties, boxcars, river rock and granite. Undulating snakes, usually made from river rock, are set into the walls and floors because Boyce believed they were symbols of protection, wisdom, and defiance. A foldout bar is made of tequila bottles cemented into the rock. His family didn't know about the castle until after his death when they moved here to care for it. The castle didn't get running water and electricity until 1971.

Mystery Castle, 800 East Mineral Rd, Phoenix, AZ 85040; ➤ 602 268 1581. *Open Thur–Sun 11.00am–4.00pm.*

As live-in environments go, this is one of *the* very best. From the moment you enter Michael Kahn and Leda Livant's world, till long after you leave it, you'll be mesmerized by what they've created in a lush desert region north of Phoenix. **Eliphante**, named after the accidental elephantine shape of the entrance tunnel, is both an art form and their home. Sprawling over three acres, their undulating, fantastical structures house themselves and their art, the land barely able to contain the exuberance that Eliphante exudes. A visit there means letting yourself play, taking in the forms, patterns, colors and textures with all your senses. Michael and Leda settled on this property in 1979, living in their truck and in a tent. Scavenging natural materials from the creek and the desert, they sculpted the first 'building', creating an art structure that became architecture. The path to it winds by a creek, topped by a canopy of driftwood. The main entrance is through a tunnel that leads to a domed chamber, every inch of which is decorated with a mosaic of glass, stone, tile, plaster, paint, and wood. Next they created their winter-time 'home', another undulating, highly idiosyncratic structure, as well as an outdoor kitchen, bathroom and shower.

Next they moved on to the largest installation on the property, Pipe Dreams, 2,500 square feet of tactile and visual adventure. You'll be in awe at what you see, an underground labyrinth inlaid with intricate wood, tile and stone mosaics. Walls and ceilings are draped with fabrics, collages, and Mylar weavings. Light streams in from secret sources. There's not a straight line in sight; everything flows, rounds, and curves. Michael's paintings hang throughout. The whole thing is topped by a giant sculpture of twisting, intertwining metal pipes, a sight any extra-terrestrial would find hard to resist. In yet another structure off to the side, the ceiling gets lower and lower until you're forced to crawl toward the light at the end of the tunnel. The room at the end is well worth it. Whatever the forces driving Leda and Michael, the end result is a truly unique, utterly extraordinary eccentric environment.

> **Eliphante**, PO Box 971, Cornville, AZ 86325; ↘ 928 634 4341; web: www.eliphante.org. *Directions: From Interstate 17 take 293W to Cornville. Go about 9 miles, cross a bridge, then go one block to Loy Rd. Left on Loy about 2¹/₂ miles, then left on Kaddomoto which dead ends at Candler. Right on Candler (dips and curves). Turn right at the Eliphante mailbox.* You must call ahead for an appointment. Sometimes Michael has to ferry you across the creek in a canoe!

A quiet residential street in Phoenix is the last place you'd expect to see a front yard filled with fanciful rock figures and stone arches inlaid with rock mosaics. **Mr Lee's Rock Garden** is a complete surprise, a delightful contrast to the sameness of his neighbor's landscaping. This colorful garden of rock and concrete sculpture, imbedded with colorful glass, stones, terracotta and smiling faces, represents 40 years of dedication.

> **Mr Lee's Rock Garden**, 4015 E McDonald, Phoenix, AZ 85018; ↘ 602 840 2684

You'd have to be a little wacky to volunteer to live inside a human terrarium with eight other people for two years, even if it was done in the interests of science. In a case of life imitating art, the experiment at **Biosphere 2** wasn't much more congenial than those survivor-type television shows. The whole thing was supposed to be a sealed, controlled environment with air, food, water and waste being endlessly recycled. Unfortunately, the project ran low on oxygen and high on carbon dioxide, so all the birds, animals and plants died and the pioneers finally stumbled out, heading for the nearest McDonald's. Temporarily operated by Columbia University, the biosphere is open for tours so you can see for yourself what they were trying to accomplish inside this biosphere designed to mimic conditions on Earth. The giant, three-acre, enclosed glass terrarium is now being used to study the greenhouse effect along with a dozen other scientific projects. The original $150 million, privately funded venture supposedly turned out to be a cult experiment by a group hoping to colonize Mars.

> **Biosphere 2**, located on Hwy 77 about 20 miles north of Tucson, AZ; ↘ 800 828 2462 or 520 838 6200; web: www.bio2.edu. *Open daily 8.30am–5.00pm except Christmas Day.*

Looking somewhat like Tinker Toys on steroids, **Arconsanti** hopes to become a model for how the world will build its cities in the future. Unlike most of the eccentric visionaries who dream up similar schemes, Paolo Soleri is a world-renowned architect. Using the concept of arcology (architecture + ecology), he hopes his prototype demonstrates that urban conditions don't have to be destructive to the planet or stressful to the psyche. Volunteers and students from around the world take a five-week workshop learning how to build the three-dimensional, pedestrian-oriented city that has been under construction since 1970. When complete, the facility is meant to house 7,000 pioneers, all hoping to avoid rush hour forever. Can a new Starbucks be far behind?

> **Arcosanti**, located in Central Arizona, 65 miles north of Phoenix, just off I-17, exit 262 (Cordes Junction). Contact HC 74, Box 4136, Mayer, AZ

86333; ↘ 520 632 7135; web: www.arcosanti.org. *Open daily 10.00am–4.00pm except Thanksgiving and Christmas. Donations suggested.*

Known as the Mountain Gnome, George Phar Legler lived in a magical kingdom inhabited by elves, fairies, trolls, wizards, and witches. At his **Valley of the Moon**, he and his imaginative creatures lived happily among the hundreds of rock and cement monuments he built at his fantasy fairyland. Three generations of children shared his fantasies, wandering among the pathways, nooks and crannies of both his environment and his fertile imagination. George's magical kingdom lives on today through the efforts of a dedicated preservation society. Especially popular are the Moon Strolls and Haunted Ruins Halloween events.

Valley of the Moon, 2544 E Ellen Rd, Tuscon, AZ 85716 (north of Prince Rd, between Tuscon Blvd and Country Club); ↘ 520 323 1331; web: www.valleyofthemoon.org

Museums and collections
Better look quick or you'll whiz right past this one. The **World's Smallest Museum,** which began life as a humble tool shed, now sports a false front and houses little themed vignettes with stuff like household implements from the 1850s and the last ever photo taken of Geronimo. But it's not so much what's inside that's of interest as much as what's outside: an assortment of large waterfalls created out of recycled stuff like tires, wheelbarrows, and washtubs. Curators Dan and Jake, who own the Buckaroo Restaurant next door, set up the fountains to attract desert birds and animals. The museum, which of course attracts customers, aims to depict the hard-working people of the region's past.

World's Smallest Museum, 1111 West US Hwy 60, Superior, AZ 85273; ↘ 520 689 5857; web: www.worldssmallestmuseum.com. *Open daily 8.00am–2.00pm. Admission free.*

Nedra Soloman's kids say she's easy to shop for. Just buy her a bug or a reptile that she can display at her **Katydid Insect Museum**. She and her family have been in the pest control business for two decades, but the 60-something's passion for bug collecting is relatively recent – just under ten years. One of her favorite gifts was a $200 Mongolian walking stick, a very skinny insect with a body a foot long. On Mother's Day she was thrilled to receive a bearded dragon, a most picturesque member of the lizard family. (Don't you wish your mother were that easy to shop for?) Once you get over the 'Ewu-u!' and 'Ick!' stage, you'll find her hobby quite fascinating. The museum has plenty of creepy-crawly activities to keep the kids busy while you try to look cool. There are 20,000 insects under glass (meaning dead), but Nedra also displays hundreds of live ones, some of which you can hold: tarantulas (including one with a ten-inch leg span); centipedes and millipedes; hissing roaches; and a collection of the world's most dangerous spiders. Reptiles include a python and leash-trained iguanas.

Katydid Insect Museum, a division of Heritage Pest Control, 5060 W Bethany Home, PO Box 1702, Glendale, AZ 85301-1702; ↘ 623 931 8718; web: www.insectmuseum.com. *Open Mon–Fri 11.00am–4.00pm, Sat noon–4.00pm, Oct–Feb.*

At the **Titan Missile Museum** a retired Air Force veteran takes you down into the control bunker of this restored missile silo to see the largest Inter-

Quirk Alert

DIAPERS FOR DUCKS

Nancy Townsend calls herself **Mother Goose** and walks diaper-wearing ducks and geese on a leash. Dressed as the fairy-tale character, she's one of the more well-known free spirits in Arizona. Nancy didn't set out to become famous for inventing the world's only known fowl diaper harness. All she wanted to do was bring her pet duck inside to live (unmessily) with the family. After many hits and misses, if you get the drift, she applied for a patent on a comfortable harness that not only allows a ten-second diaper change but also provides a convenient leash attachment. Nancy has made it possible to keep ducks and geese as house pets, a passion shared by an amazing number of like-minded people.

According to Mother Goose, ducks are environmentally sound pets, eating bad bugs and leaving the good ones to do their jobs. They'll do your yard work by killing weeds, fertilizing, and keeping your grass and plants healthy. They don't need shelter, never complain about the weather, are free of disease, provide 20% of their own food and can even provide some of yours. (We're talking duck eggs, here, not the ducks.) On top of all that, ducks are smart, learning skills and routines in just two to three days. Training requires no discipline, no commands, no orders and no rewards. Highly social and affectionate, they just want to please. When reared from birth, they imprint on humans and, according to Nancy, 'expect to wear clothes and sit on chairs like

Continental Ballistic Missile (ICBM) ever developed by the United States. In all, there were 54 Titan II missile sites, all operational in 1963 and all phased out 20 years later. This is the only site that remains intact; all the others were destroyed.

> **Titan Missile Museum**, 1580 W Duval Mine Rd, Sahuarita, AZ; ☎ 520 625 7736; web: www.pimaair.org/titan_01.htm. Directions: approximately 25 miles south of Tucson. From Tucson take I-19 south to Green Valley, exit 69 west 10 miles past La Canada to entrance. *Open daily 9.00am–5.00pm Nov 1–Apr 30 except Thanksgiving and Christmas; Wed–Sun 9.00am–5.00pm May 1–Oct 31. Admission charge.*

Just plain weird

Roy Purcell looked at 2,000 square feet of desert rock and boulders and saw an opportunity for self-discovery. Roy was taking some time off to 'find himself' 40 years ago and the rocks seemed to say, 'Look here, look here!' Using automotive paint bought for him by a friendly miner, he spent a summer creating 'The Journey', murals painted right there on the rocks. Some of the images tower 75 feet above you. You'll have to drive down a bumpy dirt road 1.3 miles to see his creation, known as **The Chloride Rocks**, but it's worth it. Today Roy is an accomplished artist, propelled into his career by way of his 'Journey'.

everyone else. Treat them like well-behaved children from a foreign country who do not speak the language,' she says, 'and they'll be quite happy.'

Cricket the Duck and Maggie and Mimi the Geese are Nancy's constant companions, becoming concerned if she's away for more than four hours. Her incredibly tolerant husband, Alan, joins her for their public appearances dressed as — who else? — Father Goose. They all have quite a wardrobe, dressing appropriately for the season and holidays. People are so surprised by the sight of them, sipping coffee with their brood on their laps or shoulders, that they often blurt our really dumb questions such as 'Is it real?' or 'Is it tame?' 'No', Nancy thinks, but does not say 'I was sitting here minding my own business when this wild duck came out of the sky and sat in my lap all dressed up! Incredible!' Instead, she invites you to pet her pets, telling you all about her life with these fascinating creatures. Maggie the Goose will even hug you, wrapping her silky long neck around yours in a gesture of affection. Once, while eating lunch on ritzy Rodeo Drive in Los Angeles, a lady from England gently told Nancy, 'You do know, dear, you're just a tad left of center.' Not at all offended, this delightful eccentric agreed.

Mother and Father Goose and their entourage appear at various Renaissance festivals in Arizona, Georgia, Colorado, Minnesota and North Carolina, including a two-month run in Arizona. You can see her pets 'hop-walk' on a leash and see Mother Goose herself reciting rhymes about her life with ducks. You're welcome to photograph and videotape; tips are appreciated.

Renaissance Fair, held every weekend in February and March in Apache Junction, AZ. Fairgrounds are located 9 miles east of Apache Junction on US Route 60; ✆ 520 631 3320; web: www.thegoosesmother.com. *Admission charge.*

The Chloride Rocks, located in the hills behind Chloride, AZ. Directions: follow US-93 about 90 miles east of Las Vegas to the Chloride turn-off just before Kingman.

Quirky cuisine

Now this is surround sound! At **Organ Stop Pizza** the music comes from the world's largest Wurlitzer theater organ. The entire restaurant was designed to house this massive 'unit orchestra', originally designed in the early 1900s to replace a live orchestra. While you're eating your pizza, the organ's centerpiece rises up from the stage floor and you're treated to a dozen or so tunes played by their staff of classical musicians. The whole experience is enhanced with lighting, dancing puppets and sing-alongs. Four huge turbine blowers, visible on the exterior of the building, power the 5,500-pipe organ. The apparatus fills the entire restaurant so you'll have no trouble hearing. Forty-three-foot ceilings allow plenty of acoustical space for the sound waves to reach your table.

Organ Stop Pizza, 1149 E Southern Ave, Mesa, AZ 85204; ✆ 480 813 5700; web: www.organstoppizza.com

If you look closely at Juan Delgadillo's business card, you'll notice 'dead chicken' listed along with shakes, sundaes and cheeseburgers. Juan, 87, is famous for his practical jokes. Eat at **Delgadillo's Snow Cap** and you're likely to find Juan handing your change to the guy behind you. Order a small Coke and he may fill your order in a thimble. The restaurant itself has handles on doors that don't open, a menu offering hamburgers without ham, and a sign that says 'Sorry, we're open'. Juan shares the eccentric spotlight with his younger brother, Angel, 76, who greets the public each day from his **Route 66 Gift Shop**/barbershop/visitor center/museum/ex-pool hall next door. Angel is likely to consult a barbering textbook just as he takes a razor to your chin. The two are well known along the route for their quirky humor and practical jokes; they've been fixtures on Route 66 for 50 years.

> **Delgadillo's Snow Cap & Route 66 Gift Shop**, 217 E Route 66, PO Box 426, Seligman, AZ 86337; ↘ 928 422 3352 or 928 422 3291; web: www.route66giftshop.com. *Open daily 8.00am–9.00pm.*

Room with a Skew

Way off the beaten path, **Cochise Stronghold Bed & Breakfast** offers a night in a straw bale lodge or in a teepee. Owners and wilderness enthusiasts John and Nancy Yates, who live in yurts on the property themselves, built these structures because they think it's important for people to be able to 'hear the quiet'. The rooms in the straw bale lodge have thick, solid, sculpted walls, wood-burning stoves, and include use of the hot tub. The teepee is tucked in a grove of juniper trees; it has fire pits both inside and out. The Yates live a sustainable lifestyle (albeit with satellite TV and computers), harvesting rainwater and grinding the corn for your cornmeal pancakes.

> **Cochise Stronghold Bed & Breakfast**, located off Forest Service Rd #84 at 2126 W Windancer Trail, Box 232, Pearce, AZ 85625; ↘ 877 426 4141 or 520 826 4141; web: www.cochisestrongholdbb.com

The Inn at Castle Rock is definitely not your normal B&B. In fact, 'We're Not Normal' is their motto. There's a koi pond in the restaurant – at the bottom of a mineshaft. Every room is decorated differently, some with funky interpretations of Western, island and Victorian themes. Then there are the ghosts, one of whom is reportedly the man responsible for all this, artist and collector Jim Babcock who died in 1997. His daughter, Jeannene, now runs the inn and hasn't changed a thing since her quirky father's death.

> **Inn at Castle Rock**, 112 Tombstone Canyon Rd, Box 1161, Bisbee, AZ 85603-2161; ↘ 800 556 4449 or 520 432 4449; web: www.theinn.org

At the **Shady Dell Trailer Park** in Arizona, you get to stay in one of eight restored aluminum travel trailers from the 40s and 50s, listening to tinny-sounding radios playing tapes of your favorite oldies. The owners are sticklers for detail: your cookies are stored in an old cookie jar, your drinks are mixed in vintage shakers, real record players still spin 45 and 78 rpm platters, and old *Life* magazines are scattered about for your reading pleasure. Some of the larger trailers have old black-and-white TVs that play movies of the era. You might also sleep in a dry-docked 1947 Chris Craft boat or a restored 1949 road bus that once belonged to a baseball team. Home-style cooking is available at Dot's, a 1957 diner relocated from Hollywood and lovingly restored to its original art deco splendor.

> **Shady Dell Trailer Park**, 1 Douglas Rd, Bisbee, AZ 85603; ↘ 520 432 3567; web: www.theshadydell.com (Be sure to include the 'the'!)

Documentaries and movies have been made at **Wigwam Village**, the famous Route 66 landmark motel. Renovated in the late 80s, the teepees have the original tile baths and hickory furniture. Color TV, though, has replaced the old coin-operated radios that gave you an hour of sound for ten cents. Classic cars are dotted around the 15-wigwam village.

> **Wigwam Village Motel**, 811 W Hopi Dr, Holbrook, AZ; ➧ 928 524 3048; web: www.wigwamgazette.info

Two White Rocks Hospitality is a cultural experience that takes place in an eight-sided native hogan (hut). Located on the Navajo Reservation, the Hogan Bed and Breakfast provides sheepskin sleeping rugs on the dirt floor and a potbellied stove for heat. You can listen to stories around the campfire and take a traditional sweat-lodge bath.

> **Two White Rocks Hospitality**, Navajo Nation, AZ. Contact: Navajo Tourism Department, PO Box 663, Window Rock, AZ 86515; ➧ 520 871 6436; fax: 520 871 7381; web: www.discovernavajo.com

The **OK Street Jailhouse** in Bisbee has a jacuzzi in a former upstairs cell and a kitchen and living-room in the former drunk tank. The heavy metal cell doors still make a satisfactory clank when they shut.

> **OK Street Jailhouse**, 9 OK St, Bisbee, AZ; ➧ 520 432 7435

Belle Starr, 77 years old, runs the **Silverado Ranch**, a wildlife preserve, bird sanctuary and botanical gardens with Old West-style cabins and RV hookups. There's a real Indian hogan and sweat lodge for purification sweats and meditation and she'll take you on a hayride tour or sing for you by the fire pit. You can pet her miniature horses, mules and donkeys and meet Lobo, her pet wolf. Star has created this ranch almost entirely on her own and she shares it freely with you, asking only for a donation for maintenance.

> **Silverado Ranch**, Hwy 80, Milepost 353 between Bisbee and Douglas, AZ; 9132 Washboard Rd, 1-40 Adamana exit 303, Holbrook, AZ 86025; ➧ 520 524 9127; web: www.bellestarr.org

UTAH

Utah is a few pews short of a church when it comes to humor. This state takes itself way too seriously and wins the *Eccentric America* award for being the state least likely to poke fun at itself.

Festivals and events

Talk about taking things too seriously…

The little town of Cedar City (pop 23,000) issued a press release in 2003 announcing the creation of a **Festival Royale of Himmeisk**, an event ostensibly designed to celebrate the city's newly discovered heritage as an ancient Viking settlement. The festival's creators, including the mayor and his cronies, concocted a complicated, long-winded yarn about Viking artifacts being discovered in a nearby cave. The implausible tale, involving volcanic eruptions and tsunamis dumping a Viking island on the desert plateau, was published in installments in the local paper, with the originators fully expecting the populace to support the new festival as a way of raising tourism revenue. Instead, to their bemusement, the tale inspired believers, with some going so far as to claim that the artifacts unearthed belonged to them. One man implored the major not to give the priceless relics to the Smithsonian; another claimed to have the molds that the iron pieces were cast from. Even when told that the tale was entirely fiction, many of the duped refused to believe it. Nevertheless, the city plans to go ahead with plans for the first annual Festival Royale in 2004, hoping for 'the idiocy of Mardi Gras without the booze or the raunch'.

> **Festival Royale of Himmeisk**, Cedar City, UT 84720; ↘ 435 586 2953; email: mayor@cedarcity.org. *Event planned for April each year.*

Eccentric environments

At least they can claim a cave dweller, one Albert Christensen, who hand-carved a home for himself out of rock. The place occupies almost 5,000 square feet and it took 12 years of blasting away to create the 14-room **Hole 'n the Rock**. He and his wife, Gladys, lived there beginning in 1952, even running a diner and gift shop at one point, until Albert took sick and died in 1957. Gladys kept up the place for 17 more years. When she died, the family left things just as they were, including Harry the donkey, a victim of do-it-yourself taxidermy. Harry stands right next to Albert's painting of Franklin Roosevelt. Roosevelt's head is also carved into the rock near the entrance to the dream home. They're both (Albert and his wife, not Roosevelt) laid to rest in a small rock cove near the home.

> **Hole 'n the Rock**, located on Hwy 191, 15 miles south of Moab, UT 11037 South Hwy 191, Moab, UT 84532; ↘ 435 868 2250; web: www.moab-utah.com/holeintherock

Attractions

The population of Dog Town averages 600; the Cat Club around 650. Along with the Bunny House (pop 230), the Bird House (130 guests) and the Happy Herd (40 horses, sheep and goats) these villages make up the animal retirement haven known as **Best Friends Animal Sanctuary**. On any given day this refuge houses, on average, 1,500 abused and abandoned animals in a style most humans would appreciate: plenty of fresh air, sunshine, exercise and tender-loving-care combined with good food and lots of companionship. Sounds like a spa or a cruise, doesn't it? This 23,000-acre ranch offers temporary care for animals deemed adoptable (82%) or, if necessary, a permanent home for those less fortunate. A tour of the ranch lets you see the cage-free environments and experience what it's like to be in the minority species-wise.

> **Best Friends Animal Sanctuary**, Kanab, UT 84741; ↘ 435 644 2001; web: www.bestfriends.org. *Tour availability should be checked in advance.*

Just plain weird

The only eccentric burp on the plains of conformity is a strange, contemporary sculpture, **Metaphor: the Tree of Utah**, stuck way out on the Bonneville Salt Flats. Created by European artist Karl Momen, it is meant as a 'hymn to our universe whose glory and dimension is beyond all myth and imagination'. There isn't so much as a place to pull over to contemplate this, however, so maybe Utah doesn't want to encourage anyone to think California-type thoughts.

> **Metaphor: the Tree of Utah**, located at milepost 26 on I-80, Salt Flats, UT.

Quirkyville

The tiny (pop 300) town of Bicknell spoofs the Sundance Film Festival each summer in their own quirky way with the **Bicknell International Film Festival** held in the town's only theater, a venue with more seats (306) than residents to fill them. Each year they choose a theme, select the movies, and launch the festival by inviting everyone to dress in costume and decorate their cars for a 65mph caravan from Torrey, eight miles away, to the theatre. The festival's motto is, 'When Good Things Happen to Bad Movies'.

Bicknell, Utah Wayne County Travel Council; ↘ 435 425 3930; web: www.waynetheatre.com

Quirky cuisine

While the words 'Utah' and 'kitsch' usually can't be found in the same sentence, let alone in the same state, the **Mayan Restaurant** is an exception. In a fake rainforest-cum-Yucatan setting that would do Florida proud, animated parrots tell jokes, iguanas sing, thunder crashes and real live 'Mayans' in Speedos dive from 30-foot high indoor cliffs in a reenactment of an ancient Mayan sacrifice. Seating more than 1,000 people, all of whom sit on different levels in the 'trees', the Mayan qualifies as the largest restaurant in Utah – and certainly the most eccentric.

Mayan Restaurant, at Jordan Commons, 9400 S State St, Sandy, UT; ↘ 801 304 4551; web: www.jordancommons.com/food/mayan. *Open Mon–Thu 11.00am–10.00pm, Fri–Sat 11.00am–11.00pm, Sun noon–9.00pm. Dive shows run every top of the hour and every 45 minutes past the hour.*

Rooms with a Skew

The romantic **Anniversary Inn** in Old Salt Lake City is an all-theme hotel with a variety of unique suites. In the Italian Gondola, you actually sleep in a gondola; in Swiss Family Robinson you sleep in a tree; and in Jackson Hole you sleep in a covered wagon. The Lighthouse has a round bed with an aquarium above it.

Anniversary Inn, located 460 South 1000 East, Salt Lake City, UT 84102; ↘ 801 863 4900 or 800 324 4152; and South Temple located 678 East South Temple, Salt Lake City, UT 84102; ↘ 801 363 4950 or 800 324 4152; web: www.anniversaryinn.com

WISCONSIN, MINNESOTA, IOWA & ILLINOIS

CANADA

Lake of the Woods
Rainy Lake
Red Lake
Grand Forks
Crookston
Bermidji
Leech Lake
Virginia
Lake Superior
Copper Harbor
Ice Box Days, International Falls
Sandpaper Museum, Two Harbors
Duluth
Marquette
Fargo
Moorhead
Polar Fest, Detroit Lakes
St Urho's Day, Menahga
Great American Think-off, New York Mills
Nordic Inn Medieval Brew & Bed, Crosby
Mille Lake
Hayward
Ironwood
MICHIGAN
Escanaba
Potato Days, Barnesville
Runestone Museum, Alexandria
Museum of Woodcarving, Shell Lake
Beef-A-Rama, Minocqua
Iron Mountain
Wisconsin Concrete Park, Phillips
Rhinelander
Menominee
Ortonville
St Cloud
Franconia Sculpture Park, Shafer
Rice Lake
WISCONSIN
Wausau
Green Bay
Willmar
World's Biggest Ball of Twine, Darwin
ST PAUL
Canoe Bay, Chetek
Hot Air Affair, Hudson
Eau Claire
Green Bay
Minneapolis
Two-Story Outhouse, Belle Plaine
General Mills Cereal Adventures, Bloomington Hills
Stevens Point
Houdini Historical Center, Appleton
Mankato
Cabela's Outfitters, Owatonna
John Michael Kohler Arts Center, Sheboygan
Sod House B&B, Sanborn
Rochester
US Watermelon Seed Championships, Pardeeville
Americanism Center Museum, Waubeka
Luverne
Albert Lea
SPAM, Austin
Ed's Museum, Wykoff
La Crosse
Tommy Bartlett's Thrill Show, Wisconsin Dells
West Bend Inn, West Bend
Sioux Falls
Jailhouse Historic Inn, Preston
Baraboo
House on the Rock, Spring Green
Milwaukee
Spencer
Britt
Bily Clocks Museum & Dvorak Exhibit, Spillville
Waterloo Workshop, Dorchester
Mt Horeb
MADISON
Watson's Wild West Museum, Elkhorn
Burlington
Mason City
Fort Crawford Museum, Prairie du Chien
Don Q Inn, Dodgeville
Grandview, Hollandale
Angel Museum, Beloit
Adventure Inn Motel, Gurnee
Grotto of the Redemption, West Bend
Dickeyville Grotto, Dickeyville
Walworth II Mailboat, Lake Geneva
Ahlgrim Acres, Palatine
IOWA
Fort Dodge
Waterloo
Lighthouse Valley View Bed & Breakfast, Dubuque
Rockford
Cermak Shopping Plaza, Berwyn
Elgin
Chicago
Life-size Butter Cow, Iowa State Fair, DES MOINES
Cedar Rapids
Toto Fest, Welton
Raven's Grin Inn, Mt Carroll
Aurora
Joliet
Squirrel Cage Jail, Council Bluffs
Tug Fest, LeClaire
Tug Fest, Port Byron
Omaha
Palmer Mansion, Davenport
Rock Island
Riverside
Max Nordeen's Wheels Museum, Alpha
Bishop Hill
LINCOLN
Beatrice
Ottumwa
Lakeview Museum's Community Solar System, Peoria
Bloomington
ILLINOIS
Marysville
St Joseph
Chillicothe
Hannibal
Museum of Funeral Customs, SPRINGFIELD
Decatur
Terre
Riley
Two Story Outhouse, Gays
Vandalia
World's Largest Bagel Breakfast, Mattoon
Junction City
Kansas City
Columbus
Alton
Olney
Vince
TOPEKA
Kansas City
MISSOURI
St Louis
Catsup Bottle Summerfest Birthday Party, Collinsville
KANSAS
JEFFERSON CITY
East St Louis
Evan
Newton
Lake of the Ozarks
Rolla
Superman Celebration, Metropolis
KY
Wichita
N
Bradt
Ft Scott
Springfield
Mississippi
Cairo
Carthage

0   150km
0   150 miles

North Central Region

WISCONSIN
Festivals and events

The **Hot Air Affair** is the country's only wintertime hot-air-balloon festival and it involves a lot more than just hot air. This Intergalactic Olympiad features several wacky competitions: armchair quarterbacks try to hit a target with a football while sitting in an easy chair and turkey bowlers try to knock down as many soda bottles as possible using a frozen game hen wrapped in duct tape. But the highlight is Smooshboarding in which four people, dressed in absurd costumes, are strapped to makeshift skis and expected to make their way around a figure-eight course – with their feet held to 2 x 4s with bungee cords. Along with the colorful balloons, they also have a costumed torchlight parade and marching kazoo bands.

> The **Hot Air Affair**, held annually in February. Contact the Hudson Hot Air Affair, PO Box 744, Hudson, WI 54016; ☎ 888 247 2332 or 715 381 2050; web: www.hudsonhotairaffair.com

The Minocque Chamber of Commerce hosts an annual **Beef-A-Rama**, an event involving a parade of beef, a beef roast cook-off, and costumed chefs. Lakeland area businesses do the grilling in front of their shops; the roasts compete for best taste, presentation and appearance. The beef parade is led by a fire truck and followed by folks proudly displaying their cooked roasts. The roasts are then carved, sliced, put on buns and served to around several thousand visitors. They cook enough roasts to serve 3,000 beef sandwiches, all of which sell out within the first hour.

> **Beef-A-Rama**, held annually in September. Contact Minocqua Chamber of Commerce, 8216 Hwy 51S, Minocqua, WI 54548; ☎ 715 356 5266 or 800 44-NORTH; web: www.minocqua.org

A contest to see who can spit watermelon seeds the farthest may seem like child's play to you, but to thousands of adults the **US Watermelon Seed-Spitting & Speed Eating Championship** is a serious reason to celebrate. This national competition attracts the best spitters – and eaters – in the country, all of them trying to break the current record of 61 feet 3 inches for spitting and $2\frac{1}{2}$lb in $3\frac{1}{2}$ seconds for eating.

> **US Watermelon Seed-Spitting & Speed Eating Championship**, held annually early September at Chandler Park on Park Lake in Pardeeville, WI. Contact Gary Koerner, PO Box 357, Pardeeville, WI 53954; ☎ 608 429 3214; web: www.pardeeville.com

ECCENTRIC CALENDAR
WISCONSIN
February	**Elm Farm Ollie Day**, Mt Horeb (page 86)
	Hot Air Affair, Hudson (page 79)
April	**Yo-Yo Convention**, Burlington (page 88)
July	**World Lumberjack Championship**, Hayward (page 82)
August	**National Mustard Day**, Mt Horeb. Held on the first Saturday in August (page 86)
	Topless Auto Tour, Madison (page 82)
September	**Beef-A-Rama**, Minocqua (page 79)
	US Watermelon Seed-Spitting & Speed Eating Championship, Pardeeville (page 79)
October	**Spin-A-Top Day**, Burlington (page 88)
November	**Whatchamacallits**, Burlington (page 88)
	Tongue Twister, Burlington (page 88)

MINNESOTA
January	**Ice Box Days**. Held annually the third weekend in January, 15 miles east of International Falls (page 92)
	Saint Paul Winter Carnival (page 94)
February	**Polar Fest**, Detroit Lakes (page 93)
March	**St Urho's Day**, Menahga (page 93)
June	**Great American Think-off**, New York Mills (page 93)
July	**SPAM™ Town USA Festival and SPAM™ Jam**, Austin (page 94)
August	**Potato Days**, Barnesville (page 93)
	Twine Ball Day, Darwin. Held the second Saturday in August (page 97)
November	**Fish House Parade**, Aitkin. Held the day after Thanksgiving (page 92)

IOWA
May/June	**Toto Fest**, Welton. Held on Memorial Day weekend (page 99)
June	**Trek Fest**, Riverside (page 101)
July/August	**Iowa State Fair** (featuring Butter Sculptures), Des Moines (page 99)
August	**National Hobo Convention**, Britt (page 99)
	Tug Fest, LeClaire, IA and Port Byron, IL (page 100)

ILLINOIS
February	**Hustle Up the Hancock**, Chicago (page 103)
June	**Superman Celebration**, Metropolis (page 103)
July	**Catsup Bottle Summerfest Birthday Party**, Collinsville (page 102)
	World's Largest Bagel Breakfast, Mattoon (page 102)
August	**Tug Fest**, Byron, IL and LeClaire, IA (page 103)
	World Freefall Convention; location varies. (page 103)
and keep in mind...	**Cardboard Boat Regattas**, held at various locations throughout the state, normally in the spring and summer. *Visit web: www.gcbr.com for details* (page 102)

MICHIGAN

February	**Outhouse Classic**, Trenary (page 108)
June	**Doo-Dah Parade**, Kalamazoo (page 111)
	World's Longest Breakfast Table, Battle Creek (page 111)
July	**International Cherry Pit Spitting Contest**, Eau Claire (page 109)
	National Baby Food Festival, Fremont (page 109)
and keep in mind...	Cardboard Boat Regattas, held at various locations throughout the state, normally in the spring and summer. *Visit web: www.gcbr.com for details* (page 109)

INDIANA

April	**Rube Goldberg Machine Contest**, West Lafayette (page 115)
July	**Pierogi Festival**, Whiting (page 115)
September	**Wizard of Oz Fest**, Chesterton (page 114)

OHIO

June	**International Washboard Festival**, Logan (page 120)
August	**Twins Days**, Twinsburg (page 119)

SOUTH DAKOTA

July	**Mashed Potato Wrestling**, Clark. Part of the annual Potato Days celebration (page 124)
August	**International Vinegar Festival**, Roslyn (page 125)
	Sturgis Motorcycle Rally, Sturgis (page 124)

NEBRASKA

January	**Avoca Quack-off**, Avoca. Held the last Saturday in January (page 127)
July	**Wayne Chicken Show and Cluck-Off Contest**, Wayne (page 127)
September	**Running of the Wieners**, Grand Island. Part of German Heritage Days (page 127)

'Bring your toys. Drop your tops. Play in the road'. That's how the invitation reads to the Convertible Classic's **Topless Auto Tour**. Combining topless cars, scenic back roads, and plenty of partying, 'Running Around Topless' is a four-day, non-competitive tour for any make or vintage convertible or open-air car. Two hundred topless cars participate, all tuning their radios to Classic Hits 94.7 to create the world's largest topless boom box.

> **Topless Auto Tour**, held annually in August. Contact WCC, PO Box 44781, Madison, WI 53744; web: www.wiautotours.com

You, along with other amateurs, can try your hand at log-rolling, chopping, and sawing at the **World Lumberjack Championship** in Hayward. But you'll be glad to leave the pole shimmying to the professional male and female lumberjacks who compete in speed sawing, speed chopping, an 80-foot pole speed climb, and log-rolling events. It's amazing how competitors can remain upright, in spiked shoes no less, on a slippery log while trying to knock their opponent into the water.

> **World Lumberjack Championship**, held annually in July. Contact the Lumberjack World Championships, PO Box 666, Hayward, WI 54843; ↘ 715 634 2484; web: www.lumberjackworldchampionships.com

Eccentric environments

The House on the Rock, located in Spring Green, looks like an architectural impossibility, perched as it is on the pinnacle of a rock in a spot so improbable that you won't believe your eyes. You'll immediately notice the most extraordinary feature of the 14-room house: the Infinity Room, a 200-foot structure with 3,000 windows that juts out precariously over the Wyoming Valley far below. What you'll see when you get up to the house is just as amazing: a peculiar, outlandish complex of rooms, streets, buildings and gardens covering 200 acres. The post-World War II house is the work of Alex Jordan, an eccentric wannabe architect who wanted most of all to be left alone to pursue his creative quirks. When he saw the rock in 1946, he knew he'd found the place of his dreams. Working alone, he built the original studio by carrying stones and mortar up to the site in a basket strapped to his back. Eventually, he built a ramp through the treetops to make the site more accessible. The studio fireplace, the largest you'll ever see, has a stairway in its flue and a secret room hidden within it.

As his fantasy grew in size, so did the curiosity surrounding it. Irritated by nosy neighbors, he thought he'd discourage gawkers by charging admission. Not only didn't this ploy work, it attracted even more attention. So Jordan used his ever-increasing income to indulge with incomprehensible thoroughness his bizarre and fertile imagination.

Over the next four decades he expanded his attraction to include dozens of strange exhibits. There are structures built just to house his collections and displays: dollhouses and dolls, suits of armour, mechanical banks, paperweights, a one million piece miniature circus, a pyramid of life-size elephants, model ships, giant organs, weaponry and oriental artifacts. He assembled the greatest collection of automated music machines in the world. The Blue Room contains the world's only mechanically operated symphony orchestra. A $4.5 million carousel boasts 240 animals, not one of them a horse. Twenty thousand lights illuminate it and hundreds of topless angels cavort overhead. In the Streets of Yesterday, he recreated the 19th century complete with a sheriff's office, carriage house, woodcarver's shop, homes and gas lamps.

Shortly before he died in 1989, he sold the House on the Rock to a long-time friend and collector who has since added a Heritage of the Sea building housing a 200-foot sea creature engaged in a titanic struggle with an octopus. Also new is the Transportation building which offers a terrific view of the house itself. At Christmas, they trot out thousands of Santas, including life-size replicas from around the world. You'll be grateful for the on-site café. You'll need sustenance to see and absorb this most eccentric of American attractions.

The House on the Rock, 5754 Hwy 23, Spring Green, WI 53588;
➘ 608 935 3639; web: www.thehouseontherock.com. *Open daily 9.00am–7.00pm Mar 15–Oct 29; also special holiday hours in Nov & Dec.*

Nick Engelbert was a dairy farmer who immigrated to America early in the last century. He led a relatively normal life – if you don't count the 40 concrete, glass, shell and stone sculptures he made in between milking the cows and making cheese. Or that he covered every inch of his farmhouse with concrete inlaid with china, glass, buttons, beads, and shells. At his home in Hollandale, which he called **Grandview**, he crafted sculptures like Snow White with five of her seven dwarfs, a lion, an eagle and an organ grinder. There's also Neptune's fountain, a lighthouse, an elephant, and a stork carrying a baby. Some of Nick's sculptures were built to pay tribute to his friends while three Swiss patriots honor his wife, a Swiss immigrant. He used the same technique for all his sculptures: arranging wooden boxes for structure, wrapping them with nets made of metal, then covering them with cement and adding the decorative touches. When he got too old to make any more sculptures, he turned to painting, producing 200 oils before his death in 1962. The environment is visible from the road during the winter months when the facility is closed, but you can call for an appointment off-season if you want to see the house.

Grandview, located on Wisconsin State Hwy 39, west of Hollandale, 30 miles southwest of Madison and 11 miles east of Mineral Point, WI. Grounds open daily year round. Contact Barb Kehrein, PEC Foundation; ➘ 608 523 4018; email: barbkehrein@yahoo.com; web: www.nicksgrandview.org. *House open daily 10.00am–4.00pm from Memorial Day to Labor Day, weekends only May and Oct or by special appointment.*

Fred Smith was an extremely prolific concrete and glass sculptor, creating 250 figures of mythical, as well as real, characters and animals at his **Wisconsin Concrete Park** in Phillips. A former logger, farmer, tavern owner and musician, he began his obsession when he retired in the late 1940s. His sculptures, made over a 14-year period as a gift 'for all the American people', all have a joyous, flamboyant quality. Some of his figures are so large they had to be made in pieces and assembled on their footings. Glass for decoration was readily available from the tavern next door as well as from supportive neighbors who brought colorful glass, bottles, and mirrors each time they visited. Fred's characters, some adorned with tail-lights, skulls or antlers, were taken from regional lore and legendary heroes. The three-and-a-half-acre park has tributes to Ben Hur, Abe Lincoln, the Indian princess Sacajawea and Paul Bunyan.

Wisconsin Concrete Park, Hwy 13, Phillips, WI. Contact Friends of Fred Smith, Price County Forestry Dept, 104 S Eyder St, Phillips, WI 54555; ☎ 715 339 6371; web: http://outsider.art.org/fred/

Politics and religion mix well at **Dickeyville Grotto**, an environment created in the 1920s and 1930s by Father Wernerus, a German-born Catholic priest with a fondness for concrete and all things that glitter. His sculptures and shrines, located in the grounds of the Holy Ghost Parish in Dickeyville, are a madcap mixture of glass, gems, pottery, shells, starfish, fossils, corals, quartz, iron and copper ore, crystals, coal, petrified wood and moss. Visitors have been flocking to this eccentric environment for 75 years, probably because its theme is as much about patriotism as it is about religion. Father Wernerus was motivated by two ideals: love of God and love of country, and the Grotto reflects a deep devotion to both. The Grotto of the Blessed Virgin, the main structure, is covered with symbols important in Catholic ritual. A Vatican flag flies at the left, an American flag at the right.

Dickeyville Grotto, located at US Rte 151 and West Main St, one block west of the 151/61 intersection, Dickeyville, WI; ☎ 608 568 3119. *Open daily 9.00am–5.00pm Apr–Nov. Donations appreciated.*

Looking like something you'd see in a *Homer Simpson meets Back to the Future* movie, **The Forevertron** is the fantasy – and the alter-ego – of Tom Every who refers to himself as Dr Evermor. Inventive in vision, and astounding in scope, the Forevertron is a gargantuan science fiction landscape, a conglomeration of contraptions designed to shoot Dr Evermor into space using some kind of 1890s' magnetic lightning beam propulsion that only he understands. The 320-ton complex is the largest metal scrap sculpture in the world and a monument to the machine age that has taken the doctor 23 years to construct. The fantastical device, six stories high, is assembled from generators, thrusters, massive machine components and factory scrap collected by this former industrial salvage dealer.

The Forevertron is well thought out, not at all random, and has such well-defined components as the Gravitron, the place where he'll de-water himself to get his weight down, before lift-off. (Since humans are made up of about 90% water, this would indeed save a lot of weight.) The Teahouse, which began life as a wrought-iron gazebo, is reserved for visiting royalty who will come to watch the event. Celestial Listening Ears, theater speakers in a former incarnation, keep an ear on the universe. Skeptics can follow the Doctor's airborne progress through an enormous telescope, just about the only thing with a recognizable function. In the Overlord control center (Houston, are you listening?) is a decontamination chamber supposedly from one of the Apollo moon missions. The good doctor himself will take off, electro-magnetically speaking, from a glass ball nestled inside a copper egg. Gathering to watch the festivities is the Big Bird Band, a playful, expectant crowd of several dozen figures made from musical instruments, old tools, gasoline nozzles, bed posts and the like. A huge scrap spider stands poised in anticipation of the event.

For all its madcap madness, Dr Evermor hopes the Forevetron will carry the message that we're scrapping a large part of our energy, and that it's important to stay connected to the stuff of our past. If the medium is the message, you may have to stay awhile if you're to understand it.

The Forevertron, located behind Delaney's Surplus on Hwy 12 just south of Baraboo, across the street from the Badger Ammunitions Plant, Baraboo, WI. Contact the Evermor Foundation, PO Box 22, Prarie Du Sac, WI 53578; web: www.drevermor.org. *Open Mon–Sat 9.00am–5.00pm, Sun noon–5.00pm.*

Museums and collections

The **John Michael Kohler Arts Center**, under the auspices of plumbing manufacturer Kohler and Company, devotes itself to some pretty unusual art. Besides preserving the work of 'outsider' (ie: self taught) artists, they offer an art-in-residence program that encourages new art forms and new ideas to flourish. Their six public bathrooms are fine examples. One portrays the social history of the world through tiles depicting architectural history from ancient Egypt to the present. Another is tiled with imagined silhouettes of arts center members who submitted their names and one-sentence bios to the artist. The bathroom in the children's studio was created by – and for – three- to five-year-olds. It has tot-sized fixtures, tiles glazed by toddlers, and clay toys made by injecting real stuffed animals with liquid clay.

> **John Michael Kohler Arts Center**, 608 New York Ave, Sheboygan, WI 53082; ❧ 920 458 6144; web: www.jmkac.org. *Open daily Mon, Wed, Fri 10.00am–5.00pm, Tue & Thu 10.00am–8.00pm, Sat & Sun 10.00am–4.00pm. Free.*

Beginning with the banishment of Adam and Eve from the Garden of Eden, the 100 life-sized woodcarvings depicting scenes from the Bible at the **Museum of Woodcarving** were done by just one man, Joseph Barta. Inspired by a series of dream revelations, Joseph spent 15 years working at his monumental task. *The Last Supper* took him four and a half years to carve.

> **Museum of Woodcarving**, 539 Hwy 63, Shell Lake, WI; ❧ 715 468 7100. *Open 9.00am–6.00pm May 1–Oct 31.*

Certified by Guinness as having the world's largest privately owned angel collection, Joyce and Lowell Berg own 13,000 of them, half of which are displayed at any given time at the world's largest **Angel Museum**. Made of every conceivable material, the angels are arranged by theme (musical, wedding, planters, glass, cornhusk, wood, and so forth) and by country of origin. Adding to the Berg's collection is that of Oprah Winfrey's. She donated 600 black angels.

> **Angel Museum**, 656 Pleasant St, Hwy 51, Beloit, WI 53512; ❧ 608 362 9099; web: www.angelmuseum.com. *Open Tue–Sat 10.00am–4.00pm Feb–Dec. Also open Sun 1.00–4.00pm Jun–Aug.*

Bernard Cigrand, a young teacher in a one-room schoolhouse in 1885, was the first to observe the birthday of the American flag by standing one in his inkwell and instructing his students to write about what the flag meant to them. His lifelong crusade to have July 14 1777 declared a national holiday is told at the **Americanism Center Museum** at the Stoney Hill School, the place where it all began. President Woodrow Wilson issued a proclamation about Flag Day ceremonies in 1916 but it wasn't until 1949 that President Harry Truman made it an official holiday.

Americanism Center Museum, County Rd I and Fredonia-Kohler Dr, Waubeka, WI; ↘ 262 692 9111; web: www.nationalflagday.com

A bizarre story is told at the **Fort Crawford Museum**. Back in 1822 a Dr Beaumont, an army surgeon, treated a patient for a deadly gunshot wound in the stomach. Not expecting the victim to survive, he studied the man's digestive process through a hole that hadn't closed. Much to everyone's surprise, the patient did, indeed, pull through and, several years later, the good doctor convinced his patient to come to Fort Crawford for further experiments. The results, *Experiments and Observations on Gastric Juices*, are told at the museum along with exhibits of 19th-century medicine and quackery.

Fort Crawford Museum, 717 S Beaumont Rd, Box 298, Prarie du Chien, WI 53821; ↘ 608 326 6960; web: www.fortcrawfordmuseum.com. *Open 10.00am–4.00pm May–Oct, 10.00am–5.00pm Jun–Aug.*

Barry Levenson was depressed. It was October 27 1986 and the Boston Red Socks had just lost the baseball World Series. While standing in the supermarket, he told himself it was ridiculous for a grown man to be depressed about a game. He decided right then and there he needed a hobby – and that's when he heard the mustards say 'Buy me, and they will come'. So he bought, and they have come, to the **Mt Horeb Mustard Museum**, where Barry has almost 4,000 different kinds of mustard from all over the world, including chocolate fudge mustard. His newsletter, the *Proper Mustard*, prints 7,000 copies twice a year, and he's the official sponsor of **National Mustard Day**, held the first Saturday in August. The whole town turns out for this festival that features painting with mustard and a mustard wheel of fortune. Hot dogs are free as long as you eat them with mustard; there's a ketchup surcharge that goes to charity. He holds a Mustard Family Reunion each June – anyone named Mustard can attend and dozens actually do.

Barry is also the man behind **Elm Farm Ollie Day**, a tribute to the first cow to fly in an airplane. This happened way back in 1930, when flying was new and daring. The St Louis International Air Exposition was looking for a gimmick to bring folks to the fair. Someone came up with the idea of taking a milk cow up in the plane, milking her, and then parachuting the milk down to the crowds below. To mark the occasion, a bovine cantata is performed every February 18 at his Mustard Museum. He'd like to see three cows go into orbit in a rocket so he could call them the 'herd shot round the world'.

Mt Horeb Mustard Museum, 100 W Main St, Mt Horeb, WI 53572; ↘ 800 438 6878; web: www.mustardmuseum.com. *Open daily 10.00am–5.00pm.*

Elm Farm Ollie Day held annually in February.

National Mustard Day held the first Saturday in August.

Those who can remember wanting to run away and join the circus can indulge their fantasy at the **Circus World Museum** in Baraboo, the world's leading repository of circus memorabilia. It's a lively place, recreating the wonder and awe inspired by the Ringling Brothers in the late 1800s. Besides letting you get up close to 200 circus wagons, the museum has demonstrations on how these wagons were loaded and how the circus train made the journey from one locale to another. Each year 750,000 people turn out to watch an old-fashioned circus parade leave Baraboo and make its way to Milwaukee, cheering on the 2,000 participants, 700 horses and 55 antique wagons, as well as the clowns, musicians, and exotic animals. The museum is also home to the one-million-piece Howard Brothers' Miniature Circus.

> **The Circus World Museum**, 550 Water St, Hwy 113, Baraboo, WI 53913; ℸ 866 693 1500; 24-hr info ℸ 608 356 0800; office ℸ 608 356 8341; web: www.circusworldmuseum.com. *Open daily 9.00am–6.00pm mid-May to Labor Day; Mon–Sat 10.00am–4.00pm, Sun 11.00am–4.00pm Labor Day to mid-May.*

Harry Houdini was a brilliant escape artist who many thought to be quite mad for taking the risks he did. The Houdini Historical Center in Appleton honors the magician and his bag of tricks, including his locks, picks, handcuffs, and straitjackets. Demonstrations and hands-on exhibits offer more opportunities to learn about his escapades and escapes.

> **Houdini Historical Center**, located in the Outagamie Museum, 330 E College Ave, Appleton, WI 54911; ℸ 920 733 8445; web: www.foxvalleyhistory.org/houdini. *Open Tue–Sat 10.00am–4.00pm; Sun noon–4.00pm. Also open Mon 10.00am–4.00pm Jun–Aug.*

The world's largest fiberglass structure will 'lure' you in at the **National Freshwater Fishing Hall of Fame** in Hayward. You can stand in a giant fiberglass musky – that's a fish – that's half a block long and four stories tall. The observation deck is in its wide-open mouth. It's also the world's largest fiberglass structure and you know you're there when it looms up in front of you from the road. This place is like one huge tackle box with 5,000 lures, whole rooms of rods and reels, outboard motors, examples of really bad taxidermy, and a couple of thousand hooks, removed by doctors, that snagged the unfortunate human holding the rod. If you're a fisherman, 400 trophies should make you tremble with excitement. The World Records Gallery is crammed with statistics of where, how, and with what, so you leave nurturing the fantasy that you could someday duplicate the feat. Outside, they've thoughtfully provided you with a number of photo ops, so you can bag a print that makes it look as if you're reeling in a big one.

> **National Freshwater Fishing Hall of Fame**, 10360 Hall of Fame Dr, Hayward, WI 54843; ℸ 715 634 4440; fax: 715 634 4440; web: www.freshwater-fishing.org. Located at the junction of State Hwy 27 and County Hwy B. *Open daily 10.00am–5.00pm Apr 15–Nov 1.*

Everyone who walks into **Watson's Wild West Museum** in Elkhorn gets a personal tour from Doug Watson, a cowboy character who captures your imagination with tall tales, cowboy poetry and humor. This replica of an 1880s' general store has thousands of artifacts and memorabilia from the cowboy era, including 2,000 branding irons, 115 saddles and a bathroom papered in wanted posters.

Watson's Wild West Museum, W4865 Potter Rd, Elkhorn, WI 53121; ❚ 262 723 7505; web: www.watsonswildwestmuseum.com. Ten minutes north of Lake Geneva, WI. *Open May–Oct Tue–Sat 10.00am–5.00pm, Sun 11.00am–5.00pm. Closed Mon.*

American culture is tied to advertising like no other culture on Earth and a visit to the new **Eisner Museum of Advertising** in Milwaukee will show you how and why. Taking you through the past, present and future of American advertising and design, the museum presents a complete history of the slogans, campaigns and logos that made America the consumer capital of the world. An interactive radio booth lets you record and play back your own advertising spot. You'll learn about 'profiling', experiencing at first hand how advertisers target their market. Other exhibits include the shopping bag as portable art and using album cover art to sell records. It's a world of pop culture in there, filled with messages and memories.

Eisner Museum of Advertising, Milwaukee Institute of Art and Design, 208 N Water St, Milwaukee, WI 53202; ❚ 414 203 0371; fax: 414 847 3299; web: www.eisnermuseum.org. *Open Wed 11.00am–5.00pm, Thu 11.00am–8.00pm, Fri 11.00am–5.00pm, Sat noon–5.00pm, Sun 1.00–5.00pm.*

Judith Schultz, curator of the **Spinning Top Exploratory Museum**, has collected 5,000 tops, yo-yos, and gyroscopes. While she only displays 2,000 or so at one time, that should be plenty to keep you entertained during the lively two-hour play session, demonstration and trick show she offers. Creator of International **Spin-A-Top Day**, a day in which fellow top enthusiasts worldwide all spin their tops at high noon, she's also the sponsor of an annual **yo-yo convention**.

But she doesn't stop at tops. Judith is also responsible for the nearby **Hall of Logic Puzzles**, a collection of vintage parlor puzzles that require brain and logic power instead of a joystick. She is so fond of vintage pastimes that she puts on contests for games like 'jacks' and 'pickup-sticks' to encourage folks to play non-electronically. The hall is also home to the **International Tongue Twister Contest** with prizes related to the twisters themselves. (You wouldn't get an entire peck of pickled peppers, but you would get something pickle related if you were to win that one.) A three-day '**Whatchamacallits**' event has you guessing what various odd and curious gizmos might be.

Spinning Top Exploratory Museum, at Teacher Place & Parent Resources, 533 Milwaukee Ave (Hwy 36), Burlington, WI 53105; ❚ 262 763 3946; web: www.topmuseu.org. *Open year-round. Advance reservations are necessary since she tailors her presentation to the needs of the group.*

Yo-yo Convention, held annually in April.

Whatchamacallits and **Tongue Twister**, both in November.

Spin-A-Top Day, held annually in October.

Attractions

They've been walking on water since 1952 at **Tommy Bartlett's Thrill Show**, a kitschy throwback to the days when families actually traveled to see such roadside attractions. A legend among tourist traps, almost two million people still come every summer to see one of the three daily water-skiing shows featuring costumed skiers doing stunts like bare-footing backwards, jumping through fire, flipping off six-foot-high jumps, and skiing in a pyramid. A dream job for the two-dozen college students who get to spend their summers showing off their skills on skis, the shows are strictly family affairs, kitsch choreographed so tightly that the management guarantees that it will take no more than 18 minutes to exit from the parking lot.

> **Tommy Bartlett's Thrill Show**, 560 Wisconsin Dells Parkway,
> Wisconsin Dells, WI 53965; ↘ 608 254 2525; web:
> www.tommybartlett.com. *Shows at 1.00pm, 4.30pm and 8.30pm May
> 23–Sept 1.*

Quirkyville

You may hear about steel-wool-bearing sheep, or about a town so small that they had to widen the street to put a line down the center of it, or about the naive couple who obeyed a sign stating: 'Clean restrooms ahead'. They're all lies, of course, which is to be expected at the world famous **Burlington Liars' Club**. The club got its start in 1929 when a local prankster, who was also a reporter for the local paper, ran a fabricated story about a contest by police and firemen to see who could tell the biggest whopper. The story, picked up by the national press, resulted in so many inquiries about the contest that the reporter decided to form a club. For a dime and a lie you could become a card-carrying, lifetime member. The fee has gone up to $1 today but you can still join and enter the annual contest. Lies can be sent in at any time. Judging is done in secret each New Year's Eve. Amateurs only, please; no politicians are allowed. You can follow a 'Trail of Lies' by picking up a map at the Burlington Area Chamber of Commerce. The trail is a walking tour, mainly downtown, that takes you to store fronts with bronze plaques containing the best lies from over the years.

> **Burlington Liars' Club**, 179 Beth Ct, Burlington, WI 53105; Burlington
> Area Chamber of Commerce, 112 E Chestnut St, Burlington, WI 53105;
> ↘ 262 763 6044; web: www.burlingtonareachamber.com

Tours

Talk about 'pier' pressure. Mail carriers give new meaning to special delivery as they jump from the side of a moving tourist boat, race up to a resident's pier, deposit the mail or newspaper, then dash back to catch the boat. Mail carriers aboard the **Walworth II Mailboat** have been delivering mail this way for 85 summers and you can watch them make 60 jumps during their daily two-and-a-half-hour cruise. The boat has been piloted by the same captain for 30 years so the team is experienced enough that the carrier rarely ends up in the water.

> **Walworth II Mailboat**. Contact Lake Geneva Cruise Line, 812 Wrigley
> Dr, PO Box 68, Lake Geneva, WI 53147; ↘ 262 248 6206; web:
> www.cruiselakegeneva.com. *Tours depart Mon–Sat 9.45am Jun 15–Sept 15.*

Just plain weird

Loy Bowlin was a real-life **rhinestone cowboy**. Inspired by the famous Glen Campbell song, he set out to transform himself from a lonely retiree into someone

Quirk Alert

Some people collect bananas, or toasters, or weird stuff like drain tiles. Don Gorske, 50, collects calories, as in Big Macs. Known as the '**Big Mac Guy**', Don has eaten more than 20,000 of the 500-calorie hamburger sandwiches, averaging two a day for 30 years while eating at McDonald's restaurants in 48 states and Canada. Ask him the price in 1972 and he can tell you: 49 cents. He keeps a meticulous calendar, carefully recording the number of each consumed (number 8,000 was on May 28 1987; number 19,000 was on March 18 2003). At 18,250 he earned the Guinness World record for Big Macs consumed. The most Big Macs ever eaten in a day? Nine. He's only missed eating a Big Mac eight days since starting his quest, being stopped only by a snowstorm, a death in the family, a work emergency, and a short vacation. The McDonald's corporation recognized him with their highest honor: a Ronald McDonald poster, shirt decal, and proclamation.

You'd think he'd weigh as much as 600 Big Macs (they're 7 ounces each) but he doesn't. He's a tall, slender six-footer, 185lb, with normal cholesterol. He just loves Big Macs and wishes he could visit a McDonald's in every city and state in America. On the days he can't actually get to a McDonald's, he eats one from the freezer, keeping a supply on hand for just such an emergency. (His brother mailed him one once from Cancun, Mexico.) So passionate is Don about his peculiar pursuit that he proposed to his wife at McDonald's.

who could make people laugh. Starting with his apparel, he covered his clothes with rhinestones, glitter and pictures of himself. Then he covered his car and then his false teeth. Happy with the results of his transformation, he turned to his house, covering every inch with polka dots, glitter, sparkling collages and Christmas ornaments. Each day he'd go into town, dressed in a different outfit, and sing and dance his way into people's hearts. His house, originally located in Mississippi, has been preserved by the John Michael Kohler Arts Center in Sheboygan.

The **Rhinestone Cowboy**, located at the John Michael Kohler Arts Center, 608 New York Ave, Sheboygan WI 53082; ✆ 920 458 6144; fax: 920 458 4473; web: www.jmkac.org. *Open Mon, Wed, Fri 10.00am–5.00pm, Tue & Thu 10.00am–8.00pm, Sat & Sun 10.00am–4.00pm.*

Quirky cuisine

If you don't know the password, you might not be allowed in – unless you're willing to make a fool of yourself by doing silly things that will appear on the big screen inside. You've arrived at the **Safe House**, a restaurant and bar with a theme so weird you just have to experience it for yourself. The term 'safe house' is used by international spies to describe a secure meeting place, usually one operating in premises disguised as a respectable business. International Exports Ltd is your safe house in this case when mystery and intrigue bring you to Milwaukee. Make sure you're not being followed, then slip inside, whisper the

Quirk Alert

A WISCONSIN TURKEY

It's a shame the **Gobbler Supper Club and Motel** no longer exists. It was one of America's finest examples of lunacy; the stretching of a theme to the outer boundaries of sanity. Billed as a 'new and exciting experience in good living', the place took itself seriously, promising a world of romance and intimacy. The lobby of the turkey-shaped building was carpeted in a custom turkey pattern, with walls, railings and doors covered with pink and purple shag carpet. In the Royal Roost Cocktail Lounge, the platform holding plastic barrel chairs rotated completely around so you could fully absorb the fine collection of turkey art, animal oils, and a rare John Wayne on velvet. The proprietors proudly referred to how the natural lava stone exterior of the building simulated ruffled turkey feathers.

The only taste this place ever exhibited was turkey: almost every item on the menu in the lavender dining-room, which sat 350 people, featured turkey in one form or another. In the motel's romantic suites, no bad idea was ever rejected, nor any good idea likely proposed. The Passion Pit had a television imbedded in the clamshell headboard but this was way before VCRs so the purpose was murky indeed unless watching bandleader Lawrence Welk on 'live' TV rang your chimes. Stereo turntables and eight-track tape players were provided, but it was strictly bring-your-own-sounds. Their brochure claimed a mission to 'enhance the role of Tom Turkey as the all-American delicacy'.

password and enter through the bookcase. The place is filled with spy-like contraptions, secret escape routes, bulletproof windows, and a CIA cover phone guaranteed to hide your whereabouts from the enemy (or spouse). A disappearing booth transports guests from the meeting facility into the restaurant.

The Safe House, 779 North Front St, Milwaukee, WI 53202; ℩ 414 271 2007; web: www.safe-house.com

Holler House, an historic corner pub, is home to the nation's oldest bowling alley, so old that you have to call ahead and arrange for a pinsetter to be on duty if you want to play at the two-lane alley in the basement. The bar is also home to a collection of underwear that hangs from the ceiling. A long-standing tradition, first time patrons are asked to leave a bra or skivvies behind to grace the rafters. If you don't want to part with your undies, you can sign the concrete wall by the bowling lanes instead.

Holler House, 2042 W Lincoln Avenue, Milwaukee, WI 53215; ℩ 414 647 9284

Rooms with a Skew

The largest hotel bed in America is the 'emperor' bed at **Canoe Bay**. This luxury resort had the seven-foot five-inch bed made so their pro-basketball clients wouldn't have to sleep diagonally in a regular king bed.

Canoe Bay, PO Box 28, Chetek, WI; ↘ 715 924 4594; web: www.canoebay.com

Fifteen FantaSuites are featured at the **Don Q Inn** in Dodgeville. Each suite has its own theme such as the Blue Room's 300-gallon copper cheese-vat tub, the Float's Viking ship waterbed and heart-shaped hydro-therapy tub and the Swinger's suspended swinging bed. Meanwhile, 25 FantaSuites are featured at the **West Bend Inn** with themes like the Arabian Nights, a suite complete with a sheikh's tent and overhead starlight mirror. The Continental suite has a 1964 Lincoln Continental bed, the Medieval Castle Dungeon sports wall shackles and oversized whirlpool, and the Teepee has a waterbed in a forest setting with a mirrored ceiling. (Well, no-one ever said Americans have taste.) Tours are held at both properties on Saturdays or Sundays at 3pm, or you can buy a video in the lobby if you're so enamored.

Don Q Inn, 3656 State Rd 23 N, Dodgeville, WI 53533; ↘ 800 666 7848 or 608 935 2321; web: www.fantasuite.com

West Bend Inn, 2520 West Washington St, West Bend, WI 53095; ↘ 800 727 9727 or 262 338 0636; web: www.fantasuite.com

MINNESOTA
Festivals and events
It's tough for folks who live in the 'Ice Box of the Nation' to find a reason to get out of bed in January. To make it easier they've created four days of organized insanity in January called **Ice Box Days** during which they go frozen-turkey bowling, play golf on the ice and run in the snow in a Freeze yer Gizzard Blizzard Run. They hold an Ode to the Cold poetry contest, a pre-school Olympics, a town-wide scavenger hunt and some Mutt Races so the dogs don't feel left out. If you can drive a tricycle and balance a pizza in one hand, you can join in the Cold Pizza Delivery race. If that doesn't appeal, there's always the Beach Party (dress appropriately), a snow sculpture contest, and the Barrel Sauna and Polar Bear Dip.

Ice Box Days, held annually the third weekend in January at Voyageurs National Park on the northern border of Minnesota, about 15 miles east of International Falls, MN and 300 miles north of Minneapolis–Saint Paul, MN. International Falls Area Chamber of Commerce; ↘ 800 325 5766 or 218 283 9400; web: www.intlfalls.org

For three months each winter, thousands of wooden fish-houses are installed on a huge, frozen lake in Aitkin. The residents play cards, watch TV, work on their computers, cook and have parties while their automatic lines go fishing for them. Some folks live on the ice for weeks. The temporary city includes ploughed streets, stores, sanitation facilities and, obviously, electricity. The houses are transported to the lake at a wacky **Fish House Parade** the day after Thanksgiving.

Fish House Parade, held annually the day after Thanksgiving in downtown Aitkin, MN. Contact Aitkin Area Chamber of Commerce, PO Box 127, Aitkin, MN 56431; ↘ 218 927 2316; web: www.aitkin.com

People from time immemorial have grappled with such questions as whether life has meaning, whether humans are inherently good or evil, and whether God exists. In more modern times man has debated whether honesty is always the best policy or if the death penalty is ethical in a civilized society. The **Great American**

Think-off, held at the Regional Cultural Center in New York Mills, ponders such weighty questions at an annual sports-like event that pits armchair philosophers against one another in a debate to win the title of America's Greatest Thinker. Each year the contest asks the nation to provide a written answer to a provocative question, in 750 words or less, based on personal experience. Real philosophers need not apply: the event is meant to encourage normal, everyday folks to have their say. The best essayists are brought to the town for the battle of the brains, with the audience deciding the ultimate winner.

> **The Great American Think-off**, held annually in June at the New York Mills Regional Cultural Center, 24 North Main Ave, New York Mills, MN 56567; ↘ 218 385 3339; web: www.think-off.org

Virtually everything you can think to do to a potato is done at the **Potato Days** festival every August in Barnesville. The spuds are picked, peeled, tossed, fried, raced, baked and even worn. Activities include loony mashed potato wrestling, a potato-sack fashion show, potato-car races, speed peeling contests, potato billiards, potato golf, a potato hunt, a potato scramble and a Mr Potato Head competition.

> **Potato Days**, held annually in August in Barnesville, MN. Contact Barnesville Potato Days, PO Box 345, Barnesville, MN 56514; ↘ 800 525 4901 or ↘ 218 354 2479; web: www.potatodays.com

Frigid temperatures mean only one thing in Detroit Lakes – it's time to celebrate. At **Polar Fest**, those courageous enough to brave the elements don their silliest costumes and beachwear and take a plunge into 33° lake water. A local dive team cuts a huge hole in the ice and then stays in the water to help the 50 or so plungers waiting their turns in the fishing houses above. The smart plungers warm up in the hot tub first but there are always a few who plunge in cold turkey (which is why they look like a plucked one when they shoot up from the water). Depending on how deep the hole, and how short the contestant, the plungers may end up going completely under. Fans cheer them on from bleachers, music blares, and everyone runs around in zany costumes.

> **Polar Fest**, held annually in February in Detroit Lakes, MN. Detroit Lakes Regional Chamber of Commerce, ↘ 218 847 9202; web: www.visitdetroitlakes.com

Menahga erected a statue of St Urho, the Finnish saint of grasshoppers, in their town center even though the saint himself is a figment of some very fertile, and probably inebriated, imaginations. Created 41 years ago after an especially festive St Patrick's Day party, the saint spawned an elaborate legend about his supposed ability to rid the land of locusts by waving a pitchfork and chanting 'Grasshopper grasshopper skoot'. Despite the obvious absurdity of the story, each year they celebrate **St Urho's Day**, reenacting the saint's supposed feat by running around in green costumes, chanting and waving pitchforks. No one cares how silly this is; they just like an excuse to party during the cold winter.

> **St Urho's Day**, held annually in March in Menahga, MN. Contact Park Rapids Area Chamber of Commerce, ↘ 800 247 0054 or 218 732 4111; web: www.gomenahga.com

Insulting Minnesotans will get you more than a cold shoulder. In the late 1800s, a New York newspaper described Saint Paul as 'another Siberia, unfit for human habitation in winter'. Highly offended, its citizens set out to prove them high-and-mighty easterners wrong by hosting a gala **Saint Paul Winter Carnival**, complete with royalty inhabiting a giant ice castle. Now in its 108th year, the 'coolest celebration on earth' is the largest cold-weather festival in the United States. In addition to parades, contests, ice golf, kite-flying, skating, and ice- and snow-sculpting contests, the festival features an Ice Palace that is built every decade or so. These mammoth structures, often six or seven stories high, take almost two months to construct and use close to half-a-million blocks of ice. The most recent was built in 2004.

> **Saint Paul Winter Carnival**, held annually in January in downtown Saint Paul, MN; web: www.winter-carnival.com

Museums and collections

SPAM™, that pink blob of gelatinous spiced ham famous the world over, was invented by Minnesota's Hormel Corporation, which has sold more than five billion cans of the stuff. (That's enough to feed three meals a day to a family of four for four and a half million years.) Hormel is so proud of its creation that it honors the blob with a SPAM™ Jamboree and with its very own **SPAM™ Museum**, a perfect blending of kitchen and kitsch. Past recipes using SPAM™ include SPAM™ strudel with mustard sauce, SPAM™ mousse, and SPAM™ cheescake'! The museum features displays pertaining not just to SPAM™, but to Hormel's other processed food products as well. You can join a simulated SPAM™ production line, play a SPAM™ game show, and watch a video of the famous Monty Python 'SPAM™, SPAM™, SPAM™' skit. The diner serves SPAM™ burgers and SPAM™ dogs.

> **SPAM™ Town USA Festival** and **SPAM™ Jam** held annually in July in Austin, MN. Austin Convention and Visitors Bureau, 104 11th Ave NW, Ste D, Austin, MN 55912; ➘ 800 444 5713 or ➘ 507 437 4563; web: www.austincvb.com

> **SPAM™ Museum**, 1937 SPAM Blvd, Austin, MN 55912; ➘ 800 588 7726 or 507 437 4563. *Open Mon–Sat 10.00am–5.00pm, Sun noon–4.00pm May 1 to Labor Day. Closed Mon from Labor Day to Apr 30. Admission is free.*

You may be looking at the finest archaeological hoax ever perpetrated. Or perhaps you're looking at evidence that the Norse, not the Italians, discovered America. Whatever conclusions you draw after viewing the Kensington Runestone at the **Runestone Museum**, you'll come away with a better understanding of this quirky neck of America's woods. The legitimacy of this stone, said to 'prove' Norse exploration of the region, has been debated, often hotly, in these parts for more than a hundred years and the debate is likely to rage for a hundred more unless scientists find a foolproof way to foil a long-dead hoaxer.

> **Runestone Museum**, 206 Broadway, Alexandria, MN 56308; ➘ 320 763 3160; web: www.runestonemuseum.org

Americans are nothing if not inventive, and nowhere is this more obvious than at the **Museum of Questionable Medical Devices**, now incorporated into the Science Museum of Minnesota. Robert McCoy, a pediatrician and connoisseur of quackery, has been collecting the devices for three decades. Phrenology machines are his special passion, these being devices resembling a spiked helmet that deduce your personality and recommend suitable careers by reading the bumps on your head. 'People fall for things,' he says, 'that are really preposterous, especially about sex.' Why anyone would buy a prostate gland warmer to improve their sex life (it had to be plugged in, no less, and then inserted!) is beyond comprehension.

It's impossible not to burst out laughing at most of these utterly absurd contraptions. The sharp metal device that was to be clamped you-know-where to prevent sex is a prime example, as is the MacGregor Rejuvenator, a machine that blasted you with magnetic waves to reverse the aging process. They remind you just how gullible we humans can be. Didn't anyone look around and say, 'Hey, if this thing works, how come there aren't more 120-year-olds walking about?' Someday, future generations will be having a good laugh at the thought of our copper bracelets, adhesive magnets, and Viagra.

Museum of Questionable Medical Devices, located in the Science Museum of Minnesota, 120 W Kellogg Blvd, St Paul, MN 55102; ⟍ 651 221 9444; web: www.smm.org. Robert McCoy's personal web: www.mtn.org/quack. *Hours vary by season, please call.*

Almost everyone knows a pack rat, a person who compulsively saves everything, no matter how useless. You may even be married to one. But no-one can be as bad as Ed Kruger, who never threw anything away for 50 years after his wife died, not even junk mail, TV guides, check registers, or his long dead cat. Ed ran the Jack Sprat Food store in Wykoff from 1933 until this death in 1989. His will left the store and its contents to the city, providing it was turned into a museum. The ladies of the Wykoff Progress Club took up the challenge, hauling away truck full after truck full of trash to make enough space to organize the mess so it could be gawked at. You can see the before and after pictures at **Ed's Museum**, along with his string collection, every toy Ed ever had, and every magazine he ever subscribed to. This place is the hen-pecked husband's ultimate revenge.

Ed's Museum, located at 100 S Gold St in downtown Wykoff, MN; ⟍ 507 352 4205. About 35 miles southeast of Rochester between Spring Valley and Preston. *Open Sat–Sun 1.00–4.00pm or by appointment Jun–Sept. Admission free, donations appreciated.*

Sandpaper just isn't glamorous, nor is the Sandpaper Museum in Two Harbors. It marks the spot where the 3M Company got its start, but if you're a Tim Allen sort, you'll probably appreciate it.

Sandpaper Museum, officially known as the 3M/Dwan Museum, 2nd Ave and Waterfront Dr, Two Harbors, MN; ⟍ 218 834 4898. *Hours: Usually Mon–Fri 12.30–5.00pm, Sat 9.00am–5.00pm, Sun 10.00am–3:00pm but will vary seasonally.*

Attractions

If you always fantasized about being the champion pictured on a box of Wheaties cereal, this is your chance to make it real. At **General Mills Cereal Adventures** you can take home your own personalized Wheaties box – with you pictured as the hero. Or, you can combine your favorite cereals to invent your very own taste, design the box, choose a name, and then take the thing home where it will more than likely remain an uneaten souvenir forever. There's also a virtual Cocoa Puffs experience, cereal games, cereal crafts, and a restaurant serving all 50 varieties of General Mills cereals. You can eat while watching old TV cereal commercials or a cooking demonstration.

General Mills Cereal Adventures, 376 N Garden, Mall of America, Bloomington Hills, MN 55425; ↘ 952 814 2900; web: www.cerealadventure.com

Tours

You'll follow your nose – literally – on this twin cities 'smell tour', an experience devised by a group of urban design professors at the University of Minnesota. After identifying 50 distinctive odors, they put them on a map, hoping people will embark on an olfactory scavenger hunt. You can also experience the city's various decibel levels with their sound map and audio CD. It charts citywide decibel levels and chronicles residents' sonic stories of the city. Their objective is to increase awareness of the need for better urban planning. You can get a copy of *Odorama: A Smell Map* and *50 Sound Stories + 466 Decibel Readings* at the Design institute.

Smell & Sound Knowledge Maps, available by mail from the Design Institute, 149 Nicholson Hall, 216 Pillsbury Dr SE, Minneapolis, MN 55455; ↘ 612 625 3373; web: www.design.umn.edu/go/document/ TCDC.03.KMap.mappage. You can purchase them in person at the Minneapolis College of Art & Design Bookshop (The Art Cellar), 2501 Stevens Ave S, Minneapolis, MN 55404; ↘ 612 874 3775.

Your gangster guide confesses, exposing the corrupt politicians, the crooked police force, and the underworld leaders who actually ran the city of St Paul in the 1920s and 1930s. The **St Paul Gangster Tour** takes you to all the sites of the famous clubs, kidnappings and gun battles.

St Paul Gangster Tours depart from the Wabasha Street Caves, 215 Wabasha St S, St Paul, MN; ↘ 612 292 1220; fax: 651 224 0059; web: www.wabashastreetcaves.com. *Bus outings operate Sat in the warm-weather months, less frequently in the winter.*

Just plain weird

In Belle Plaine you can see a two-story outhouse, constructed by a man with too many children and too few holes. All told, the outhouse is a 'five-holer'.

Two-Story Outhouse, Belle Plaine, MN. Contact Belle Plaine Historical Society, ↘ 952 873-6109; web: www.belleplainemn.com

The small field with the strange objects that sits along Highway 8 has a name: **Franconia Sculpture Park**. It's a place where artists can unleash their desires in the most uninhibited, and public, of ways. Funded by a foundation that supports emerging artists, Franconia awards more than a dozen live/work fellowships each year, permitting a lot of art to emerge in such an enabling environment. Along with the work of interns and self-funded artists, 30 or so new pieces are erected each year while just as many older ones are removed. The sculptures are massive and the guided tours that attempt to explain them are free. Or you can just wander. Franconia is open every day of the year from dawn to dusk.

Franconia Sculpture Park, 29815 Unity Ave, Shafer, MN 55074; ↘ 651 465 3701; web: www.franconia.org. *Open daily from dawn until dusk. Free.*

Darwin, population 262, has been attracting visitors to their tiny town for generations with their oddball claim to fame – the **World's Biggest Ball of Twine**. The attraction, almost nine tons of it, resides in a glass-enclosed gazebo off Main Street, waiting to rope in visitors who are willing to spend money on souvenirs and refreshments. The ball's creator, Francis Johnson, was raised not to waste so, besides pencils and nails, he hoarded twine. One day, as the story goes, he wrapped some twine around his fingers and then just kept at it until, 29 years later, the ball was 11 feet high and 40 feet around. As the thing grew Johnson had to use boxcar jacks to move it around. When Ripley's Believe It or Not! wanted to buy the ball, the town was thrilled – until they discovered that Ripley's wanted to take the ball away for good. No sale. A new museum dedicated to the ball and to Darwin's history has just opened in the old railroad depot that was moved next to the gazebo. There you can see Johnson's other waste-not collections like pencils, nails, tools and nutcrackers as well as his seven-foot wood carving of a pair of pliers.

World's Biggest Ball of Twine, located at First and William Sts in Darwin, MN; web: www.geocities.com/Hollywood/Theater/5805/main.html.

Twine Ball Day is held annually the second Saturday in August.

The **dueling elves** are fighting it out to capture the hearts of the city's children. For eight years there was only one place the kids could leave cards and letters during the summer addressed to a mysterious elf – inside his little arched door carved into the foot of a tree on the lake's southern shore. Mr Little Guy, as he signs his name, would respond with personalized answers to their letters on tiny, dated, silver cards. But recently another elf took up residence in a nearby tree, building a little door of his own and competing for the children's letters. The new elf answers with computer printed messages, obviously hoping to attract the more tech-savvy kids.

The **dueling elves** can be found at the bottom of two trees near the Lake Harriet band shell in Minneapolis, MN.

Odd shopping

What kind of store would need parking for 800 cars plus spaces for boats, caravans and semi-trucks? Try Cabelas, a 150,000-square-foot showroom for hunting, fishing and outdoor gear that's so big it takes several thousand employees to run it. Inside stands a mountain, covered with a hundred North American game mounts. Walk through museum-quality dioramas depicting the circle of life, practice target shooting and archery in the virtual reality range and dine on game delicacies in the restaurant. The grounds are so extensive that they lead tours; the annual sidewalk sale is so famous that many folks fly in for it.

Cabela's Outfitters, 3900 Cabela Dr, Owatonna, MN 55060; ➤ 507 451 4545; web: www.cabelas.com. *Open Mon–Sat 8.00am–9.00pm, Sun 10.00am–6.00pm.*

Quirky cuisine

The **Newsroom Restaurant** is divided into various newspaper sections, each with décor consisting of articles and headlines based on a theme. As an added bonus, there's no need to take anything into the bathroom to read. In fact, the path to the bathroom gradually turns gender-specific and guides you to the appropriate destination. Inside a surprise awaits: one-way mirrors look into the bathroom of the opposite sex next door. The Travel Channel rates The Newsroom bathroom as one of their Top 10 Outrageous Bathrooms.

Newsroom Restaurant, 990 Nicolet Mall, Minneapolis, MN 55402; ⌕ 612 343 0073

Rooms with a Skew

Richard Schmidthuber, aka Steinarr Elmerson, the Crazy Viking, is well suited to his role as head Norseman of the **Nordic Inn Medieval Brew and Bed**. A large, burly man, he's quite convincing in his persona – you can almost picture him thrusting a lance while mounted on a white steed. At this inn you travel back in time, soaking up the atmosphere in the theme rooms: the feminine Freya's Boudoir; the decidedly not-so-feminine Jaris' Den; the Pauper's Lookout (in the belltower); and Odin's Loft. Meals are taken at a huge table, family style. If enough people show up, you'll become part of a Viking Feast interactive dinner theater performance.

Nordic Inn Medieval Brew and Bed, 210 1st Ave NW, Crosby, MN 56441; ⌕ 218 546 8299; web: www.vikinginn.com

The **Sod House Bed and Breakfast** in Minnesota encourages you to dress in prairie clothes, read by oil lamps, and play old-fashioned games while sleeping in a prairie sod house. In fact, you have no choice but to be old fashioned since there is no electricity, thus no phones or TV. Wood burning stoves provide heat in the one-room house and the hosts will bring you breakfast. You can also visit their replica dugout sod house, now a historical exhibit.

Sod House Bed and Breakfast, 12598 Magnolia Ave, Sanborn, MN 56083; ⌕ 507 723 5138; web: www.sodhouse.org

Thirty fantasy suites are featured at Quality Inns and Suites in Burnsville. Each suite has its own theme; there's a sheikh's tent with a waterbed and overhead mirror, a thatched jungle hut with mosquito netting over the waterbed and a queen-size whaling dinghy waterbed with a whirlpool behind the mouth of a whale. Waterbeds went out in the 1970s but today's 20-somethings probably don't know that. Tours are held any Saturday or Sunday at 3pm or you can buy a video in the lobby.

Quality Inns and Suites, 250 N River Ridge Circle, Burnsville, MN 55337; ↘ 952 890 9550 or 800 666 STAY; web: www.fantasuite.com

Travelers with conviction stay at the **Jailhouse Inn** in Preston, an 1869 jailhouse converted into a bed and breakfast. In the 'cell block' you can sleep behind bars. Or choose the 'master bedroom' that was the sheriff's personal quarters.

Jailhouse Inn, 109 Houston St NW, Preston, MN 55965; ↘ 507 765 2181; web: www.jailhouseinn.com

IOWA
Festivals and events

The National Hobo Convention is the nation's largest gathering of hobos, ie: vagabonds who ride the rail system on freight trains. Drawing both real and faux hobos, the event draws around 30,000 people. Spectators are invited to vote for their favorite hobo and hobo-ess; those elected king and queen are rewarded with flowing robes and tin-can crowns. The hobos get together to sing, trade and act out the drama of their lives in the Hobo Theater. The Hobo Museum is housed in an old movie house purchased with funds left to the foundation in a hobo's will.

National Hobo Convention, held annually in August in Britt, IA. Contact Hobo Foundation, PO Box 413, Britt, IA 50423; ↘ 641 843 9104 or 641 843 3840; web: www.hobo.com.

The Hobo Museum, also in Britt, is open daily during the convention; by appointment at other times.

The yellow brick road leads to **Toto Fest**, a celebration honoring all things *Wizard of Oz*-ly, with real life Munchkins Margaret Pellegrini (the sleepyhead one) and Clarence Swensen (the soldier) lending their movie personas to the festivities. There's a Dorothy look-alike contest and also one for Toto, with prizes for the dog that not only 'looks most like Toto', but that also looks 'a little like Toto', and 'nothing like Toto'. Everyone sings Oz songs and plays Oz Toz Across and *Wizard of Oz* Bingo.

Toto Fest, held annually Memorial Day Weekend. Contact Annie M's Nostalgic Collectibles, 411 Main St, Box 70, Welton, IA 52774; ↘ 563 659 2424; web: www.anniems.com

Since 1911 the **Iowa State Fair** has featured a 600lb **life-size butter cow**. They've also had a butter-sculpted John Wayne, an Elvis, and the entire *Last Supper*, the last consisting of 1,700 buttery pounds worth of Jesus and his disciples seated around a butter table. Norma 'Duffy' Lyon, 74, carved the sculptures for 44 years, outdoing herself in 2003 with a butter Harley Davidson to celebrate the motorcycle company's 100th anniversary. Norma has finally hung up her knives, but her legacy is being carried on by Nancy Hise who's been carving cheese herself for more than a decade. You can see her work outside the refrigerated display case in the John Deere Agriculture Building.

Life-size butter cow, Iowa State Fair, Des Moines, IA; ↘ 515 262 3111; web: www.iowastatefair.com

It's America's biggest tug-of-war. The Mississippi River separates the towns of LeClaire, Iowa and Port Byron, Illinois. At the annual **Tug Fest**, ten teams of 20 pull against one another with a 2,400ft, 680lb rope. The winning town gets to keep the prize statue of a bald eagle in flight for the next year.

Tug Fest, held annually in August in LeClaire, IA and Port Byron, IL; web: www.tugfest.com

Eccentric environments

Father Paul Dobberstein made a vow to the Virgin Mary that he'd build her a shrine if she'd cure him of pneumonia. She delivered, and so did he. Over a period of 42 years, winter and summer, he built the **Grotto of the Redemption** near Fort Dodge. Setting ornamental rocks and gems into concrete, he created an entire city block portraying scenes from the life of Christ. Eventually nine towering structures were built, making the grotto the largest of its kind in the world. It has a geological value of over $5 million and one of the largest concentrations of minerals in any one spot on Earth. After the Father died, his assistant picked up the trowel and carried on for another eight years. For the last six years, Father Gerald Streit has been continuing construction and maintenance.

Grotto of the Redemption, West Bend, IA 50597. Located northwest of Fort Dodge, between State Hwys 18 and 20; ↘ 800 868 3641 or 515 887 5591; web: www.westbendgrotto.com

Jill and Michael Stephenson lead a very unusual life. They live, by choice, without modern conveniences at their **Waterloo Workshop** in Dorchester. Ten years ago, following a stint of subsistence farming, they bought an old log home that had never been equipped with electricity. Having limited funds to set up their farm, they decided to forgo electricity along with a few other modern trappings of life in America. Jill says, 'It's just a matter of learning to do things more directly. If we need water, we walk 100 feet to the pump and fill the pail.' They have nine grown children who today live in conventional houses. The Stephensons earn a living doing what they love: Michael is a woodcarver and Jill weaves baskets and makes jam. They like the idea that they're living with minimal negative impact on the earth and hope to be an inspiration to others looking for a way to simplify their life. They're almost always home so you can drop in any time. But if you want to be absolutely sure they'll be there, you'll have to send a note, by snail mail, of course.

Waterloo Workshop, 369 Waterloo Creek Dr, Dorchester, IA 52140

Museums and collections

Winters are long and cold in Iowa and having a hobby helps pass the time. In the early 1900s farm boys Frank and Joseph Bily decided that carving clocks would become theirs. It took them two years to build the Apostle Clock, and four years to create the American Pioneer History Clock. Church clocks followed, and the brothers carved until the late 1950s, leaving behind 40 clocks ranging in size from ten inches to over ten feet tall. Each clock chimes, plays music and has moving figures dancing about. Oddly enough, the museum in Spillville is called the **Bily Clocks Museum and Dvořák Exhibit**, partly in honour of the Bily boys' collection and partly reflecting the composer's visit to the town in 1893.

> **Bily Clocks Museum and Dvořák Exhibit**, 323 Main St, Spillville, IA 52168; ✎ 563 562 3589; web: www.bilyclocks.org. *Open daily 8.30am–5.00pm May–Oct; Sat–Sun only 10.00am–4.00pm Mar & Nov; closed Dec–Feb.*

B J Palmer, son of the founder of chiropractic medicine, not only ran the then-controversial Palmer School of Chiropractic, but also assembled a cornucopia of strange collections. Elephant representations fascinated him and his wife, as did idols, lamps, knives, and Abraham Lincoln memorabilia. When four white oak trees had to be cut down to make room for a classroom, they couldn't stand to see them chopped up for firewood. Instead they incorporated the trunks into a rustic room, carving them with a parade of elephants, an assortment of dogs and a variety of oriental objects. You can visit their strange home, called the **Palmer Mansion**, by making an appointment.

> **Palmer Mansion**, 1000 Brady St, Davenport, IA 52803-5287; ✎ 563 884 5714; web: www.palmer.edu. *By appointment only.*

Just plain weird

It's amazing what a determined 'trekkie' can accomplish. Steve Miller, of Riverside City, convinced the city council to declare Riverside the '**Future Birthplace of Captain Kirk**'. Of course it helped that he was a council member himself at the time. Remembering that Kirk supposedly hailed from a small town in Iowa, he impulsively proposed the theme during discussion of an upcoming celebration. The result is **Trek Fest**, Riverside's annual tribute to the future. The town's motto used to be 'Where the best begins'. With Kirk's impending conception just 228 years off, the motto was revised to read 'Where the Trek begins'. While it's not clear just who will bring the future Kirk into the world, it is clear where it will happen – behind the barbershop.

> **Future Birthplace of Captain Kirk**, Trek Fest held annually in June in Riverside, IA. Hwy 218, 20 miles south of I-80/Iowa City. Contact the Riverside Area Community Club, PO Box 55, Riverside, IA 52327; ✎ 319 648 KIRK; web: www.trekfest.com

It's been called the Lazy Susan Jail, the **Squirrel Cage Jail**, and the Human Rotary Jail. This bizarre experiment in jail architecture was invented in 1885, creating a jail that wouldn't require contact between prisoners and guards. The structure, virtually a three-story lazy susan with ten pie-shaped cells, was operated by just one deputy whose chair rotated to allow a view of all the cells. The facility eventually closed in 1969 due to safety regulations.

> **Squirrel Cage Jail** (also called the Lazy Susan Jail or Human Rotary Jail), 226 Pearl St, Council Bluffs, IA; ✎ 712 323 2509; web: www.mountpleasantbeautiful.com/iowa/article_396.shtml. *Hours vary Apr–Oct; closed Nov–Mar.*

Rooms with a Skew

It's one thing to have a fixation with lighthouses. It's quite another to build one – on the Iowa prairie, no less. But Bill Klauer, who had researched and visited hundreds and hundreds of lighthouses, didn't let a small thing like the absence of an ocean deter him from fulfilling his dream. In 1991, with the full support of his wife, Jill, he built his lighthouse tower, a slender white structure that can be seen from 16 miles away during the day. Its light can be seen for 22 miles at night. The structure doesn't guide any ships but it can guide you to a stay at the **Lighthouse Valley View Bed and Breakfast**.

> **Lighthouse Valley View Bed and Breakfast**, 15931 Lore Mound Rd, Dubuque, IA 52002; ☎ 800 407 7023 or 563 583 7327; web: www.lighthousevalleyview.com

ILLINOIS
Festivals and events

Now in its 19th year, bagel manufacturer Lender's sponsors the **World's Largest Bagel Breakfast**, serving some 60,000 bagels to 25,000 people and holding a Bagel Bow Wow in search of the best-dressed bagel dog. In 1977 they baked the Guinness world record bagel: 12½ inches high, 563lb and 59³/₁₆ inches in diameter.

> **World's Largest Bagel Breakfast**, held annually in July as part of BagelFest. Contact the Mattoon Chamber of Commerce, 500 Broadway Ave, Mattoon, IL 61938; ☎ 217 235 5661; web: www.mattoonchamber.com

What's unique about Collinsville is not that they've lived in the shadow of the world's largest catsup bottle for 53 years but that they hold a citywide event to celebrate it. They honor the 170-foot tall water-tower bottle, built in 1949, at the **Catsup Bottle Summerfest Birthday Party**. The family-style games are all catsup related: Pass the Catsup, Spin the Bottle, and Pin the Landmark on the Map. They go catsup-bottle bowling, play musical chairs in the downtown streets and hold a taste test to see if anyone can actually tell the difference among the different brands of catsup.

> **Catsup Bottle Summerfest Birthday Party**, held annually in July. Contact the World's Largest Catsup Bottle International Fan Club, PO Box 1108, Collinsville, IL 63334; ☎ 618 345 5598; web: www.catsupbottle.com

Illinois is really fond of cardboard boats, holding no fewer than six **Cardboard Boat Regattas**. The challenge is to build a human-powered craft out of cardboard, paper tape, paint and glue that is capable of completing three trips around a 200-yard course. Awards are given for the most spectacular or prettiest-looking boat; the most creative design and best use of corrugated cardboard; the best-dressed, most creatively costumed team; the most spirited and best organized team, regardless of how bad the boat looks or performs; and the Titanic Award for the most spectacular sinking. To qualify for the coveted Titanic the team must salvage the remains completely. Past designs included a computer with a mouse that trailed in the water, a raft with a trailing shark fin, and a floating outhouse.

> **Cardboard Boat Regattas**. Visit the Great Cardboard Boat Regatta website at www.gcbr.com for dates and times of rallies in Illinois and throughout the country.

Running a marathon is impressive enough – but doing it vertically? During **Hustle Up the Hancock**, runners compete in the marathon of all stair climbs – 1,632 of them to be exact – up to the 94th floor. One of the tallest stair climbs in the world, the event takes place in two of the mammoth building's many stairwells. Thousands of climbers participate, taking off in ten-second intervals. Competitive racers can finish in around 15 minutes. There a gentler, 42-flight event for the less vertically inclined.

Hustle Up the Hancock, held annually in February. Contact the American Lung Association of Metropolitan Chicago, 1440 W Washington Blvd, Chicago, IL 60607; ↘ 800 LUNG USA or 312 243 2000; web: www.lungchicago.org

It's America's biggest tug-of-war. The Mississippi River separates the towns of LeClaire, Iowa and Port Byron, Illinois. At the annual **Tug Fest**, ten teams of 20 pull against one another with a 2,400-foot, 680lb rope. The winning town gets to keep the prize statue of a bald eagle in flight for the next year.

Tug Fest, held annually in August in LeClaire, IA and Port Byron, IL; web: www.tugfest.org

At an isolated Quincy airfield, around 5,000 adrenaline junkies every year attend the World Freefall Convention, a display of kamikaze, freestyle skydiving in which participants compete in sky surfing and accelerated, freefall speed dives. Each day of the event includes several religious services, which is understandable considering how extremely dangerous the sport is.

World Freefall Convention, held annually in August. Location varies. Contact World Free Fall Convention Headquarters, 1659 Hwy 104, Quincy, IL 62035; ↘ 217 222 5867; fax: 217 885 3141; web: www.freefall.com

Museums and collections

Superman comes to the aid of Metropolis tourism in the form of an obsessed collector who's amassed more than 100,000 pieces of the man of steel's memorabilia. Curator of the **Super Museum and Gift Shop**, Jim Hembrick has been instrumental in seeing that the small town lives up to its potential. At the annual **Superman Celebration**, the town of Metropolis puts on a mock bank robbery that gives Superman the opportunity, once again, to triumph over evil even if he has to do so on the ground instead of in the air. Superman slogans abound, with practically every business in town finding some way to align itself with the cartoon, television and movie legend that has endured for more than 60 years. After all, isn't tourism an important component of truth, justice and the American way?

Super Museum and Gift Shop, 517 Market St, Metropolis, IL 62960; ↘ 618 524 5518; web: www.supermuseum.com

Superman Celebration, held annually in June in Metropolis, IL. Contact Metropolis Chamber of Commerce, 607 Market St, Metropolis, IL 62960; ↘ 800 949 5740 or 618 524 2714; web: www.metropolischamber.com

Statues of the doctors who actually used the implements displayed in the **International Museum of Surgical Science** stand silent and imposing in the

Hall of Immortals. Gruesome paintings of surgeries long past join devices dating from ancient and not so ancient times. The X-ray room has an X-ray shoe fitter that was routinely used in the 1950s – before the dangers of X-rays were known – to see exactly how your foot fitted in your shoe.

> **International Museum of Surgical Science**, 1524 N Lake Shore Dr, Chicago, IL; ↘ 312 642 6502; web: www.imss.org. Located along 151 bus route, few blocks north of Clark/Division elevated train stop. *Open Tue–Sat 10.00am–4.00pm Oct–Apr; Tue–Sun 10.00am–4.00pm May–Sept. Closed Mon.*

Lucky for us that Dr William M Scholl had an obsession with feet. The creator of foot comfort products, the story of Dr Scholl is told at an entertaining exhibit called **Feet First: the Scholl Story** at the Scholl College of Podiatric Medicine. The good doctor was a master marketer in the 1920s and 1930s, long before marketing became fashionable. He would try anything to reach customers, including always carrying a skeleton of the foot in his pocket and setting up free foot screenings outside the local druggist's emporium. An early innovator in corporate training, he wrote company songs and slogans to motivate his sales staff; the company motto was 'early to bed, early to rise, work like hell, and advertise'. You'll learn all about your foot at the interactive exhibits and see the world's biggest shoe, an astounding size 44 worn by the world's tallest man, Robert Wadlow, who was eight foot 11 inches tall. Call ahead if you'd like a personal tour given by curator David McKay.

> **Feet First: the Scholl Story**, located at the Finch University of Health Sciences. 3333 Green Bay Rd, N Chicago, IL 60064; ↘ 847 578 3000; web: www.finchcms.edu/SCPM/feetfirst/index.cfm. *Tours by appointment.*

Here's a museum that doesn't look or feel like one. The **Rolling Meadows Historical Museum** is designed so you feel as if you just walked into a 1950s' suburban tract home, a guest of the family 'living' there – Fred, Mildred and their three kids. Mildred even has cake and coffee set out for you. Everything in the home is straight out of the 50s right down to the contents of the cupboards and closets. The building itself is a replica of the houses built by Rolling Meadows developer Kimball Hill. If you're over 50 the non-museum museum will be a trip down memory lane; much younger and you'll feel like you're watching *Leave It To Beaver* or Andy Griffith on TV.

> **Rolling Meadows Historical Museum**, 3100 Central Rd, Rolling Meadows, IL 60008; ↘ 847 577 7068; web: www.ci.rolling-meadows.il.us/historical_museum.htm. *Open Wed 10.00am–2.00pm, Sun 1.00–4.00pm (admission free) or call for appointment ($3pp).*

Max Nordeen's Wheels Museum, so-called because he loves anything pertaining to wheels, is a bit off the beaten track, so he doesn't get a lot of visitors. When he does, Max loves to talk about his collections, a strange mixture of just about anything and everything that's appealed to him during a lifetime of collecting. He's got a story behind each piece, all 3,700 of them, so plan to stay awhile. You'll see a chunk of coal and a steward's badge from the doomed Titanic, a petrified leech, a chunk of glass rubble from the Chicago Fire of 1871 and a prostitute mannequin holding a $100 bill and a key to a hotel room. One of his wheels is more than 12 feet in diameter and weighs 18 tons. From war trinkets to naughty key chains, from spark plugs to gear-shift knobs, Max has it.

Max Nordeen's Wheels Museum, 6400 N 400 Ave, Alpha, IL 61413; ↘ 309 334 2589. *Best to call first as hours vary.*

Presenting the social history of funerals, **The Museum of Funeral Customs** documents the history of Americans funerals as well as maintaining a library of funeral practices worldwide. Displays of caskets and coffins (there *is* a difference!) represent our changing tastes in style along with plenty of embalming equipment, port-mortem photography, and mourning articles. A visit to this museum will answer such questions as why pallbearers are called that, why coins were placed on the eyes of the dead and why small-town furniture stores ran the local funeral home and ambulance service. There's a replica of President Lincoln's casket and a model of his tomb so you can learn all about his funeral and burial before visiting his nearby tomb.

The **Museum of Funeral Customs**, 1440 Monument Ave, Springfield, IL 62702; ↘ 217 544-3480; web: www.funeralmuseum.org. *Open Tue–Sat 10.00am–4.00pm, Sun 1.00–5.00pm. Closed Mon and holidays.*

Attractions

Jim Warfield doesn't just work in a haunted house, he lives in one. As eccentric as they come, he turned a decrepit old mansion, **Raven's Grin Inn**, into a permanent haunted house open practically every day of the year. While the tour of his bizarre house relies more on the creative-goofy than on the standard gruesome, it certainly has it share of scary moments. The house is said to be genuinely haunted, with Jim adding to the experience with pitch-dark passageways, mazes, tunnels, trapdoors, and a 60-foot slide leading from the upper story to the basement. (You can also take the stairs.)

Raven's **Grin Inn**, 411 N Carroll St., Mount Carroll, IL 61053; ↘ 815 244 4746; web: www.hauntedravensgrin.com

Quirkyville

Olney has a leash law – for cats. The law is needed to keep them from preying on the rare albino squirrel population for which the town is famous. The townsfolk are so proud of their white squirrels that they've been passing laws to protect them since 1925. The critters have right of way on all city streets as well as their own crosswalks. Hit one with your car and you'll pay a hefty fine. Don't even think about taking one out of town; you could go to jail. There's a likeness of the bushy-tailed creatures on the police department's insignia patch.

Olney, IL. Contact the Olney Chamber of Commerce, 201 E Chestnut St, Olney, IL 62450; ↘ 618 392 2241; web: www.olneychamber.com

Known as one of the most haunted small towns in America, **Alton** builds on its ghostly reputation with two 'hauntrepreneurs': **Antoinette's Haunted History Tours** and Troy Taylor's **History and Haunting Tours**. Both are dead serious about their ventures, offering tours led by professional ghost hunters. Antoinette focuses on educating you about such things as the differences between apparitions and ghosts, how to identify them, and, most importantly, if they can hurt you. Meanwhile, Troy focuses on telling the history of Alton through its haunted places. Note for would-be ghost hunters: Troy also gives tours for ghost hunters-in-training, teaching you the secrets of ghost hunting. You wouldn't think that a town with a population of just 31,000 could support this many ghost hunters so there just may be some substance behind Alton's claim to fame.

Antoinette's Haunted History Tours. Contact Right Brain Activities, PO Box 10, Alton, IL 62002; ☎ 618 462 4009; web: www.hauntedalton.com

History and Haunting Tours. Contact the History & Hauntings Book Co, 515 E 3rd St, Alton, IL 62002; ☎ 888 446 7859 or 618 465 1086; web: www.prairieghosts.com

The **Lakeview Museum's Community Solar System** spreads over 60 miles of central Illinois, making it the largest complete solar system model in the world. The sun, 36 feet across, is at the museum itself. Saturn and its rings, nearly eight feet across, is in a grocery store in East Peoria; the Earth, a mere four inches, hangs in a gas station. The original Pluto was stolen from its furniture store orbit in Kewanee, replaced with a gumball until the museum made a ³/₄-inch replacement. If you visited all the planets, with a stop for lunch in historic Peoria, you'd travel the equivalent of 25 billion miles, or 200 miles by car. Want to ride the Jupiter–Saturn–Jupiter bike trail? You'll ride 1.5 billion miles, or 12 miles. For directions to all nine planets, email the creator of the solar system, Sheldon Schafer, at sschafer@lakeview-museum.org.

Lakeview Museum's Community Solar System. 1125 W Lake Ave, Peoria, IL 61614-5985; ☎ 309 686 7000; web: www.lakeview-museum.org

Tours

Chicago Neighborhood Tours takes you to parts of the city you probably wouldn't find on your own, exploring themes and neighborhoods with tours like the Great Chicago Fire (it takes you around on a fire truck), the Great Cemeteries of Chicago and an eclectic sampling of neighborhoods.

Chicago Neighborhood Tours, 78 E Washington St, Chicago, IL 60602; ☎ 312 742 1190; web: www.chgocitytours.com

Dennis McKenna is a retired cop who just likes showing folks around his town. Coming from the unique perspective of someone who's seen and heard it all, Dennis loves taking individuals and small groups around his city, using public transportation just like the locals. With Dennis you become immersed in the life of the city, coming to understand its cultural quirks. He'll also help you with plans for the rest of your visit if you see him early on.

See Chicago With a Cop, Dennis McKenna; ☎ 312 988 9479 or 312 315 6374

Chicago was once home to notorious felons like Al Capone and James Dillinger. On the **Untouchables Tour** you'll go back to the time of the 1920s and 1930s. Shifty and South Side are your guides, acting out the gangster's parts. This two-hour theater-on-wheels brings to life the bizarre and frightening legends of hoodlums, brothels, gambling dens and gangland shoot-outs.

Untouchables Tour, 10924 S Prospect Ave, Chicago, IL 60643; ☎ 773 881 1195; web: www.gangstertour.com

Just plain weird

It's an eight-car pile up – on a skewer, that is. In a Berwyn parking lot at the Cermak Plaza Shopping Center stands an odd piece of art called the 'Spindle'. The cars are skewered on a 50-foot spike, with a red Volkswagen 'Beetle' topping it off like a cherry. The object of much controversy, some think it's delightfully refreshing, while others view it more like garbage on a skewer. The center is also home to other bizarre art such as the 'Pinto Pelt' on the wall near Walgreen's. Some Berwyn citizens have soundly criticized the center's owner, David Bermant, for his artistic taste – or lack of it – and they voted, in a non-binding referendum, to tear down a previous sculpture that was on the site. Fortunately, the art sits on private property so David can display whatever he wants. The cars on a spike, created by artist Dustin Shuler, cost $75,000 in 1989.

Cermak Plaza Shopping Center, Cermak Road and Harlem Ave, Berwyn, IL

It's not all grim at Ahlgrim's funeral home, Palatine. In the basement of this mortuary is a macabre miniature golf course called **Ahlgrim Acres**. Started 35 years ago as a pastime for family and employees, word of mouth brought service clubs, scouts and other organizations to play the unique course. Hole #1 is a sand trap with a red-light-blinking skull. Hole #2 is an old casket shipping box with twisting troughs for the ball inside. Other challenges include a guillotine, a haunted house, a pinball-like gravestone bounce and the crematorium. If your ball falls into a grave, you lose. There's no charge to play but you do need to call for a reservation. In the event of a funeral you'll have to reschedule.

Ahlgrim Acres, located at Ahlgrim's Funeral Home, 201 N Northwest Hwy, Hwy 14, Palatine, IL 60067; ✆ 847 358 7411

Images of **Robert Wadlow**, the world's tallest man, can be seen in museums and attractions all across the USA. But it was here, in Alton, that Wadlow was born, educated and buried. In kindergarten he was five-and-a-half-feet tall. At the age of 20 he earned a living by touring the states for a shoe company that supplied him with his size 37 shoes. When he died from an infected blister in 1940 at the tender age of 22, he weighed 490lb. Today there are drugs to control this freakish physical condition. On the grounds of SIU Dental School, a life-size, eight-foot eleven-inch statue of him makes a terrific photo op. Remember to hold your camera vertically.

Alton Museum of History and Art, 2809 College Ave, Alton, IL 62002; web: www.altonmuseum.com. *Open Mon–Fri 10.00am–4.00pm, Sat–Sun 1.00–4.00pm.*

A two-story outhouse is the pride of the town of Gays, home to the double-decker privy since its construction in 1869. You'll have to see for yourself how two people could use it at the same time!

Quirk Alert

GRANDIOSE SCHEMES

Several dreamers and schemers have attempted to build Meccas to their religions in America. With the exception of the Mormons in Utah, all have failed, leaving behind the architectural skeletons of dashed hopes and dreams. Eric Jason of Sweden was one of those failed visionaries. He and his band of Jasonists settled in **Bishop Hill** in 1846. Life was harsh, and made even harsher by Jason, who insisted on three- to four-hour services twice daily and three times on Sundays. When a cholera epidemic invaded the colony, Jason refused to allow doctors in, telling his flock they were dying because they lacked faith. A disgruntled colonist finally murdered him. His believers, expecting him to arise from the dead, didn't bury him until the smell convinced them he wasn't coming back. The colony disbanded several years later. All that's left of Eric Jason's tyranny is the little town called Bishop Hill where you can visit the Bishop Hill Museum.

Bishop Hill Museum, PO Box D, Bishop Hill, IL 61419; ↘ 309 927 3345; web: www.bishophill.com. *Hours vary seasonally.*

Two-Story Outhouse, Gays, IL. Located above the SF Gammill General Store.

Quirky cuisine

The ladies' loo at **Pasha Restaurant and Club** was honored by the Travel Channel as having the 'World's Best Ladies Room'. Candlelight, a stocked bar and a singing bartender enhance the lush pink and mahogany décor. This is not a quick stop to powder your nose.

Pasha Restaurant and Club, 642 N Clark St, Chicago, IL 60610; ↘ 312 397 0100; web: www.pasharest.com

Rooms with a Skew

The **Adventure Inn Motel** in Gurnee claims the world's largest selection of 'FantaSuites'. In the Hollywood Motel section you'll find two dozen way-off-the-wall suites, including the Igloo, an ice and penguin fantasy, and Area 51 (referring to Nevada's famed UFO sites), which simply have to be seen to be believed. Other over-the-top themes are the Roman Empire, Under the Sea, Gotham City, Signs of the Zodiac, Jewel of the Nile and Knight Moves. Tours are offered at 2pm weekdays for the over-21 set.

Adventure Inn Motel, 3740 Grand Ave, Gurnee, IL 60031; ↘ 800 373 5245 or 847 623 7777; web: www.adventureinninc.com

MICHIGAN
Festivals and events

Entries in the winter **Outhouse Classic** in Trenary are built from wood and/or cardboard, installed with a toilet seat and a roll of toilet paper, mounted on skis, then pushed 500 feet down Main Street. Some of the entries are built for speed, some for laughs and some are so elaborate you wouldn't mind having them in your backyard. The annual event started out with 20 entries a decade ago; now it attracts at least 60. A past humor award went to the costumed 'nuns', who pushed the outhouse while praying and slapping people with their rulers; their list of ten commandments included, 'thou shalt not leave the seat up, thou shalt not spray, and thou shalt not take thy farts in vain'. Thirty-five hundred spectators show up for this event and the little town boasts the only 'outhouse parking' signs in Michigan. Past entries included the Hawaiian Pu Pu Inna Hola, and a house powered by pitted prunes. The event also features Snow Volleyball.

Outhouse Classic, held annually in February in Trenary, MI. Contact Outhouse Classic, PO Box 271, Trenary, MI 49891; ↘ 906 446 3504; web: www.jldr.com/ohraces2002.html

When you eat a cherry, you have to get rid of the pit, right? At the **International Cherry Pit Spitting Contest**, they do that by eating the cherry and then spitting the pit as far as possible along a plywood platform marked with measurement grids. The pit that goes the furthest, including the roll, wins. Rick 'Pellet Gun' Krause, 47, has taken the championship for 12 of the competition's 30-year history. His son, 'Young Gun', and wife, 'Machine Gun', also compete. Rick's record is 72 feet 7½ inches; his son finally beat him with a 72 foot 11 inch spit. Denture racks are provided for those who wish to remove their teeth.

International Cherry Pit Spitting Contest, held annually in July. Contact Tree-Mendus Fruit, 9351 E Eureka Rd, Eau Claire, MI 49111; ↘ 269 782 7101; web: www.treemendus-fruit.com

Michigan is pretty fond of cardboard boats, holding three **Cardboard Boat Regattas**. The challenge is to build a human-powered craft out of cardboard, paper tape, paint, and glue that is capable of completing three trips around a 200-yard course. Awards are given for the most spectacular or prettiest-looking, boat; the most creative design and best use of corrugated cardboard; the best-dressed, most creatively costumed team; the most spirited and best organized team, regardless of how badly the boat looks or performs; and a Titanic Award for the most spectacular sinking. To qualify for the Titanic the team must salvage the remains completely. Past entries included a monster truck, a curly-tailed pig and a cow. Even the mayor gets involved, once going down with his ship along with ten city employees.

Cardboard Boat Regattas, held throughout the summer in various locations in Michigan; web: www.gcbr.com

Remember the days when it seemed that more baby food ended up on the floor than it did in your baby? Being on the bib end of the experience isn't all that easy as the adults involved in the **National Baby Food Festival** soon find out. During the baby-food-eating contest, adults work in pairs, trying to get through jars of baby food in the least amount of time. Here's the catch: the person doing the feeding is blindfolded, leaving the person being fed to do all the work. Adults also race tricycles and compete in diaper-changing contests using their own babies. But the cutest competition, by far, is the baby crawl. Carrying on like idiots, parents go to any length to entice their babies to crawl across the finish line. During the week the festival runs, this town of 4,000, home of Gerber Baby Foods, brings in 125,000 people.

National Baby Food Festival, held annually in July. Contact the Fremont Area Chamber of Commerce, 9 E Main St, Fremont, MI 49412; ↘ 231 924 0770; web: www.nbff.org

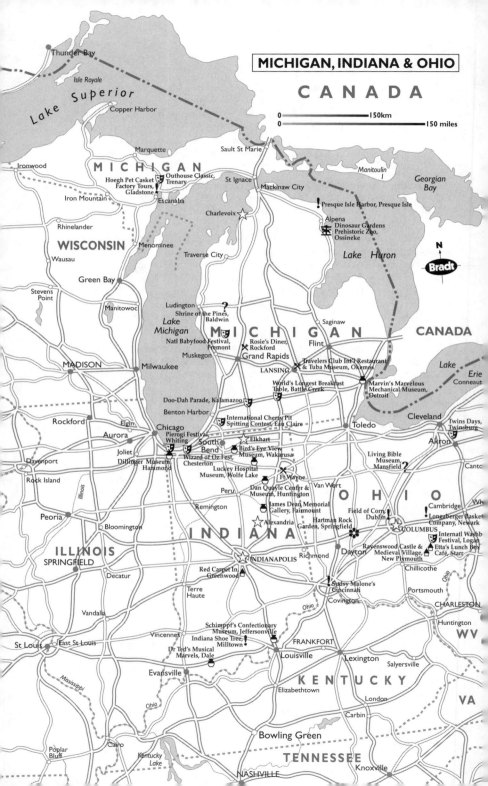

MICHIGAN, INDIANA & OHIO

CANADA

0   150km
0   150 miles

Thunder Bay

Isle Royale

Lake **Superior**

Copper Harbor

Ironwood

M I C H I G A N

Marquette

Sault St Marie

St Ignace

Mackinaw City

Manitoulin I

Georgian Bay

Hoegh Pet Casket Factory Tours, Gladstone
Outhouse Classic, Trenary
St Ignace
Iron Mountain
Escanaba
Charlevoix
Presque Isle Harbor, Presque Isle
Alpena
Dinosaur Gardens Prehistoric Zoo, Ossineke

Rhinelander

WISCONSIN

Menominee

Wausau

Traverse City

Lake Huron

CANADA

N

Bradt

Green Bay

Stevens Point

Manitowoc

Ludington
Shrine of the Pines, Baldwin

Lake Michigan

Saginaw

Lake Erie
Conneaut

MADISON

Milwaukee

Natl Babyfood Festival, Fremont
Muskegon
Rosie's Diner, Rockford
Grand Rapids
LANSING
Flint
Travelers Club Int'l Restaurant & Tuba Museum, Okemos

M I C H I G A N

Marvin's Marvelous Mechanical Museum, Detroit

World's Longest Breakfast Table, Battle Creek

Rockford

Elgin

Aurora

Doo-Dah Parade, Kalamazoo

Benton Harbor

Cleveland

Twins Days, Twinsburg

Akron

Chicago
Pierogi Festival, Whiting
Joliet
Dillinger Museum, Hammond

Davenport

Rock Island

International Cherry Pit Spitting Contest, Eau Claire

Toledo

South Bend
Elkhart
Bird's Eye View Museum, Wakarusa
Wizard of Oz Fest, Chesterton
Luckey Hospital Museum, Wolfe Lake
Ft Wayne

Living Bible Museum, Mansfield

Canton

Peoria

Bloomington

Peru

Remington

Dan Quayle Center & Museum, Huntington
Van Wert

O H I O

Cambridge

ILLINOIS
SPRINGFIELD

Decatur

I N D I A N A

James Dean Memorial Gallery, Fairmount
Alexandria

Hartman Rock Garden, Springfield

Field of Corn, Dublin
COLUMBUS

Longaberger Basket Company, Newark
Internat'l Washb Festival, Logan
Etta's Lunch Box Café, Starr

Terre Haute

INDIANAPOLIS
Richmond
Red Carpet Inn, Greenwood

Dayton

Ravenswood Castle & Medieval Village, New Plymouth

Chillicothe

Portsmouth

CHARLESTON

Vandalia

Sudsy Malone's, Cincinnati
Covington

Ohio

Huntington

WV

St Louis
East St Louis

Vincennes

Schimpff's Confectionary Museum, Jeffersonville
Indiana Shoe Tree, Milltown
Dr Ted's Musical Marvels, Dale

FRANKFORT

Louisville

Lexington

Salyersville

VA

Evansville

K E N T U C K Y

Elizabethtown

London

Carbin

Poplar Bluff

Cairo

Kentucky Lake

Mississippi

Ohio

TENNESSEE

Bowling Green

NASHVILLE

Knoxville

Any town named Kalamazoo would have to have a sense of humor, and its **Doo-Dah Parade** each June proves that it does. Do-Dah is a salute to silliness, a parade that spoofs parades. It's an annual event that draws 1,300 participants and as many as 50,000 spectators. The Keggers, a local nightclub, has its employees form a Keggers Drill Team, performing with empty kegs, rolling and throwing them in formation.

> **Doo-Dah Parade**, held annually in June in Kalamazoo, MI. Contact Kalamazoo County Convention and Visitors Bureau, 346 W Michigan Ave, Kalamazoo, MI 49007; ↘ 800 530 9192 or Cumulus Broadcasting WKFR; ↘ 616 344 0111; web: www.kazoofun.com

Battle Creek is known as the cereal capital of the world. Each year the Kellogg Company, the famous maker of breakfast cereals, pushes 300 picnic tables together and serves a free breakfast for up to 60,000 people at the **World's Longest Breakfast Table**. The company's Cereal City USA™ is an entertaining attraction about the history of cereal and the part it has played in American culture.

> **World's Longest Breakfast Table**, 171 W Michigan Ave, Battle Creek, MI 49017; ↘ 616 962 6230; web: www.battlecreek.org/whats-new/chamber/cereal_festival/

Eccentric environments

As a boy, **Earl Young** liked to collect rocks, much like young boys everywhere. Only for Earl, the rocks became an obsession. Prowling the shores of Lake Michigan and the woods surrounding his hometown of Charlevoix, he collected stones that 'spoke' to him, for Earl firmly believed that each stone had a distinctive personality. The houses he built with these stones and boulders have been called variously, 'gnome', 'mushroom', 'fairy' and 'elf' homes. Earl, with no training as an architect, managed to create a career building these strange, undulating houses that seem to sprout from the earth like mushrooms. No two houses were ever alike, for Earl built to the site, never cutting down trees. Instead, his houses flowed into the setting, undulating and weaving in a mating dance between man and landscape. He built into the hillsides and into the trees, planning each meticulous detail. A stone's 'personality', and how it would get along with the stone next to it, dictated the placement of each. The results were whimsical and eccentric, both fluid and chunky, with wavy roofs, massive fireplaces and free-form contours that melted into the setting. Sometimes Earl would find a stone or boulder, then go to great effort to bury it until he found a place for it. He once dropped a nine-ton boulder into the lake and, 26 years later, knew exactly where to retrieve it. Twenty-six of his houses can be seen on a self-guided walking tour.

> **Earl Young Gnome Homes**. Information: pick up a brochure and map at the Charlevoix Area Chamber of Commerce, 408 E Bridge St, Charlevoix, MI 49720; ↘ 231 547 2101; web: www.charlevoix.org. *You can find most of the houses by taking Bridge St to the Pine River Channel. Immediately south of the channel take Park Ave west and south to see a triangular block full of his homes. You can walk, bike, or drive past the houses.*

Museums and collections

Marvin Yagoda has somehow crammed his masses of historical and modern arcade machines, side-show wonders and curiosities into every square inch of

Quirk Alert

THE HEIDELBERG PROJECT

It happened on Heidelberg Street. One man, working alone, painted polka dots on his house, his car, the trees and the trashcans. Using his blighted neighborhood as his canvas, and a compelling vision as his tools, Tyree Guyton rebuilt the spirit of his riot-torn community through art. The street has been a living kaleidoscope, bursting with exuberant color and pattern. Polkadots are everywhere, joined by an abundance of found and broken objects, including whole houses, transformed into art. People came from all over the world to visit the Heidelberg Project (web: www.heidelberg.org) and experience for themselves Guyton's message of hope penetrating the blight. Unfortunately, the city of Detroit didn't see the street through artistic eyes: all they saw were condemned buildings, which they've twice torn down since Guyton began in 1986. Still inspired to rebuild and expand, he's usually in his outdoor studio each day. Today a non-profit organization manages the project, working to clean up abandoned lots and properties and running the community art center. Web: www.heidelberg.org

available floor space at **Marvin's Marvelous Mechanical Museum** in Farmington Hills. Marvin, a 65-year-old pharmacist known for his outlandish wardrobe and tattooed teeth, admits the museum is a hobby that went way-y-y out of control. You'll see fascinating old coin-operated games, like the gypsy fortune-teller, right alongside modern video games. Here are neon, robots, and animation; signs, dummies, and planes, all clicking and clacking at once in a madhouse filled with his passion gone wild. Most amazing is that Marvin manages to keep all the games in operating condition so you can play around here for hours. He also has a wicked sense of humor. There's a naked pin-up poster of Burt Reynolds with a wooden figleaf covering his privates. Lift up the hinged leaf and a flash bulb goes off in your face.

Marvin's Marvelous Mechanical Museum, 31005 Orchard Lake Rd, Farmington Hills, MI 48334; ↘ 248 626 5020; web: www.marvin3m.com. *Open: Mon–Thu 10.00am–10.00pm, Fri–Sat 10.00am–11pm, Sun 11.00am–9.00pm. Free.*

Attractions

Dinosaur Gardens Prehistorical Zoo in Ossineke features a welcome by Jesus, huge concrete dinosaurs and a sprinkling of cavemen hunting for their supper. A Mr Domke, who colored his creatures green, grey, and brown, built these strange

Quirk Alert

Detroit is headquarters for **Hair Wars**, an extravaganza that pits hair designers against one another in a battle to see who can produce the most outrageous, bizarre, over-the-top hairstyle. Primarily a fantasy-hair fashion show for those who style African-American hair, the events attract thousands of attendees in cities across the country. Flamboyant, flashy, and certainly not for introverts, the hair-dos out-do themselves in the weirdness department. How weird? Try the 'hairy copter', a battery-assisted hair structure that included flashing lights and miniature rotating helicopter blades. Then there's the zipper man who, each year, unzips the hairdo to retrieve a surprise. In years past it's been a live four-foot python, two white doves, and a bottle of champagne with two glasses. A show held during a Tigers' game featured baseball-themed styles. Not all the styles are this gimmicky, of course, but they're all works of art, however fleeting they may be. Up to a hundred models strut their structures during each production, often in costume, and each wearing creations that may have taken two days to craft.

Hair Wars. Contact David Humphries ✆ 313 534 8318; email: humpthegrinder@ameritech.net. Hair Wars are held throughout the country.

sculptures in the 1950s. The current owner, Jean Cousineau, has repainted them in bright, cheerful colors. The effect is curious indeed.

Dinosaur Gardens Prehistoric Zoo, US 23S, Ossineke, MI; ✆ 989 471 5477. *Open daily 9.00am–6.00pm in the summer.*

Raymond W Overholzer was so enamored of the white pine that he built a cabin, complete with furnishings, as a tribute to the tree. At the **Shrine of the Pines**, the furniture is chiseled from tree stumps and roots that were scraped with broken glass and wire brushes, then finished with sandpaper, resin, and deer hide. You'll see chairs, chandeliers, tables, beds, and candlesticks – more than 200 items in all – in a tranquil setting on the banks of the Pere Marquette River in Baldwin. It's the largest collection of rustic white-pine furniture in the world.

Shrine of the Pines, located 2 miles south of Baldwin in the Manistee National Forest; ✆ 616 745 7892; web: www.baldwin.localis.com/shrineopine. *Open Mon–Sat 10.00am–6.00pm, Sun 1.30–6.00pm May 15–Oct 15.*

Just plain weird

Three Depression-era drinking buddies from **Presque Isle Harbor** give the expression 'drop dead' a whole new meaning. It seems that Fred Piepkorn, Charlie Priest and Bill Green agreed, in honor of their friendship, that as each pal passed away, the others would remember him by pouring a drink into the earth at his gravesite. At the town's **cemetery**, you can see three cement slabs next to one another, each drilled with a hole – the better for the drop to drip down to the departed chums. Local folks still drink with them.

Presque Isle Harbor Cemetery, 455 N Seventh St, Marquette, MI; ➘ 906 228-0471. Contact Marquette County Convention and Visitors Bureau; ➘ 800 544 4321; web: www.marquettecounty.org

You can view the manufacture of pet caskets and tour a model pet cemetery at the **Hoegh Pet Casket Factory** tours in Gladstone. The casket showroom has velvet paintings of wide-eyed puppies along with caskets from shoebox size on up. The sewing room displays memorial pet plaques after which you'll see the actual manufacturing and quality control process. You end the tour outside in the model pet cemetery.

Hoegh Pet Casket Factory Tours, 311 Delta Ave, Gladstone, MI 49837; ➘ 906 428 2151; web: www.hoeghpetcaskets.com

Rosie's Diner in Rockford is about two things: food and art. Jerry Berta and his wife, Madeline, bought a decrepit diner for $2,000, moved it to a vacant lot they owned and restored it for use as an art studio and gallery in which to make and show their work. They did such a good job spiffing up the diner that folks thought it was a restaurant and flocked there to eat. So they put up a sign saying, 'No Food, Just Art', but folks still kept coming, buying art and asking for food. So Jerry found another diner, moved it to his lot, and looked for someone to run the food side of the business since he knew absolutely nothing about it. Finding no-one, he decided to run it himself and they hung a sign one morning announcing the opening of the diner. By that evening they had to take down the sign; people were lining up to get in. During the last 15 years they have served more than a million customers.

The art part is obvious when you see the miniature golf course they've set up. The holes have two themes: food and art. You can play through slabs of ribs, hamburgers, hot dogs, a teapot, tubes of paint, a brush and a palette. Jerry specializes in outrageous, often bizarre ceramic and neon sculptures such as a domesticated, Godzilla-like figure zapping the kitchen sink with neon rays. He also likes to keep things hopping now that he's finally found someone to take over the diner part. He ran for office under the slogan 'I'm not a lawyer'.

Rosie's Diner, 4500 14 Mile Rd, Rockford, MI 49341; ➘ 616 866 2787; web: www.rosiesdiner.com

The **Travelers Club International Restaurant and Tuba Museum** in Okemos is an eclectic little place run by Jennifer Boorke and William White. The travel theme is attributed to Jennifer, whose affinity for exotic food is reflected in the restaurant's menu. The tuba part is William's, whose passion for the instrument is evident in the collection.

The **Travelers Club International Restaurant and Tuba Museum**, 2138 Hamilton Rd, Okemos, MI 48864; ➘ 517 349 1701; web: www.travelerstuba.com

INDIANA
Festivals and events
There are real Munchkins to be seen at Duneland's annual **Wizard of Oz Festival**. Each year around 75,000 people converge on the little town to meet half a dozen of the actors who portrayed the original Munchkins in the *Wizard of Oz* movie and watch them lead the Oz Fantasy Parade in downtown Chesterton. The festival features Oz character look-alike contests, autograph sessions, town crier competitions and a collector's swap meet.

Wizard of Oz Fest, held annually in September in Chesterton, IN. Contact Duneland Chamber of Commerce, 303 Broadway, Chesterton, IN 46304; ↘ 219 926 5513; web: www.chestertonchamber.org

The late cartoonist Rube Goldberg specialized in drawing implausible, wacky and complex machines to perform simple tasks. Today colleges hold yearly, regional competitions culminating in a national event, **The Rube Goldberg Machine Contest**, in which students are challenged to build such machines according to a specific theme. The rules are complicated even though the task itself is simple. For example, the contraptions might be required to raise and wave a flag, pour a cup of coffee, pitch a can into a recycling bin, or screw in a light bulb – all in 20 or more steps. The machine must be no larger than five feet by six feet by five feet; must do its job in no more than two minutes per run; must use at least 20 steps (there are no maximums); and can't use live animals. Teams have to have at least four student members. Judging is based on timing, functionality, team chemistry and how well they exemplify the Rube Goldberg spirit. The audience is allowed to vote for their favorite contraption and invited on stage for a closer look while the ballots are being counted and the judges are calculating the results.

Rube Goldberg Machine Contest, held every April. Contact Willie Karashin, National Machine Contest Chairmen, at ↘ 765 743 2461; web: www.rubemachine.com

It's all about polka, potatoes and Poland at Whiting's annual **Pierogi Festival**. Most everyone in the downtown area gets involved, starting with a Polka Parade on Friday night that features the Twirling Babushkas, the World's Original Lazy-Boy float, the Precision Lawn Mower Drill Team and the Pierogi Queen and her court. Then Mr Pierogi and his Pieroguettes (Misses Potato, Cheese, Mushroom, Berry, Beef, Apricot, and Sauerkraut) perform at the Pierogi Musicale, singing such tunes as 'Anything You Can Eat, I Can Eat More Of'. Other activities include polka bands (lots and lots of them), a pierogi toss, and Eastern Blok Jeopardy. The region is home to many of Polish and Slovakian descent and the festival is their way of honoring both their heritage and their favorite comfort food.

Pierogi Festival, held annually in July. Contact the City of Whiting, 1443 119th St, Whiting, IN 46394; ↘ 877 659 0292 or 219 659 7700; web: www.whitingindiana.com/pierogi.html

Museums and collections
More than 40% of the recreational vehicles and motor homes in the US are made in Indiana and they're so proud of that fact that there's a hall of fame, museum, and library to prove it. The **RV/MH Heritage Museum and Hall of Fame** displays travel trailers and RVs in kitschy vignettes paying tribute to the open-road lifestyle. You'll see the first RV ever made (c1915), sleek Airstreams, and clunky not-so-travel-worthy models along with the very earliest trailers, one of which was designed to be towed behind a carriage. The library archives thousands of magazines and manuals often used by owners seeking their unit's origin and design. Most interesting is a scale model of a utopian 'trailer high-rise', a concept whereby you could stack RVs 20 stories high, allowing entire communities of them to live vertically in the cities. It never caught on, of course, defeating the purpose of owning a portable home to begin with.

RV/MH Heritage Museum and Hall of Fame, 801 Benham Ave, Elkhart, IN 46516; ❧ 800 378 8694 or ❧ 574 293 2344; web: www.rv-mh-hall-of-fame.org. *Open Mon–Fri 9.00am–4.00pm; weekends by appointment.*

Trying to convince the world that outlaw John Dillinger was actually a good guy was the life's work of one Joe Pinkston, an eccentric who amassed enough Dillinger memorabilia to open the **Dillinger Museum**. He crammed the place solid with artifacts honoring the criminal's bloody saga, explaining each display with single-spaced, full-page typewritten descriptions. He considered his museum so provocative that he even had a sign warning those with faint hearts to stay out. When he died in 1996 his collection was bought by the Lake County Convention and Visitors Bureau, which houses it today in their new exhibition hall. They've redesigned the exhibits into an interactive experience, giving you a snapshot of history from the early 1900s up through the 1960s as if seen through the eyes of John Dillinger. You can still see the life-size wax diorama of the outlaw on the morgue slab, his tombstone, his tommy gun and his jailhouse letters.

Dillinger Museum, located at the Lake County Convention and Visitors Bureau, 7770 Corinne Dr, Hammond, IN 46323; ❧ 800 ALL LAKE or ❧ 219 989 7770; web: www.johndillingermuseum.com. *Open Mon–Fri 8.00am–6.00pm, Sat–Sun 9.00am–6.00pm from Memorial Day to Labor Day; Mon–Fri 8.00am–5.00pm, Sat–Sun 9.00am–5.00pm Labor Day to Memorial Day.*

Shirley Hite and her sister Mary Adams, both retired nurses, have been collecting discarded, outdated medical equipment for 25 years, part of which they display in a non-operating, 20-bed hospital they own in this tiny, no-stoplight town. The **Luckey Hospital Museum** takes up part of the first floor, showcasing their most unusual collection of medical instruments and equipment. Here the sisters have recreated period rooms from the 1700s to the 1900s including furnished examples of a surgical suite, an exam room, a doctor's office and a library. Though the museum has been open informally just a short time, the entire medical community is behind this effort to preserve a little part of their heritage. If all goes well, the sisters will be adding a 'circa 1931' costumed tour, responding only when spoken to in 1931 language. For now, you need to call for an appointment to see their museum.

Luckey Hospital Museum, on the corner of State Route 109 and US 33 in the center of Wolfe Lake, IN. Call Shirley Hite for tour information, ❧ 260 635 2214.

Schimpff's has been making candy for 110 years and they're so fond of doing it the old-fashioned way that they have a museum honoring old-fashioned sweets right there in the manufacturing plant. At **Schimpf's Confectionary Museum** you'll see thousands of pieces of American candy memorabilia including things like a hand-cranked popcorn popper and an 1890s rabbit-fur candy container (shaped like a chicken, of all things) that will make you appreciate modern microwaves and packaging. Besides the museum they have a large candy demonstration room where you can watch candy being made on turn-of-the-century equipment. They still make hard candy lozenges on drop rollers 100 years old and still pour fudge and toffee from antique copper kettles.

Schimpff's Confectionary Museum, 347 Spring St, Jeffersonville, IN 47130; ❧ 812 283 8367; web: www.schimpffs.com. *Open Mon–Fri*

10.00am–5.00pm, Sat 10.00am–3.00pm. Closed Dec 23–Jan 1 and major holidays. Free.

The **Dan Quayle Center** at the United States Vice Presidential Museum in Huntington is a curious tribute to a former vice president who made little contribution except for his occasional displays of brain-dead aphorisms. He was famous for such Quayle-isms as 'If we don't succeed, we run the risk of failure' and 'What a waste it is to lose one's mind'. Many feel he couldn't pour water out of a boot even if the instructions were printed on the heel. Others think he's been terribly misjudged by an unforgiving press intent on reporting his every tongue-twisted blooper. The museum, which is also a fascinating look at the vice presidency as a whole, is located on the Highway of Vice Presidents, so-called because three of them hailed from this 100-mile section of Indiana 9. One of the displays contains Dan's law diploma, torn to shreds by the family dog.

Dan Quayle Center, United States Vice Presidential Museum, 815 Warren St, PO Box 856, Huntington, IN 46750; ☏ 260 356 6356; fax: 260 356 1455; web: www.quaylemuseum.org. *Open Tue–Sat 10.00am–4.00pm, Sun 1.00–4.00pm. Closed Mon and major holidays.*

DeVon Rose's hobby started innocently enough with some props for his son's train layout. Forty years later, he's still building miniatures out of toothpicks, popsicle sticks, wooden grape boxes, cardboard, candy wrappers and whatever other odds and ends strike his creative fancy. He uses steel wool, all fluffed out and spray painted, to make trees. Black pantyhose serve as screening material. His work is so detailed that he's been known to break a toothpick into 13 pieces and still have a piece left over.

After getting hooked on the hobby, he began a model of his hometown, just as it was in the 1960s, right down to broken windows and construction mistakes. Finished with that, he added buildings surrounding the town, then decided to add landmark buildings from each of the 92 counties in Indiana. Numbering 200 now, his buildings are accurately scaled re-creations of such state landmarks as the Dan Quayle Center and the courthouse in Greensburg that has trees growing out of its tower. His most recent accomplishment is the Bag Factory Building; it took 2,438 toothpicks, 588 popsicle sticks and five months of 40- to 60-hour weeks to complete it. At this rate he could end up with the entire state of Indiana in miniature. You can visit his 'town', fully equipped with lights, fences, signs and streetlights, at his **Bird's Eye View Museum of Miniatures** in Wakarusa. During your tour he'll dim the lights so you can see the intricate lighting he installs in his buildings. His figures of people are all characters with personalities; he delights in telling you their 'stories'.

Bird's Eye View Museum of Miniatures, 325 S Elkhart St, Wakarusa, IN 46573; ☏ 574 862 2367; web: www.wakarusachamber.com. *Tours by appointment.*

Made from toothpicks, 421,000 of them to be exact, is a six-foot-long, fully detailed steam locomotive. Weighing in at 50lb, it took builder Terry Woodling seven years to construct. See it at the **National New York Central Railroad Museum** in Elkhart.

National New York Central Railroad Museum, 721 S Main St, Elkhart, IN 46515; ☏ 574 294 3001; web: www.nycrrmuseum.org. *Open Tue–Sat 10.00am–4.00pm, Sun noon–4.00pm. Closed Mon and major holidays.*

Dr Ted's Musical Marvels in Dale is the local doc's personal collection of self-playing musical instruments from around the world. His huge collection includes nickelodeons, music boxes, gramophones, player pianos, street organs and an enormous 24-foot by 12-foot dance organ.

Dr Ted's Musical Marvels located at Exit 57, Hwy 231 ($\frac{1}{2}$ mile north of I-64), Dale, IN. Contact RR 2, Box 30A, Dale, IN 47523; ☎ 812 937 4250. *Open Mon–Sat 10.00am–6.00pm, Sun 1.00–6.00pm.*

James Dean, popular movie star and culture icon of the 1960s, was born and buried in Grant County. At Fairmount's James Dean Memorial Gallery, David Loehr, an all-time Dean guru, has assembled the largest collection of Dean memorabilia in the world. Besides hundreds of novelty items with the actor's likeness, such as lighters, snow domes and key chains, his address book, his school papers, his motorcycle and his Oscar are all here; and he has a copy of the speeding ticket Dean received just hours before his fatal accident.

James Dean Memorial Gallery, 425 N Main St, PO Box 55, Fairmount, IN 46928; ☎ 765 948 3326; fax: 765 948 3389; web: www.jamesdeangallery.com. *Open daily 10.00am–5.00pm.*

Quirkyville

It takes balls, two of them actually, to put **Alexandria** on the map. First there was the 200lb hairball, coughed up by the town's sewer system and promoted, supposedly, as one of the world's largest. But you can only coast on a hairball for so long. That's where Mike Carmichael, a house painter, comes in. For 26 years he's unknowingly been working on the town's next big tourist attraction: the **World's Largest Ball of Paint**.

It all started out innocently enough with a regular 1lb baseball, nine inches in circumference. Seventeen thousand, three hundred coats of paint later, the ball is 104 inches around and weighs 1,100lb. Mike has been painting a single coat of

Quirk Alert

When Sam Crane bought a run-down farmhouse, he didn't expect to find himself living without electricity and water for 15 years. But life has a strange way of turning out, as Sam would tell you if he used a phone, or fax, or email, which he doesn't. He lives an almost pure, c1843 existence – by choice. He cooks on a wood stove, reads by oil lamp, draws water from the well, visits the outhouse, sews clothes on a foot-pedalled sewing machine, burns firewood for heat (splitting it himself, of course), washes his clothes on a scrub board, and bathes in a galvanized tub in water heated on the wood stove.

He didn't plan this when he bought the farmhouse at the age of 53. Divorced and depressed, he just started fixing up the farm, using 19th-century tools out of respect for the property. The months turned into years and the longer he lived without electricity and running water, the less he missed them as well as all other modern conveniences. He only drives once a month to pick up supplies, mainly canned food and dried meat. Other than that, he's completely self sufficient, staying busy what with strangling chickens, writing with a quill pen and pulling his own teeth.

paint on that ball every day since 1977, keeping meticulous records as to how many layers of each of 20 colors the ball contains. (Blue is the most common, with 2,029 layers; silver the least with only two layers). It's finally gotten big enough that he and the mayor are hopeful that the ball will become Alexandria's next claim to fame. Can a Big Balls Festival be far behind? Mike will accept email requests if you want to have a layer painted in your honor.

World's Largest Ball of Paint, 10696 N 200 W, Alexandria, IN 46001; ☎ 765 724 4088; web: www.ballofpaint.com/BOP/index.shtml. Contact the Chamber of Commerce, 119 N Harrison, Alexandria, IN 46001; ☎ 765 724 3144; web: www.alexandriachamber.com

Just plain weird

The **Indiana Shoe Tree** has been featured in newspapers, and on television and radio, for most of the 35 years in which it has been collecting thousands of pairs of shoes and other footwear. Originally local folks shoed it just for fun, but now that it's famous, people come from all over to tie their old laces together, then hurl their old shoes up into the white oak tree. Some people put their name and date on the soles before tossing them skyward. In winter you can truly see just how many shoes reside in the tree since there is no foliage to hide its contents.

Indiana Shoe Tree, located along County-1, 6 miles south of Milltown, IN. Contact Maxine Archibald, Maxine's Market, 402 W Main St, Milltown, IN 47145; ☎ 812 633 4251

Rooms with a Skew

FantaSuites in Greenwood at the Red Carpet Inn has 24 suites, each decorated with its own theme. The Alien Invasion suite has a flying saucer bed surrounded by rock formations, Cinderella has a queen-size, horse-drawn carriage bed and glass slipper whirlpool, while Cupid's Corner has a heart-shaped bed and mirrored ceiling. Tours are held any Saturday or Sunday at 3pm or you can buy a video in the lobby.

Red Carpet Inn and Fantasuites, 1117 E Main St, Greenwood, IN 46143; ☎ 800 444 7829 or ☎ 317 882 2211; web: www.fantasuite.com

When you spend the night at the Indianapolis **Crowne Plaza Union Station**, a porter will show you to your Pullman sleeper car, just like in the old days. Each of the 26 cars has its own distinctive décor as was standard for the Pullman cars of the railroad era. The accommodations are roomier than you'd expect.

Crowne Plaza Union Station, 123 W Lousiana St, Indianapolis, IN 46225; ☎ 800 2CROWNE or 317 631 2221; web: www.ichotelsgroup.com/h/d/hicp/hd/inddt

OHIO
Festivals and events

You'll be seeing double in Twinsburg during **Twins Days**, the world's largest annual gathering of twins. The event makes for terrific people-watching as 3,000 sets of twins, triplets, quads and more march in the Double Take Parade and compete in contests for the most alike, the least alike, the oldest pair and the youngest. You don't have to be a twin to watch.

Twins Days, held annually in August in Twinsburg, OH. Contact the Twins Days Festival Committee, PO Box 29, Twinsburg, OH; ✎ 330 425 3652; web: www.twinsdays.org

There's only one company in America still making washboards and you can tour their factory during the **International Washboard Festival**. The festival's focus is on music and all the performing bands have at least one musician playing the washboard. While no-one today except the Amish still use washboards for actually washing clothes, the factory still produces them both for playing and for collecting.

International Washboard Festival, held annually in June. Contact the Columbus Washboard Co, 14 Gallagher Ave, Logan, OH 43138; ✎ 740 380 3828; web: www.washboardfestival.com

Eccentric environments

H G Hartman turned his back yard into a rock garden, devoting the seven years prior to his death to creating dozens of rock displays of castles, cathedrals and scenes from American history. Containing approximately 20,000 stones, the **Hartman Rock Garden** has models of the White House, a tribute to boxer Joe Louis, and another to the Dionne Quintuplets, all surrounded by religious scenes and statues. You're welcome to wander the back yard, no need to call.

Hartman Rock Garden, located at the corner of McCain and Russell Sts in Springfield, OH. Contact the Springfield Area Convention & Visitors Bureau, 333 N Limestone St, Ste. 201, Springfield, OH 45503; ✎ 800 803 1553 or 937 325 7621; web: www.springfield-clarkcountyohio.info/hartman_rock_garden.htm. *Open year-round. Admission free.*

Attractions

At the **Living Bible Museum** in Mansfield, you take a 'walk of faith' through the Bible, encountering along the way 41 dioramas made of wax. Divided into Old Testament and New Testament tour sections, the audio recordings, made by volunteers, bring God's words to life. The museum was inspired by Pastor Richard Diamond's 1970s' vision of such a place. He and his wife Alwilda began searching for figures that could turn their dream into reality. Discouraged that new wax and fiberglass figures were so costly, they prayed they'd find some used ones. Hearing of a defunct outdoor Bible walk, they made contact with the owner, who miraculously agreed to donate his 22 weathered figures to the cause. Church members donated their skills, framing the scenes, reconstructing the figures, making the costumes, styling the hair, writing the scripts, and recording the audio. The museum is maintained through the efforts of dozens of dedicated volunteers

There's also a large collection of Votive Folk Art, ie: jewelry, hat pins, tie pins, beadwork, cuff links, collar studs and coins all with biblical scenes.

Living Bible Museum, 500 Tingley Ave, Mansfield, OH; ✎ 419 524 0139; web: www.livingbiblemuseum.org. *Hours vary seasonally.*

Just plain weird

Doing your laundry can't get much wilder than at **Sudsy Malone's**, billed as the world's finest laundry and libation emporium. There's no sitting on a plastic chair reading an old issue of *Soap Opera Digest* here. Instead they provide Maytags, Michelob and enough cutting-edge musical acts to make you want to wash your sheets every week.

> **Sudsy Malone's**, 2626 Vine St, Cincinnati, OH 45219; ↘ 513 751 2300; web: www.sudsys.com

Any basket that can hold 500 people is one B-I-G basket – big as in occupying seven stories and 180,000 square feet, with 84 windows and weighing in at 9,000 tons. The basket, complete with handles and a 25-foot logo tag, is actually a building housing the home offices of the **Longaberger Basket Company** in Newark; it's undoubtedly the largest – and only – basket building in the world. The building itself represents the company's most popular market basket. (A short distance away, the company has built the largest basket monument in the world, a replica of their famous apple basket.) If it seems strange to you that a company would go to such trouble to memorialize a basket, consider this: LBC's basket fans come from all over to worship at the basket shrines and to have their own baskets autographed by the company. The Longaberger Experience involves a tour of the manufacturing campus; a visit to the gift shop; a tour of the Homestead, a mini theme park that pays tribute to the company and their values; and a tour of the basket building. The company even owns and operates its own hotel, The Place off the Square, and its own golf course. This is corporate quirkiness at its finest.

> **Longaberger Basket Company**, 1500 East Main St, Newark, OH 43055; ↘ 740 322 5588; web: www.longaberger.com

What distinguishes the **Field of Corn** in Dublin from thousands of others is that 109 of the ears are human-size sculptures made of concrete. The field is meant to dramatize the plight of farms being overrun with urban development.

> **Field of Corn**, located at Sam and Eulalia Frantz Park, Dublin, OH. Contact Greater Dublin Chamber of Commerce, 129 South High St, Dublin, OH 73017; ↘ 614 889 2001; web: www.dublinchamber.org

Quirky cuisine

Ladora Quesley didn't know what to do with her ever-growing collection of lunchboxes so she decided to display them in an appropriate setting: her own diner. Called **Etta's Lunch Box Café**, the restaurant is decorated with 400 of them. If you point out the lunchbox you remember carrying, Ladora will tell you the year you went to school as well as the background on that particular lunchbox.

> **Etta's Lunch Box Café**, located at the intersections of S Rte 56 and S Rte 38 in Starr, OH; ↘ 740 380 0736

Rooms with a Skew

Breakfast and dinner are served by candlelight in the great hall at **Ravenwood Castle and Medieval Village**. Anglophiles Sue and Jim Maxwell built the 12th-century-style castle and surrounding cottages from scratch, creating a Sherwood Forest-type experience. Each cottage has its own theme: Spinster, Woodcutter, Merchant, Cinderella's Coach House and Celtic Legends. Two gypsy wagons, available for camping, lend an authentic aura to the setting. They put on an original murder mystery weekend several times each year.

Ravenwood Castle and Medieval Village, 65666 Bethel Rd, New Plymouth, OH 45654; ↘ 800 477 1541 or 740 596 2606; web: www.ravenwoodcastle.com

NORTH DAKOTA
Museums and collections

Some of Paul Broste's sculptures at his **Rock Museum** in Parshall look like floor lamps gone bad, while the building itself, which houses his life-long obsession with boulders, rocks, and crystals, looks like a psychedelic version of medieval. The farmer turned artist built his museum in the hope that people would come to appreciate his hundreds of sculptures, painting, poems and, of course, rocks. All manner of rocks and minerals were his passion, and his collection grew to include some of the finest specimens from all over the world. He cut, ground, and polished them into spheres and slabs, then suspended them, science project style, in space and swirling up the walls. In the hexagonal Infinity Room, he used mirrors to reflect the spheres, so they appear to be forever floating in endless space.

Paul Broste's Rock Museum, ND Hwy 1804 and ND Hwy 37, Parshall, ND; located south of Hwy 23 in central ND; 701 862 3264; e-mail: pbrostemuseum@hotmail.com; web: www.parshallndak.com/rockmuseum.htm. *Open Tues–Sun 10.00am–5.00pm, May 1–Oct 1; email the curator for an appointment Oct 2–Apr 30.*

Attractions

During the heyday of the railroads, hobos had a secret 'language', leaving markings around rail yards that only other hobos could understand. Sometimes the markings were warnings, sometimes greetings. When the railroad put up a storage shed in the town of Lamert, it became a hobo version of email. When a tramp wanted to leave a message, he'd carve it in the wood, then move on. Today, the **Hobo House** resides in McHenry, an old-fashioned reminder that communication wasn't always so instantaneous. Each year the town holds an annual Hobo Festival, with everyone dressing like tramps and eating hobo stew.

Hobo House, located at the McHenry Railroad Loop, Museum, and Hobo House, Main St N, Prairies, ND 58464; ↘ 701 785 2333

Just plain weird

Along the 32 miles of highway between Regent and Gladstone, you'll see the most unlikely of giant metal creatures. The sculptures, ranging from 40 to 50 feet in height, reside along the **Enchanted Highway**, the brainchild of sculptor Gary Greff, a former schoolteacher who set out to give folks a reason to visit the region. You'll see giant grasshoppers, a tin family, a flock of pheasants and another of flying geese, and a silhouette of Teddy Roosevelt on a horse. Each year a new sculpture is added with the idea of creating a tourist Mecca that would benefit the towns at both ends of the highway. A gargantuan spider-web is planned in the future.

The **Enchanted Highway** begins at Interstate 94, Exit 72 to Gladsone, ND and runs 32 miles to Regent.

Quirky cuisine

The **Hunter's Table and Tavern** in Rhame is a unique roadhouse constructed of 16-inch-thick walls made from masonry that resembles stacks of logs. Light pours in through the wine bottles cemented into the walls. Sawdust provides the insulation. An all-female construction crew built the structure in 1983.

Hunter's Table and Tavern, located on Hwy 12 Rhame, ND 58651; ↘ 701 279 6689; web: www.plainsfolk.com/oases/oasis7.htm

SOUTH DAKOTA
Festivals and events

At the annual **Potato Days Festival** in Clark, the most popular event is **Mashed Potato Wrestling**. The festival also features a potato parade and potato sculptures.

> **Mashed Potato Wrestling**, held annually during Potato Days in July in Clark, SD. Contact Clark Area Chamber of Commerce, PO Box 163, Clark, SD 57225; web: www.clarksd.com/potato.htm

For the 285,000 motorcycle enthusiasts who invade the town of Sturgis every August, the **Sturgis Motorcycle Rally** is the ultimate experience of the open road. Sixty years old, the annual event started with a small motorcycle race and stunt competition. As the cycling lifestyle gained in popularity, more and more riders flooded to the scenic rally. Today, the festival draws enthusiasts from every walk of life, dispelling the notion that motorcyclists are only big brutes just itching for a brawl. The crowd creates a tidal wave of bikes and people, participating in competitions and cruising to such scenic sites as Mount Rushmore, the Crazy Horse Monument, and the Badlands of the Black Hills region.

> **Sturgis Motorcycle Rally**, held annually in August in Sturgis, SD. Contact the City of Sturgis, Rally Department, 2030 Main St, Sturgis, SD 57785; ↘ 605 720 0800; web: www.sturgismotorcyclerally.com

Museums and collections

There are way more shoes than normal in Webster, South Dakota thanks to Mildred O'Neil, a former librarian who moved her 8,000-plus shoe collection to the tiny town in 1994. With a population of just 2,000 souls, Webster welcomed Mildred and her collection to the Wildlife, Industry, and Science Museum by building the **Shoe House**, a two story, shoe-shaped building, to house her collection of soles. Every shoe has its own card, describing its acquisition and its history, in her meticulously kept card catalog. The collection grows monthly as folks from all over send her more shoes. Mildred's been collecting shoes and shoe-related items since her teens. She's in her late seventies now, which pretty much makes her a world authority on the subject. The shoes, ranging in size from miniature to clown size, are classified into 22 categories, including jewelry, cowboy, sport, straw, children's and baby shoes. Her workshop displays old shoemaking techniques as well as a cobbler's sign, shaped like a boot, that has a bullet hole in it. She once got together with two other major collectors; they found only three duplicate pairs of shoes. During the season, Mildred can often be found at the museum, dusting the displays and rearranging the objects of her affection. Occasionally she even dresses up as 'The Old Woman who Lived in a Shoe'. During the winter she'll be happy to meet you at the museum if you call ahead for an appointment.

> The **Shoe House**, located at the Museum of Wildlife, Industry, and Science, 760 W Highway 12, Webster, SD 57274; ↘ 605 345 4751; web: www.sdmuseum.org. Open Mon–Fri 9.00am–5.00pm, Sat–Sun 1.00–5.00pm May 1–Oct 31, or by appointment.

All you'll ever need (or want) to know about vinegar is explained for you at the **International Vinegar Museum** whose mission is to educate visitors about the 'sour power' of vinegar. You'll learn how vinegar is made in factories, villages and homes all over the world, see vinegar paper, taste vinegars made from all kinds of plants and shop at the most complete vinegar store on the planet. They sponsor an International Vinegar Festival each August.

International Vinegar Museum and Festival, Roslyn, SD. Contact Vinegar Connoisseurs International, 104 W Carlton Ave, Box 41, Roslyn, SD 57261; ↘ 800 342 4519; web: www.vinegarman.com. *Open Tue–Sat 10.00am–6.00pm Jun 1–Oct 31. Festival held annually in August.*

Do six items constitute a museum? They do if they're outhouses and six examples probably cover the subject pretty thoroughly. Each of the outdoor toilets (used in the days before indoor plumbing) is named, with a story behind it, at the **South Dakota Outhouse Museum** in Gregory.

South Dakota Outhouse Museum, Napers Emporium, 520 Main St, Gregory, SD 57533; ↘ 605 835 8002

The **Petrified Wood Park and Museum** in Lemmon consists of strange, man-made formations built in the 1930s from petrified wood. The sculptors were unemployed and untrained in art; they worked in exchange for food. There's a castle, a wishing well, a water fountain, and numerous ugly pyramids. The museum itself is also petrified wood.

Petrified Wood Park and Museum, 500 Main Ave, Lemmon, SD 57638; ↘ 605 374 5716 or 5760; fax: 605 374 5332; web: www.dakota-web.com/lemmon/about/see/ppark/park.htm

Attractions

It's been said that as many people have heard of **Wall Drug** as have heard of Monica Lewinsky. Now that's a lot of people. But Wall Drug spent 70 years building its reputation and it didn't take television to do the job. Instead, the word was spread with old-fashioned signage, beginning back in the Depression years when cars didn't come with air conditioning. In 1931 Ted and Dorothy Wall opened a tiny drugstore in the middle of nowhere. Business was slow, so Dorothy suggested tempting people by putting up a sign advertising free ice water. Ted thought the idea silly, but he listened to her anyway and the rest is history.

Folks showed up in droves to cool down. Once Ted saw the value of signs, he went sign-crazy, plastering the landscape coast to coast with billboards advertising his drug store. The whole point of stopping at Wall Drug became, well … stopping at Wall Drug. By the time they added five-cent coffee, Wall Drug had become a must-see rest stop on the road across the plains. (Isn't there a lesson in here somewhere for husbands?) But the signage didn't stop with billboards. He printed up souvenir signs, giving them away and imploring folks to post them anywhere and everywhere. They've ended up in some of the most remote places on Earth. Servicemen from the States post them all over the globe, as does almost every visitor who's been there in the last 60 years. The sight itself does America proud as a tourist trap, offering the best in roadside activities: plenty of funky photo ops, giant animals, an arcade, clean rest rooms, lots of shopping, food, and, of course, free ice water and five-cent coffee. When the freeway was built, bypassing Wall Drug, they erected an 80-foot dinosaur just in case you missed the signs leading to it.

Wall Drug Store, 510 Main St, Wall, SD 57790; ↘ 605 279 2175; fax: 605 279 2699; web: www.walldrug.com

David Adickes gives new meaning to the term 'heads of state'. He's personally sculpted giant presidential busts of each of our 43 presidents and they're all chronologically arranged, complete with biographical panel, in the sculpture garden he built at his **Presidents Park**. Representing five years of work, David, now in his seventies, made each of the 16-foot-high, all-white busts from molds and Portland cement, spending about a month and a half creating each likeness. He got the idea after visiting nearby Mt Rushmore and coming away disappointed that he couldn't get closer to the heads. As he's fond of saying, 'From George W to George W, they're all here.'

Presidents Park, 4 miles south of Lead/Deadwood, SD on Hwy 85 at Deer Mountain; ↘ 866 584 9096; web: www.presidentspark.com. *Hours vary by season.*

Yabba-dabba-doo! Flintstones – meet the Flintstones – at their **Bedrock City** theme park in Custer. Just like the cartoon, the park has all the familiar rock buildings along with Fred, Barney, Wilma, Betty, Pebbles and Dino. There's a Flintmobile, a drive-in serving Brontoburgers and Dino Dogs, an animated show and Mount Rockmore, a spoof of the big guys down the road.

Bedrock City, US Hwys 16 & 385, Box 649, Custer, SD 57730; ↘ 800 992 9818 or 605 673 4079; web: www.flintstonesbedrockcity.com. Located southwest of Custer, SD near Hwy US 16 and 385.

In Mitchell the world's only **Corn Palace** has been drawing visitors for a hundred years. The palace, shaped like a castle topped with minarets, is 'upholstered' on the exterior with corn, grain, and grass – 3,000 bushels worth. Each year, the designs are redone and colorful new murals go up depicting the current theme. The palace was built in 1892 to prove how rich the soil is in the region.

Corn Palace, 601 N Main, Mitchell, SD 57301; ↘ 866 273 CORN or 605 996 5031; web: www.cornpalace.com. *Open varied hours year-round; call for information. Admission free.*

The **Black Hills Maze** in Rapid City is a 37,000-square-foot, two-story high labyrinth. This is for serious mazeophiles who have to conquer the towers and then try to escape. Real addicts can load up for paintball games.

Black Hills Maze, located 3 miles south of Rapid City on Hwy 16 on the left; ↘ 605 343 5439; web: www.blackhillsmaze.com. *Open 8.30am–9.00pm May 1–Sept 30 (weekends only in May and Sept).*

Just plain weird

Porter Sculpture Park in St Lawrence features the work of Wayne Porter, a welder who sculpts creatures from scrap metal in his spare time. In the tiny park outside his shop you can see his fantastic creations, including a gigantic fish that spurts water, playful dragons, delicate ballerinas and a host of other colorful characters.

Porter Sculpture Park, PO Box 127, St Lawrence, SD 57573; ↘ 605 853 2266; web: www.portersculpturepark.com. *Open from 8.00am–6.00pm, Memorial Day through Labor Day.*

NEBRASKA
Festivals and events

It doesn't get much nuttier than the **Wayne Chicken Show.** At the show's **Cluck-Off Contest**, each contestant imitates either a rooster or a hen. Hopeful champs have to strut their stuff for at least 15 seconds, trying mightily to sound like a chicken, be heard like a chicken and act like a chicken, all while remembering to stop in under 60 seconds. Hen-picked judges declare the winner. The 1999 champ appeared on Jay Leno's famous late-night talk show. The Chickendale Male Dancers, wearing paper bags over their heads to conceal the identity of these less-than-physically fit, chicken struttin'

bods, are a sight to behold. And the weekend wouldn't be complete without the chicken hat contest; the most beautiful beak and chicken legs competitions; the bare-handed egg-drop catch – raw eggs dropped from 40 feet up; and a hardboiled egg-eating contest. The festival even has a chicken coupe – a 1967, egg-yolk yellow, Cadillac Coupe de Ville with a 12-foot rooster mounted on the trunk.

Wayne Chicken Show and Cluck-Off Contest, held annually in July in Wayne, NE. Contact Wayne Chamber of Commerce, 108 W 3rd St, Wayne, NE 68787; ✆ 402 375 2240 or 888 587 3961; web: www.chickenshow.com.

Beer and boredom are responsible for the **Avoca Quack-Off**, an annual event involving around 100 ducks and an ice-covered tennis court. Humans, who may do anything except touch the ducks to get them across the finish line, shout encouragement and verbally prod clipped-wing ducks across the ice. The event began 24 years ago with three ducks, three guys and a substantially higher number of beers. There isn't a lot to do mid-winter in this tiny town of 254 people, and the idea of a duck race became mighty appealing. Today, the Quack-Off fundraiser almost triples the town's population as folks come from all over to rent a duck and watch a gang of duck jockeys make fools of themselves on the Webb Foot Raceway.

Avoca Quack-off, held annually the last Saturday in January in Avoca, NE. Contact David Seay ✆ 402 275 3221; email: g-s@alltel.net

They're off, they're running, well, sort of... With their stubby little legs and limited attention spans, entrants in the **Running of the Wieners** aren't exactly built for speed. Part of German Heritage Days, this event brings out around 130 dachshunds, some decked out with chequered scarves. Their owners come equipped with squeaky toys, treats, or whatever they think might entice their dog to go for gold. While some dogs make it to the finish line, others run backwards or in circles, their owners chasing them all over the field. The musical theme from the *Lone Ranger* (the *William Tell Overture*) plays during each heat.

Running of the Wieners held during German Heritage Days each September at the Platt-Duetsche Society, 1315 West Anna Street, Grand

Island, NE. Contact Grand Island Area Chamber of Commerce, 309 W
2nd St, PO Box 1486, Grand Island, NE 68802-1486;
↘ 308 382 9210; web: www.gichamber.com/home_site.htm

Museums and collections

How odd can odds and ends get? Try the **Museum of the Odd** in Lincoln, where
Charlie Johnson displays oddities that cover almost every square inch of his house,
including floors, walls, and ceilings. What makes this such an astounding place is
not that the objects themselves are so odd, but rather that the sheer number of them
is so overwhelming. Charlie's life-long collection of bric-a-brac includes Beta
video-cassette tapes, severed doll heads, squeaky rubber animals, comic books,
bubble-bath containers, plastic banks, religious icons, macabre trinkets and so very,
very much more, all meticulously organized. Dennis the Menace was Charlie's role
model as a child, so it's not surprising he'd be up to such mischief himself.

Museum of the Odd, 701 Y Street, Lincoln, NE; ↘ 402 476 6735. *Free.*

Bill's Food Mart in Howells displays the owner Bill Wisnieski's collection of 900
cookie jars, representing three decades of collecting. Dating from 1930, you can see
Disney cookie jars, such as Goofy driving a school bus, along with jars depicting
cowboys Roy Rogers, Gene Autry, and Hopalong Cassidy. No free cookies to go
along with these jars, but you might pick up a donut.

Bill's Food Mart, 112 S 3rd St, Howells, NE; ↘ 402 986 1141. *Open
Mon–Sat 7.30am–6.00pm.*

Just plain weird

Carhenge, near Alliance, is a replica of Britain's Stonehenge, only this one is
made out of cars that are very nearly the same dimensions as those of the famous
stones. The cars, 1950s' and 1960s' models, are planted trunk down in the
ground with the capstone cars perched on top. The 38 grey-painted cars, welded
together in formation, exactly match the number of stones at the real
Stonehenge. The structure is one of the most eccentric in America.
Surprisingly, more than half of the visitors to Carhenge don't even know that
it's a spoof of one of the world's most mysterious monuments. Jim Reinders,
who originated the idea and lived on the farm on which it sits, dedicated
Carhenge on the summer solstice of 1987. Two years later it was in danger of
being declared a junkyard and in violation of zoning regulations. When the site
was threatened with destruction, thousands of people rallied to its defense.
Eventually Carhenge gained government approval and was formally elevated in
rank from junkyard to tourist attraction.

Carhenge, located north of Alliance, NE, along Hwy 87. Contact Friends
of Carhenge, PO Box 464, Alliance, NE 69301; web: www.carhenge.com

Quirky cuisine

Burger King, eat your heart out. The whopper hamburger served at **Sioux
Sundries** in Harrison is 28 ounces of meat, topped with cheese, onions, lettuce,
pickles and tomatoes, with chips on the side. The Coffeeburger, as it's called, was
named for rancher Bill Coffee who didn't want his ranch hands going hungry.

Sioux Sundries, located at 201 Main St, Harrison, NE; ↘ 308 668 2577.
Open Mon–Fri 7.00am–5.30pm, Sat 7.00am–5.00pm.

South Central Region

TEXAS
Festivals and events

Oatmeal, Texas is a tiny burg with fewer than a thousand people. But during the **Oatmeal Festival**, its population swells up to around 10,000, with festivities that include an oatmeal cook-off and an oatmeal eat-off. The highlight of the event is when 1,000lb of oatmeal is dropped from an airplane on to the crowd (assuming it's not raining!). The Cow-Chip Kick-Off is literally that – one kicker, one holder, and a prize for the team whose fragment goes the farthest. There's also an Oatmeal Box Stacking Contest, Cow Chip Bingo, an Oatmeal Cookie Eating Contest, an Egg Toss, a Pet Parade, a Grand Parade, and all the barbeque you can eat.

> **Oatmeal Festival**, held annually Labor Day weekend (September) in Bertram, TX. Contact the Oatmeal Festival Association, PO Box 70, Bertram, TX 78605; ✆ 512 355-2197; web: www.bertramchamber.com

Hormel, the corporate parent responsible for foisting millions of cans of SPAM™ upon an unsuspecting world, is very sensitive about anyone making fun of their potted pork product. You can imagine their reaction, then, when David Arnsberger and Dick Terry held the first **SPAMARAMA™** in Austin back in 1976. Hormel let the guys know, in no uncertain terms, that taking the can's name in vain, without using ALL CAPITALS and the trademark insignia, could have serious legal consequences. That explains why there are so many CAPS and little '™'s in this entry. Officially called the Pandemonious Potted Pork Festival, SPAMARAMA™ draws 10,000 people with a highly refined sense of humor to one of the wackiest festivals in America. Held each year in Austin on a weekend close to April Fool's Day, the festival is famous for making rollicking good fun of a product folks either love or love to hate. The cooking entries are divided into two divisions: the open, in which anyone can enter serious or joke dishes; and the professional, which is limited to chefs and restaurateurs. Awards are given not just for the best – and worst-tasting – concoctions, but for showmanship as well. Past entries have included various flavors of SPAM™ ice cream, Moo Goo Gai SPAM™, GuacaSPAMole™, and SPAMalama™ Ding

ECCENTRIC CALENDAR
TEXAS

March	**SPAMARAMA™**, Austin. Held the weekend closest to April Fool's Day (page 131)
	Rattlesnake Round-up and Cook-off, Sweetwater (page 134)
May	**O Henry Pun-Off World Championships**, Austin (page 133)
	Orange Show Foundation Art Car Weekend, Houston (page 135)
June	**Watermelon Thump**, Luling. Held the last full weekend in June (page 133)
August	**Austin Chronicle Hot Sauce Competition**, Austin (page 134)
August/ September	**Oatmeal Festival**, Bertram. Held annually Labor Day weekend (page 131)
October	**Corn Dog Festival**, Dallas (page 134)
	Fire Ant Festival, Marshall (page 135)
	Hands on a Hardbody, Longview (page 133)
	Hogeye Festival, Elgin (page 134)

NEW MEXICO

February	**World Snow Shovel Race**, Angel Fire (page 144)

June	**Elfego Baca Shoot**, Socorro (page 147)
	Roswell UFO Encounter Festival and Intergalactic Fashion and Food Extravaganza, Roswell (page 146)
	Taos Poetry Circus, Taos (page 146)
	World's Richest Tombstone Race (also known as Billy the Kid's Tombstone Race), Fort Sumner. Held during Old Fort Days (page 146)
July	**Muck and Mud Derby**, Rio Rancho (page 144)
September	**Burning of Zozobra Fiestas de Santa Fe**, Santa Fe. Normally held theThursday following Labor Day (page 144)
	Whole Enchilada Fiesta, Las Cruces. Held the last weekend in September (page 147)

COLORADO
January	**Fruitcake Toss**, Manitou Springs (page 151)
	International Snow Sculpting Championships, Breckenridge (page 154)
February	**Snowdown**, Durango (page 152)
February/March	**In-Drag Race**, Telluride (page 155)
March	**Cardboard Box Derby**, Arapahoe Basin (page 153)
	Frozen Dead Guy Day, Nederland (page 153)
April	**Flauschink**, Crested Butte (page 154)
May	**Kinetic Sculpture Race**, Boulder (page 152)
	Mike the Headless Chicken Days, Fruita (page 150)
July	**Nothing Festival**, Telluride (page 154)
	Rolling River Raft Race, Pueblo (page 152)
August	**Mushroom Festival**, Telluride (page 155)
September	**Vinitok**, Crested Butte (page 154)
October	**Emma Crawford Coffin Races**, Manitou Springs (page 152)

KANSAS
February/March	**International Pancake Race**, Liberal. Held on Shrove Tuesday (page 158)

OKLAHOMA
March/April	**Waynoka Rattlesnake Hunt**, Waynoka. Held the first weekend after Easter (page 162)
April	**Waikrua Rattlesnake Hunt**, Waikrua (page 162)
	Apache Rattlesnake Festival, Apache (page 162)
April 20	**World Cow Chip Throwing Contest**, Beaver (page 162)
May	**Okeene Rattlesnake Hunt**, Okeene (page 162)
September	**State Prison Outlaw Rodeo**, McAlester (page 163)
October	**Spooky Goofy Golf Tournament**, Antlers (page 163)

MISSOURI
July	**Tom Sawyer Days**, Hannibal (page 166)

ARKANSAS
May	**Toad Suck Daze**, Conway (page 172)
July	**World Championship Cardboard Boat Festival**, Heber Springs (page 171)
October	**Mountain View Bean Festival**, Mountain View (page 171)
	Yellville Turkey Trot, Yellville (page 171)

LOUISIANA
January–March	**Mardi Gras events**, New Orleans (page 175)
May	**Authentic Bonnie and Clyde Festival and Museum**, Gibsland. Held on the weekend nearest May 23 (page 177)
November	**Giant Omelette Celebration**, Abbeville (page 178)

Dong, a concoction made with the pink colored meat, whipped cream, and chocolate. You can even buy a recipe book full of different ways to make this gelatinous pink stuff palatable.

Judges of the SPAM™ cook-off have to actually taste all the dishes entered, although they're allowed three passes during the judging. Additionally, they have the right to require the contestant to take a bite first, minimizing some of the risk. Being thoroughly tanked is a great help. Imagine how you'd react to SPAMish™ fly, a delightful mix of diced SPAM™, cheddar cheese, mayonnaise and flies of raisins. The creator of this dish was so incensed when he didn't win that he froze it and returned each year with the same entry. That was before they instituted the last-place-even-if-there-were-a-hundred entries award in his honor.

Other events include the SPAM™ Cram, a potted pork pig-out with predictable consequences. The SPAM™ carving display usually involves themes based on current events, body parts, or animals such as the SPAMagator™. The SPAM™ calling contest is a riot, as is the SPAM™ toss. Fun to win, but not to lose, is the Tug of War across a pit filled with SPAM™ jelly. SPAMARAMA™ gives adults a chance to play with their food, paint their bodies with SPAM™ themes, and to sing along to SPAMish™ Eyes and This SPAM™ is my SPAM™'!

SPAMARAMA™, held annually the weekend closest to April Fool's Day in Austin, TX. Location varies. Information from the charitable beneficiary of the event, Disability Assistance of Central Texas: ↘ 512 834 1827; web: www.spamarama.com

Once u-pun a time (sorry!) a group of courageous pundits came out of the closet, daring to expose their penchant for wretched pun-play to the groans of pun worshipers everywhere. Now in its 23rd year, the **O Henry Pun-Off World Championships** in Austin delight and dismay 2,000 punsters who brave a day of preposterous puns perpetrated by limber linguists who perform this lowest form of humor in high style.

O Henry Pun-Off World Championships, held annually in May in Austin, TX. Contact O Henry Museum, 409 E 5th St, Austin TX 78701; ↘ 512 472 1903 or 512 973-9929; web: www.ci.austin.tx.us/parks/ohenry.htm

Each year in Longview, a local Nissan dealer holds a bizarre competition called **Hands on a Hardbody**. Two dozen quirky contestants, anxious to win a new pickup, compete to see who can stand the longest with their hand placed firmly on the surface of a new Hardbody truck. They get one five-minute break each hour and a 15-minute break every six hours. No leaning is permitted, and no-one gets sleep time. The contest is a test of endurance, stamina and physical as well as mental strength, all qualities Texans pride themselves on having in abundance. The previous competition lasted 102 hours, so this isn't for sissies. A very funny documentary focusing on the contestants' various strategies for winning was made of the 1995 event.

Hands on a Hardbody, held annually in September in Longview, TX; web: www.hohb.com

The record distance for spitting a watermelon seed stands at 75 feet 2 inches, a feat recorded in the *Guinness Book of Records*. At the annual **Watermelon Thump** in Luling, 20,000 folks descend on this little town of 4,500 residents to watch the contest, celebrate at the carnival and dance in the streets.

Watermelon Thump, held annually the last full weekend in June in Luling, TX. Contact Luling Watermelon Thump, 421 E Davis St, PO Box 710, Luling, TX 78648; ↘ 830 875 3214 ex 2; web: www.watermelonthump.com

The annual **Hogeye Festival** in Elgin pays tribute to porkers by staging greased-pig chases, a Pearls Before Swine art show, a children's costume and pet parade, a hog calling contest, a BBQ cook-off, and the crowning of King Hog or Sowpreme Queen. The cow patty bingo event has a big payoff as the downtown street is painted with 1,500 one-foot by one-foot squares. Three cows are let loose, and the owner of the square where the first one plops wins the jackpot.

Hogeye Festival, held annually in October in Elgin, TX. Contact City of Elgin, Texas at 310 N Main St, Box 591, Elgin, TX 78621; ↘ 512 281 5724; web: www.elgintx.com/

Thirty thousand people show up to hunt rattlesnakes and then eat them at the annual Sweetwater Jaycee's **Rattlesnake Round-up and Cook-off**. In the 40 years since the event was organized as a way to control the deadly snake population, more than 220,000 tons of rattlesnakes have ended up deep fried, barbecued, or otherwise recycled into less-threatening form. There are demonstrations of snake-handling, snake-milking, and a Miss Snake Charmer Queen contest. The squeamish might want to sit this one out.

Rattlesnake Round-up and Cook-off, held annually in March in Sweetwater, TX. Contact: Rattlesnake Roundup, PO Box 416, Sweetwater, TX 79556; ↘ 915 235 5488 or 915 235 8938; web: www.rattlesnakeroundup.com.

It's an evening of wacky fun at the **Corn Dog Festival**, a styling competition designed to bring out the hidden nature of this cornbread-wrapped hot-dog-on-a-stick. The decorated doggies compete for the titles of the biggest, best dressed, weirdest, most traveled and celebrity look-alike. You can eat the less fortunate corn dogs that have been deprived of the opportunity to express themselves.

Corn Dog Festival, held annually in October in Dallas, TX; web: www.corndogfestival.com

First the preliminary judges have to sample all the hot sauce entries to weed out those deemed just too hot for human consumption. (How do you ever get volunteers for that job?) Then celebrity judges step in, ready to choose a winner in the *Austin Chronicle* **Hot Sauce Competition**. Under a blazing August sun, hundreds of hot sauce contenders have their homemade and restaurant sauces judged for flavor, aroma and looks, hoping they've concocted the next great hot sauce to grace the shelves of hot sauce emporiums across the country.

Austin Chronicle **Hot Sauce Competition**, held in August. Contact The *Austin Chronicle*, PO Box 49066, Austin, TX 78765; ↘ 512 454 5766; web: www.austinchronicle.com.

Making fun of the pesky fire ant, the **Fire Ant Festival** is famous for its wacky and zany events. There's a fire ant calling contest; rubber chicken chunking; gurning (ugly-face making); a diaper derby, and a men's Crazy Legs contest.

> **Fire Ant Festival**, held annually in October. Contact the Marshall Chamber of Commerce, 213 W Austin, Marshall, TX 75671; ☎ 800 953 7868 or 903 935 7868; web: www.marshall-chamber.com

Eccentric environments

When it comes to weird, Houston does more than its part as far as the sheer number of ultra-eccentric people, places and objects it champions. The **Orange Show Foundation**, named after the environment described below, keeps a nationwide database of eccentric artists and their creations as well as maintaining the monument itself and sponsoring folk-art educational programs. As coordinators of the **Everyones Art Car Parade**, it keeps track of hundreds of art cars around the country. It also sponsors a series of tours to other visionary art installations, seeking out folk-art and folk-art environments worldwide. Their **Eyeopener Tours** visit such places as historic cemeteries, eccentric environments, public art installations, unique markets, artists' studios, and quirky architectural wonders.

Houston is the only large city in the country that doesn't have the kind of zoning restrictions that normally discourage budding eccentrics from building their strange environments. The **Orange Show Monument** itself is an outlandish place, handmade over a period of 25 years of intense, single-handed labor by Jeff McKissack. McKissak used to deliver oranges in the south during the Depression, becoming fond not only of their taste, but of their attributes as well. Believing them to provide a long, healthy, productive life, he worked obsessively to build a monumental tourist attraction, hoping that the whole city would turn out to honor his creation. When he finally did throw open the gates, the expected crowds failed to materialize and he died just a few months later, possibly of a broken heart. The Orange Show is a riot of color, especially orange. Made from concrete, brick, steel, gears, tiles, wagon wheels, mannequins, tractor seats and statuettes, it lurches maze-like from the arena to the stage, from the pond to the gift shop. Lettered tiles spell out his philosophy and urge visitors to watch their step, love oranges and enjoy the show. The site serves as a chapel for weddings and as a venue for funky dances, art workshops, films, multi-media events and – once – for McKissak's funeral. His ashes were scattered there.

> **The Orange Show Foundation & Monument**, 2402 Munger St, Houston, TX 77023; ☎ 713 926 6368; web: www.orangeshow.org. *Open Sat & Sun noon–5.00pm mid-Mar–mid-Dec; also open Wed–Fri 9.00am–1.00pm Memorial and Labor Day.*

> The **Everyones Art Car Parade** is held in May. For parade information, and for **Eyeopener Tours**, contact the foundation.

John Milkovisch was blessed with a very patient wife who put up with his compulsion to cover the exterior of their house with beer cans. Beginning in 1968, and working at a rate of more than a six-pack a day for 18 years, **John Milkovisch's Beer Can House** has long beer-can garlands hanging from the eaves, garlands made from pull tabs, can tops, and can bottoms. The fencing uses the whole can, the siding is made from riveted sheets of flattened beer-can labels, while concrete and marble sculptures use the seams of the cans. His handiwork stopped at the door; he wasn't allowed to decorate inside. When the wind blows, you can hear the house before you see it. Fourteen thousand marbles are set in concrete in the garden. Ripley's Believe It or Not estimated that Milkovisch drank 50,000 cans while working on his eccentricity. John and his wife both died recently and the house has been bought by The Orange Show Foundation. They're refurbishing it and plan to open the interior to the public in the future. Meanwhile, you can still drive by anytime.

> **John Milkovisch's Beer Can House**, 222 Malone St, north off
> Memorial Dr between Shepherd Dr and Loop 610, Houston, TX 77007;
> The Orange Show Foundation, ↘ 713 926 6368; web:
> www.orangeshow.org.

Museums and collections

Displaying scientific 'evidence' for Creation, the **Creation Evidence Museum** is devoted to answering such questions as 'How did all the animals fit on Noah's Ark?' and 'How did kangaroos get from Australia to the ark and back again?' The museum's founder and curator, Dr Carl Baugh, has been researching evidence to support the theory of Creation for 40 years, excavating and acquiring fossils and artifacts that he and his followers feel can prove, among other things, that men and dinosaurs could have lived at the same time. To wit: a hammer embedded in a rock; a giant footprint supposedly made by a giant, the size of all humans before the biblical flood; a fossilized human finger that looks very much like a teeny loaf of bread; a fossilized foot in a boot; and an iron cup in coal.

A video by Dr Baugh explains all the artifacts in the museum while you browse, including his work investigating the original, pre-flood biospheric conditions on Earth. He's built the 'world's first hyperbaric biosphere' model right there on site, where he performs experiments only he understands, and he's hard at work on a giant biosphere in the hope of one day growing dinosaurs in it. In fact, some of Bayou Bob's rattlesnakes (see page 140) have spent time in the biosphere although the results were somewhat vague. The museum is in a cramped, temporary facility while funds are being raised to complete the partially constructed permanent building.

> **Creation Evidence Museum**, PO Box 309, Glen Rose, TX 76043;
> ↘ 254 897 3200; fax: 254 897 3100; web: www.creationevidence.org.
> Open Tue–Sat 10.00am–4.00pm.

If you're not already paranoid, you will be after a visit to the **Conspiracy Museum**. Underwritten by a retired architect and self-proclaimed 'assassinogolist', this private exhibition aims to convince you that there has been only one conspiracy to control the presidency since 1940 – and that sole conspiracy is responsible for eight assassinations. You'll learn that President Lincoln's assassin may have lived into the 20th century; that Ted Kennedy's famed Chappaquiddik incident was really a diabolical frame-up to destroy his chance at the White House; and that it was really a security guard's gun that killed RFK, not Sirhan Sirhan's.

> **The Conspiracy Museum**, 110 S Market St, Dallas 75202; ↘ 214 741
> 3040. Open 10.00am–6.00pm.

The 'gunman's nest' in the Texas School Book Depository building is the most chilling exhibit at the **Sixth Floor Museum**, offering the view of the streets below that Lee Harvey Oswald saw through his rifle scope. Examining the life, times, death and legacy of President John F Kennedy, the museum has hundreds of photos, artifacts, and films. Displays build up in suspense, ending with the famous film of the President collapsing into Jackie's arms.

Sixth Floor Museum, 411 Elm St, Dallas, TX 75202; ↘ 214 747 6660; web: www.jfk.org. *Open daily 9.00am–6.00pm.*

Supreme court justice Sandra Day O'Connor was one. So was artist Georgia O'Keefe and singer Patsy Cline. They're all honored in the **National Cowgirl Museum and Hall of Fame**, representing distinguished women who exemplify the pioneering spirit of the American West. Paying homage to gritty, independent females, the two-story museum tells the story of women such as writer Laura Ingalls Wilder (*Little House on the Prairie*), slave Clara Brown and the great sharpshooter Annie Oakley. Kids can ride a spring-powered bronco while a videotape of their ride is speeded up and spliced into footage from an old-fashioned rodeo.

National Cowgirl Museum and Hall of Fame, 111 W 4th St, Ste 300, Fort Worth, TX 76102; ↘ 817 336 4475; fax: 817 336 2470; web: www.cowgirl.net. *Open Tue 10.00am–8.00pm, Wed–Sat 10.00am–5.00pm, Sun noon–5.00pm.*

Nicknamed the 'Garage Mahal', the **Art Car Museum** displays highly eccentric, one-of-a-kind cars decorated and built by their equally eccentric owners. These cars, flamboyant expressions of their owners' quirky personalities, usually make a political or personal statement. Some owners have been known to dress like their cars, covered in stuff like buttons or pennies. Some are representative, like the Roachster or Rex Rabbit, or follow a theme like the Swamp Mutha. Others are plastered with all manner of things from toys to beadwork. You really have to see these cars to understand what would drive these artists to express themselves in this gentle, yet extroverted way.

The Art Car Museum, 140 Heights Blvd, Houston, TX 77007; ↘ 713 861 5526; web: www.artcarmuseum.com. *Open Wed–Sun 11.00am–6.00pm.*

Old Sparky is the star attraction at the **Huntsville Texas Prison Museum**, having played host to 361 condemned prisoners over a 40-year period. The electric chair, now retired, is a stark reminder that Texas executes more prisoners than any other state in the union and that Texas has the country's second largest prison population after California. The inmate who built the chair never had to test it out; he was eventually released, un-fried. The museum paints a fascinating portrait of prison life, showcasing the peculiar, often bizarre ways inmates coped with the culture inside the walls. Confiscated weapons, fashioned from anything from forks to toothbrushes, could be amazingly deadly. Toilet-paper art helped pass the time, as did lifting weights, visiting the chapel and working in the laundry. One inmate carved a sculpture with 20 different animals and faces, completing it during several prison stints interrupted by periods of parole. The prison hardware, such as whips and balls and chains, make you glad you followed the path of righteousness – or at least didn't get caught. A letter from gangster Clyde Barrow, of Bonnie and Clyde fame, written to Henry Ford, praises the V8 engine as an excellent choice for a getaway car. You can try on a nine-foot by six-foot cell for size (and get your picture taken in it) and pick up a copy of the **Prison Driving Tour** so you don't miss anything, like the arena used for prison rodeos until insurance difficulties shut it down in 1986. The gift shop sells 'death-row caps', prisoner-made items like wallets and belts, and books like *Texas Prisons: The Longest Hotel Chain in Texas*.

Huntsville Texas Prison Museum, 491 SH 75 N, Huntsville, Texas 77320; ☎ 936 295 2155; web: www.txprisonmuseum.org. *Open Mon–Sat 10.00am–6.00pm; Sun noon–5.00pm.*

Barney Smith is a master in the art of decorating toilet seats and he's got 616 examples hanging in his garage museum to prove it. His **Toilet Seat Art Museum** is a real traffic stopper as he swings open the doors, exposing his artistic endeavors for all the world to see. A retired master plumber, Barney, now in his eighties, has been painting 'theme' toilet seats as a hobby for 32 years. Along with discarded seats, plumbing supply houses send him their damaged seats and he decorates each one with something special. Each seat is numbered, catalogued, and then documented with information about the materials he used for decoration, who might have donated the materials and what inspired the idea. His seats display, among other things, volcanic ash from Mount St Helens, a piece of the Berlin Wall, barbed wire from a World War II concentration camp, and a piece of insulation from the Challenger Space Shuttle explosion. Less infamous art includes arrowheads, license plates, Pokemon cards, casket handles and tributes to all the service clubs in America. Be sure to sign his guestbook; he's had visitors from 44 countries.

Toilet Seat Art Museum, 239 Abiso Ave, San Antonio, TX; ☎ 210 824 7791; web: www.unusualmuseums.org/toilet. Located in the Alamo Heights area of San Antonio; at 6021 Broadway; go around behind the bank to Argo Street, go 2 blocks to Arbutus, then left one half block to Abiso. If you see the flag and welcome sign, he's open. *If you call ahead he'll be sure to be there to show you around.*

The **Devil's Rope Museum** is dedicated solely to barbed-wire fencing, the invention that finally tamed the American West. Exhibits containing almost 700 different kinds of barbed wire explore the evolution of the cowboy, the history of brands and branding, the kinds of wire used in range warfare, and demonstrations in the art of making barbed wire. Strangely enough, barbed wire is collectible. In order to get a patent, every wire manufacturer had to submit a design that included a completely original 'twist' to the barb. Collectors are a determined bunch, seeking to locate hundreds of unique specimens. They even have a magazine, the *Barbed Wire Collector*.

Devil's Rope Museum, PO Box 290, McLean, TX 79057; ☎ 806 779 2225; web: www.barbwiremuseum.com. Located in McLean, Texas, 75 miles east of Amarillo, on I-40 and Old Route 66. Directions: take exits 141, 142 and 143 to 'The Heart Of Old Route 66' at 100 Kingsley St.

Presenting the Dr Pepper story as an example of how wonderful the free enterprise system is, the **Dr Pepper Museum and Free Enterprise Institute** in Waco is a strange mix of capitalism and patriotism. The cherry-flavored cola beverage was introduced in 1904, about the same time as the hamburger, the hot dog and the ice-cream cone. In true American fashion, the product went through many advertising incarnations, including a stint in the 1920s when it was billed as the 'drink a bite to eat at 10, 2, and 4' beverage, referring to new research that shed light on sugar's ability to give you an energy lift. The museum, which defines free enterprise as 'the freedom of individuals and businesses to operate and compete with a minimum of government interference or regulation', aims its exhibits at school-age children, hoping to plant the seeds of entrepreneurial initiative and libertarianism early on in life. Part of the museum's mission is to use the soft-drink industry to show how Americans do business.

Dr Pepper Museum and Free Enterprise Institute, 300 S 5th St, Waco, TX; ↘ 254 757 1025; web: www.drpeppermuseum.org. Directions: take IH35 into Waco, exit at the 4th and 5th sts exit, turn west on 4th St, go to Mary Ave, turn left on Mary. The museum is on the corner of 5th St and Mary.

Pest control specialist Michael Bohdan, aka Cockroach Dundee, has one heck of a show-and-tell exhibit. He's appeared with his **Cockroach Hall of Fame** on every major television and news channel in the country and is the author of *What's Buggin You*, a book covering his 20 years spent chasing down creepy-crawlies. With four-inch-long roaches that hiss on command, a safari hat covered with roaches, and roaches dressed up in costumes, Michael makes for an entertaining guest. Look for Liberoachi, a roach (dead, of course) wearing a white mink cape and sitting at an itty-bitty piano. Or a spike-heeled, blonde-wigged Marilyn Monroach. Each August he has a contest that draws 2,000 entries for the largest roach of the year as well as the most sensational roach of art. The winners get a cash prize while the bugs get to reign on a throne in the Hall of Fame. The museum is located in Plano.

Cockroach Hall of Fame, The Pest Shop, 2231-B W 15th St, Plano, TX 75075; ↘ 972 519 0355; web: www.pestshop.com. *Open Mon–Fri 12.15–5.00pm, Sat noon–3.00pm. Admission free.*

An eye-opening look at American funeral customs is graphically presented at the **National Museum of Funeral History** in Houston. From icebox caskets, which kept the body 'fresh' in pre-embalming days, to the bizarre, such as the casket built for three, and the ostentatious, like the all-glass casket which proved too heavy for even ten pallbearers to lift, the museum is a fascinating look at the history of burial customs. Mourning attire, jewelry made from the deceased's hair, memorabilia of the funerals of the rich and famous, death wagons and hearses, along with a video on the Value of the Funeral, make this a memorable place to spend a few hours dealing with the inevitable. The entrance to the museum has a 'Find a Famous Grave' kiosk that leads you electronically to the remains of the previously famous. A recent addition is the collection of fantasy coffins from Ghana, where elaborate versions are designed to capture the essence of the dead they contain. On display are coffins depicting a KLM airplane, a Mercedes car, various boats, animals and even an outboard motor. You can pass the time on the next leg of your journey trying to imagine what would happen if this custom caught on here.

National Museum of Funeral History, 415 Barren Springs Dr, Houston, TX 77090; ↘ 281 876 3063; web: www.nmfh.org. *Open Mon–Fri 10.00am–4.00pm, Sat–Sun noon–4.00pm.*

Attractions

Bob Popplewell, aka 'Bayou Bob', is seriously addicted to rattlesnakes, so much so that he surrounds himself with them – live, dead, skinned ... whatever. Bob appears fearless as he shows you around his **Rattlesnake Ranch**/museum/gift shop, hauling slithering snakes out of garbage cans and buckets for your closer inspection. (Most folks don't take him up on it.) Dried snakeskins hang everywhere and a crate of live mice wiggle around prior to becoming the reptilian version of a McNugget. This is hardly a pretty, or nice-smelling, place but you can learn an awful lot about rattlers from Bob if you're so inclined.

Rattlesnake Ranch, Interstate Hwy 20 and US Hwy 281, PO Box 1655D, Weatherford, TX 76086; ☎ 940 769 2626; web: www.wf.net/~snake

There are probably as many dinosaurs in Moscow, Texas as there are people. A lonely attraction, **Dinosaur Gardens** has 11 of the fiberglass beasts laid out along a woodsy trail behind Donald Bean's home. He saved up for 20 years to build his dinosaur dreamland, much to the dismay of his wife who has to work to support his obsession since the attraction has failed to attract many visitors. Bean spends all his time playing in his garden, creating sound effects, hiding speakers in trees and experimenting with environmental settings like jungles and swamps.

Dinosaur Gardens, located on US 59 near intersection of FM 62, Moscow, TX. *Open daily 10.00am–6.00pm Jun–Labor Day; weekends 10.00am–6.00pm Sep–Oct and Mar–May. Closed Nov–Feb.*

Most everything is larger than life in Texas, and Billy Bob's is no exception. Known as the **World's Largest Honky Tonk** (dance hall), the Fort Worth attraction has 40 bar stations, real bull-riding, a photo 'bull' for the less adventurous and a dancefloor big enough to hold several jumbo jets. Besides hosting rodeos, livestock auctions and country music concerts inside the enormous facility, Billy Bob's has served as a setting for numerous movies and television shows. Six thousand people can fit inside.

Billy Bob's World's Largest Honky Tonk, 2520 Rodeo Plaza, Fort Worth, TX 76106; ☎ 817 624 7117; web: www.billybobstexas.com

The last thing you'd expect to see in Texas is a scaled-down version of ancient China, but **Forbidden Gardens**, an outdoor cultural center in Katy, is just that. Complete with zither music and koi fish, the garden has remarkable replicas of the Forbidden City and of the 7,000 terracotta soldiers of Emperor Qin's army; they're modeled in fiberglass at about one-third the size of those in Xi'an. Highlights of China's history are portrayed throughout the 40-acre, $16 million garden, featuring intricately detailed people and buildings. Financed by reclusive Hong Kong-born millionaire Ira Poon, who lives in Seattle, the project gets a new exhibit every few years or so, built in China and installed by the Chinese artisans who make it. Park employees have little contact with their eccentric benefactor – he's only visited the park a few times since it opened in 1996.

Forbidden Gardens, 23500 Franz Rd, Katy, TX 77493; ☎ 281 347 8000; web: www.forbidden-gardens.com. *Open year-round Fri–Sun 10.00am–5.00pm.*

Texans do everything up B-I-G, and the **Buckhorn Saloon & Museum** in San Antonio proves it. If you counted, you'd find 4,000 antlers in just one of their chandeliers. Formerly known as the Hall of Horns, the saloon opened in 1881 with a standing offer to all patrons – 'Bring in your deer antlers and you can trade them for a shot of whiskey or a beer'.

Buckhorn Saloon & Museum, 318 E Houston St, San Antonio, TX 78205; ℺ 210 247 4000; fax: 210 247 4020; web: www.buckhornmuseum.com. *Open daily 10.00am–6.00pm (or later – call for exact closing time) Memorial Day–Labor Day; 10.00am–5.00pm (or later – call for exact closing time) Labor Day–Memorial Day.*

Quirkyville

There's one hippo for every 57 people in **Hutto**, a situation causing dissent among the town's 5,000 residents. Eighty-seven of the huge concrete creatures adorn the sidewalks and public spaces, the result of a hippo-crazed mayor's obsession with the beasts and his determination to bring tourism to Hutto. Half the townsfolk are embarrassed by the bulbous figures; the other half takes delight in decorating them and dressing them up. The state legislature recently declared Hutto the Hippo Capital of the World.

Hutto Hippos. Contact Hutto Chamber of Commerce, PO Box 99, Hutto, TX 78634; ℺ 512 759 4400; web: www.hutto.org

Tours

Austin's **Graveyard Chronicles** tour van goes out once a month to explore four cemeteries filled with history and intrigue from Austin's past. And every weekend, **Austin Promenade Tours** offers Ghosts, Murder and Mayhem, a walking tour of the sinister side of Austin.

Graveyard Chronicles tour van goes out once a month, Austin, TX; ℺ 512 498 4686; web: www.promenadetours.com

Austin Promenade Tours, ℺ 512 695 7297; web: www.promenadetours.com

Just plain weird

It's hard to resist the urge to play hide-and-seek among the stones at **Stonehenge II**, a retirement project that kept Doug Hill and Al Shepperd busy for nine months building it. Using steel posts, rebar, mesh, concrete and plaster, the pals created a smaller-scale version of the real thing in a field by the highway, causing many a car to slam on its brakes – and its occupants to stare in disbelief – at the totally unexpected sight. They did it just for the fun of it and you're welcome to walk

through an opening in the fence and play like a kid among the ruins. The site also contains two replicas of the statues found on Easter Island.

Stonehenge II, located in Hunt, TX; web: www.alfredsheppard.com/stonehenge/untitled.html

Ten million head of cattle were driven from south Texas through Fort Worth in the 1880s on their way to the railheads in Kansas. Today, a herd of 15 are still driven through the stockyards district twice daily on the **Fort Worth Cattle Drive**. Funded by the city, the drive is run by real cowboys, regular municipal employees responsible for driving the longhorn cattle 300 yards each way, each day. Weather permitting, you can view the drive from the herd observation deck on the northeast side of the Exchange Building, in front of the Stockyards Visitor Center or Livestock Exchange Building, or from any Stockyards Station restaurant with outdoor seating.

Fort Worth Cattle Drive, Fort Worth Livestock Exchange Bldg, 131 E Exchange Ave, Ste 215, Fort Worth, TX 76106; ↘ 817 336 HERD; web: www.fortworthherd.com. *Cattle drives occur daily at 11.30am and 4.00pm.*

In honor of Route 66, the American Mother Road, millionaire Stanley Marsh III planted ten Cadillac cars, fin ends up, noses down, into the ground on a Texas plain west of Amarillo. The spectacle, known as **Cadillac Ranch**, has become a shrine to the open road, accessible for worship in Amarillo day and night. All the 1949–64 cars came from junkyards or used-car lots and had their hubcaps and wheels welded on to minimize vandalism. Graffiti artists have their way with them, which only adds to their charm. In 1977, Marsh had to dig them up and move them a couple miles further away from the fast encroaching city.

Cadillac Ranch, located near Love's Truck Stop at Arnot Rd in Amarillo, TX. The ranch is one of The Hampton Inn's ongoing Route 66 Save-A-Landmark renovation projects.

Quirky cuisine
How much money does it take to motivate someone to eat a 72-ounce steak plus a potato, salad, shrimp cocktail, dinner roll and dessert in under an hour? Not much! If you succeed at the steak challenge at the **Big Texan Steak Ranch**, all you get is a free meal, a T-shirt and a place in their hall of fame. Fail, and you have to pay for your meal, about 50 bucks. Thirty-five thousand people have taken them up on the challenge since 1960, but only 6,000 have succeeded. Of those, few are women; approximately two succeed each year of the four or five who attempt the feast. The oldest person to eat the steak was a 69-year-old grandmother, the youngest an 11-year-old boy. Nine and a half minutes was the fastest time although one contestant consumed *two* of the 5,200-calorie dinners in the time allotted. If you're too stuffed to drive home afterward, the restaurant has a motel where you can sleep it off. The website records all the statistics, including the winner's height, weight and age.

Big Texan Steak Ranch, 7700 I-40 E, Amarillo, TX 79112; ↘ 800 657 7177 or 806 372 7000; web: www.bigtexan.com

Odd shopping
Beauty and the Book, one of the only bookstores in this rural corner of Texas, is a bookstore and beauty parlor in one. Located in the garage of her house,

owner/stylist Kathy Patrick gave up an intense career as a publisher's rep to spend more time with her family. Dusting off her (very) old cosmetology degree, Kathy not only runs the salon/bookstore, she reigns over the Pulpwood Queens Book Club whose members sport tiaras and leopard-print scarves. Authors get the goddess treatment when they come for readings, even signing their books while getting a pedicure. With a motto like 'the higher the hair, the closer to God', you know the place just has to be in Texas.

Beauty and the Book, Rte 4, Box 285, Jefferson, TX 75657; ☏ 903 665 7520; web: www.beautyandthebook.com

You can hock your gun, buy your fiancée a diamond ring and marry her, all in the same place at the same time. Ted Kipperman runs the only **pawn shop/wedding chapel** in the world. A mail-order chaplain, Kipperman will rent you everything you need for a memorable ceremony under a plastic flower canopy.

Ted Kipperman's Pawn Shop/Wedding Chapel, 6120 Bellfort St, Houston, TX; ☏ 13 734 2543

Quirk Alert

FERTHAIRLIZER!

Barber Bill Black (web: www.ferthairlizer.com) has a novel obsession. He's hoping to help feed, clothe, and house poverty-stricken areas of the world using human hair. His vision is utterly unique: to make productive use of the mountains of hair clippings disposed of each day in a product he calls FertHAIRlizer, a 20/80 hair-to-soil mix that he claims is superior to other fertilizers on the market today. He'd also use hair in adobe bricks in place of straw, and would even weave it into bolts of cloth. Bill's epiphany sprang from observing that the house plants in his barbershop that received daily doses of airborne hair clippings were thriving despite being otherwise neglected. After testing his hypothesis and seeing his FertHAIRlizer out-perform the competition, he tried to interest investors, without success, in his concept. His idea sounded so far-fetched, however, that he drew the attention of the media, garnering publicity in print, radio, and television, including Jay Leno and David Letterman. Happy to get anyone to listen, he proudly talks about his hair bikini, hair undies, hair clip-on ties, vests and hair shirts, all of which are lined with cotton for comfort and all of which are made to pique curiosity about his ideas. While he's quite accepting of the ridicule that often comes his way, he hasn't given up hope that, someday, we'll see the light and turn our obsession with the hair on our heads into one more way of serving mankind. Meanwhile he'd like to create the world's largest hairball as a way to recycle hair.

Rooms with a Skew

At **Cibolo Creek Ranch** you can experience what it was like to live in a fort designed to protect its inhabitants from Indian attacks. The luxury ranch, just north of the Mexican border, manages to let you experience the rugged isolation of the Texas frontier despite its five-star reputation for quality, pampering and price. Restoration of the three-fort complex was meticulous, with no visible evidence of modern conveniences anywhere; some bathrooms even have to be entered through a fake armoire.

> **Cibolo Creek Ranch**, Box 44, Shafter, TX 79850. Located 20 miles north of the Mexico/Texas border on Hwy 67; ↘ 866 496 9460 or 915 229 3737; web: cibolocreekranch.com

NEW MEXICO
Festivals and events

He's big, he's ugly and he gets bigger and uglier with each passing year. Volunteers spend 1,500 hours creating the monster, only to see their efforts go up in smoke at the culmination of the annual **Burning of Zozobra Fiestas de Santa Fe**. The gruesome effigy, an animated wooden and cloth marionette, is ceremoniously strung up then set aflame, taking with him all of Santa Fe's troubles for another year. The festival, celebrated since 1712, is America's oldest civic celebration. The puppet became a symbol of the Fiestas de Santa Fe in 1924; a community service club, the Kiwanis, has sponsored the burning since 1963. It takes two weeks to build Zozobra. He waits behind city hall, illuminated by green fires, for the procession of Kiwanians dressed in black robes and hoods. The mayor proclaims the death sentence, the green fires change to red and Zozobra is toast. The Kiwanis throw off their robes and emerge in costume, leading a torch light parade to the tune of 'La Cucaracha'.

> **Burning of Zozobra Fiestas de Santa Fe**, held annually in September, usually the Thu following Labor Day, in Santa Fe, NM. Contact Santa Fe Visitor Bureau, ↘ 800 777 2489 or 505 955 6200; web: www.zozobra.com and www.santafefiesta.org

It's slimy, dirty and yucky and the kids love it. Rio Rancho's Muck and Mud Derby lets kids indulge in behavior they'd do naturally if their mothers would only let them. The parks and recreation department sets up an annual obstacle course in mud; kids compete against others in their age group to see who can finish the slimy course in the fastest time.

> **Muck and Mud Derby**, held annually in July. Contact the Rio Rancho Convention and Visitors Bureau, PO Box 15550, Rio Rancho, NM 87174; ↘ 888 746 7262 or 505 891 7258; web: www.rioranchonm.org

If riding a snow shovel down a slope sounds like child's play, think again. Shovel racing is a daredevil sport and shovel athletes have been clocked going 76 mph. The World Snow Shovel Race in Angel Fire has three race categories. Basic production

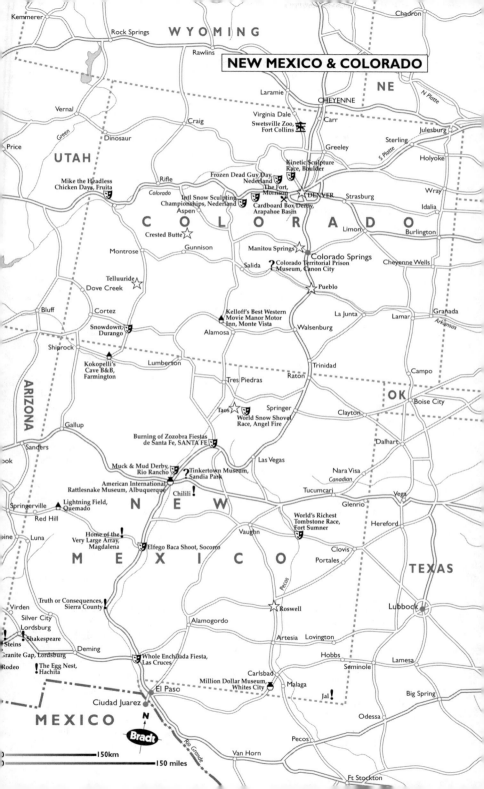

is where you simply nestle into the scoop of a standard shovel, place the handle between your legs, and shoot down the 1,000-foot course, desperately flailing or dragging your hands to gain some semblance of control. The modified class attaches the shovel to a contraption such as a bobsled, luge or dragster framework, while the modified unique class can be either hi-tech or supremely wacky. An entire living-room has gone down the 1,585-foot slope at 40mph, followed by a doghouse, only to be beaten by a chicken sandwich. The sport has its origins as a competition among trail maintenance crews who discovered that riding their work shovels down the mountain at the end of the day was the quickest way home after a long day of work.

World Snow Shovel Race, held annually in February in Angel Fire, NM. Contact Angel Fire Resort, Angel Fire, NM; ➘ 505 377 4207; web: www.angelfireresort.com

The **Taos Poetry Circus** is a nine-day extravaganza of poetry competitions. Readings are scored competitively and there are both individual and team events. The audience is invited to hoot and holler at the dramatic presentations, attracting folks who would normally prefer root canal surgery to a poetry reading.

Taos Poetry Circus, held annually in June in Taos, NM. Contact World Poetry Bout Association, 5275 NDCBU, Taos, NM 87571; ➘ 505 758 1800; web: www.poetrycircus.org

America's obsession with aliens is abundantly evident at the **Roswell UFO Encounter Festival and Intergalactic Fashion and Food Extravaganza**. This event celebrates the mysterious crash of an unidentified flying object (UFO) in Roswell on July 8 1947. At first the government claimed that the fallen debris was really a spaceship. Days later it retracted the story, claiming it was really a weather balloon. Fifty years later, in 1997, it changed its story once again, claiming it was really a secret spy satellite. Regardless of what the government says, thousands of people believe it was really a spaceship. Countless documentaries claim that space creatures were killed in the crash and that the government has been covering it up all these years. At the festival, you'll hear all about breeding experiments and alien autopsies and see the world's largest UFO Parade. An alien costume contest, a trade show and homemade spaceships will keep your camera snapping up the atmosphere. The Intergalactic Fashion and Food Extravaganza caps off the activities. The event draws thousands of abductees, conspiracy theorists, skeptics, believers, and just plain folk who gather to enjoy the weirdness. Be prepared to shed some of your skepticism; the evidence and hype can be pretty persuasive.

Roswell UFO Encounter Festival and Intergalactic Fashion and Food Extravaganza, held annually in June in Roswell, NM. Contact Roswell Chamber of Commerce, PO Box 70, Roswell, NM 88202; ➘ 877 849 7679 or 505 623 5695; web: www.uforoswell.com

The infamous outlaw, Billy the Kid, is buried behind the old Fort Sumner Museum. During its annual festival, the museum puts on the **World's Richest Tombstone Race**. Since Billy the Kid's tombstone has been stolen three times, once spending 27 years in a Texas boxcar, the Fort gives each entrant a replica of the actual tombstone that weighs 80lb. They have to carry the thing up to an obstacle, throw it over to the other side, jump the obstacle themselves, pick up the tombstone again and come back. Women get to race with a 20lb stone. Entrants are really motivated to win – the prize is $1,000 cash.

World's Richest Tombstone Race (also known as Billy the Kid's Tombstone Race), held annually in June during Old Fort Days in Fort Sumner, NM. Contact Fort Sumner Chamber of Commerce, 707 N 4th St, Fort Sumner, NM 88119; ↘ 505 355 7705; web: www.ftsumnerchamber.com

Robert Estrada gives new meaning to the expression 'the whole enchilada'. The **Whole Enchilada Fiesta** in Las Cruces is a three-day event centered around the making of the world's largest enchilada. Estrada designed the technique and equipment needed to make the monster tortilla. The dough, 250lb worth, is pressed on a tray; it takes 14 men to carry it to a cooking vat. The tortilla is cooked in 550° oil in a trampoline-size vat. Then Robert ladles on the three layers of chili sauce, cheese and onions. Two-and-a-half hours later, the enchilada is ready to be shared by the hundreds of spectators.

Whole Enchilada Fiesta, held annually in September, PO Box 8258, Las Cruces, NM 88006; ↘ 505 571 5510; web: www.twefie.com

The **Elfego Baca Shoot** is long-distance golf played from a mountaintop with the starting hole on a 7,280 foot peak. Each golfer gets ten specially painted balls at the start along with a scorekeeper and three spotters who attempt to keep track of their golfer's balls. Since the average distance to a hole is two and a half miles as the crow flies, the spotter's role is crucial. During play a ball can be moved up to 50 feet laterally from the hole to improve position. All in all, it takes about two and a half hours to play the 'course' and the players move from hole to hole in 4WD vehicles. A low gross score and the lowest ball count determines the winner.

Elfego Baca Shoot, held annually in June in Socorro, NM. Located on I-25 approx 65 miles south of Albuquerque. Contact New Mexico Institute of Mining and Technology; ↘ 505 835 8211; web: www.hiltonopen.com/Elfego0402.htm

Museums and collections

White City's **Million Dollar Museum** is a dilapidated relic of American roadside culture, a throwback to the days when a collection of odd collections was worthy of a family outing. If you've visiting Carlsbad Caverns, you're bound to stop at the tourist junction and the museum makes for a nice, if musty, distraction. Claiming 30,000 items, 50 collections and several real mummies, the place meanders through almost a dozen basement rooms displaying curiosities like two-headed creatures, mummified skeletons and a possible alien baby left over from the Roswell incident. The collections include branding irons, saddles, dollhouses, clocks, and typewriters.

Million Dollar Museum, located at White's City Resort, 17 Carlsbad Caverns Hwy, White City, NM 88268; ↘ 505 785 2291; web: www.whitescity.com. *Hours vary seasonally.*

Before the bald eagle was adopted as America's symbol, the rattlesnake had that honor. During the Revolution soldiers waved flags at the British that pictured a big rattlesnake with 13 rattles and the phrase, 'Don't Tread On Me'. You can see this flag, and more than 30 kinds of rattlesnakes, at the **American International Rattlesnake Museum** in Albuquerque. Bob Meyers, a former biology teacher, opened the museum to promote a kindlier, gentler attitude toward this much-maligned snake. The museum dispels the myths that rattlesnakes go after people, that you'll die from a rattler bite, and that the number of rattles tells a snake's age. All those statements are false. These snakes attack only when they're threatened and their warning rattle has been ignored. Only a handful of deaths result each year from their venom, and the number of their rattles has nothing to do with their age. In fact, the most dangerous rattlesnakes are the immature ones that haven't developed rattles yet and have very little experience making objective judgements. Sounds like the average teenager.

American International Rattlesnake Museum, 202 San Felipe NW, Suite A, Albuquerque, NM 87104; ↘ 505 242 6569; web: www.rattlesnakes.com. *Open daily 10.00am–6.00pm. Closed major holidays.*

Both the **UFO Enigma Museum** and the **International UFO Museum and Research Center** claim to have authentic debris found at this well-known UFO crash site. Photos, re-creations, videos, books and displays – some compelling and some ludicrously unbelievable – provide you with an entertaining look at the whole UFO phenomena. The gift shops are equally amusing.

UFO Enigma Museum, Roswell, located near the entrance of Walker Air Base; ↘ 505 347 2275

International UFO Museum and Research Center, 114 N Main St, Roswell, NM 88203; ↘ 505 625 9495; fax: 505 625 1907; web: www.iufomrc.com. *Open daily 9.00am–5.00pm. Admission free; donations accepted.*

Attractions

Tinkertown Museum in Sandia Park started off as a hobby 40 years ago when Ross Ward began carving an animated, miniature Western town. When he'd finished the town, he built an entire three-ring circus, a circus parade, a menagerie and a side-show. But he still wasn't done and he needed a place to put all this. Fifty thousand recycled bottles later, he had his buildings. Ross got the inspiration for his first creations as a nine year old, visiting Knott's Berry Farm and coming home with a desire for an Old West town of his very own. The bottle idea came while visiting Grandma Prisby's Bottle Village, a famous Simi Valley, California site. Ross is just a born tinkerer; he even tinkered as a profession, painting carnival rides and fun houses all over the country. When he and his wife Carla retired, they built the kind of place that had always attracted them in their own travels.

Tinkertown Museum, Sandia Park, NM; ↘ 505 281 5223; web: www.tinkertown.com. Directions: take I-40 and NM 14 on NM 536, 17 miles east of Albuquerque to the Turquoise Trail. *Open daily 9.00am–6.00pm Apr–Nov.*

Quirkyville

You see them way off in the distance: cowboys driving cattle across the barren, desolate landscape. As you get closer to **Jal**, a dusty place with 2,000 hearty souls, you notice that the horses and cows aren't moving. That's because they're made of steel: 17 enormous silhouettes created by artist Brian Norwood. Each of the cowboy, horse and cow silhouettes was cut from a ten-foot by 40-foot piece of steel, weighing 4,000lb apiece. Jal raised the funds to install the 400-foot sculpture, hoping to encourage tourists to stop in the town. Brian also created an 80-foot by 100-foot map of the United States on an elementary school playground. Each state is outlined in the parking lot's white paint; the states themselves are painted in color. Alaska alone required over a gallon of red paint

> **Jal**, located in Lea County, southeast corner of New Mexico. Contact Jal Chamber of Commerce, 100 W Idaho Ave, Jal, NM 88252; ☏ 505 395 2620; web: www.jalnewmexico.org.

Just plain weird

New Mexico is home to several ghost towns, relics of the short-lived boom towns that flourished during the silver rush of the 1870s. The Hill family gives weekend tours of **Shakespeare**, where Billy the Kid supposedly worked as a dishwasher. The place feels eerie, like a movie set waiting for folks to come back and pick up their lives where they left off. **Steins**, an old railroad town of the 1900s, lies just off the highway. In 1988, Larry Link stopped by and found an old coot with a shotgun keeping looters away. Larry and his wife, Linda, ended up buying Steins; the whole place is like a museum. Meanwhile, **Granite Gap**, owned by Klondike Mike and Jackass Jill, provides a look at the turn-of-the-century tunnels that honeycomb through Granite Mountain. In Hachita, the **Egg Nest** is a restaurant and shop featuring museum-quality music boxes made out of unfertilized eggshells. Marlene and Pat Harris have been making them for 15 years. The ghost town of **Rodeo** boasts a collection of 2,000 license plates at Kathy's gift shop. And owner Lois Bernard doesn't print a menu at Rodeo's tavern restaurant. She'd rather stand there and talk to you. Now that's really eccentric.

> Information on these and other New Mexico ghost towns is available from the Lordsburg-Hidalgo Chamber of Commerce, 208 E 2nd St, Lordsburg, NM 88045; ☏ 505 542 9864; web: www.hidalgocounty.org/ lordsburgcoc

Chilili boasts a cemetery in which dozens of the tombstones are made of tin sheets mounted on marble pedestals. The memorials were made by Horace McAfee, today a cemetery resident, who laboriously punched out the entire wording on the tins using just a nail. McAfee was also responsible for the tin angels and the tin sheet explaining his own views on the afterlife.

> **Chilili, NM**. Contact Albuquerque Visitors Bureau, PO Box 26866, Albuquerque, NM 87125; ☏ 800 284 2282 or 505 222 4304; web: www.abqcvb.org

The arid desert plains near Magdalena are home to the **Very Large Array** near Socorro, the most powerful radio telescope in the world. Its 27-dish antennas, ten stories high and spread out over 22 miles in a 'Y' formation, can detect extremely faint radio transmissions from distant stars. Astronomers and other scientists apply each year for observing time. UFO types hope the first 'ET phone home' signal will come through here. The visitor center offers a slide show, displays, and a self-guided tour.

> **Very Large Array**, located in Magdalena in southwest New Mexico along US Hwy 60. Contact National Radio Astronomy Observatory Public Information Office, PO Box O, 1003 Lopezville Rd, Socorro, NM 87801; ☏ 505 835 7000; fax: 505 835 7027; web: www.vla.nrao.edu. *Guided tours given once a quarter and in the summer on weekends; contact the NRAO for times. Admission free.*

Rooms with a Skew

They call it 'biotecture', sustainable buildings in an array of shapes and sizes made from recycled and inexhaustible materials like tires, aluminum cans, bottles, and mud. At the **Greater World Earthship Community** several of the community's earthships for are rent, including the Nautilus, a spiral, seashell, island-themed design, and the Hut, which is really two pods connected with a greenhouse. Earthships are completely self-sustainable, functioning without any connection to water, sewage, or electricity.

> **Greater World Earthship Community**, I Earthship Way, PO Box 1041, Taos, NM 87571; ↘ 505 751 0462; web: www.earthship.org

Kokopelli's Cave Bed and Breakfast in Farmington is a luxury cliff dwelling north of Farmington near Mesa Verde National Monument. Located 70 feet below the surface, you reach this subterranean B&B by way of a sandstone path, steps carved in the rock, and a short ladder. The 1,600-square-foot cave was originally built to house a resident geologist. It's completely furnished with carpeting, southwestern furnishings, plumbing, electricity, a full kitchen and laundry, a waterfall shower, and a flagstone hot tub. The setting is unique – isolated and spectacular – but you really have to want to stay there since the climb can be somewhat arduous and there are no bellmen. You carry your own luggage to the site.

> **Kokopelli's Cave Bed and Breakfast**, 3204 Crestridge Dr, Farmington, NM 87401; ↘ 505 325 7855; web: www.bbonline.com/nm/kokopelli. *Open Mar–Nov. Closed Dec–Feb.*

The **Lightning Field** is like a giant garden of lightning rods. The remote isolated art installation consists of 400 stainless steel poles arranged in a rectangular grid about a mile long. To fully appreciate the impact of the project, you need to view it over an extended period of time. Thus, up to six visitors can reserve the three-bedroom log cabin located on the site. It's the only way you can see it.

> **The Lightning Field**, in Quemado, NM, off Route 117 S. Contact Dia Center for the Arts, PO Box 2993, Corrales, NM, 87048; ↘ 505 898 3335; fax: 505 898 3336; web: www.lightningfield.org. Directions: The Dia office is a three-hour drive from Albuquerque. *Open May 1–Oct 31. Reservations required.*

COLORADO
Festivals and events

Organizing an event around a headless chicken may sound odd to anyone outside of Fruita, Colorado, but as history shows, festivals arise out of many unusual occurrences. **Mike the Headless Chicken Days** celebrates the 1945 saga of farmer Lloyd Olsen and the chicken that refused to become his dinner. It all began when Lloyd, who was particularly fond of chicken neck, lopped off the head of a rooster up near the base of its skull. To Lloyd's astonishment, the bird didn't seem to mind losing his head. Fluffing up his feathers, he went right on doing what he'd done all his life: pecking for food. True, he could only go through the motions, but that didn't stop him one bit. It didn't even stop him from crowing, although the sound that came out was more like a gurgle. When Lloyd found the rooster still alive the next morning, he used an eye dropper to put food and water directly down its gullet. After a week of successful feedings, he took the bird, now named Mike, to a university where they determined Mike had just enough brain stem left to live to continue acting like a chicken.

Lloyd, knowing a good thing when he spotted it, signed on as Mike's public relations agent and took him on the road making personal appearances. The decapitated bird gained fame and fortune, posing for *Life* magazine and making it into the *Guinness Book of World Records*. He lived two profitable years before choking to death on a kernel of corn in 1947. Others tried to create their own Mikes, but the best of the copybirds lived only 11 days. A statue of Mike, made from rakes, axes and other sharp implements, now stands proudly in town, providing an especially weird photo op. The events at Mike the Headless Chicken Days include a Run Like a Headless Chicken race, egg tosses, Pin the Head on the Chicken, a Cluck Off, Rubber Chicken Juggling and, of course, the Chicken Dance. Chicken bingo is played with chicken droppings on a grid and everyone eats great quantities of chicken. You can even buy a bar of headless chicken soap. In election years they run Mike for president.

Mike the Headless Chicken Days, held annually in May in Fruita, CO; ☎ 970 858 0360; web: www.miketheheadlesschicken.org

Toss it, hurl it, launch or drive it. One way or another, you'll get rid of that dreadful fruitcake during the January **Fruitcake Toss**. You've got several ways to get the inedible mass out of your life. Launching requires some kind of mechanical device capable of thrusting the thing into the air; tossing involves throwing it; and hurling gets you one fling on the official catapult. If you're a golfer, you get one swing to see who can drive their cake the furthest without hitting it out of the park. There's a fruitcake carving event, a fruitcake relay race and recognition for the fruitcake that traveled the most miles to take part in the festivities. If you think you have the ugliest or the most beautiful fruitcake, you might want to save it for the glamour competitions If you weren't lucky enough to get your very own concoction of glacé fruit, nuts and flour during the holidays, you can rent one for a quarter. Ditto the golf club. Parking tip: Fruitcakes travel from west to east, so don't park on the east side of the event.

Fruitcake Toss, held annually in January in Manitou Springs, CO. Contact Manitou Springs Chamber of Commerce, 384 Manitou Ave, Manitou Springs, CO 80829; ☎ 800 642 2567 or 719 685 5089; web: www. manitousprings.org

The legend of Emma Crawford lives on in Manitou Springs when coffins, complete with Emmas riding inside, race up the town's main street during the **Emma Crawford Coffin Races** in October. The races are the legacy of one Emma Crawford, a 19th-century spiritualist who thought she saw her Indian spiritual guide waiting for her on a mountaintop. When she died of illness at a tragically young age, she was buried at the spot where she'd seen the vision and there she remained until a powerful storm washed the coffin down into town. A team of four mourners pulls a coffin that is mounted on tiny wheels; the fastest and most creative coffins and teams get a prize. That evening 'ghosts' lead a tour of Emma's favorite haunts, telling tall tales and spinning yarns.

> **Emma Crawford Coffin Races**, held annually in October in Manitou Springs, CO. Contact Manitou Springs Chamber of Commerce, 384 Manitou Ave, Manitou Springs, CO 80829; ☎ 800 642 2567 or 719 685 5089; web: www.manitousprings.org

Thirty thousand people are on hand each spring to witness human-powered handmade machines conquer the deep water and muddy beaches of the Boulder Reservoir at the **Kinetic Sculpture Race**. Prior to the race itself, a parade is held to judge the strange crafts for popularity and style and the participants for costumes and theme creativity. The course is three miles long, two-thirds of it on water. A few craft sink right off the bat, leaving the rest to flounder and splash while trying to sink a competitor's vessel. If they make it across the water, they face an obstacle course with the final challenge being a plunge down a water slide.

> **Kinetic Sculpture Race**, held annually in May in Boulder, CO. Contact Boulder Visitor Bureau; ☎ 303 442 2911, or the sponsors, KBCO Radio; ☎ 303 444 5600; web: www.kbco.com/kinetics/index.html

At the July **Rolling River Raft Race** in Pueblo, contestants build their rafts out of recycled materials, then try to race them three and a half miles down the river. Racers with the best speed, best costumes, best use of materials and most creative raft are awarded prizes.

> **Rolling River Raft Race**, held annually in July in Pueblo, CO. Contact Pueblo Chamber of Commerce, 302 N Santa Fe, Pueblo, CO 81003; ☎ 800 233 3446 or 729 542 1704; web: www.pueblochamber.org

To beat the midwinter doldrums, Durango locals indulge in some pretty weird behavior at their annual **Snowdown** festival. The five days of shenanigans take place all over town and involve 60 events, give or take a few, that range from the ridiculous to the absurd. One of the most popular is the Grand Mashers Cream Pie Hit Squad. A 'contract' is placed, for a fee, on your intended victim. The squad then notifies the target, offering 'protection' for a price. Anyone whose protection has lapsed, or who is uninsured on hit day, will get his or her just desserts. At the Golf Tournament, bars round town each set up their own miniature indoor golf holes. Golfers, four to a team and dressed in costume, make their way from watering hole to watering hole with predictable results. Bribery is encouraged to improve your score. Down at the river there's a portable steam room. To take the Animas River Plunge, you jump into the icy waters, then scramble up the bank to a warm reception. Shop Til You Drop involves a shopping scavenger hunt sponsored by local stores. For the infamous Follies production townspeople try out in December, hoping their silly, goofy act will survive the final cut.

The Grocery Games involve SPAM™ carving contests, timed shopping-cart events and frozen-turkey bowling. The local hotels sponsor the Bed Races, providing two twin beds on casters. Contestants compete in bed-making speed and bed-racing competitions. Guys have their own beauty contest, the Male Review, at which they strut their stuff in beach wear. If there's enough snow, you can join the Snow Sculpture Contest. Other events include a waiters-waitress race, a bartender's contest, a dos and don'ts fashion show, a jokedown, a snow shoveling contest, skijoring (where a horse and rider pull the skier through an obstacle course), a pet fashion show, and an owner/pet look-alike contest. Although it's hard to imagine, they also play ski softball and race kayaks and mountain-bikes downhill. Indoors there's a spelling bee, a dance contest and a blackjack freeze-out tournament. The events are numerous and you can sign up for most of them right then and there. Snowdown culminates with the explosion of a single firework left over from July 4th festivities.

Snowdown, held annually in late Jan/early Feb in Durango, CO. Contact SNOWDOWN Durango, Inc, PO Box 1, Durango, CO 81302; ✆ 970 382 3737; web: www.snowdown.org

The February **Cardboard Box Derby** at Arapahoe Basin ski resort brings 10,000 people to the slopes to watch a derby of wacky crafts made solely out of paper, string, glue, tape and cardboard. The event has grown so popular that entries are limited to the first 150 folks who sign up. Prizes are given for originality, costumes and construction. An Empire State Building that won in a prior year was more than 30-feet high and crashed about ten feet from the starting line. Another, King Kong, came complete with screaming movie star on the monster's 35-foot 'sky scrapper' entry.

Cardboard Box Derby, held annually in March in Arapahoe Basin, CO. Contact Arapahoe Basin Resort, PO Box 8787, Keystone, CO 80435; ✆ 888 ARAPAHOE or 970 468 0718; web: www.arapahoebasin.com

'Grandpa Bredo' has been grandfathered in – he's the only corpse in town allowed to hang out on private property. Since 1989 the 89-year-old body has been resting at his grandson's house in an ice-encased shed in the back yard, his blanket of dry ice replenished monthly with 1,500lb of the stuff to keep him properly frozen. And since 1989 the town has been trying to pass an ordinance prohibiting Grandpa from remaining a resident. As the story goes, Tygve Bauge, a devoted grandson, had Grandpa's body shipped from Norway when he died and put on ice in hopes of resurrecting him in the future.

Unfortunately, Tygve was deported shortly afterward following an immigration dispute, but Grandpa was allowed to stay, cared for by a secretive caretaker. The town reacted by passing a law making it illegal to store dead bodies on private property but they couldn't make it retroactive to cover the existing situation. Giving up the fight, they now celebrate **Frozen Dead Guy Day**. While no-one has seen the actual body in years, that doesn't stop the town from celebrating their decidedly weird claim to fame. Festival day includes a coffin race, a snow-sculpting contest, a parade, tours to the shed, a frozen dead van smash, and 'Bride of Grandpa and Grandma' look-alike contests. 'He's a champion of the rights of the temporarily dead,' says Kathy Beeck, producer of *Grandpa's Still In The Tuff Shed*, a documentary screened frequently during the festival.

> **Frozen Dead Guy Day**, held annually in March. Contact the Nederland Chamber of Commerce, PO Box 85, Nederland, CO 80466; ✆ 800 221 0044 or 303 258 3936; web: www.nederlandchamber.org

Crested Butte, a tiny close-knit community of no more than 2,500 people, really knows how to throw a community-wide party. Twice each year they celebrate the seasons with the zany festivals of **Flauschink** and **Vinitok**. Flauschink literally means 'flushing out winter and welcoming spring', an interpretation made obvious when you see the king and queen carrying their royal toilet plungers as scepters. The event, now in its 35th year, is always held during the last weekend of the ski season and kicks off with the telling of the tale (often quite a tall one) in a local bar. Next comes the Royal Coronation Ball, held in another bar, at which the king and queen of Flauschink are crowned.

There's always a polka band because polka is huge in Crested Butte. The next day all the townsfolk turn out for the parade, bowing on their knees to their new royalty. Immediately behind the royal couple comes the 'truck full of has beens', all the ex-kings and queens from the past. That evening is the Royal Promenade during which the royal party goes to every bar in town for a drink. (Are you sensing a theme here?) Finally, on Sunday, everyone skis to Flushing Hill to build snow benches and watch naked skiers honor the king and queen. Meanwhile, to celebrate the autumn equinox, Vinitok honors the region's East European heritage. This festival kicks off with a Liar's Night tall-tale storytelling contest, held, of course, at a bar, followed by the annual procession, trial, and ceremonial burning of a creature they call the Great Grump.

> **Flauschink**, held annually in April and **Vinitok**, held annually in September. Contact the Crested Butte Chamber of Commerce, PO Box 1288, Crested Butte, CO 81224; ✆ 800 545 4505 or 970 349 6438; web: www.crestedbuttechamber.com

Teams from all over the world compete in the **International Snow Sculpting Championships**. Using only hand tools like vegetable peelers, saws, and chisels, these four-person teams transform 12-foot-high, 20-ton blocks of man-made snow into mammoth sculptures, working a maximum of 65 hours during a five-day period. Depending on the weather, the results last for a week or more.

> **International Snow Sculpting Championships**, held annually in January. Contact the Breckenridge Resort Chamber, 311 S Ridge St, PO Box 1909, Breckenridge, CO 80424; ✆ 970 453 2913; web: www.gobreckevents.com

Telluride has three festivals worthy of note. A famous resort destination, the town is the site of endless events, so many, in fact, that the festival-weary populace declares one week each summer to be festival free. Started by accident in 1991 when a local resident sarcastically requested a non-festival festival permit, the Telluride **Nothing Festival** features T-shirts that have become a favorite of collectors: each year a new cartoon graphic proclaims nothingness and the festival's motto, 'Leave Me Alone!'. With no crowds and no traffic, folks just hang out, lounging in the middle of Main Street on lawn chairs under the Nothing Festival banner. Planned events include sunrises, sunsets, gravity as usual, and a search for a sense of humor. The website thanks you for not participating.

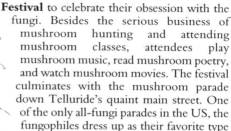

Several hundred fungophiles gather during August's peak mushroom season at Telluride's **Mushroom Festival** to celebrate their obsession with the fungi. Besides the serious business of mushroom hunting and attending mushroom classes, attendees play mushroom music, read mushroom poetry, and watch mushroom movies. The festival culminates with the mushroom parade down Telluride's quaint main street. One of the only all-fungi parades in the US, the fungophiles dress up as their favorite type of mushroom, painting their faces like mushrooms and dressing up their dogs to match. Winter in Telluride brings the AIDS benefit **In-Drag Race**, a skiing spectacle in which the most outrageous drag outfit wins.

Nothing Festival, held every July in Telluride, CO. Contact the Telluride Visitor Bureau; ☏ 888 605 2578; web: www.telluridenothingfestival.com

Mushroom Festival, held every August in Telluride, CO. Contact the Telluride Visitor Bureau; ☏ 888 605 2578; web: www.visittelluride.com

In-Drag Race, held every February/March in Telluride, CO; ☏ 800 801 4832; web: www.visittelluride.com

Eccentric environments

It's not easy being God's tool. Even Jim Bishop has trouble understanding why he was chosen to work up to 72 hours a week chopping down trees, making his own timbers and hauling 1,000 tons of rock and concrete up to his elaborate, ten-story- high, medieval-style castle. Constructed by hand, his only assistance is a system of winches, pulleys, and ropes that he operates with the aid of his pickup. He refuses any outside help on the castle itself, accepting help only with a retaining wall. According to Jim, his is the 'world's biggest – with the help of God – one man, physical project. Always open, always free to the public, it's a place of liberty, freedom, and justice. A poor man's Disneyland.' He's been building **Bishop's Castle** for 35 years now and has big plans for the future, like adding an orchestra balcony, a tunnel through the mountain, a moat and drawbridge, and maybe a second castle for his long-suffering wife. His massive stone and iron structure is, as he says, a monument to hard-working people – a castle to satisfy every man's desires. Now in his 60s, he's still going strong, driven by voices only he can hear.

Bishop's Castle, 1529 Claremont Ave, Pueblo, CO 81004; ☏ 719 485 3040; web: www.bishopcastle.org. *Open daylight hours every day. Free.*

Attractions

Bill Swets has been building funny, strange, whimsical critters out of junk since he retired from farming 14 years ago. His bizarre menagerie, known as the **Swetsville Zoo**, has 160 insects, birds, dinosaurs and robots, all made from scraps of metal, car parts, farm equipment tools and machinery. This quirky roadside stop is famous for its dinosaurs, dragons, bugs and other odd creatures. It's a labor of love for Bill and he's just in it for the fun of it; it doesn't cost you anything to enjoy his obsession.

Swetsville Zoo, 4801 E Harmony Rd (exit 265 off I-25), Fort Collins, CO 80525; ↘ 970 484 9509; web: www.ftcollins.com/ Media%20Center%20Pages/family.htm. *Open daylight hours. Admission free.*

That strange, submarine-looking thing sitting out front of the **Museum of Colorado Prisons** is a real gas chamber. Thirty-two of the 77 men executed at this notorious prison met their maker in that chamber. Known as the 'Hell Hole', this prison had the distinction of housing the only man ever convicted of cannibalism in the United States. (You can sit in his cell and wonder about his unique brand of takeout.) Thirty-two cells are filled with exhibits and life-sized models that bring life behind bars in the Old West all too alive. One of them belongs to an 11-year-old convicted murderer. If the gruesome artifacts and stories get to be too much for you, lighten the mood with the photo ops the museum thoughtfully provides.

Museum of Colorado Prisons, PO Box 1229, Canon City, CO 81215; ↘ 719 269 3015; web: www.prisonmuseum.org. Directions: Hwy 50 to 1st St, 2 blocks to museum and signs for parking. Museum is next to the prison. *Open daily 8.30am–6.00pm summer; Fri–Sun 10.00am–5.00pm winter.*

Just plain weird

The Jeppes Terminal at the Denver International Airport has two large maps by artist and airline employee Gary Sweeney titled **'America, Why I Love Her'**. Fascinated by America's bizarre tourist haunts, Gary made the maps, with photos to illustrate each oddity, to commemorate his visits to hundreds of eccentric sites.

'America, Why I Love Her', located at the Jeppes Terminal at the Denver International Airport, 8500 Peña Blvd, Denver, CO 80249; ↘ 303 342 2000; web: www.flydenver.com

Quirky cuisine

All the animal parts you can eat – and more. That what you'll find at **The Fort**, a restaurant serving authentic, well-researched pioneer, cowboy, and mountain man dishes. Originally built by owner Sam Arnold as his home, the mud and straw-brick building is a replica of an actual 1833 fort. He had to open the restaurant in 1963 to help pay the mortgage on the building. Sam carefully researches his recipes, finding ideas in old cookbooks, diaries and in the journals of the pioneers. The Fort is famous for buffalo dishes, delicacies like buffalo tongue, buffalo sausages, and grilled buffalo bones. The grilled bones are cracked; you extract the marrow to spread on toast. (Famous chef Julia Child is said to have ordered seconds of the bones, one of their most popular dishes.) They also serve wild boar chops, elk chops, and Rocky Mountain Oysters (bull testicles).

The place itself is like a museum, filled with artifacts from the Old West. Sam has been known to open champagne bottles with a tomahawk. For those celebrating special events, the wait staff, dressed in period clothing, beat a ceremonial Indian drum throughout the dining-room. Then the celebrant receives a buffalo horn or coyote headdress along with a piece of chili chocolate cake. Everyone joins in a hip-hip-huzzah while they take a picture to post on their website so customers can share the event with family and friends.

The Fort, 1912 Hwy 8, Morrison, CO 80465; ↘ 303 697 4771; web: www.thefort.com

Previous page Red Stiletto by David Crow (HB) page 279
Above Sweet Potato Queens in all their finery (TJ) page 250 © 2004 SPQ Inc
Right Mashed potato wrestling at Potato Days in South
Dakota (CC) page 124

Above The *Mega-sore-ass* dinosaur machine crossing the Eel River and traveling to Ferndale in the Annual World Championship, Great Arcata to Ferndale Cross-Country Kinetic Sculpture Race (DF) page 31

Below Surf and Turf, in front of the College of the Redwoods (RF) page 31

Above North Carolina is home to the world's largest chest of drawers (HP) page 249

Right Headquarters of the Longaberger Basket Company in Ohio (OH) page 121

Above Dr Evermor plans to shoot himself into space in his Wisconsin Forevertron (LH) page 84

Left Arachna Artie one of many large-scale, recycled metal sculptures in Dr Evermor's Sculpture Site, Wisconsin (AP) page 84

Above Salvation Mountain, a tribute to God made entirely
of adobe and paint in Southern California (LH) page 41

Below A Piece of Cake: a winner in the Cardboard Boat
Race, Crosswell, Michigan (NC) page 109

Above Bunny Slippers at Burning Man, 2002 (LB) page 62
Below The Temple of Rudra by Pepe Ozan, Burning Man, 1998 (HK) page 62

Left A caravan of art cars visits the world's largest dinosaur statues, near Cabazon, California. Art-car gatherings nationwide are listed at www.artcarscalendar.com (TK) page 278

Below Harrod Blank and his *Camera Van* at Carhenge (LBI) page 128

You can't miss it from the road. A statue of an Aztec king atop a bell-shaped tower atop a Spanish mansion is certain to make heads turn. But this is nothing compared with the dining experience awaiting you inside **Casa Bonita**. Ten themed dining areas, including a mineshaft with a snoring miner and a cavern with water dripping off ceiling stalactites, serve up Mexican food in a setting that can only be described as incredible. But the bizarre part is yet to come, for the restaurant is famous for its indoor cliff divers. The divers, often in strange costumes, execute a variety of jumps and spins while hurling themselves off 15- and 30-foot platforms into 14 feet of water. If you tire of this, Black Bart's Hideout awaits, a set-up geared for children and for adults brave enough to act like children. Add in the puppets and the pinatas and you can see why you'll never get bored. You may even forget to eat.

Casa Bonita, 6715 W Colfax Ave, Lakewood, CO; ↘ 303 232 5115; web:www.casabonitadenver.com. *Open Sun–Thu 11.00am–8.30pm, Fri–Sat 11.00am–10.00pm.*

Game is on the walls as well as on the menu at the **Buckhorn Exchange**. This famous restaurant serves real guy food, like rattlesnake, rocky mountain oysters, fried alligator tail, buffalo and elk. Deceased relatives of the animals that contribute to your eating pleasure line the walls. Almost 500 of them give you glassy-eyed stares as you dine.

Buckhorn Exchange, 1000 Osage St, Denver, CO; ↘ 303 534 9505; email: info@buckhorn.com; web: www.buckhorn.com

Rooms with a Skew

Kelloff's Best Western Movie Manor Motor Inn is a movie motel with 54 rooms facing a giant outdoor movie screen. Sound is piped into your room and you have a good view of the screen through a large picture window. If you feel like climbing out of bed, you can visit the snack bar for popcorn and other goodies. Open from mid-May through September, the motel shows new G, PG, and PG-13 releases. You can also drive your car to the movies, listening through drive-in style speakers.

Kelloff's Best Western Movie Manor Motor Inn, 2830 W US Hwy 160, Monte Vista, CO 81144; ↘ 800 771 9468 or 719 852 5921; fax: 719 852 0122; web: www.bestwesternmoviemanor.com

Jerry Bigelow, owner of the **Claim-Jumper B and B** in Crested Butte, can't let an empty space stay empty for long. Claiming he never throws anything away, the six guest rooms at his inn are decorated with all manner of unexpected stuff. Soda Creek boasts 300 Coke bottles from 50 countries along with a working Coke machine. Prospector's Gulch looks just like a miner's cabin complete with helmets, lamps and pickaxes hanging about. In Captain Corrigan's Cabin you'll sleep with a mounted marlin named Brando. In Ethyl's room you'll discover the fabulous 1950s with automobile memorabilia, including a gas pump and a Studebaker sign. You enter Jack's Cabin through a secret bookcase door. The sporty Fanatic Room houses Jerry's lifelong sporting collection, with many of the items autographed. The dining area has a couch made from the back end of a 1957 De Soto, a biplane hanging from the rafters and mannequins of presidents Nixon and Gorbachev.

Claim-Jumper B and B, 704 Whiterock Ave, Crested Butte, CO 81224; ↘ 970 349 6471; web: www.visitcrestedbutte.com/claimjumper

KANSAS
Festivals and events

In an event shared with the town of Olney, England, the annual **International Pancake Race** in Liberal commemorates a 500-year-old legend that began when an Olney housewife, engrossed in using up cooking fats forbidden during Lent, rushed to the shriving service with her pancakes and skillet still in hand. In subsequent years neighbors got into the act and it became a tradition for women to race to the church with their skillets. Since 1950 the race has been held on Shrove Tuesday on both sides of the pond with an international winner declared after transatlantic comparisons of the race results. To date Liberal has 28 wins; Olney, 24. The record time to run the 415-yard, S-shaped course, skillet and pancake in hand, is just under 59 seconds. On the weekend preceeding the race there's a pancake flipping and eating contest; the record here is 66 flips in one minute.

> **International Pancake Race**, held annually on Shrove Tuesday (February/March) in Liberal, KS. Contact International Pancake Day, PO Box 665, Liberal, KS 67905 or the Liberal Convention and Tourism Bureau, ☏ 620 624 6423; web: www.pancakeday.com

Eccentric environments

The **Garden of Eden** in Lucas is frontier eccentricity at its most splendid, the history of the world according to one Samuel Dinsmoor who was gripped by a severe case of concretia dementia in 1905 at the age of 64. Almost defying description, the garden represents Dinsmoor's love of freedom, hatred of big government and big business, and his literal interpretation of the Bible. At the front of his faux log cabin, in actuality limestone carved to look log-like, Adam and Eve greet you with outstretched arms, forming a gateway to his weird world. A concrete serpent coils in a tree above the pair while a concrete devil watches from a nearby rooftop. A concrete apron, placed there to appease the neighbors, discreetly covers Adam's genitalia. An American flag made of red, white and blue concrete flies above.

Everywhere you look is concrete; 113 tons of it formed into primitive sculptures over a period of 22 years. Dinsmoor's garden has 40-foot trees, huge flags mounted on ball bearings, and hundreds of figures, from bugs to birds to the eye of God. Storks with babies under their wings have light bulbs in their mouths to light their way; children run from demons. More modern history includes Indians, soldiers, and his quirky tribute to the food chain. Big business and government are lambasted in the Crucifixion of Labor, featuring a doctor, lawyer, banker and preacher nailing the Christ-like figure of Labor to a cross-like tree. Dinsmoor died in 1933, fully prepared for this event. His mausoleum is in a 40-foot-tall building in a corner of his garden; he, himself, is in a glass-sided coffin for all the world to see.

> **Garden of Eden**, 305 E 2nd St, Lucas, KS 67648; ☏ 785 525 6395; email: questions@garden-of-eden-lucas-kansas.com; web: www.garden-of-eden-lucas-kansas.com. *Open daily 10.00am–5.00pm May–Oct; 1.00–4.00pm Nov–Apr.*

Museums and collections

Devoted to preserving and documenting outsider art environments, the **Kansas Grassroots Art Center** exhibits and promotes the work of self-taught artists, artists about whom the term 'crazy' is frequently applied. The term 'grassroots' or 'outsider' art refers to people with no formal artistic training, people who usually

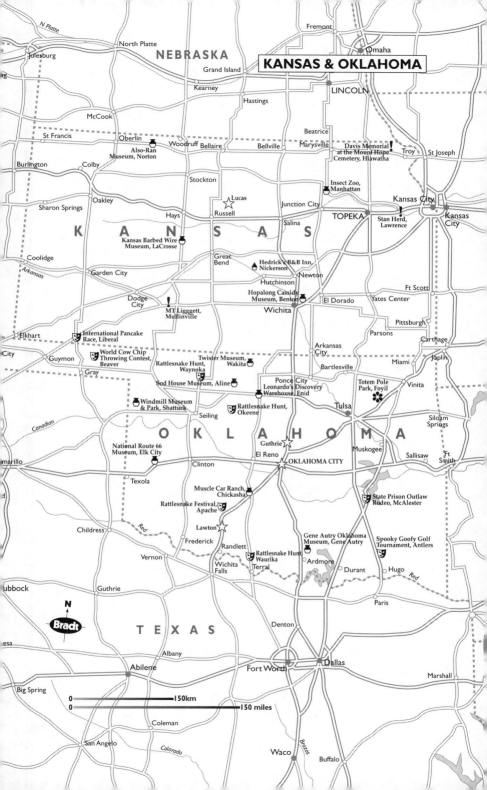

begin compulsively producing their work around retirement age. They use ordinary and found materials in extraordinary ways, often spending decades building a bizarre environment that suits them. The center's galleries display the work done by outsider artists of the region: strange stone- and wood-carvings, aluminum pull-tab sculptures (think chairs and motorcycles), metal totems, convoluted machines and glass-studded concrete sculptures. Kansas ranks third in America in the number of grassroots art sites, also called eccentric environments, after Wisconsin and California.

Kansas Grassroots Art Center, 213 S Main St, Box 304, Lucas, KS 67648; ↘ 785 525 6118; web: home.comcast.net/~ymirymir/index2.htm. *Art Center hours vary seasonally.*

Flies on the drain board. Roach-filled cabinets. Giant cockroaches. They're all part of the **Insect Zoo** at the Kansas State University. The kitchen display is meant to get you thinking about how clean your kitchen really is and about how to prevent creepy infestations. There's also a bug-petting zoo where you can get more up close and personal than you probably want to with creatures like tarantulas. Eeuuw … the kids will love it.

Insect Zoo, located in the Kansas State University Gardens in Manhattan, KS; ↘ 785 532 2122; web: www.ksu.edu/butterfly. *Open Mon, Wed & Fri 10.00am–4:00pm, Sat 11.00am–2.00pm. Admission free; donations appreciated.*

Known as the King of the Merchandising Cowboys, Hopalong Cassidy was a famous early-television cowboy hero whose persona appeared in and on every form of media and advertising of the time. From lunchboxes to bedroom suites, Western outfits to bikes and wagons, they're all displayed at the new **Hopalong Cassidy Museum**. Besides the huge collection of memorabilia, the museum theater has continuous showings of all Hopalong's TV shows as well as his 66 feature films.

Hopalong Cassidy Museum, 15231 SW Parallel Rd, Benton, KS 67017; ↘ 316 778 2121; web: www.prairierosechuckwagon.com. *Open Mon–Sat 11.00am–6.00pm.*

Barbed wire changed the course of Western history and the **Kansas Barbed Wire Museum** in La Crosse explains how it happened. The West was nothing but wide open spaces when the settlers arrived. Over time, farmers and ranchers – who got along about as well as oil and water – divided up the land. When barbed wire was invented, farmers were finally able to fence their land to prevent herds of livestock from trampling it. Whenever the wire went up, a range war usually ensued. The museum has 700 varieties of the stuff and barbed wire is now a collector's item, fetching up to $400 per section of strand.

Kansas Barbed Wire Museum, 120 W 1st St, La Crosse, KS; ↘ 785 222 9900; web: www.rushcounty.org/barbedwiremuseum. *Open Mon–Sat 10.00am–4.30pm May–mid-Sep.*

Here's a bank with a quirky sense of humor. In the tiny town of Norton, the First State Bank houses the **Also-Ran Museum**, a collection dedicated to those who ran for president but didn't win. You'll see a portrait of each loser, along with a description of the election they didn't win. The gallery was started in 1965 by then

Quirk Alert

The idea of using the land as his canvas just cropped up one day for **Stan Herd** (web: www.stanherd.com). Stan is a crop artist, meaning he uses plants, rocks, flowers and vegetables to create giant earthworks best appreciated from the air. Given the geography of Kansas, you'll see he couldn't have chosen a better place. Using a tractor as his brush, he's completed 15 images in 20 years. Some of his work, such as the Absolut vodka bottle he did for a liquor distributor, is for commercial clients, which helps pay the bills. Some is just for the challenge of it, like the landscape image he created on a vacant Trump property in Manhattan. It was strange to work in the shadow of skyscrapers instead of in the open air of a field, but he had help from an unusual source: the homeless. The vegetables he used in his 'painting' also served as a free supermarket for the needy that harvested the vegetables as they ripened. Better yet, he didn't have to be in a plane to appreciate his efforts; eight stories up worked just fine. Usually his art lasts for just a single season; occasionally for up to three. But the Amelia Earhart Earthwork is his first attempt at a permanent work of art. An entire acre in size, it's on a hillside near Atchison's International Forest of Friendship. He also created a five-acre, interactive corn maze in the shape of a turtle for Pendelton's Country Market. The 'Stalk of the Town', 5,000 visitors had played in the turtle maze by the time it closed at harvest.

bank president W W Rouse who was inspired after reading Irving Stone's book about losing presidential candidates.

Also-Ran Museum, First State Bank, 105 W Main St at Hwy 283, Norton, KS 67654; ☎ 785 877 3341; web: www.firstatebank.com. *Open during regular bank hours.*

Just plain weird

They don't get much bigger, at least in cemeteries, than the gargantuan grave memorial left by John Davis, a childless eccentric determined to spend his every dime rather than see his wealth go to his deceased wife's children. The **Davis Memorial at the Mount Hope Cemetery** in Hiawatha contains ten life-sized Italian marble statues depicting Davis' life with his beloved wife who predeceased him in 1930. The statues portray the early years of their marriage, then progress to their life together as they aged, finally ending with Mr. Davis seated next to a 'vacant chair', symbolizing his loneliness after his wife died. At his sparsely attended funeral, the preacher commented, 'Well, everybody has their peculiarities …' As for John himself, he defended spending his fortune by stating, 'It's my money; I spent it the way I pleased.' Amen.

Davis Memorial, at the Mount Hope Cemetery, Hiawatha, KS. Contact Hiawatha Chamber of Commerce, 602 Oregon, Hiawatha, KS 66434; ☎ 785 742 7136

M T Liggett of Mullinville uses the fields along Highway 154 to make his opinions known. He's planted dozens and dozens of kinetic wind-powered junk sculptures (he calls them 'totems') that mock local and national politicians. His field has become a three-dimensional editorial page, with strange figures such as the Stool Brothers, who have a toilet bowl for a head, and Monica's famous blue dress made out of scrap metal painted blue with dabs of white. The figure of a joker represents a judge with whom he disagrees. With a never-ending supply of current events to fuel his imagination, this irascible artist continues to add figures to his crop. If he's around when you arrive, he'll happily take you on a highly opinionated tour of his sculptures. Liggett, who isn't afraid of speaking up, is fond of saying, 'A man is never remembered for the words he didn't say.'

> **M T Liggett**, Mullinville, KS 67109; ✆ 620 548 2597; web: www.midway.net/greensburg/default.htm. Located along Hwy 154 on west edge of Mullinvlle.

Rooms with a Skew

Hedrick's Bed and Breakfast Inn in Nickerson is part of an exotic animal farm that hand-raises giraffe, zebra, llama, kangaroo, camel, ostrich and emu. Each of its seven rooms is decorated after an animal and its country; you can pet, feed and even kiss the animals during your stay.

> **Hedrick's Bed and Breakfast Inn**, 7910 N Roy L Smith Rd, Nickerson, KS 67561; ✆ 316 422 3245 or 888 489 8039; fax: 316 422 3766; web: www.hedricks.com

OKLAHOMA
Festivals and events

A chip is the part of a bovine's meal that goes 'plop' as it hits the ground. Early settlers discovered that the buffalo chips, and later cow chips, left by the animals after summer grazing made excellent cooking fuel. So the chips were collected each fall, with whole communities setting out in wagons to load up with their winter fuel. Tossing the chips into the wagon evolved into friendly competitions and today the **World Cow Chip Throwing Contest** in Beaver celebrates this strange art of slinging dung. Contestants get two chips each, the goal being to throw the chip the farthest. If the poop pops in mid air, the piece that goes the farthest counts. The chips are provided by the county, have to be at least six inches diameter, and can't be altered in any way. The variety of throwing styles will vary depending upon wind direction and speed. Some toss underhanded, others use a Frisbee fling or an Olympic-style shot-put. The record of 182 feet 3 inches has been standing since 1979.

> **World Cow Chip Throwing Contest**, held annually every April 20 in Beaver, OK. Contact Beaver County Chamber of Commerce, 33 W 2nd St, Beaver, OK 73932; ✆ 580 625 4726.

Rattlesnake hunts are so popular in Oklahoma that the state offers five of them, organizing the reptile round-ups to protect livestock and ranchers from the plentiful and venomous creatures. Steeped in tradition, the spring events bring as many as 45,000 spectators and participants to each round-up. Some come to display their bravado, competing for bragging rights by capturing the longest, heaviest and most rattle-enhanced specimens. But most just come to watch others clamber about in the snake pit, content to watch safely from a distance or to have their picture taken with a de-fanged snake wrapped around their neck. Opposed by some animal rights activists who claim the hunts are excessive, proponents dismiss their concerns, claiming the dangerous creatures would pose significant hazards to humans and animals alike if their populations weren't controlled. The events offer guided hunts, a butcher's shop, milking demonstrations, snake auctions, booths selling rattlesnake delicacies and souvenirs, carnivals, and entertainment. Okeene, which sponsors the longest running round-up (62 years), also features pro bull riding, a tug of war, a staged train robbery, a greased pig contest, and a demolition combine derby.

Waikrua Rattlesnake Hunt, held annually in April. Contact Little Rattler, PO Box 224, Waurika, OK 73573; ➤ 580 228 2553; web: www.rattlesnakehunt.com

Apache Rattlesnake Festival, held annually in April. Contact Verla Thompson at ➤ 580 588 2880.

Waynoka Rattlesnake Hunt, held annually the first weekend after Easter. Web: www.outdoorguide.net/rattlesnake

Okeene Rattlesnake Hunt, held annually in May. Contact the Okeene Diamondback Club, 217 N Main, Okeene, OK 73763; ➤ 580 822 3174; web: www.maxpages.com/diamondback

At the Antlers Springs Golf Course in Antlers, they hold a **Spooky Goofy Golf Tournament** at which you tee off toilets, shoot the ball from cannons and slingshots, and use brooms, baseball bats and cue sticks as clubs. The second nine holes are played after dark with glow balls. Local undertaker Jim Bob Sims and owner Butch Morris originated the event. Jim Bob has since moved on but Butch keeps coming up with wacky new ways to keep the tournament interesting.

Spooky Goofy Golf Tournament, held annually in October. Contact the Antlers Springs Golf Course, Antlers, OK 74523; ➤ 580 298 9900.

You've got to be on your good behavior to participate in this rodeo; one screw-up and you're not only off the team, you could be sent to solitary. The Oklahoma **State Prison Outlaw Rodeo** in McAlester is the world's only rodeo that takes place behind prison walls and it's the only time every seat in the prison's 12,000-seat arena is filled. It's not just for state prison inmates either. Inmates from other correctional facilities participate, as do free cowboys from the outside. Real life, tough-as-nails cowpokes go up against real life, tough-as-nails felons, and it isn't always a pretty site. Calf-roping, bull-riding, steer-wrestling, and barrel-racing keep you on the edge of your seat, as does an inmate-only event which involves grabbing a $100 bill (four months' salary in prison currency) from between the horns of a very irritated bull. At least you can count on the crowd to be reasonably well-behaved; it's just you and the prisoners, no alcohol allowed.

State Prison Outlaw Rodeo, held annually in September at Oklahoma State Penitentiary in McAlester, OK. Contact the McAlester Chamber of Commerce and Agriculture, 10 S 3rd Street, PO Box 759, McAlester, OK 74501; ➤ 918 423 2550; fax: 918 423 1345; web: www.mcalester.org

Eccentric environments

Ed Galloway spent his retirement years building a unique monument to the American Indian known as **Totem Pole Park**. The totem poles inside don't look like any you've seen before. These are made from stones and concrete, lumpy but colorful, ranging in size from petite to over 90 feet tall. The largest pole sits atop a giant turtle and served as an observation tower from which to look out over the plains. Birds, coyotes and squirrels cavort on these brightly colored poles. Totem poles, however, weren't Ed's only obsessions. So were violins. This unlikely duo shared Ed's imagination and you'll be astounded when you see inside the 11-sided Fiddle House. Violins line every wall, hundreds of them. Some are works of art, delicately inlaid with designs and patterns. Others are made from hundreds of tiny pieces of wood. These delicate instruments are quite a contrast to the chunky totem poles outside.

> **Totem Pole Park**, SH 28A, 4 miles E of Foyil, OK; ✎ 918 287 4803; web: www.claremore.org/historicalsociety/totem.htm. *Admission free; donations accepted.*

Museums and collections

Oklahoma is tornado territory and it's where the movie *Twister* was filmed. It's inevitable, this being America, that some enterprising soul would find value in the debris and memorabilia left over after the filming. At the **Twister Museum** in Wakita, they saved some furnishings from Aunt Meg's home, the Elm Street sign used in the movie and a windmill sculpture from Aunt Meg's front yard. Residents have plans to develop a Twister Park across the street, but for now you'll have to be content with pictures of the storefronts and houses used as sets for the movie. They're displayed on pedestals in front of the now mostly empty lots.

> **Twister Museum**, 101 Main St, Wakita, OK 73771; ✎ 580 594 2312

The National Cowboy & Western Heritage Museum is a tribute to the men and women who contributed so much to America's cultural heritage. This huge facility features enormous art, such as a 16,000lb white marble cougar and an 18-foot sculpture called End of the Trail, as well as a turn-of-the-century Western town, a rodeo gallery and galleries devoted to firearms and Western performers.

> **National Cowboy & Western Heritage Museum**, 1700 NE 63rd St, Oklahoma City, OK 73111; ✎ 405 478 2250; web: www.nationalcowboymuseum.org. *Open daily 9.00am–5.00pm. Closed Thanksgiving, New Years, and Christmas Day.*

Leonardo's Discovery Warehouse in Enid is an unusual museum devoted to hands-on experiences in the arts and sciences. You can build your own castle in the carpentry shop, get lost in a warren of tunnels, bridges, and mazes, fly to the moon in a simulated space shuttle, dig for fossils, and plunge down a three-story-high slide.

Leonardo's Discovery Warehouse, 200 E Maple, Enid, OK 73701; ↘
580 233 2787; fax: 580 237 7574; web: www.leonardos.org. *Open
Tue–Sat 10.00am–5.00pm, Sun 2.00–5.00pm.*

A 70-acre open-air museum, **Muscle Car Ranch** is devoted to souped-up cars,
antique auto signs, vintage motorcycles and classic Mack trucks. The Ranch hosts
a huge annual Car Swap Meet that attracts collectors from all over the world. The
site itself is an early 1900s' dairy farm with all the original barns providing a novel
backdrop for the cars and trucks.

Muscle Car Ranch, 3609 S 16th, Chickasha, OK 73108; ↘ 405 222
4910; web: www.musclecarranch.com. *Open Mon–Fri 8.00am–5.00pm or
by appointment. Admission free; donations accepted.*

Almost every American over the age of 40 can remember movie stars flicking
open their Zippo lighter in such a way that its flame illuminated the emotion of
the moment. The **National Lighter Museum** in Guthrie has hundreds of old
lighters from table models to pocket ones, from Zippos to Ronsons and from
85,000-year-old fire-starters to modern plastic flicks. The museum's mission is
to preserve the history of the evolution of lighters, and to that end they've given
the plain old lighter a more politically correct name: the 'mechanical pyrotechnic
apparatus'. Thirty thousand such apparatuses are in this museum, which is
owned by Ted and Pat Ballard; they live next door to the biggest collection of
fire-starters in the world. If Ballard can't convince someone to keep their
lighters, then he wants to buy them for his collection. If he had his way, he'd
have everyone looking through their basements and attics for the things,
especially the ones used for advertising or to commemorate special occasions.
Years ago, lighters were as common as pens and pencils, and Ted thinks their
heritage is too important to lose.

National Lighter Museum, 5715 S Sooner Rd, Guthrie, OK 73044; ↘
405 282 3025; web: www.natlitrmus.com. *Best to call for an appointment
if you want to be sure they're home.*

Besides the museums described above, Oklahoma is home to a variety of other
off-the-wall collections and halls of fame. The **Percussive Art Society
Museum** in Lawton displays only percussion (striking) instruments from
around the world. The **Gene Autry Museum** in the town that bears his name
honors the famous Old West cowboy-movie and television star. College and
Olympic wrestling is the theme at the **National Wrestling Hall of Fame and
Museum** in Stillwater. The original sod house built in 1894 is furnished and
preserved at the **Sod House Museum** in Aline. In Shattuck is an outdoor
display of rare and restored windmills at the **Shattuck Windmill Museum
and Park**. The **99s Museum of Women Pilots** in Oklahoma City honors past
and present female aviators. A museum that focuses on the people who lived,
worked, and traveled America's mother road, the **Route 66 Museum** in Elk
City, takes you along the road through eight states. The **National Four String
Banjo Hall of Fame Museum** in Guthrie is for and about nothing but banjos,
banjo recordings and banjo players.

The Percussive Art Society Museum, 701 NW Ferris Ave, Lawton,
OK 73507-5442; ↘ 580 351 1455; fax: 580 353 1456; web: www.pas.org.
Open Mon–Fri 8.00am–5.00pm, Sat–Sun 1.00–4.00pm.

Gene Autry Oklahoma Museum, 601 Praire St, Gene Autry, OK
73436; ↘ 580 294 3047; web: www.cow-boy.com/museum.htm. *Open
Mon–Sat 10.00am–4.00pm. Admission free.*

National Wrestling Hall of Fame and Museum, 405 W Hall of Fame
Ave, Stillwater, OK 74075; ↘ 405 377 5243; fax: 405 377 5244; web:
www.wrestlinghalloffame.org. *Open Mon–Fri 9.00am–4.00pm. Admission
free.*

Sod House Museum, State Hwy 8 S, Aline, OK 73716; ↘ 580 463 2441.
Open Tue–Fri 9.00am–5.00pm, Sat–Sun 2.00–5.00pm. Admission free.

Shattuck Windmill Museum and Park, 1100 S Main, Shattuck, OK
73858; ↘ 580 938 2818; web: www.shattuckwindmillmuseum.org. *Open
daily, outdoor exhibit.*

99s Museum of Women Pilots, 4300 Amelia Earhart Rd, Oklahoma
City, OK 73159; ↘ 405 685 9990; web: www.ninety-
nines.org/museum.html. *Open Tue–Thu 10.00am–4.00pm. Please call
before visiting.*

National Route 66 Museum, US 66 and Pioneer Rd, PO Box 542, Elk
City, OK 73648; ↘ 580 225 6266; web: www.elkcitychamber.com/
route66.asp. *Open Mon–Sat 9.00am–5.00pm, Sun 2.00–5.00pm.*

National Four String Banjo Museum and Hall of Fame, The
International Banjo College, 116 E Oklahoma Ave, Guthrie, OK 73044;
↘ 405 260 1323; web: www.banjomuseum.com. *Open Tue–Sat
10.00am–5.00pm.*

MISSOURI
Festivals and events
Mark Twain made Hannibal, Missouri famous. On **Tom Sawyer Days** they have
fence-painting contests for pre-teens and adults, a Tom and Becky competition
that is only for pre-teens and, of course, frog-jumping contests.

Tom Sawyer Days, held annually in July in Hannibal, MO. Contact
Hannibal Jaycees, PO Box 484, Hannibal, MO 63401; web:
www.hannibaljaycees.org/tomsawyer.htm

Museums and collections
With more than a million marbles, Cathy Runyan-Svacina and her husband Larry
aren't in any danger of losing theirs anytime soon. But they do keep their collection
in a safe place: the newly opened **Marble Room** at the **Toy and Miniature
Museum** of Kansas City. Cathy, known as the Marble Lady, may be obsessive
about the smooth, glittering orbs but she manages to keep a balanced perspective
on their role in the universe. She wears a T-Shirt proclaiming, 'Life is Marbelous.
Play It For Keeps', and takes her 'Shoot Marbles, Not Drugs' program into schools.
    Their collection of one million marbles (they stopped counting at the million
mark) refers to only those considered collectible. The common, non-collectible
variety end up imbedded in their concrete walkway, used for speaking
engagements, or simply given away to those they encourage to be playing with
them. The first woman to represent America in international competition, Cathy
organized, according to Guinness, the largest marble tournament ever held in
Missouri. Over the past 25 years she's taught over a million kids and adults how to

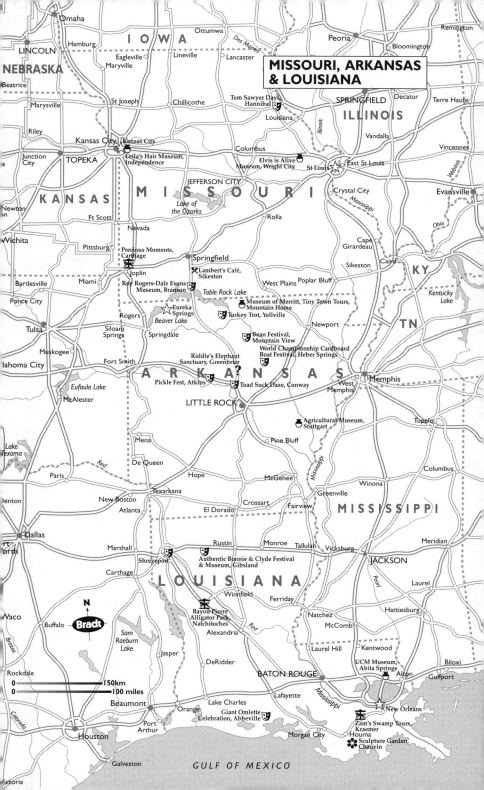

play the game. Before the museum opened, she and Larry kept the collection in their home. Moving it into the museum took a horse trailer and a 50-car caravan of helpers.

Marble Room, located at the Toy and Miniature Museum, 5235 Oak St, Kansas City, MO 64112; ↘ 816 333 2055; web: www.umkc.edu/tmm/. *Open Wed–Sat 10.00am–4.00pm. Closed major holidays and the two weeks following Labor Day.*

Roy Rogers, the famous King of the Cowboys, liked to save things and his famous horse, Trigger, was one of the things he saved. Displayed at the Roy Rogers-Dale Evans Museum in Branson, Trigger knew more than 100 tricks, including opening gates, dancing the rhumba, and refraining from lifting his tail indoors. When the horse died at 33 years of age, Roy had him mounted in his most famous position: rearing up on his hind legs. You can see him (Trigger, that is) in all his glory at the museum, which houses the memories and treasures of some of America's most beloved icons. The Roy and Dale husband and wife duo was noted for its clean-cut, all-American movies and television shows. Every child of the 1940s and 1950s knew their theme songs, 'Happy Trails' and 'Tumbling Tumbleweeds'. Their images, along with Trigger's, appeared on hundreds of Western toys, hobbyhorses and lunchboxes. The museum is filled with memories and mementos of the spirit of the West, including his showy Pontiac Bonneville car with its tooled leather interior, coins imbedded in the upholstery, guns for handles and rifles on the hood.

Roy Rogers-Dale Evans Museum, 3950 Green Mountain Dr, Branson, MO 65616; ↘ 417 339 1900 (24-hour recording) or 417 339 1925; web: www.royrogers.com. *Open daily 9.00am–6.00pm. Closed Easter, Thanksgiving, Christmas.*

Inquiring minds want to know: Did Elvis ever really leave the building? According to Bill Beeny, 75, curator of the **Elvis is Alive Museum**, the King is alive, well, and living peaceably out of the limelight. How can he prove it? DNA, of course. It seems, according to Bill, that samples from Elvis don't match up with samples from the body they buried in his place. It also seems that the real Lisa Marie Presley was placed in a foster home and a fake Lisa Marie brought in at age 18 to sign over her wealth to Priscilla. The fake Lisa also married Michael Jackson. (Don't quibble about details, just accept the facts.) Bill has several theories as to why Elvis is alive and why he's hiding from the world. Prime among them is that Elvis was a secret FBI informer who had to fake his death and/or that he was working undercover for the Drug Enforcement Agency, exposed a mob drug ring, and had to fake his death to save his life. Besides, he was tired of all the hype and just wanted to live out the rest of his live in peace and quiet. (Yea, that Elvis certainly could blend right into a crowd.) This tiny museum, where you can buy a roll of Elvis toilet paper, is a shrine to Beeny's convictions, loaded with evidence that the King lives. Elvis sightings are well documented, and Elvis' wax figure, lying in a coffin, suggest that a dummy was buried in the King's place.

Elvis is Alive Museum & Restaurant, I 70 exit, Wright City, MO; ↘ 636 745 3107. *Open Mon–Sat 10.00am–5.00pm.*

Back before cameras could record family history, it wasn't unusual for family hair to be woven into keepsakes like rings, necklaces, bracelets, brooches, hat-pins, bookmarks, and cuff links. Multiple generations, as well as happy occasions, were memorialized in elaborate hair wreathes and woven hair art. Sometimes a hair ring would be sent to a friend or relative who couldn't attend the funeral of a loved one. **Leila's Hair Museum** in Independence displays the collection that the cosmetology school owner has been collecting for 40 years. Once she got hooked on hair art, now a lost craft, she had to stash her purchases out of sight of her husband so he wouldn't know how much she was spending. Coming out of the closet with the museum in 1992, she doesn't regret the time or money she's spent. It's been a labor of love.

> **Leila's Hair Museum**, 815 W 23rd, Independence, MO 64055; ↘ 816 252 HAIR; web: www.hairwork.com/leila

It's hard to know where to begin in a place that has no end. The **City Museum** in St Louis is – all at once – an outrageous environment, an innovative event and a madcap museum that has everyone behaving as if they're kids. The museum grabs children at the entrance and lets them loose only when they've reluctantly admitted they've had enough stimulation for the day. For grown-ups, it's an irresistible opportunity to shed the confines of maturity and just play along. It's like a giant erector set; a warehouse of wacky adventures and outlandish events waiting to happen. Founded by Bob Cassilly, a delightful rebel who needed a bigger playpen for his toys, this three-floor museum gives him the freedom to create whatever his fertile imagination propels him to do. For instance, the entire museum is built with recycled materials, including the concrete, the bricks, the rooftops and even the sidewalks. Two thousand steel squirrel-cages line the exterior bathroom walls. The Brontosaurus staircase banisters are made of conveyor-belt rollers. An enormous whale has ribs of scrap-metal shelving units while recycled water from the aquarium comes crashing down into caves to the delight of squealing children. In the restaurant, mosaics are created from springs, plastic watchbands, pencils, shells and floor sweepings from industrial plants. Aside from this astonishing visual assault, a jumble of startling experiences await. Kids disappear into a whale's mouth only to reappear over the aquarium. A dinosaur with a staircase on its back leads upwards to the upper floors; you come down in a slide shoot, which is a lot more fun. A maze-like network of caves is crawling with kids; in fact, anyone can crawl through anything in this place, as long as you can fit through. There are tunnels, secret passageways, waterfalls, streams, an enchanted forest, a crawl-through bird's nest and a jungle gym of ropes and screens. Quirky events spring up all around you: an everyday, interactive circus, life-size chess and checkers games, recycled art workshops, an express mini-train, a toddler mini city with chalk and magnetic walls and a youth city where kids from ages three through eight play in gravel pits with trucks, tools, and blocks. Then there are the special events, like the annual Fiber Day, when hairdressers and pet groomers harvest human and animal hair to weave into rugs and art. The Really Big Shoe Show showcased what happens when you tell 50 artists to have a go at it: a shoe of nails made a political statement about women's footwear; while an 18-foot, one-and-a-half-ton stiletto pump, made of 2,000 cast aluminum pumps, was big enough to stand in. Every visit is different, stirring up activity and energy you didn't know you had. Interactive without computers or electronics of any kind, the City Museum is an experiential breath of fresh air in a world of entertainment given over to virtual reality. It's the real thing.

> **City Museum**, 701 N 15th St, St Louis, MO; ↘ 314 231 2489; web: www.citymuseum.org. *Hours vary seasonally.*

Attractions

Collectors of the angelic Precious Moments bisque porcelain figurines will be enchanted by the **Precious Moments** chapel complex near Carthage. If you're not a collector, you can't help but be impressed by this shrine to the work of artist Sam Butcher who combines art and ministry while producing some of the world's most popular collectibles. The Chapel Center has overtones of Las Vegas; it's an eccentric attraction designed to part you from your money while making you feel good about doing it. The chapel itself has 52 biblical murals, 30 stained-glass windows, and bronze relief panels all done in the Precious Moments art style. The Fountain of Angels Show is pure glitz, with one of the world's largest show fountains featuring 252 bronze sculptures made by Butcher. Victorian Wedding Island sits on a lake in a storybook setting that would give any Vegas chapel a run for its money. A honeymoon mansion and bridal cottage nestle near by. To make you feel really, really romantic, the aroma of freshly baked bread and pastries emanate from the Royal Delights Café and Sammy's Sweet Shoppe. Naturally, there's a convenient gift shop. You can even sleep in the complex at the Best Western Precious Moments Hotel decorated, of course, with Precious Moments art. The place is so large that it offers a shuttle service to take you from place to place. With half a million collectors worldwide, it's obvious that art, ministry and manufacturing can go well together.

> **Precious Moments**, 4321 Chapel Rd, Carthage, MO 64836; ↘ 800 543 7975; web: www.preciousmoments.com

Just plain weird

Talk about leaving a lasting impression! You've just got to check out the **J Stephen Memorial Restroom** at Waldo's Pizza in Kansas City. This audaciously bold farewell gesture was supposed to be Joe's swan song, a way for his pizza-slinging days to be remembered in the employee bathroom after he'd quit to seek fame and fortune in California. The idea germinated when Joe, suffering from a bought of the flu, got a fever-enhanced vision for the memorial bathroom. Thinking his idea was brilliant, if not quite mad, he set about gathering mementos of his not-very-distinguished life, framing them, and then making up museum-type placards describing his egocentric flotsam. His next challenge was to covertly mount the exhibits so as not to alert his boss as to his intentions. Enlisting the help of fellow employees, he got the memorial installed by having his cohorts distract the boss during Joe's going-away party. When the boss used the restroom the next day, he had what Joe describes as a 'humorously surreal experience'. The exhibits stayed put and evolved, according to Joe, 'like a virus in a Petri dish'. His friends added things like a biography, a newspaper clipping lauding Joe's candidacy for Waiter of the Year, a polka dot floor, fluorescent ceiling, disco balls and hot-pepper Xmas lights. Today it remains an entertaining chronicle of an ordinary, if eccentric, man's life. And Joe is back at his old job, having added a pair of singing fish, a doorbell, a fountain and a library to his memorial restroom.

> **J Stephen Memorial Restroom**, located at Waldo Pizza, 7433 Broadway, Kansas City, MO 64114; ↘ 816 363 5242. *Optimal viewing times Sun–Thu 2.00–4.00pm. Offerings for the shrine appreciated.*

Quirky cuisine

The hot rolls flying through the air astound people eating at **Lambert's Café** for the first time. It all started back in 1976 when the owner got tired of saying, over and over, 'Would you care for a hot roll?' One day a customer called out to her,

'Just throw the damn thing.' She did, and everyone else joined in. They've been throwin' 'em ever since, an average of more than two million a year. The 'Home of the Throwed Rolls' is also famous for its hubcap cinnamon rolls. There are two locations in Missouri: Sikeston and Ozark as well as one in Foley, AL.

> **Lambert's Café**, 1800 W Hwy J, Ozark, MO 65721; ➤ 417 581 7655, also 2515 E Malone, Sikeston, MO 63801; ➤ 573 471 4261, and 2981 S McKenzie, Foley, AL 36535; ➤ 334 943 7655; web: www.throwedrolls.com

ARKANSAS
Festivals and events

Bill Clinton's home state puts on some very strange events, the most notorious of which is the **Yellville Turkey Trot**. To understand the history of this event you need to know that wild turkeys can fly and domestic turkeys cannot. When the festival started decades ago in this tiny town (pop 2,000), they threw live wild turkeys off the courthouse roof in a turkey-shooting contest. Then someone got the bright idea of tossing the turkeys out of a low-flying airplane and the so-called Turkey Shoot took on a whole new life. Eventually the animal rights people got wind of this, the tabloids had a field day and, by the 1980s, the shooting had pretty much stopped and the chasing had begun. As the turkeys landed, the sport became to capture them so you had people running all over the place trying to catch their trophy turkey. Today, of course, the chamber won't include the airborne turkeys in their schedule of events, but the practice mysteriously persists. This is a big weekend in Yellville, with parades, bands, and pageants galore. The Turkey Trot is famous for its renowned turkey-calling contest along with the Miss Drumsticks beauty contest that is judged by seeing only the legs of the girls lined up on stage. A Lip Sync contest, a Turkey Trot race and a turkey dinner round out the festivities. Expect crowds; 20,000 folks show up for this festival.

(A popular sitcom TV show of the 1970s, *WKRP in Cincinnati*, did a spoof of the event, the premise being that the fictional radio station would drop Thanksgiving turkeys, domestic of course, as a charitable gesture. The publicity stunt went down in a hail of feathers and screaming children, the turkeys hitting the ground like sacks of wet cement.)

> **Yellville Turkey Trot**, held annually in October in Yellville, AR. Contact Yellville Area Chamber of Commerce, PO Box 369, Yellville, AR 72687; ➤ 800 832 1414 or 870 449 4676; web: www.yellville.com

The highlight of the **Mountain View Bean Festival** in October is the championship outhouse race. Following – appropriately – a free beans-onion-cornbread feed, the bizarrely bedecked outhouse toilets are paraded through the streets. Once the prizes for most original outhouse and best costumes are handed out, the outhouses compete in a drag race by being pulled, not pushed, along the racecourse by two-person teams. The frolic continues with a Tall Tale Telling Contest and a Talent Competition.

> **Mountain View Bean Festival**, held annually in October in Mountain View, AR. Contact Mountain View Area Chamber of Commerce, ➤ 870 269 8068; web: www.mountainviewcc.org

You only have to know how to swim to compete in the **World Championship Cardboard Boat Festival** in July. The boats, which can be of any shape and design, have to be constructed entirely of cardboard, glue and duct tape. Then they're painted and waterproofed and the costumed skippers try to stay afloat for 200 yards using any form of human propulsion. The first boat to cross the finish line wins regardless of how much time it takes its crew to get there. The Titanic award is given for the most spectacular sinking. It looks as wacky as it sounds.

> **World Championship Cardboard Boat Festival**, held annually in July in Heber Springs, AR. Contact the Heber Springs Chamber of Commerce, 1001 W Main St, Heber Springsb AR 72543; ↘ 800 774 3237 or 501 362 2444; web: www.heber-springs.com

At Conway's **Toad Suck Daze**, the Toad Master, sporting a bright green jacket, jump-starts the festivities with a baby crawl race. Then the toad store opens and it's time to select the your little toad jock for the frog jumping contest. With proper care and training, your toad may win you a fleeting moment of fame. The secret is in the crickets: a few of those tasty morsels before the race gets the old toad blood-sugar going. After their tour of duty, all participating toads are carefully returned to their habitat. Frog legs aren't on the menu, but food on a stick is. If it can be eaten with your hands, or put on a stick, you'll find someone selling it at Toad Suck Daze. A Tour de Toad bike race and a Mardi Daze parade round out the festivities. Be sure to hear the Toad Suck Drum and Kazoo Corps play 'When the Toads Go Marching In'. The Toad Suck event got its name in reference to the boatmen who refreshed themselves so copiously at the local tavern that they were said to suck on the bottle 'til they swelled up like toads'. Anyone for alligator on a stick?

> **Toad Suck Daze**, held annually in May in Conway, AR. Contact Conway Area Chamber of Commerce, 900 Oak St, Conway, AR 72032; ↘ 501 327 7788; fax: 501 327 7788; web: www.toadsuck.org

Eccentric environments

If you think living in a lumber shed with five children is tough, try living in a chicken house. Tired of her husband's procrastination in building her a decent house, Elsie Quigley tore down the shed they were living in when hubby wasn't home and moved the whole family into the chicken house. That got his attention and he started building her the 'castle' she'd designed years earlier. Elsie was a flower child long before the hippies of the 1960s adopted the name and she'd been collecting rocks since childhood. She used those rocks to cover the entire exterior of the abode. Over the next 50 years she added more rocks, covering benches, ponds and bird baths, and planted 400 flower varieties in her garden. Tropical plants grow in the soil on the ground floor inside the house. She even found an ingenious way to sleep in the treetops. By far, **Quigley's Castle** is the Ozark's strangest dwelling; it also houses Mrs Quigley's extraordinary collections of butterflies, fossils, crystals, arrowheads and glassware.

> **Quigley's Castle Ark**, 23 S Eureka Springs, AR; ↘ 501 253 8311; web: www.quigleyscastle.com. *Open Mon–Wed, Fri–Sat 8.30am–5.00pm Apr 1–Oct 31.*

Museums and collections

They're obviously big on frogs in these parts and Louise Mesa has 7,000 of the knick-knack kind at her **Frog Fantasies Museum** in Eureka Springs. This ever-expanding collection represents 60 years' worth of collecting. The Frog Lady, as she is known, hosts conventions for frog enthusiasts. Fifty to 100 of the country's more than 5,000 frogophiles convene annually to buy, sell and trade their Kermit brethren. It's a chance to show off your finest in frog-wear and jewelry and to spend time with peers who share a fascination with these creatures. When you ask her the obvious question – 'Why?' – she'll tell you all about the mythological and literary history of the frog. It has been a symbol of prosperity, wealth and abundance in many cultures; and a symbol of fertility in others. No wonder there are so many frog collectors.

Frog Fantasies Museum, 151 Spring St, Eureka Springs, AR; ↘ 479 253 7227; web: www.frogfantasies.com

The **Stuttgart Agricultural Museum** has one of the most bizarre coats you'll ever see: a coat made entirely of duck heads. That's right, duck heads. The late Ruby Abel, two-time women's world champion duck caller and professional duck dresser, saved 450 of the mallard heads she'd chopped off at work. She painstakingly skinned them, tanned the hides, and hand stitched them together to make a coat. Ruby actually wore the thing while appearing as a contestant on television's *What's My Line* game show in the 1960s. A fetching duck-feather hat completed her ensemble. Not even Madonna could have dreamed this one up.

Stuttgart Agricultural Museum, 921 E 4th, Stuttgart, AR 72160; ↘ 870 673 7001. *Open Tue–Sat 10.00am–4.00pm. Closed Sun, Mon and legal holidays.*

Tedna Merritt knows a lot about little things. Over a period of 60 years she's amassed one of the largest private collections of miniatures in the world – more than 100,000, including a 19-room replica of Tara, the famous *Gone With the Wind* plantation house and a bake shop with food made from buttons. At her **Museum of Merritt**, **Tiny Town Tours**, in the tiny town of Mountain Home, she also offers her poetry and art work free for the asking.

Museum of Merritt, Tiny Town Tours, 2113 Hwy 62 East, Mountain Home, AR 72653; ↘ 870 425 4979. *Open Mon–Fri 10.00am–4.00pm, Sat & Sun by appointment.*

Attractions

A six-story-tall King Kong, holding a life-size Fay Ray, greets you at **Dinosaur World** near Beaver Dam, the largest dinosaur park in the world. By largest, they're referring to the setting: about 70 acres of meadow and lake. Dotted randomly throughout the park are about a hundred life-size, concrete dinosaurs along with a few cavemen thrown in for anthropological atmosphere. About the only thing that's 'actual' about these creatures is their size. Their bright colors are a reflection of the theory that dinosaurs could see color and thus might have been colorful themselves. It's a very strange Kodak moment.

Dinosaur World, located on Hwy 187, 8 miles west of Eureka Springs, AR; ↘ 479 253 8113; web: www.dinosaurworld.info. *Open daily 7.00am–7.00pm Apr–Oct; daily 9.00am–4.00pm Nov–Dec.*

All aboard the soul tram for a guided, narrated tour of the **New Holy Land** in Eureka Springs, complete with the only known, life-sized, fully furnished reproduction of Moses' Tabernacle in the Wilderness. The driver communicates with exhibit guides by walkie-talkie, saying such things as 'Holy Land to Simon Peter, we're nearing the Sea of Galilee.' Costumed guides enthusiastically portray key biblical characters. Each of the 40 exhibits and settings is 'authentically' replicated with historical accuracy, but you'll have to judge for yourself how successful they've been at achieving this. A Bible Museum and Sacred Arts Center complete the complex.

New Holy Land Tours, PO Box 471, Eureka Springs, AR 72632; ↘ 479 253 8559; web: www.greatpassionplay.com. *Tours leave every 15 minutes Mon–Sat beginning at 9.00am.*

Riddle's Elephant Sanctuary is a pachyderm paradise. Serving as a cross between an orphanage and a rest home for stray and unwanted elephants, Riddle's takes in any elephant regardless of previous health or behavioral problems. Owners Scott and Heidi Riddle are passionate about protecting and expanding the number of Indian and Asian elephants in the sanctuary. Besides caring for these gentle creatures, they offer a two-week school in elephant management and care, as well as weekend elephant treks through the Ozarks. The Elephant Experience Weekend has you feeding, watering, bathing and perhaps even trimming the toenails of these gentle, giant creatures. Mary, an Asian elephant, even paints pictures.

Riddle's Elephant Sanctuary, PO Box 715, Greenbrier, AR 72058; ↘ 479 589 3291; web: www.elephantsanctuary.org

Quirkyville

Eureka Springs is the name, quirky is its game. The town, referred to as 'the place where misfits fit' by the *New York Times*, is where 'Woodstock meets livestock meets Birkenstock meets the stock market'. An authentic 1900s Victorian town nestled in the Ozarks, it plays host to almost a million tourists a year. There are no traffic lights, no streets that cross at right-angles, and so many hills that one hotel had a different address for each of its four floors. The town boasts an above-average number of psychics, palm readers, tarot card readers, white witches, hypnotists, astrologists and other new-age types. It's not unusual to see some of the town's 25 massage therapists setting up shop in the city parks. It's also host to an annual UFO Conference and a Dowser's Convention. More than 4,000 wedding licenses are issued each year in the 'town that lovers love'. You can get married in a treehouse, on horseback, or in an all-glass chapel in the woods. They claim to have more bed and breakfast inns than any other city or town in the country. They even elected a dead mayor, a candidate who died before the election; the townsfolk were so disenchanted with the alternative candidates that they voted for the deceased anyway. Past mayor, Beau Satori, who is very much alive, will happily tie his below-the-waist ponytail into a bun and take you on a tour of the town. You can also take an historic haunted mansions and cemeteries tour.

Eureka Springs is located in the Ozarks region of Arkansas. Contact Eureka Springs Chamber of Commerce Visitors Information Center, 137-B W Van Buren, Eureka Springs, AR 72632; ↘ 479 253 8737; fax: 479 253 5037; web: www.eurekaspringschamber.com

LOUISIANA
Quirkyville: New Orleans

New Orleans is where America kicks off its shoes and lets its hair down. Unlike the corporate eccentricity of Las Vegas, New Orleans is genuinely oddball, with behavior ranging from peculiar to outrageous; from quirky to preposterous; and from madcap to downright loony. Where else can one million people party like there's no tomorrow, face themselves in the mirror the next day, then go out and do it all over again when tomorrow comes? Even on an ordinary day, New Orleans looks like a carnival. It's the only city in America, besides Las Vegas, with no closing laws. Stay out as late as you like, for you'll always have company. Eat as much as you wish, for good food is cherished here and never eaten in a rush. The most European in feeling of American cities, it's a vast stew of curious religions, secretive societies and delightfully daft characters. N'awlins, as it's properly pronounced, prizes itself on idiosyncrasy. With 3,000 bars, 41 cemeteries and 700 churches, it's a mixture of Disneyland, Times Square and a religious tent revival. If America were to select one city as its national theme park, New ORR-le-ins, the only other correct pronunciation, would likely win hands down.

Festivals and events

Mardi Gras is the biggest bash in North America. Carnival season begins on January 6 and goes through Fat Tuesday, the day before the start of the austere Lenten season. Mardi Gras also refers to the last two weeks of carnival when 60 parades take place morning, noon and night. Two of the biggest parades alone involve five dozen marching bands, 250 floats and units and 2,300 'krewe' members throwing, literally, millions and millions of trinkets to the crowd. Spectators jostle for position, crying out 'Throw me something, mister!'

Mardi Gras has its own unique vocabulary. 'Krewes' are private membership societies that throw elaborate carnival parades and masked balls, many costing upwards of $100,000. The 'throws' they toss include cups, beads and medallions with the krewe's logo and motto. Costumed float riders are called 'masquers'. The strange-sounding krewe names, like Proteus and Bacchus, are mostly taken from mythology. Each krewe goes to great lengths to keep its theme a secret, and being chosen king or queen to reign over a krewe's parade is a great honor. A 200-member krewe might have up to 3,000 participants, including band members, dance teams, clowns and other costumed groups.

> **Mardi Gras**, events held January through March; web:
> www.mardigrasneworleans.com

Don't even try to make sense of Mardi Gras without **Arthur Hardy's Mardi Gras Guide**, an indispensable companion to parade goers for 24 years. You can buy a copy practically anywhere in the city.

Attractions

New Orleans is famous for music, with jazz, rhythm and blues, new-age rock and gospel all playing an important role in its culture. The historic Storyville district got its name from one Sidney Story, a city councilman who proposed zoning the district for houses of ill repute. Mr Story thought it would be best to keep the red-light district all in once place so such businesses wouldn't bring down property values in other parts of the city. Well, it became America's first red-music district; the first place where European brass and African drums mixed it up. The brothels, dancehalls and clubs were filled with the new sound of jazz and Storyville became a notorious night and day hot spot.

You'll hear music coming from most every doorway, even from the bowling alley. At **Mid-City Lanes Rock 'n' Bowl**, the air is filled with the sounds of rolling balls, falling pins, crashing drums and honking saxophones. Rock 'n' Bowl started quite by accident. Owner John Blanchard's bowling alley was facing a bleak future when he decided to book a band for the weekend. People started dancing even while they were bowling and John decided that offbeat was the secret. Today, there's a full bar, good food like fried alligator sausage and New Orleans street scenes painted on the walls. On St Patrick's Day he offers Shamrock and Bowl; Thanksgiving is Pluck and Bowl. An Elvis impersonator emerges from behind the pins in a cloud of smoke twice each year, once on Elvis' birthday and once on his 'deathday'.

> **Mid-City Lanes Rock 'n' Bowl**, 4133 Carrolton Ave, New Orleans, LA;
> ℄ 504 482 3133; web: www.rockandbowl.com

A tour of **Blaine Kern's Mardi Gras World** takes you behind the scenes where artists, painters and sculptors work in full view all year long creating the sensational props, costumes and giant figures that make the festival so colorfully flamboyant. After seeing a historical video of the spectacle, you can gaze in amazement at the costumes and floats and even dress up in costume yourself. This is a definite Kodak moment.

> **Blaine Kern's Mardi Gras World**, 233 Newton St, New Orleans, LA
> 70114; ℄ 800 362 8213 or ℄ 504 361 7821; web:
> www.mardigrasworld.com

Tours

New Orleans sits an average of five feet below sea level, which makes being buried six feet under an almost impossible task. In the days before they built above-ground tombs, holes would have to be drilled in the underside of a coffin so gravediggers, armed with poles, could push the casket down into the muck before it floated to the surface. This gruesome practice was thankfully dispensed with when elaborate mausoleums began to be constructed topside instead.

A **Cities of the Dead Cemetery Tour** is an absolute must and is one of the most fascinating excursions offered in the city. There are 42 cemeteries, with Metairie Cemetery considered the most varied and unique. It is also home to the tallest privately owned monument in the country, its 85-foot height making it visible from the freeway. It was built by Daniel Moriarty who wanted his wife buried where she could look down on the blue bloods who had snubbed her during her life.

> **Cities of the Dead Cemetery Tours**. Contact Save Our Cemeteries;
> ℄ 888 721 7493 or 504 525 3377; web: www.saveourcemeteries.org

In the mid-19th century, voodoo was all the rage, much like today's new-age movement. Brought here by the slaves, voodoo has many variations involving strange and exotic ceremonies. Numerous **voodo tours**, guaranteed not to be run-of-the-mill experiences, take you into this mysterious and secretive world of sorcery, curses and black magic. 'Mojos' (good luck charms) along with dead bits of reptiles, birds, animals and humans are still used today as part of voodoo rituals designed to fix that problematic someone or something. With names like the

Mourning Tour, the Voodoo/Cemetery tour, the Tour of the Undead and the Singing Bones Tour, you're sure to remember these spooky experiences.

Bloody Marys Tours, ↘ 504 915 7774; web: www.bloodymarystours.com

New Orleans Spirit Tours, ↘ 866 314 1224 or 504 314 0806; web: www.neworleanstours.net

Historic New Orleans Tours, ↘ 504 947 2120; web: www.tourneworleans.com

Haunted History Tours, ↘ 504 861 2727; web: www.hauntedhistorytours.com

Museums and collections
The **Historic Voodoo Museum** is a small, comprehensive museum of voodoo lore and memorabilia. A tour through the crowded rooms yields all manner of altars, statues, masks, dolls and potions, plus an opportunity to buy Gris Gris bags, concoctions meant to bring success in love or work, or perhaps get rid of a pesky neighbor. Sports fans buy the bags in hopes of bringing salvation to their losing teams. Curator John Martin offers specialized readings by appointment in his third-floor temple but you need to be prepared to hang out with his uncaged reptiles, a 260lb, 18-foot python and a smaller albino one, just 60lb and nine feet long.

Historic Voodoo Museum, 724 Rue Dumaine, New Orleans, LA 70116; ↘ 504 581 3824; web: www.voodoomuseum.com

Quirky quarters
The **Dive Inn Guest House** in New Orleans has aquatic-themed rooms with toilets situated in outlandish places such as in a phone booth or a shower. This six-room, off-the-wall establishment has a swimming pool in the lobby.

Dive Inn Guest House, 4417 Dryades St, New Orleans, LA 70115; ↘ 888 788 DIVE or 504 895 6555; web: www.thediveinn.com

Louisiana, outside of New Orleans
Festivals and events
Bonnie and Clyde, the bank robber lovebirds, met their maker near Gibsland. The town celebrates their infamous fame and couplehood at the **Authentic Bonnie and Clyde Festival and Museum** with reenactments of both the FBI ambush and the duo's death scene. The bad guys are perpetually more popular than the FBI and their bandit memorabilia is more in demand than that of the good guys.

Authentic Bonnie and Clyde Festival and Museum, held annually on the weekend nearest May 23. Hwy 154, Gibsland, LA; ↘ 318 843 6141. Contact Sharon Washington at email: townofgibsland@lausa.net. *Museum open by appointment.*

Eccentric environments
Feeling no need to show his work to the world, recluse bricklayer Kenny Hill quietly transformed his bayou property into an environment densely packed with more than a hundred concrete sculptures. A riot of Cajun colors, his **Chauvin Sculpture Garden** is an odd achievement, evidence of a man driven to sculpt

fantastical figures and creatures mostly inspired by the Bible. Dozens of figures cling to the outside of a 45-foot-tall brick lighthouse: soldiers, cowboys, images of God and of Kenny Hill himself. Angels are everywhere, lifting and guiding. In 2000, after a decade of work, Kenny had a dispute with his landlord and simply abandoned the property, leaving a sign 'Hell is here. Welcome'.

> **Chauvin Sculpture Garden**, located near Chauvin in Terrebonne Parish, about 90 minutes south of New Orleans. Web: www.kohlerfoundation.org/chauvin.html. Contact the NSU Folk Art Studio at ➤ 985 594 2546 or Prof Donald Sipiorski at ➤ 985 448 4595 to arrange a tour.

Five thousand eggs makes for a pretty awesome omelette. At Abbeville's **Giant Omelette Celebration**, they cook up a big one each year to celebrate their French heritage and their membership in a worldwide fraternity of cultural exchange cities known as the confrerie. Every year foreign representatives from member cities are knighted as chefs to help prepare the Cajun-style omelette that is eaten by happy spectators. Besides the eggs, the omelette takes 50lb of onions, two gallons of parsley, six-and-a-half gallons of milk, 52lb of butter, three boxes of salt, two boxes of black pepper, and Tabasco Pepper Sauce 'to taste'.

> **Giant Omelette Celebration**, held annually in November in Abbeville, LA. Contact Confrerie d'Abbeville, PO Box 1272, Abbeville, LA 70511; ➤ 337 893 0013 or 337 898 588; web: www.giantomelette.org.

Museums and collections

The whimsical **UCM Museum** ('You-see-em Mu-se-um', get it?) in Abita Springs is the work of eccentric curator John Preble. Every day John asks himself, 'What would be fun?', then answers his own question by making whatever strikes his playful fancy. His intricately carved, animated scenes of Southern life are impossibly detailed, and made with more than 50,000 found and recycled objects. Rocks, bottle caps, license plates, springs, motors; you name it, John has probably used it. A pull tab becomes a tail-light; a plastic fork becomes a tractor grill. It's all housed in a clump of old buildings, including a vintage gas station, an old Creole cottage, and the famous House of Shards which is covered with tens of thousands of itty bitty pieces of tiles, pottery, mirrors and glass.

> **UCM Museum**, 22275 Hwy 36, Abita Springs, LA 70420; ➤ 985 892 2624; web: ucmmuseum.com. One block east on Hwy 36 from the town's only traffic light.

Attractions

A variety of swamp tours explore the muck and marshes that surround New Orleans. You'll see alligators, egrets and wild animals in moss-covered swamps that once were home to Indians and pirates. If you prefer your alligators live, **Bayou Pierre Alligator Park** in Natchitoches has hundreds of them, ranging in size from petite four-footers to huge 1,000-pounders. You can feed 'em, touch 'em and eat 'em all in one place.

> **Bayou Pierre Alligator Park**, 380 Old Bayou Pierre Rd, Natchitoches, LA 71457; ➤ 877 354 7001 or 318 354-0001; web: www.alligatorshow.com. Directions: Old Bayou Pierre Rd, about 10 minutes north of Natchitoches on Hwy 1 N. Look for the Alligator School Bus.

Northeastern Region

NEW YORK STATE
Eccentric environments

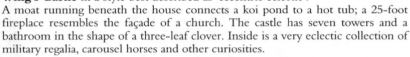

Over a 30-year period, Peter and Toni Wing have constructed their very own stone castle using mostly salvaged materials and the remains of historic buildings. Hauling the rubble from all over the state to their parent's old dairy farm, they've built **Wing's Castle** in a style best described as 'eccentric eclectic'. A moat running beneath the house connects a koi pond to a hot tub; a 25-foot fireplace resembles the façade of a church. The castle has seven towers and a bathroom in the shape of a three-leaf clover. Inside is a very eclectic collection of military regalia, carousel horses and other curiosities.

> **Wing's Castle**, Bangall Rd, Dutchess County, Millbrook, NY 12545; ↘ 845 677 9085. Located 5 miles north of Millbrook on Bangall Rd, 1.2 miles north of Rte 57. *Open Wed–Sun noon–5.00pm Jun 1–Labor Day; weekends noon–5.00pm Labor Day–Oct 31; call for hours Nov–Dec; by appointment Jan–May.*

Museums and collections

Topped by the world's largest metal kazoo, the **Original American Kazoo Company** museum showcases the history of the kazoo as well as the 88-year history of the factory. Kazoos, those quirky, often irritating noise-making instruments that most anyone can play are made the same way today as they were in 1916. The museum has hundreds on display, including liquor-bottle-shaped ones that celebrated the end of prohibition.

> **Original American Kazoo Company**, 8703 S Main St, Eden, NY 14057; ↘ 716 992 3960; web: www.kazooco.com. *Open Mon–Sat 10.00am–5.00pm, Sun noon–5.00pm. Admission free.*

They take their Lucy very seriously in Jamestown, Lucille Ball's birthplace, claiming a **Lucy-Desi Museum** and celebrating not one, but two Lucy events. On her birthday weekend they hold a grape-stomping competition and an *I Love Lucy* trivia contest. During Lucy-Desi Days they throw an **I Love Lucy Masquerade Ball** where guests dress up like their favorite characters from the TV series. Both events have art exhibits, film fests, fan reunions, memorabilia auctions, outdoor movies, and some sort of contest based on her antics on the show: grape-stomping, chocolate- wrapping, or egg-stuffing. Lucytown Tours offer drive-bys of her birthplace, her childhood home and of the schools she attended. The museum, open year-round, tells the story of the famous comedy couple through displays of their personal belongings, interactive exhibits and

ECCENTRIC CALENDAR
NEW YORK

January	**Matzo Ball Eating Contest**. Held at various Ben's Deli locations (page 186)
May/June	**Desi-Lucy Days**, Jamestown. Held on Memorial Day weekend (page 181)
June	**Mermaid Parade**, Coney Island. Held the first Saturday following the summer solstice (June 21) (page 186)
September	**BARC Animal Parade**, Brooklyn (page 186)

VERMONT

March	**Odor-Eaters International Rotten Sneaker Contest**, Montpelier (page 194)
August	**Zucchini Fest**, Ludlow (page 194)

NEW HAMPSHIRE

September	**Mud Bowl Championships**, North Conway (page 197)

MAINE

January	**White, White World Week**, Carrabassett (page 201)
February	**Moose Stompers Weekend**, Houlton (page 200)
June	**Lindbergh Crate Day**, Canaan (page 199)
July	**Central Maine Egg Festival**, Pittsfield (page 198)
	Moxie Days Festival, Lisbon (page 199)
	Potato Blossom Festival, Fort Fairfield (page 200)
August	**Potato Feast Days**, Houlton (page 200)
October	**Festival of Scarecrows**, Rockland (page 199)
	Fryeburg Fair, Fryeburg (page 198)
	National Wife Carrying Championships, Bethel (page 199)

MASSACHUSETTS

October	**Fantasia Fair**, Provincetown (page 202)

plenty of videos. According to the museum, 'Lucy's face has been seen by more people than any other human who ever lived'.

Lucy-Desi Museum, 212 Pine St, Jamestown, NY 14701; ↘ 716 484 0800; web: www.lucy-desi.com. *Hours vary seasonally*. The I Love Lucy Masquerade Ball is part of Desi-Lucy Days, held annually on Memorial Day weekend.

You would hardly consider drainage tiles worthy of collecting, but Mike Weaver, a drainage and irrigation engineer, collected more than 350 of them. Displayed at the **Mike Weaver Drain Tile Museum** in Geneva, his collection is, not surprisingly, the world's largest. The oldest tile dates from about 500BC. Weaver started collecting the tiles in 1950 and eventually opened the museum in the restored home of John Johnston, the man who brought the idea of drainage tiles from Scotland to the United States.

RHODE ISLAND

January I	**Penguin Plunge**, Jamestown (page 206)
July 4	**Ancient and Horribles Parade**. Held at 4.30pm in the village of Chepachet in Glocester (page 206)
August	**Fools Rules Regatta**, Jamestown (page 206)

CONNECTICUT

July 4	**Boom Box Parade**, Willimantic (page 207)

NEW JERSEY

August	**Weird Contest Week**, Ocean City. Held the third week of August (page 210)

PENNSYLVANIA

January	**Wing Bowl**, Philadelphia (page 214)
January I	**Mummers' Parade**, Philadelphia (page 213)
February	**Ice Tee Golf Tournament**, Lake Wallenpaupack, Hawley (page 214)
March	**Amish Mud Sales** (page 215)
May	**Stink Fest**, Bradford (page 214)
July	**Bark Peeler's Convention**, Galeton (page 214)

MARYLAND

April	**Kinetic Sculpture Race**, Baltimore (page 221)
June	**HonFest**, Baltimore (page 224)

DELAWARE

November	**Punkin' Chunkin'**, Georgetown (page 224)

Mike Weaver Drain Tile Museum, Hwy 5, Geneva, NY; ✆ 315 789 3848 or 315 789 5151; web: www.genevahistoricalsociety.com/ Johnston.htm. Directions: Go to the Rose Hill mansion located on Rte 96A 1 mile south of rtes 5 and 20 for escorts to the museum. *Open Mon–Sat 10.00am–3.00pm May–Oct, Sun 1.00–4.00pm; or by appointment.*

Inside the Ossining/Caputo Visitor Center is a display of prison-made weapons, shanks and shivs confiscated from convicts residing in the notorious **Sing Sing Prison**. The exhibit also has two real-life jail cells, positioned in a mirrored hall, to give you an idea of just how big the 'big house' is. You can have your picture taken in one of the cells or beside 'Sparky', the electric chair, an exact replica of the real sizzler that was made by the prison's vocational class.

Sing Sing Prison, Ossining Visitor Center, 95 Broadway, Ossining, NY 10562; ✆ 914 941 3189

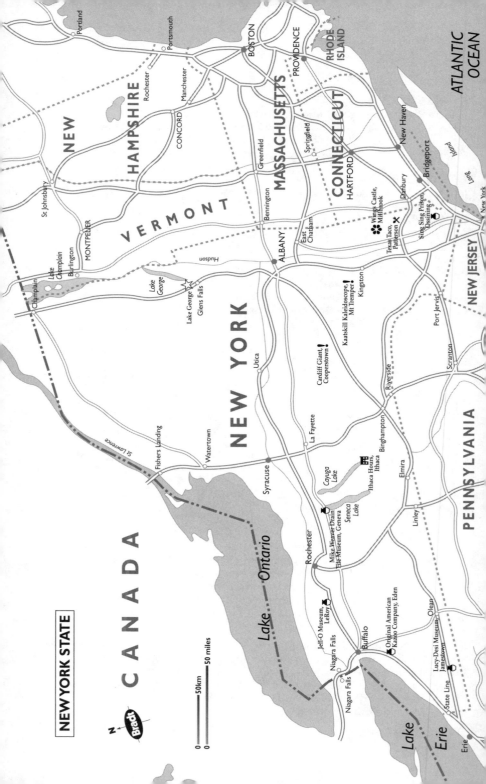

Jell-O, America's favorite dessert, sells 1.1 million boxes a day, or 13 boxes every second. But when a young carpenter selling patent medicines invented the wobbly fruit-flavored gelatin in 1897, no-one was buying. The dejected inventor sold the trademark to Orator Woodward, the wealthiest man in town, for $450. Woodward, too, had trouble convincing American housewives to try the dessert, so he in turn tried to sell the company to his plant manager (for $35), who also turned him down. Determined to recoup his investment, Woodward hired a team of stylishly dressed salesmen who showed up in horse-drawn carriages at every fair, picnic, tea, wedding, and church social in the region. Bowls of Jell-O were handed out to immigrants passing through Ellis Island, and he spent $335 for an ad in *Ladies' Home Journal* proclaiming Jell-O 'America's Most Famous Dessert'. He concocted recipes, such as Shredded Wheat Jell-O Apple Sandwich, and convinced doctors to endorse his product. And he took to the streets, selling Jell-O door-to-door and printing recipe books in Spanish, Swedish, German, and Yiddish.

Woodward's Jell-O molds became a key element in his brilliant marketing strategy. He gave them away free, emphasizing not just Jell-O's taste, but its aesthetic appeal as well. Those molds, along with Jell-O boxes, posters, advertisements, and giveaways, are an important part of the **Jell-O Museum** run by the LeRoy Historical Society. Today Jell-O is still designing molds that it sells on its website, including a Super Bowl version, alphabet cutters and a map of the United States. The company even has a Make It Now link: tell them what you have on hand and they'll tell you how to use it in Jell-O. (Can you imagine the requests they must get?) The museum is home to the world's only Gelometer, a device that measures the jigglyness of Jell-O.

Jell-O Museum, 23 E Main St, LeRoy, NY 14882; ✆ 585 768 7433 (LeRoy Historical Society); web: www.jellomuseum.com. *Open May 1–Nov 2.*

Attractions

Frankenstein isn't the only monster at the **House of Frankenstein Wax Museum** in Lake George. A gruesome cast of torturers, taking obvious delight in decidedly anti-social behavior, joins the monster in 52 all-too-realistic vignettes. Audio-enhanced with screams of terror and pain, some of the exhibits get even weirder with figures that move and talk. The experience is memorable, as is the artistic quality. Sweet dreams.

House of Frankenstein Wax Museum, 213 Canada St, Lake George, NY 12845; ✆ 518 668 3377; web: www.frankensteinwaxmuseum.com. *Open mid-April–Oct.*

The sign at **Magic Forest Amusement Park's Fairy Tale Trail and Safari Ride** claims to have Lake George's only diving horse. You'd think it would also be the world's only horse that dived off a platform into a pool, but it turns out that Atlantic City used to have such a tourist attraction as well. The man responsible for Rex the diving horse is Jimmy Brown, who also puts on a live bird show and a magic act. During the season Brown does three shows a day, every day, for three months straight. Rex doesn't seem to mind, pausing for effect at the top of his platform before plunging in. The park has several dozen rides and theme trails based on nursery rhymes and fairy tales.

Magic Forest Fairy Tale Trail and Safari Ride, PO Box 71, Lake George, NY 12845; ✆ 518 668 2448; web: www.magicforestpark.com. *Open 9.30am–6.00pm Jun–Sep.*

Quirkyville

The town of Ithaca, population 30,000, is famous for its local currency. Called **Ithaca Hours**, the currency is just as valid as US dollars, but instead of being issued by the government, the Hours are issued by community organizations and used only within the town itself. Each Hour is worth one hour of basic labor pegged at a value of $10 per Hour; denominations are available for as little as one eighth of an Hour. They're called Hours to remind the citizens that the real source of a currency's value is measured by people's time, skills and energy. Individuals and businesses accept the Hours based on the rate at which they can reliably spend them elsewhere. The program is so popular that some employees even accept Hours as a small part of their pay.

> **Ithaca Hours**, PO Box 6731, Ithaca, NY 14851; ↘ 670 272 3738; web: www.ithacahours.org

Just plain weird

The **Kaatskill Kaleidoscope** is the world's largest, built inside a converted grain silo by members of the Brewster Society, a group of kaleidoscope craftsmen. To see the show, you lean back against padded boards equipped with neck supports, then enjoy 15 minutes of inventive sound and imagery.

> **Kaatskill Kaleidoscope**, Catskill Corners, Mt Tremper, Ulster County, NY; ↘ 914 688 5300; web: www.catskillcorners.com/marketplace/ kaleidoworld/kworld.htm. *Open Sun–Thu 10.00am–5.00pm, Fri–Sat 10.00am–7.00pm.*

It's nice when you have the money to pull off a really good practical joke. And it's even nicer when the joke earns back hundreds of times what you spent. Often referred to as America's Greatest Hoax, **The Cardiff Giant** in Cooperstown is the 1868 work of George Hull. It seems that Hull was ticked off when a fundamentalist minister stubbornly refused to interpret the Bible, choosing instead to take the scripture literally. So when Hull came upon Genesis 6:4: 'There were giants on the earth in those days, and also afterward, when the sons of God had relations with the daughters of men, who bore children to them', he couldn't resist. He purchased an acre of gypsum-rich land in Iowa and quarried an enormous block of blue-veined stone. Claiming that he was making an Abraham Lincoln memorial destined for Washington, DC, he hauled the stone, with great difficulty, to the railway station where he sent it on its way to a sculptor in Chicago. Hull himself followed so he could serve as the model for his 12-foot 'giant', as well as direct the aging process that would render the giant a genuine antiquity. When his 'giant' was suitably aged, he hauled the thing back to New York and buried it behind the barn of William 'Stub' Newell, a relative and fellow co-conspirator.

A year later they professed to need a new well, hiring diggers to commence work. Sure enough, the diggers 'discovered' the buried giant and the trap was sprung. By afternoon, a tent had been erected over the giant's 'grave' and curious visitors were paying 25 cents to view the remains. Word spread far and wide; the price doubled to 50 cents, then doubled again to $1, a huge sum in those days. Speculation as to the origin of the Cardiff Giant, as it was called, also raged far and wide, with clergy, academics, and politicians postulating all kinds of far-fetched theories. The giant was, depending on your viewpoint, a Jesuit missionary from the 1500s, an ancient Onondaga Iriquois Indian, or a petrified man just as described in the Bible. A letter from a Chicago sculptor claiming to have made the giant was dismissed as the ramblings of a crackpot. One geologist proclaimed 'It has the mark of ages stamped upon every limb and feature, in a manner and with a distinctness which no man can imitate.'

P T Barnum, America's greatest showman of the time, got wind of the giant and offered Hull $60,000 to rent him for three months. Hull turned him down, so Barnum petulantly made his own giant, claiming to have bought him from Hull, and that Hull's giant was now a copy of his. Hull sued Barnum for copying his fake and for calling him a fraud; in court he gleefully admitted that it was all a hoax. The court ruled that Barnum couldn't be sued for calling Hull's giant a fraud because it was, indeed, a fraud. One of Hull's partners testified, 'there's a sucker born every minute', a remark mistakenly attributed to P T Barnum. You can see the Cardiff Giant at the Cooperstown Farmers' Museum where you'll have to pay a bit more than a quarter.

The **Cardiff Giant**, located at New York State Historical Society Farmers' Museum, State Hwy 80, Cooperstown, NY; ✆ 888 547 1450 or 607 547 1400; web: www.farmersmuseum.org/cardiff.htm

Quirky cuisine

At **Texas Taco** in Patterson, the fence is made of tricycles and the entire place is a mosaic, covered with beads and ceramics. Rosemary, the proprietress, is all aglitter with her purple hair, signature overalls, false eyelashes, and spray-painted tennis shoes. Even the parking lot, where you can see her school bus decorated with seashells, radio knobs, and doll heads, is festooned with swirls of color. 'Every day is like being on stage', says Rosemary, who started out in 1970 with a pushcart on Fifth Avenue. The prices haven't changed much since then; there's nothing over $3.

Texas Taco, Rural Route 22, Patterson, NY 12563; ✆ 845 878 9665. *Open daily 11.00am–8.45pm.*

NEW YORK CITY
Manhattan and the boroughs

You'd need a lot more than this chapter to even scratch the surface of Manhattan's eccentrics and eccentricities. The city is a mosaic of creative madness, with weird people and strange businesses in virtually all neighborhoods. They come and go, often quickly, taking their quirkiness to a new street corner or to the newest cutting-edge locations. To fully appreciate the vast cornucopia of curious characters, bizarre businesses, peculiar pastimes and loony lifestyles the city has to offer, get your eyes off the pages of the guidebooks and on to the street where life is being lived by delightfully daft folks quite unlike you and me.

Festivals and events

Free to watch and open to everyone, the annual **BARC Animal Parade** is testament to New Yorkers' obsessive fondness for their dogs and their cats. Hundreds show up in costume – themselves *and* their pets – to show off in the parade and compete in various pet pageants. There are definite Kodak moments as prizes are awarded for the best butt, the gruffest-looking dog with the sweetest temperament, the best kisser, the best dressed, the best owner-dog look-alikes, and (aw, shucks…) the Greatest Benefit to Humanity.

> **BARC Animal Parade**, held annually in September. Contact the Brooklyn Animal Resource Coalition, 253 Wythe Ave (at N 1st St), Brooklyn, NY 11211; ✆ 718 486-7489; web: www.barcshelter.org

On the first Saturday after the summer solstice, thousands of spectators converge on Coney Island to watch the **Mermaid Parade**, a funky spectacle of mermaids, mermen, merbabies, and merpets. Anything goes, costume-wise, as long as it's fish related. In the past, retired mermaids in wheelchairs paraded with Evian water drips and one woman's top consisted only of artfully placed rubber lobsters. There's enough flesh and boisterous behavior to last you quite a while.

> **Mermaid Parade**, held the first Saturday following the summer solstice (June 21) in the Coney Island section of Brooklyn, NY, 11 miles from lower Manhattan; ✆ 718 372 5159; web: www.coneyislandusa.com/mermaid.shtml

Some of the world's biggest eaters complete in Ben's Annual Charity **Matzo Ball Eating Contest**. Held at various Ben's Deli locations, the quest for the $2,500 prize, as well as for the coveted matzo ball eating trophy, has been sought by many of the world's most competitive eaters, winners of records for eating boiled eggs, burritos, donuts, hot dogs, sushi, spaghetti, and pizza. You can watch them in action as they wolf down as many of Ben's matzo balls as possible in two minutes and 50 seconds.

> **Matzo Ball Eating Contest**, held annually in January at various Ben's Deli locations; web: www.bensdeli.net

Attractions

Step right up, folks … see freaks, wonders, and human curiosities! Sideshows by the Seashore at **Coney Island Circus** is the last place in the country where you can see an old-fashioned circus sideshow performance. They're all here – the snake charmers, human blockheads, and sword swallowers of the past. Not only can you see them, you can even learn to be like them, should you be so inclined, if you sign up for Sideshow School.

> Sideshows by the Seashore is part of the **Coney Island Circus**, 1208 Surf Ave, Brooklyn, NY 11224; ✆ 718 372 5159; web: www.coneyisland.com. *Open Easter weekend, and primarily weekends from Memorial Day–Labor Day. Contact for specific hours and dates.*

Museums and collections

When you first come upon the building housing the **Museum of Sex**, you might think the place is still under construction. Inspired by the body's skeletal system, the exterior façade is meant to evoke undulating human ribs, an effect achieved (or not!) by stretching spandex fabric over aluminum 'ribs' and letting the wind tug suggestively at the fabric. Once inside, you'll delve into the history of prostitution, burlesque, birth control, obscenity, fetish, and more. The museum also presents the city's sexual subcultures and offers a variety of novel tours. The gift shop is more tantalizing than the displays, however, offering an intriguing selection of salt and peppershakers as well as tastefully presented merchandise of the sort you'd usually need a password and credit card to view. You must be over 18 to visit this museum.

Museum of Sex, 233 5th Ave (at 27th St), New York, NY 10016; ↘ 212 689 6337; web: museumofsex.com. *Open Sun–Fri 11.00am–6.30pm, Sat 11.00am–8.00pm. Closed Thanksgiving and Christmas Day. Visitors under 18 not permitted.*

Seven thousand people from 20 different countries lived in the tenement building that now belongs to the **Lower East Side Tenement Museum**. For most European immigrants, overcrowded tenements (multi-family apartment buildings) were the first stop in their quest for the American dream. The museum offers three tours that trace the lives of immigrant families through layers of wallpaper and household furnishings. The regular weekday tour explores the lives of the many families who lived there. On weekends, the Confino Family Tour is led by a costumed interpreter who welcomes you as if you were newly arrived in this country in 1916, giving you a unique opportunity to experience immigrant life. You can even reserve the tenement after hours for an offbeat dinner party in the tenement kitchen that comes complete with enamel-topped tables and authentic décor.

Lower East Side Tenement Museum, 90 Orchard St at Broome St, New York, NY 10002; ↘ 212 431 0233; fax: 212 431 0402; web: www.tenement.org

The world's largest architectural scale model, built for the 1964 World's Fair, is on display at the Queens Museum of Art. **The Panorama**, built at a scale of one inch to one hundred feet, has every building in NYC as well as the city's topography, parks and transportation: 895,000 structures covering 320 square miles displayed in 9,335 square feet. Lester and Associates, the original model builders, reconstructed and restored the Panorama and now keep it up to date. A plane even takes off regularly from LaGuardia airport. The margin of error is less than 1%.

The Panorama, located at the Queens Museum of Art, New York City Bldg, Flushing Meadows Corona Park, Queens, NY 11368; ↘ 718 592 9700; web: www.queensmuse.org. *Open Tues–Fri 10.00am–5.00pm, Sat–Sun noon–5.00pm Sep–Jun; Wed–Sun 1.00pm–8.00pm Jul–Aug.*

Thanks to Thomas Edison, the folks at Luna Park on Coney Island were able to electrocute an elephant. This was in 1903, and Edison had been publicly electrocuting cats and dogs to prove that his direct current electrical system (DC) was safe, while a competing system, alternating current (AC) being touted by Westinghouse, was not. When an elephant named Topsy was sentenced to death for killing three men in three years, Edison volunteered to fry Topsy as a way to prove his point. With a film crew recording the grisly event, the elephant was led to a special platform and ten seconds later Topsy was toast. You can see the film at the **Coney Island Museum**.

Coney Island Museum, 1208 Surf Ave, Brooklyn, NY 11224-2816; ↘ 718 372 5159; web: www.coneyislandusa.com

Tours

In a city as physically dense and culturally diverse as Manhattan, walking is the best way to explore its neighborhoods. There are hundreds of guides offering walking tours of areas they know and love. The following tours explore some of the more offbeat aspects of life in the Big Apple, with tour guides who are known for their knowledge, showmanship and ability to make you feel comfortable in some mighty strange surroundings. Most of these guides will do a custom tour for you (for a price, of course), based on your interests. The Friday *New York Times* lists dozens of tours for the upcoming weekend, as does the magazine *Time Out New York* which comes out on Thursdays.

Led by a group alarmed by the increasing presence of surveillance cameras, the **Surveillance Camera Outdoor Walking Tours** cover most Manhattan neighborhoods, meeting Sundays, rain or shine, for the one-and-a-half-hour tours. The leaders, known as the Surveillance Camera Players, share a great deal of history on the subject as well as pointing out the technological capacities of the various types of cameras.

> **Surveillance Camera Outdoor Walking Tours (SCOWT)** meet on Sundays at 2.00pm sharp in various neighborhoods. Check the website for details; web: www.notbored.org/scowt.html. *Free.*

Michael Kaback has carved out a curious niche for himself in the tour business. If you're nostalgic for those carefree childhood days, join him on **Games of The Lower East Side**, an afternoon spent playing street games like stoop ball, hopscotch, jump rope and kick the can. Building on a life-long familiarity with the garment trade, he also offers a walking tour of the **Garment District**, dodging 'sidewalk locomotives' laden with clothes, patterns and rolls of fabric. Michael is full of juicy stories about store buyers, truckers, 'knock-off' artists (who copy designer clothes and sell them for substantially less), and the characters and criminals behind the scenes of this cut-throat trade. On this tour you get to shop for bargains among the cancelled orders, overproduction, unsold inventory and one-of-a-kind salesman samples. Cold cash, along with Kaback's advice on bargaining, can net you some outstanding deals on high-end fashion. Then there's the **Bizarre and Eccentric Tour of the East Village**, a voyeuristic evening of tattoo parlors, body piercing, sex shops and vampire haunts. Not for the faint of heart, you get up close to the kind of folks who have hair color usually associated with polyester as well as jewelry on body parts usually seen only by that special someone.

> **Bizarre and Eccentric Tour of the East Village** and **Garment District Tour**, Michael Kaback Walking Tours, 305 E 40th St, Apt 9F, New York, NY; ↘ 212 370 4214. *Call for tour dates and times.*

Arthur Marks is in a class by himself, the kind of character you'd love to have for a neighbor if you lived in Manhattan. Often referred to as a living landmark, Arthur has been giving tours for 30 years. He doesn't just tell you stuff, he sings it, breaking into song as the mood strikes. He offers an astounding variety of decidedly offbeat tours, dispensing fascinating anecdotes along with his own unique perspective on history. With Arthur, you can explore east side, west side, and all around the town, giving yourself to Broadway and peeking into the lives of past and present New Yorkers. He knows history and legend, fact and fantasy, whether boring or interesting, and the difference between them. Seeing Manhattan through his eyes is like peering into an urban kaleidoscope, always in motion, always changing.

Arthur Marks Tours for All Seasons, 24 5th Ave, New York, NY 10011; ↘ 212 673 0477

Something Old, Something New is a walking tour of the Lower East Side's Orchard Street, the city's first discount retail district. The tour takes you deep into this bustling shopping area, exploring a former public bathhouse, a Romanian-American congregation, and a shop devoted entirely to umbrellas.

Something Old, Something New meets at Katz's Delicatessen, 205 E Houston St at Ludlow St; ↘ 212 226 9010; web: www. lowereastsideny.com. *Sun 11.00am, Apr–Dec. Tour lasts about an hour and a half. Free.*

The **Charles Simon Center for Adult Life and Learning** provides an intriguing series of summer excursions. Join an archeological excavation in Brooklyn, an all-night July 4th walking tour, a pre-Rosh Hashanah Lower East Side tour, Chinatown's herb markets, or a social history of baseball in New York. The walking and riding tour of historic subway routes takes you to Brooklyn and Coney Island.

Charles Simon Center for Adult Life and Learning, New York, NY; ↘ 212 415 5433; web: www.92y.org

If it's happening in Manhattan, **iMar** knows. They can hook you up with a truly astounding variety of eccentric tours and experiences, both in the city and elsewhere in the region. Fancy a midnight drive with a cop, a personal shopping trip with a fashion model, or a World Trade Center tour with an emergency worker? They can do it. How about a Harlem Gospel Sunday Brunch? From an after-hours ride with a cabbie to nightclubbing with a DeeJay, this booking service offers over 300 unique tours and services.

iMar, ↘ 212 239 1124; web: www.iMar.com

Author and political activist Bruce Kayton puts a left-wing spin on his **Radical Walking Tours of New York City**. You can buy his book of 13 self-led tours or go along with him on several tours, including a radical lovers tour of Greenwich Village, a 1960s' political/protest tour of the Village, a radical Jews tour of the lower east side, or a tour of Harlem with a left-wing twist. Other tours cover money and other evils; riots, prohibition, and 'trees, grass, and the working class' in Central Park.

Radical Walking Tours of New York, Bruce Kayton; ↘ 718 492 0069; web: www.he.net/~radtours. *No reservations required.*

The dead of centuries past lie below today's bustling downtown neighborhoods. **Joyce Gold** takes you to four graveyards of lower Manhattan on a 'Where they came to rest' tour. In Little Italy she presents a walking tour of crime, describing how the Mafia began, how Prohibition changed the picture, who the main families were, which mobsters owned which restaurants, where the bullets are and why rivals were rubbed out in front of their families. The 'Tory Story in Lower Manhattan' celebrates Independence Day (July 4th) by looking at the revolution through British eyes. She also offers a 'Macabre Greenwich Village' tour, exploring graveyards, the hangman's house and tree, famous murders, ghosts and hauntings; the 'New Meat Market' tour featuring butchers, bakers and art- scene makers; and a 'Hell Ain't Hot' tour – this here's Hell's kitchen.

Joyce Gold History Tours of New York, 141 W 17th St, New York, NY 10011; ☎ 212 242 5762; web: www.nyctours.com

The real life **Kenny Kramer** (upon whom the quirky character of the TV comedy *Seinfeld* was based) gives a hugely entertaining, slick and professional tour of the people and places that populated the television show about nothing. He unabashedly admits to being a celebrity without accomplishment and to making money for being indirectly famous – not for his own talent, but because he lived across the hall from someone who became famous. (His neighbor was Larry David, co-creator of the show and the personality behind the character of George Costanza.) He does this in such a good natured way that you fall in love with the real Kramer the same way you fell in love with his character on the show. Following a funny stand-up routine, you hop on his bus from where he'll show you the real-life places where so many of the show's story lines took place, and tell you all about the real-life characters depicted in *Seinfeld*. At Tom's restaurant (called Monk's on the show) he patiently spends as many Kodak moments as it takes to satisfy his guests. The bus portion is funny, non-stop commentary and he'll answer any question you ask. The tour ends with a slice of pizza and a chance to buy the dozen or so Kramer products that he also hawks on his website.

Kenny Kramer Reality Tour, starts at The Producers Club, 358 W 44th St, New York, NY; ☎ 800 KRAMERS or 212 268 5525; web: www.kennykramer.com. *Reservations required.*

Paul Zukowski lives and breathes gangsters. He knows where they got their start, how they rose to power and fame, their infamous accomplishments and where they met their ends. As a kid he pretended to be Al Capone, read every book he could get his hands on about the bad boys, and watched every movie and television show that had gangsters. He's a walking encyclopedia of gangsterdom, a dapper young man who conducts his **Gangland Tour** around New York City in a limousine that would do Capone proud. What makes Paul's passion so extraordinary is that he

grew up in Poland, exposed by propaganda only to the bad, evil side of America. Leaving his homeland just a few years ago, he's managed to chase and catch the American dream by turning his hobby into a business. Explaining that it was a lack of opportunity – a tight job market – that had young men turning to crime, he takes you past the Irish, English, German, Jewish, and Italian sites where so much of gangland activity took place. He can barely contain his enthusiasm for his subject and you'll leave his tour reeling from the stories he tells.

Gangland Tours, New York, NY; ↘ 212 239 1124; email: ganglandtours@aol.com

Escape reality, if only for a few hours, with an **On Location Tour**, tracing the footsteps of your favorite TV and movie characters. Like *Sex and the City*? See where Carrie and the girls live, drink, and shop, including the bakery where Miranda gorges on cupcakes. *The Sopranos*? See dozens of locations, including the diners and strip clubs where the bad guys do their business. From Manhattan, you'll get a trip through the Lincoln Tunnel to the tune of 'Woke Up This Morning', just like the trip Tony takes in the opening sequence. *Seinfeld* locations? They're included in the TV & Movie Tour, along with those from *Friends, Will & Grace*, and *The Cosby Show*. The bookstore from *You've Got Mail* is also on this tour. The guides, who all take pride in their extensive knowledge of shows and films, entertain you with gossip and trivia. Bring your camera; you'll want lots of pictures sitting and standing where the famous have planted their feet and rear ends.

On Location Tour. Contact Zerve at ↘ 212 209 3370 for reservations; web: www.sceneontv.com

For a really innovative way to experience the city, especially its museums, take a **Scavenger Hunt** with Watson Adventures. Participants are divided into teams for hunts on Wall Street and the Bronx Zoo, as well as at various art and natural history museums. They also offer movie hunts in Central Park and in various neighborhoods where you can sleuth out the locations of scenes from the movies. Stand-up comedians often lead the tours.

Scavenger Hunts with Watson Adventures, ↘ 212 726 1529; web: www.watsonadventures.com

Off-beat field trips, walking tours and workshops are offered by many other tour companies, including the **American Museum of Natural History**, that offers tours of such locations as Central Park West, the new Times Square, and urban forest walking tours. **Art Tours of Manhattan** visits the eclectic, eccentric village art scene, while **Doorway to Design** visits village houses and creative firms. **Big Apple Greeter** matches you with a volunteer escort to show you around. **Big Onion Walking Tours** goes where mainstream tours don't, with a Gay and Lesbian History walk, a Multi-Ethnic Eating tour, and a Riot and Rebellion tour. The **Municipal Art Society** offers tours from a unique perspective, that of architects and urban planners. **Nosh Walks** takes you into a dozen different neighborhoods, letting you experience the food within the cultural context of the community.

American Museum of Natural History, Central Park W at 79th St, New York, NY 10024; ↘ 212 769 5200; web: www.amnh.org

Art Tours of Manhattan, 63 E 82nd St, New York, NY 10028; ↘ 609 921 2647. *Groups only.*

Big Apple Greeter, 1 Centre St, # 2035, New York, NY 10007; ☎ 212 669 8159; web: www.bigapplegreeter.org

Big Onion Walking Tours, 476 13th St, Brooklyn, NY 11215; ☎ 212 439 1090; web: www.bigonion.com

Doorway to Design, 1441 Broadway, New York, NY 10018; ☎ 212 221 1111 or 718 339 1542; web: www.doorwaytodesign.com

Municipal Art Society, 457 Madison Ave, New York, NY 10022; ☎ 212 935-3960; web: www.mas.org

Nosh Walks, 771 West End Avenue #12J, New York, NY 10025; ☎ 212 222 2243; web: www.noshwalks.com

Odd shopping

Bats, cats, and rats are favorites at **Evolution**, a very strange store where you can buy freeze-dried mice, replicas of velociraptor claws, skull casts of extinct species, lollipops with bugs inside, a mounted bat in a frame, and stuffed snakes. Folks who cook bugs and eat them, keep them as pets, or steam and mount them buy their supplies here.

Evolution, 120 Spring St, New York, NY 10012; ☎ 212 343 1114 or ☎ 800 952 3195; fax: 212 343 1815; web: www.evolutionnyc.com

If you can dream it up, **Abracadabra** will rent it to you. This store/museum/freak show/costume shop has every bizarre object in it that anyone has ever requested, along with everything and anything that appeals to owner Bob Blum, a character himself who walks around his domain with a parrot named Nairobi on his shoulder. Bob claims to have the largest selection of props in the world, a very believable claim considering the thousands and thousands of things crammed into his two-level shop. From feather boas to body parts, from lighting to special effects, from magic to the macabre, Abracadabra has it all. The place is wild, with figures and animals of every description made of materials ranging from rubber to stone. Around Halloween, the place is even wilder as hundreds of costume hunters descend on a selection of costume rentals extensive enough to outfit a small city. Blum says it's 'the coolest place on the planet'.

Abracadabra, 19 W 21st St, New York, NY 10010; ☎ 212 627 5194; web: www.abracadabrasuperstore.com

Skeleton collectors flock to **Maxilla & Mandible**, the world's first osteological store, where you can buy penis-bone earrings and order amusing custom skeletons. Mostly of interest to scientists, museums, artists, designers, doctors and photographers, the just plain curious are also welcome in this bone collector's paradise, a haven of museum-quality bone, fossil and other natural history specimens. Be sure to ask them how the bones get so clean.

Maxilla & Mandible, 451 Columbus Avenue, New York, NY 10024; ☎ 212 724 6173; web: www.maxillaandmandible.com

Quirky cuisine

Well, this is McStrange – a **McDonald's** with class. Located in the financial district, this McQuirky restaurant has real marble tables, real silverware, and staff dressed in tuxedo shirts and berets. During prime dine-times a doorman greets you and a piano player provides soothing background music. If you reserve the private dining-room, waiters take your orders and hostesses circulate with silver trays piled high with condiments. There's even been a wedding there. McWeird, huh?

McDonald's, 160 Broadway, NY, NY 10038, across from Ground Zero.

An intergalactic, virtual-reality shuttle speeds you to **Mars 2112** for an extraterrestrial culinary and interactive event. Dubbed 'eatertainment', Mars 2112 in Times Square weaves fantasy and reality through state-of-the-art technology. Kids love the place because of the Red Planet décor, strolling Martians, video games, and kid-friendly food. Adults love it because the kids stay entertained while they enjoy surprisingly good grown-up food.

Mars 2112, 1633 Broadway, New York, NY 10019; ↘ 212 582 2112; fax: 212 489 7955; web: www.mars2112.com

Tacky by intention, the **Trailer Park Bar & Grill** doesn't aim to impress. The antithesis of haute, it's the height of kitsch with its yard sale and plastic laundromat décor. From Elvis on velvet to old road signs, from record album jackets to plastic patio lights, the walls and ceilings are plastered with stuff that wouldn't even sell at a flea market. The stools are disco orange and the tables are festooned with condiments and rolls of paper towels. There's a real trailer, cut in half and embedded in a wall. Owner Tom McKay calls it a 'good natured parody of questionable taste'.

Trailer Park Lounge & Grill, 271 W 23rd St, New York, NY 10011; ↘ 212 463 8000

Rooms with a Skew

If you like your quirky classy, Manhattan offers two fine choices: The Muse and The Library hotels. **The Muse** sets the standard for cutting edge and chic guest programs, offering celebrity make-up artists, themed pajama parties and shopping with fashion models. No wish is too big for their Dream Coordinators who can even make fantasies such as dancing a Bob Fosse number or playing at Julliard come true. If you'd rather play than perform, the hotel's 'Sex and the City' package provides for a gaggle of girlfriends to hit some of the famous TV foursome's favorite haunts – like shoe shopping at Jimmy Choo's – before indulging in in-room massages and midnight milk and cookies.

The Muse, 130 W 46th St, New York, NY 10036; ↘ 877 NYC MUSE or 212 485 2400; web: www.themusehotel.com

The Library, as the name suggests, takes a more soothing approach, dedicating each floor to one of the ten major categories of the Dewey Decimal System. Each room comes with art and books relevant to one of the topics within the category of floor it occupies. (Neil Armstrong stayed in the astronomy room.) The reading room and poetry garden are delightfully peaceful, classical music plays softly in the background, and you can borrow films from the video library.

The Library, 299 Madison Ave at 41st St, New York, NY 10017; ↘ 877 793 7323 or 212 983 4500; web: www.libraryhotel.com

During the Westminster Kennel Club Dog Show, held each February, the **Hotel Pennsylvania** becomes the preferred quarters for canines. With doggie concierge Urmas Karner's help, the ballroom is transformed into the largest indoor dog grooming and comfort station in all of New York, if not the world. They house up to a thousand dogs, plus their handlers, during the event, sleeping up to four pooches to a room. According to Urmas, the dogs are delightful guests, often better behaved than their human counterparts. While most of the rooms are reserved for show participants during that week, it's still possible to book a room, if you do so early enough, so you can enjoy the most unusual elevator and lobby companions in Manhattan. The rest of the year the hotel is pet friendly, too.

> **Hotel Pennsylvania**, 401 7th Ave at 33rd St (across from Madison Square Garden), New York, NY 10001; ↘ 212 502 8128; web: www.hotelpenn.com

The Gershwin is all about pop culture with its artsy bohemian hallways, simple rooms, underground theater performances, and stand-up comedy weekends. Fiberglass art canopies and sconces, called 'Tongues and Flames', make the exterior look like it's on fire.

> **The Gershwin**, 7 E 27th St, New York, NY 10016; ↘ 212 545 8000; web: www.gershwinhotel.com

VERMONT
Festivals and events
Thanks to the **Odor-Eaters International Rotten Sneaker Contest**, kids from all over the country get to show off their grungiest, grossest, stickiest, foulest sneakers, hoping to win the grand prize of $500 savings bond and prove to their parents that cleanliness isn't always a virtue. Shoes can be entered in an online contest or at one of about a dozen regional events, the winners of which go nose to nose for the honor of having their sneakers enshrined in the Hall of Fumes. Judges look for the worst tongue, laces and heels; the actual sniffing is done by a 'certified nose', a NASA space agency master sniffer. The winner also gets a year's supply of Odor-Eater products that probably go unused until adulthood.

> **Odor-Eaters International Rotten Sneaker Contest**, held annually in March in Montpelier, VT. Montpelier Recreation Department, ↘ 802 223 5141; web: www.odoreaters.com

For four days each year the folks around Ludlow make fun of the lowly zucchini at the **Zucchini Fest**, carving it into weird shapes, racing it, flying it, making creative dishes with it and making up limericks about it. Zucchini chunk ice cream? Oh, yum!

> **Zucchini Fest**, held annually in August in Ludlow, VT. Contact Ludlow Area Chamber of Commerce, PO Box 333, Clock Tower, Okemo Marketplace, Ludlow, VT 05149; ↘ 877 668 1852 or 802 228 5830; web: www.vacationinvermont.com

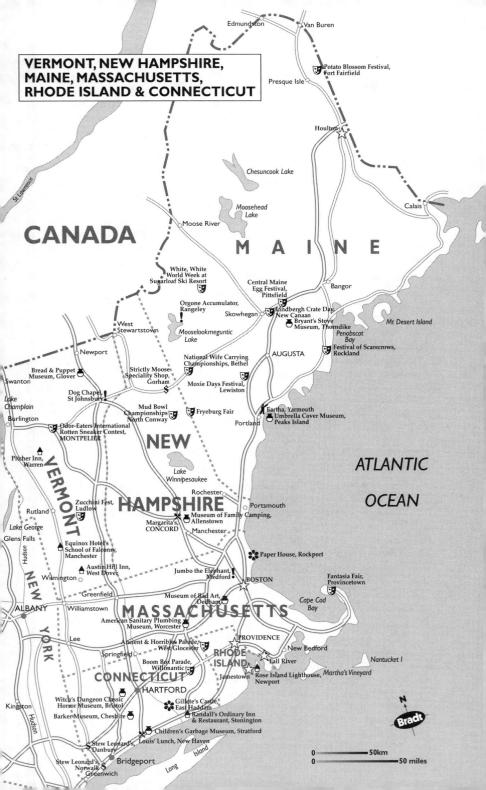

Museums and collections

The **Bread and Puppet Museum** contains one of the biggest collections of large puppets in the world, all past 'actors' in Bread and Puppet theater productions. Grouped according to theme, color, or size, the puppets represent scenes from past shows put on by the theater company famous for its political, satirical, and outrageous treatment of contemporary social issues. A visit to this massive collection, housed in an unheated barn, is a weird, surreal type of experience as the puppets, depicting figures from every walk of life, are crammed into every nook and cranny as well as hanging from the rafters. What's really bizarre, though, is that the museum staff *expects* its inventory to slowly decay, eschewing the traditional notions of preservation. The museum and theater company gets its funny name from originator Peter Shumann who thought art was as essential as bread and should be cheap and available to everyone. At the end of each performance free, freshly baked bread was given to the audience. If you happen to visit on a baking day you, too, get bread.

> **Bread and Puppet Museum**, Route 122, Glover, VT 05875; ➘ 802 525 1271; web: www.theaterofmemory.com. Located between Hardwick and Barton off I 91 and Rte 16. *Open daily 10.00am–5.00pm Jun–Nov 1.* *Free; donations appreciated.*

Just plain weird

This chapel is non-denominational – any breed is welcome. Situated on Dog Mountain, **Dog Chapel** is open to dogs and to people of any belief system. Built by dog artist Stephen Huneck, the chapel looks like any small New England church until you get up close. Then you see the Labrador with wings turning in the wind on the steeple, the ring of Greek columns topped with dog's heads, and the stained-glass windows portraying dogs eating ice cream. Stephen built the chapel after having a vision, resulting from a near-death experience, about the spiritual bond people have with their dogs. Visitors often leave photographs of beloved pets that have gone on to pet heaven.

> **Dog Chapel**, at Dog Mountain, Spaulding Rd, St Johnsbury, VT 05819; ➘ 802 748 2700; web: www.dogchapel.com. *Open Mon–Sat 10.00am–5.00pm, Sun 11.00am–4.00pm Jun–Oct. Also by appointment.* *Free.*

Rooms with a Skew

The **Equinox Hotel's School of Falconry** is one of the only certified places in the country where you can learn the art of handling large birds of prey. (Washington, DC must be the other.) The falconry package includes private instruction.

> **Equinox Hotel's School of Falconry**, located at 3567 Main St, Manchester Village, VT 05254; ➘ 800 362 4747 or 802 362 4700; web: www.equinox.rockresorts.com

The elegant **Pitcher Inn** has a whimsical, unexpected ambience. Décor in the 11 rooms emphasizes a different adventure in each one, all part of a history of Vermont theme. Among them is a Masonic lodge, a 19th-century schoolroom, a mountain cabin, a hayloft, and the most luxurious duck blind ever imagined. The Trout Room is octagonal with a bed made of tree trunks, a headboard carved with ferns and tree roots that spread out on the floor. A flying trout hangs from a ceiling that is ribbed like the sides of a boat. Add a fireplace, a collection of oars, a fly-tying desk and a porch over a rushing stream and you have a delightfully eccentric experience.

Pitcher Inn, 275 Main St, Warren, VT 05674; ☏ 802 496 6350 or 888 867 4824; web: www.pitcherinn.com

They come dressed to kill at **Austin Hill Inn**, home to almost a dozen of the country's most intriguing mystery weekends. What sets these weekends apart from the 'staged' variety is that the guests play all the roles and the 'script' is customized to accommodate the individual sizes and personalities of the scheduled participants. When you sign up, hosts John and Debbie Baily will ascertain your approximate age, gender, sense of humor and how introverted or extroverted you seem to be. Weeks before the scheduled event you'll receive a 'for your eyes only' packet in the mail containing secrets about the character you'll be playing as well as secrets about the other characters involved in the mystery. Costumes are suggested, most of which you can assemble easily just by rummaging around a bit, or you can rent a costume in town. The plot unfolds without anyone needing to memorize a script, starting with a reception during which you mingle, bribe, and blackmail to gain information. At dinner you continue to behave in character. Then someone dies – perhaps you. Or you may be the killer. In any case the evening continues until a round of secret balloting determines the culprit and his or her motive. Sunday morning sees the awards for Best Dressed, Best Actors, and, of course, the Most Clueless.

Austin Hill Inn, Rte 100, Box 859, West Dover, VT 05356; ☏ 800 332 7352 or 802 464 5281; web: www.murdermysteryweekend.com

NEW HAMPSHIRE
Festivals and events

Here's a football tournament that would put any detergent to the test: the **Mud Bowl Championships**. Played in North Conway in the only mud football stadium in the eastern US, this touch football tournament requires big beefy guys to wallow in the knee-deep muck while playing a game they hope resembles the real thing. On the first two days of the event, eight barefoot teams slosh it out in the elimination rounds; the winning two teams go whole hog during the

Sunday championship. Each year this charity event has a different theme, such as 'Mud Bowl Goes Hollywood', with competing teams performing skits based on the year's theme. The famous lawn-chair precision drill team always performs at the theme parade.

Mud Bowl Championships, held annually in September in North Conway, NH. Contact New Hampshire Division of Travel and Tourism Development, 172 Pembroke Rd, PO Box 1856, Concord, NH 03302; ☏ 800 FUN IN NH or 603 271 2665; web: www.visitnh.gov

Museums and collections

If your kid's idea of roughing it is a high-tech tent, featherlite sleeping bags and state-of-the-art cooking gear, then take him to see the **Museum of Family Camping**. After a good look at the early trailers and primitive camping gear of the mid-1900s, perhaps he'll appreciate that roughing it means more than taking off the headphones.

> **Museum of Family Camping**, located in Bear Brook State Park, Allenstown, NH; ↘ 603 485 3782; web: www.ucampnh.com/museum. *Open daily 10.00am–4.00pm, Memorial Day–Columbus Day.*

Odd shopping

Shish Ka Poop, dehydrated moose dung on a Skewer, and Moosletoe, a festive cluster of droppings, are among the thousand moose-related items sold at **Strictly Moose** in Gorham. These ungainly creatures, often described as proof that God has a sense of humor, grace everything from mugs to candles. Try the Moosturd jar – the poopun of choice – or the moose-butt mug. For connoisseurs of moose poop, it's important to collect only winter droppings; their summer diet isn't conducive to the manufacture of moose poop earrings.

> **Strictly Moose**, 129 Main St, Gorham, NH; ↘ 877 250 6713 or 603 466 9417; web: www.strictlymoose.com

Quirky cuisine

At **Margaritas Mexican Restaurant and Watering Hole** meals are served in your cell. Located in the town's former police station and jail, the 16 jail cells are now individual dining 'cells' complete with iron doors. The hostess welcomes you from the former witness box; the lounge is in the former courtroom. Presidential hopefuls hang out here during the primaries, leading to all kinds of sarcasm about how appropriate the accommodations are for politicians, to say nothing of Enron executives and Martha Stewart.

> **Margaritas Mexican Restaurant and Watering Hole**, 1 Bicentennial Square, Concord, NH 03301; ↘ 603 224 2821; web: www.margs.com/concord.htm

MAINE
Festivals and events

The folks in Pittsfield like to cook up quite an egg fry at their **Central Maine Egg Festival** by using one of the world's largest frying pans: five feet in diameter and weighing 300lb. The Alcoa Company made the Teflon-coated pan back in 1973; it's heated by gas on its own specially designed burners. The festival also features the Egglympics, with all kinds of run-with-an-egg-on-a-spoon-type games, and a parking lot chalk-art contest.

> **Central Maine Egg Festival**, held annually in July. Contact Central Maine Egg Festival Committee, 12 Hartland Ave, Pittsfield, ME 04967; ↘ 207 487 3520; web: www.pittsfield.org/eggfes.htm

Lumberjacks do for fun what most of us wouldn't, or couldn't, do for a million dollars. During the Woodsmen Field Day at the **Fryeburg Fair**, they compete in a sort of lumberjack rodeo, trying to out do each other in buck sawing, ax throwing, tree-felling, chain-sawing and log-rolling competitions. The springboard chop event sends competitors hacking their way to the top of a tall pole. There's also a skillet-throwing contest.

Fryeburg Fair, held annually in October. Contact W Oxford Agricultural Society, Fryeburg Fair Association, PO Box 78, Fryeburg, ME 04037; ⤳ 207 935 3268 or 207 935 3662; web: www.fryeburgfair.com

Rockland is home to the Farnsworth Art Museum, a facility that specializes in innovative community-based art. Each year they, and the local chamber of commerce, co-sponsor the **Festival of Scarecrows**, resulting in dozens of scarecrows popping up all over town. Anyone can enter: businesses, groups, families and individuals. A parade, barn dance, pumpkin hunt and street bazaar add to the festivities.

Festival of Scarecrows, held annually in October at the Farnsworth Art Museum, Rockland, ME. Contact the Farnsworth Art Museum at ⤳ 207 596 6256; web: www.farnsworthmuseum.org

Moxie was the nation's most popular soft drink prior to World War II, a curative 'nerve' tonic invented in Maine in 1884. Today you can still buy it in Maine, but it's definitely an acquired taste. The town of Lisbon has been honoring the drink for 20 years with a medieval-themed **Moxie Days Festival** featuring a parade, a medieval personal insulter, human chess, an 'Ugliest Knees in a Kilt' contest and a wench-carrying competition.

Moxie Days Festival, held annually in July. Contact the Androscoggin Chamber of Commerce, 179 Lisbon St, PO Box 59, Lewiston, ME 04243; ⤳ 207 783 2249; web: www.moxiefestival.com

Larry Ross, a middle school teacher, has a charming, eccentric way of inspiring children to reach for their dreams. He uses the packing crate that once carried Lindbergh's *Spirit of St Louis* plane back to America after Lindbergh made his first solo transatlantic flight. Larry bought the decaying crate, which had been converted into a rustic cabin, in 1990 for $3,000, hauling it from New Hampshire to his home in Maine. After restoring the structure, he began filling it with Lindbergh and early aviation memorabilia, including photos, scrapbooks, letters and news clippings. Beginning in 1992, on the 65th anniversary of Lindbergh's famous flight, Larry started holding an annual **Lindbergh Crate Day** on the last day of the school year, using the crate as an inspirational message to kids of what they, too, can achieve.

Lindbergh Crate Day, held annually in June. Contact the Lindbergh Crate Museum, Easy St, New Canaan, ME 04924; ⤳ 207 474 9841.

It's hard enough to get a guy to carry out the trash; how on earth do you convince him to carry his wife 278 yards uphill, jump over obstacles, and wade through a water trough, all the while carrying her on his back? Maybe he'll do it for the prizes at the **National Wife Carrying Championships**: five times the wife's weight in cash plus her weight in beer and other goodies. This wacky contest is based on the practices of a 19th-century Finnish band of robbers who were known to run off with the townsfolk's wives during their raids; new recruits were expected to prove their prowess by running with sacks of flour. The event has proven so popular that competitions are popping up in other states, with the winners going to the national championships in Maine, then on to the world championships in Europe.

> **National Wife Carrying Championships**, held annually in October. Contact the Sunday River Resort, PO Box 04217, Bethel, ME 04217; ❧ 207 824 3000; web: www.wifecarrying.com

It doesn't last for very long – just two hours – but the opportunity to wrestle in mashed potatoes during the **Potato Blossom Festival** draws about a hundred fans each year, half of whom join in the fray. Anyone who shows up can wrestle in the foam-padded enclosure filled with a mixture of freeze-dried potato flakes and water. The goop first attracts the kids, then older teens as they lose their inhibitions, and finally adults willing to have a go at it.

> **Potato Blossom Festival**, held annually in July. Contact the Fort Fairfield Chamber of Commerce, 232 Main St, Ste 4, Fort Fairfield, ME 04742; ❧ 207 472 3802; web: www.potatoblossom.org

Three days of potato worship take place each August in Houlton at the **Potato Feast Days**. There's a potato-picking contest, potato relay races, potato-peeling contests and a potato-barrel-rolling competition in addition to potato carving and tasting. You'll learn a lot of interesting potato trivia, such as that inferior potatoes used to feed farm animals are called hog, or pig, potatoes.

> **Potato Feast Days**, held annually in August. Contact Greater Houlton Chamber of Commerce, 109 Main St, Houlton, ME 04730; ❧ 207 532 4216 or 207 532 4217; web: www.greaterhoulton.com

The winter **Moose Stompers Weekend** in Houlton will have you watching human dog-sled races (two people pull, one rides), human curling, a wiffle snowball tournament, and a half-dollar scramble that has kids diving in the snow for coins. A giant bonfire and fireworks display tops off the event.

> **Moose Stompers Weekend**, held annually in February. Contact Greater Houlton Chamber of Commerce, 109 Main St, Houlton ME 04730; ❧ 207 532 4216 or 207 532 4217; web: www.greaterhoulton.com

Paul Schipper isn't the first person to dream of buying a ski lodge and skiing every day, but he's probably the most determined. Now in his eighties, the former World War II fighter pilot has skied every day for 3,600 (and counting) consecutive ski days since 1981. If Sugarloaf Ski Resort is open, Paul's there. Nothing stops him, not even pneumonia, liver cancer, or the triple by-pass surgery he postponed until after ski season. When he broke his thumb, the doctor fashioned a special cast to fit around his ski-pole grip. Weather doesn't stop him either. When high winds closed the lifts, he just hiked up the ski hills and dodged moose on the way down. Once he had to ski at midnight by the light of a snow blower to maintain his streak. He's been profiled in *People* magazine and featured on television's *Good Morning America*. 'The Streak', as he calls it, started as a challenge instituted between Paul's friends and himself. The goal was to ski throughout the entire 1981–82 ski season without missing a single day. Paul was the only one who succeeded. Not wanting to let anyone down, Paul continued the feat, learning to adjust his schedule.

Sugarloaf holds **White, White World Week** in January with a snow sculpture contest and a toga party. The Dummy Dump is the highlight of the week, with an award given for the most creative and stylish 'flying' on the part of a dummy that needs to land with all pieces intact. A downhill body slide, a waiter and waitress race, and the crowning of Miss Sugarloaf and King of the Mountain conclude the event.

Paul Schipper's Streak, Sugarloaf Ski Resort

White, White World Week, held annually in January at the Sugarloaf Ski Resort, RR1 Box 5000, Carrabassett Valley, ME 04947; ↘ 800 THE LOAF or 207 237 2000; web: www.sugarloaf.com

Museums and collections

It started out innocently enough 50 years ago with just one old wood-burning stove. Bea Bryant brought the thing home and her husband, Joe, set about restoring it. They were so pleased with the results that one thing led to another and now, a lifetime later, they're delighted to show you around **Bryant's Stove Museum**. There are hundreds and hundreds of them dating from the 1750s to the 1850s, all lovingly restored. But they didn't stop at stoves. Joe added antique cars and a massive collection of piano-type music machines: calliopes, hurdy-gurdys, organ grinder's box-organs, nickelodeons and player pianos. (More than likely you'll find yourself singing golden oldies as Joe pumps out old tunes.) But the couple didn't stop there either. Bea got fixated on dolls and toys and Joe just couldn't resist making mechanical contraptions to interact with them. The result is the Doll Circus, a gigantic room of toys moving, dancing, and flying about. Ferris wheels, merry-go-rounds, music and lights … Bea and Joe are perpetually at play. Aren't they lucky?

Bryant's Stove Museum, 27 Stovepipe Alley, Thorndike, ME 04986; ↘ 207 568 3665; web: www.uninet.net/~bryants/. *Open Mon–Sat 8.00am–4.30pm.*

An entire museum devoted to umbrella covers? Just the covers? You mean those little sleeves that cover the folded umbrella when you buy it? Yup, that's it. The world's first – and only – **Umbrella Cover Museum** is the passion of one Nancy Hoffman, a musician from Peak's Island, a 20-minute ferry ride from Portland, ME. Nancy got the idea for the museum when she was cleaning out closets and came across seven umbrella covers. Curious as to what others do with their covers, she started asking around. Now, years later, she's accumulated enough covers, and enough umbrella cover trivia, to open her own museum. She has 400 of the things, from 32 countries, and folks from around the world keep sending her more. They range in size from a two-and-a-half-inch Barbie doll cover to a six-foot patio umbrella sleeve. Nancy has dedicated the museum to the appreciation of the mundane in everyday life. 'It's about finding wonder and beauty in the simplest of things,' she says, ' and about knowing that there is always a story behind the cover.' Amen.

Umbrella Cover Museum, 62-B Island Ave, Peaks Island, ME 04108; ↘ 207 766 4496; web: umbrellacovermuseum.tripod.com. Directions: Take the Casco Bay Lines ferry to Peaks Island. From the dock, walk up the hill to the first street (Island Ave) and turn left. *Open summers only; contact for exact dates and times.*

Attractions

This globe is so big that California is almost three and a half feet tall. Dubbed **Eartha**™, this is officially the world's largest revolving globe. Over 41 feet in diameter with a surface area of 5,542 square feet, it rotates just like the real thing and features the largest image of Earth ever created. It revolves in a three-story glass atrium in the lobby of the DeLorme Mapping Company and was built by the map publisher using a database that took two years to compile.

Eartha™, located at DeLorme Headquarters, Two DeLorme Dr, PO Box 298, Yarmouth, ME 04096; ➧ 800 642 0370 or 207 846 7000; web: www.delorme.com. *Lobby open 7 days a week. Free.*

Just plain weird

The **Orgone Energy Accumulator** in Rangaley Lakes was the bizarre, 'scientific' invention of a Dr Wilhelm Reich. In 1948, the doctor became fascinated by Freud's concepts and set out to find the physical basis for his theory of neurosis. It was Reich's belief that our species' energy, which he named 'orgone', becomes trapped in the body following traumatic human events. By sitting in his device, a six-sided box of organic materials and metals, you could regain lost orgone. Not everyone agreed with Reich's theories, however. In fact, the government charged him with all sorts of violations and ordered the accumulator destroyed. He was jailed for contempt of court after an associate refused to obey the order to destroy the accumulator, and Reich died in his jail cell of heart failure. In his will he asked that his work be sealed for 50 years, at which time, he hoped, the world would see the error of its ways and embrace the 'technology' he'd developed. That was in 1957; in 2007 perhaps we'll get a chance to see things his way.

Orgone Energy Accumulator, Orgonon-Dodge Pond Rd, PO Box 687, Rangeley, ME 04970; ➧ 207 864 5156 or ➧ 207 864 3443; web: www.orgone.org/unvsci-00reich.htm. *Open Wed–Sun 1.00–5.00pm Jul–Aug; Sun 1.00–5.00pm Sept.*

MASSACHUSETTS
Festivals and events

The Annals of Improbable Research organizes the **Ig Nobel Prizes**, a tongue-in-cheek event co-sponsored by various Harvard science associations. Now in its second decade, ten prizes are awarded annually for 'achievements that cannot or should not be reproduced'. All the awards are given for actual scientific research, the results of which have been published in reputable journals. Past recipients include scientists who fed Prozac to clams; explained why buttered toast always falls buttered side down; and reported on the relationship among height, penile length, and foot size. One winner trained pigeons to discriminate between the paintings of Picasso and those of Monet; another explored the sociology of Canadian donut shops. Also honored were the inventors of the pink plastic flamingo, a self-perfuming business suit, and an auto burglar alarm consisting of a detection circuit and a flamethrower. The awards are given good-naturedly and to receive one is considered an honor among scientists and inventors. Recipients show up at the awards ceremony wearing funny hats and costumes.

Ig Nobel Prizes. Contact the Annals of Improbable Research, PO Box 380853, Cambridge, MA 02238; ➧ 617 491 4437; web: www.improbable.com

Also known as Transgender Week, the annual **Fantasia Fair** in Provincetown is the Super Bowl of make-up and dress-up for cross-dressers, transsexuals and gays. Educational and social programs fill the week, but the highlights are the Follies and the Fashion Show at which the Queen and King of Fantasia are chosen. Unlike most beauty pageants in politically correct America, talent and brains don't really count, only costuming, and the crown goes to those with the greatest skill and creativity in hair, make-up, and walking in heels.

Fantasia Fair, held annually in October in Provincetown, MA; web: www.fantasiafair.org

Eccentric environments

Today it could be accepted as a novel way to recycle newspapers, but back in the 1920s building a house out of newspapers was, well, odd to say the least. Elis Stedman, an engineer who designed the machinery that makes paper clips, started experimenting with paper as a building material for his summer home. At his **Paper House** in Rockport, the framework and the floors are wood, but the walls are made of pressed paper about an inch thick. Stedman used an estimated 100,000 newspapers in the two-room cabin, pressing layers and layers together with glue and varnish. A normal roof protects the house from weather. Once the walls were up and he was living there, he couldn't ignore the little voice that told him to keep pasting. So he made the furniture, all of it, out of smaller paper logs around a half-inch thick. When he couldn't figure out a way to make a paper piano, he simply covered a real one in newsprint instead. He also made a grandfather clock, using a paper from each of the nation's 48 state capitals. The house was built with the regular electricity and plumbing of the day, meaning no indoor toilets. And, no, the outhouse wasn't made of paper.

Paper House, 52 Pigeon Hill St, Rockport, MA 01966; ↘ 978 546 2629; web: www.essexheritage.org/visiting/placestovisit/ listofsitesbycommunity/paper_house.shtml. Directions: On entering Rockport follow 127 to Pigeon Cove, after Yankee Clipper Inn take second left on to Curtis St, then left onto Pigeon Hill St. *Open daily 10.00am–5.00pm; Apr 1–Oct 31. Donations appreciated.*

Attractions

For a really unique view of the world, try standing inside the 30-foot, stained-glass globe room in The Christian Science Publishing Society. From a glass bridge inside the **Mapparium**, you experience the whole world surrounding you, just like standing inside a globe. There are 608 brightly colored glass panels, each representing ten degrees of latitude and longitude, and illuminated by a computer-controlled light show. Constructed in the 1930s, it's the only one of its kind in the world.

Mapparium, located at the Mary Baker Eddy Library, 200 Massachusetts Ave, Boston, MA 02115; ↘ 888 222 3711 or 617 450 7000; web: www.marybakereddylibrary.org

Museums and collections

You may take toilets for granted, but it's a good thing for us that someone takes them seriously. Charles Manoog, a successful plumbing wholesaler, wanted to pay tribute to his trade when he retired, so he began collecting all manner of plumbing parts and pieces, the results of which reside in the **American Sanitary Plumbing Museum**. Today his son carries on the family tradition of attending to all things washable and flushable. Plumbing industry people are enthralled by the hundreds of tools, pipes, sinks, showerheads, tubs and toilets scattered about the museum. Older folks are inspired to tell stories from the pre-potty and early-potty days. By the time youngsters realize what the moat that surrounded the castle was for, they stop smirking and begin to realize how good they have it nowadays. The museum's library can tell you everything you'd ever want to know about the business end of the pipes. Now if they could just do something about plumber's crack...

> **American Sanitary Plumbing Museum**, 39 Piedmont St, Worcester, MA 01610; ↘ 508 754 9453. *Open Tue & Thu 10.00am–2.00pm, or by appointment. Closed Jul & Aug.*

Some things are just so bad that they become good and you can see why for yourself at the **Museum of Bad Art**. Here, art that's too bad to be ignored is collected from artists who've had a bad brush day or are just so incompetent that they deserve recognition. Dubbing it 'A great monument to the work of unrecognized bad artists everywhere', museum founder Jerry Reilly looks for sincere attempts at art gone bad. If it's not sincere it doesn't have a chance of gracing the gallery's walls. You'll laugh all the way through this museum, especially at the titles given the paintings: 'Lucy In the Field With Flowers' and 'Sunday on the Pot With George'. Look closely and you'll become aware that bad art shares some common characteristics: distorted body parts, Skewed perspective, impossible settings and unfortunate choices of materials.

In addition to the collection, preservation, exhibition and celebration of bad art in all its forms and in all its glory, the museum holds special events in the Boston area. Some past exhibitions include 'Know what you like/ Paint what you feel', 'Fine Wine, Bad Art' and 'Gallery in the Woods', an art-goes-out-the-window theme that hung from trees in the woods. It's hard to believe, but only one piece in ten submitted to them actually meets their extremely low standards. If you have a unique and spectacular work of bad art and would consider donating it to MOBA, they'd be happy to consider it. Plain brown-paper wrappers are expected.

> **Museum of Bad Art**, 580 High St, Dedham, MA 02026 (in the basement of the movie theater); ↘ 617 325 8224; web: www.glyphs.com/moba. *Open Mon–Fri 6.00–10.00pm, Sat–Sun and holidays 1.00–10.00pm. Free with substantial discounts to anyone with a business card in Comic Sans Font.*

Just plain weird

Celebrities often meet strange deaths and **Jumbo the Elephant** was no exception. The 'largest elephant on earth' gained fame and fortune in the late 1800s. Unfortunately, he was run over and killed by a freight train. His owner, circus magnate P T Barnum, had the huge beast stuffed and put on display at Tufts University in Medford where he became the school mascot. When a fire destroyed him yet again, an enterprising administrator scooped the ashes into a peanut butter jar, and there he remains for Tufts athletes to rub the jar for good luck before their sporting events.

Quirk Alert

Glenn Johanson collects dirt, as in the stuff beneath your feet. He has jars and jars of it at his **Museum of Dirt** (web: www.planet.com/dirtweb), collected from places as far flung as Mt Fuji and the Amazon. He's got the dirt from Martha Stewart's house, the grit from Times Square following New Year's Eve and the grime from O J Simpson's former estate. Glenn is picky about his dirt and not just any old dirt will do. It needs to be distinctive, color-wise, and contain bits of something interesting. It can come from an exotic place or have some deeper meaning that only the donor can provide. For example, he has the whitest sand, the reddest and the bluest dirt, as well as the pinkest. Celebrities dish out their dirt. Chef Julia Child and entertainers Bob Hope, Mick Jagger, and Dick Clark have all contributed. So have Picasso, Belushi, Versace, and Liberace, although they don't know it. Dave Barry sent lint. You can also submit your own idea for dirt by filling out the online form and explaining why your dirt is so special.

Jumbo the Elephant's remains, located at Tufts University in Medford, MA 02155; ☎ 617 628 5000; web: www.tufts.edu. (A peanut butter jar holding ashes currently rests in the office of Athletic Director Bill Gehling.)

Quirky cuisine

Like the old popular song says, 'everybody plays a fool', but nobody plays it with more outrageous delight than the fool at **Medieval Manor** in Boston, just one of the zanies who run amok in this spoof of the Dark Ages. The manor houses an assortment of oafs, wenches, minstrels and its very own king, who remains benevolent as long as you play by his rules. Songs, stories and assorted antics fill the evening while you consume a six-course meal medieval-style – with your hands. You have your elbows on the table, crumbs fly, and your fingers are in everything. It's fun to act like a toddler again. Dress to mess.

Medieval Manor, 246 E Berkeley St, Boston, MA 02118; ☎ 617 423 4900; web: www.medievalmanor.com

Rooms with a Skew

Youth groups can sleep in genuine navy bunks in the crew quarters of the **Battleship Massachusetts** docked in Fall River. Chow is served navy style and classes in Morse code keep the spirit of the fighting ship alive.

Battleship Massachusetts, Battleship Cove, Fall River, MA 02721; ☎ 508 678 1100; web: www.battleshipcove.com

'Lizzie Borden took an axe and gave her mother 40 whacks; and when she saw what she had done, she gave her father 41.' Almost every child in America learns this little ditty that describes the 1892 murder of Lizzie's parents, presumably by Lizzie although this was never proven conclusively. At the **Lizzie Borden Bed and Breakfast and Museum** in Fall River, you can stand where Lizzie stood and, if you're brave enough, sleep where Mom and Dad did. Overnight guests are treated to a special after-hours tour and served the same breakfast that the victims probably ate. The museum is open for tours during the day.

> **Lizzie Borden Bed and Breakfast and Museum**, 92 Second St, Fall River, MA; ↘ 508 675 7333; web: www.lizzie-borden.com

RHODE ISLAND

Rhode Island is known as the vampire capital of America. Researchers have documented at least five deaths attributed to the vampire myth in the early settlement days. By the late 1800s, when embalming practices finally reached rural areas, the idea of digging up bodies to suck their blood clearly lost appeal and the 'vampires' died of starvation.

Festivals and events

The **Fools Rules Regatta** in Jamestown is a zany race of 'anything that floats'. Entrants get two hours at the beach to build their boats from non-marine items such as an old doghouse, car parts, hay bales and packing crates. The crafts are assigned classes depending upon the number of 'fools' intending to board them and then the crews prod their reluctant vessels downwind for 500 yards.

> **Fools Rules Regatta**, held annually in August in Jamestown, RI. Contact Jamestown Yacht Club, PO Box 562, Jamestown, RI 02835; web: www.jyc.org

The **Ancient and Horrible's Parade** on Independence Day (July 4) dates back to 1926 and features several hundred participants dressed in zany, horrible or patriotic costumes. The ancient aspect refers to the past when the youths dressed up as historical figures; the horrible part gives folks today an excuse to be as wacky as possible. Many of the entries spoof current events or reflect 'Rhode Island humor', defined as something 'you just have to live here to understand'. Twenty-five thousand folks turn out for the event.

> **Ancient and Horribles Parade**, held annually on July 4 at 4.30pm in the village of Chepachet in Glocester, RI. Contact Glocester Town Hall; ↘ 401 568 6206; web: www.glocesterri.org

The **Penguin Plunge** involves 300 tuxedo-clad swimmers brave enough to take a frigid plunge each New Year's Day.

> **Penguin Plunge**, held annually on New Year's Day (Jan 1) in Mackerel Cove, Jamestown, RI; ↘ 401 823 7411

Just plain weird

The **Big Blue Bug** that sits atop the New England Pest Control Building has become a Providence landmark. The 58-foot-long, 9-foot-high subterranean termite – named Nibbles Woodaway – is almost 1,000 times the actual size of a termite. The bug gets dressed up with hats and props to celebrate holidays and events.

> **Big Blue Bug**, New England Pest Control Building, 161 O'Connell St, Providence, RI; ↘ 888 BLUEBUG; web: www.bigbluebug.com

Odd shopping

Oop! is a whimsical and zany gift store with two locations: one in the heart of Providence's historic College Hill district and one in the Providence Place Mall next to Nordstrom. It bottles its own drink called OOP!Juice, offering customized holiday flavors like Ghoulade at Halloween and Turkey Slurpee at Thanksgiving. The stores carry one-of-a-kind knick-knacks, home furnishings, jewelry, toys and trinkets such as naked people candles, nose-shaped pencil sharpeners and fly-swatter clocks. Their motto, 'Shopping for Good, Clean Fun', refers to their inventive in-store games, contests, and special events. They celebrate 'days' like National Sarcasm Day and Kiss and Make Up Day, as well as stars' birthdays and competitions like National Grouch Day where the grumpiest scowl wins a prize. The stores personify wackiness; their employees are given personas like 'Diva' and 'Manager of the Inner Child'.

> **Oop!**, 297 Thayer St and Providence Place Mall, Providence, RI 02906; ↘ 800 281 4147; fax: 401 751 9055; web: www.oopstuff.com

Rooms with a Skew

At the **Rose Island Lighthouse**, the two keepers' bedrooms are available for overnight guests after the museum closes at 4.00pm each day. Restored right down to the pitcher pump at the sink, the lighthouse is furnished with everything you need to play keeper – a gas hot plate, a barbecue, a water pump, solar shower and pollution-free, wind-powered electricity. You have to change the bed and clean the place up by the time the museum opens at 10.00am. They also offer week-long programs where you perform real keeper duties like flag raising, data recording and maintenance and repairs.

> **Rose Island Lighthouse**, PO Box 1419, Newport, RI 02840; ↘ 401 847 4242; fax: 401 847 7262; web: www.roseislandlighthouse.org

CONNECTICUT

Festivals and events

July 4th, Independence Day, means parades and noise, lots of it. In Willimantic they celebrate with the **Boom Box Parade**, an all-ages procession requiring only a red, white and blue outfit and a cranked-up boom box to enter. No other kind of music is allowed – just powerful radios that are tuned to station WILI. The event, which began in 1986 when no marching band could be found for the parade, is known for its wacky costumes and floats. The parade's Grand Marshall has worn boom boxes as shoes and towed a bus-sized boom box while skating on roller blades. The precision drill team wields power drills.

> **Boom Box Parade**, held annually on July 4 in Willimantic, CT. Contact wili 14 AM, The Nutmeg Broadcasting Company, 720 Main St, Willimantic, CT 06226; ↘ 860 456 1400; fax: 860 456 9501; web: www.wili.com

Eccentric environments

William Gillette was an early 1900s' theater actor and playwright who took his role as Sherlock Holmes very personally; so personally, in fact, that he built a replica of 221B Baker Street in the eccentric **Gillette Castle** he built in Hadlyme. With 24 rooms, this rock and cement eccentricity includes twisting passageways, 47 intricately carved doors equipped with special locking mechanisms, and mirrors strategically placed so he could time his grand entrances for maximum impact. A

Quirk Alert

THE NUT LADY

The Nut Lady, as they say in England, was one of life's full-on nutters. Elizabeth Tashijian elevated nuts to a god-like status for 30 years, turning her estate into an ode to the nut. She sang about nuts, wrote about nuts, painted nuts, and plugged the power of nuts on radio and television. Of the opinion that nuts are of primeval existence, and that nutcrackers are the nut's worst enemy, her **Nut Museum** in Old Lyme was a sanctuary for abused nuts and a shrine to the virtues of her favorite seed. Sadly, at age 88, she was taken ill and sent to a nursing home. Her house was condemned, but much of her art was rescued by the Lyman Allyn Art Museum in New London, CT. Elizabeth, now 92, is an occasional guest speaker at the museum.

Nut Art located at the Lyman Allyn Art Museum, 625 Williams Street, New London, CT 06320; tel: 860 443 2545; web: www.lymanallyn.org. Nut lady web: www.roadsideamerica.com/nut/

miniature railway that once carried visitor Albert Einstein used to surround the property.

> **Gillette's Castle**, 67 River Rd, East Haddam, CT; ☎ 860 526 2336; web: www.cttourism.org. *Open daily 10.00am–5.00pm May–Oct.*

Museums and collections

The **Children's Garbage Museum** in Stratford makes its point in a big way – big as in a 24-foot-long, 12-foot-high dinosaur made entirely of trash. The Trash-o-saurus very graphically illustrates how the solid waste monster can grow to overwhelm us. Here, children and adults learn how to reduce, reuse, recycle and rethink our throw-away lifestyles through 15 most unusual, hands-on exhibits.

> **Children's Garbage Museum**, 1410 Honeyspot Rd Extension, Stratford, CT 06615; ☎ 800 455 9571 or 203 381 9571; fax: 203 377 1930. *Open Wed 1.00–3.00pm Jul–Aug.*

The heroes of horror are honored in style at the **Witch's Dungeon Classic Movie Museum** in Bristol. This one-of-a-kind horrorium features life-size recreations of monster stars in their most famous roles. Cortland Hull, the creator of these creepy dioramas, began molding his characters in 1966 when he was just 13 years old. Frankenstein, Dracula, the Mummy, and the Phantom of the Opera, are among those depicted in movie settings that use actual props from their films. Special voice tracks recorded by the famous voices of horror bring the sets eerily to life. Cortland uses real-life casts of the actors and works endlessly on each and every detail. You might say his 30-year pursuit of vampires and other monsters is in his blood.

> **Witch's Dungeon Classic Horror Museum**, 90 Battle St, Bristol, CT 06010; ☎ 860 583 8306; web: www.ndeavor.com/www_ndeavor_com/dungeon/home.htm

The **Barker Character, Comic, and Cartoon Museum** is a nostalgic trip back in time. With its staggering 65,000 items, this Cheshire museum is the lifetime dream of Herb and Gloria Barker, passionate animation collectors for three decades. Their strange hobby has resulted in the most complete tribute to American animation and pop culture existing in the USA today. Besides showcasing movie, television and cartoon characters along with their memorabilia, they've acquired advertising characters such as the Pillsbury Doughboy, the Hershey Kisses, Gumby and the California Raisins. They'll go anywhere, anytime in search of their piece of Americana, and especially to Florida, the mother-lode of kitsch. Where else would you find a Lone Ranger cereal-box ring, a Bing Crosby ice-cream box, or a Beatles bobbin' head doll? Nothing in the museum is for sale, but everything is marked with its current market value to collectors. A cartoon theater on the grounds shows old-time cartoons on a big screen. This is a place for sharing childhood memories and gratitude for this couple's obsession.

> **Barker Character, Comic, and Cartoon Museum**, 1188 Highland Ave, Rte 10, Cheshire, CT 06410; ℩ 800 995 CELS or 203 699 3822; web: www.barkermuseum.com. *Open Wed–Sat 11.00am–5.00pm.* *Admission free.*

Odd shopping
Now here's something really weird – a supermarket grocery store that goes out of its way to make shopping fun. That's fun, as in a little farmyard zoo out front, staff dressed as cows and chickens, displays that go 'moo' when you push a button, a free ice-cream cone if your bill totals more than $100 and televisions above the check-out stations to keep you pacified if you have to wait. With locations in both Norwalk and Danbury, the staff at **Stew Leonard's** are fond of saying, 'profit is the applause of happy customers'. They must be getting standing ovations because the *Guinness Book of World Records* cites them as having the highest per-square-foot retail sales in the world.

> **Stew Leonard's**, 100 Westport Ave, Norwalk, CT 06851; ℩ 203 847 7214; and 99 Federal Rd, Danbury, CT 06881; ℩ 203 790 8030; also located at 1 Stew Leonard Dr, Yonkers, NY 10710; ℩ 914 375 4700; web: www.stew-leonards.com

Quirky cuisine
For a hamburger with attitude, visit the tiny building housing **Louis' Lunch**. Owned by the same family for 106 years, the place is famous for inventing the very first hamburgers in US history. Louis Lassen opened the lunch stop in 1895, serving steak sandwiches. One day he got an order from a customer in a rush that wanted something he could eat on the run. Louis had been grinding up left over steak bits so he grilled them, stuck them between two pieces of toast and sent the man on his way. And so a legend was born, one honored in the Congressional Record on their 105th anniversary. A sign on the wall says, 'This is not Burger King. You don't get it your way. You take it my way or you don't get a damn thing'. They still serve it the same way they always have, with a choice of just three garnishes: cheese, tomato, and onion. Don't even think of asking for ketchup or mustard. But do ask for a tour of the bricks, each one with a tale to tell. When they were threatened with demolition to make way for a high-rise, folks from all over sent bricks to aid in the reconstruction when the tiny building was moved to a new location.

Louis' Lunch, 261-263 Crown St, New Haven, CT 06510; ↘ 203 562 5507; web: www.louislunch.com

Rooms with a Skew

Randall's Ordinary Inn and Restaurant is anything but. Owner Bob Gillmore, dressed in 17th-century knee britches, cotton shirt and vest, starts the day by kindling a roaring fire in a 300-year-old hearth over which he cooks all the inn's food. His staff and waitresses, all in period attire too, circulate through the Hearth Room, stoking the fire, cooking with a variety of old-fashioned utensils and regaling the guests with stories of Colonial-era life. Home to ten generations of the Randall family, Bob bought the inn and converted it to a guest facility in 1986. Besides the unusual manner of cooking, the rooms in the house and barn are decorated with the charm and simplicity of the 1600s; the barn houses the lobby and more guest rooms. The silo honeymoon suite comes with a domed hot tub loft.

> **Randall's Ordinary Inn and Restaurant**, Rte 2 N, Stonington, CT 06359; ↘ 877 599 4540 or 860 599 4540; web: www.randallsordinary.com

NEW JERSEY
Festivals and events

Ocean City devotes an entire week to weirdness during its **Weird Contest Week**. Even tots are invited to participate. Kids from three to five years old get to demonstrate their abilities to bang on pots and pans, hammer wooden pegs, jingle and jangle bells and generally create a racket. The noisiest kids are crowned Little Miss and Little Mister Chaos. At the Saltwater Taffy Sculpting event, contestants attempt to create works of art from the sticky but pliable candy; past entries have featured Ferris wheels,  unicorns, computers and a pair of wearable eye glasses. Participants can also try their hands at french fry and pie sculpting. The wet T-shirt competition doesn't include wearing one; rather, it involves throwing one the farthest.

> **Weird Contest Week**, held annually the third week in August. Contact Public Relations Office; ↘ 609 525 9300; web: www.oceancity-nj.com

Museums and collections

Space Farms Zoo and Museum in Sussex, named after the Space family, is an odd place filled with old stuff: a miniature circus here, old cars over there; toy collections, Indian skulls, dinosaur bone displays and an antique merry-go-round. Dead animals in jars and the mounted remains of Goliath, supposedly the world's largest bear, join the live animals in the petting zoo. With more than 100 species, the zoo claims to be the largest private collection of North American wild animals.

> **Space Farms Zoo and Museum**, 218 Route 519, Sussex, NJ 07461; ↘ 973 875 5800; web: www.spacefarms.com. *Open daily 9.00am–5.00pm May–Oct.*

You get to play detective at a crime scene at the **New Jersey State Police Museum** in West Trenton. In the kitchen set-up, complete with blood, a chalk

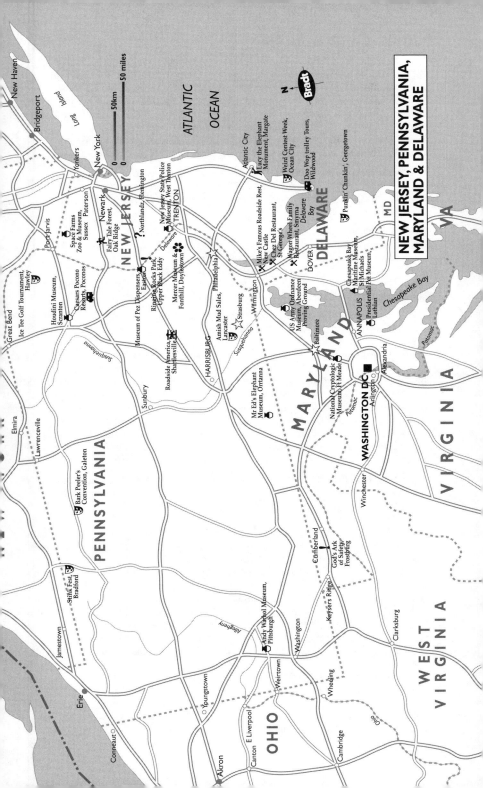

NEW JERSEY, PENNSYLVANIA, MARYLAND & DELAWARE

outline and yellow crime scene tape, you're supposed to look for clues that will lead to the murderer. Luckily, a video helps you spot what would be obvious to a real detective and you can examine the fingerprints under a microscope. Other displays exhibit an array of confiscated weapons, details on how tough State Trooper training is, the chillingly real Lindberg kidnapping ransom note and an explanation of why America's government was hard at work during the 1930s tattooing chickens to curb the theft of the birds by the hungry unemployed.

New Jersey State Police Museum, PO Box 7068, River Rd, W Trenton, NJ 08628; ☎ 609 882 2000, ext 6400; web: www.njsp.org/about/museum.html. *Open Mon–Sat 10.00am–4.00pm.*

Attractions

She's six stories tall and weighs 90 tons. Her name is **Lucy**, and she's an elephant monument built in 1881 to draw tourists to the Jersey Shore. A million pieces of wood went into her construction, wood that began showing its age in the 1960s. A 'Save Lucy' committee raised half a million dollars to get Lucy the plastic surgery she needed. (We should all be so lucky.) She's now open for tours.

Lucy the Elephant Monument, 9200 Atlantic Ave, Margate, NJ; ☎ 609 823 6473; web: www.lucytheelephant.org

Fairy Tale Forest is a kiddie attraction frozen in time. Dating back to 1957, this delightfully quirky park has winding pathways leading past two-dozen child-size buildings. Depicting nursery rhymes and fairy tales, as well as a few other odd tableaux, the village includes Peter and his pumpkin, the old lady and her shoe, Robin Hood and his merry gang, Goldilocks and the three bears, and the big, bad wolf of Little Red Riding Hood fame. Children's tunes play throughout the park and storytellers read while sitting in Mother Goose's nest. Santa has his workshop, with elves making presents and playing Christmas carols even in the summer. The place is a real throwback to kinder, gentler days.

Fairy Tale Forest, 140 Oak Ridge Rd. Located south of Route 23, Oak Ridge, NJ 07834; ☎ 973 697 5656; web: www.fairytaleforest.com. *Hours vary seasonally.*

Bruce Zaccagnino has a compulsion to build little bridges, bridges that need to span something if they're to make sense. So Bruce builds little gorges, mountain passes and rivers. Then his little trains, 135 of them, have something to do as they run around his not-at-all little **Northlandz** miniature railroad in Flemington, home of the **Great American Railway, Doll Museum, and Art Gallery**. Northlandz trains run along eight miles of miniature track as you walk an entire mile through Bruce's world, gaping at the 10,000 freight cars winding their way among 4,000 buildings nestled among mountains and bridges soaring as high as 40 feet. It's hard to take in all the detail before you because, in addition to the scenic backdrop, Bruce has added thousands of people going about their lives in this vertical world including – improbably – ones escaping from a downed airliner by climbing down little ladders. While the attraction advertises a tour through some of the 'finest scenery in America', you won't see scenery like this anywhere on the planet. His world of cliffs and canyons couldn't possibly be home to cities and towns, so it's best just to appreciate the massive scope of his 30-year effort and leave feeling somewhat inadequate that you're compulsion-deprived. Don't be surprised if you hear organ music during your tour; Bruce often plays one of the

Wurlitzer organs he installed in the middle of his vast, other-worldly empire. Once outside you can ride a real, ⅔-scale steam train.

Northlandz, Great American Railway, Doll Museum, and Art Gallery, 495 Hwy 202 S, Flemington, NJ 08822; ↘ 908 782 4022; web: www.northlandz.com. *Open Mon–Fri 10.30am–4.00pm; Sat–Sun 10.00am–6.00pm.*

Tours
Relive the felt poodle skirt and duck-tail era of the 1950s on the **Doo Wop Trolley Tours of the Wildwoods**. You'll see chrome-plating, pastel neon, and plastic palm trees reminiscent of Elvis-era architecture; buildings with pointy parts, boomerang rooflines, thatched roofs, Kon-Tiki heads, glass walls, and Jetson fins. You'll also experience the social glitter of the entertainment district, playground of such stars as Liberace, Connie Francis and Johnny Mathis.

Doo Wop Trolley Tours, Wildwood, NJ. Contact Doo Wop Preservation League, 3201 Pacific Ave, Wildwood, NJ 08260; ↘ 609 729 4000; web: www.doowopusa.org

PENNSYLVANIA
Festivals and events
It can last ten hours, be two miles in length, and involve 10,000 marchers who spend the better part of each year planning for this most eccentric of parades. Every New Year's Day, Philadelphia's **Mummers' Parade** takes to the streets with elaborate costumes, comedy, music, and revelry. Continuing a tradition dating back to colonial times, the parade has its roots in the noisy welcoming of the New Year with firearms and masked processionals. Rowdy revelers would go house to house, chanting, 'Here we stand by your door, as we stood the year before. Give us whiskey, give us gin, open the door and let us in.' It got so out of hand that a law was passed in 1808 declaring such parades to be public nuisances. The celebrations were quieted, but never stopped; today they've evolved into a massive event unifying the various neighborhood groups of yesteryear.

The parade consists of four divisions: the Comics, the Fancies, the String Bands and the Fancy Brigades. The Comic clubs exist to make people laugh. Experts at satire, they dance their wacky way along the route, making fun of anyone and everything. Nothing escapes their mockery: politics, pop culture and current events are all fair game. They're judged on originality and how well they play out their chosen theme. The Fancy division, named for their mission, brings dazzling displays of color, form and texture to life. Magnificent in size, extraordinary in execution, their beauty is stunning. They're judged on color, grandeur and theme; the captain of each club competes in a best-dressed competition. Fancy Brigades are groups, rather than individuals, presenting choreographed shows in elaborate costumes depicting a theme. Broadway-like stage scenery is carried along on flatbed trucks and assembled each time the brigade stops to perform. How effectively and spectacularly they portray their theme is the criterion for judging. The String Bands compete for prizes based on their music, their presentation and their costumes. Unusual or unique combinations of instruments may be used, including the addition of accordions, drums, bells, and saxophones to the stringed instruments. While the core band moves in unison, breakaway groups do specialty acts. Rivalry among bands is quite intense.

You can see and hear all about mummery at the **Mummer's Museum**, open year around. A mummer is defined as any man, woman or child who participates in the parade, which they do by joining any of the mummer's clubs. Tremendously varied, each club has its own unique style. A truck driver may find himself wearing feathers; while a stodgy judge just might be the clown behind the mask. You'll see some of the past costumes that cost upwards of $20,000 each.

Mummers' Parade, held annually on New Year's Day (Jan 1) in Philadelphia, PA; web: www.mummers.com. Contact Mummer's Museum, 1100 S 2nd St, Philadelphia, PA 19147; ↘ 215 336 3050; web: www.riverfrontmummers.com/museum/html. *Hours vary seasonally.*

Just because there's two feet of snow outside doesn't mean you can't play golf. At the **Ice Tee Golf Tournament**, Lake Wallenpaupack is turned into a challenging course complete with tree-lined fairways, greens, water traps, obstacles and roughs. Golfers are limited to two clubs and one putter.

Ice Tee Golf Tournament, held annually in Februray at Ehrhardt's Waterfront, Route 507, Lake Wallenpaupack, Hawley, PA; ↘ 570 226 3191; web: www.ehrhardts.com

Promoted as an event with absolutely no redeeming value, radio station WIP's **Wing Bowl** is a celebration of gluttony and eye candy. The Wing Bowl started a decade ago as a simple enough chicken-wing-eating contest and grew into the extravaganza it is today, one attracting 15,000 spectators. To qualify to enter the eating competition, each contestant has to do an eating stunt, live on the air and video recorded for play on the website. The stunts aren't pretty: one contestant ate a bowl of dog food, another a jar of mayonnaise. Twenty-six are eventually chosen to compete along with 56 Wingettes, women chosen for their ability to look sexy while cheering on guys stuffing themselves with chicken wings. There are bizarre parades of cheering fans as well as the crowning of Top Wingette. The prizes are significant enough to motivate people to behave this way: a car for the top eater and a five-day beach vacation for the top Wingette.

Wing Bowl, held annually in January. Contact Sports Radio 610 WIP, 441 N 5th St, Philadelphia, PA 19123; ↘ 215 922 5000; web: www.610wip.com

Woodsmen show off their lumberjack skills, ax throwing, crosscut sawing and camp cooking skills at the **Bark Peeler's Convention** at the Pennsylvania Lumber Museum. Besides demonstrating useful skills, they also compete in tobacco spitting, frog jumping, lugging and carrying, and greased pole contests.

Bark Peeler's Convention, held annually in July. Contact the Pennsylvania Lumber Museum, 5660 US 6 West, Box 239, Galeton, PA 16922; ↘ 814 435 2652; web: www.lumbermuseum.org

It's not a humdrum supermarket leek you'll smell at **Stink Fest**. We're talking about the real thing here, an incredibly pungent wild onion that smells so strong that schoolchildren are sent home if teachers smell it on their breath. Leek dip and leek soup contests are part of the culinary delights, but the real fun is the outhouse race where various tasks, like threading toilet paper on plungers, challenge the contestants along the route.

Stink Fest, held annually in May. Contact Stink Fest, PO Box 1004, Bradford, PA 16701; ↘ 814 362 4322

You can buy a buggy ($5,000), a quilt ($400) and the kitchen sink at the annual **Amish Mud Sales**. So named because they take place at the beginning of spring when the ground is muddy, the four March Mud Sales are an opportunity to mingle with this most elusive group of Americans. Each sale offers everything an Amish family might need and that a non-Amish might covet or collect. Thousands of people attend each sale, getting caught up in the multiple auctions going on around them or buying from tarps spread out on the ground. Tools, socks, canned goods, farm equipment, pressure washers, wooden toys, and sleigh bells … whatever, it's all there along with good food and interesting company.

Amish Mud Sales. Contact the Pennsylvania Dutch Convention & Visitors Bureau, 501 Greenfield Rd, Lancaster, PA 17601; ↘ 800 PADUTCH or 717 299 8901; web: www.padutchcountry.com

Eccentric environments

Unlike most self-taught visionary artists who create bizarre surroundings out of misshapen concrete, Henry Mercer used concrete artfully, constructing three architecturally outstanding buildings in the early 1900s to house his twin obsessions: tools and tile. His **Mercer Museum** in Doylestown was built specifically to showcase his extensive collection of tools and work objects, which, he theorized, could tell the story of human progress through their evolution and use. He classified all tools into 12 categories: tools that made other tools, tools used for food, shelter, clothing and transportation; those that aided language, such as books; and the tools used in religion, business, government, art, science, and amusement. Angered that others, especially local historians, didn't embrace his theories, he designed and built the seven-story structure himself, using just a handful of assistants and a single horse for hauling heavy loads. The tools of 60 trades, some 50,000 of them, including cider-making, blacksmithing, printing and shoemaking, are displayed en masse, leaving you to draw your own conclusions as to whether his theory makes sense. Mercer's obsession with tile led him to build the Moravian Pottery and Tile Works in 1910. Now acknowledged as an artistic leader in the arts and crafts movement of the time, his tiles were used in buildings across America. But it's his home, Fonthill, built in 1908, that gave free reign to his vivid imagination. He built the 44-room structure room by room, stopping only when he'd run out of ideas for more rooms. Fonthill has been called a 'concrete castle for the New World', an amazing tribute to his artistic visions of concrete and tiles. He died in 1930, a lonely and disillusioned eccentric.

Mercer Museum and Fonthill Historical Society, Headquarters, 84 S Pine St, Doylestown, PA 18901; ↘ 215 345 0210; web: www.mercermuseum

Museums and collections

If you weigh as much as 500,000 fireflies, your doctor may want you on a diet. Try Cheddar-flavored worm larvae; it's only nine calories a serving and loaded with protein. Barley and bee salad is good, too; just keep away from the chocolate-covered grasshoppers for dessert. Cooking with bugs is just one of the weird things you can experience at the **Insectarium** in Philadelphia, the country's only interactive, all-bug museum. You'll see 100,000 insects, 10% of them alive and kicking. The petting corner, where you get to hold Vinnie the tarantula and pet a hissing beetle, may be more personal than you'd care to get but, compared to the cockroach kitchen and bath, it may suddenly seem the lesser of two evils. The kitchen and bath display is the museum's *pièce de résistance*, sitting squarely in the middle of the room surrounded by electrified plexiglass walls and the squeals of the squeamish. Roaches by the hundreds lounge here and there, but flip open the cupboards or sprinkle some water and thousands and thousands more swarm from their dark hiding places. There's never been an escape, or even an escape attempt – why bother when you're living in the buggy version of heaven? Still, the cockroaches eventually die, but don't worry – replacements are bred in cans of garbage behind the scenes.

The Insectarium is the brainchild of Steve Kanya, head bugmeister and former cop, who turned to stamping out bugs instead of crime. Always fascinated with insects, he started displaying his 'catch of the day' in the window of his exterminating business. The display attracted so much attention that he moved to a three-story building so he could have his pest execution business on the ground floor and put the museum on the upper two floors. Today half a dozen school groups visit every day, and it takes a staff of ten just to manage the bugs and visitors. It's a favorite place for kids' birthday parties: they're booked months in advance. Some years they hold a Bug Olympics. Ants have a weight-lifting competition. Other species, such as roaches, beetles and walking sticks (some grow to a foot in length) get their own racing event; an all-species race is the finale. At Halloween they have a bug costume contest and Spider Walk scavenger hunt. Downstairs in the gift shop you can buy lunchboxes, ties, aprons, and picnic cloths festooned with various critters, while their website showcases 500 buggy items for sale.

Insectarium, 8046 Frankford Ave, Philadelphia, PA; ❧ 215 338 3000; web: www.insectarium.com. *Open Mon–Sat 10.00am–4.00pm.*

The **Andy Warhol Museum** in Pittsburgh lives up to its eccentric namesake's reputation. Along with displaying the famous Campbell Soup Can paintings, the cow wallpaper and the double exposures of Elvis, the museum also serves as a sort of living pop culture venue, holding events as strange as the art it contains. Transsexuals have given tours, Tibetan monks have practiced dance routines amid the exhibits, and Friday night happy hours bring in an eclectic mix of Pittsburgh's avant-garde along with the just plain curious. Performance art is planned for the future, along with offbeat symphonic concerts and operas.

Andy Warhol Museum, 117 Sandusky St, Pittsburgh, PA, 15212; ❧ 412 237 8300; web: www.warhol.org. *Open Wed–Sun 10.00am–5.00pm, Fri 10.00am–10.00pm.*

The elephant potty chair is probably the most memorable item in **Mr Ed's Elephant Museum**. Or maybe it's the elephant hairdryer or, perhaps, the life-size talking elephant that greets you roadside. One of the largest elephant collections in the world, 6,000 and counting, Ed Gotwalt has been collecting everything elephant for 35 years, ever since he received one as a good-luck gift on his wedding day. His museum displays them all, from tiny to gigantic, from serious to playful, made from just about every substance known to man.

Mr Ed's Elephant Museum, 6019 Chambersburg Rd, Orrtanna, PA 17353; ❧ 717 352 3792; web: www.mistereds-elephantmuseum.com. Directions: located two miles east of Caledonia State Park on US Rte 30, 12 miles west of Gettysburg. *Open daily 10.00am–5.00pm. Admission free.*

Opened in 1829 as part of a controversial movement to change the behavior of inmates through 'confinement in solitude with labor', **Eastern State Penitentiary** in Philadelphia was the most expensive – and most copied – prison building of the era. Willie Sutton, the 'gentleman bandit' and Al Capone were among its involuntary guests. So was the governor's dog, sentenced in 1924 to life in prison for murdering his wife's precious cat. All contact between prisoners was prohibited, and full facemasks were worn in the rare instances a prisoner was taken out of his cell. Each cell was equipped with feed doors, isolated exercise yards, and sky-lit ceilings. This system was formally abandoned in 1913 after it was determined to constitute cruel and unusual punishment. The prison itself was remodeled over the years before being finally closed in 1971. You can experience a taste of this bizarre and now lost and crumbling world on tours of the facility. Accompanied by a guide, you'll be taken through the central rotunda, the solitary confinement yards, the baseball diamond and death row. Special events are occasionally scheduled such as Willie Sutton's Birthday, when actors portray the convict's doomed tunnel escape. The Bastille Day Party sees French revolutionaries, armed with muskets and cannon, storm the wall of the prison and capture 'Marie Antoinette' who tosses Twinkies from medieval-style towers. Ignoring her cries of 'Let them eat TastyKake', they drag her to a real, functioning guillotine. The watching crowd decides her fate. Some parts of the prison can be explored without a tour.

Eastern State Penitentiary, 22nd St and Fairmount Ave, Philadelphia, PA; ✆ 215 236 3300; web: www.EasternState.org. *Open Wed–Sun 10.00am–5.00pm mid-April–Nov.*

Houdini lives on, thanks to Bravo the Great and the First Lady of Magic, aka curators John Bravo and Dorothy Dietrich. Their **Houdini Museum** in Scranton showcases their dedication to the magician and escape artist. Houdini, whose real name was Eric Weiss, began performing magic at the age of 12, once running away for a time to join the circus. By the time he was in his 20s, his career as a master illusionist and escape artist was well on its way. Later in life he testified before Congress, debunking phony spiritualists and fake mediums. For years after his death, his wife held yearly séances, trying to contact him with a secret code they'd worked out earlier. She never did get through to him.

Houdini Museum, 1433 N Main, Scranton, PA 18508; ✆ 570 342 5555; web: www.houdini.org. *Hours vary seasonally.*

The **Easton Museum of Pez Dispensers**, located just next door to the Crayola Factory, is one of three Pez museums in the country. The little candy dispensers have become increasingly popular as collectibles during the last decade, sometimes fetching upwards of hundreds of dollars for a single container. This museum has around 1,500 of them on them on display, imaginatively arranged by theme. All the Halloween dispensers are in a haunted house; the psychedelic ones are arranged around a real Volkswagon Beetle car that appears to be crashing through a wall.

Easton Museum of Pez Dispensers, 15–19 Bank St, Easton, PA; ✆ 610 253 9795. *Open daily 10.00am–6.00pm.*

You need to schedule a visit to Temple University's School of Podiatry in Philadelphia in advance if you want to see the **Shoe Museum**, part of the school's History of Foot Care and the Foot Wear Center. Several hundred of their 800-plus shoe collection are displayed at any given time. You'll be blessing your Nikes when you see the 200-year-old wooden shoes from France, called 'sabots', that gave rise to the expression 'sabotage', as well as the Chinese foot-binding exhibit. The miniature salesman's samples are fun, as is the size 18 shoe worn by a circus giant. Sally Struthers donated the six-inch platforms she wore in the 1970s sitcom, *All in the Family*. Platform shoes have surfaced regularly throughout history, reaching absurd heights of up to two feet in the 16th century. Wearing the things required two servants to keep Madame upright and looking fashionably frail and dependent.

> **Shoe Museum**, Temple University School of Podiatric Medicine, Philadelphia, PA; ➤ 215 625 5243; web: www.podiatry.temple.edu/ shoe_museum/shoe_museum.html. *Reservations required.*

Voted number one as the 'best place to break the ice on a first date', the **Mütter Museum** in Philadelphia is brimming with bodily oddities too incredible to be kept to yourself. Impeccably displayed at the College of Physicians, this collection of medical specimens from the 1800s includes the result of terminal constipation – a grossly distended colon measuring five feet long and almost a foot in diameter. The 20,000 items, including fluid preserved specimens, obsolete medical instruments, skeletons, bones and wax models of diseases, combine the collections of many individual doctors. One such doctor in the 1920s carefully catalogued 2,000 objects, removed from the human body, that got there either by swallowing or inhaling: buttons, pins, needles, jewelry, coins, toy jacks, nails and even a bullet. Another collection is a series of wax models showing every disease of the human eye known at the time.

These medical specimens weren't saved for their shock value; they were the teaching and research tools of the 19th and early 20th centuries, 3D models of the real, not virtual, kind. And knowledge of anatomy wasn't limited just to medical students. The social elite attended medical lectures as well; it was an upscale thing to do. The museum has some famous body parts, including a tumor removed from President Cleveland's jaw, the thorax of John Wilkes Booth (who assassinated President Lincoln), and bladder stones removed from a Supreme Court justice. Among the most riveting exhibits are those relating to conjoined twins, both dead and still alive, who have been the subject of many a documentary. As disquieting as the displays can be, they're a fascinating look behind our own scenes.

> **Mütter Museum**, College of Physicians of Philadelphia, 19 S 22nd St, Philadelphia, PA 19103; ➤ 215 563 3737; web:
> www.collphyphil.org/muttpg1.shtml. *Open daily 10.00am–5.00pm except Thanksgiving, Christmas and New Year.*

Attractions

While some men get obsessed with building concrete sculptures, others get obsessed with models, and **Roadside America** is a fine example of the latter. Representing 50 years of labor, Lawrence Gieringer built the 'World's Greatest Indoor Miniature Village', a model display representing rural, small-town America. This 8,000-square-foot display has 300 buildings, 4,000 people, 10,000 shrubs and trees, running water and running trains and trolleys. Every half-hour there's a patriotic and religious slideshow that begins with the village fading into dusk and emerging with lights ablaze. Gieringer died in 1963 and Roadside America is exactly as he left it. Family members maintain it today.

> **Roadside America**, Interstate 78 and Rte 22, Shartlesville, PA 19554; ➤ 610 488 6241; web: www.roadsideamericainc.com. *Open Mon–Fri 9.00am–6.30pm, Sat–Sun 9.00am–7.00pm Jul–Labor Day; Mon–Fri 10.00am–5.00pm, Sat–Sun 10.00am–6.00pm Sep–Jun.*

Here's an obsession that spans two generations. People have been coming to the **Choo Choo Barn** for 44 years to see George Groff's 1,700-square-foot miniature train layout. Twenty-one trains along with 150 animated figures and vehicles populate his vision of the Amish countryside. There are skiers, a three-ring circus, an Amish barn raising, and a fire truck, sirens blaring, racing to put out a house on fire. For years prior to opening the Choo Choo Barn, George and his wife Florence had been letting visitors into their basement to admire the elaborate layout, but it wasn't until they needed money to send their kids to college that they moved the model to the barn and starting charging admission. When the Groff's retired, their youngest son Thomas, and his wife Linda, took over the barn, adding the model train hobby shop famous among model builders for offering the same items that his father created for the layout.

Choo Choo Barn, Rte 741 East, Box 130, Strasburg, PA 17579; ➘ 716 687 7911; web: www.choochoobarn.com. *Choo Choo Barn open Apr–Dec; shops open year-round. Visit the website or call for details.*

Just plain weird

Artist Cheryl Capuzzuti wants your lint. No, not the belly-button kind, the kind you get from the lint screen on your clothes dryer. She sculpts the lint into small figures and then returns the sculpture to the donor. Through her **National Lint Project**, which she acknowledges is 'dangerously close to laughable', she attempts to make the point that everyday life is found within mundane, material fluff and that, by transforming such a discardable material, we might take more delight in the discarded moments of everyday life. Cheryl exhibits her work, conducts free art classes and produces theatrical performances regularly at the **Duds 'N' Suds Laundromat**. In the past the laundromat has displayed lint puppets up to ten feet tall as well as showing an animated film made by launderers inspired by her work. Then there was a 'happening' in which performers did laundry and talked to the audience about daily chores we take for granted. You can usually find Cheryl there between November and April but be sure to check her website for actual dates and times.

National Lint Project, web: www.studiocapezzuti.com

Duds 'N' Suds Laundromat, 5430 Centre Ave, Pittsburgh, PA; ➘ 412 362 1024

If you bring a hammer with you when you hike in the woods near Upper Black Eddy you can play the ringing rocks. **Ringing Rocks Park** has a field of boulders, around eight acres worth, that sound as if they're metal and hollow if you strike them with a hammer or with another rock. One hundred and fifteen years ago the Pleasant Valley Band played what may be the first ever rock concert there.

Ringing Rocks Park, located in Bridgeton Township 2 miles west from Upper Black Eddy on Ringing Rocks Rd. Directions: Take Rte 611 south out of Easton to Rte 32 South (near Kintersville). Follow Rte 32 four miles, then turn right on Bridgeton Hill Rd. Follow to Ringing Rocks Rd and turn right. The park is about ½ mile up on the right.

Quirky cuisine

Chocolate body parts are big sellers at **Chocolate by Mueller** in Philadelphia. The anatomically correct chocolate heart is popular with cardiologists and their patients as well as being the Valentine gift you don't quite know how to react to. 'Oops, I thought you said a dozen noses' explains the chocolate bunch of nostrils. An ear with a chunk bitten out of it is the Mike Tyson special. For the person who's sweet on the outside, but nasty on the inside, send a chocolate covered onion. Brains, bagels, tool sets, dentures, lab rats and lungs; the selection is always evolving.

> **Chocolate by Mueller**, Reading Terminal Market, 12th and Arch sts, Philadelphia, PA; ☎ 800 848 5601; web: www.chocolatebymueller.net

Rooms with a Skew

A seven-foot champagne glass whirlpool bath for two awaits you at **Caesars Pocono Resorts**. Famous for their honeymoon packages, the three resorts in Cove Haven, Paradise Stream, and Pocono Palace are for couples only. A fourth resort in Brookdale welcomes families. There are two-dozen different themes in the suites, each of which have four levels, fireplaces, and in-room pools and whirlpools, heart-shaped and otherwise. Couples go through 60,000 fireplace logs, 40,000 bottles of bubble bath, 30,000 candles, 20,000 bottles of champagne and 13,000 disposable cameras each year. Frequent guests become members of the Forever Lovers Club.

> **Caesars Pocono Resorts**, Caesars Pocono Resorts, Poconos, PA; ☎ 877 822 3333 or 570 226 2101; fax: 570 226 6982; web: www.caesarspoconoresorts.com

Leave the city behind and awake to a rooster instead of a garbage truck on one of **Pennsylvania's Family Farms**. Member farms offer bed, breakfast and a chance to play farmer for a day or two.

> **Pennsylvania's Family Farms**, Pennsylvania Farm Vacation Association, Inc; ☎ 888 856 6622; web: www.pafarmstay.com

Sleep in one of 49 restored train cabooses at the **Red Caboose Lodge** in Strasburg. The lodge is the result of an absurdly low bid, made on a dare, to buy snow-bound rolling railroad stock following a 1970 blizzard. The place is listed in the *Guinness Book of World Records*.

> **Red Caboose Lodge**, PO Box 175, Strasburg, PA 17579; ☎ 888 687 5505 or 717 687 5000; web: www.redcaboosemotel.com

The **Fulton Steamboat Inn** in Lancaster County recalls the glory days of river boating. On the promenade deck are nautically themed family cabins with queen beds and bunks for the kids, as well as a pool. The observation deck has the Captain's Quarters, while the sun deck offers adult-only staterooms.

> **Fulton Steamboat Inn**, PO Box 333, Strasburg, PA 17579; ☎ 717 299 9999 or 800 922 2229 (reservations only); web: www.fultonsteamboatinn.com

MARYLAND
Festivals and events

A kinetic sculpture is an imaginative, often wacky – but always ludicrous – contraption designed to travel along a 15-mile obstacle course on land, through mud and over deep harbor waters. These machines can be simple crafts piloted by a single person, or they can be quite complex, well-engineered vehicles powered by a team of pilots. Used bicycles, gears and machine scraps usually play a big role in their construction, as do a lunatic sense of humor and a wildly inventive brain. The American Visionary Art Museum sponsors the **Baltimore Kinetic Sculpture Race**, the winner of which races in the world championship. The 30-year-old race has been nominated for a Nobel Peace Prize for recognizing unsung genius, promoting non-polluting transport and lifting the spirit of the communities that hold the race. Past entries included a 14-foot poodle, a 15-foot frog, a leaping beaver, a giant scorpion, Dr Seuss, a flying pig, the world's largest mobile wine-making cask and the world's largest seesaw, bearded nurses, and the Philadelphia Dumpster Divers.

There are a number of quirky race rules. The personal security rule requires that each sculpture carry a comforting item of psychological luxury, namely a homemade sock creature made from a not-too-recently washed sock. Another stipulates that each vehicle must be totally human powered, with no pulling, pushing or paddling allowed (except by pilots and pit crew), although the natural power of water, wind, sun and gravity can be used. The sculptures must also fit on public roads and follow the rules of the open road. Mom's high anxiety clause dictates a quick exit strategy. The honk-and-pass politeness rule requires yielding the right of way to another sculpture that wants to pass. (A one-finger salute is expected.) Time penalties are incurred for rule infractions, while time bonuses are given for carrying a passenger, called a barnacle, along the entire course. The Mediocre Award is given for finishing exactly in the middle. The Next to Last Award is highly coveted, making the end of the race particularly exciting. Awards are also given for best costume, the most memorable breakdown and the most interesting water entry. The winner of the Speed Award gets to be addressed as 'Most Visionary Professor'.

> **Kinetic Sculpture Race**, held annually in April. Contact American Visionary Art Museum, 800 Key Hwy, Baltimore, MD 21230; ↘ 410 244 1900; web: www.avam.org/kinetic

Museums and collections

Outsider artists have a home away from home at the **American Visionary Art Museum** in Baltimore. Outsider art is made by people who are driven to create, but who are usually unaware they're making art. Such artists are obsessive about their creations, use unusual materials, and have little or no knowledge of the mainstream art world. The museum's ever-changing collection is understandably eclectic and ranges from the delightfully naive to the decidedly bizarre. They've had a life-size interactive chess set populated with angels and aliens, and an art car contributed by psychic Uri Geller that consists of 5,000, psychically bent spoons and forks, many of which were used or touched by celebrities. They hold off-the-wall workshops where you can create your own wacky inventions out of trash and special events like the double wedding of life-size robot families. Throughout this book you'll find many descriptions of the self-made 'eccentric environments' referred to at the museum. The Visionary Art Museum also sponsors a Strut Your Stuff Pet Parade with prizes awarded for the best pet and owner look-alikes and for the animal 'least likely to succeed as a pet'. Any kind of creature is welcome.

American Visionary Art Museum, 800 Key Hwy, Baltimore, MD
21230; ☎ 410 244 1900; fax: 410 244 5858; web: www.avam.org. *Open
Tue–Sun 10.00am–6.00pm. Admission charge.*

Kids: If you want to grow up to be president, you'd do well to like pets. According
to Claire McLean, founder of the **Presidential Pet Museum**, all but four of our
43 presidents knew the value of pets when it came to tugging at voter's heartstrings.
Claire became addicted to the presidential pet pursuit after a White House stint
grooming the Reagan's dog, Lucky. Secreting some of the dog's furry clippings in
her purse, she had her first memento, eventually having a portrait made of Lucky
adorned with its own fur. Along with the portrait, Claire's museum, in a small
building next door to her house, tells the story of 400 presidential pets ranging
from the common – horses, dogs, and cats – to the more exotic – a tobacco-eating
goat, leash-trained raccoons and an elephant.

Presidential Pet Museum, 1102 Wrighton Rd, Lothian, MD 20711;
☎ 410 741 0899; web: www.presidentialpetmuseum.com. *Open Tues–Sun
11.00am–4.00pm.*

Great Blacks in Wax in Baltimore may not be the glitziest wax museum you'll
ever see, but it certainly has the most heart. Owners Elmer and Joanne Martin have
been nurturing their museum along since 1980 when it consisted of just four
figures in the back of their truck. Determined to instill pride in black culture and
history, they took their show on the road, visiting schools and churches to get their
message across. Eventually they were able to open an actual museum, with almost
two-dozen figures, in 1983. Today they have 130 of them, representing key figures
in American black history and culture. The most gripping display is a slave ship
documenting the horrid conditions the slaves had to endure as they were
imprisoned and sent to America in slave ships. Rosa Parks, who triggered the civil
rights movement by refusing to sit in the back of the bus, is shown being arrested
by white officers as she stepped off the bus. Former black congresswoman Shirley
Chisholf donated two of her outfits, one for winter and one for summer. To make
their figures economically, the owners construct only the black heads and hands of
their models; the bodies are those of white mannequins.

Great Blacks in Wax Museum, 1601 E N Ave, Baltimore, MD;
☎ 410 563 3404 or 410 569 6416; fax: 410 675 5040; web:
www.greatblacksinwax.org

This place just oozes with testosterone. Grown-up GI Joes are transported back to
childhood, or war time, as they climb all over the rockets, cannons and tanks
displayed at the **US Army Ordnance Museum** in Aberdeen. The 25 acres of
rusted, used equipment give you some idea of how the Pentagon spends our money.

US Army Ordnance Museum, Bldg 2601, Aberdeen Proving Ground,
MD 21005; ☎ 410 278 3602 or 410 278 2396; fax: 410 278 7473; web:
www.ordmusfound.org. *Open daily 10.00am–4.45pm. Closed national
holidays except Armed Forces Day, Memorial Day, July 4, Veterans Day.
Admission free; donations appreciated.*

Cryptology is a hidden world, shrouded in secrecy if it succeeds and steeped in
despair when it fails. The **National Cryptologic Museum**, which opened its
doors in 1993, welcomes the public to look behind the curtain at the people – and

the machines they invented – that were responsible for transmitting and intercepting secure communications. While computers have transformed the field, it would still be difficult today to break a code based on an obscure language that only a few people speak, as was the case with the Navajo Code Talkers of World War II.

> **National Cryptologic Museum**, located at the intersection of Maryland Route 32 and Maryland Route 295; ↘ 301 688 5849; web: www.nsa.gov/museum. *Open Mon–Fri 9.00am–4.00pm, 1st and 3rd Sat 10.00am–2.00pm.*

How many people does it take to change 60,000 light bulbs? Hugh Hicks, a retired dentist, probably knew the answer. He'd been collecting electric light bulbs since he was a child. At his Mount Vernon **Museum of Incandescent Lighting** he'd amassed a phenomenal collection of bulbs, the largest of which was a 50,000-watt, three-foot-diameter giant made for a 1933 fair; it took ten minutes to reach full brilliance. The smallest bulb, made for missile instrumentation, was a tiny, tiny speck only visible under a microscope. The most expensive bulbs ever made were ordered by the government (naturally!) and cost $28,000 apiece. He also had an exhibit of Christmas lighting from around the world; a dashboard light from the Enola Gay; the plane that dropped the atomic bomb on Hiroshima; and the 15-watt fluorescent bulb that illuminated the table on which the Japanese signed the surrender ending World War II. He also had bulbs shaped like Disney characters, bulbs in bottles, and bulbs imbedded in men's ties. Once, in a Paris subway in the 1960s, he surreptitiously unscrewed a bulb from an art deco fixture, plunging the station into darkness. Dr Hicks, who died in 2002, was most proud of his Edison Case, an unbroken history of the rapid evolution of lighting from 1879 to 1892. Developments happened every week, a situation similar to the high-tech revolution we experience today. The collection, previously located in his townhouse in the basement of his dental office, is now displayed at the Baltimore Museum of Industry.

> **Museum of Incandescent Lighting**, seen at the Baltimore Museum of Industry, 1415 Key Hwy, Inner Harbor S, Baltimore, MD 21230; ↘ 410 727 4808; web: www.thebmi.org. *Open Mon–Sat 10.00am–4.00pm.*

Just plain weird

Pastor Greene had a vision: a large ark, located on a hillside, with people the world over flocking to see it. When (and if) it finally gets built, God's Ark of Safety will serve as a church and as a sign from God that Jesus will soon be coming. The pastor had his vision in 1974. The completion date is dependent on a schedule set by God, who doesn't seem to be in an awfully big hurry to get this thing built. At this point all you can see are the steel beams forming the structure of the ark, which will be 450 feet long, 75 feet wide, and 45 feet high. Funds to build the ark come from folks donating their time, talent and money. When finished, it will house a Christian school, a Bible college, a 2,000-seat auditorium, conference facilities, a history room, a counseling center and radio and television equipment. As God provides financing, the pastor's flock moves ahead with construction. Snails will probably be the first in line to board.

> **God's Ark of Safety**, PO Box 52, Frostburg, MD 21532; ↘ 301 689 3551; web: www.godsark.org. Located off I-68, MD Rte 36, left on Cherry Lane.

Quirky cuisine

Don't be surprised when a total stranger calls you 'hon' in Baltimore. A cultural quirk, the term is short for 'honey', an endearment extended to one and all. And don't be surprised if the person calling you 'hon' is sporting big hair – really big hair. It's another quirk of the city's reputation for wackiness. And nowhere can more 'hons' be found that at **Café Hon**, ruled over by head hon Denise Whiting. You can't miss her – she's the one with the towering blonde beehive hairdo, the black stretch pants, the high heels and the faux-leopard stole. The café is famous for its comfort food as well as its wacky **HonFest**, an annual event featuring zany contests and the crowning of Baltimore's Best Hon. During the fest you can get a real 'hon' makeover or compete in the fashion show, the 'Bawlmerese' talking contest, or for the title of best all-around 'hon'. The SPAM™ bowl uses cans of SPAM™ in place of bowling pins.

> **Café Hon**, 1002 W 36th St, Baltimore, MD 21211; ☎ 410 242 1230; web: www.cafehon.com. *Open Mon–Thu 7.00am–9.00pm, Fri–Sat 9.00am–10.00pm, Sun 9.00am–8.00pm.*

> **HonFest** (web: www.honfest.net), held annually in June.

Rooms with a Skew

Youth groups can bring their sleeping bags and stay overnight at the **Chesapeake Bay Maritime Museum** in St Michaels. Addressing each other as 'Keeper so and so', they learn about the lifestyle of lighthouse keepers. Everyone performs all the traditional duties of a keeper, including standing watch. The overnight program is offered weekends in April, May, September and October. During the summer, families can stay, too, during one of the three public lighthouse programs.

> **Chesapeake Bay Maritime Museum**, Mill St, PO Box 636, St Michaels, MD 21663; ☎ 410 745 2916; fax: 410 745 6088; web: www.cbmm.org. *Hours vary seasonally.*

DELAWARE
Festivals and events

Delaware's home-grown insanity event goes by the name of **Punkin' Chunkin'**, an annual November occasion pitting man against pumpkin. It started back in 1986 when some guys with way too much time on their hands came up with a challenge to see who could design a machine to throw a pumpkin the farthest. Of the three original contraptions, the winning chunker, with a 128-foot throw, was a bunch of garage door springs connected to a car frame. The losers had to pack up their ropes, tubes, pulleys, springs, and poles and slink off into the night. Today, 48 teams and 30,000 spectators form the world's largest hurling party. There are only four rules: all the pumpkins must weigh between eight and ten pounds, pumpkins must leave their machine intact, no part of the machine can cross the starting line and no explosives are allowed. The chunkers themselves have several categories, including human powered, unlimited, centrifugal, catapult, air cannon and pneumatic. Even the wimpiest of contraptions manages over 250 feet today, while the most sophisticated can hurl a pumpkin almost 3,700 feet. On two earlier occasions the activity had to be moved to larger quarters when the machines became so effective that the pumpkins started out-distancing the fields in which the event was held.

Punkin' Chunkin', held annually in November in Georgetown, DE. Contact Pumpkin Chunk Association, Box 132, 4590 Hwy 1, Rehoboth Beach, DE 19971; web: www.punkinchunkin.com

Quirky cuisine

The owner of **Mike's Famous Roadside Rest**, Mike Schwartz, knows how to get you to shop at his Harley-Davidson motorcycle dealership. He'll feed you at his restaurant and entertain you with museum-type displays. Then he'll introduce you to the joys of a Harley. This huge facility houses one of the busiest dealerships in the country, not at all surprising seeing as the restaurant, The Warehouse Grill, is a popular roadside stop. Set inside the 40,000-square-foot building, the cafeteria has turn-of-the-century factory décor complete with a view of the mechanics working in the service bays. The Dave Barr Room lovingly portrays life on two wheels, featuring the only Harley ridden around the world. Dave Barr, a paraplegic, rode it on an 83,000-mile journey in 1972.

Mike's Famous Roadside Rest, 2160 New Castle Ave, New Castle, DE 19720; ☏ 800 FAMOUS HD or 302 658 8800; web: www.mikesfamous.com

If you've got a hankering for muskrat, two restaurants can oblige: **Ches Del Restaurant** in St George's and the **Wagon Wheel Restaurant** in Smyrna. Wonder if you can ask for a muskrat bag for leftovers?

Ches Del Restaurant, US 13 N, St George's, DE; ☏ 302 834 9521

Wagon Wheel Family Restaurant, 110 S Dupont Blvd, Smyma, DE 19977; ☏ 302 653 1457

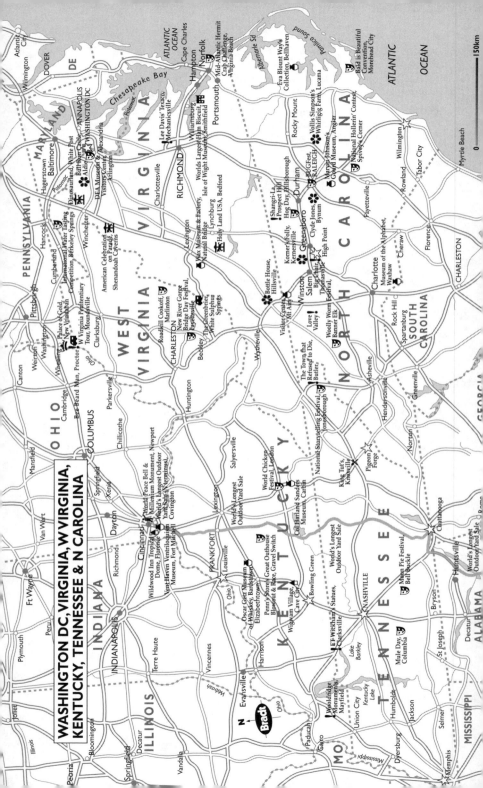

WASHINGTON DC, VIRGINIA, W VIRGINIA, KENTUCKY, TENNESSEE & N CAROLINA

Southeastern Region

6

WASHINGTON, DC
Museums and collections

Squished penny souvenirs have been around for more than a hundred years. They're coins flattened into take-away trinkets, made by mashing – or squishing – the penny between die-imprinted rollers. Collecting these things is more than a hobby for Christine Henry and Petey Moore; they'll actually invite you into their home to visit their **Squished Penny Museum** and tell you all kinds of stories about squashed, mashed, and mangled coins. You'll have to call first for an appointment; try to give them a few days' notice. They love having visitors – really!

> **Squished Penny Museum**, ❧ 202 986 5644; web: www.squished.com.
> *Open by appointment only.*

The **International Spy Museum** is the only museum in the country dedicated solely to international espionage. You'll see real artifacts that seem decidedly unreal, things like shoe transmitters, a wristwatch camera, a lipstick pistol, escape boots and a camera designed to take pictures through walls. At the entrance you can choose an 'identity', memorize facts about yourself, and then hope you remember the details when a video-screen border guard quizzes you. Once inside you look for drop sites, spot suspicious activities, watch movie and TV spy clips, and try to break codes. The interactive exhibits are among the most intriguing, letting you test your potential as a spy. Look at a photo, then watch surveillance camera videotape and try to find that person in the photo. (It's not as easy as it sounds.) Or try to find camouflaged fighter jets in satellite pictures, or pick up on suspicious behavior just by looking at an ordinary photo of a city block. Exhibits include a School for Spies, the Secret History of History, and the War of the Spies.

> **International Spy Museum**, 800 F St NW, Washington, DC 20004;
> ❧ 866 SPY MUSEUM or 202 393 7798; web: www.spymuseum.org

Tours

See Washington the way insiders do – as one nice, big, juicy scandal. **Gross National Product**, a local satirical comedy troupe, runs seasonal **Scandal Tours**, impersonating political characters from Richard Nixon to Monica Lewinsky. Their Scandal Van takes you to almost a hundred infamous sites from where many news reporters had to spend endless days and nights bringing you the story, over and over and over again.

> **Scandal Tours**, ❧ 202 783 7212; web www.gnpcomedy.com/
> ScandalTours.html. Tour departs from the Old Post Office Pavilion, 1100

ECCENTRIC CALENDAR

VIRGINIA

July	**Mid-Atlantic Hermit Crab Challenge**, Virginia Beach (page 230)

WEST VIRGINIA

February	**International Water Tasting Competition**, Berkeley Springs (page 233)
September	**Roadkill Cookoff**, Marlinton (page 233)
October	**New River Gorge Bridge Day Festival**, Fayetteville. Held on the third Saturday in October (page 233)

KENTUCKY

April	**Kentucky Derby Festival**, Louisville (page 236)
August	**Duncan Hines Festival**, Bowling Green (page 236)
	World's Longest Outdoor Yard Sale. Held at various locations throughout the state (page 235)
September	**World Chicken Festival**, London (page 236)
October	**Great Outhouse Blowout and Race**, Gravel Switch (page 235)

TENNESSEE

April	**Mule Day**, Columbia (page 239)
June	**Moon Pie Festival**, Belt Buckle (page 239)
August	**World's Longest Outdoor Yard Sale**. Held at various locations throughout the state (page 239)
October	**National Storytelling Festival**, Jonesborough (page 239)

NORTH CAROLINA

June	**Hillsborough Hog Day**, Hillsborough (page 245)
	National Hollerin' Contest, Spivey's Corner (page 245)
August	**BuGFest**, Raleigh (page 246)
September	**Bald is Beautiful Convention**, Morehead City (page 245)
	Mayberry Days, Mt Airy. Held the last weekend in September (page 248)
October	**Banner Elk Woolly Worm Festival**, Banner Elk (page 246)

MISSISSIPPI

March 17	**Mal's Patrick's Day Parade** (featuring the Sweet Potato Queens), Jackson (page 250)
April	**World Championship Anvil Shooters Classic**, Bay Springs (page 252)

ALABAMA

August	**World's Longest Outdoor Yard Sale**. Held at various locations throughout the state (page 254)
September	**Key Underwood Coon Dog Graveyard Festival**. Held on Labor Day (page 255)

GEORGIA

July   **Redneck Games**, Dublin (page 256)

SOUTH CAROLINA

April   **World Grits Festival**, St George (page 259)

September   **Kudzu Festival**, Blythewood (page 260)

November/   **Chitlin Strut**, Salley. Held the Saturday after Thanksgiving
December   (page 259)

FLORIDA

January   **Gasparilla Parade and Pirate Fest Festival**, Tampa. Held
               the last Saturday in January (page 265)

March/April   **Underwater Easter Egg Hunt**, Key Largo. Held on
               Easter Sunday (page 265)

April   **Conch Republic Independence Celebration**, Key
               West/Conch Republic (page 263)
               Interstate Mullet Toss, Pensacola. Held the last Friday in
               April (page 265)

May   **Old Island Days ends**, Key West. Events run
               November–May (page 263)

June   **Billy Bowlegs Festival**, Fort Walton Beach (page 266)

July   **Hemingway Days**, Key West Underwater Music Festival,
               Key West (page 263)

August   **Dog Days of Summer**, Key West (page 263)

September   **Womenfest**, Key West (page 263)

October   **Fantasy Fest**, Key West Underwater Pumpkin Carving,
               Key Largo (page 263)

November   **Bug Jam**, Spring Hill. Held the second Saturday in
               November (page 266)
               Old Island Days begins, Key West. Events run
               November–May (page 263)
               Pirates in Paradise, Key West (page 263)

December   **King Mango Strut**, Coconut Grove. Held the first Sunday
               after Christmas (page 266)

Pennsylvania Ave 12th St side (across from the Federal Triangle Metro Stop). *Sat 1.00pm April Fool's Day–Labor Day. May run on request for groups of 4 or more. Reservations required.*

Long considered the spy capital of the world, America's capital is still home to clandestine operations. According to the retired agents who lead the **Spydrive Tour of Washington, DC**, someone is likely spotting potential recruits, photocopying or stealing secret documents, using dead drops, evading surveillance, writing up intelligence reports, sending coded messages or living a double life at any given moment. The two-and-a-half-hour tour, led by real ex-spies from the FBI (Federal Bureau of Investigation), the CIA (Central Intelligence Agency), and the KGB covers 30 sites involving major spy cases over the past 50 years. Seeing the actual places where unnoticed events had deadly consequences will give you a whole new perspective on James Bond movies.

Spydrive Tour of Washington, DC, ➘ 1 866 SPYDRIVE; web: www.spydrive.com. *Tours are held one Saturday per month; call for dates.*

VIRGINIA
Festivals and events

You wouldn't normally associate hermit crabs with beauty pageants except during the **Mid-Atlantic Hermit Crab Challenge**. The pet creatures get all dressed up and decorated – some of them as Disney characters – and then they compete in the Miss Curvaceous Crustacean Beauty Pageant. Prizes are given in categories such as friendliest, most athletic, most traveled, shyest and, of course, best-looking crabs. Then, antennae waving, they compete in the Crustacean 500, a race to see which crab can be the first to claw its way from an inner to an outer circle. You can adopt a hermit crab at the festival; they make popular pets, each having their own unique colorful shell and personality.

Mid-Atlantic Hermit Crab Challenge, held annually in July. Contact Beachevents, 205 Laskin Rd, Virginia Beach, VA 23451; ➘ 757 491 SUNN; web: www.beacheventsfun.com.

Eccentric environments

Pharmacist John Hope estimated he'd saved about 10,000 bottles back in the 1940s that he used to build the **Bottle House**, a one-room cottage his children used as a playhouse. The walls were formed using bottles of all kinds – clear, colored, gallon- size and pint-size – which were laid so that flat bottle bottoms are on the inside and the uneven bottle tops are on the exterior. The bottles light up when the sun shines through; at night a blue bottle chandelier provides illumination.

Bottle House, located behind 1551 N Main St, Hillsville, VA. To arrange a tour contact Katy Dalton, Carroll County Chamber; ➘ 276 728 5397; web: thecarrollchamber.com.

In 1980 John Miller told everyone he was going to build a castle. Being a man of his word, he followed through – with a 7,000-square-foot castle built to withstand attack. **Bull Run Castle** in Aldie is for real, complete with an armory, two portcullis barricades, tunnels and arrow slits. The dungeon is accessed through a trapdoor. While John, now in his 70s, doesn't expect to have to defend his castle, he is a stickler for details. 'Just like I wouldn't build a bike I couldn't ride, I wouldn't build a castle that couldn't be defended,' he said. The fortress, with its 89 windows and 14 closets, has served as the meeting site for a vampire group, for a couple of medieval weddings and for a few masquerade parties now and then. If you're so inclined you can spend the night.

Bull Run Castle, 24600 James Monroe Hwy, Aldie, VA 20105; ✆ 703 327 4113; web: www.dupontcastle.com/castles/bullrun.htm. Located on Route 15, two miles south of Gilberts corner where Route 15 intersects with Route 50. *Tours are available for a small fee.*

Museums and collections

One-hundred-and-twenty-five wax figures come together to narrate historical vignettes at the **Wax Museum and Factory** in Natural Bridge. Aided by electronic animation, light and sound, the figures act out scenes from Virginia history, including those of the founding fathers, Confederate soldiers and generals, and moon-shiners. You take a seat for the theatrical presentation of *The Last Supper*. A tour of the wax factory follows.

Wax Museum and Factory, PO Box 57, Natural Bridge, VA 24578; ✆ 800 533 1410 or 541 291 2121; web: www.naturalbridgeva.com

You wouldn't expect the US Drug Enforcement Agency to have a museum but they do. The **DEA Museum and Visitors Center** originally began as an exhibit depicting the DEA's history, enhanced by a special agent's collection of early narcotics agents' badges. That inspired other employees to begin collecting things relating to their drug enforcement jobs, too, leading to a museum that now encompasses the history of drug abuse, addiction, and law enforcement in America.

DEA Museum & Visitors Center, 700 Army Navy Dr, Arlington, VA; ✆ 202 307 3463; web: www.usdoj.gov/dea/deamuseum. *Open Tue–Fri 10.00am–4.00pm.*

Attractions

They may not be anatomically correct, but the 35 quasi-realistic beasts at **Dinosaur Land** in White Post do have a certain quirky appeal. Dating from the early 1970s, when scientists believed dinosaurs were slow, squatty and stupid, the creatures in this prehistoric forest are still worthy of a Kodak moment, if only for the nostalgia of it all. A more up-to-date addition is a scene involving a T-Rex ripping the flesh from a screaming herbivore that bleeds from an invisible tube that pumps out a stream of blood through its gaping wounds. It's enough to make you appreciate the oldies. And while it may not make a lot of scientific sense that King Kong, a 20-foot cobra and a giant octopus all share forest quarters with dinosaurs, it does make tourism sense.

Dinosaur Land, Rte 1, Box 63A, White Post, VA 22663; ✆ 540 869 2222; fax: 540 869 0951; web: www.dinosaurland.com. *Open 9.30am–5.30pm Mar 1–Memorial Day and Labor Day–Nov 1; 9.30am–6.30pm Memorial Day–Labor Day; 9.30am–5.00pm Nov 2–Dec 31. Closed Jan–Feb.*

Don't just show up at **Holy Land USA** in Bedford unless you plan to walk three miles through the life and deeds of Jesus Christ. It's best to schedule a journey well in advance and to allow about three-and-a-half hours to complete it. Holy Land itself is a nature sanctuary dedicated to the journeys and deeds of Christ. Two hundred and fifty acres contain replicas – or representations – of the biblical lands in Israel, Syria and Jordan. The trail winds from Bethlehem to Jericho to Galilee, then on to Jerusalem, to Lazarus and back again to Bethlehem. You have plenty of choices as to the type of journey you can take: walking with a guide; riding with a guide in an air-conditioned and heated vehicle; riding in a set of farm wagons pulled by a 4WD vehicle; riding in a bus with or without air conditioning; riding in an air-conditioned van; riding in a hay wagon; or (whew!) riding in a truck. A Holy Land guide accompanies your journey.

> **Holy Land USA**, 1060 Jericho Rd, Bedford, VA 24523; ➥ 540 586 2823;
> web: www.holyland.pleasevisit.com

Parades pass by so quickly that you hardly get a chance to really appreciate the floats. Earl Hargrove, a float contractor, displays the floats he's built for presidential inaugurals, the Rose Parade and for various Thanksgiving Day processions at his **American Celebration on Parade**. Inside this huge attraction you'll see the story behind every float and prop, and learn what it takes to operate these complicated floating exhibits. Many floats require operators to spend prolonged periods inside cramped quarters in less-than-comfortable positions.

> **American Celebration on Parade**, 397 Caverns Rd, Shenandoah
> Caverns, VA 22847; ➥ 540 477 4300; web:
> www.shenandoahcaverns.com. *Open daily except Christmas Day;*
> *9.00am–6.15pm Jun 16–Labor Day; 9.00am–5.15pm Labor Day–Oct 31 and*
> *Apr 15–Jun 15; 9.00am–4.15pm Nov 1–Apr 14.*

Quirkyville

Smithfield, known as the ham capitol of the world, baked the **World's Largest Ham Biscuit**, a mega biscuit stuffed with 500lb of their famous Smithfield ham. Baked to commemorate the town's 250th anniversary, the biscuit – eight feet wide and 12 inches high – cooked in a specially built, glass-walled oven in a specially built, eight-and-a-half-foot spring-form pan. It baked for 14 hours, its progress eagerly monitored by onlookers. Cooled by dry ice and fans for three hours, it then took an hour, with the aid of a forklift, to ease the 1,000lb top off the biscuit. The biscuit stayed on display for a day and then, sadly, was ground up for fertilizer but not before being tasted by the town fathers who had to certify it as edible for the *Guinness Book of World Records*. You can see half the pan it was baked in (the whole pan wouldn't fit through the door) along with a video of the event at the town's **Isle of Wight Museum**. You'll also get to see their infamous 102-year-old ham.

> **World's Largest Ham Biscuit**, Isle of Wight Museum, 103 Main St,
> Smithfield, VA 23430; ➥ 757 357 7459; web: www.co.isle-of-
> wight.va.us/museum.html. *Open Tue–Sat 10.00am–4.00pm.*

Just plain weird

Gas station bathrooms in America are hardly noted for their appeal but the ones at **Lee Davis' Texaco** are the exception. Voted the 'Paragon of Pit Stops' by the Travel Channel, these potties don't just look terrific, they smell nice, too, thanks to the seasonal flower arrangements and homemade air-fresheners supplied by owners Patricia and Donald Pike. The walls are adorned with murals and the floors with hand-knitted rugs. Lighted candles are a further clue that this is not your average pit stop.

> **Lee Davis' Texaco**, 7039 Mechanicsville Turnpike, Mechanicsville, VA
> 23111; ➥ 804 746 8944

WEST VIRGINIA
Festivals and events

The spa town of Berkeley Springs came up with a novel way to promote itself. It holds an annual **International Water Tasting Competition**, part of a three-month-long Winter Festival of the Waters, and it's the largest water-tasting competition in the world. Municipal waters from several dozen states compete for the honor of best-tasting tap and bottled waters. They compete not only for taste but for best packaging honors as well. The awards presentation itself is a 'black tie or bib-overall' optional event. Taste is rated in three categories – flavor, aftertaste and mouth-feel – and is judged by journalists from magazines and newspapers around the country.

> **International Water Tasting Competition**, held annually in February in Berkeley Springs, WV. Contact Travel Berkeley Springs, ➤ 800 447 8797 or 304-258-9147; web: www.berkeleysprings.com

One day each year, the world's longest, single-arch-span bridge is closed to traffic and open to 100,000 people who gather to watch several hundred hardy souls fling themselves off it into the water 1,000 feet below. Known as BASE jumpers (bridge, antenna, spans and earth-fixed-objects) they consider the **New River Gorge Bridge Day Festival** in Fayetteville to be their annual convention. Beneath the bridge, rock climbers practice their skills and the roads leading up the bridge are filled with several hundred vendors ready for a feeding frenzy of funnel cakes, corn dogs, barbecue and handmade ice-cream.

> **New River Gorge Bridge Day Festival**, held annually the third Saturday in October in Fayetteville, WV. Contact New River Convention and Visitors Bureau, ➤ 800 927 0263 or 304 465 5617; web: www.wvbridgeday.com

Several years ago, when the state of West Virginia made it legal to take home – and use – animals killed by cars, the **Roadkill Cookoff** in Marlinton was born. Dishes with names like Thumper Meets Bumper, Asleep at the Wheel Squeal, One Ton Wonton, Rigormortis Bear Stew, Tire Tread Tortillas and Deer on a Stick are judged for their taste – or lack of it. Citizens of the state had been picking up, and cooking, roadkill long before they named a festival in honor of the practice.

> **Roadkill Cookoff**, held annually in September in Marlinton, WV. Contact the Pocahontas County Tourism Commission, Box 275, Marlinton, WV 24954; ➤ 800 336 7009; web: www.pocahontascountywv.com

Tours

The **Greenbrier** is an ultra-posh hotel with a secret: it has an underground cold war facility designed to house congressional members in the event of a nuclear strike on Washington, DC. Called the Government Relocation Center, the bunker was equipped to house 1,100 congressmen, their staffs, government officials and their families. Payroll, social security and health documents were stored there so citizens could still get their monthly checks. A stay in the bunker would have been

Quirk Alert

GRANDIOSE SCHEMES

Dubbed 'America's Taj Mahal', the **Palace of Gold** at the Hare Krishna's New Vrindaban complex near Moundsville is an impressive example of faith-based architecture. Built by self-taught followers of Srila Prabhupada, the inventor of the 'religion' best known for its robed, shaved-head devotees, this Indian-style palace is an extravagant, ornate and bizarre structure. Certainly the most unusual and startling building in the state, it was built specifically to draw tourists to the teachings of Krishna. The rose, black and gold palace is topped with a 22-karat gold-leaf dome and furnished with ornate carved panels, gold bath fixtures, crystal murals and chandeliers, stained-glass windows and four dozen varieties of marble, onyx and other stones.

The palace contains rooms supposedly used by the guru but in fact he died before its completion. A life-size idol of his guru-ness sits on a platform above a figure of Christ, who is portrayed sitting in the lotus position. Devotees, who have renounced all their worldly possessions, worship at the idol's feet. At the peak of the Hare Krishna movement in the 1980s, hundreds of followers lived at the complex, dominated by a man who called himself Bhaktipada. Until he (and his cohorts) received long prison sentences for murder and racketeering in 1996, he ruled his kingdom with an iron fist, establishing rigid rules and regulations and meting out punishments – such as days of silence – for transgressions. Every act of coitus had to be authorized by Bhaktipada. Today just a few dozen believers remain at the compound, keeping the tourism fires burning and trying to rebuild the sect's tattered image.

Palace of Gold, Rd I NBU#24, Moundsville, VW 26041; ↘ 304 843 1812; web: www.palaceofgold.com. Directions: From I-70 exit to Wheeling I-470, take exit 2 (Bethlehem) south to Rte 88, right on Rte 88 to end and stop sign, turn left, look for signs for Palace of Gold, approximately 4 miles to left at fork in road. Open 10.00am–8.00pm Apr–Aug 10.00am–5.00pm Sep–Mar.

very strange indeed, especially considering what would be going on topside. Everyone in the contamination-free facility would have dressed in green jumpsuits, slept in bunk beds and shared meals of freeze-dried foods in the cafeteria. An electronic media production room would have allowed this elite group to stay in touch with survivors, assuming there were any. The bunker was maintained at top readiness for 34 years. The mechanical systems were tested each week and food supplies rotated. Even the magazines were kept current. They give guided tours daily, March through December. Information about the Greenbrier was the basis for a $1 million question on *Who Wants to be a Millionaire?*

Greenbrier Hotel, 300 W Main St, White Sulphur Springs, WV 24986; ↘ 800 453 4858 or 304 536 1110; web: www.greenbrier.com

Staff on the **West Virginia Penitentiary Tour** treat you like inmates, loading you on the prison bus, fingerprinting and photographing you on arrival, then leading you into your impossibly tiny cell and slamming the door shut. (You can skip this part if you want to.) Later, you'll see prison art, the gallows and an electric chair. The Gothic-style fortress, built with convict labor, was closed in the mid-1990s at which point these very experiential and memorable tours were instituted. The prison gift shop sells tin cups, prison garb and handcuffs.

West Virginia Penitentiary Tour, 818 Jefferson Ave, Moundsville, WV 26041; ℡ 304 845 6200; web: www.wvpentours.com. *Tours available Tue–Sat 10.00am–4.00pm Apr–Nov, by appointment Dec–Mar. Closed Easter Sunday, Christmas Day and Thanksgiving Day.*

Just plain weird

Steve Conlon has a mighty peculiar talent. He takes a queen bee, puts her in a tiny box on his chin and then waits for the thousands of bees that follow her to form a huge beard of bees on his chin and neck. Known as the **Bee-Beard Man**, Steve has been doing this for more than a decade and claims to love every minute of it. He appeared on Jay Leno's famous late-night talk show where he endured an unusually high number of stings – about 50 or 60. Steve and his wife, Ellie, raise honey bees and produce honey on their farm, Thistledew, in Proctor. He and his bee beard can be seen at the annual Honey Festival in Parkersburg, occasionally at other events around the state, and at his Thistledew Farm.

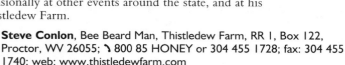

Steve Conlon, Bee Beard Man, Thistledew Farm, RR 1, Box 122, Proctor, WV 26055; ℡ 800 85 HONEY or 304 455 1728; fax: 304 455 1740; web: www.thistledewfarm.com

KENTUCKY
Festivals and events

Penn's Store, the oldest country store in America, holds the **Great Outhouse Blowout and Race** in Gravel Switch each fall. The event was started when the store, previously potty deprived, celebrated the installation of an outhouse for customer use in 1992. The store still doesn't have indoor plumbing.

Great Outhouse Blowout and Race, held annually in October in Gravel Switch, KY. Contact Penn's Store, 257 Penn's Store Rd, Gravel Switch, KY 40328; ℡ 859 332 7715 or 859 332 7706; web: www.pennsstore.com

Some people plan their vacations around the **World's Longest Outdoor Yard Sale**. Stretching 450 miles from Gadsden, Alabama, through Tennessee, and all the way to Covington, KY, the sale runs along scenic highways and through historic towns and villages. The event, which began as a way to get travelers off the interstate, now attracts thousands of vendors selling art, crafts, collectibles, farm equipment, antiques, food and your average everyday junk.

World's Longest Outdoor Yard Sale, held annually in August. Contact the Fentress County Chamber of Commerce, 114 Central Ave W, PO Box 1294, Jamestown, TN 38556; ℡ 931 879 9948; web: www.127sale.com

They race more than horses at the Kentucky Derby. During the **Kentucky Derby Festival** they also race beds, taking the event pretty seriously. Attended by 10,000 fans, the bed race is one of the festival's most popular and colorful events. Called 'Bedlam in the Streets', the event features dozens of wildly decorated beds racing around the Louisville Motor Speedway. The rules are quite specific at the start but rarely in evidence at the end: each bed must have four wheels touching the ground; each bed must include a mattress and steering mechanism; and each must meet certain size specifications. The winning beds appear in the festival's Pegasus Parade.

> **Kentucky Derby Festival**, held annually in April. Contact Kentucky Derby Festival, 1001 S 3rd St, Louisville, KY 40203; ↘ 502 584 6383; web: www.kdf.org

What weighs 950lb and measures 29 feet by 12 feet? The world's biggest fresh-baked brownie. Every year the folks at the **Duncan Hines Festival** try to outdo themselves by baking either a giant cake or a giant brownie. On Friday evening they assemble the ingredients. For the brownie this means 615 packages of brownie mix (Duncan Hines, of course), nine-and-a-half gallons of water, 1,845 eggs, 19 gallons of oil, and 615lb of frosting. Saturday is bake day. The giant batch of brownies takes 325 hours of baking at 350°, the equivalent of 13 full days of baking. More than 250 volunteers assemble, bake and decorate the brownie that serves about 12,000 people. Don't try this at home.

> **Duncan Hines Festival**, held annually in August in Bowling Green, KY. Contact Bowling Green Convention and Visitors Bureau, ↘ 800 326 7465 or 270 782 0800; web: www.duncanhinesfestival.com

The annual **World Chicken Festival** is a 'finger-lickin' good' tribute to Colonel Sanders, founder of Kentucky Fried Chicken. A quarter of a million folks attend the four-day event at which 30,000 chickens get fried in the world's largest skillet. The thing measures ten-and-a-half feet in diameter by six-inches deep, weighs 700lb and boasts a handle eight feet long. It can cook 600 chicken quarters at one time. Contests abound, including competitions in the Survival Egg Drop, Chicken Wing Eating, Best Chicken Costume, Chick-O-Lympics, Rooster Crowing, Strutting, and Clucking and Colonel Sanders Look-a-Like events.

> **World Chicken Festival**, held annually in September in London, KY; ↘ 800 348 0095 or 606 878 6900; web: www.chickenfestival.com

Museums and collections

Whether you prefer yours original or extra crispy, you're sure to crave Kentucky Fried Chicken by the time you finish touring **Colonel Harland Sanders Museum** in Louisville. The Colonel was 65 years old and flat broke when he parlayed his fried chicken recipe into a worldwide phenomenon. He became so famous that his body lay in state at the capitol when he died. A yellow line leads the way to his gravesite at the Cave Hill Cemetery.

> **Colonel Harland Sanders Museum**, 1441 Gardiner Lane, Corbin, KY; located off US-25E (I-75, exit 29); ↘ 606 528 2163. *Open daily 10.00am–10.00pm.*

Walk into the **Vent Haven Ventriloquism Museum** in Fort Mitchell and 1,000 eyes belonging to 500 dummies will stare back at you. The collection belonged to

William Berger, a man who became enamored with the business as a child after his actor father entertained him with hand puppets. Berger mastered throwing his voice as a teenager, but he didn't get serious about collecting until after his retirement. The dummy heads are supported on poles and can spit, salute, move their eyes and eyebrows, cry and wiggle their noses and ears. As a matter of fact, they can do almost anything except speak. The ventriloquist doesn't actually 'throw' his voice. The 'vent' is an illusion in which the performer changes his or her tone of voice, playing on the imagination and willingness of the audience to go along with the charade. It's the only museum in the world devoted to ventriloquism.

Vent Haven Ventriloquism Museum, 33 W Maple Ave, Fort Mitchell, KY 41011; ↘ 859 341 0461; web: www.venthaven.com. *Open Mon–Fri May–Sep by appointment only.*

Located in a boarding house in which he once lived, the **Thomas Edison House** commemorates the career of America's most prolific – and eccentric – inventor. To wit: he proposed to his wife by using Morse code on the palm of her hand; lived on an all-liquid diet in his later years; used the nursery rhyme 'Mary Had a Little Lamb' to test his first phonograph; and built a nap platform in his factory office since he slept only four hours a night.

Thomas Edison House, 729-31 E Washington St, Louisville, KY 40202; ↘ 502 585 5247; web: www.edisonhouse.org. *Open Tue–Sat 10.00am–2.00pm and by appointment.*

Kentucky is famous for its whiskey as well as for its Prohibition-era stills. The **Oscar Getz Museum of Whiskey History** takes you through the history of the whiskey industry from pre-colonial days through the 1960s. You'll see a copper still that once belonged to George Washington and an 1854 E C Booze bottle, the brand from which the word 'booze' originated. One of the decanters claims that whiskey is 'the best medicine ever used'.

Oscar Getz Museum of Whiskey History, Spalding Hall, 114 N 5th St, Bardstown, KY; ↘ 502 348 2999; web: www.visitbardstown.com. *Open Mon–Sat 9.00am–5.00pm, Sun 1.00–5.00pm May–Oct; Tue–Sat 10.00am–4.00pm, Sun 1.00–4.00pm Nov–Apr. Admission free.*

Attractions

This is one BIG bell: it's 12 feet high, 12 feet wide and weighs in at 66,000lb. Named the **World Peace Bell**, the world's largest bell resides at the world's largest monument, the **Millennium Monument** in Newport. Ascend to the top and you can have the very freaky experience of stepping out on to a glass floor and looking through it to the ground a thousand feet below. In case that isn't scary enough for you, try the 200-foot, vertical SpaceShot ride.

World Peace Bell and the Millennium Monument, 403 York St, Newport, KY 41071; ↘ 859 655 9500. *Hours vary. Usually open mid-morning–early evening.*

Just plain weird

It's a group of very stoned people, all marching in line but going nowhere. Called the 'strange procession that never moves', the 18 life-sized stone statues mark the gravesite of Colonel Henry Wooldridge. The good colonel commissioned the statues of his parents, sisters, brothers, nieces and that of his childhood sweetheart who died tragically young before they could marry. The **Wooldridge Monuments** at Maplewood Cemetery in Mayfield are all carved of granite; only the colonel himself is carved out of marble. His statue shows him mounted on his faithful horse, Fop.

> **Wooldridge Monuments**, located US 45 N, Mayfield, Graves County, Mayfield, KY. Contact Mayfield-Graves County Chamber of Commerce, 201 E College St, Mayfield, KY 42066; ↘ 270 247 6101; fax: 270 247 6110; web: www.mayfieldchamber.com.

Quirky cuisine

If you get impatient waiting for your food at **Lynn's Paradise Café** in Louisville, she'll probably tell you to be quiet and play with your toys. The Paradise is a place where guests wearing banana noses can play with potato guns as they sit under a giant, egg-decorated tree in her zany dining-room-cum-playhouse. Visitors are encouraged to play, climb on the animals in the colorful cement 'zoo' and take their pictures beside a larger-than-life coffee pot that pours 'coffee' into a giant cup. Each year Lynn sponsors the 'ugliest lamp contest' at the Kansas State Fair. Since both the winners and losers tend to end up at the restaurant, you have an idea of what the place must look like. A huge eight-foot-by-24-foot mural made entirely of colored corncobs decorates the side of the building; the mural's theme is changed annually. There's always something going on that's bound to delight as she unleashes her off-the-wall imagination on her restaurant and her guests.

> **Lynn's Paradise Café**, 984 Barret Ave, Louisville, KY 40204; ↘ 502 583 3447; fax: 502 583 0211; web: www.lynnsparadisecafe.com. *Open Mon 8.00am–2.30pm, Tue–Fri 7.00am–10.00pm, Sat–Sun 8.00am–10.00pm.*

Rooms with a Skew

The **Wildwood Inn Tropical Dome and Spa** in Covington takes the theme concept to the extreme. The Cave Suite has stalagmites, stalactites and a waterfall spa. In the *Happy Days* Suite, you sleep in the back of a 1950 Caddy in a room decorated like a 1950s' diner. Other outrageous suites include the Safari, Contemporary, Western, Champagne, Cupid and Nautical. In the Shi-Awela Safari Village, you can sleep in a hut complete with mosquito net, spa, mini kitchen and a projection television system with surround sound. The main dome has a lagoon pool, steam-room and sauna, along with billiard and ping-pong tables.

> **Wildwood Inn Tropical Dome and Theme Suites**, 7809 US 42 Florence, KY 41042; ↘ 859 371 6300 or 800 758 2335; fax: 859 525 0829; web: www.wildwood-inn.com

Wigwam Village in Cave City is the original roadside attraction, now restored, that had kids clamoring to sleep in its teepees. The 15 concrete wigwams, arranged in a semi-circle, have the original hickory bark and cane furniture dating back to 1937.

> **Wigwam Village**, 601 N Dixie Hwy, Cave City, KY 42127; ↘ 270 773 3381; web: www.wigwamvillage.com. *Open Mar–Nov.*

TENNESSEE
Festivals and events

It's **Mule Day** in Columbia, and mules stretch as far as the eye can see. Back in the 1930s when the parade started, there could be as many mules as there were people.

Today, folks celebrate the hardy, if grumpy, creatures by throwing a party in their honor, complete with a parade, liar's contest, mule-driving show and mule-pulling competition.

Mule Day, held annually in April. Contact Mule Day Office, 1018 Maury Co Park Dr, Columbia, TN 38401; ✎ 931 381 9557; web: www.muleday.com. *Mule Day Offices open Jan–Apr.*

The story of storytelling is told at the International Storytelling Center, sponsor of the **National Storytelling Festival**. Now in its 32nd year, the festival fosters interest nationwide in storytelling as entertainment and today there are events all across the country. The center offers a year-round schedule of storytelling, including a summertime 'teller-in-residence' program.

National Storytelling Festival, held annually in October. Contact the International Storytelling Center, 116 W Main St, Jonesborough, TN 37659; ✎ 800 952 8392 or 423 753 2171; web: www.storytellingcenter.com

The phrase 'RC Cola and a Moon Pie™' is as Southern as cornbread and chitlins. A gooey pastry made of marshmallow squished between soft, flat cookies and then coated with icing, the moon pie has its own **Moon Pie Festival** in the tiny town of Bell Buckle, population 391.

Moon Pie Festival, held annually in June. Contact the Bell Buckle Chamber of Commerce, PO Box 222, Bell Buckle, TN 37020; ✎ 931 389 9663; web: www.bellbucklechamber.com or www.bellbuckletn.org/rcmoonpie.shtml

Some people plan their vacations around the **World's Longest Outdoor Yard Sale**. Stretching 450 miles from Gadsden, Alabama, through Tennessee, and all the way to Covington, KY, the sale runs along scenic highways and through historic towns and villages. The event, which began as a way to get travelers off the interstate, now attracts thousands of vendors selling art, crafts, collectibles, farm equipment, antiques, food and your average everyday junk.

World's Longest Outdoor Yard Sale, held annually in August. Contact the Fentress County Chamber of Commerce, 114 Central Ave W, PO Box 1294, Jamestown, TN 38556; ✎ 931

Museums and collections
Butler, Tennessee was a town that refused to die. In 1948, the powers that be revoked the town's charter, dammed up a nearby river, and drowned the whole town under Watauga Lake. Many citizens of the day didn't take kindly to the event, moving quite a few of the town's buildings to higher ground before the flooding took place. Today, a museum tells the whole story and the town celebrates Old Butler Days the second weekend in August. Once every 20–30 years the lake level is dropped so repairs can be made to the dam, revealing the 'old town'; the next drop should take place sometime in the next three to six years. You can take a boat tour of the submerged city during the summer months on a six-person craft equipped with an underwater camera, your guide pointing out the sights below.

Butler Museum, 123 Selma Curtis Rd, Butler, TN 37640; ✎ 423 768 2432 or 423 768 2911, or the Johnson County Welcome Center at

↘ 423 727 5800. *Open Sat–Sun 1.00–4.00pm or by appointment.* For boat tours contact Wally Bender at Outdoor Adventures (↘ 423 768 2548) or through Fish Springs Marina (↘ 423 768 2336). *Boat tours run May–Oct.*

The **Willie Nelson Museum** is a quaint little place that's all heart, much like the country-western singer it honors. In addition to the normal memorabilia and artifacts you'd expect to find, you'll see a replica of his tour bus, 'Honeysuckle Rose', inside of which are photos of the musicians who make up his road family. All told there are 19 showcases, as well as a movie room, paying tribute not just to Willie but also to all the performers who've been part of his life.

> **Willie Nelson Museum**, 2613-A McGavock Pike, Nashville, TN 37214;
> ↘ 615 885 1515; web: www.audiemurphy.com/willie.htm

You don't give much thought to a tow truck until you need one, but there are people who take towing and recovery very seriously, so much so that there's an **International Towing and Recovery Hall of Fame and Museum** in Chattanooga, the birthplace of the tow truck. The industry got its start in 1916 after Ernest Holmes, Sr, along with ten helpers, spent a frustrating night trying to haul a Model A out of a creek using only ropes and blocks tied to trees. The museum is filled with tow trucks and equipment, and you'll come away with a greater appreciation for AAA the next time you need a tow.

> **International Towing and Recovery Hall of Fame and Museum**,
> 3315 Broad St, Chattanooga, TN 37408; ↘ 423 267 3132; web:
> www.internationaltowingmuseum.org. *Open Mon–Sat 9.00am–5.30pm,
> Sun 11.00am–5.00pm Apr–Dec; Mon & Fri 10.00am–4.30pm, Sat–Sun
> 11.00am–5.00pm Dec–Apr.*

Country music is endemic to Southern culture and its performers and their lyrics are known for eccentricity. Celebrating this quirky genre is the **Country Music Hall of Fame and Museum**, a million-item collection illustrating its history. In addition to a huge number of exhibits, the theater shows a film exploring the impact of country music around the world, live songwriters and pickers explaining their craft, and the dancefloor has steps imprinted on it for those with two left feet.

> **Country Music Hall of Fame and Museum**, 2222 5th Ave S, Nashville,
> TN 37203; ↘ 800 852 6437 (reservations) or 612 416 2001; web:
> www.halloffame.org. *Open daily 10.00am–6.00pm. Closed Thanksgiving,
> Christmas and New Year's Day.*

The **Peabody Ducks** are award-winning fowl, not because of any pedigree but rather for their marching abilities. The hospitality industry's Lifetime Achievement Award went to the birds for their twice daily red-carpet 'march' from their rooftop quarters to the travertine fountain in the lobby and back again.

> **Peabody Ducks at The Peabody Memphis**, 149 Union Ave, Memphis,
> TN 38103; ↘ 800 PEABODY or 901 529 4000; web:
> www.peabodymemphis.com

Headless statues lurk eerily by the roadside, erected by a man named **E T Wickham**. They're part of a memorial he made to his family who are laid to rest in the nearby cemetery. Depicting assorted people and animals, including a 'gallery' of great Americans, they reside in an overgrown tangle of brush and weeds beside the road near Palmyra.

E T Wickham's statues. Contact Clarksville-Montgomery County Convention and Visitors Bureau, Economic Development Council, PO Box 883, 312 Madison St, Clarksville, TN 37041; ↘ 800 530 2487 or 931 648 5780; web: www.clarksville.tn.us

Attractions

If there were a list of the top-ten mass eccentricities exhibited worldwide, the adulation of a dead rock-and-roll singer would have to be on it. Nowhere is this more evident than in Tennessee, where Elvis Presley's birth, death, and every detail of his life is celebrated, mourned, and examined. **Graceland** in Memphis is the home, and final resting place, of the phenomenon known as Elvis. 'The image is one thing, and the human being is another,' he said in 1972, 'and it's very hard to live up to an image.' Maybe for him it was, but not for his fans in America, who have long since exceeded living up to his image. They now live way, way beyond it – past legend and into the realm of worship. Even if you aren't an Elvis fan, a visit to Graceland is worthwhile if only for a glimpse into the psyche of true fans. People gape, they gasp, they tear up, they sob. They gaze lovingly up at the mansion while waiting for their turn for a tour, one of which begins every three minutes and lasts for two hours. Elvis lived in this mansion for the last 20 years of his all-too-short life, and every detail of his lifestyle, including what should be none-of-your-business stuff, is exposed for all to venerate. From what he ate, to how he ate it, from where he sat and with whom; to where he slept and with whom, it's all absorbed in hushed awe.

The most memorable rooms in the main house are probably his jungle room, with its waterfall and green shag carpeting, and his mirrored television room. After the house, the tour continues in the trophy room where fans can reminisce to their heart's content surrounded by the largest privately owned collection of gold records in the world. Then it's on to the meditation garden, the racquetball court where he spent some of his last moments, the pool area, and the nearby grave site. Fans the world over send fresh flowers every day. They also leave messages, some quite intimate, on the long fieldstone wall. John Lennon once said, 'Before Elvis, there was nothing.' But after Elvis there sure is plenty.

Every August they host **Elvis Week**, also known as Death Week, a time when thousands upon thousands of fans from the world over descend upon Memphis to pay tribute to their King. In ceremonies normally reserved for royalty, Elvis is

mourned, memorialized and idolized in a manner no real member of royalty has ever enjoyed. There are cruises, fan reunions, tours, fashion shows, concerts, tributes, dance parties, gospel brunches, art and trivia contests, and enough Elvis impersonators to keep your eyes popping for days. The ultimate tribute, though, is the candlelight vigil. Rain or shine, everyone lines up, lights a candle, and joins a seemingly endless processional past his grave.

> **Graceland**, 3734 Elvis Presley Blvd, Memphis, TN 38186; ❧ 800 238 2000 or 901 332 3322; web: www.elvis.com. *Open daily (except Tue Nov–Feb). Closed Thanksgiving Day, Christmas Day and sometimes on New Year's Day. Call for other holiday hours.*

Talk about off the wall – you'll be literally bouncing off padded ones at **Flyaway Indoor Skydiving**. Flapping around like a bird stuck in a silo, you'll 'fly' in a vertical wind tunnel, floating upon updrafts generated by a turbine engine mounted in the floor. But first you need to attend flight school. Here you learn how to position your body for maximum uplift, practice the 'tuck and roll' – which is how you exit the updraft safely – and learn the communication hand-signals. Then you'll watch a lawyerly video explaining all the ways you could be hurt or killed (no-one ever has) and sign your life away on the liability release form.

After that, it's into your flight suit, knee and elbow pads, helmet, ear plugs and goggles. Then it's into the wind tunnel with up to four of your soon-to-be-best friends. Since your body isn't likely to agree with your decision to leap into a void, your flight suit has handles so your trainer can pull you into and out of the maelstrom. The tunnel itself is a giant, padded, cylindrical tube. The first person to fly flings themselves off the side and on to the air current. Or at least that's the idea; your mind is willing, but your feet may stay firmly planted along the outer rim. That's where the handles come in and, before you know it, you really are flying. Exiting the air current isn't quite as scary as entering it and once you get the hang of it, you're ready to go again and again. For an extra charge they'll record a video of your flight.

> **Flyaway Indoor Skydiving**, 3106 Parkway, Pigeon Forge, TN 37863; ❧ 877 293 0639 or 865 453 7777; web: www.flyawayindoorskydiving

Tours

It's all about Elvis in this part of the country and Mike Freeman and Cindy Hazen are a part of that culture. Depending on how passionate your interest is in the King and his life, they'll customize an Elvis tour for you, spending a full day showing you where Elvis lived, went to school, ate his meals, went to church, where he worked and where he played. If you're not up to a full day, their company, **Memphis Explorations**, also offers a half-day tour of Elvis' Memphis. So committed are they to Elvis that they bought the home the rock star lived in when he was 21, the same year he recorded *Hound Dog* and *Teddy Bear*. Die-hard fans positively swoon when they find out that their tour leaders reside so close to greatness. If you're lucky they'll give you a tour.

> **Memphis Explorations**, 1034 Audubon Dr, Memphis, TN 38117; ❧ 901 761 1838; web: www.memphisexplorations.com. *By appointment only.*

Billed as the wackiest tour in Nashville, **Nash Trash Tours** is a two-act, 90-minute comedy on wheels in a bright pink bus. Brenda Kay Wilkins and Sheri Lynn Nichols sing and dance their way through Nashville pop culture on a tour so entertainingly offbeat that you don't even mind learning that their Southern accents are phony. Nor will you object to being served hors d'oeuvres consisting of Cheese Whiz (foam-like cheese that squirts out of a can) and stale crackers. The two sisters are the personification of poor white trash, dishing out the dirt on not-so-squeaky-clean stars and filling you in on all the latest gossip. There's no charge for make-up and styling tips.

Nash Trash Tours, Nashville, TN; ℘ 800 342 2132 or 615 226 7300; web: www.nashtrash.com. Tours leave from the south end of the Farmers Market, next to the Bicentennial Mall; look for the Big Pink Bus! *Tours depart daily: Thu–Fri 10.30am, Sat–Sun 9.00am and 11.30am Jun–Sept; and Sat–Sun 11.00am and 2.00pm Oct–May.*

Odd shopping

A Schwab has been on Beale Street since 1876, the oldest family-owned general store in the mid-South. Their slogan, 'If you can't find it at A Schwab, you are better off without it!' becomes self-evident as you gape at the shelves and tables stacked with piles of merchandise: ladies underpants in sizes so big that the elastic stretches to arm's width; 44 kinds of suspenders; bow ties, spats, and top hats; crystal balls; garters, long-johns, and bloomers; straight razors; men's pants to size 74; ladies dresses to size 60; and the largest selection of hats and caps in Memphis. The store has hardly changed in 127 years, creaky wood floors, ancient displays and all. Upstairs is a museum of sorts with artifacts from Schwab's glory days. Be sure to look at the display of lucky mojo and voodoo merchandise to the left of the front door. There you can buy merchandise to influence your luck, things like money-drawing candles, jinx-removing bath washes, and fast-luck sprays.

A Schwab, 163 Beale St, Memphis, TN 38103; ℘ 901 523 9782

Right next door to A Schwab is **Tater Reds**. They, too, sell lucky mojo merchandise, but with a twist. Owner Leo 'Tater Red' Alred designed his own line of potions with names like 'Keep Away Elvis Impersonators'; 'Other Lawyer Be Stupid'; 'Get My Ass Out Of Trouble'; 'Dump That Chump'; 'Ex-Wife Stay Away'; and his best seller, 'Bitch Be Gone'. The bottles make great souvenirs.

Tater Reds, 153 Beale St, Memphis, TN 38103; ℘ 901 578 7234; web: www.taterredsluckymojos.com

Quirky cuisine

It's pretty rare to find a restaurant owner so committed to earning repeat business that he'll perform magic tricks, lead a conga line through the tables, and invite you to bring in your own music so he can play for you while you dine. Mo Girgis, owner of **King Tut's**, has you drinking out of vases or jars instead of cups in his tiny restaurant (capacity 38) located in the living-room of his old house. While the family cooks, he entertains, singing, dancing, telling jokes and serving your food. And just when you think it can't get any quirkier, he'll pull out toy musical instruments and make everyone part of an orchestra. On Saturday nights he dresses the place up with tablecloths and lights the dining-room only with candles.

King Tut's, 40132 Martin Mill Pike, Knoxville, TN 37920; ℘ 865 573 6021

While you're waiting for your hamburger at **Huey's Downtown** you can count the toothpicks in the ceiling or write graffiti on the walls. Every year they have a contest

Quirk Alert

With a passion for purple, Sonia Young is Chattanooga's resident eccentric. Known simply as **'The Purple Lady'** (she's even listed that way in the phone book), Sonia lives, breathes, and eats purple. In the home she shares with her purple-tolerant husband and three purple-collared pups, most everything is purple: floors, walls, furniture, counters, draperies, towels and bedding. But her passion for the color goes much further than that. She buys purple foods, like beans, vegetables, and M&Ms; cooks with purple foods, pork in plum sauce, for example; grows purple plants and flowers like petunias and orchids; and keeps a purple Christmas tree, covered with purple ornaments, displayed all year in her atrium. Active in civic organizations, often raising considerable sums for charity with her persona, the Purple Lady is recognized everywhere she goes. Her favorite restaurants decorate her table with purple flowers and serve her on purple plates.

to guess how many toothpicks have been shot up into the ceiling with straws. You can shoot some up there yourself or scribble slogans wherever you can find an opening on walls dense with graffiti. Even the bathrooms are covered with it.

Huey's Downtown, 77 S 2nd St, Memphis, TN 38103; ↘ 901 527 2700

Leave it to Elvis to start a restaurant. **Elvis Presley's Memphis** serves comfort food, some made from Elvis' mother's recipes, as well as Elvis' favorite dishes. The infamous fried peanut butter and banana sandwich is the signature dish. Designed the give diners the feeling of being close to 'him', the restaurant displays memorabilia and a ceiling studded with stars – the gold one is Elvis.

Elvis Presley's Memphis, 126 Beale St, Memphis, TN 38186; ↘ 901 527 9036; web: www.elvis.com

Rooms with a Skew

It's inevitable that you'd find a **Heartbreak Hotel** in Memphis. The standard rooms feature the expected 1950s' décor and Elvis photos. The suites, however, are appropriately gaudy, inspired by various aspects of Elvis' life, career and personal style. The Graceland suite lets you pretend to be living at Graceland itself; The Hollywood pays homage to his movie-star persona; the Gold and Platinum is rock 'n' roll retro, and the Burning Love is a red-and-gilt tribute to his image as a romantic idol.

Heartbreak Hotel, Memphis, TN; ↘ 800 238 2000 or 901 332 3322; web: www.elvis.com

Forty-eight train cars make up a portion of the **Chattanooga Choo Choo Holiday Inn** in Chattanooga. Each 'room' is in all or part of a restored passenger car. The hotel also has a model railroad museum featuring a layout that took 33,000 man-hours to build.

Chattanooga Choo Choo Holiday Inn, 1400 Market St, Chattanooga, TN 37402; ↘ 423 266 5000 or 800 TRACK29 (reservations); fax: 423 265 4635; web: www.choochoo.com

NORTH CAROLINA
Festivals and events

According to Guinness, it's official: the largest number of attendees – 48,000 – at a one-day barbecue. The annual **Hillsborough Hog Day** broke Sydney, Australia's Guinness record in 2000 as three-dozen teams cooked up 9,000lb of barbecue while live, dressed-up porkers competed for the title of Best Dressed Pig. The show just keeps getting bigger each year with additional contests for the best hog-hollerer and the best ham-hock tosser.

Hillsborough Hog Day, held annually in June in Hillsborough, NC. Contact Hillsborough Chamber of Commerce, 121 W Margaret Ln, Hillsborough, NC 27278; ↘ 919 732 8156; web: www.hogdays.com

Hollerin' is much more than just yelling; it's a lost art that's been celebrated for 32 years at the **National Hollerin' Contest** in Spivey's Corner. Long before modern communications, folks in rural areas communicated by hollering over long distances to express distress, call in the livestock, or just plain 'chat'. Some hollerers rhymed in a sing-song way. Every morning each family would holler to let others nearby know all was well. If someone failed to check in, neighbors would come to investigate. During the event each contestant has four minutes to demonstrate his or her hollerin' skills. Finding a place to practice is problematic as anyone nearby is easily startled by the ruckus. Last year's winner appeared on David Letterman's talk show. You have to wonder if old-time politicians campaigned by hollering, 'Vote for Joe!'

National Hollerin' Contest, held annually in June in Spivey's Corner, NC; ↘ 910 567 2600; web: www.hollerincontest.com

Bald-headed men of America (BHMA) unite at the **Bald is Beautiful Convention** in Morehead City (get it?). The Bald Pride organization sponsors National Rub a Bald Head Week, publishes *Chrome Dome*, a periodic newsletter, operates a bald hall of fame and generally champions the position that bald men have that extra-special something. Their slogans, appearing on caps, mugs, and T-shirts, include Bald is Beautiful, Bald is Bold, Hairless Hunks and The Few! The Proud! The Bald! Twenty-thousand guys (and a few women) belong to BHMA, adding up to a considerable number of the follically challenged.

Bald is Beautiful Convention, held annually in September in Morehead City, NC. Contact Bald-Headed Men of America, 102 Bald Dr, Morehead City, NC 28557; ↘ 252 726 1855; email: jcapps4102@ aol.com; web: http://science.howstuffworks.com/framed.htm?parent=hairreplacement.htm&url=http://members.aol.com/BaldUSA/index.html

Open wide – it's time for bug-filled food and games at **BuGFest**, the country's largest one-day insect extravaganza. You'll see the Bee-Beard Man, Mike Stanghellini, demonstrate how he creates his very own living beard of bees. You can also taste such goodies as ant-i pest-o salad, arthropod stew, banana worm nut bread, ant-chilladas, and hush grubbies at the Café Insecta. Dozens of other offbeat insect activities, including the Roach 500 Races, make it a day you won't soon forget even if you wish you could.

> **BuGFest**, held annually in August at the North Carolina Museum of Natural Sciences, 11 W Jones St, Raleigh, NC 27601; ↘ 877 4NATASCI or 919 733 7450; web: www.naturalsciences.org or www.bugfest.org

Worms racing? Yup, they race upwards on 'lanes' of string, their coaches hoping to win fame and fortune (how does $1,000 sound?) at the **Banner Elk Woolly Worm Festival**. The victorious caterpillar is then examined by forecasters who predict what kind of winter they're facing by interpreting the colors of the winning worm's bands. The worms supposedly have had an 85% weather forecasting accuracy record over a 24-year period.

> **Banner Elk Woolly Worm Festival**, held annually in October. Contact the Avery/Banner Elk Chamber of Commerce, PO Box 335, Banner Elk, NC 28604; ↘ 828 898 5605; web: www.woollyworm.com or www.averycounty.com

Eccentric environments

Korner's Folly, so dubbed by a neighboring farmer as he gazed askance upon the strange house 120 years ago, is an odd place indeed. Victorian (sort of), Romanesque (sort of), and Queen Anne (ditto), the 22-room mansion is an excellent example of what happens when form and function collide. The three-story house has seven different floor levels, ceiling heights that vary from under six feet to over 25 feet, a smoking room with windows that don't open, eight sizes of handmade bricks, and no two of anything that match. Built by eccentric decorator Jule Gilmer Korner, the house originally had both his living quarters and his stable inside until his soon-to-be wife insisted he choose between her and the horses. Some of the windows are shared by rooms on two levels. Tunnels under the house lead to flooring vents linking 20 fireplaces to just four chimneys, a system that failed miserably when it came to heating the convoluted spaces. The top level contains the first-known home theater in the country, built so the town's children could perform plays. Statuary in the master bedroom becomes progressively undressed as you move around the room.

> **Korner's Folly**, 413 S Main St, Kernersville, NC 27284; ↘ 336 996 7922; web: www.kornersfolly.org. Open Thu–Sat 10.00am–3.00pm, Sun 1.00–5.00pm.

Clyde Jones is a lucky man, for he has very few needs. He makes his living mowing lawns, and makes his art because it makes him feel good. An old mill house in Bynom is his home, but it's his yard that will attract you. It's filled with hundreds and hundreds of his 'critters': wood and scrap creatures that he's lovingly crafted using a chain saw. Seeing animals and faces in wood stumps and fallen logs, Jones carves out their personalities, resulting in critters with amazingly lifelike expressions. Balls, film canisters, tin cans; you name it, all are put to use in bringing his critters to life. Nails become teeth, plastic flowers become eyes. No two of his works are ever alike. You can't buy one of his pieces, for he rarely sells them. You may, however, be given one, which is the only way he parts with his pets except for the occasional museum exhibition or art show. He's been known to turn down thousands of dollars. Once, world-famous dancer Mikhail Baryshnikov pulled up in a white limo. After touring the yard, he asked, 'How much?' Jones glanced over at the limo and said something like 'It don't look to me like you need one.' Eventually he sent one, free of charge, to the dancer after he found out who his visitor had been. In 2002 the county held a ClydeFest in his honor.

Clyde Jones, web: www.narrowlarry.com/nlclyde.html. Located south of Carroboo/Chapel Hill. Directions: Go south on 15-501 heading towards Pittsboro, turn left on Thompson Rec Road. Clyde's is the fourth house on the right, just after the ball field.

Vollis Simpson's Whirligig Farm in Lucama is a riot of color and motion. The metal figures, massive contraptions whirling in the wind, are made by the 84-year-old Simpson who creates them to keep busy. Some of the sculptures are five and six stories high, looming over the field where he's planted at least 20 of the fruits of his labor. The cacophony of jangling and clinking metal, pie pans, ice-cream scoops, old signs and bicycle wheels turn the field into a menagerie of laughing giants. There was nothing in Simpson's past to suggest this eccentric talent would blossom in later life; he was a farmer, a household mover and a repairman. During World War II, however, he did collect parts from a wrecked plane and built a wind-powered washing machine. Except for those two instances, he waited until 1985 to unleash his creativity. The art world, though, has gotten wind of his creations and his work has been exhibited from coast to coast.

Vollis Simpson's Whirligig Farm, Wiggins Mill Rd, Lucama, NC 27851. Contact Wilson Visitor Bureau, 124 E Nash St, Wilson, NC 27893; ↘ 800 497 7398; web: www.narrowlarry.com/nlvollis.html/ www.sci.mus.mn.us/sln/vollis/theyard/yard.html. *Open daylight hours.*

Museums and collections

You might wonder how an entire museum could be devoted just to the alphabet. But we're not talking just 26 letters here. We're talking about thousands of the world's alphabets. The **Museum of the Alphabet** shows you graphically what most of us take for granted: the importance of having one to begin with. Exploring the development of writing and writing systems worldwide, you'll come away with a greater appreciation of what a transforming difference it makes when a culture gets a formalized set of squiggles that allows it to develop a written language. The museum is on the campus of the Jaars Center, an organization that, in addition to providing Bible translations, trains people to develop alphabets for groups of speakers who have none. Of the 6,809 identified languages in the world, 3,000 have no written form, leaving about 400 million people with no way to write Dear Abby.

Museum of the Alphabet, 6409 Davis Rd, Waxhaw, NC 28173; ↘ 704 843 6066; web: www.jaars.org/museum/alphabet. *Open Mon–Sat 9.00am–noon & 1.00–3.30pm. Admission free; donations requested.*

Pack-rat-itis is a common trait of eccentrics, and **Eva Blount Way's Collection** at the Belhaven Museum is one of the strangest of all. How about 30,000 buttons, arranged into maps of the United States, labeled as 'vitamins', and glued onto geometrically arranged cards? Or a series of glass jars, filled with formaldehyde, containing a pig with one eye, a two-headed pig, an eight-legged pig, a 10lb tumor, and rattlesnakes, lots of them. Eva, who died in 1962, was proud to have personally killed three to five rattlesnakes each year, using a hoe, for the 40 years she lived on a farm. She made a necktie from snakeskin as well as jewelry from snake bones. She saved everything that ever came her way: porcelain dolls, typewriters, a dress belonging to a 700lb woman who had to be taken out of her window with a crane when she died, ingrown toenails, cataracts and a jar of her chicken fat.

> **Eva Blount Way's Collection**, located at the Belhaven Memorial Museum, 210 E Main St, PO Box 220, Belhaven, NC 27810; ↘ 252 943 6817 or 252 943 3055; web: www.beaufort-county.com/Belhaven/ museum/Belhaven.htm. *Open Thu–Tue 1.00–5.00pm. Closed major holidays. Admission free.*

There are gourds as small as robin's eggs, gourds taller than a man and gourds so strong you can stand on them. At **Marvin Johnson's Gourd Museum** in Angier, you can see more than 200 different kinds of gourd, all grown by Marvin at one time or another. Back in 1964, his wife, Mary, told him to get the gourds out of the house, so he built the museum behind his home. There's a Last Supper made out of gourd seeds, a gourd Popeye and gourd reptiles, elephants, and dinosaurs. He was a world authority on gourds, never selling any, just sharing them with fellow craftspeople. Marvin died in 2002 at age 97; his nephew Mark maintains the museum.

> **Marvin Johnson's Gourd Museum**, US 401 and Hwy 55 W, Angier, NC; web: twincreek.com/gourds/museum.htm. Located off 55 between Fuquay-Varina and Angier in the Kennebeck community just opposite the Fuquay-Angier Airport. *Open year-round during daylight hours. Free.*

The visitor center in Mount Airy is home to the **Andy Griffith Museum** containing Emmett Forrest's collection of Andy Griffith memorabilia. Forrest has been collecting all things Andy for three decades, putting his high school friendship with TV star Andy Griffith to good use. Andy himself donated the suit he wore while playing a lawyer on his *Matlock* television series. You can see Andy's childhood slingshot as well as his comic books and bubblegum cards. The town is so appreciative of Andy that you can get a haircut at Floyd's or celebrate **Mayberry Days** with them. Four thousand people show up for games and talks by the actors who played in the series. There's even an Andy Griffith Show Rerun Watchers Club.

> **Andy Griffith Museum**, Mt Airy Visitor Center, 615 N Main St, Mt Airy, NC 27030; ↘ 800 576 0231 or 336 789 4636; web: www.visitmayberry.com. *Open Mon–Sat 9.00am–5.00pm, Sun 11.00am–4.40pm. Mayberry Days held the last weekend in Sep.*

Tours

John Hirchak traded a business suit for undertaker garb and now leads a nightly **Ghost Walk of Old Wilmington** tour. Dressed as a 19th-century undertaker, he'll lead you by lantern light through the back streets and alleyways, introducing you to the lost souls who still haunt the city. All of John's staff are actors, historians, and, sometimes, genuine ghost hunters.

> **Ghost Walk of Old Wilmington**, departs rain or shine from the riverfront at Market and Water Sts. ↘ 910 602 6055; web: www.hirchak.com/ghostwalk.html. *Tour nights and departure times vary seasonally. Reservations required.*

Just plain weird

If you like big chests and curvy legs, you'll love the area around High Point, North Carolina. The heartland of American furniture manufacturing, this region is home to the world's largest chair, largest bureau, and largest highboy. These three nearby sites are part of a friendly, long-term rivalry among east coast municipalities, all of whom want to lay claim to having the world's largest piece of furniture. Starting life in the 1920s as the 'bureau of information', the 18th-century-style dresser at the intersection of Hamilton and Westwood streets in downtown High Point stands 40 feet tall, twice as high as the house next door. A human can only reach as high as the top of legs on the **world's largest bureau**. The socks hanging from the third drawer are six feet long.

Thomasville's Big Chair, Duncan Phyfe style, has hosted the seats of governors, beauty queens and even President Lyndon Johnson. Once you enter the town, just roll down your window and ask anyone, 'Where's the chair?' Everyone knows and will happily point the way to the downtown square area. Built in 1948 out of steel and concrete to replace the 1920s' wood version that had disintegrated, the chair stands 30 feet high from the bottom of the base to the top. The seating area is ten and a half feet wide but you won't be able to pose up there unless you can manage to scale the 12-foot high base. A bench is thoughtfully provided in front of the structure so you get the proper perspective in your photo. Not to be outdone, nearby Jamestown entered the competition in January, 1999 with the world's largest highboy on the façade of the world's largest home furnishings showroom, **Furnitureland South**. Eighty-five feet tall, the underside of the chest serves as a roof for the outdoor seating area. You can sit on the ball-and-claw foot for a picture and imagine stacking cars three deep, with room left over for a few sofas, underneath the chest. The gold-leaf handles alone are three feet wide.

> **World's Largest Bureau**, houses the High Point Jaycees, 508 N Hamilton St, High Point, NC 27262; ✆ 336 883 2016; web: www.highpoint.net/hp-jaycees
>
> **Thomasville's Big Chair**, located in the square downtown, Thomasville, NC. Thomasville Tourism Commission, ✆ 800 611 9907; web: www.thomasvilletourism.com/attractions/bigchair.htm
>
> **Furnitureland South**, 5635 Riverdale Dr, Jamestown, NC 27282; ✆ 336 841 4328; web www.furniturelandsouth.com/highboy.shtml

Shangri-La is a miniature 'town' by the side of the road, built over a period of many years by farmer Henry Warren prior to his death in 1977. This collection of two-dozen concrete, brick, and stone 'buildings' is marked by a plaque reading 'Let me live in a house by the side of the road and be a friend to man'. You can't tour his village but you can admire it from the road.

> **Shangri-La** is located on old Rte 86, 3 miles south of the intersection of Rte 119, Prospect Hill, NC.

Quirkyville

Andy Barker is the mayor of **Love Valley**, a town where you won't find any cars, fast food, or drive thrus of any kind. What you will find are horses, cowboys, wood sidewalks, hitching posts, a saloon and a dance hall. But this isn't a movie set or a tourist trap; this real, live Western town, smack dab in the eastern US Love Valley, was a quirky dream that Barker has turned into reality, complete with a marshall to keep the peace. You can do anything you like in Love Valley – as long as you do it Barker's way.

> **Love Valley**, located on Fox's Mountain in northwest Iredell County, NC. Contact Andy Barker, Box 265, Love Valley, NC 28677; ➘ 704 592 7451; web: www.lovevalley.com

Odd shopping

The European trolls of legend were always ugly, scary monsters ready to snatch up a misbehaving child. At **US Trolls** in Wilmington, they've been creating friendly trolls, each with a cute story, for 50 years. Kids are welcome to write to the trolls and they'll be thrilled when they get a response from them. Troll story readings are held daily; on Saturdays, a life-size troll may make a guest appearance.

> **US Trolls**, 2505 Market St, Wilmington, NC 28403; ➘ 910 251 2270; web: www.trollforest.com

MISSISSIPPI
Festivals and events

The popularity of the **Sweet Potato Queens** is best summed up by their motto: 'Never wear panties to a party'. Known far and wide for their audacious, outrageous, mostly-for-show personas, queens from all over the country descend on Jackson in their red wigs, sleazy green dresses, sparkly sunglasses, and tacky crowns to march in the **St Patrick's Day Parade**. Never mind that most of them are usually normal, well-behaved women of a certain age. To a SPQ, it's the inner harlot that counts.

What makes the queens such a phenomenon is that any woman can declare herself one simply by joining any of the thousands of chapters that sprang up worldwide following the publication in the late 90s of the *Sweet Potato Queens' Book of Love*, a book/cookbook by author Jill Connor Browne. Boss queen Jill's manifesto about love, life and men stressed the importance of knowing, among other belle-like things, the magic words guaranteed to get any man to do your bidding; the five men you absolutely have to have in your life at all times; men who, quite frankly, may need killing; and the secret of 'The Promise'. More books, calendars and SPQ merchandise have since followed and queens everywhere can buy all the trappings of royalty on the irreverent SPQ website.

The queens' participation in the parade preceded the book, however, beginning when Jill and her friends, looking for a way to express their frustration at not having the chance to wear majorette boots during childhood, latched onto the St Patrick's Day parade for no reason other than they were allowed to participate. Riding in the back of a pickup truck, wearing their fantasy garb, they tossed sweet potatoes to the crowd. From this quirky beginning, today's parade could be mistaken for a drag queen convention except that most of the partygoers are women, and quite heterosexual ones at that.

Men are allowed to play along, but only as Spud Studs. The weekend's festivities include a Sweet Potato Queen Ball and lots of parties in addition to the parade on Saturday. Just be sure you wear your wig, boots, and sunglasses with *attitude*. After all, as the queens are fond of saying, 'Well behaved women rarely make history.'

> **St Patrick's Day Parade**, held annually in Jackson, MS. Contact Hal & Mal's Restaurant and Brewery, 200 S Commerce St, Jackson, MS 39201; ➘ 601 948 0888; web: www.halandmals.com

> **Sweet Potato Queens** on the web: www.sweetpotatoqueens.com

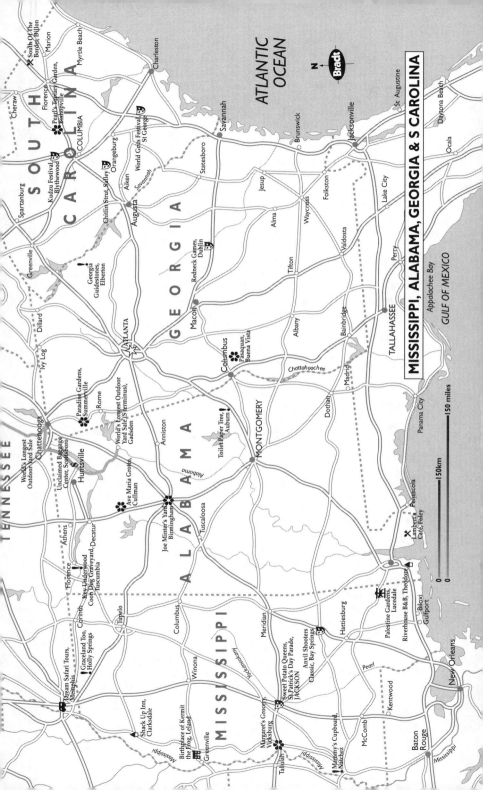

Mike 'Shine' Stringer shoots anvils into the air just for fun, hosting the **World Championship Anvil Shooters Classic** at his farm in Bay Springs. One of a handful of anvil shooting competitions, this emerging sport involves packing explosive black powder under the 100lb anvils, lighting a fuse, and then launching them into the air. The competition is judged both for height and for landing accuracy; the closer the anvil lands to the platform, the better the score. The current champion in the 'traditional' class shot his anvil 175 feet in the air and made it land only 22 inches from where it started. Mike, however, is the 'super modified' champion, having shot his 500 feet into the air and landing it just 26 feet from the base. Winners get a trophy – a 100lb anvil. If you're wondering why anyone would want to shoot an anvil anywhere, let alone up in the air, there is a precedent for this. During the Civil War, Union soldiers swept through the region destroying metalworking capabilities so the enemy couldn't produce weapons. In their attempts to destroy anvils they blew them up by stuffing gunpowder in between a pair of them.

> **World Championship Anvil Shooters Classic**, held annually in early April in Bay Springs, MS. Contact Mike Stringer, 5107 Hwy 531, Bay Springs, MS 39422; ↘ 601 725 4613; email: Shine1@teleclipse.net. Directions: Mike's farm is off Interstate 20 between Jackson and Meridian, MS. Look for the town of Newton, then go south on Hwy 15 about 30 miles to Bay Springs, then west on Hwy 18 about two miles, then left on Hwy 531 for 7 miles. Look for the mailbox with the anvil.

Eccentric environments

Widow Margaret Dennis of Vicksburg operated what was once a small, unassuming roadside snack store. Unassuming, that is, until the Reverend Dennis came along in 1980 and made her a promise she couldn't refuse: 'Marry me, and I'll turn your store into a castle.' She accepted the offer, which was pretty courageous seeing as how she would be the Reverend's fifth wife, and **Margaret's Grocery** was thrust into the realm of the strange and wacky. Reverend Dennis turned the place into a red-and-white cinder-block version of a castle. Friendly religious messages pop up everywhere; the sign as you enter proclaims his philosophy: 'All is welcome, Jews and Gentiles here at Margaret's Grocery & Mkt. & Bible Class.' While you're no longer able to shop in the grocery, you're still welcome. He preaches out front in a bus that's been converted into a church complete with pulpit and pews. And what a church it is: all metallic paint, tin foil, and duct tape – a true 'reflection' of heaven.

> **Margaret's Grocery**, Route 4, Box 219, Hwy 61, Vicksburg, MS

Without a doubt, **Graceland Too** is *the* strangest collection – and Paul McLeod is *the* most obsessed collector – you'll ever visit. Open 24 hours a day, every day, this is one seriously weird place. Whew … where to begin?

Every square inch of this faux mansion is covered with Elvis memorabilia. But not just any memorabilia, for Paul has devoted his life to keeping a record of every instance of an Elvis mention ever made, in any media, since the beginning of Elvis time and continuing, presumably, until Paul feels his mission has been accomplished. The entry is stacked with TV guides, with each Elvis mention getting its own highlight or sticky flag. Look up and the ceilings are papered with Elvis posters, trading cards, and visitor's comments taken from his guestbook. Everywhere are records, record jackets, and trinkets to say nothing of trunk after trunk, bin after bin of magazines and newspapers, all with a mention of Elvis. Part of one room is devoted to video media; he keeps half a dozen VCRs going all day and night, recording every TV channel they can get. Then, believe it or not, he watches the tapes, saving and cataloging every Elvis sighting. And then there are the shrines, brief interruptions dotting the visual chaos where you can rest your eyes for a moment and focus on just one thing, Elvis' face.

Paul himself talks non-stop at a rapid-fire pace as he takes you through his house. Grabbing a fistful of magazines, he waves them in the air, asking if you know anyone at the Smithsonian. Pointing randomly, he'll launch into story after story, one leading to the next, and the next, and the next, it all blending together in a bewildering, often incomprehensible monologue that, at first, you'll politely try to follow. After a while you realize it's best to give up trying to make sense of it and just go with this most bizarre of experiences, past the framed carpet squares from a long-ago Elvis game room, past the recording equipment where he'll croon Elvis songs for you, past the Polaroid camera with which he takes your picture.

Paul had a wife at one time ('Either I go or Elvis goes'), but before she went they had a son, naming him Elvis Aron Presley McLoud. Just imagine growing up with a name like that. Elvis, a young adult now, helps his dad out with his enormous undertaking. This is one building Elvis (the real one) is most certainly not going to be leaving anytime soon.

Graceland Too, 200 E Gholson Ave, Holly Springs, MS 38635;
↘ 601 252 7954 or 601 252 1918; web: www.rockabillyhall.com/
ElvisLives.html. *Open 7 days a week 24 hours a day.*

Attractions

A scale model of the Holy Land awaits you at **Palestine Gardens** near Lucedale, an attraction built by the late Reverend Jackson. He and his wife filled their 20-acre plot with their own version of the Promised Land. At a scale of one yard per mile, you can walk where Jesus walked, cross the River Jordan, see the Dead Sea, and stroll past two-dozen other biblical sites.

Palestine Gardens, 201 Palestine Gardens Rd, Lucedale, MS; ↘ 601 947
8422; web: www.palestinegardens.org. Located 12 miles north of
Lucedale, 5.5 miles off US 98 near West Lucedale exit. *Open Mon–Fri
9.00am–4.00pm, Sat 9.00am–6.00pm, Sun 1.00–5.00pm.*

Quirkyville

Leland's claim to fame is its exalted status as the **Birthplace of Kermit the Frog**. Reportedly born on Deer Creek, the beloved Muppet puppet has his own exhibit, courtesy of the Jim Henson Company, in the Leland Chamber of Commerce building. The exhibit documents Kermit's life history with froghood photos and early froghood videos. Kermit's creator, Jim Henson, grew up right here, playing with his boyhood friend Kermit Scott, the inspiration for his Muppet character. The exhibit also features a room of Muppet memorabilia as well as a gift shop.

Birthplace of Kermit the Frog, located at the Leland Chamber of
Commerce, PO Box 67, Leland, MS 38756; ↘ 888 307 6364 or 662 686
2687; web: www.lelandms.org

Tours

American Dream Safari takes you on an eight-hour 'blues and blacktop' tour in a 1955 Cadillac, driving along the Delta regions of Mississippi and Tennessee through the birthplace of the blues.

American Dream Safari, PO Box 3129, Memphis, TN 38173; ↘ 901
527 8870; web: www.americandreamsafari.com

Just plain weird

Today you couldn't even get a drafting student, let alone an architect, to draw up the plans for **Mammy's Cupboard** in Natchez, a restaurant so politically incorrect that it's become a pop culture icon. Picture this – a 30-foot high building in the shape of a large buxom black woman, wearing a full-length skirt, with a pill-box hat on her head. You eat in the skirt part while the upper body is sort of like a huge chimney on the top. This racist stereotype, built in the 1940s, pays homage to the Southern vision of the 'Mammy' as the idealized servant.

Mammy's Cupboard, 555 Hwy 61 S, Natchez, MS 39120; ☎ 601 445 8957; web: www.gethep.net/road/dine-mammy.html

Rooms with a Skew

Situated on an old plantation, the **Shack Up Inn** rents authentic sharecropper shanties in a setting eerily reminiscent of the Old South. Superbly tacky, the rickety, no-frills shotgun shacks (so named because you could shoot a shotgun straight through them from one end to the other), with their corrugated tin roofs and cypress wood walls, have been restored only enough to meet modern expectations – the functional, not aesthetic ones. The funky mismatched kitschy décor fits the ambiance as you sit a'rockin on your front porch, sippin' a cold one, and listenin' to an all-blues music channel, the only reception your ancient TV gets. Musicians looking for inspiration hang out here, as do groups looking for a novel place to hold parties and reunions. Tommy Polka, one of the owners, describes the shanties as 'twelve-pack architecture with six-pack construction'. Rusted old tractors and an ancient cotton gin contribute to the atmosphere, as does the commissary-cum-dance hall.

Shack Up Inn, 001 Commissary Circle, Clarksdale, MS 38614; ☎ 662 624 8329 or 615 385 4345; web: www.shackupinn.com

ALABAMA
Festivals and events

Some people plan their vacations around the **World's Longest Outdoor Yard Sale**. Stretching 450 miles from Gadsden, Alabama, through Tennessee, and all the way to Covington, KY, the sale runs along scenic highways and through historic towns and villages. The event, which began as a way to get travelers off the interstate, now attracts thousands of vendors selling art, crafts, collectibles, farm equipment, antiques, food and your average everyday junk.

World's Longest Outdoor Yard Sale, held annually in August. Contact the Fentress County Chamber of Commerce, 114 Central Ave W, PO Box 1294, Jamestown, TN 38556; ☎ 931 879 9948; web: www.127sale.com. Or the Southern Segment Coordinator at ☎ 256 549 0351

Eccentric environments

Brother Joseph had a real thing for cold-cream jars, glass fragments, shells, tiles, stones, marbles and concrete. At the three-acre **Ave Maria Grotto** in Cullman, he constructed 125 miniature versions of religious and Holy Land buildings, including the Hanging Gardens, the Tower of Babel and Noah's Ark. And he did it all from picture postcards, never having had the chance to travel abroad. Brother Joseph, a Benedictine monk, worked incessantly for almost 30 years on his creations, often referred to as 'sermons in stone'. Next to his model of Bethlehem you'll see the Tower of Thanks, built to show his gratefulness to all the folks worldwide who sent him bits of glass, shells and fisherman's glass balls. He died in 1961 and is buried on the property.

Ave Maria Grotto, located at St Bernard Abbey, 1600 St Bernard Dr SE, Cullman, AL 35055; ↘ 256 734 4110; web: www.avemariagrotto.com. Snacks available, free picnic grounds adjacent. *Open daily 7.00am–7.00pm Apr–Sep; 7.00am–5.00pm Oct–Mar. Closed Christmas Day.*

Joe Minter's Yard in Birmingham is filled with visionary sculptures depicting his African heritage. His Garden of Memory is ablaze with monuments, huts, placards and sculptures adorned with historical, biblical and political messages that Joe says he receives from God. African warriors, their heads fashioned from the hoods of old hair dryers, stand tall amid sculpture made from thrift-shop cast-offs, scraps of wood and bits of metal. A moving memorial to four children killed in the 1963 bombing of a church consists of signs with each child's name and four empty folding chairs. A jail cell surrounds an old toilet, representing Dr Martin Luther King, Jr's famous incarceration during the civil rights era. The names of folks who died in race-related violence are posted on a tree. Downplaying the creativity that characterizes the garden, Joe simply says, 'All of this is really just the hand of God.' You can drive by anytime but to meet Joe and enter the yard, an appointment is appreciated.

Joe Minter's Yard, Birmingham, AL. For appointments contact Dilcy Windham Hilley, Greater Birmingham Visitor and Convention Bureau, ↘ 800 458 8085 or 205 458 8000. Directions: I-65 south from downtown Birmingham, turn right at Green Springs Ave exit, left on Martin Luther King Blvd, right on Nassau to the dead end.

Just plain weird

At the **Key Underwood Coon Dog Graveyard** in Tuscumbia, grieving owners honor their pets by erecting headstones resembling dogs treeing their prey. Every year on Labor Day coon hunters and their dogs pay tribute to their fallen brethren and mourn the demise of the good old raccoon-hunting days. On Labor Day (early September) they hold a **Coon Dog Cemetery Celebration** with barbeque, singing and dancing, and a liar's contest. *Open daily. Free.*

Key Underwood Coon Dog Graveyard, located 7 miles west of Tuscumbia on Hwy 72, left on Alabama Hwy 247, then approximately 12 miles, turn right and follow signs; ↘ 256 383 0783. Park is equipped with picnic area, restrooms and a pavilion.

Coon Dog Cemetery Celebration, held early September

Auburn University's sports fans certainly aren't wishy-washy about their team. Every time they win, fans rush to the **Toilet Paper Tree** in the city center and unfurl toilet paper rolls up into the tree. As many as 50,000 people have been seen celebrating at the tree. Auburn is the only city in the country to have a line item in its budget for cleaning up toilet paper.

Toilet Paper Tree, located downtown Auburn, AL, following an athletic win by an Auburn University sports team.

Odd shopping

Lost luggage doesn't go to some mysterious carousel in the sky: it ends up very much alive, if not especially well, at the **Unclaimed Baggage Center** in Scottsboro. More than a million items a year pass through their doors, not all of them easily identifiable. Guessing what something might be is part of the fun of shopping there and you can't help but wonder about the owner and how on Earth they ever managed to get along without the contents of their suitcases. New stuff is brought out dozens of times a day and priced 50–80% off retail. The place is huge, covering an entire city block and many locals shop for bargains there at least once a week. Look for the tiny museum that displays, among other things, a Stetson cowboy hat signed by Muhammad Ali and a puppet from a Jim Henson Muppets movie.

Unclaimed Baggage Center, 509 West Willow St, Scottsboro, AL 35768; ↘ 256 259 1515; web: www.unclaimedbaggage.com. *Open Mon–Fri 9.00am–6.00pm, Sat 8.00am–6.00pm.*

Quirky cuisine

The hot rolls flying through the air come as a surprise to people eating for the first time at **Lambert's Café** in Foley. It all started back in 1976 when the owner got tired of holding a basket and saying, over and over again, 'Would you care for a hot roll?' One day a customer called out to her, 'Just throw the damn thing.' She did, and everyone else joined in. They've been throwin' 'em, at an average of more than two million a year, ever since. The Home of the Throwed Rolls is also famous for its hubcap cinnamon rolls.

Lambert's Café, 2981 S McKenzie, Foley, AL 36535; ↘ 334 943 7655; web: www.throwedrolls.com

Rooms with a Skew

You'll sleep in a sewer pipe at the **Riverhouse Bed and Breakfast** in Mobile. Owner Mike Sullivan made all the furniture – beds, tables, night stands, and fountains – from plastic PVC pipe. Oprah loved it.

Riverhouse Bed and Breakfast, Box 614, Theodore, AL 36590; ↘ 251 973 2233 or 800 552 9791; web: www.riverhousebedandbreakfast.com

GEORGIA
Festivals and events

Georgia is the heart of America's redneck territory, so it's no surprise that the **Redneck Games** are held here in East Dublin. This is stereotypical beer, barbeque and arm fart country, a place where bent coat-hangers with aluminum foil serve as antennas and good ol' country boys keep both dogs and wallets on chains. Originally dubbed the Bubba-Olympics in 1995, the event is an outrageous, politically incorrect spoof of the real 1966 Olympics held in Atlanta. Country radio station WQZY started the games as a promotional stunt, garnering so much publicity that newspapers and television stations all over the country started covering them. Of the 10,000 folks who attend today, very few are true rednecks. Most are just faux rednecks that return to their mainstream lives come Monday morning.

The games themselves are down-and-dirty events like bobbing for pig's feet, seed spitting, dumpster diving, hubcap hurling, bug zapping by spitball, an armpit serenade and a big-hair contest. The defining moment, though, is the mud pit belly flop, mostly entered by those with beer bellies and peek-a-boo butt cracks. The trophy is a crushed and mounted Bud Light can, disappointingly empty. L-Bow, the grand guru of the event, claims they're 'just plain good ol' boys and gals who'd give you the shirt off their back, although it's doubtful you'd want it'. Fried alligator on a stick is a favorite festival treat.

Redneck Games, held annually early July in Dublin, GA. Contact radio station WQZY; ☎ 800 688 0096 or ☎ 478 272 4422; web: www.wqzy.com

Eccentric environments

Howard Finster of Summerville set out to build his vision of the Garden of Eden. For the foundation he filled in a swamp that had been used as a dump. That took seven years. From then until his recent death he spent 36 more years building **Paradise Garden**, a chaotic masterpiece of junk sculptures, rambling buildings and glittery mosaics, cemented not only by sand, ash and water, but by his abiding faith that his sacred grounds could make a heavenly difference. Discovered by the media and the art world in the early 1980s, it's clear that he did make a difference, particularily to the tourism industry in Summerville. He's honored at an annual Howard Finster Fest.

For the thousands who visit the garden each year, his work is both entertainment and inspiration. A combination of biblical text and visual cacophany, the garden is playfully evangelical. An eight-foot concrete shoe bears the verse, 'And your feet shod with the preparation of the gospel of peace'. Waste cans implore you to keep the world as clean as your house, which may or may not be a good idea depending upon your housekeeping skills. As you wander the three-acre garden, you'll marvel at structures like the sculpted bicycle tower and museum, which leads to the Tomb of the Unknown Body. There's a meditation building, a renowned people mural, and a cement bed of roses and plants. Walkways are lined with mirrors and bits of jewelry. Howard never met a person he didn't love, a common characteristic of cement visionaries. Visitors swear his spirit joyfully follows them around much as Howard did when he was alive.

Paradise Garden, 84 Knox St, Summerville, GA 30747; ☎ 706 857 2926 or 270 424 9987; web: www.finster.com. *Open Sat 10.00am–5.00pm Apr–Oct, or by appointment anytime.*

One of the South's most eccentric figures, Edward Martin was also known as St EOM, the Wizard of Pasaquan. The self-described 'Bodacious Mystic Badass of

Buena Vista' left behind a legacy of behavior so bizarre that he was often ostracized and shunned during his lifetime. The son of a poor sharecropper, his eclectic youth was spent wandering the country, and eventually the globe, as a merchant seaman. When he had seen enough of a world he considered deprived, he paid heed to the voice in his head that told him to come home and build a compound to house a visionary religion called **Pasaquan**. St EOM told fortunes to finance the totems, tires, pagodas and paintings that make up his curious compound. The walls are studded with huge guardian figures while concrete pipes painted with the mythical occupants of Pasaquan kept him company. Rumors of trained rattlesnakes and devil worship swirled about the turbaned man who decorated himself with tattoos and dressed in jeweled robes and feathered headdresses. Cats, dozens of them, came when he called. Dogs stayed by his side. His beard, stiffened by rice syrup, was shaped upward as an antenna to the universe; his hair remained uncut for more than 40 years. Eventually, misunderstood and alone, he took his own life at the age of 77.

> **Pasaquan**, County Rd 78, Buena Vista, GA; ➘ 229 649 9444; web: www.pasaquan.com. Directions: From the Town Square in Buena Vista, GA, drive north on Hwy 137, take fork in the road to the left, take second paved road to the right, County Rd 78. Pasaquan appears brightly on your right. *Tours by appointment only, please call.*

Just plain weird

The handful of people that know who's responsible for the **Georgia Guidestones** aren't telling. The enormous cluster of stones, inscribed in eight languages with advice for the preservation of mankind, sits on a 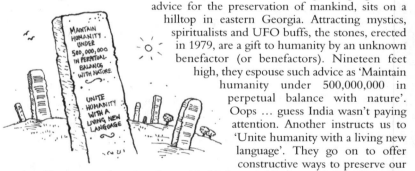 hilltop in eastern Georgia. Attracting mystics, spiritualists and UFO buffs, the stones, erected in 1979, are a gift to humanity by an unknown benefactor (or benefactors). Nineteen feet high, they espouse such advice as 'Maintain humanity under 500,000,000 in perpetual balance with nature'. Oops ... guess India wasn't paying attention. Another instructs us to 'Unite humanity with a living new language'. They go on to offer constructive ways to preserve our species: 'Protect people and nations with fair laws and just courts', 'Let all nations rule internally, resolving external disputes in a world court', and 'Avoid petty laws and useless officials'. Oops, again ... there go half our politicians.

> **Georgia Guidestones**, Hwy 77, Elberton, GA. Contact The Elbert County Chamber of Commerce, 148 College Ave, Elberton, GA 30635; ➘ 706 283 5651; web: www.elbertga.com

Quirky cuisine

The landmark **Varsity Restaurant** in Atlanta is where you go for a 'lube job', that is, to fill up on greasy chili dogs, onion rings and fried fruit pies. A sign implores you to 'Have your money in your hand and your order in your mind' when you approach the 150-foot-long counter. The Varsity staff put on quite a show as they chant, 'What'll you have? What'll you have?' and 'Next, next ... next'. Every day they serve two miles of hot dogs, 2,500lb of potatoes and 5,000 fried pies. The maze of dining-rooms are named after television broadcasters so you can eat with the media personality of your choice. In the gift shop you can buy their famous pin honoring the Olympics: a formation of five sacred onion rings. The Varsity still has a drive-in (the world's largest) with carhop service and the highest Coca-Cola consumption in the world: three million servings annually.

> **Varsity Restaurant**, 61 N Ave NW, across the Interstate from Georgia Tech, Atlanta, GA 30308; ↘ 404 881 1706; web: www.thevarsity.com. *Open Sun–Thu 10.00am–11.30pm, Fri–Sat 10.00am–12.30am.*

Talk about starving artists! You never know who will be on hand to entertain you during your meal – and thus earn theirs – at **Cafe Tu Tu Tango**. This theme restaurant is designed like an artist's loft in Barcelona, only here fine art and performance artists work and create while you dine on selections from the appetizers-only menu. The décor is upscale artist-garret and all the artwork is for sale. You may see salsa-dancing stilt walkers, tarot card readers, belly dancers, strolling musicians, singers, and, of course, artists working at their easels. Their service motto is: 'You don't have to cut off your ear to get attention here'. One of half a dozen in this unique chain, each restaurant has its own local artists and entertainers working for their supper.

> **Cafe Tu Tu Tango**, 220 Pharr Rd, Atlanta, GA 30305; ↘ 404 841 6222; web: www.cafetututango.com

SOUTH CAROLINA
Festivals and events
They're literally rolling in grits at the **World Grits Festival** in St George. A local supermarket discovered that people in the low coastal plains of the state consume unusually high portions of the cooked cereal, a fact confirmed by the country's main supplier, the Quaker Oats Company. Every April, 50,000 people attend an event that includes contests for corn-shucking, grits-eating and the crowning of Miss Grits. But the highlight is the Rolling-in-the-Grits competition involving a vat of grits and a 10-second timer. Contestants are first weighed and then they roll in the gooey grits, attempting to emerge with as many pounds of grits clinging to their clothes and body as possible. The contender that adds the most weight (15–20lb is average) is the winner.

> **World Grits Festival**, held annually in April in St George, SC. World Grits Festival Headquarters at ↘ 843 563 7943; web: www.worldgritsfestival.com

It's hard to believe that 50,000 folks turn out to consume 15,000lb of chitlins, but they do. Chitlins, or chitterlings, are boiled and fried hog intestines and they're so popular around these parts that a festival honoring them, the **Chitlin Strut**, has been held in Salley (pop 490) for more than three decades. A parade officially begins the festivities, then it's on to the main event: boiling the guts, battering them, cutting them into strips, frying them, and then (gulp!) eating them. There are other events, like a hawg-calling contest and beauty pageant, but it's the chitlins that take center stage. If you're not kindly disposed towards them, the festival does offer alternative fare.

> **Chitlin Strut**, held annually the Saturday after Thanksgiving. Contact the Town of Salley, 161 Railroad Ave N, Box 484, Salley, SC 29137; ↘ 803 258 3487; web: www.chitlinstrut.com

What is there to celebrate about a weed, called kudzu, that is so prolific it will grow unchecked over any object in its path? Entire houses, barns, cars and trucks, if abandoned, fall victim to it, as can campers if they sleep too late in the woods. In Blythewood, however, they figure, 'Why not make the best of it?' So every year since 1975 they've honored the vine-like weed at a **Kudzu Festival**, celebrating the few good things you can do with the stuff. For example, you can make jelly, syrup, art, clothing, and baskets with it. You can also eat it, as long as you choose only the tender, small leaves, as they do at the Leaf Eating Contest. Folks sing about it, twine it into their hair, and buy official kudzu Bible bookmarks. The parade features a hayride, using bales of kudzu hay, as well as kudzu costumes, some of which actually keep growing from year to year.

> **Kudzu Festival**, held annually in September in the Blythewood IGA parking lot, 135 Blythewood Rd, Blythewood, SC 29016; web: www.geocities.com/kudzufest/

Eccentric environments

Mr Pearl Fryar was so enamored of gardening that his goal in life became winning the 'Yard of the Month' award in his hometown of Bishopville. A self-taught topiary artist with a background in math, Pearl turned his three-acre garden into a fanciful field of spirals, pom-poms and other geometric forms, winning the award he coveted not once, but three times. So extraordinary are his sculptures of living plant material, seen at **Pearl's Topiary Garden,** that he's been featured on many national television shows. His yard even appeared in a book for children, *America's Weirdest Homes, Volume 4*. One of Pearl's favorite quotes is: 'He or she who does no more than average never rises above the average.' You're welcome to wander his garden alone, but he'll treat you to an above-average tour if he's there.

> **Pearl's Topiary Garden**, 145 Broad Acres Dr, Bishopville, SC 29010; web: www.fryarstopiaries.com

Quirky cuisine

It's not like the looming, 100-foot figure of Pedro comes as any surprise; after all, he's been beckoning you by billboard for hundreds of miles. Ditto the 200-foot sombrero or any of the other photo-op fiberglass figures that populate **South Of The Border**, a tourist Mecca that reaches new levels of kitsch. As the billboards claim, 'Pedro has *sometheeng* for every *juan*' and they're not kidding. Indoor miniature golf; a parachute drop, Ferris wheel and bumper cars; arcade games; a nightclub, a mega complex of gift shops, half a dozen restaurants, and a motel and campground in case you spend too much time at what you thought would be a quick stop for gas. Take the elevator to the top of the sombrero's observation deck for an expansive view of pretty much nothing.

> **South Of The Border**, I-95-U.S. 301-501, Dillon, SC 29536; ☎ 800 845 6011 or 843 774 2411; web: www.pedroland.com

FLORIDA
Quirkyville: Key West

If a vote were taken for the wackiest town in America, the win would probably go to **Key West** although it's unlikely that many of the town's 25,500 residents would take notice let alone bother to vote. The ultimate quirkyville, this is one strange place, an end-of-the-road town so over-the-top that its inhabitants think nothing of living in a place that celebrates something weirdly at least one week of every month. And when they're not holding some kind of kooky festival, they've got provocative theater and street drama to keep them entertained. That and plenty of booze. A night-time town, the streets are filled with laughter and vitality, with people enjoying life at sidewalk cafés and at the legendary open-air bars. What's not to like about living on the edge? The road runs out here in Key West, the southernmost point in the United States and you can't get any further away than this and still remain a citizen of the US. It's a Mecca for eccentrics looking for freedom of expression, and express they do, in ways that would shock even San Franciscans.

Only in Key West does the sun shine brightest when it sets. Everyone gathers for the never planned, always varied **Sunset Celebration** on Mallory Dock where jugglers, mimes, artists, musicians and street performers send it on its way. Watch Parrot Bill with his sidekick birds, or Dominique with his flying house cats, or one of a dozen other bizarre acts and you'll start to understand the kind of folks this place attracts. Where else can you get married underwater, shop for gifts in a store populated with rescued chickens, and party at a host of bizarre festivals?

Katha Sheehan, owner of **The Chicken Store,** ran for mayor on the platform 'I Will Do Nothing', representing the kind of government most Key Westians prefer. Her gift shop sells everything chicken, except, that is, for the dozen or so live ones peck-peck-pecking around the merchandise. Katha is famous for rescuing endangered chickens, claiming each of them has a unique personality. The décor is tres-chick – sawdust floors, roosting ledges and lots of local chicken art.

Key West is famous for gays, ghosts, and grog. Every Saturday morning there's a **Gay and Lesbian Trolley Tour**, a 70-minute ride that takes you past the official and not-so-official gay hot spots, explaining the impact that gay culture has had on the politics and economy of the city. They're also famous for pirates and ghosts. A walking tour, the **Ghosts and Legends of Key West**, explores the quirky legends, voodoo superstitions and pirate lore of this remote tip-of-the-country port. Once known as Bone Island, the town has a past as bizarre as its present. And drinking is so much a part of Key West culture that an entire tour is devoted to it. The **Key West Pub Crawl** takes you to the most entertaining – and infamous – pubs on the island with guides who are all too familiar with the antics of the bar scene.

Key West's official tourism videographer has the enviable job of taping the town's never-ending series of wacky festivals. He goes underwater for the Underwater Music Festival, the Underwater Pumpkin Carving contest, and the underwater Easter Egg Hunt. He also gets to tape events featuring drag queens racing in heels, naked lobster chefs, pet masquerades, and 150 Hemingway look-alikes who populate the town every summer.

Fantasy Fest is probably the most outrageous festival in America outside of Nevada's Burning Man. During Fantasy Fest a legal dress code stipulates that body paint does not constitute a costume, a regulation largely ignored in favor of the old standard that decreed the minimum 'legal' female costume to be any kind of bottom covering and at least a painted top. These are issues of great importance to the tens of thousands of revelers who attend this adults-only costume event. Key West is an extremely tolerant town, the kind of place where the unusual is the norm, but during Fantasy Fest they leap way, way over the top as far as outrageous behavior goes. During the ten days of the festival there are several dozen events, including numerous parades, costume contests and street fairs guaranteed to raise even California brows. Pets get involved, too, dressing up as people while their owners dress as pets for the Pet Masquerade and Parade.

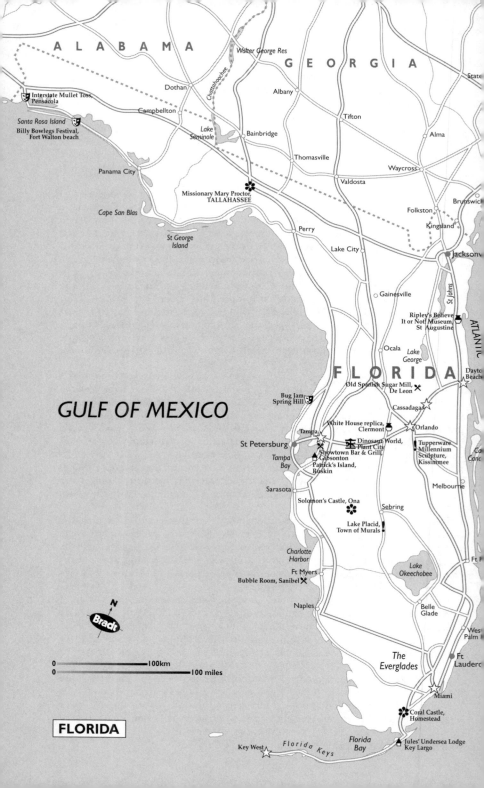

A L A B A M A

Walter George Res

G E O R G I A

Dothan

Chattahoochee

Albany

State

Interstate Mullet Toss,
Pensacola

Campbellton

Tifton

Santa Rosa Island
Billy Bowlegs Festival,
Fort Walton beach

Lake
Seminole

Bainbridge

Alma

Panama City

Thomasville

Waycross

Cape San Blas

Missionary Mary Proctor,
TALLAHASSEE

Perry

Valdosta

Folkston

Kingsland

Brunswick

St George
Island

Lake City

Jacksonv

GULF OF MEXICO

Gainesville

St Johns

Ripley's Believe
It or Not! Museum,
St Augustine

ATLANTIC

Ocala

Lake
George

F L O R I D A

Dayto
Beach

Old Spanish Sugar Mill,
De Leon

Cassadaga

Bug Jam
Spring Hill

White House replica,
Clermont

Orlando

Ca
Cana

Tampa

St Petersburg

Dinosaur World,
Plant City

Showtown Bar & Grill,
Gibsonton

Patrick's Island,
Ruskin

Tupperware
Millennium
Sculpture,
Kissimmee

Tampa
Bay

Melbourne

Sarasota

Solomon's Castle, Ona

Sebring

Lake Placid,
Town of Murals

Charlotte
Harbor

Lake
Okeechobee

Ft M

Ft Myers

Bubble Room, Sanibel

Naples

Belle
Glade

N

Bradt

West
Palm

The
Everglades

Ft
Lauderd

0   100km
0   100 miles

Miami

Coral Castle,
Homestead

FLORIDA

Key West

Florida Keys

Florida
Bay

Jules' Undersea Lodge
Key Largo

The costumes and floats are the main attractions, becoming ever more creative and bizarre from year to year. The first parade two decades ago saw a float with a human hood ornament wearing only bikini bottoms and silver paint. Today's floats can be incredibly complex and high tech, with themes such as the landing of an alien spacecraft, a fire-breathing dragon or an entire tropical jungle village with huts, trees, a volcano, a waterfall and prehistoric creatures. The whole spectacle is like Vegas on wheels – and on Ecstasy. The costumes range from the comic, such as giant M&Ms (she was plain, he was with nuts); to the risqué, such as the extension cord (she was the socket, he the plug); to the flamboyant, such as a living coral reef. Feathers and sequins are everywhere as are body parts not normally seen in public. The events include a Ripley's Believe It or Not Sideshow and Circus, a mask-as-art exhibition, a building façade competition, a headdress ball, a toga party, fetish events, a celebrity look-alike contest, and umpteen costume and parade extravaganzas. If this all sounds too weird to believe, you can buy a 90-minute video (R to X rated) from their website and see for yourself.

This oasis of oddity hosts a host of other zany festivities throughout the year, with almost every event starting or ending at a bar. **Pirates in Paradise** is a ten-day extravaganza involving a hundred historic reenactors, improvisational actors and combative stuntmen, all bedecked in colorful pirate garb, who invade the town and cause continuous chaos and revelry. Lots o' vittles an' grog keep the party going. Thousands of women show up for a five-day **Womenfest** party, a lesbian festival featuring scuba, snorkeling, comedy nights, a scavenger hunt, full-body painting, and the 'Reality Is A Drag' show. **Old Island Days** runs for months with theatrical productions, musical performances, a children's pageant, and the famous conch shell-blowing contest.

The **Conch Republic Independence Celebration** (pronounced 'konk') recalls the Florida Key's protest of a US Border Patrol roadblock on US Highway 1 in 1982. Cut off from the rest of the country, to say nothing of tourism dollars, they seceded from the union, declaring themselves an independent Conch Republic. They promptly declared war on the US, then just as promptly surrendered and applied for foreign aid. The yearly celebration symbolizes the citizen's fierce sense of independence with tattoo contests, a drag race (with drag queens in hot rods), and the world's only parade that can claim a route stretching from the Atlantic Ocean to the Gulf of Mexico. There's also a naval parade and mock battle, a fiddlers' contest, the bed races, and a pedicab downhill invitational race.

One of the weirdest sensations is to be in the thick of things during the ten-day **Hemingway Days Festival** when an average of 150 Hemingway look-alikes converge for days of partying, readings, short story competitions, and the famous key lime pie-eating contest. Despite July's blisteringly hot weather, the sweater- and safari-clad competitors roam the streets, keeping cool with cold libations. Finally, not to be ignored, resident canines travel the streets in bike baskets and swim at their own private beach, they have their own week-long festival. **Dog Days of Summer** features even more indulgences than normal, with businesses going all out to welcome dogs and everyone entering their pets in contests. It ends with a Dog Day Tea by the Sea, a dance for doggies (and their owners).

Several other Key communities also offer their own taste of weirdness. The Lower Keys **Underwater Music Festival** has an underwater bistro with serenades by underwater Elvi and service by underwater waiters. Hundreds of divers and snorklers show up each year to hear the underwater music staged by a local radio station. Key Largo contributes the **Underwater Pumpkin Carving** contest each Halloween as well as the **Underwater Easter Egg Hunt**.

Even the dead still have their say. The **Key West Cemetery** is filled with humorous headstones like the one simply stating, 'I told you I was sick'. Guided tours of the densely populated cemetery are available through the Historic Florida Keys Preservation Board. There are two to three times as many cemetery inhabitants are there are live residents of this quirkyville.

Sunset Celebration, held nightly at Mallory Square; ☎ 305 292 7700; web: www.sunsetcelebration.org

The Chicken Store, 1229 Duval St, Key West, FL 33040; ☎ 305 294 0070; web: www.thechickenstore.com

Gay and Lesbian Trolley Tour, ☎ 305 294 4603; web: www.gaykeywestfl.com/trolleytour

Ghosts and Legends of Key West, 429 Caroline St, Key West, FL 33040; ☎ 888 419 4467 or 305 294 1713; web: www.keywestghosts.com

Key West Pub Crawl, 422 Fleming St, Key West, FL 33040; ☎ 305 744 9804; web: www.islandwesttours.com

Fantasy Fest, held annually in October in Key West, FL. Contact Fantasy Fest, PO Box 230, Key West, FL 33041; ☎ 305 296 1817; fax: 305 294 3335; web: www.fantasyfest.net

Pirates in Paradise, held annually in November. Contact Pirates in Paradise, 201 William St, Key West, FL 33040; ☎ 305 296 9694; web: www.piratesinparadise.com

Womenfest, held annually in September. Contact the Atlantic Shores Resort, 510 South St, Key West, FL 33040; ☎ 800 526 3559 or 305 296 4238; web: www.womenfest.net

Old Island Days, held from November to May in Key West old town. Contact the Old Island Restoration Foundation, ☎ 305 294 9501; web: www.fla-keys.com

Conch Republic Independence Celebration, held annually in April. Contact the Office of the Secretary General, 509 Whitehead St, Ste 1, Key West, Florida/Conch Republic 33040; ☎ 305 296 0213; web: www.conchrepublic.com

Hemingway Days Festival, held in July. Contact the Ernest Hemingway Home and Museum, 907 Whitehead St, Key West, FL 33040; ☎ 305 294 4440; web: www.hemingwaydays.com

Dog Days of Summer, held annually in August. Contact Dog Days of Summer; ☎ 305 304 2400; web: www.mypetkeywest.com

Underwater Music Festival, held in July. Contact Lower Keys Chamber of Commerce, 31020 Overseas Highway, Big Pine Key, FL 33043; ☎ 305 872 2411; web: www.lowerkeyschamber.com

Underwater Pumpkin Carving (held annually in October) and
Underwater Easter Egg Hunt (held annually on Easter Sunday).
Contact the Amoray Dive Resort, 104250 Overseas Hwy, Key Largo, FL
33037; ☎ 800 426 6729 or 305 451 3595l; web: www.amoray.com

Key West Cemetery Tours, Historic Florida Keys Preservation Board,
☎ 305 292 6829; web: www.key-west.com/cemetery

Couples literally dive into matrimony at **Key West Underwater Weddings**. The
Mermaid package includes a day-dive for up to ten, a professional underwater
photographer, and cake and champagne – served topside. The ceremony itself is
performed underwater by a notary who displays the couple's vows on laminated
cards, then has them sign their 'I dos' on an underwater slate. For an extra charge
owners Kelly Friend and her mother, Gloria Wilson, will provide mermaid and
manatee costumes or an underwater Elvis impersonator.

Key West Underwater Weddings, web:
www.keywestunderwaterweddings.com

FLORIDA: THE REST OF THE STATE
Festivals and events

Seven hundred grown men, dressed in knickers and eye patches and wearing their
wives' gold hoop earrings, swarm their way over the decks of a fully-rigged pirate
ship, sail up the channel with cannons
booming, and capture the Invasion Brunch
bunch waiting at the Tampa
Convention Center. With their
crêpes and eggs Benedict held
high, the faux pirates then
invade downtown for the
**Gasparilla Parade and Pirate Fest
Festival**. After flinging beads and
doubloons to the cheering crowd, they
hunt for treasure at the Pirate Chest Arts and
Crafts Festival. The rowdy event has been a fixture of Tampa Bay for 100 years.
Named after the legendary pirate Jose Gaspar, the event also has live entertainment
and one of the largest fireworks displays in the country.

Gasparilla Parade and Pirate Fest Festival, held annually the last
Saturday in January in Tampa, FL; web: www.gasparillapiratefest.com

There's an art to tossing a dead fish, an art practiced by thousands each year who
hope to win the Interstate **Mullet Toss**, a festival that involves throwing a 1lb dead
fish from a ten-foot circle in Florida across the state line into Alabama. Local
celebrities toss the first fish, followed by 15 groups of age-ranked competitors.
Each tosser grabs a mullet from a water bucket, gives it the old heave-ho, then
must retrieve the fish and return it to the bucket, whole or in pieces as the case may
be. Experienced tossers know to ball the fish up in their hand before letting it fly.
The longest toss to date is 159 feet. Local seabirds love the event, recycling the
results throughout the day.

Interstate Mullet Toss, held annually the last Friday in April. Contact
the Flora-Bama Lounge, 17401 Perdido Key Dr, Pensacola, FL 32507;
☎ 850 492 0611 or 251 980 5118; web: www.florabama.com

While most of the country's old Volkswagens end up in sheds and junkyards, the most dedicated of owners bring theirs to **Bug Jam**, a one-of-a-kind parade of Volkswagens. Every year the show features nearly 400 Volkswagens, built between 1949 and today, including Beetles, Microbuses, Classics, and Pickups. Their owners compete in categories ranging from vintage and restoration to cosmetically challenged. Contests include shooting a VW bus with a paintball gun, an 'engine blow' (guessing when an engine, drained of oil, will quit running), and a VW tattoo contest.

> **Bug Jam**, held annually the second Sunday in November. Contact the Florida Bug Jam Administrative Office, 12309 US HWY 41, Spring Hill, FL 34610; ☏ 813 996 6306; web: www.floridabugjam.com

Commemorating a notorious scoundrel and pirate who once crowned himself King of Florida, the **Billy Bowlegs Festival** centers around a mock invasion of Fort Walton Beach. Every year, at least for the last 48, the pirate has been successful at seizing the town from the mayor. The festivities begin on a Friday night when Billy and his krewe, in their first attempt to take the city by ship, are met with a dazzling display of fireworks. They escape, only to return Saturday afternoon with their armada. In a fierce mock battle they defeat the town militia and claim a weekend of revelry. Treasure hunts are organized to search for Billy's booty and plenty of beads and candy fly through the air.

> **Billy Bowlegs Festival**, held annually in June. Contact the Greater Fort Walton Chamber of Commerce, 34 SE Miracle Strip Pkwy, Fort Walton Beach, FL 32549; ☏ 850 244 8191; web: www.fwbchamber.org

The **King Mango Strut** is one weird parade. In fact, they bill themselves as the 'Weirdest Parade in the Universe'. It's completely home-grown and free from such pesky irritants as commercial sponsors that might censor their outrageous shenanigans. Anything goes, the funkier the better, as this parody of the Orange Bowl parade struts its stuff down the streets of CocoNUT Grove. The strut has been making fun of the big parade since 1982, ever since its application to march in the Orange Bowl parade was rejected as 'unsuitable'. Around 5,000 people turn out to watch the parade, famous for biting political satire that spoofs the year's newsmakers. Anyone and anything that happened during the last year is fair game for the 500 marchers who express their political sentiments in irreverent – often tasteless – but always funny ways.

The theme of 2003 was 'Weapons of Mass Distraction' featuring Cuban Eye for the Gringo Guy, an animal reality show with a 'stud' and 25 'bitches' vying for his love, a Rush to Repent revival, and the Citizens Revolt Against Politics (the CRAP party).

In 2002 it was 'Florida-Duh' and featured priests with a lawyer running behind them handing out hush money and holding a sign reading 'Abstinence makes the church grow fondlers'. Usually the parade kicks off with the ceremonial dropping of a banana but that year saw the ceremonial dropping of Michael Jackson's 'baby' off a balcony. Osama Bin Ladens danced to the song 'Staying Alive' while Martha Stewart look-alikes dressed in jail garb.

Security was tight at 2001's event with everyone fondled and groped by officers of the newly formed Office of HomeBoy Security. King Mango's own HAZMAT team swept and decontaminated the strut route from petrified dog poop, suspicious bubble gum and really ugly people. That year also saw a Wake of the Dead Dot Coms and Harry PotHead and the Sluts. The Grand Marshall for 2000 was Wayne Brehm, an ardent parade participant who had died two weeks earlier.

His last wish was to be in the strut 'one way or another', so his urn led the parade and he was allowed to make an ash of himself one last time.

True to their political mission, the 2000 parade also included a 'Million Chad March' and a butterfly ballot flyover in which presidential candidate 'Gore' tries to catch votes with a butterfly net. For the millennium parade they featured the Y2Kmart – hoard now, pay later – led by 'Martha Stewart' demonstrating how to make unique campaign contribution baskets and kick-back arrangements. Presidential candidate Dave Barry, a renowned humor columnist, 'ran' under the slogan 'We'll get those damn stickers off your fruit'.

The event is always held the weekend preceding New Years. Their mission: 'To keep the NUT in CocoNUT Grove'.

King Mango Strut, held annually the first Sunday after Christmas (December) in Coconut Grove, FL. Contact Antoinette Baldwin; ↘ 305 401 1171 or the Coconut Grove Chamber of Commerce, 2820 McFarlane Rd, Coconut Grove, FL 33133; ↘ 305 444 7270; web: www.coconutgrove.com

Eccentric environments

Unrequited love was a powerful motivator for Ed Leedskalnin. Jilted by his fiancée on the eve of their wedding, Ed, just 26 years old, wandered aimlessly for several years before settling in Homestead in south Florida, determined to build a monument to his lost love. Single-handedly, the five-foot-tall, 100lb man labored for 20 years cutting and carving 1,100 tons of coral into a **Coral Castle**. At one point, when a housing development threatened his privacy, he moved 16 years' worth of carvings ten miles away to their present site using only a truck and tractor. When the carvings were all in place, he erected the castle walls, leveraging the 13,000lb blocks into place by himself. The really weird thing is that he never let anyone see him working, and his feat baffles scientists and engineers even to this day. He wrote several pamphlets, including *Mineral, Vegetable and Animal Life*, which explain his beliefs on the cycle of life. He died at the age of 64, leaving behind a memorial to a broken heart.

Coral Castle, 28655 S Dixie Hwy, Homestead, FL 33033; ↘ 305 248 6345; web: www.coralcastle.com. *Open daily 7.00am–9.00pm.*

Mary Proctor of Tallahassee has spent most of her life around junk. Following a tragic fire that killed three family members, Mary heeded a voice telling her to paint one of the doors in her junkyard. Before long, she was painting everything in the yard with scenes from her life and messages she was driven to share with others. Calling her former junkyard her Folk Art Museum, **Missionary Mary Proctor**, as she is now called, uses just about any small scrap that comes along to decorate the larger scraps she paints. Stuff is glued on her paintings to give them dimension; sentiments and sayings surround her subjects. Her Hall of Presidents is quite extraordinary: life-size replicas of every single US president made out of cut-up Coke cans, complete with a history and a quote about each one. Lately she's been working on garage doors. Mary loves showing visitors around her domain and she's busy making new things each day.

Missionary Mary Proctor's Folk Art Museum, 3919 Woodville Hwy, Tallahassee, FL 32311; ↘ 850 656 2879; email: proctort@talgov.com; web: www.marysart.com. *If you call first she'll be delighted to give you a tour.* Her environment is very visible from the road.

Solomon's Castle in Ona is big and shiny, which is no wonder considering the exterior is completely covered with reflective aluminum printing plates. Complete with towers, stained-glass windows and a moat with a restaurant boat in it, the castle was constructed entirely by one man, Howard Solomon, who has been building it since 1972. The 8,000-square-foot castle houses his family and pieces of his sculpture that are for sale.

> **Solomon's Castle**, 4533 Solomon Rd, Ona, FL 33865; ↘ 863 494 6077; web: www.solomonscastle.com. *Open Tue–Sun 11.00am–4.00pm. Closed Jul–Sep.*

Museums and collections

Eighty-four million dollars can lead to quite a buying spree. Mitchell Wolfson, Jr got such a windfall from the sale of his family business and set off on an extraordinary, decades-long quest accumulating 70,000-plus objects made from 1885 to 1945 that he feels reflect the moral and aesthetic ideas of their time. His collection, dubbed the **Wolfsonian**, showcases his magnificent obsession with the idea that meaning lies beneath the surface of material objects and that the design of everyday things both shape and influence our experiences. The exhibits in this impeccably displayed museum deal with how objects reflect such compelling themes as nationalism, political persuasion, propaganda, social change, consumerism and advertising. After visiting this museum you will certainly give the design of your telephone and toaster a bit more thought.

> **Wolfsonian Museum**, 1001 Washington Ave, Miami Beach, FL 33139; ↘ 305 531 1001; web: www.wolfsonian.fiu.edu

John Zweifel is one of the most patriotic men in America. Not only does he wear America's colors, right down to his socks and underwear, he's devoted the last 40 years of his life to building an enormous **White House replica** which, when it isn't on display somewhere else in the country, is housed in his **House of Presidents**. The replica isn't just a dollhouse, either. It's huge, 60 feet by 20 feet, weighs ten tons, and travels by semi-truck. John and his team of helpers, including his wife Jan, have spent hundreds of hours over the years measuring the real house, then half a million hours – and counting – building the miniature version.

Built at a scale of one inch to the foot, the White House is an exact replica – and we're talking exact here – of the real thing, right down to the cracks in the ceiling, cigar burns on the furniture, and coffee stains on the rugs. Amazingly, John calls the White House curator every few weeks to see what has changed. Perhaps a lamp has been moved, or a carpet replaced. John will make the same changes in his model, assuring up-to-date accuracy. TVs work, toilets flush, phones ring and computers glow. Every piece of furniture is built precisely to scale and carved from the same wood as the original; every rug is hand stitched; every painting and photograph painstakingly miniaturized.

You'd think that would be enough to keep John busy but he also lavishes attention on his House of Presidents, soon to become the President's Hall of Fame. There are life-like statues of all 43 presidents and their wives (the more modern ones cast in wax), each with their own display of memorabilia. When the White House model is on tour a documentary about it plays continuously in the museum. From presidential Christmas cards to a state dining-room display set for dinner, the four rooms in the house pay tribute not just to the presidents, but also to John's obsession. This is his gift to the people of America, one we should be grateful to receive.

White House replica, located at the House of Presidents, 123 N Hwy 27, Clermont, FL 34711; ℩ 352 394 2836 or 407 876 3631. *Open daily 9.30am–6.00pm.*

Harry Sperl sleeps on a hamburger-shaped waterbed and drives a hamburger motorcycle, both of which are sensible things to own if you also have the world's only **Hamburger Museum**. Originally from Germany, Harry collects hamburger items because they're American icons and because he loves Americana. The museum, located in his home, houses more than a thousand hamburger-related items. He's got hamburger banks, jars, clocks, magnets, and music boxes; hamburgers made from tin, ceramic, glass, cloth, clay, and plastic; and signs, posters, T-shirts, towels, and calendars. His bed is covered with a sesame-seed spread. His famous hamburger motorcycle has neon lighting, steam that rises from the patty, and a stereo that plays the sound of sizzling burgers. The bike was created on a Harley chassis using Styrofoam and fiberglass. Harry is so fond of car parts that they decorate his home along with the hamburgers. A Chrysler grille lights the living room with its headlights. A 350 Chevy V8 engine serves as an end table; a door from a 63 Ford Fairlane hangs on the wall. He and an architect have designed a burger-inspired building to house the International Hamburger Hall of Fame. But for now you'll have to visit him at home.

Hamburger Museum, Harry Sperl, Hamburger Collector, 1000 N Beach St, Daytona Beach, FL 32117; ℩ 356 254 8763; web: www.burgerweb.com. *Open by appointment only.*

Robert Ripley was probably one of the more eccentric people in history, gaining fame in the early 20th century for his daily cartoon called '**Ripley's Believe It or Not!**'. Seeking out the bizarre and unusual to illustrate his cartoons, he acquired unbelievable souvenirs along the way, eventually amassing a huge collection of oddities. The museum in St Augustine was his first and contains more than 800 entertaining exhibits.

Ripley's Believe It or Not! Museum, 19 San Marco Ave, St Augustine, FL 32084; ℩ 904 824 1606; web: www.ripleys.com

Attractions

Billing itself as a park 'where humans are caged and monkeys run wild', **Monkey Jungle** is unique to Florida with 35 species of monkeys running free while visitors walk among them through screen-lined walkways. Joseph and Grace DuMond conceived this unconventional arrangement in the 1930s during their studies of free-ranging monkeys. Today almost 400 animals (plus countless birds) frolic about while you stay in the maze of walkways. There's also a pair of expressive orang-utans and a gorilla named King. King has his own island and lives in a luxurious, air-conditioned enclosure complete with TV and VCR. His favorite video is the one about Koco, the ape that learned to communicate with sign language.

Monkey Jungle, 14805 SW 216th St, Miami, FL 33170; ℩ 305 235 1611; web: www.monekyjungle.com

The world's largest dinosaur attraction, **Dinosaur World** in Plant City, lets you wander among the hundred or so accurately modeled beasts whose construction reflects current theories about dinosaur colors and behavior. Arranged chronologically in a variety of settings, the atmosphere is so spookily realistic that you can practically see them moving through the trees and swamps.

Dinosaur World, 5145 Harvey Tew Rd, Plant City, FL 33565; ↘ 813 717 9865; fax: 813 707 9776; email: florida@dinoworld.net; web: www.dinoworld.net. *Open daily 9.00am–dusk. Children under three and dogs on leashes are free.*

You can't miss the entrance to **Gatorland** in Orlando, a kitschy, open-jaw welcome that could hold a dozen people at once in its gaping mouth. Famous for its gator-wrestling and dead-chicken-snatching show, the 50-year-old park is also the site of the annual **Gator Cook-off** that brings cooks from all over the country to compete for the best gator sausage, gator linguini, gator gumbo and gator pizza. The attraction is a little slice of 1950s' life; a reminder of what touristic Florida was like before Mickey Mouse and his corporate competitors arrived. Their voice mail system is most entertaining.

Gatorland, 14501 S Orange Blossom Trail, Orlando, FL 32837; ↘ 407 855 5496 or 800 393 JAWS; web: www.gatorland.com. *Open daily 9.00am–6.00pm, rain or shine.*

It's not easy becoming a mermaid. First you have to pass an interview, then a formal audition. After that, there's a year of on-the-job, underwater tail-wiggling and smile training. Finally, there's a tank test: you have to hold your breath for two-and-a-half minutes while changing costumes in a 72° spring. Fewer than half make the final cut and become genuine mermaids at **Weeki Wachee Springs Water Park** in Tampa. Set in America's only underwater lagoon theater, the park has been operating since the 1940s when Newton Perry got the idea for hose-breathing, a technique that lets the mermaids stay underwater for prolonged periods by breathing through air hoses. The Mermaid Museum next door tells the whole story, with photos, costumes and props from the past, as well as showing videos of the park's history. You can also get your picture taken with a mermaid and watch mermaids-in-training. The attraction includes a waterslide park and wilderness river cruise.

Quirk Alert

'It's all about the alligator,' says Kristie Cash. 'Without a passion for these animals, you can't call yourself an alligator wrestler.' Kristie knows what she's talking about. One of just a handful of women who have ever performed this dangerous job, she's a member of that elite club of mostly-male adrenaline junkies who jump on a giant alligator's back, wrestle it into various poses in front of gawking tourists, then get out of the way – fast. Starting out as a Gatorland cashier, she worked her way 'up' to the alligator pit. She's a mother too. Can you imagine what it must be like on 'Take Your Daughter To Work' day?

Weeki Wachee Springs Water Park, located 45 minutes north of Tampa, FL at intersection of Hwy 19 and State Rd 50; ➘ 877 GO WEEKI or 352 596-2062; web: www.weekiwachee.com. *Open daily 10.00am–4.00pm.*

The **Peabody Ducks** became world-famous back in the 1930s when the manager of the Peabody Hotel in Memphis, along with his hunting buddies, had a bit too much whiskey and decided it would be funny to put their live duck decoys in the hotel's lobby fountain. Today at the Peabody Hotel in Orlando, the ducks are world-renowned for their twice-daily duck march from their rooftop quarters down to the fountain and back again.

Ducks at the Peabody, Orlando, Peabody Hotel, 9801 International Dr, Orlando, FL 32819; ➘ 407 352 4000 or 800 PEABODY; web: www.peabodyorlando.com

Tours

David Brown is passionate about the 'other Miami', the vast city of eclectic immigrant neighborhoods outside the fashionable art deco and beach districts. His **Specialty Tours of Miami & South Florida** takes you through vibrant cultural communities like Little Havana, Little Dominica and Little Haiti, from places like botanicas selling live chickens and good luck sprays to a city farm where the owners live a totally organic lifestyle that includes living in a treehouse. David, whose license plate reads 'CULTOURS', considers Miami a 'living laboratory of cultural diversity'. His knowledgeable, lively commentary brings the real Miami into focus, including stories of how the eccentric beach district emerged from this wild mix. It's a day you'll long remember and a Miami you'll never forget. As well as taking you to some of his favorite quirky places, David also offers architectural tours of South Beach and surrounding areas, an urban parks tour, and the Miami River by boat. All his tours are by appointment and customized to your interests.

Specialty Tours of Miami & South Florida. Contact David Brown; ➘ 305 663 4455; email: db3227@aol.com; web: www.members.tripod.com/david.c.brown. *Tours by appointment only.*

Just plain weird

Every two seconds, somewhere in the world, someone is having a Tupperware party and the ubiquitous plastic ware has its own monument at the company's headquarters in Kissimmee. Known as the **Millennium Sculpture**, this 100-foot-tall tower is made entirely of the company's plastic bowls ringed by a circle of plastic cups at its base. It glows in all its pastel glory by day and at night when it's illuminated by underground lights.

Tupperware Millennium Sculpture, 14901 S Orange Blossom, Kissamee, FL. Directions: located along US 441 between the Central Florida Greenway (FL417) and the Osceola Parkway.

The little town of Lake Placid has big designs on tourism, several dozen of them, in fact. Known as the **Town of Murals**, the large-scale scenes are painted around town on the sides of buildings and on concrete abutments. Even trashcans are painted to match the murals' themes that usually tell the story of some historical event in the region's past. Some of the murals have motion-activated sound effects.

The town even has a moving billboard: murals promoting the murals are painted on the sides of a long-haul truck trailer that carries the town's message throughout the South and Midwest. The mural project is the passion of Harriet Porter, who founded the Lake Placid Mural Society. Inspired by a similar project she'd seen in Canada, she's the spark behind the murals; the lady with the vision that pulled the town out of its economic slump. The Chamber of Commerce displays renderings of all the murals and the story behind each one.

Town of Murals, Lake Placid, FL. Contact Lake Placid Mural Society, PO Box 336, Lake Placid, FL 33862; ↘ 800 557 5224 or 863 465 4331; web: www.lpfla.com

If the village of Cassadaga seems unusually tranquil, it's because half of the hundred or so people living there are practicing psychics or mediums, mellow people who can 'read' your present situation by channeling their spirit guides or using some other form of divination such as palmistry or tarot-card reading. The area, known as the **Cassadaga Spiritualist Camp**, was established a century ago by George Colby whose Indian spirit guide informed him during a séance that he was meant to establish a haven for spiritualists in the South. Colby searched the wilds of Florida until he found a spot that looked exactly like the vision he'd had during the séance and he set up camp there as a winter haven for visiting spiritualists. Today it's their year-round home where they offer private readings, seminars, workshops and educational programs for believers and skeptics alike. At Cassadaga you can delve into astrology, numerology, palmistry, runes, tarot cards, dream analysis, spiritual contact and past life regression.

Cassadaga Spiritualist Camp, located between Orlando and Daytona Beach, FL. Contact Cassadega Spiritualist Camp, 1325 Stevens St, PO Box 319, Cassadaga, FL 32706; ↘ 386 228 3171 or 386 228 2880; web: www.cassadaga.org. *Directions: From I-4 use exit 54 (SR 472) travel west to CR 4101 (Dr Martin Luther King Beltway), turn right to CR 4139, right again into town.*

Quirky cuisine

For a real taste of quirky, visit **Showtown Bar & Grill** in Gibsonton. The town was once home to off-duty circus performers like Lobster Boy and Percilla the Monkey Girl. During its heyday the town had the only post office with a special counter for midgets and offered special zoning laws that allowed residents to keep elephants in their yards and circus trailers in their driveways. The Showtown still caters to such circus folk, its exterior painted with satirical trompe l'oeil murals. Inside are more circus-theme murals, the bar, and a cluster of tables and chairs that serves as the restaurant and karaoke center. It's the combination of character and characters that make this place so intriguing.

Showtown Bar & Grill, 10902 US Hwy 41 S, Gibsonton, FL 33534; ↘ 813 677 5443

Miami's South Beach nightlife is all about looking good in the right place at the right time and **B.E.D.** offers one of the best places to do that. This novel concept in dining involves a room full of elegantly appointed white beds adorned with fashionably appointed diners for each of the two nightly seatings, called 'lays'. Some of the beds can 'lay' up to ten, others a more intimate two to four. The wait staff is dressed in pajamas and soup isn't on the menu. Each night has a different theme (erotica, Euro-trash, hip-hop, ladies, and industry) and each brings in a different crowd. The special event décor, managed by 'Barbarella', the resident art director and drag queen, can be anything from island to hippie, sometimes involving elaborate performance art. B.E.D. is inside an old storefront and there's no sign out front. The guest list is on a priority basis but they do accept same-day reservations if space is available. As the last dinner seating is finishing up, the place seamlessly transforms into a nightclub with fashion-police admission policies.

> **B.E.D.**, 929 Washington Ave, Miami Beach, FL 33139; ↘ 305 532 9070; web: www.bedmiami.com

Talk about starving artists! You never know who will be on hand to entertain you during your meal – and thus earn theirs – at **Cafe Tu Tu Tango**. This theme restaurant is designed like an artist's loft in Barcelona, only here fine art and performance artists work and create while you dine on selections from the appetizers-only menu. The décor is upscale artist-garret and all the artwork is for sale. You may see salsa-dancing stilt walkers, tarot-card readers, belly dancers, strolling musicians, singers and, of course, artists working at their easels. Their service motto is: 'You don't have to cut off your ear to get attention here'. One of half a dozen in this unique chain, each restaurant has its own local artists and entertainers working for their supper.

> **Cafe Tu Tu Tango**, located at 3015 Grand Ave, Ste 250, Coconut Grove, FL 33133; ↘ 305 529 2222 and 8625 International Dr, Orlando, FL 32819; ↘ 407 248 2222; web: www.cafetututango.com

The **Tantra Restaurant and Lounge** in Miami Beach is no place to come without a lover. With its aphrodisiac menu, fresh-cut grass on the floor, soothing waterfall, fiber-optic starlight and vanilla-scented candles, the place is designed to awaken all five senses. Tantric (Indian) food is supposed to make men more virile and women more receptive and the pointedly sensual atmosphere paves the way to a (hopefully) predictable result.

> **Tantra Restaurant and Lounge**, 1445 Pennsylvania Ave, Miami Beach, FL 33139; ↘ 305 672 4765; fax: 305 672 4288; web: www.tantrarestaurant.com

A sign on the wall of the **Desert Inn** in Daytona Beach makes its philosophy perfectly clear: 'Tinkers, pig stye keepers, bankers, hair salesmen, newspaper people, cess pool engineers, card sharks, and interior designers will not be served.' A leering male mannequin hangs out in the ladies room, poised to invite the lowering of his zipper; give in to the impulse and the zipper alarm sounds, resounding throughout the inn. Plastic spiders and bats hang from the ceiling, controlled by a barman who delights in lowering them on unsuspecting guests. A plastic tarantula lurks, hidden, somewhere in the men's room. It's a quirky place, with chickens running loose, a resident mongoose, a bordello museum and jackasses being raised in the back. Turtle, gator and frog are on the menu, while the bar serves an 'Ass Grinder', a drink packing the kick of a mule.

> **Desert Inn**, 900 N Atlantic Ave, Daytona Beach, FL 32118; ↘ 800 826 1711 or 386 258 6555; web: www.desertinnresort.com

The **Bubble Room** in Sanibel is unlike anything you've experienced before – or likely will again. A sensory overload of twinkling lights, fairy tales, Christmas and

Quirk Alert

GRANDIOSE SCHEME

If you're set on recreating the Garden of Eden, Florida's a good place to try, possessing all the requisite foliage and serpents you could ask for. In 1869, a 30-year-old Chicago physician, believing himself to be the Messiah, changed his name from Teed to Koresh and founded Koreshanity, a religion he hoped would supersede Christianity. In 1894 he convinced a small band of believers to follow him to Florida to build New Jerusalem, a city that was supposed to house ten million Koreshanites. With his 200 or so helpers, Teed built an economically independent community in Estero that supplied all their needs and then some. Women had equal rights, a concept almost unheard of at the time. Arts and crafts flourished, a print shop put out a weekly newspaper, and evenings saw classical and Shakespearean performances in the Art Hall.

Teed supplied scientific enlightenment with his theory that the Earth was a hollow orb with the continents and oceans on the inside. The sun, moon, and stars were just reflections in the ball of gas that constituted the orb's core. He also thought that celibacy created immortality, so men and women lived separately and children were raised communally. Obviously, celibacy wasn't strictly observed, nor was immortality. When Teed died, his followers propped him up on the Art Hall stage, assuming he'd resurrect himself after the customary three-day waiting period. Then they waited, and waited ... and waited. Eventually the health inspector insisted they dispose of the body, so they put him in a mausoleum by the beach. Thinking he was just being stubborn, or perhaps delayed by some kind of heavenly construction project, they kept up a 24-hour vigil for 13 years until his body was washed to sea by a hurricane. The last remaining Koreshan died in 1982.

Hollywood, this famously insane restaurant was a happy accident waiting to happen. Twenty years ago, when Jamie and Katie Farkmusen bought this building, they put everything they had into opening a restaurant. Unfortunately – or fortunately, as it turned out – everything they had wasn't quite enough. As opening day approached, they still hadn't decorated the place and barely had enough money for food. So Katie, who had just inherited some antique bubble-type Christmas tree lights, hung them up, along with several hundred old black-and-white movie pictures she'd cut out of magazines while growing up. Jamie set up his Lionel trains to run through the restaurant, then threw in his wind-up Victrola, which played old 78rpm records, for atmosphere. They told their waitress to wear something funky; she showed up in her girl scout uniform.

Now that you know the background, try to picture this: the roofs and siding of the three-story building are purposely crooked so the place looks like it's in motion; the paint job is five pastel colors while the awnings are bright circus colors. A yellow brick road leads across yellow bridges; gnomes, elves, mermaids and frogs abound. Santas are everywhere, as are the pulsating lights. Chandeliers spin, festive music from the 1930s and 1940s adds nostalgic ambiance, and antique toys are everywhere, even set into the glass-top dining tables. The servers wear khaki, decorating their uniforms and hats to express their personalities. It can't get more unpredictable than this, especially since customers are always contributing more stuff to add to the décor.

Bubble Room, 15001 Captiva Dr, Captiva Island (near Sanibel), FL 33924; ✎ 239 472 5558; web: www.bubbleroomrestaurant.com

OK, so it's corporate kitsch, but it still counts as weird. The **Monster Café** at Universal Studios beckons you with rotating monsters on top of the building. Frankenstein's monster holds a menu, Wolf Man holds a pizza, and the Creature is frosting a cake with a boat oar. Inside, each dining area has a theme like the Mummy's tomb, Frankenstein's Lab, and Dracula's Mansion. Monster rock fills the air, classic images line the walls, videos play trailers and out-takes and monster displays are everywhere. What's really strange is that, disconcertingly, everything's in color even though the original monster flicks were always in black and white.

Monster Café, 1000 Universal Studios Plaza, Orlando, FL 32819; ✎ 407 363 8000; web: www.usf.com

The **Old Spanish Sugar Mill** in Deleon Springs puts a unique spin on its pancakes: you cook them at your own table griddle. They give you pitchers of pancake batter, along with all the toppings you could want, and leave the cooking to you. Just watch where you flip. They do offer other food besides pancakes.

Old Spanish Sugar Mill, 601 Ponce Deleon Blvd, Deleon Springs State Recreation Area, Deleon Springs, FL 32130; ✎ 386 985 5644; fax: 386 985 3315; web: www.planetdeland.com/sugarmill. Located 1 hour north of Orlando and half an hour west of Daytona Beach. *Open Mon–Fri 9.00am–4.00pm, Sat–Sun 8.00am–4.00pm. Closed Thanksgiving and Christmas Day.*

Rooms with a Skew

A blow-up red-and-white beach ball sits playfully on your stark white bed at the trendy 'cheap-chic' **Townhouse**, a boutique hotel famous for its rooftop terrace. Up there a glow-in-the-dark water tower substitutes for a pool, spraying mist on guests lounging on red waterbeds shaded by huge red umbrellas. The red-and-white theme runs throughout this 'upscale dormitory' with exercise and laundry equipment awaiting your use in the hallways as well as puzzles and board games in the do-it-yourself breakfast lounge.

Townhouse, 150 20th St, Miami, FL 33139; ☎ 877 534 3800 or ☎ 305 534 3800; web: www.townhousehotel.com

On **Patrick's Island** at Ruskin you'll be the only guests in the only house on the island. You can go fishing, boating, or just lounge around your very own fantasy island.

Patrick's Island, Contact Pat and Rick Spears, Proprietors, 7341 Nebraska Way, Longmont, CO 80501; ☎ 303 684 9626; fax: ☎ 303 774 1398; web: www.cruising-america.com/patricksisland/island3.html

The **Pelican Hotel** in Miami is decorated in high Fellini-esque kitsch with 30 witty, one-of-a-kind rooms sporting names like Best Whorehouse, Psychedelic Girl, the Executive Fifties, and Jesus Christ, Megastar. The Pelican Penthouse, at $2,000 a night, features a canary yellow dining-room, a round tropical fish tank, a round bed, his and hers walk-in closets and a nine-screen video wall. The ultra-friendly place is a favorite with the fashion, music and publishing set.

Pelican Hotel, 826 Ocean Dr, Miami Beach, FL 33139; ☎ 800 7 PELICAN or 305 673 3373; fax: ☎ 305 673 3255; web: www.pelicanhotel.com

You have to scuba dive to stay at **Jules' Undersea Lodge** in Key Largo. The entire hotel is built in a 30-foot-deep lagoon that it shares with an underwater research facility. One of only two such habitats in the world, certified divers enjoy unlimited diving with a continuous air supply from 120-foot lines. You can stay more than one night but don't plan on flying for 24 hours after surfacing. Gourmet food is part of the many dive packages the hotel offers.

Jules' Undersea Lodge, 51 Shoreland Dr, Mile Marker 103.2, Oceanside, Key Largo, FL 33037; ☎ 305 451 2353; fax: 305 451 4789; web: www.jul.com

The **Cassadaga Hotel** is the psychic center of a spiritualist camp where you can take advantage of on-site new-age pursuits such as astral projection, reincarnation and other parapsychology offerings.

Cassadaga Hotel Spiritualist Camp, 355 Cassadaga Rd, Cassadaga, FL 32706; ☎ 386 228 2323; web: www.cassadagahotel.com

Cross-Country Quirks

Some weirdness knows no bounds, skipping across state lines with abandon. From peculiar pursuits to bizarre behaviors, eccentric experiences are taking place all across America.

A CAR-CRAZED CULTURE

Nowhere else on earth has the car played such a significant role in shaping a society as it has in America. While other countries had to integrate automobiles into long-established cities and cultures, Americans were able to create a brand-new infrastructure based solely on their cars, integrating them so completely into society that the car influenced not only their behavior, but also the very architecture of the country itself.

Embracing their cars with fervor, Americans took to the open road and, in typical American style, entrepreneurs followed, determined to make the journey as much fun as the destination. During the 1930s and 1940s, billboards, diners, motels and gas stations sprang up, all competing in a mad scramble to get the attention of a Ford or Chevy. Eccentric buildings, in the shape of whatever product was being peddled, proliferated, as did theme attractions and amusement parks. Giant roadside oranges, donuts, chickens, dinosaurs, and mythical figures promoted themselves miles in advance with billboards promising incredible adventures, messages aimed not only at adults, but at the 2.3 children clamoring to escape from the back of a station wagon. While a giant dinosaur might be deemed by the authorities to be out of place near the Eiffel Tower, there were no such restraints along American roads.

In the 1950s, defense fears resulted in the building of a massive, coast to coast, interstate highway system that could also be used to land airplanes. Faster highways, with their limited on-and-off access, paved the way for the rise of the now ubiquitous homogenized franchises. One by one, bits of what became off-road Americana fell into ruin and the roadside, with its quirky façades, was lost to history. Today, you can still see some remnants of the roadside glory days while meandering down back roads, and preservationists are rushing to preserve what's left of the odd architecture, gargantuan figures and advertising icons. Meanwhile, Americans have found new ways to worship their wheels. Besides dozens of museums and restaurant chains devoted solely to cars, trucks, and motorcycles, you'll find an astounding variety of competitions, rallies, races, events and parades honoring the various sub-cultures of Americans on wheels.

IT'S A GUY THING

Nothing gets the testosterone flowing like a good car crushing, which is exactly what you'll get at **Monster Truck Rallies and Demolition Derbies**. Events like these symbolize America's worship of motorized power and are, not surprisingly, almost exclusively male domains. With names like Bigfoot, Grave Digger and King

Krunch, monster trucks are preposterously modified, 4WD vehicles that compete by driving off an elevated ramp and seeing how many cars they can crush beneath them before grinding to a stop. The truck body sits way, way up on top of tires six feet high and almost four feet wide. Far too absurd for the road, they're towed to stadium racetracks where they battle it out for superiority. Between 15 and 25 cars are crushed during the average rally, an event attended by tens of thousands of rabid fans. The resulting auto carnage leaves the stadium looking like a cross between a battlefield and a junkyard, which is where the crushed cars came from in the first place.

Demolition Derbies are carnage of a different kind: the place to smash, crash, wreck and otherwise destroy junk cars that no longer have any business being on the road. Thousands of these events are held each year during which drivers bump, ram and hammer their cars into each other until only one vehicle is left operating. To begin, drivers line up their cars in a circle on a dirt field surrounded by a four-foot-high wall of mud. As the siren sounds, the cars begin crashing into each other and the air is filled with the sound of satisfying crunches. Auto parts fly everywhere as, one by one, the cars bite the dust. Helmets and seat belts are the only safety requirements for these modern day gladiators. Good sense is optional.

Part of the entertainment on the car scene is funny cars: cars with eccentric shapes, styles and sizes. Some sport enormous horsepower and hurtle at speeds up to 300 miles per hour. Others are huge, lumbering monsters such as Robosaurun, a 40-foot tall, 60,000lb dinosaur that breathes fire while cooking and eating cars. Various bikini and beauty contests are part of this world – are you surprised?

Monster Truck Rallies, web: www.truckworld.com/mtra

Demolition Derbies, web: www.DENTUSA.com

At **School Bus Figure 8 Races**, real-life and only-in-it-for-the-race bus drivers negotiate the figure 8 course, trying to avoid hitting each other in the crossover, blowing an engine, or tipping over in the turns. The buses are often decorated with graffiti and cartoons of screaming kids painted in the windows.

School Bus Figure 8 Races, web: www.members.tripod.com/ seat_slasha/f8.html

Lawn Mower Drag Racing involves guys, ages 16 to 80, who modify riding lawn mowers so they can accelerate up to 70mph in three seconds and reach top speeds up to 127mph. The only rule is that modifications cannot be made to more than 50% of the original lawn mower.

Lawn Mower Drag Racing, web: www.letsmow.com

ART CARS

America's love affair with the car has some creative extroverts converting their objects of affection into moving art. **Art cars** are vehicles that have been transformed into mobile, public folk-art, their owners merging their adoration for their car with their need to express themselves in a very public way. Art car events are quite the opposite of the testosterone-driven pursuits described above. Steered by highly individualistic and artistic men and women, they slowly cruise the highways on their way to the dozens of art car parades held every year.

There are several hundred art cars nationwide as well as a few art boats and art motorbikes. Many have an American flag somewhere on the vehicle as a symbol of personal freedom, the very sentiment that encourages such eccentricity to flourish

Quirk Alert

HARROD BLANK, ART CAR DESIGNER AND PHOTOGRAPHER

Harrod Blank (web: www.cameravan.com and www.artcaragency.com), art car photographer and filmmaker, created the Camera Van, one of America's most famous art cars. The van is covered with almost 2,500 cameras, some of which flash randomly to draw attention to the van (just in case no-one noticed!) and some of which are strategically mounted so as to capture the astonishment and disbelief on people's faces when they see him coming. According to Harrod, the van is 'both the bait and the snare that catches the prey, both the fascination and the flash'. His intent is to record that 'magical instant of reflex reaction, of surprise, bewilderment, wonder, of curiosity in action'. Not surprisingly, the Camera Van also had folks gawking in amazement in England, Canada and Germany.

In addition he owns Pico De Gallo, a VW Bug transformed into a playable tribute to rock and roll, complete with working instruments and an interactive sound system. Typical of art car owners, Harrod thrives on the attention driving an art car brings. Driving into a town, he honks the horn just in case people aren't paying attention. Highly individualistic, art car creators tend to be open, curious and gregarious, unconventional folk who invite adventure and mystery. 'Time stands still', says Harrod when he's driving one of his art cars. He only drives his regular car when he's in a hurry, which isn't very often.

Harrod likes to think of himself as a 'conduit to understanding the weird'. In a 1992 film, *Wild Wheels*, he documented four-dozen artists and their cars; a book by the same name followed. His second book, *Art Cars*, was published in 2002 and he produced another art car documentary in 2003. He's also working on a film about Burning Man, the alternative arts festival.

here Some artists like to dress like their cars: the 'Button Man' covered his mailbox, toilet, coffin and clothing, as well as his car, in buttons. The 'Ambulance to the Future', by Peter Lochren, has an alien recovering in an oxygen chamber on the roof; its sides are painted with underwater, robotic alien scenes, and he and his co-pilot always wear matching protective gear. Artist Jan Elftmann saved over 20,000 corks while working as a waitress to make her 'Cork Truck'; she has a dress to match. Other art cars, like the 'Buick of Unconditional Love' owned by Philo Northrup, make a social statement – his features a spawning, mummified fish on the hood, a live garden on the back; and Betty Boop making love with a Buddha on the roof. 'Danger', by Reverend Charles Linville (and his dog) is covered with everything that is bad for you, from hazardous industrial equipment to red meat.

Some cars simply reflect their owner's quirky personality. The 'Graffiti Beamer', by Marilyn Dreampeace, invites you to play on her car that is covered with interactive musical toys. The 'Duke', by Rick McKinney, transformed an old 1970s' car into one piled high with antique trunks, a typewriter (reflecting his career as a writer), tons of beads, baubles, bones, robotic arms, graffiti and autographs of celebrities he's come across while driving it. Inside there's a live ferret and a working model train set. 'Cowasaki' is a motorbike converted into a cow. The 'Guitar Cycle' is a rolling guitar; singer Ray Nelson drove it across the country, singing in honky tonks along the way. And then there's 'Funomena' (fa-nom-en-na – get it?). This mobile museum of the weird and strange also tours with the art cars. Actually, anything on wheels, from unicycles to lawnmowers, can be decked out and join the parades. Log on to the art car websites below to find out about art car parades and events nationwide.

Art Cars, web: www.artcarworld.com, www.artcarfest.com and www.artcaragency.com

PECULIAR PURSUITS

'Forward into the past' is the motto of the **Society for Creative Anachronism**, an organization of people who research and recreate the Middle Ages. Not to be confused with dungeons and dragons role-playing games, these aficionados take their history very, very seriously. From authentic costumes to faking an authentic death on the battlefield, these knights and warriors are exacting in their practice of medieval culture and customs. Feudal society is a lifestyle for its members, many of whom hail from the diametrically opposite high-tech field. Events take place almost every weekend around the country.

Society for Creative Anachronism, web: www.sca.org

Forty years ago California was the birthplace of the first **Renaissance Faire**, now a network of 152 countrywide medieval festivals celebrating the work, play, music, religion and superstition of the English Renaissance. Featuring reenactments and historically based entertainment, foods and crafts, these fairs have spawned an industry of guilds and clans eager to play at all things medieval. Men in tights and women in coarse cloth roam the streets portraying constables, peasants, cutpurses (pickpockets), gypsies, knights and barons. There are swordfights, jousting knights on horseback and plenty of brew masters to keep things lively.

Renaissance Faires, web: www.faires.com

Historical Reenactors are a zealous bunch, recreating historic war battles with fanatical realism. Some go so far as to live on a soldier's diet so they'll be appropriately gaunt, or practice bloating out their bodies so they appear to have been dead for a day or two. They sleep outside in the rain, subsist on scavenged food and have trouble explaining to their loved ones why they do such asinine things. Passionate imposters like these often join associations such as that of Lincoln Presenters, the Gunfight Reenactors Association, the American Federation of Old West Reenactors, and Reenactors of the American Civil War.

Historical Reenactors, web: 'Google' reenactors for specific time periods and wars

The **Friends of the Society of Primitive Technology** goes back way, way further than the reenactors above. These folks teach primitive skill workshops where you can learn seven ways to make a fire (flicking your Bic lighter isn't one of them), craft primitive tools and weapons, and make shelters out of natural materials (we're not talking cotton and linen here). They conduct workshops in various locations across the country, teaching classes in such subjects as 'Brain-Tanned Buffalo Hides'; 'Deer Hoof Rattle'; 'Four Hour Kayak'; and 'Was Agriculture a Good Idea or an Act of Desperation?'

Society of Primitive Technology, web: www.primitiveways.com

According to their website, the **Rainbow Nation** is the largest non-organization of non-members in the world. Nobody represents them and the website itself is unofficial, describing them as 'into non-violence, community building, and alternative life styles', which is pretty much the same as saying they're still living in the 1960s. They hold regional gatherings throughout the year and an annual gathering each summer somewhere in a forest – out of sight of anyone who doesn't appreciate mind-altering substances. 'Focalizers' (there are no leaders) facilitate consensus when needed. Aging and wanna-be hippies, Deadheads and chickie-poos (young, beautiful things) drink from bliss cups, speak when holding 'the feather', and pray for peace here on Earth. Aren't you relieved that somebody is looking out for your welfare?

Rainbow Nation Gatherings, held annually in regional locations; web: www.welcomehome.org

Beware the attack of the closet eccentrics, for they strike when you least expect it, leaving behind the stuff of urban legends. Who are they? Members of **cacophony societies**, loosely structured groups of people who band together to metaphorically give the finger to the more pompous aspects of American culture. Their pranks, public buffoonery, performance art and field trips are all about making noisy spectacles of themselves and providing cultural feedback that society hasn't asked for. They claim to be 'nonpolitical, nonprophet, and nonsensical', part-time eccentrics misbehaving for the greater good. According to their entertaining website, you may already be a member.

Cacophony Societies, web: www.cacophony.org

Tattoo conventions include body art contests along with an exhibit floor where artists sell their merchandise and tattooing skills. Unadorned folks attend for many reasons, but the main one is the opportunity to be immersed in a strange, foreign world while having the freedom to stare at other people's tattoos without being considered rude. You also get a unique chance to ask someone with dozens of body piercings or tattoos why on Earth they do it. Tattoo contest categories include the best black and white, most unusual, best tribal, best portrait and best overall. Binoculars are acceptable: it makes it easier to appreciate the body art up close.

Tattoo conventions, web: www.tattoodirectory.com/calendr2.htm

Pretending they're scientists living on Mars, members of the **Mars Society** volunteer for two-week stints in habitats they hope simulate conditions likely to be encountered by explorers to the red planet. One of the 'habs', as they're called, is in the Utah Desert near Hanksville. Looking very much like a giant silo, the structure houses would-be colonists who must act in accordance with strict mission protocols during their simulation. The team keeps meticulous records and ventures outside only while wearing their spacesuits: helmets made from plastic light fixtures and trash-can lids, and canvas suits trimmed with duct tape. The society has around 5,000 members worldwide, all sincerely dedicated to the cause of human Mars exploration. They're no dummies, either; many are NASA employees. Another 'hab' station is in Canada and more are planned for Iceland and the Artic.

Mars Society, web: www.marssociety.org

The popularity of the **Sweet Potato Queens** is best summed up by their motto: 'Never wear panties to a party'. At least that's what they want you to think. Known far and wide for their audacious, mostly-for-show personas, queens from the country's 1,700 chapters don wigs, sleazy dresses, sparkly sunglasses, majorette boots and tacky crowns and give themselves permission to behave outrageously, if only for a few hours. Never mind that most of them are usually normal, well-behaved women of a certain age. To a Sweet Potato Queen, it's the inner harlot that counts. The website is a hoot.

Sweet Potato Queens, web: www.sweetpotatoqueens.com

More sedate and more plentiful than the queens above are the members of the **Red Hat Society**, a 'disorganization' of women 50 and older that get together for outings wearing red hats and clashing purple clothes. Each of the country's 14,000 chapters has a queen mother who enforces 'suggestions' (there aren't any rules), one of which is that members under 50 stick to pink hats and lavender clothing until THAT birthday.

Red Hat Society, web: www.redhatsociety.com

The summer and fall maze season (August through early November) offers hundreds of opportunities to get lost among the corn stalks. Known as 'agritainment', these human-size **cornfield labyrinths** have become increasingly complex, often taking two to three hours to exit if you're too embarrassed to raise the white flag. Some of the more ambitious mazes are two stories high with slides and tunnels added to the twists and turns.

Cornfield Mazes, web: www.CornMaze.net/get-in-touch.htm; www.cornfieldmaze.com/site_list.html or www.AmericanMaze.com

Murder Mystery events take place at country inns, downtown hotels, on cruise ships and on trains. Carefully crafted and cunningly executed, these dinner and weekend experiences range in complexity from simple audience participation to costumed and role-playing involvement. The food is often linked to the theme of the event, and all mysteries end with prizes being awarded to the most clever and most clueless sleuths.

Murder Mysteries, web: www.murdermystery.com/

If **sleeping with ghosts** and **prowling haunted places** appeals to you, there are several websites to help you find your elusive prey. Prairieghosts.com is all things ghostly, providing information and links to hundreds of ghost tours, cemetery tours and haunted sites. Around Halloween time, BedandBreakfast.com has links to members offering close encounters of the ghostly kind. Click on the specials button, and then use the drop-down menu to choose the theme.

Ghosts & Hauntings, webs: www.prairieghosts.com; www.BedandBreakfast.com

Quirk Alert

TOTALLY ABSURD INVENTIONS

Eccentric inventors, convinced of the brilliance and marketability of their individual creations, spend big money to get a patent. Totally Absurd Inventions explores the funnier side of America's inventive nature on a delightfully daft website at www.totallyabsurd.com. Some of the stranger inventions include the following:

- A nose wipe for skiers that controls irritating nose drip without having to resort to cumbersome tissues that are never available when you need them. This nifty wrist attachment protects your sleeves without any trouble or bother, preventing interruption of or delay in your sporting activity. Snot a bad idea.

- An easy-on, easy-lift 'hospital happiness flap' covers that embarrassing part of your anatomy exposed by the diabolical, rear-opening hospital gown. Think what a favor you're doing the hospital staff.
- A motorized ice-cream cone. Using your tongue for repeated licking actions can become tiresome. Modern technology saves you the bother: simply put your cone into a holder, flip a switch, and *voilà!* – your tongue stays still while your cone spins around.
- A boob tube to protect yourself from the weather at sporting events. Umbrellas block another's view and can cause umbrella wrist syndrome. Instead, slip into your own little tube complete with arm slits and a built-in hood. If it were made from yellow slicker material, you'd be mistaken for a corn dog.
- A hijacker injector, a device to be installed under every airline seat that would allow the pilot to remotely activate a syringe, filled with sedative or poison, to eject its contents into the hijacker's butt.

Other genius inventions on the site include bulletproof buttocks, a wearable doghouse, toilet landing lights, a kissing shield and pogo shoes. Ted VanCleave, originator of the site, came upon the idea by accident when he was applying for a patent in 1997 for his inflatable greetings cards. You can while away hours and hours here.

Anybody can create a 'day' in America. You simply proclaim it, then promote it to establish it. You can even register it online at the **National Special Events Registry**. Ever since the government backed out of the special events business in

1994, it's been open season for holidays. For example, we have Sneak Some Zucchini Onto Your Neighbor's Porch Night; Buy a Musical Instrument Day; National Juggling and Kitchen Klutzes of America Day; Cuckoo Warning Day; and National Nude Day. If a day isn't enough, you can name a week or even a month. March is National Noodle Month; April belongs to Welding; May is Fungal Infection Month. For thousands more curious, nutty and peculiar holidays, visit the websites below.

National Special Events Registry, web: www.celebratetoday.com; www.chases.com

There's more to the 'sport' of **competitive eating** than cramming in food and letting loose with a few hearty belches. For those who criss-cross the country entering eating contests at food festivals, this is serious business indeed because the prize winnings can be considerable. Except for one iron-clad rule – 'If you heave, you leave' – competitors are on their own to devise winning strategies and to train effectively. For example, pickles require more jaw stamina than do hotdogs, especially if you dunk the buns in water to cut chewing time. Some prefer to fast before gorging; others work on expanding their stomachs in the days prior to an event. Referred to as 'athletes' by their brethren, these glutton gladiators compete by eating everything from beef tongue to butter, cow brains to matzo balls. The website has listings of events countrywide.

International Federation of Competitive Eaters (IFOCE), web: www.ifoce.com

PET PURSUITS

Canine freestyle dancing is actually an athletic sport, healthy for both people and dogs. Instructors help you select music suitable for your dog's style and temperament (they really do perk up when music appeals to them!), then choreograph your dance routines, planning the steps and movements that make up your 'dance'. Add costumes coordinated with the theme of the music you've chosen and you're ready to rock. There are lots of local and regional classes and events if you just want to have fun while getting Fido in shape. If you get really good you can go on to the national competitions.

Canine freestyle dancing, web: www.canine-freestyle.org; www.worldcaninefreestyle.org

If you're determined to spend your vacation with your dog, log on to **dog-play.com** for links to all kinds of activities you and your dog can enjoy together. This comprehensive site is an amazing resource for dog lovers, covering, among other things, dog camps, carting and scootering, flygility, performance trick art and rollerblading. If you need accommodation along the way, check out petswelcome.com

Dog-Play.com, webs: www.dog-play.com; www.petswelcome.com

If your mother always complained you didn't have enough sense to come in out of the rain, then a **storm chasing tour** might be for you. Led by weather fanatics with state-of-the-art storm finding equipment, these tours last from one to two weeks during prime storm-chasing season in May and June. Most of them originate out of Oklahoma City and can travel thousands of miles in search of the perfect storm in the multi-state region known as Tornado Alley. Don't expect a rain check if skies stay clear.

Quirk Alert

The **Museum of Menstruation and Women's Health** (web: www.mum.org) is looking for a permanent home. Planned displays include an actual menstrual hut, the history of menstrual objects, customs and advertising, and current women's health issues. Until recently the museum was in the private home of a bachelor, but folks were reluctant to visit the museum in that location. The museum's founder, Harry Finley, has amassed 4,000 items relating to the subject.

Storm Chasers, webs: www.silverliningtours.com; www.cloud9tours.com; www.stormchasing.com; www.tempesttours.com

CURIOUS COLLECTIONS

Scattered all over the states, **Ripley's Believe It or Not museums** can be found in heavily touristed areas. Each museum's displays, housed in 27 museums in ten countries, are 90% unique and different. Robert Ripley, a modern-day combination of Marco Polo and Indiana Jones, collected unbelievable (but true), inexplicable, and one-of-a-kind oddities over a period of 40 years.

Ripley's Believe It or Not museums, web: www.ripleys.com

KEEP AN EYE OUT...

Shoe trees, not the type you put in your shoes, are the kind you throw your shoes up and into. Shoe trees, and sometimes shoe fences, pop up from time to time on back roads where trees still line the highway. No one really knows how or why a particular tree is selected, but all of a sudden there'll be shoes and boots hanging from it. You won't find most of them listed in this guide, though, because nature often has her way with them. So just keep your eyes out or, better yet, start your own.

Street performers work the heavily touristed areas of America's cities, delighting passers-by with their antics while earning a living of sorts. Louis Armstrong, BB King, Bob Dylan, Johnny Carson, and Robin Williams all got their start on the street. From chain-saw juggling to flying house cats to living statues, there's some fine – and wacky – talent to be found out there.

CORPORATE KUDOS

You wouldn't normally associate 'quirky' with 'corporate' but in the case of **Hampton Inns & Hotels**, you'd have to make an exception. This hotel chain, part of the Hilton family, has made it their mission to renovate and preserve roadside landmarks all across America. Dubbed '**Save-A-Landmark**', the program was launched in 2000 as a way to bring the 1,000 Hampton hotels together on a single-focused, service-oriented cause. They identified hundreds of beloved American landmarks – historical, fun, and cultural – in need of repair, most of them built in the 30s, 40s, and 50s. A million dollars later, they're making a real difference, fixing up icon after icon. Inn employees and volunteers do the actual work. In 2003 they turned their attention to Route 66, fixing up landmarks in eight states and donating 100 route markers.

The corporation also has a fondness for festivals and events, maintaining a comprehensive website, '**Year of 1,000 Weekends**', of the most unique, entertaining, quirky, educational and enjoyable events happening each weekend in cities and towns across America. Organizing them into ten different categories of interest, the most eccentric events can be found in the 'really different' section of the website.

Save A Landmark, Hampton Inns & Hotels; web:
www.hamptoninn.com/landmarks

Hampton's Year of 1,000 Weekends, web:
www.hamptoninnnweekends.com

Appendix

FURTHER READING
Series of note
Avant Guides: Las Vegas, New York City, New Orleans, and San Francisco
Off The Beaten Path, state-by-state guides, Globe-Pequot Press
Curiosities, state-by-state guides, Globe-Pequot Press

Books

America Bizarro: A Guide to Freaky Festivals, Groovy Gatherings, Kooky Contests and other Strange Happenings Across the USA, Nelson Taylor, St Martin's Griffen, 2000

America's Strangest Museums: A Traveler's Guide to the Most Unusual and Eccentric Collections, Sandra Gurvis, Carol Publishing Group, 1996

An American Festival of 'World Capitals' From Garlic Queens to Cherry Parades: Over 300 'World Capitals' of Arts, Crafts, Food, Culture and Sport, Laura Bergheim, John Wiley and Sons, Inc, 1997

Calling Texas Home, Calling the Midwest Home & Calling California Home, Wells Teague, Wildcat Canyon Press, 1996-2000

Culture Shock USA: A Guide to Customs and Etiquette, Esther Wanning, Graphics Arts Center Publishing, 1991

The Banana Sculptor, the Purple Lady, and the All Night Swimmer: Hobbies, Collecting, and Other Passionate Pursuits, Susan Sheehan and Howard Means, Simon & Schuster, 2002

The Darwin Awards: Evolution in Action, Wendy Northcutt, E P Dutton, 2000

Dear Elvis: Graffiti from Graceland, Daniel Wright, Mustang Publishing, 1996

Eat Your Way Across the USA, Jane & Michael Stern, Broadway Books, 1997

Eccentric Britain, Benedict le Vay, Bradt Publications, 2000

Eccentrics: A study of Sanity and Strangeness, Dr. David Weeks, Villard Books, 1996

Field Guide to Elvis Shrines, Bill Yenne, Renaissance Books, 1999

Frommer's Irreverent Guide to Manhattan, 3rd Edition, Ian McMahan, IDG Books Worldwide, 2000

Frommer's Irreverent Guide to San Francisco, 3rd Edition, Liz Barrett, IDG Books Worldwide, 2000

Fun Along the Road: American Tourist Attractions John Margolies, Bulfinch, 1998

The Fun Also Rises: Fun Seekers North America Alan Davis, Greenline Publications, 1999

Fugitives and Refugees: A Walk in Portland, Oregon, Chuck Palahniuk, Crown Publishers, 2003

The Good, the Bad, and the Mad: Weird People in American History, E. Randall Floyd, harbor House, 1999

Great American Motorcycle Tours, Gary McKechnie, John Muir Publications, 2000

Great Little Museums of the Midwest, Christine des Garennes, Trails Books, 2002

The Great San Francisco Trivia and Fact Book, Janet Bailey, Cumberland House, 1999

Greatest Hits Maps by AAA: Route 66:The Best of the Mother Road; Southern California Car Culture Landmarks, AAA Western Travel Publications, 2002

Gullible's Travels, Cash Peters, Globe-Pequot, 2003

Holding On: Dreamers, Visionaries, Eccentrics and Other American Heroes, David Isay and Harvey Wang, W W Norton and Company, 1997

How to Talk American: A Guide to our Native Tongues, Jim 'the Mad Monk' Crotty, Houghton Mifflin Company, 1997

Idaho Loners Hermits, Solitaires and Individualists, Cort Conley, Backeddy Books, 1994

LA Bizarro: The Insider's Guide to the Obscure, the Absurd, and the Perverse in Los Angeles, Anthony R Lovett and Matt Maranian, St Martin's Press, 1997

The Last of the Mountain Men: The True Story of an Idaho Solitary, Sylvan Hart, Backeddy Books, 1969

Little Museums: Over 1,000 Small (and Not-So-Small) American Showplaces, Lynne Arany and Archie Hobson, Henry Holt and Company, 1998

The Mad Monks' Guide to California, James Crotty and Michael Lane (The Monks), Macmillan Travel, 2000

The Mad Monks' Guide to New York City, James Crotty and Michael Lane (The Monks), Macmillan Travel, 1997

Main Street Festivals: Traditional and Unique Events on America's Main Streets, Amanda B West, The National Main Street Center of the National Trust for Historic Preservation, John Wiley and Sons, Inc, 1998

Making America: The Society and Culture of the United States, edited by Luther Leudtke, University of North Carolina Press, 1992

The Museum of Hoaxes, Alex Boese, E P Dutton, 2002

Nevada off the Beaten Path: A Guide to Unique Places, Donna Peck, The Globe Pequot Press, 1997

The New Roadside America: The Modern Traveler's Guide to the Wild and Wonderful World of America's Tourist Attractions, Mike Wilkins, Ken Smith and Doug Kirby, Fireside, 1992

Oddball Illinois: A Guide to Some Really Strange Places, Jerome Pohlen, Chicago Review Press, 2000

Oddballs and Eccentrics, Karl Shaw, Carroll & Graf Publishers, 2000

Odd Jobs, Portraits of Unusual Occupations, Nancy Rica Schiff, Ten Speed Press, 2002

Off the Beaten Aisle: America's Quirky Spots to Tie the Knot, Lisa Primerano, Carol Publishing Group, 1998

OffBeat Food: Adventures in an Omnivorous World, Alan Ridenour, Santa Monica Press, 2000

Offbeat Museums: The Collections and Curators of America's Most Unusual Museums, Saul Rubin, Santa Monica Press, 1997

On The Back Roads: Discovering Small Towns of America, Bill Graves, Addicus Books Inc, 1999

Only In Mississippi: A Guide for the Adventurous Traveller, Lorraine Redd and Jack E Davis, Quail Ridge Press, 1993

The Outrageous Atlas: A Guide to North America's Strangest Places, Richard D Rogers and Laurine Rogers, Citadel Press, 1993

Philly Firsts: The Famous, Infamous and Quirky of the City of Brotherly Love, Janice L Booker, Camino Books Inc, 1999

Quack! Tales of Medical Fraud from the Museum of Questionable Medical Devices, Bob McCoy, Santa Monica Press, 2000

Radical Walking Tours of New York City, Bruce Kayton, Seven Stories Press, 1999

The Rhode Island Guide, Barbara Radcliffe Rogers and Stillman D Rogers, Fulcrum Publishing, 1998

Roadfood: The Coast-to-Coast Guide to 500 of the Best Barbeque Joints, Lobster Shacks, Ice Cream Parlors, Highway Diners, and Much More, Jane Stern, Broadway, 2002

Roadtrip, USA: Cross-Country Adventures on America's Two-Lane Highways, Jamie Jensen, Avalon Travel Publishing, 2002

San Francisco Bizarro: A Guide to Notorious Sights, Lusty Pursuits and Downright Freakiness in the City by the Bay, Jack Boulware, St Martin's Press, 2000

Sense of Place: American Regional Cultures, edited by Barbara Allen and Thomas J Schlereth, University Press of Kentucky, 1990

Slanguage: A Cool, Fresh, Phat, and Shagadelic Guide to All Kinds of Slang, Mike Ellis, Hyperion Books, 2000

South Dakota, T D Griffith, Photographs by Paul Horsted, Compass American Guides, 1994.

USA by Rail, John Pitt, Bradt Travel Guides, 2003

Wacky Chicks: Life Lessons from Fearlessly Inappropriate and Fabulously Eccentric Women, Simon Doonan, Simon & Schuster, 2003

Watch it Made in the USA: A Visitor's Guide to the Companies that Make your Favorite Products, Karen Axelrod and Bruce Brumbert, Avalon Travel Publications, October 2002

Way out in West Virginia: A Must-have Guide to the Oddities and Wonders of the Mountain State, Jeanne Mozier, Quarrier Press, 1999

Wet and Wired: A Pop Culture Encyclopedia of the Pacific Northwest, Randy Hodgins and Steve McLellan, Taylor Publishing Company, 2000

Why People Believe Weird Things, Michael Shermer, W H Freeman, 1997

Wild Chicago, Will Clinger, Mindy Bell, & Harvey Moshman, Globe-Pequot Press, 2003

Whatnots!, Thirty Fascinating People Share Their Extraordinary Collections, Eileen Birin, Neelie Publishing, 2002

COMING SOON...
Eccentric Mini Guides

This expansion of the Bradt Eccentric series into a new Mini Guide series focuses on popular British and Irish cities that have strongly individual identities. Loved by tourist and locals alike, these cities have a wealth of curious ceremonies, bizarre buildings and peculiar people to discover. Benedict le Vay, author of Bradt's *Eccentric Britain* and *Eccentric London*, extracts the extraordinary from the mundane.

New for 2004
Eccentric Edinburgh

This new guide is the essential source on all that is offbeat, bizarre and absurd in the Scottish capital, featuring eccentric pastimes and an eccentric calendar, and including the annual Edinburgh Festival. Trace the ghosts, murders and mayhem of macabre Edinburgh, meet the wacky characters who make the modern city tick and find the hidden gems that other guides ignore. (July 2004 publication)

Eccentric Oxford

Benedict le Vay delves into the medieval back alleys of this cultural gem and comes up with a fascinatingly fresh look at a city of contrasts. Behind the picturesque façade discover where batty Oxford dons and eccentric characters have lived and the hidden secrets of the 'city of dreaming spires'. (November 2004 publication)

We have Eccentric Mini Guides to Bath, Cambridge and Dublin in the pipeline.

More from Jan Friedman: In 2005 *Eccentric Florida* and *Eccentric California* will kick-off a series focusing on American regional eccentricities.

ECCENTRIC LONDON
The Bradt Guide to Britain's Crazy and Curious Capital
Benedict le Vay

'Positively pulsating with crackpot customs, transport trivia and a whole host of unbelievable stuff!' *Essex Courier*

Meet a man who listens to Tube trains from the road above with a large hearing-trumpet, the inventor who made giant ships out of ice, a chap who rides down the river in an Edwardian bath chair, the guy with the world's biggest collection of pillar boxes...

These are just a few of the colourful characters to be found in *Eccentric London*, the fascinating follow-up to Benedict le Vay's sell-out book, *Eccentric Britain*. Here the London-born author revisits his childhood stomping grounds and devises a district-by-district guide to everything compelling, curious, bizarre, absurd or hilarious. Plus the oddest shops, museums, jobs, pubs and people you could possibly imagine.

MORE BRADT ECCENTRICS

Eccentric Britain
The Bradt Guide to Britain's Follies and
Foibles
Benedict le Vay

'A wonderfully barmy guide' *Scotland on
Sunday*

'Benedict le Vay's splendid indulgence is
occasionally a bit of an eye-popper but
mostly a chuckle, and his obvious affection
for the odd and the oddball shines through.'
Observer

'A truly great guide. Perhaps the most unique guidebook
around.' *TNT*

Eccentric France
The Bradt Guide to French Farces and
Frolics
Piers Letcher

'Compulsive reading' *The Times*

From outrageous artists and ridiculous
royalty to bizarre buildings and fabulous
festivals, *Eccentric France* covers an
eclectic range of people, places and
events. The ultimate collection for anyone with a taste for the
extraordinary, this guide includes a 'nuts and bolts' section on
travel practicalities.

*Bradt Guides are available from all good bookshops,
or by post, fax, phone or internet direct from*

Bradt Travel Guides Ltd
19 High Street, Chalfont St Peter, Bucks SL9 9QE, England
Tel: 01753 893444 Fax: 01753 892333
Email: info@bradtguides.com
Web: www.bradtguides.com

State Index

ALABAMA 254–6
Ave Maria Grotto, Cullman 254
Coon Dog Cemetery Celebration, Tuscumbia 255
Joe Minter's Yard, Birmingham 255
Key Underwood Coon Dog Graveyard, Tuscumbia 255
Lambert's Café, Foley 256
Riverhouse B&B, Theodore 256
Toilet Paper Tree, Auburn 255
Unclaimed Baggage Center, Scottsboro 256
World's Longest Outdoor Yard Sale 254

ARIZONA 67–75
Arcosanti, Cordes Junction 70
Bed Races, Oatman 66
Biosphere 2, Tucson 70
Chloride Rocks, Chloride 72
Cochise Stronghold B&B, Pearce 74
Cow Pasture Golf, Springerville 68
Delgadillo's Snow Cap, Seligman 73
Egg Fry, Oatman 66
Eliphante, Cornville 69
Great Cardboard Boat Regatta, Tempe Town Lake 68
Ghost Town, Oatman 66
Katydid Insect Museum, Glendale 71
Mr Lee's Rock Garden, Phoenix 70
Mother Goose at Renaissance Fair, Apache Junction 72
Mystery Castle, Phoenix 69
Organ Stop Pizza, Mesa 73
Route 66 Gift Shop, Seligman 73

Ostrich Festival, Chandler 68
Silverado Ranch, Holbrook 75
Titan Missile Museum, Sahuarita 71
Two White Rocks Hospitality, Navajo Nation 75
Valley of the Moon, Tucson 71
Wigwam Village Motel, Holbrook 75
World's Smallest Museum, Superior 71

Bisbee 74, 75
Inn at Castle Rock 74
OK Street Jailhouse 75
Shady Dell RV Park 74

ARKANSAS 171–4
Agricultural Museum, Stuttgart 173
Bean Festival, Mountain View 171
Museum of Merritt, Mountain Home 173
Riddle's Elephant Sanctuary, Greenbrier 174
Toad Suck Daze, Conway 172
Turkey Trot, Yellville 171
World Championship Cardboard Boat Festival, Heber Springs 171

Eureka Springs 172, 173, 174
City of 174
Dinosaur World 173
Frog Fantasies Museum 172
New Holy Land Tours 174
Quigley's Castle Ark 172

CALIFORNIA 21–53
Northern California 21–38
Bone Room, Berkeley 36
Bonfante Gardens Family Theme Park, Gilroy 35
Boonville, Town of 35
BraBall 37

Calaveras County Fair and Jumping Frog Jubilee, Angels Camp 32
Carmel, City of 36
Castlewood Cottages, Big Bear Lake 37
Ciao Bella!, Ben Lomond 36
di Rosa Preserve, Napa 34
Fashion Police, Mill Valley 35
Forestiere Underground Gardens, Fresno 33
Horned Toad Derby, Coalinga 32
How Berkeley Can You Be? Parade, Berkeley 32
Kinetic Sculpture Museum, Ferndale 31
Kinetic Sculpture Race, Ferndale 31
Lake Haven Motel and Resort, Clearlake Oaks 38
Litto's Hubcap Ranch, Pope Valley 34
Lucky Mojo Curio Company, Forestville 36
Museum of Pez Memorabilia, Burlingame 34
National Yo-Yo Championship, Chico 34
National Yo-Yo Museum, Chico 34
Poison Oak Show, Columbia 33
Railroad Park Resort, Dunsmuir 37
Safari West Wildlife Preserve & Tent Camp, Santa Rosa 37
Toad Tunnel, Davis 35
Vision Quest Safari B&B, Salinas 37
Winchester Mystery House, San Jose 33
World Pillow Fighting Championship, Kenwood 31

San Francisco Area 21, 24, 26, 27–8, 29–31

Bay to Breakers Race 21
Beach Blanket Babylon 30
Cartoon Art Museum 26
Chinese New Year's Treasure
 Hunt 21
City Guides Neighborhood
 Walks 27
Cruisin' the Castro Tour 27
Defenestration 29
Emperor Norton 30
Exotic Erotic Halloween Ball 26
Fire Engine Tours and
 Adventures 28
Flower Power Haight-Ashbury
 Walking Tour 28
Foot! Tours 29
Footstock Festival 21
Ghost Hunt Walking Tour 27
Haight-Ashbury Street Fair 26
Hallowe'en 24
How Weird Street Faire 21
Precita Eyes Mural Arts Center
 28
Red Vic B&B 30
St Stupid's Day Parade 26
San Francisco Zoo Valentine's
 Day Sex Tours 29
Street Retreats 29
Wax Museum 27

Southern California 38–53
Amargosa Opera House, Death
 Valley Junction 42
Ballantines Hotel, Palm
 Springs 53
Blessing of the Dates, Riverside
 County 40
Bubble Gum Alley, San Luis
 Obispo 49
Bulldozer Building, Turlock 49
Cafe Tu Tu Tango, Orange &
 Universal City 51
Cowboy Memorial & Library,
 Caliente 43
Donut Hole, La Puente 49
Doo Dah Parade, Pasadena 39
Fabulous Palm Springs Follies,
 Palm Springs 48
Golf Cart Parade, Palm Desert
 39
Grandma Prisbrey's Bottle
 Village, Simi Valley 42
Historical Burlesque Museum
 and Hall of Fame,
 Helendale 45
International Banana Club,
 Altadena 44
Lobster Festival, Redondo
 Beach 40

Lompoc Valley Mural Project,
 Lompoc 48
Madonna Inn, San Luis Obispo
 52
Miss Exotic World, Helendale
 45
Moon Amtrak, Laguna Niguel
 38
Mud Run, Camp Pendleton 39
Museum of Jurassic
 Technology, Culver City 44
National Date Festival,
 Riverside County 40
Noah Purifoy Desert Art
 Environment, Joshua Tree
 41
Oasis of Eden Inn & Suites,
 Yucca Valley 52
Pageant of Masters, Laguna
 Beach 38
Perry's Beach Café & Rentals,
 Santa Monica 50
Port of Los Angeles Lobster
 Festival, San Pedro 40
Randy's Donuts, Inglewood 49
Salvation Mountain, Niland 41
Scotty's Castle, Death Valley 47
Toy Piano Festival, La Jolla 39
Typhoon Restaurant, Santa
 Monica Airport 52
Underwater Pumpkin Carving
 Contest, San Diego 41
Witch's House, Beverly Hills 49

**Hollywood 45–7, 49–50, 51,
 53**
Frederick's of Hollywood
 Lingerie Museum and
 Celebrity Lingerie Hall of
 Fame 45
Guinness World Records
 Museum 46
Hollywood History Museum
 46
Ripley's Believe It or Not
 Museum 46
Standard Hotel 53
Tail o' the Pup 49
Wacko 51

**Los Angeles 43, 46–7, 48,
 50–1, 52**
Angelyne 47
Farmacia Million Dollar
 Botanicas 50
Galco's Old World Grocery 50
Hotel Bel Air 52
L Ron Hubbard Life
 Exhibition 46

Petersen Automotive Museum
 47
Re-Mix Shoe Company 50
Skeletons in the Closet 51
Standard Hotel 53
Take My Mother★Please (★or
 any other VIP) Tours 48
Watts Towers 43

Venice 49–50
Abbot's Habit, Venice 49
Audrey's Good Vibrations,
 Venice 50
Binocular Building, Venice
 Beach 49
Perry's Beach Café & Rentals
 50
Venice Beach 49

COLORADO 150–7
America, Why I Love Her,
 Denver International
 Airport 156
Bishop's Castle, Pueblo 155
Buckhorn Exchange, Denver
 157
Cardboard Box Derby,
 Arapahoe Basin 153
Casa Bonita, Lakewood 157
Emma Crawford Coffin Races,
 Manitou Springs 152
Frozen Dead Guy Day,
 Nederland 153
Fruitcake Toss, Manitou
 Springs 151
International Snow Sculpting
 Championships,
 Breckenridge 154
Kelloff's Best Western Movie
 Manor Motor Inn, Monte
 Vista 157
Kinetic Sculpture Race,
 Boulder 152
Mike the Headless Chicken
 Days, Frutia 150
Museum of Colorado Prisons,
 Canon City 156
Rolling River Raft Race,
 Pueblo 152
Snowdown, Durango 152
Swetsville Zoo, Fort Collins
 155
Fort, The, Morrison 156

Crested Butte 154, 157
Claim-Jumper B&B 157
Flauschink 154
Vinitok 154

Telluride 154
In-Drag Race 154
Mushroom Festival 154
Nothing Festival 154

CONNECTICUT 207–10
Barker Character, Comic, &
  Cartoon Museum, Cheshire
  209
Boom Box Parade, Willimantic
  207
Children's Garbage Museum,
  Stratford 208
Elizabeth Tashijian, Nut Lady
  XII, 208
Gillette's Castle, East Haddam
  207
Louis' Lunch, New Haven 209
Nut Art, New London 208
Nut Museum 208
Randall's Ordinary Inn &
  Restaurant, Stonington 210
Stew Leonard's, Norwalk &
  Danbury 209
Witch's Dungeon Classic
  Horror Museum, Bristol 208

DELAWARE 224–5
Ches Del Restaurant,
  StGeorge's 225
Mike's Famous Roadside Rest,
  New Castle 225
Punkin' Chunkin',
  Georgetown 224
Wagon Wheel Family
  Restaurant, Smyrna 225

DISTRICT OF
  COLUMBIA 227–30
Gross National Product 227
International Spy Museum 227
Scandal Tours 227
Spydrive Tours 230
Squished Penny Museum 227

FLORIDA 260–76
Billy Bowlegs Festival, Fort
  Walton Beach 266
Bubble Room, Captiva Island
  273
Bug Jam, Spring Hill 266
Café Tu Tu Tango, Coconut
  Grove 273
Cassadaga Hotel 276
Coral Castle, Homestead 267
Desert Inn Resort Motel &
  Suites, Daytona Beach 273
Dinosaur World, Plant City
  269

Gasparilla Parade & Pirate Fest
  Festival, Tampa 265
Hamburger Museum, Daytona
  Beach 269
House of Presidents, Clermont
  268
Interstate Mullet Toss,
  Pensacola 265
Jules' Undersea Lodge, Key
  Largo 276
King Mango Strut, Coconut
  Grove 266
Koreshanity 274
Missionary Mary Proctor's
  Folk Art Museum,
  Tallahassee 267
Old Spanish Sugar Mill,
  Deleon Springs 275
Patrick's Island 276
Ripley's Believe It or Not!
  Museum, St Augustine 269
Showtown Bar & Grill,
  Gibsonton 272
Solomon's Castle, Ona 267
Spiritualist Camp, Cassadaga
  272
Town of Murals, Lake Placid
  271
Tupperware Millennium
  Sculpture, Kissamee 271
Weeki Wachee Springs Water
  Park, Tampa 270
White House replica, Clermont
  268

Key West 260–5
Cemetery Tours 265
Chicken Store 261
City of 260
Conch Republic Independence
  Celebration 263
Dog Days of Summer 263
Fantasy Fest 261
Gay & Lesbian Trolley Tour
  261
Ghosts and Legends of Key
  West 261
Hemingway Days Festival 263
Old Island Days 263
Pirates in Paradise 263
Pub Crawl 261
Sunset Celebration 261
Underwater Easter Egg Hunt
  263
Underwater Music Festival 263
Underwater Pumpkin Carving
  263
Underwater Weddings 265
Womenfest 263

Miami 268, 269, 271, 272–3,
  275–6
B.E.D. 272
Monkey Jungle 269
Pelican Hotel 276
Specialty Tours of Miami &
  South Florida 271
Tantra Restaurant & Lounge
  273
Townhouse 275
Wolfsonian Museum 268

Orlando 270, 271, 275
Ducks at the Peabody 271
Gatorland 270
Gator Cook-off 270
Monster Café 275

GEORGIA 256–9
Café Tu Tu Tango, Atlanta 259
Guidestones, Elberton 258
Paradise Garden, Summerville
  257
Pasaquan, Buena Vista 258
Redneck Games, Dublin 256
Varsity Restaurant, Atlanta 258

IDAHO 10–12
Anniversary Inn, Boise 12
Bed Race & Parade, Preston 10
Dog Bark Park, Cottonwood
  12
National Old Time Fidddlers'
  Contest, Weiser 10
Oasis Bordello Museum,
  Wallace 11
Richard Zimmerman (Dugout
  Dick), Elk Bend 12
Spud Day, Shelley 10
World Potato Exposition,
  Blackfoot 11

ILLINOIS 102–8
Adventure Inn Motel, Gurnee
  108
Ahlgrim Acres, Palatine 107
Bishop Hill Museum, Bishop
  Hill 108
Cardboard Boat Regattas 102
Catsup Bottle Summerfest
  Birthday Party, Collinsville
  102
Cermak Plaza Shopping
  Center, Berwyn 106
Historical Museum, Rolling
  Meadows 104
Lakeview Museum's
  Community Solar System,
  Peoria 106

Max Nordeen's Wheels Museum, Alpha 104
Museum of Funeral Customs, Springfield 105
Olney, Town of 105
Raven's Grin Inn, Mount Carroll 105
Super Museum & Gift Shop, Metropolis 103
Superman Celebration, Metropolis 103
Tug Fest, Port Byron 103
Two-Story Outhouse, Gays 107
World Freefall Convention 103
World's Largest Bagel Breakfast, Mattoon 102

Alton 105–6, 107
Antoinette's Haunted History Tours 105
History & Haunting Tours 105
Museum of History & Art 107
Town of 105
Wadlow, Robert (world's tallest man) 107

Chicago 103–4,106,108
Feet First: the Scholl Story 104
Hustle Up the Hancock 103
International Museum of Surgical Science 103
Neighborhood Tours 106
Pasha Restaurant & Club 108
See Chicago with a Cop 106
Untouchables Tour 106

INDIANA 114–19
Alexandria, City of 118
Bird's Eye View Museum of Miniatures, Wakarusa 117
Crane, Sam 118
Crowne Plaza Union Station, Indianapolis 119
Dan Quayle Center, Huntington 117
Dillinger Museum, Hammond 116
Dr Ted's Musical Marvels, Dale 118
Indiana Shoe Tree, Milltown 119
James Dean Memorial Gallery, Fairmount 118
Luckey Hospital Museum, Wolfe Lake 116
National New York Central Railroad Museum, Elkhart 117

Pierogi Festival, Whiting 115
Red Carpet Inn & Fantasuites, Greenwood 119
Rube Goldberg Machine Contest 115
RV/MH Heritage Museum & Hall of Fame, Elkhart 115
Schimppf's Confectionary Museum, Jeffersonville 116
Wizard of Oz Fest, Chesterton 114
World's Largest Ball of Paint, Alexandria 119

IOWA 99–102
Bily Clocks Museum and Dvorak Exhibit, Spillville 101
Future Birthplace of Captain Kirk, Riverside 101
Grotto of the Redemption, West Bend 100
Hobo Museum, Britt 99
Life-size butter cow sculpture (Iowa State Fair), Des Moines 99
Lighthouse Valley View B&B, Dubuque 102
National Hobo Convention, Britt 99
Palmer Mansion, Davenport 101
Squirrel Cage Jail, Council Bluffs 101
Toto Fest, Welton 99
Trek Fest, Riverside 101
Tug Fest, LeClaire 100
Waterloo Workshop, Dorchester 100

KANSAS 158–62
Also-Ran Museum, Norton 160
Barbed Wire Museum, La Crosse 160
Davis Memorial at the Mount Hope Cemetery, Hiawatha 161
Garden of Eden, Lucas 158
Grassroots Art Center, Lucas 158
Hedrick's B&B Inn, Nickerson 162
Hopalong Cassidy Museum, Benton 160
Insect Zoo, Manhattan 160
International Pancake Race, Liberal 158
M T Liggett, Mullinville 161

Stan Herd, Lawrence 161

KENTUCKY 235–8
Colonel Harland Sanders Museum, Corbin 236
Duncan Hines Festival, Bowling Green 236
Great Outhouse Blowout & Race, Gravel Switch 235
Millennium Monument, Newport 237
Oscar Getz Museum of Whiskey History, Beardstown 237
Vent Haven Ventriloquism Museum, Fort Mitchell 236
Wigwam Village, Cave City 238
Wildwood Inn Tropical Dome & Theme Suites, Florence 238
Wooldridge Monuments, Mayfield 237
World Chicken Festival, London 236
World Peace Bell, Newport 237
World's Longest Outdoor Yard Sale 235

Louisville 236, 237, 238
Kentucky Derby Festival 236
Lynn's Paradise Café 238
Thomas Edison House 237

LOUSIANA 175–8
Authentic Bonnie and Clyde Festival & Museum, Gibsland 177
Bayou Pierre Alligator Park, Natchitoches 178
Giant Omelette Celebration, Abbeville 178
Sculpture Garden, Chauvin 177
UCM Museum, Abita Springs 178

New Orleans 175–7
Blaine Kern's Mardi Gras World 176
Bloody Marys Tours 176
Cities of the Dead Cemetery Tours 176
City of 175
Dive Inn Guest House 177
Haunted History Tours 176
Historic New Orleans Tours 176

Historic Voodoo Museum 177
Mardi Gras 175
Mid-City Lanes Rock 'n Bowl 175
Spirit Tours 176

MAINE 198–202
Bryant's Stove Museum, Thorndike 201
Central Maine Egg Festival, Pittsfield 198
Eartha™, Yarmouth 201
Festival of Scarecrows, Rockland 199
Fryeburg Fair, Freyberg 198
Lindbergh Crate Day, New Canaan 199
Moose Stompers Weekend, Houlton 200
Moxie Days Festival, Lewiston 199
National Wife Carrying Championships, Bethel 199
Orgone Energy Accumulator, Rangeley 202
Paul Schipper's Streak, Sugarloaf Ski Resort 200
Potato Blossom Festival, Fort Fairfield 200
Potato Feast Days, Houlton 200
Umbrella Cover Museum, Peaks Island 201
White, White World Week, Sugarloaf Ski Resort 200

MARYLAND 221–4
Chesapeake Bay Maritime Museum, St Michaels 224
God's Ark of Safety, Frostburg 223
National Cryptologic Museum 223
Presidential Pet Museum, Lothian 222
US Army Ordnance Museum, Aberdeen Proving Ground 222

Baltimore 221–2, 223, 224
American Visionary Art Museum 221
Café Hon 224
Great Blacks in Wax Museum 222
Honfest 224
Kinetic Sculpture Race 221
Museum of Incandescent Lighting 223

MASSACHUSETTS 202–6
American Sanitary Plumbing Museum, Worcester 203
Battleship Massachusetts, Fall River 205
Fantasia Fair, Provincetown 202
Ig Nobel Prizes, Cambridge 202
Jumbo the Elephant's remains, Medford 204
Lizzie Borden B&B & Museum, Fall River 205
Museum of Bad Art, Dedham 204
Paper House, Rockport 203

Boston 203, 205
Mapparium 203
Medieval Manor 205
Museum of Dirt 205

MICHIGAN 108–14
Cardboard Boat Regattas 109
Dinosaur Gardens Prehistoric Zoo, Ossineke 112
Doo-Dah Parade, Kalamazoo 111
Gnome Homes, Charlevoix 111
Hair Wars, Detroit 113
Heidelberg Project 112
Hoegh Pet Casket Factory Tours, Gladstone 114
International Cherry Pit Spitting Contest, Eau Claire 109
Marvin's Marvelous Mechanical Museum, Farmington Hills 111
National Baby Food Festival, Fremont 109
Outhouse Classic, Trenary 108
Presque Isle Harbor Cemetery, Marquette 113
Rosie's Diner, Rockford 114
Shrine of the Pines, Baldwin 113
Travelers Club International Restaurant & Tuba Museum, Okemos 114
World's Longest Breakfast Table, Battle Creek 111

MINNESOTA 92–9
Cabela's Outfitters, Owatonna 97
Ed's Museum, Wykoff 95
Fish House Parade, Aitkin 92

Franconia Sculpture Park, Shafer 96
General Mills Cereal Adventures, Bloomington Hills 95
Great American Think-Off, New York Mills 92
Ice Box Days, International Falls 92
Jailhouse Inn, Preston 99
Lake Street USA 98
Nordic Inn Medieval Brew & Bed, Crosby 98
Polar Fest, Detroit Lakes 93
Potato Days, Barnesville 93
Quality Inns and Suites, Burnsville 98
Runestone Museum, Alexandria 94
St Urho's Day, Menahga 93
Sandpaper Museum (3M/Dwan Museum), Two Harbors 95
Sod House B&B, Sanborn 98
Twine Ball Day, Darwin 97
Two-Story Outhouse, Belle Plaine 96
World's Biggest Ball of Twine, Darwin 97

Austin 94
SPAM™ Jam 94
SPAM™ Museum 94
SPAM™ Town USA Festival 94

Minneapolis/Saint Paul 93, 94–5, 96, 97
dueling elves 97
Museum of Questionable Medical Devices 94
Newsroom Restaurant 97
Saint Paul Winter Carnival 93
St Paul Gangster Tours 96
Smell & Sound Knowledge Maps 96

MISSISSIPPI 250–4
American Dream Safari 253
Birthplace of Kermit the Frog, Leland 253
Graceland Too, Holly Springs 252
Mal's St Patrick's Day Parade, Jackson 250
Mammy's Cupboard, Natchez 254
Margaret's Grocery, Vicksburg 252

Palestine Gardens, Lucedale 253
Shack Up Inn, Clarksdale 254
Sweet Potato Queens 250
World Championship Anvil Shooters Classic, Bay Springs 252

MISSOURI 166–71
City Museum, St Louis 169
Elvis is Alive Museum & Restaurant, Wright City 168
Lambert's Café, Ozark & Sikeston 170
Leila's Hair Museum, Independence 168
Precious Moments, Carthage 170
Roy Rogers–Dale Evans Museum, Branson 168
Tom Sawyer Days, Hannibal 166
Kansas City 166–8, 170
J Stephen Memorial Restroom 170
Marble Room 166
Toy & Miniature Museum 166

MONTANA 17–19
Bear Creek Saloon Pig Races, Bear Creek 19
Cardboard Classic, Red Lodge 18
Furniture Races, Whitefish 18
Iron Horse Rodeo, Red Lodge 17
Mission Mountain Testicle Festival, Carlo 18
Running of the Sheep, Reed Point 18
Testicle Festival, Clinton 18
Testicle Festival, Ryegate 18
York Bar's Go-Nuts Testicle Festival, York 18

NEBRASKA 127–8
Bill's Food Mart, Howells 128
Carhenge, Alliance 128
Chicken Show, Wayne127
Cluck-Off Contest, Wayne 127
Museum of the Odd, Lincoln 128
Quack-off, Avoca127
Running of the Wieners, Grand Island 127
Sioux Sundries, Harrison 128

NEVADA 53–66
Area 51, Rachel 66

Beatty Burro & Flapjack Races, Beatty 63
Camel Races, Virginia City 63
Dooby Lane, Gerlach 64
Extraterrestrial Highway, 66
Festival in the Pit, Battle Mountain 64
Gold Well Open Air Museum, Beatty, 65
Kit Carson Trail Ghost Walk, Carson City 63
Little A 'Le' Inn & Motel, Rachel 66
National Cowboy Poetry Gathering, Elko 63
New Millennium Holy Land, Mesquite 65
Shoe Tree, Middlegate 64
Thunder Mountain, Imlay 64
US 50 (the Loneliest Road in America) 53

Black Rock Desert 62
Black Rock Desert Self-Invitational Golf Tournament 62
Burning Man 62
Lucifer's Anvil golf course 62

Las Vegas 53–62
Attic, The 57
Aureole Restaurant 60
Bonanza Gifts 58
Casino Legends Hall of Fame 55
Elvis-o-Rama Museum 55
Elvis Impersonator Contest & Fan Convention 54
Fetish & Fantasy Ball 54
Flyaway Indoor Skydiving 56
Fremont Street Experience 56
Gambler's General Store 57
Gameworks Showcase 56
Guinness World of Records Museum 55
Harley-Davidson Café 58
Integriton 61
Liberace Museum 54
Lion Habitat 59
Madame Tussaud's Celebrity Encounter Wax Museum 60
Main Street Station Casino, Brewery & Hotel 61
Mandalay Bay Resort & Casino 60
Neon Museum 55
Rain Forest Café 59
Ray's Beaver Bag 58
Red Square Restaurant 60

Rio Suite Hotel & Casino's Masquerade in the Sky 59
Serge's Showgirl Wigs 57
Star Trek Experience 60
Thrillseekers Unlimited 57
Treasure Island Buccaneer Bay Sea Battle 61
Viva Las Vegas Wedding Chapel & Hotel 58

NEW HAMPSHIRE 197–8
Margarita's Mexican Restaurant & Watering Hole, Concord 198
Mud Bowl Championships, Concord 197
Museum of Family Camping, Allenstown 198
Strictly Moose, Gorham 198

NEW JERSEY 210–13
Doo Wop Trolley Tours, Wildwood 213
Fairy Tale Forest, Oak Ridge 212
Lucy the Elephant Monument, Margate 212
New Jersey State Police Museum, W Trenton 210
Space Farms Zoo & Museum, Sussex 210
Weird Contest Week, Ocean City 210

Flemington 212–13
Art Gallery 212
Doll Museum 212
Great American Railway 212
Northlandz 212

NEW MEXICO 144–50
American International Rattlesnake Museum, Albuquerque 147
Burning of Zozobra Fiestas de Santa Fe, Santa Fe 144
Chilili, Town of 149
Egg Nest, Ghost Town 149
Elfego Baca Shoot, Socorro 147
Granite Gap, Ghost Town 149
Greater World Earthship Community, Taos 150
Jal, Town of 148
Kokopelli's Cave B&B, Farmington 150
Lightning Field, Quemado 150
Million Dollar Museum, White City 147
Muck & Mud Derby, Rio Rancho 144

Poetry Circus, Taos 146
Rodeo, Ghost Town 149
Shakespeare, Ghost Town 149
Steins, Ghost Town 149
Tinkertown Museum, Sandia
    Park 148
Very Large Array, Magdalena
    140
Whole Enchilada Fiesta, Las
    Cruces 147
World Snow Shovel Race,
    Angel Fire 144
World's Richest Tombstone
    Race (aka Billy the Kid's
    Tombstone Race), Fort
    Sumner 147

Roswell 146, 148
International UFO Museum &
    Research Center, Roswell
    148
UFO Encounter Festival &
    Intergalactic Fashion &
    Food Extravaganza, Roswell
    146
UFO Enigma Museum,
    Roswell 148

NEW YORK 179–94
Cardiff Giant, Cooperstown
    184
House of Frankenstein Wax
    Museum, Lake George 183
Ithaca Hours, Ithaca 184
Jell-O Museum, LeRoy 183
Kaatskill Kaleidoscope 184
Magic Forest Fairy Tale Trail
    & Safari Ride, Lake George
    183
Mike Weaver Drain Tile
    Museum, Geneva 180
Original American Kazoo
    Company, Eden 179
Stew Leonard's, Yonkers 209
Sing-Sing Prison, Ossining 181
Texas Taco, Patterson 185
Wings Castle, Milbrook 179

Jamestown 179
I Love Lucy Masquerade Ball
    179
Lucy-Desi Days 179
Lucy-Desi Museum 179

New York City 185–94
Abracadabra 192
American Museum of Natural
    History 191
Art Tours of Manhattan 191

Arthur Marks Tours for All
    Seasons 188
BARC Animal Parade 186
Big Apple Greeter 191
Big Onion Walking Tours 191
Bizarre & Eccentric Tour of
    the East Village 188
Charles Simon Center for
    Adult Life & Learning 189
Coney Island Circus 186
Coney Island Museum 187
Doorway to Design 191
Evolution 192
Games of the Lower East Side
    188
Gangland Tours 190
Garment District Tour 188
Gershwin Hotel 194
Hotel Pennsylvania 193
iMar 189
Joyce Gold History Tours 190
Kenny Kramer Reality Tour
    190
Library Hotel 193
Lower East Side Tenement
    Museum 187
Mars 2112 193
Matzo Ball Eating Contest 186
Maxilla & Mandible 192
McDonald's 192
Mermaid Parade 186
Municipal Art Society 191
Muse Hotel 193
Museum of Sex 187
Nosh Walks 191
On Location Tour 191
Panorama, The, 187
Radical Walking Tours 189
Scavenger Hunts by Watson
    Adventures 191
Sideshows by the Seashore 186
Something Old, Something
    New 189
Surveillance Camera Outdoor
    Walking Tours 188
Trailer Park Lounge & Grill
    193

**NORTH CAROLINA
245–50**
Andy Griffith Museum, Mt
    Airy 248
Bald is Beautiful Convention,
    Morehead City 245
Big Chair, Thomasville 249
BuGFest, Raleigh 246
Clyde Jones, Pittsboro 246
Eva Blount Way's Collection,
    Bellhaven 247

Furnitureland South, High
    Point 249
Ghost Walk, Wilmington 248
Hog Day, Hillsborough 245
Korner's Folly, Kernsville 246
Love Valley 249
Mayberry Days, Mt Airy 248
Marvin Johnson's Gourd
    Museum, Angier 248
Museum of the Alphabet,
    Waxhaw 247
National Hollerin' Contest,
    Spivey's Corner 245
Shangri-La, Prospect Hill 249
US Trolls, Wilmington 250
Vollis Simpson's Whirligig
    Farm, Lucama 247
Woolly Worm Festival, Banner
    Elk 246
World's Largest Bureau, High
    Point 249

NORTH DAKOTA 123–4
Enchanted Highway 123
Hobo House, Jamestown 123
Hunter's Table & Tavern,
    Rhame 123
Paul Broste's Rock Museum,
    Parshall 123

OHIO 119–23
Etta's Lunch Box Café, Starr
    121
Field of Corn, Dublin 121
Hartman Rock Garden,
    Springfield 120
International Washboard
    Festival, Logan 120
Living Bible Museum,
    Mansfield 120
Longaberger Basket Company,
    Newark 121
Ravenwood Castle & Medieval
    Village, New Plymouth 121
Sudsy Malone's, Cincinnati 121
Twins Days, Twinsburg 119

OKLAHOMA 162–6
99s Museum of Women Pilots,
    Oklahoma City 165
Gene Autry Museum, Gene
    Autry 165
Leonardo's Discovery
    Warehouse, Enid 164
Muscle Car Ranch, Chickasha
    165
National Cowboy & Western
    Heritage Museum,
    Oklahoma City 164

National Four String Banjo Museum and Hall of Fame, Guthrie 165
National Lighter Museum, Guthrie 165
National Route 66 Museum, Elk City 165
National Wrestling Hall of Fame & Museum, Stillwater 165
Percussive Art Society Museum, Lawton 165
Rattlesnake Festival, Apache 162
Rattlesnake Hunt, Okeene 162
Rattlesnake Hunt, Waurika 162
Rattlesnake Hunt, Waynoka 162
Sod House Museum, Aline 165
Spooky Goofy Golf Tournament, Antlers 163
State Prison Outlaw Rodeo, McAlester 163
Totem Pole Park, Foyil 164
Twister Museum, Wakita 164
Windmill Museum & Park, Shattuck 165
World Cow Chip Throwing Contest, Beaver 162

OREGON 13–17
da Vinci Days Festival, Corvallis 13
Funny Farm, Bend 16
Hart's Reptile World, Canby 15
Oregon County Fair, Eugene 13
Out 'n' About Treesort, Takilma 17
Petersen's Rock Garden, Redmond 13
Prehistoric Gardens, Port Orford 15
Sylvia Beach Hotel, Newport 17

Portland 14–16
Alien Museum 14
American Advertising Museum 14
Kennedy School Hotel 16
Kidd's Toy Museum, Portland 14
Mill End's Park (world's smallest park) 15
Rimsky-Korsakoffee House 16
Stark's Vacuum Cleaner Museum 14
Underground Tour 15

PENNSYLVANIA 213–20
Amish Mud Sales, Lancaster 215
Andy Warhol Museum, Pittsburgh 216
Bark Peeler's Convention, Galeton 214
Caesars Pocono Resorts, Poconos 220
Duds'N' Suds Laundromat, Pittsburgh 219
Houdini Museum, Scranton 217
Ice Tee Golf Tournament, Lake Wallpaupack 214
Mercer Museum & Fonthill Historical Society, Doylestown 215
Mr Ed's Elephant Museum, Orrtanna 216
Museum of Pez Dispensers, Easton 217
National Lint Project 219
Pennsylvania's Family Farms 220
Ringing Rocks Park, Bridgeton Township 219
Roadside America, Shartlesville 218
Stink Fest, Bradford 214

Philadelphia 213–14, 216–17, 218
Chocolate by Mueller 219
Eastern State Penitentiary 216
Insectarium 215
Mummer's Museum 213
Mummers Parade 213
Mütter Museum 218
Shoe Museum 217
Wing Bowl 214

Strasburg 219, 220
Choo Choo Barn 219
Fulton Steamboat Inn 220
Red Caboose Lodge 220

RHODE ISLAND 206–7
Ancient & Horrible's Parade, Glocester 206
Big Blue Bug, Providence 206
Fools Rules Regatta, Jamestown 206
Oop!, Providence 207
Penguin Plunge, Mackerel Cove 206
Rose Island Lighthouse, Newport 207

SOUTH CAROLINA 259–60
Chitlin Strut, Salley 259
Kudzu Festival, Blythewood 260
Pearl's Topiary Garden, Bishopville 260
South of the Border, Dillon 260
World Grits Festival, St George 259

SOUTH DAKOTA 124–6
Bedrock City, Custer 126
Black Hills Maze, Rapid City 126
Corn Palace, Mitchell 126
International Vinegar Museum, Roslyn 124
Mashed Potato Wrestling, Clark 124
Motorcycle Rally, Sturgis 124
Outhouse Museum, Gregory 125
Petrified Wood Park & Museum, Lemmon 125
Porter Sculpture Park, St Lawrence 126
Potato Days Festival, Clark 124
Presidents Park, Deer Mountain 126
Shoe House, Webster 124
Vinegar Festival, Roslyn 124
Wall Drug Store, Wall 125

TENNESSEE 238–45
Butler, Town of 239
E T Wickham's statues, Clarksville 240
Flyaway Indoor Skydiving, Pigeon Forge 242
King Tut's, Knoxville 243
Moon Pie Festival, Bell Buckle 239
Mule Day, Columbia 238
Museum, Butler 239
National Storytelling Festival, Jonesborough 239
World's Longest Outdoor Yard Sale 239

Chattanooga 240, 244–5
Chattanooga Choo Choo Holiday Inn 244
International Towing & Recovery Hall of Fame & Museum 240
Purple Lady 244

Memphis 240, 241–2, 243–4
A Schwab 243
Elvis Presley's Memphis 244
Elvis Week 241
Graceland 241
Heartbreak Hotel 244
Huey's Downtown 243
Memphis Explorations 242
Peabody Ducks 240
Tater Reds 243

Nashville 240, 242–3
Country Music Hall of Fame
& Museum 240
Nash Trash Tours 242
Willie Nelson Museum 240

TEXAS 129–44
Beauty & the Book, Jefferson
142
Big Texan Steak Ranch,
Amarillo 142
Buckhorn Saloon & Museum,
San Antonio 140
Cadillac Ranch, Amarillo 142
Cibolo Creek Ranch, Shafter
144
Cockroach Hall of Fame,
Plano 139
Creation Evidence Museum,
Glen Rose 136
Devil's Rope Museum,
McLean 138
Dinosaur Gardens, Moscow
140
Dr Pepper Museum & Free
Enterprise Institute, Waco
138
Ferthairlizer 143
Fire Ant Festival, Marshall
135
Forbidden Gardens, Katy 140
Hands on a Hardbody,
Longview 133
Hogeye Festival, Elgin 134
Huntsville Texas Prison
Museum, North Huntsville
137
Hippos, Hutto 141
Oatmeal Festival, Bertram 129
Rattlesnake Ranch,
Weatherford 140
Rattlesnake Round-up &
Cook-off, Sweetwater 134
Stonehenge II, Hunt 141
Toilet Seat Art Museum, San
Antonio 138
Watermelon Thump, Luling
133

Austin 131, 133, 134, 141
Chronicle Hot Sauce
Competition 134
Graveyard Chronicles 141
O Henry Pun-Off World
Championships 133
Promenade Tours 141
SPAMARAMA™ 133

**Dallas/Fort Worth 134,
136–7, 140, 142**
Billy Bob's World's Largest
Honky Tonk 140
Cattle Drive 142
Conspiracy Museum, Dallas
136
Corn Dog Festival, Dallas 134
National Cowgirl Museum &
Hall of Fame, Fort Worth
137
Sixth Floor Museum, Dallas
136

Houston 135–6, 137, 139, 143
Art Car Museum 137
Everyones Art Car Parade 135
Eyeopener Tours 135
John Milkovisch's Beer Can
House 135
National Museum of Funeral
History 139
Orange Show Foundation 135
Orange Show Monument 135
Ted Kipperman's Pawn
Shop/Wedding Chapel 143

UTAH 75–7
Anniversary Inn, Salt Lake City
77
Best Friends Animal Sanctuary,
Kanab 76
Festival Royale of Himmeisk,
Cedar City 75
Hole 'n the Rock, Moab 76
International Film Festival,
Bicknell 77
Mayan Restaurant, Sandy 77
Metaphor: the Tree of Utah,
Salt Flats 76

VERMONT 194–7
Austin Hill Inn, West Dover
197
Bread & Puppet Museum,
Glover 196
Dog Chapel, St Johnsbury 196
Equinox Hotel's School of
Falconry, Manchester
Village 196

Odor-Eaters International
Rotten Sneaker Contest,
Montpelier 194
Pitcher Inn, Warren 196
Zucchini Fest, Ludlow 194

VIRGINIA 230–2
American Celebration on
Parade, Shenandoah
Caverns 232
Bottle House, Hillsville 230
Bull Run Castle, Aldie 230
DEA Museum & Visitors
Center, Arlington 231
Dinosaur Land, White Post 231
Holy Land USA, Bedford 231
Isle of Wight Museum,
Smithfield 232
Lee Davis' Texaco,
Mechanicsville 232
Mid-Atlantic Hermit Crab
Challenge, Virginia Beach
230
Wax Museum and Factory,
Natural Bridge 231
World's Largest Ham Biscuit,
Smithfield 232

WASHINGTON 1–11
Banana Museum, Auburn 5
Carr's One-of-a-Kind
Museum, Spokane 4
Cedar Creek Treehouse,
Ashford 10
Codger Pole, Colfax 7
Copper Creek Lodge, Ashford
10
Combine Demolition Derby,
Lind 1
D B Cooper Party, Aerial 1
Dick and Jane's Art Spot,
Ellensburg 4
Ex-Nihilo Sculpture Park, Elbe
4
Gerhke's Windmill Garden,
Electric City 7
House of Poverty Museum,
Moses Lake 5
Kinetic Sculpture Race, Port
Townsend 3
Leavenworth, Town of, 7
Loggers Jubilee, Morton 2
Mon-Railroad, Moses Lake 5
Mystery Weekend, Langley 2
Olympic Game Farm, Sequim
5
Richart's Ruins, Centralia 4
Row of exercise bikes, Vashon
Island 8

Self-Kicking Machine,
    Rockport 7
Stonehenge, Goldendale 8
TipiTrek, Lake Forest Park 9
World's Largest Lava Lamp,
    Soap Lake 8
World's longest diary, Pullman
    11

Seattle 1, 3, 6, 7, 8–9
5 Spot 9
Bug Blast 3
Experience Music Project 6
Fremont Neighborhood 6
Fremont Rocket 6
Fremont Troll 6
Gum wall 8
Lenin statue 6
Milk Carton Derby 1
Outdoor cinema 6
Pike Place Fish 9
Private Eye on Seattle Tour 7
Sunday Market 6
Solstice Parade 6
Underground Tour 7
Waiting for the Interurban 6
Ye Olde Curiosity Shop 9

WEST VIRGINIA 233–5
Bee Beard Man, Proctor 235
Greenbrier Hotel, White
    Sulphur Springs 233
International Water Tasting
    Competition, Berkeley
    Springs 233
New River Gorge Bridge Day
    Festival, Fayetteville 233
Palace of Gold, Moundsville
    234
Roadkill Cookoff, Marlinton
    233
West Virginia Penitentiary
    Tour, Moundsville 234

WISCONSIN 79–92
Americanism Center Museum,
    Waubeka 85
Angel Museum, Beloit 85
Beef-A-Rama, Minocqua 79
'Big Mac Guy' 90
Canoe Bay, Chetek 91
Circus World Museum,
    Baraboo 87
Dickeyville Grotto, Dickeyville
    84
Don Q Inn, Dodgeville 92
Eisner Museum of Advertising,
    Milwaukee 88
Forevertron, Baraboo 84

Fort Crawford Museum,
    Prairie du Chien 86
Gobbler Supper Club & Motel
    91
Grandview, Hollandale 83
Holler House, Milwaukee 91
Hot Air Affair, Hudson 79
Houdini Historical Center,
    Appleton 87
House on the Rock, Spring
    Green 82
Kohler Arts Center, Sheboygan
    85
Museum of Woodcarving,
    Shell Lake 85
National Freshwater Fishing
    Hall of Fame, Hayward 87
Rhinestone Cowboy,
    Sheboygan 89
Safe House, Milwaukee 9
Tommy Bartlett's Thrill Show,
    Wisconsin Dells 89
Topless Auto Tour, Madison
    82
US Watermelon Seed-Spitting
    & Speed Eating
    Championship, Pardeeville
    79
Walworth II Mailboat, Lake
    Geneva 89
Watson's Wild West Museum,
    Elkhorn 87
West Bend Inn, West Bend 92
Wisconsin Concrete Park,
    Phillips 83
World Lumberjack
    Championship, Hayward 82

Burlington 88, 89
Hall of Logic Puzzles 88
International Tongue Twister
    Contest 88
Liars' Club 89
Spin-A-Top Day 88
Spinning Top Exploratory
    Museum 88
Whatchamacallits 88
Yo-yo Convention 88

Mt Horeb 86–7
Elm Farm Ollie Day 86
National Mustard Day 86
Mustard Museum 86

WYOMING 19–20
Ames Brothers Pyramid,
    Laramie 20
Carbon County Museum,
    Rawlins 19

Cosimo Cavallaro, Powell 20
Frontier Prison Old West
    Museum, Rawlins 19
Grand Encampment Museum
    Complex, Encampment 19
Gunslingers, Cheyenne 20

Alphabetical Index

5 Spot, Seattle, WA 9

99s Museum of Women Pilots, Oklahoma City, OK 165

A Schwab, Memphis, TN 243

Abbot's Habit, Venice, CA 49

Abracadabra, New York City, NY 192

Adams, Mary 116

Adventure Inn Motel, Gurnee, IL 108

Agricultural Museum, Stuttgart, AR 173

Ahlgrim Acres, Palatine, IL 107

albino squirrels 105

Alexandria, IN 118

Alien Museum, Portland, OR 14

Also-Ran Museum, Norton, KS 160

Alton, IL 105

Amargosa Opera House, Death Valley Junction, CA XII, 42

America, Why I Love Her, Denver International Airport, CO 156

American Advertising Museum, Portland, OR 14

American Celebration on Parade, Shenandoah Caverns, VA 232

American Dream Safari, MS 253

American International Rattlesnake Museum, Albuquerque, NM 147

American Museum of Natural History, New York City, NY 191

American Sanitary Plumbing Museum, Worcester, MA 203

American Visionary Art Museum, Baltimore, MD 221

Americanism Center Museum, Waubeka, WI 85

Ames Brothers Pyramid, Laramie, WY 20

Amish Mud Sales, Lancaster, PA 215

Ancient & Horrible's Parade, Glocester, RI 206

Andy Griffith Museum, Mt Airy, NC 248

Andy Warhol Museum, Pittsburgh, PA 216

Angel Museum, Beloit, WI 85

Angelyne, Los Angeles, CA 47

Anniversary Inn, Boise, ID 12

Anniversary Inn, Salt Lake City, UT 77

Antoinette's Haunted History Tours, Alton, IL 105

Arcosanti, Cordes Junction, AZ 70

Area 51, Rachel, NV 66

Art Car Museum, Houston, TX 137

art cars, 135, 278

Art Gallery, Flemington, NJ 212

Art Tours of Manhattan, New York City, NY 191

Arthur Marks Tours for All Seasons, New York City, NY 188

Attic, The, Las Vegas, NV 57

Attractions, XVI

Audrey's Good Vibrations, Venice, CA 50

Aureole Restaurant, Las Vegas, NV 60

Austin Hill Inn, West Dover, VT 197

Authentic Bonnie and Clyde Festival & Museum, Gibsland, LA 177

Ave Maria Grotto, Cullman, AL XII, 254

B.E.D., Miami, FL 272

Bald is Beautiful Convention, Morehead City, NC 245

Ballantines Hotel, Palm Springs, CA 53

Banana Museum, Auburn, WA 5

Bannister, Ken XII, 44

Barbed Wire Museum, La Crosse, KS 160

BARC Animal Parade, New York City, NY 186

Bark Peeler's Convention, Galeton, PA 214

Barker, Andy 249

Barker Character, Comic & Cartoon Museum, Cheshire, CT 209

Barsody, Sister Carmen 29

Battleship Massachusetts, Fall River, MA 205

Bay to Breakers Race, San Francisco, CA 21

Bayou Pierre Alligator Park, Natchitoches, LA 178

Beach Blanket Babylon, San Francisco, CA 30

Bean Festival, Mountain View, AR 171

Bear Creek Saloon Pig Races, Bear Creek, MT 19

Beatty Burro & Flapjack Races, Beatty, NV 63

Beauty & the Book, Jefferson, TX 142

Beckett, Marta XII, 42

Bed Race & Parade, Preston, ID 10

Bed Races, Oatman, AZ 66

Bedrock City, Custer, SD 126

Bee Beard Man, Proctor, WV 235

Beef-A-Rama, Minocqua, WI 79

Beeny, Bill 168

Ben's Deli, 186

Berg, Joyce & Lowell 85

Best Friends Animal Sanctuary, Kanab, UT 76

Big Apple Greeter, New York City, NY 191
Big Blue Bug, Providence, RI 206
Big Chair, Thomasville, NC 249
Big Mac Guy, WI 90
Big Onion Walking Tours, New York City, NY 191
Big Texan Steak Ranch, Amarillo, TX 142
Bigelow, Jim 157
Bill's Food Mart, Howells, NE 128
Billy Bob's World's Largest Honky Tonk, Dallas, TX 140
Billy Bowlegs Festival, Fort Walton Beach, FL 266
Bily Clocks Museum and Dvorak Exhibit, Spillville, IA 101
Binocular Building, Venice Beach, CA 49
Biosphere 2, Tucson, AZ 70
Bird's Eye View Museum of Miniatures, Wakarusa, IN 117
Birthplace of Kermit the Frog, Leland, MS 253
Bishop, Jim 155
Bishop Hill Museum, Bishop Hill, IL 108
Bishop's Castle, Pueblo, CO 155
Bizarre & Eccentric Tour of the East Village, New York City, NY 188
Black, Bill 143
Black Hills Maze, Rapid City, SD 126
Black Rock Desert, NV 62
Black Rock Desert Self-Invitational Golf Tournament, NV 62
Blaine Kern's Mardi Gras World, New Orleans, LA 176
Blank, Harrod 279
Blessing of the Dates, Riverside County, CA 40
Block, Anne 48
Bloody Marys Tours, New Orleans, LA 176
Bohdan, Michael 139
Bonanza Gifts, Las Vegas, NV 58
Bone Room, Berkeley, CA 36
Bonfante Gardens Family Theme Park, Gilroy, CA 35

Boom Box Parade, Willimantic, CT 207
Boonville, CA 35
Boorke, Jennifer 114
Bottle House, Hillsville, VA 230
BraBall, 37
Bread & Puppet Museum, Glover, VT 196
Brother Joseph XII, 254
Brown, David 271
Browne, Jill Connor (The Sweet Potato Queen) 250
Bryant's Stove Museum, Thorndike, ME 201
Bubble Gum Alley, San Luis Obispo, CA 49
Bubble gum wall, Seattle, WA 8
Bubble Room, Captiva Island, FL 273
Buckhorn Exchange, Denver, CO 157
Buckhorn Saloon & Museum, San Antonio, TX 140
Bug Blast, Seattle, WA 3
Bug Jam, Spring Hill, FL 266
BuGFest, Raleigh, NC 246
Bull Run Castle, Aldie, VA 230
Bulldozer Building, Turlock, CA 49
Burning Man, Black Rock Desert, NV 62
Burning of Zozobra Fiestas de Santa Fe, Santa Fe, NM 144
Butler, TN 239
Button Man, 279

Cabela's Outfitters, Owatonna, MN 97
Cacophony Societies, 281
Cadillac Ranch, Amarillo, TX 142
Caesars Pocono Resorts, Poconos, PA 220
Café Hon, Baltimore, MD 224
Cafe Tu Tu Tango, Orange & Universal City, CA 51
Café Tu Tu Tango, Coconut Grove, FL 273
Café Tu Tu Tango, Atlanta, GA 259
Calaveras County Fair and Jumping Frog Jubilee, Angels Camp, CA 32
Camel Races, Virginia City, NV 63
canine freestyle dancing, 284
Canoe Bay, Chetek, WI 91

Capuzzuti, Cheryl 219
Carbon County Museum, Rawlins, WY 19
cardboard boat races/regattas, 68, 102, 109, 171
Cardboard Box Derby, Arapahoe Basin, CO 153
Cardboard Classic, Red Lodge, MT 18
Cardiff Giant, Cooperstown, NY 184
Carhenge, Alliance, NE 128
Carmel, CA 36
Carmichael, Michael, 118
Carr, Marvin 4
Carr's One-of-a-Kind Museum, Spokane, WA 4
Carsey, Gene 16
Cartoon Art Museum, San Francisco, CA 26
Casa Bonita, Lakewood, CO 157
Cash, Kristie 270
Casino Legends Hall of Fame, Las Vegas, NV 55
Cassadaga Hotel, FL 276
Castlewood Cottages, Big Bear Lake, CA 37
Catsup Bottle Summerfest Birthday Party, Collinsville, IL 102
Cattle Drive, Dallas, TX 142
Cedar Creek Treehouse, Ashford, WA 10
Cemetery Tours, Key West, FL 265
Central Maine Egg Festival, Pittsfield, ME 198
Cermak Plaza Shopping Center, Berwyn, IL 106
Charles Simon Center for Adult Life & Learning, New York City, NY 189
Chattanooga Choo Choo Holiday Inn, Chattanooga, TN 244
Ches Del Restaurant, St.George's, DE 225
Chesapeake Bay Maritime Museum, St Michaels, MD 224
Chicken Show, Wayne, NE 127
Chicken Store, Key West, FL 261
Children's Garbage Museum, Stratford, CT 208
Chilili, NM 149
Chinese New Year's Treasure Hunt, San Francisco, CA 21

Chitlin Strut, Salley, SC 259
Chloride Rocks, Chloride, AZ 72
Chocolate by Mueller, Philadelphia, PA 219
Choo Choo Barn, Strasburg, PA 219
Chronicle Hot Sauce Competition, Austin, TX 134
Ciao Bella!, Ben Lomond, CA 36
Cibolo Creek Ranch, Shafter, TX 144
circus trees, 35
Circus World Museum, Baraboo, WI 87
Cities of the Dead Cemetery Tours, New Orleans, LA 176
City Guides Neighborhood Walks, San Francisco, CA 27
City Museum, St Louis, MO 169
Claim-Jumper B&B, Crested Butte, CO 157
Cluck-Off Contest, Wayne, NE 127
Clyde Jones, Pittsboro, NC 246
Coble, Goody 16
Cochise Stronghold B&B, Pearce, AZ 74
Cockroach Hall of Fame, Plano, TX 139
Codger Pole, Colfax, WA 7
Colonel Harland Sanders Museum, Corbin, KY 236
Combine Demolition Derby, Lind, WA 1
Compher, John & Leslie 10
Conch Republic Independence Celebration, Key West, FL 263
Coney Island Circus, New York City, NY 186
Coney Island Museum, New York City, NY 187
Conklin, Francis 12
Conlon, Steve 235
Conspiracy Museum, Dallas, TX 136
Coon Dog Cemetery Celebration, Tuscumbia, AL 255
Copper Creek Lodge, Ashford, WA 10
Coral Castle, Homestead, FL 267

Corn Dog Festival, Dallas, TX 134
Corn Palace, Mitchell, SD 126
cornfield mazes, 282
Cosimo Cavallaro, Powell, WY 20
Country Music Hall of Fame & Museum, Nashville, TN 240
Cow Pasture Golf, Springerville, AZ 68
Cowasaki, 279
Cowboy Memorial & Library, Caliente, CA 43
Crane, Sam IN 118
Creation Evidence Museum, Glen Rose, TX 136
Cross-County Quirks, XVII, 277
Crowne Plaza Union Station, Indianapolis, IN 119
Cruisin' the Castro Tour, San Francisco, CA 27

D B Cooper Party, Aerial, WA 1
da Vinci Days Festival, Corvallis, OR 13
Dan Quayle Center, Huntington, IN 117
Davidson, Chris 55
Davis, John XII
Davis Memorial at the Mount Hope Cemetery, Hiawatha, KS 161
de Fonville, Paul & Virginia 43
DEA Museum & Visitors Center, Arlington, VA 231
Defenestration, San Francisco, CA 29
Delgadillo's Snow Cap, Seligman, AZ 73
Demolition Derbies, 278
Desert Inn Resort Motel & Suites, Daytona Beach, FL 273
Devil's Rope Museum, McLean, TX 138
di Rosa, Rene 34
di Rosa Preserve, Napa, CA 34
Dick and Jane's Art Spot, Ellensburg, WA 4
Dickeyville Grotto, Dickeyville, WI 84
Dillinger Museum, Hammond, IN 116
Dinosaur Gardens, Moscow, TX 140
Dinosaur Gardens Prehistoric Zoo, Ossineke, MI 112

Dinosaur Land, White Post, VA 231
Dinosaur World, Plant City, FL 269
Dinosaur World, Eureka Springs, AR 173
Dive Inn Guest House, New Orleans, LA 177
Doo-Dah Parade, Kalamazoo, MI 111
Dog Bark Park, Cottonwood, ID 12
Dog Chapel, St. Johnsbury, VT 196
Dog Days of Summer, Key West, FL 263
Dog-Play.com, 284
Doll Museum, Flemington, NJ 212
Don Q Inn, Dodgeville, WI 92
Donut Hole, La Puente, CA 49
Doo Dah Parade, Pasadena, CA 39
Doo Wop Trolley Tours, Wildwood, NJ 213
Dooby Lane, Gerlach, NV 64
Doorway to Design, New York City, NY 191
Doss, Gary & Nancy 34
Dr Pepper Museum & Free Enterprise Institute, Waco, TX 138
Dr Ted's Musical Marvels, Dale, IN 118
Dreampeace, Marilyn 279
Ducks at the Peabody, Orlando, FL 271
Duds'N' Suds Laundromat, Pittsburgh, PA 219
dueling elves, Minneapolis, MN 97
Duffy, Emily 37
'Dugout Dick' XII, 12
Duncan Hines Festival, Bowling Green, KY 236

E T Wickham's statues, Clarksville, TN 240
Eartha™, Yarmouth, ME 201
Eastern State Penitentiary, Philadelphia, PA 216
Eccentric Environments, XV
Ed's Museum, Wykoff, MN 95
Egg Fry, Oatman, AZ 66
Egg Nest, NM 149
Eisner Museum of Advertising, Milwaukee, WI 88
Elfego Baca Shoot, Socorro, NM 147

Elftmann, Jan 279
Eliphante, Cornville, AZ 69
Elliott, Dick 4
Elm Farm Ollie Day, Mt
    Horeb, WI 86
Elvis Fan Club, 54
Elvis Impersonator Contest &
    Fan Convention, Las Vegas,
    NV 54
Elvis is Alive Museum &
    Restaurant, Wright City,
    MO 168
Elvis Presley's Memphis,
    Memphis, TN 244
Elvis Week, Memphis, TN 241
Elvis-o-Rama Museum, Las
    Vegas, NV 55
Emma Crawford Coffin Races,
    Manitou Springs, CO 152
Emperor Norton, San
    Francisco, CA 30
Enchanted Highway, ND 123
Equinox Hotel's School of
    Falconry, Manchester
    Village, VT 196
Etta's Lunch Box Café, Starr,
    OH 121
Eureka Springs, AR 174
Eva Blount Way's Collection,
    Bellhaven, NC 247
Every, Tom 84
Everyones Art Car Parade,
    Houston, TX 135
Evolution, New York City, NY
    192
Ex-Nihilo Sculpture Park,
    Elbe, WA 4
Exotic Erotic Halloween Ball,
    San Francisco, CA 26
Experience Music Project,
    Seattle, WA 6
Extraterrestrial Highway, NV
    66
Eyeopener Tours, Houston,
    TX 135

Fabulous Palm Springs Follies,
    Palm Springs, CA 48
Fairy Tale Forest, Oak Ridge,
    NJ 212
Faithful Fools Ministry 29
Fantasia Fair, Provincetown,
    MA 202
Fantasy Fest, Key West, FL 261
Farmacia Million Dollar
    Botanicas, Los Angeles, CA
    50
Fashion Police, Mill Valley, CA
    35

Fassbinder, Jim 17
Feet First: the Scholl Story,
    Chicago, IL 104
Ferthairlizer 143
Festival in the Pit, Battle
    Mountain, NV 64
Festival of Scarecrows,
    Rockland, ME 199
Festival Royale of Himmeisk,
    Cedar City, UT 75
Festivals & Events xv
Fetish & Fantasy Ball, Las
    Vegas, NV 54
Field of Corn, Dublin, OH 121
Finster, Howard 257
Fire Ant Festival, Marshall, TX
    135
Fire Engine Tours and
    Adventures, San Francisco,
    CA 28
First Church of the Last Laugh
    26
Fish House Parade, Aitkin,
    MN 92
Flauschink, Crested Butte, CO
    154
Flower Power Haight-Ashbury
    Walking Tour, San
    Francisco, CA 28
Flyaway Indoor Skydiving,
    Pigeon Forge, TN xvi, 242
Flyaway Indoor Skydiving, Las
    Vegas, NV xvi, 56
Fools Rules Regatta,
    Jamestown, RI 206
Foot! Tours, San Francisco,
    CA 29
Footstock Festival, San
    Francisco, CA 21
Forbidden Gardens, Katy, TX
    140
Forestiere Underground
    Gardens, Fresno, CA 33
Forevertron, Baraboo, WI 84
Fort Crawford Museum, Prarie
    du Chien, WI 86
Fort, The, Morrison, CO 156
Franconia Sculpture Park,
    Shafer, MN 96
Frederick's of Hollywood
    Lingerie Museum &
    Celebrity Lingerie Hall of
    Fame, Hollywood, CA 45
Freeman, Mike 242
Fremont neighborhood,
    Seattle, WA 6
Fremont Rocket, Seattle, WA 6
Fremont Street Experience, Las
    Vegas, NV 56

Fremont Troll, Seattle, WA 6
Friends of the Society of
    Primitive Technology, 280
Frog Fantasies Museum,
    Eureka Springs, AR 172
Frontier Prison Old West
    Museum, Rawlins, WY 19
Frozen Dead Guy Day,
    Nederland, CO 153
Fruitcake Toss, Manitou
    Springs, CO 151
Fryeburg Fair, Freyberg, ME
    198
Fulton Steamboat Inn,
    Strasburg, PA 220
Funny Farm, Bend, OR 16
Funomena 280
Furniture Races, Whitefish,
    MT 18
Furnitureland South, High
    Point, NC 249
Future Birthplace of Captain
    Kirk, Riverside, IA 101

Galco's Old World Grocery,
    Los Angeles, CA 50
Gambler's General Store, Las
    Vegas, NV 57
Games of the Lower East Side,
    New York City, NY 188
Gameworks Showcase, Las
    Vegas, NV 56
Gangland Tours, New York
    City, NY 190
Garden of Eden, Lucas, KS 158
Garment District Tour, New
    York City, NY 188
Garnier, Michael 17
Gasparilla Parade & Pirate Fest
    Festival, Tampa, FL 265
Gator Cook-off, Orlando, FL
    270
Gatorland, Orlando, FL 270
Gay & Lesbian Trolley Tour,
    Key West, FL 261
Gene Autry Museum, Gene
    Autry, OK 165
General Mills Cereal
    Adventures, Bloomington
    Hills, MN 95
Gerhke's Windmill Garden,
    Electric City, WA 7
Gershwin Hotel, New York
    City, NY 194
Ghost Hunt Walking Tour,
    San Francisco, CA 27
Ghost Town, Oatman, AZ 66
Ghost Walk, Wilmington, NC
    248

Ghosts & Hauntings 282
Ghosts and Legends of Key West, Key West, FL 261
Giant Omelette Celebration, Abbeville, LA 178
Gillette's Castle, East Haddam, CT 207
Gnome Homes, Charlevoix, MI 111
Gobbler Supper Club & Motel, WI 91
God's Ark of Safety, Frostburg, MD 223
Gold, Joyce 190
Gold Well Open Air Museum, Beatty, NV 65
Golf Cart Parade, Palm Desert, CA 39
Gorske, Don (Big Mac Guy) 90
Graceland, Memphis, TN 241
Graceland Too, Holly Springs, MS 252
Grand Encampment Museum Complex, Encampment, WY 19
Grandma Prisbrey's Bottle Village, Simi Valley, CA 42
Grandpa Bredo, 153
Grandview, Hollandale, WI 83
Granite Gap, NM 149
Grassroots Art Center, Lucas, KS 158
Graveyard Chronicles, Austin, TX 141
Great American Railway, Flemington, NJ 212
Great American Think-Off, New York Mills, MN 92
Great Blacks in Wax Museum, Baltimore, MD 222
Great Cardboard Boat Regatta, Tempe Town Lake, AZ 68
Great Outhouse Blowout & Race, Gravel Switch, KY 235
Greater World Earthship Community, Taos, NM 150
Greenbrier Hotel, White Sulphur Springs, WV 233
Greff, Gary 123
Groggin, Brian 29
Gross National Product, Washington, DC 227
Grotto of the Redemption, West Bend, IA 100
Guidestones, Elberton, GA 258
Guinness World of Records Museum, Las Vegas, NV 55

Guinness World Records Museum, Hollywood, CA 46
gum wall, Seattle, WA 8
Gunslingers, Cheyenne, WY 20
Guyton, Tyree 112

Haight-Ashbury Street Fair, San Francisco, CA 26
Hailey, Trevor 27
Hair Wars, Detroit, MI 113
Hall of Logic Puzzles, Burlington, WI 88
Hallowe'en, San Francisco, CA 24
Hamburger Museum, Daytona Beach, FL 269
Hampton's Year of 1,000 Weekends 285
Hands on a Hardbody, Longview, TX 133
Hargrove, Earl 232
Harley-Davidson Café, Las Vegas, NV 58
Hart, Mary Esther 15
Hartman Rock Garden, Springfield, OH 120
Hart's Reptile World, Canby, OR 15
Haunted History Tours, New Orleans, LA 176
Hazen, Cindy 242
Heartbreak Hotel, Memphis, TN 244
Hedrick's B&B Inn, Nickerson, KS 162
Heidelberg Project, MI 112
Hemingway Days Festival, Key West, FL 263
Henson, Jim 253
Hill, Cortland 208
Hippos, Hutto, TX 141
Hirchak, John 248
Hise, Nancy 100
Historic New Orleans Tours, New Orleans, LA 176
Historic Voodoo Museum, New Orleans, LA 177
Historical Burlesque Museum and Hall of Fame, Helendale, CA 45
Historical Museum, Rolling Meadows, IL 104
Historical Reenactors, 280
History & Haunting Tours, Alton, IL 105
Hite, Shirley 116
Hobo House, Jamestown, ND 123

Hobo Museum, Britt, IA 99
Hoegh Pet Casket Factory Tours, Gladstone, MI 114
Hoffman, Nancy 201
Hog Day, Hillsborough, NC 245
Hogeye Festival, Elgin, TX 134
Hole 'n the Rock, Moab, UT 76
Holler House, Milwaukee, WI 91
Hollywood History Museum, Hollywood, CA 46
Holm, Monte 5
Holy Land USA, Bedford, VA 231
Honfest, Baltimore, MD 224
Hopalong Cassidy Museum, Benton, KS 160
Hopkins, Rich 57
Horned Toad Derby, Coalinga, CA 32
Hot Air Affair, Hudson, WI 79
Hotel Bel Air, Los Angeles, CA 52
Hotel Pennsylvania, New York City, NY 193
Houdini Historical Center, Appleton, WI 87
Houdini Museum, Scranton, PA 217
House of Frankenstein Wax Museum, Lake George, NY 183
House of Poverty Museum, Moses Lake, WA 5
House of Presidents, Clermont, FL 268
House on the Rock, Spring Green, WI 82
How Berkeley Can You Be? Parade, Berkeley, CA 32
How Weird Street Faire, San Francisco, CA 21
Huey's Downtown, Memphis, TN 243
Huie, Wing Young 98
Hunter's Table & Tavern, Rhame, ND 123
Huntsville Texas Prison Museum, North Huntsville, TX 137
Hustle Up the Hancock, Chicago, IL 103

I Love Lucy Masquerade Ball, Jamestown, NY 179
Ice Box Days, International Falls, MN 92

Ice Tee Golf Tournament, Lake Wallpaupack, PA 214

Ig Nobel Prizes, Cambridge, MA 202

iMar, New York City, NY 189

Indiana Shoe Tree, Milltown, IN 119

indoor skydiving XVI, 56, 242

In-Drag Race, Telluride, CO 154

Inn at Castle Rock, Bisbee, AZ 74

Insect Zoo, Manhattan, KS 160

Insectarium, Philadelphia, PA 215

Integriton, Las Vegas, NV 61

International Banana Club, Altadena CA XII, 44

International Cherry Pit Spitting Contest, Eau Claire, MI 109

International Federation of Competitive Eaters, 284

International Film Festival, Bicknell, UT 77

International Museum of Surgical Science, Chicago, IL 103

International Pancake Race, Liberal, KS 158

International Snow Sculpting Championships, Breckenridge, CO 154

International Spy Museum, Washington, DC 227

International Tongue Twister Contest, Burlington, WI 88

International Towing & Recovery Hall of Fame & Museum, Chattanooga, TN 240

International UFO Museum & Research Center, Roswell, NM 148

International Vinegar Museum, Roslyn, SD 124

International Washboard Festival, Logan, OH 120

International Water Tasting Competition, Berkeley Springs, WV 233

Interstate Mullet Toss, Pensacola, FL 265

Iron Horse Rodeo, Red Lodge, MT 17

Isle of Wight Museum, Smithfield, VA 232

Ithaca Hours, Ithaca, NY 184

J Stephen Memorial Restroom, Kansas City, MO XVII, 170

Jailhouse Inn, Preston, MN 99

Jal, NM 148

James Dean Memorial Gallery, Fairmount, IN 118

Jell-O Museum, LeRoy, NY 183

Joe Minter's Yard, Birmingham, AL 255

John Milkovisch's Beer Can House, Houston, TX 135

Johns, Lawrence 14

Johnson, Francis 97

Johnson, Charlie 128

Jones, John 10

Jorgensen, Reverend Ken 29

Joyce Gold History Tours, New York City, NY 190

Jules' Undersea Lodge, Key Largo, FL 276

Jumbo the Elephant's remains, Medford, MA 204

Just Plain Weird XVI

Kaatskill Kaleidoscope, NY 184

Kaback, Michael 188

Kahn, Michael XII, 69

Katydid Insect Museum, Glendale, AZ 71

Katzman, Robert & Marilyn 28

Kayton, Bruce 189

Keister, Doug 63

Kelloff's Best Western Movie Manor Motor Inn, Monte Vista, CO 157

Kennedy School Hotel, Portland, OR 16

Kenny Kramer Reality Tour, New York City, NY 190

Kentucky Derby Festival, Louisville, KY 236

Key Underwood Coon Dog Graveyard, Tuscumbia, AL 255

Key West, FL 260

Kidd's Toy Museum, Portland, OR 14

Kinetic Sculpture Museum, Ferndale, CA 31

Kinetic Sculpture Race, Ferndale, CA 31

Kinetic Sculpture Race, Boulder, CO 152

Kinetic Sculpture Race, Port Townsend, WA 3

Kinetic Sculpture Race, Baltimore, MD 221

King Mango Strut, Coconut Grove, FL 266

King Tut's, Knoxville, TN 243

Kit Carson Trail Ghost Walk, Carson City, NV 63

Klauer, Bill 102

Klennert, Dan 4

Knight, Leonard 42

Kohler Arts Center, Sheboygan, WI 85

Kokopelli's Cave B&B, Farmington, NM 150

Koreshanity 274

Kornbluth, Bill 52

Korner's Folly, Kernsville, NC 246

Kramer, Kenny 190

Kudzu Festival, Blythewood, SC 260

L Ron Hubbard Life Exhibition, Los Angeles, CA 46

Lake Haven Motel and Resort, Clearlake Oaks, CA 38

Lake Street USA 98

Lakeview Museum's Community Solar System, Peoria, IL 106

Lambert's Café, Foley, AL 256

Lambert's Café, Ozark & Sikeston, MO 170

Langley, WA 2

Lawn Mower Drag Racing 278

Leavenworth, WA 7

Lee Davis' Texaco, Mechanicsville, VA 232

Leila's Hair Museum, Independence, MO 168

Lenin statue, Seattle, WA 6

Leonardo's Discovery Warehouse, Enid, OK 164

Levenson, Barry 86

Liars' Club, Burlington, WI 89

Liberace Museum, Las Vegas, NV 54

Library Hotel, New York City, NY 193

life-size butter cow sculpture (Iowa State Fair), Des Moines, IA 99

Lighthouse Valley View B&B, Dubuque, IA 102

Lightning Field, Quemado, NM 150

Lindbergh Crate Day, New Canaan, ME 199

Linville, Charles 279

Lion Habitat, Las Vegas, NV 59

Little A 'Le' Inn & Motel, Rachel, NV 66

Litto's Hubcap Ranch, Pope
Valley, CA 34
Livant, Leda XII, 69
Living Bible Museum,
Mansfield, OH 120
Lizzie Borden B&B & Museum,
Fall River, MA 205
Lobster Festival, Redondo
Beach, CA 40
Lochren, Peter 279
Loggers Jubilee, Morton, WA 2
Lompoc Valley Mural Project,
Lompoc, CA 48
Longaberger Basket Company,
Newark, OH 121
Louis' Lunch, New Haven, CT
209
Love Valley, NC 249
Lovell, Ann 5
Lower East Side Tenement
Museum, New York City,
NY 187
Lucifer's Anvil Golf Course,
NV 62
Luckey Hospital Museum,
Wolfe Lake, IN 116
Lucky Mojo Curio Company,
Forestville, CA 36
Lucy the Elephant Monument,
Margate, NJ 212
Lucy-Desi Days, Jamestown,
NY 179
Lucy-Desi Museum,
Jamestown, NY 179
Lucytown Tours, Jamestown,
NY 179
Lynn's Paradise Café,
Louisville, KY 238
Lyon, Norma 'Duffy' 100

M T Liggett, Mullinville, KS 161
Madame Tussaud's Celebrity
Encounter Wax Museum,
Las Vegas, NV 60
Madonna Inn, San Luis
Obispo, CA 52
Magic Forest Fairy Tale Trail
& Safari Ride, Lake George,
NY 183
Main Street Station Casino,
Brewery & Hotel, Las
Vegas, NV 61
Mal's St Patrick's Day Parade,
Jackson, MS 250
Mammy's Cupboard, Natchez,
MS 254
Mandalay Bay Resort &
Casino, Las Vegas, NV 60
Mapparium, Boston, MA 203

Marble Room, Kansas City,
MO 166
Mardi Gras, New Orleans, LA
175
Margaret's Grocery, Vicksburg,
MS 252
Margarita's Mexican
Restaurant & Watering
Hole, Concord, NH 198
Marks, Arthur 188
Mars 2112, New York City,
NY 193
Mars Society, 281
Martin, Elmer & Joanne 222
Marvin Johnson's Gourd
Museum, Angier, NC 248
Marvin's Marvelous
Mechanical Museum,
Farmington Hills, MI 111
Mashed Potato Wrestling,
Clark, SD 124
matzo ball eating contest, New
York City, NY 186
Max Nordeen's Wheels
Museum, Alpha, IL 104
Maxilla & Mandible, New
York City, NY 192
Mayan Restaurant, Sandy, UT
77
Mayberry Days, Mt Airy, NC
248
McCoy, Robert 95
McDonald's, New York City,
NY 192
McKenna, Dennis 106
Mckinney, Rick 279
McKissack, Jeff 135
McLeod, Paul 252
Medieval Manor, Boston, MA
205
Memphis Explorations,
Memphis, TN 242
Mercer Museum & Fonthill
Historical Society,
Doylestown, PA 215
Mermaid Parade, Brooklyn,
NY 166
Merritt, Tedna 173
Metaphor: the Tree of Utah,
Salt Flats, UT 76
Mid-Atlantic Hermit Crab
Challenge, Virginia Beach,
VA 230
Mid-City Lanes Rock 'n Bowl,
New Orleans, LA 175
Mike the Headless Chicken
Days, Frutia, CO 150
Mike Weaver Drain Tile
Museum, Geneva, NY 180

Mike's Famous Roadside Rest,
New Castle, DE 225
Milk Carton Derby, Seattle,
WA 1
Mill End's Park (world's
smallest park), Portland, OR
15
Millennium Monument,
Newport, KY 237
Miller, John 230
Million Dollar Museum, White
City, NM 147
Miss Exotic World, Helendale,
CA 45
Mission Mountain Testicle
Festival, Charlo, MT 18
Missionary Mary Proctor's
Folk Art Museum,
Tallahassee, FL 267
Monkey Jungle, Miami, FL
269
Mon-Railroad, Moses Lake,
WA 5
Monster Café, Orlando, FL
275
monster truck rallies, 278
Moon Amtrak, Laguna Niguel,
CA 38
Moon Pie Festival, Bell Buckle,
TN 239
Moose Stompers Weekend,
Houlton, ME 200
Mother Goose (Nancy
Townsend) XII, XVII, 72
Mother Goose at Renaissance
Fair, Apache Junction, AZ
XII , 72
Motorcycle Rally, Sturgis, SD
124
Moxie Days Festival, Lewiston,
ME 199
Mr Ed's Elephant Museum,
Orrtanna, PA 216
Mr Lee's Rock Garden,
Phoenix, AZ 70
Muck & Mud Derby, Rio
Rancho, NM 144
Mud Bowl Championships,
Concord, NH 197
Mud Run, Camp Pendleton,
CA 39
Mule Day, Columbia, TN 238
Mummer's Museum,
Philadelphia, PA 213
Mummers Parade,
Philadelphia, PA 213
Municipal Art Society, New
York City, NY 191
Murder Mysteries, 282

Muscle Car Ranch, Chickasha, OK 165
Muse Hotel, New York City, NY 193
Museum, Butler, TN 239
Museum of Bad Art, Dedham, MA 204
Museum of Colorado Prisons, Canon City, CO 156
Museum of Dirt, Boston, MA 205
Museum of Family Camping, Allenstown, NH 198
Museum of Funeral Customs, Springfield, IL 105
Museum of History & Art, Alton, IL 107
Museum of Incandescent Lighting, Baltimore, MD 223
Museum of Jurassic Technology, Culver City, CA 44
Museum of Menstruation & Women's Health 285
Museum of Merritt, Mountain Home, AR 173
Museum of Pez Dispensers, Easton, PA 217
Museum of Pez Memorabilia, Burlingame, CA 34
Museum of Questionable Medical Devices, St Paul, MN 94
Museum of Sex, New York City, NY 187
Museum of the Alphabet, Waxhaw, NC 247
Museum of the Odd, Lincoln, NE 128
Museum of Woodcarving, Shell Lake, WI 85
Museums & Collections, xv
Mushroom Festival, Telluride, CO 154
Mustard Museum, Mt Horeb, WI 86
Mütter Museum, Philadelphia, PA 218
Mystery Castle, Phoenix, AZ 69
Mystery Weekend, Langley, WA 2

Nash Trash Tours, Nashville, TN 242
National Baby Food Festival, Fremont, MI 109
National Cowboy & Western Heritage Museum, Oklahoma City, OK 164

National Cowboy Poetry Gathering, Elko, NV 63
National Cowgirl Museum & Hall of Fame, Fort Worth, TX 137
National Cryptologic Museum, MD 223
National Date Festival, Riverside County, CA 40
National Four String Banjo Museum and Hall of Fame, Guthrie, OK 165
National Freshwater Fishing Hall of Fame, Hayward, WI 87
National Hobo Convention, Britt, IA 99
National Hollerin' Contest, Spivey's Corner, NC 245
National Lighter Museum, Guthrie, OK 165
National Lint Project, PA 219
National Museum of Funeral History, Houston, TX 139
National Mustard Day, Mt Horeb, WI 86
National New York Central Railroad Museum, Elkhart, IN 117
National Old Time Fidddlers' Contest, Weiser, ID 10
National Route 66 Museum, Elk City, OK 165
National Special Events Registry 283
National Storytelling Festival, Jonesborough, TN 239
National Wife Carrying Championships, Bethel, ME 199
National Wrestling Hall of Fame & Museum, Stillwater, OK 165
National Yo-yo Championship, Chico, CA 34
National Yo-Yo Museum, Chico, CA 34
Neighborhood Tours, Chicago, IL 106
Nelson, Ray 279
Neon Museum, Las Vegas, NV 55
New Holy Land Tours, Eureka Springs, AR 174
New Jersey State Police Museum, W Trenton, NJ 210
New Jerusalem, 274

New Millennium Holy Land, Mesquite, NV 65
New Orleans, LA 175
New River Gorge Bridge Day Festival, Fayetteville, WV 233
Newsroom Restaurant, Minneapolis, MN 97
Noah Purifoy Desert Art Environment, Joshua Tree, CA 41
Nordic Inn Medieval Brew & Bed, Crosby, MN 98
Northlandz, Flemington, NJ 212
Northrup, Philo 279
Nosh Walks, New York City, NY 191
Nothing Festival, Telluride, CO 154
Nut Art, New London, CT 208
Nut Museum, CT 208

O Henry Pun-Off World Championships, Austin, TX 133
Oasis Bordello Museum, Wallace, ID 11
Oasis of Eden Inn & Suites, Yucca Valley, CA 52
Oatmeal Festival, Bertram, TX 129
Odd Shopping XVII
Odor-Eaters International Rotten Sneaker Contest, Montpelier, VT 194
OK Street Jailhouse, Bisbee, AZ 75
Old Island Days, Key West, FL 263
Old Spanish Sugar Mill, Deleon Springs, FL 275
Olney, IL 105
Olson, Windsor 7
Olympic Game Farm, Sequim, WA 5
On Location Tour, New York City, NY 191
O'Neil, Mildred XII, 124
Oop!, Providence, RI 207
Orange Show Foundation, Houston, TX 135
Orange Show Monument, Houston, TX 135
Oregon County Fair, Eugene, OR 13
Organ Stop Pizza, Mesa, AZ 73
Orgone Energy Accumulator, Rangeley, ME 202

Original American Kazoo Company, Eden, NY 179
Orleman, Jane 4
Oscar Getz Museum of Whiskey History, Beardstown, KY 237
Ostrich Festival, Chandler, AZ 68
Out 'n' About Treesort, Takilma, OR 17
outdoor cinema, Seattle, WA 6
Outhouse Classic, Trenary, MI 108
Outhouse Museum, Gregory, SD 125

Pageant of Masters, Laguna Beach, CA 38
Palace of Gold, Moundsville, WV 234
Palestine Gardens, Lucedale, MS 253
Palmer Mansion, Davenport, IA 101
Panorama, The, New York City, NY 187
Paper House, Rockport, MA 203
Paradise Garden, Summerville, GA 257
Pasaquan, Buena Vista, GA 258
Pasha Restaurant & Club, Chicago, IL 108
Patrick, Kathy 143
Patrick's Island, FL 276
Paul Broste's Rock Museum, Parshall, ND 123
Paul Schipper's Streak, Sugarloaf Ski Resort, ME 200
Peabody ducks, Memphis, TN 240
Peabody ducks 240, 271
Pearl's Topiary Garden, Bishopville, SC 260
Pelican Hotel, Miami, FL 276
Penguin Plunge, Mackerel Cove, RI 206
Pennsylvania's Family Farms, PA 220
Percussive Art Society Museum, Lawton, OK 165
Perry's Beach Café & Rentals, Santa Monica, CA 50
Perry's Beach Café & Rentals, Venice, CA 50
Petersen Automotive Museum, Los Angeles, CA 47
Petersen's Rock Garden, Redmond, OR 13

Petrified Wood Park & Museum, Lemmon, SD 125
Pierogi Festival, Whiting, IN 115
Pike Place Fish, Seattle, WA 9
Pirates in Paradise, Key West, FL 263
Pitcher Inn, Warren, VT 196
Pitkin, David & Christine 9
Poetry Circus, Taos, NM 146
Poison Oak Show, Columbia, CA 33
Polar Fest, Detroit Lakes, MN 93
Poppelwell, Bob 140
Port of Los Angeles Lobster Festival, San Pedro, CA 40
Porter, Wayne 126
Porter Sculpture Park, St Lawrence, SD 126
Potato Blossom Festival, Fort Fairfield, ME 200
Potato Days, Barnesville, MN 93
Potato Days Festival, Clark, SD 124
Potato Feast Days, Houlton, ME 200
Preble, John 178
Precious Moments, Carthage, MO 170
Precita Eyes Mural Arts Center, San Francisco, CA 28
Prehistoric Gardens, Port Orford, OR 15
Presidential Pet Museum, Lothian, MD 222
Presidents Park, Deer Mountain, SD 126
Presque Isle Harbor Cemetery, Marquette, MI 113
Private Eye on Seattle Tour, Seattle, WA 7
Promenade Tours, Austin, TX 141
Pub Crawl, Key West, FL 261
Pulpwood Queens Book Club, 143
Punkin' Chunkin', Georgetown, DE 224
Purple Lady, Chattanooga, TN 244

Quack-off, Avoca, NE 127
Quality Inns & Suites, Burnsville, MN 98
Quesley, Ladora 121
Quigley's Castle Ark, Eureka Springs, AR 172

Quirk Alerts, XVII
Quirky Cuisine, XVII
Quirkyville, XVI

Radical Walking Tours, New York City, NY 189
Railroad Park Resort, Dunsmuir, CA 37
Rain Forest Café, Las Vegas, NV 59
Rainbow Nation Gatherings 281
Randall's Ordinary Inn & Restaurant, Stonington, CT 210
Randy's Donuts, Inglewood, CA 49
Rattlesnake Festival, Apache, OK 162
Rattlesnake Hunt, Okeene, OK 162
Rattlesnake Hunt, Waurika, OK 162
Rattlesnake Hunt, Waynoka, OK 162
Rattlesnake Hunts/Festivals/Museums 134, 140, 147, 162
Rattlesnake Ranch, Weatherford, TX 140
Rattlesnake Round-up & Cook-off, Sweetwater, TX 134
Raven's Grin Inn, Mount Carroll, IL 105
Ravenwood Castle & Medieval Village, New Plymouth, OH 121
Ray's Beaver Bag, Las Vegas, NV 58
Red Caboose Lodge, Strasburg, PA 220
Red Carpet Inn & Fantasuites, Greenwood, IN 119
Red Hat Society 282
Red Square Restaurant, Las Vegas, NV 60
Red Vic B&B, San Francisco, CA 30
Redneck Games, Dublin, GA 256
Re-Mix Shoe Company, Los Angeles, CA 50
Renaissance Faires, 280
Rhinestone Cowboy, Sheboygan, WI 89
Richart's Ruins, Centralia, WA 4
Riddle's Elephant Sanctuary, Greenbrier, AR 174

Rimsky-Korsakoffee House, Portland, OR 16
Ringing Rocks Park, Bridgeton Township, PA 219
Rio Suite Hotel & Casino's Masquerade in the Sky, Las Vegas, NV 59
Ripley's Believe It or Not! Museum, Hollywood, CA 46
Ripley's Believe It or Not! Museums, 285
Ripley's Believe It or Not! Museum, St Augustine, FL 269
Riverhouse Bed and Breakfast, Theodore, AL 256
Roadkill Cookoff, Marlinton, WV 233
Roadside America, Shartlesville, PA 218
Rodeo, NM 149
Rolling River Raft Race, Pueblo, CO 152
Rooms with a Skew XVII
Rose, DeVon 117
Rose Island Lighthouse, Newport, RI 207
Rosie's Diner, Rockford, MI 114
Ross, Larry 199
Route 66 Gift Shop, Seligman, AZ 73
Row of exercise bikes, Vashon Island, WA 8
Roy Rogers-Dale Evans Museum, Branson, MO 168
Rube Goldberg Machine Contest, IN 115
Runestone Museum, Alexandria, MN 94
Running of the Sheep, Reed Point, MT 18
Running of the Wieners, Grand Island, NE 127
RV/MH Heritage Museum & Hall of Fame, Elkhart, IN 115

Safari West Wildlife Preserve & Tent Camp, Santa Rosa, CA 37
Safe House, Milwaukee, WI 9
Saint Paul Winter Carnival, St Paul, MN 93
Salvation Mountain, Niland, CA 41
San Francisco Zoo Valentine's Day Sex Tours, San Francisco, CA 29

Sandpaper Museum (3M/Dwan Museum), Two Harbors, MN 95
Save A Landmark 285
Scandal Tours, Washington, DC 227
Scavenger Hunts by Watson Adventures, New York City, NY 191
Schimppf's Confectionary Museum, Jeffersonville, IN 116
Schipper, Paul 201
School Bus Figure 8 Races 278
Schultz, Judith 88
Schwatz, Mike 225
Scotty's Castle, Death Valley, CA 47
Sculpture Garden, Chauvin, LA 177
See Chicago with a Cop, Chicago, IL 106
Self-Kicking Machine, Rockport, WA 7
Serge's Showgirl Wigs, Las Vegas, NV 57
Shack Up Inn, Clarksdale, MS 254
Shady Dell RV Park, Bisbee, AZ 74
Shakespeare, NM 149
Shangri-La, Prospect Hill, NC 249
Sheehan, Katha 261
Shields, Reverend Robert 11
Shoe House, Webster, SD XII, 124
Shoe Museum, Philadelphia, PA 217
shoe museums 124, 217
Shoe Tree, Middlegate, NV 64
Shoe Trees 64, 119
Showtown Bar & Grill, Gibsonton, FL 272
Shrine of the Pines, Baldwin, MI 113
Sideshows by the Seashore, New York City, NY 186
Silverado Ranch, Holbrook, AZ 75
Sing-Sing Prison, Ossining, NY 181
Sioux Sundries, Harrison, NE 128
Sixth Floor Museum, Dallas, TX 136
Skeletons in the Closet, Los Angeles, CA XVII, 51

Smell & Sound Knowledge Maps, Minneapolis, MN 96
Smith, Barney 138
Snowdown, Durango, CO 152
Society for the Creative Anachronism 280
Sod House B&B, Sanborn, MN 98
Sod House Museum, Aline, OK 165
Soleri, Paolo 70
Soloman, Nedra 71
Solomon's Castle, Ona, FL 267
Solstice Parade, Seattle, WA 6
Something Old, Something New, New York City, NY 189
South of the Border, Dillon, SC 260
Space Farms Zoo & Museum, Sussex, NJ 210
SPAM™ Museum, Austin, MN 94
SPAM™ Jam, Austin, MN 94
SPAM™ Town USA Festival, Austin, MN 94
SPAMARAMA™, Austin, TX 133
Specialty Tours of Miami & South Florida, Miami, FL 271
Speidel, Bill 7
Sperl, Harry 269
Spin-A-Top Day, Burlington, WI 88
Spinning Top Exploratory Museum, Burlington, WI 88
Spirit Tours, New Orleans, LA 176
Spiritualist Camp, Cassadaga, FL 272
Spooky Goofy Golf Tournament, Antlers, OK 163
Spud Day, Shelley, ID 10
Spydrive Tours, Washington, DC 230
Squirrel Cage Jail, Council Bluffs, IA 101
Squished Penny Museum, Washington, DC 227
St Paul Gangster Tours, St Paul, MN 96
St Urho's Day, Menahga, MN 93
St. Stupid's Day Parade, San Francisco, CA 26
Stan Herd, Lawrence, KS 161

Standard Hotel, Hollywood, CA 53

Standard Hotel, Los Angeles, CA 53

Stanghelllini, Mike (Bee-Beard Man) 246

Star Trek Experience, Las Vegas, NV 60

Stark's Vacuum Cleaner Museum, Portland, OR 14

State Prison Outlaw Rodeo, McAlester, OK 163

Steins, NM 149

Stephenson, Michael & Jill 100

Stew Leonard's, Norwalk & Danbury, CT 209

Stew Leonard's, Yonkers, NY 209

Stink Fest, Bradford, PA 214

Stonehenge, Goldendale, WA 8

Stonehenge II, Hunt, TX 141

Storm Chasers, 284

Street Retreats, San Francisco, CA 29

Strictly Moose, Gorham, NH 198

Stringer, Mike 252

Sudsy Malone's, Cincinnati, OH 121

Sullivan, Dennis 12

Sunday Market, Seattle, WA 6

Sunset Celebration, Key West, FL 261

Super Museum & Gift Shop, Metropolis, IL 103

Superman Celebration, Metropolis, IL 103

Surveillance Camera Outdoor Walking Tours, New York City, NY 188

Sweeney, Gary 156

Sweet Potato Queens, MS 250

Sweet Potato Queens 282

Swets, Bill 155

Swetsville Zoo, Fort Collins, CO 155

Sylvia Beach Hotel, Newport, OR 17

Tail o' the Pup, Hollywood, CA 49

Take My Mother*Please (*or any other VIP) Tours, Los Angeles, CA 48

Tantra Restaurant & Lounge, Miami, FL 273

Tashijian, Elizabeth (the Nut Lady) XII, 208

Tater Reds, Memphis, TN 243

tattoo conventions 281

Ted Kipperman's Pawn Shop/Wedding Chapel, Houston, TX 143

testicle festival, Clinton, MT 18

testicle festival, Ryegate, MT 18

testicle festivals 18

Texas Taco, Patterson, NY 185

Thomas Edison House, Louisville, KY 237

Thrillseekers Unlimited, Las Vegas, NV 57

Thunder Mountain, Imlay, NV 64

Tinkertown Museum, Sandia Park, NM 148

TipiTrek, Lake Forest Park, WA 9

Titan Missile Museum, Sahuarita, AZ 71

Toad Suck Daze, Conway, AR 172

Toad Tunnel, Davis, CA 35

Toilet Paper Tree, Auburn, AL 255

Toilet Seat Art Museum, San Antonio, TX 138

Tom Sawyer Days, Hannibal, MO 166

Tommy Bartlett's Thrill Show, Wisconsin Dells, WI 89

Topless Auto Tour, Madison, WI 82

Totally Absurd Inventions 283

Totem Pole Park, Foyil, OK 164

Toto Fest, Welton, IA 99

Tours XVI

Town of Murals, Lake Placid, FL 271

Townhouse, Miami, FL 275

Townsend, Nancy (Mother Goose) XII, 72

Toy & Miniature Museum, Kansas City, MO 166

Toy Piano Festival, La Jolla, CA 39

Tracy, Richard "Richart" 4

Trailer Park Lounge & Grill, New York City, NY 193

Travelers Club International Restaurant & Tuba Museum, Okemos, MI 114

Treasure Island Buccaneer Bay Sea Battle, Las Vegas, NV 61

Trek Fest, Riverside, IA 101

Tug Fest, Port Byron, IL 103

Tug Fest, LeClaire, IA 100

Tupperware Millennium Sculpture, Kissamee, FL 271

Turkey Trot, Yellville, AR 171

Twine Ball Day, Darwin, MN 97

Twins Days, Twinsburg, OH 119

Twister Museum, Wakita, OK 164

Two White Rocks Hospitality, Navajo Nation, AZ 75

two-story outhouse, Gays, IL 107

two-story outhouse, Belle Plaine, MN 96

Typhoon Restaurant, Santa Monica Airport, CA 52

UCM Museum, Abita Springs, LA 178

UFO Encounter Festival & Intergalactic Fashion & Food Extravaganza, Roswell, NM 146

UFO Enigma Museum, Roswell, NM 148

Umbrella Cover Museum, Peaks Island, ME 201

Unclaimed Baggage Center, Scottsboro, AL 256

Underground Tour, Portland, OR 15

Underground Tour, Seattle, WA 7

Underwater Easter Egg Hunt, Key West, FL 263

Underwater Music Festival, Key West, FL 263

Underwater Pumpkin Carving, Key West, FL 263

Underwater Pumpkin Carving Contest, San Diego, CA 41

Underwater Weddings, Key West, FL 265

Untouchables Tour, Chicago, IL 106

US 50 (the Loneliest Road in America), NV 53

US Army Ordnance Museum, Aberdeen Proving Ground, MD 222

US Trolls, Wilmington, NC 250

US Watermelon Seed-Spitting & Speed Eating Championship, Pardeeville, WI 79

Valley of the Moon, Tucson, AZ 71

VanCleave, Ted 283

Varsity Restaurant, Atlanta, GA 258

Venice Beach, CA 49

Vent Haven Ventriloquism Museum, Fort Mitchell, KY 236

Very Large Array, Magdalena, NM 140

Vinegar Festival, Roslyn, SD 124

Vinitok, Crested Butte, CO 154

Vision Quest Safari B&B, Salinas, CA 37

Viva Las Vegas Wedding Chapel & Hotel, Las Vegas, NV 58

Vollis Simpson's Whirligig Farm, Lucama, NC 247

Wacko, Hollywood, CA 51

Wadlow, Robert (world's tallest man), Alton, IL 107

Wagon Wheel Family Restaurant, Smyrna, DE 225

Waiting for the Interurban, Seattle, WA 6

Wall Drug Store, Wall, SD 125

Walworth II Mailboat, Lake Geneva, WI 89

Warfield, Jim 105

Waterloo Workshop, Dorchester, IA 100

Watermelon Thump, Luling, TX 133

Watson Adventures, 191

Watson's Wild West Museum, Elkhorn, WI 87

Watts Towers, Los Angeles, CA 43

Watts Towers Art Center, 43

Wax Museum, San Francisco, CA 27

Wax Museum and Factory, Natural Bridge, VA 231

Weeki Wachee Springs Water Park, Tampa, FL 270

Weeks, David XI

Weird Contest Week, Ocean City, NJ 210

West Bend Inn, West Bend, WI 92

West Virginia Penitentiary Tour, Moundsville, WV 234

Whatchamacallits, Burlington, WI 88

White, William 114

White House replica, Clermont, FL 268

White, White World Week, Sugarloaf Ski Resort, ME 200

Whiting, Denise 224

Whole Enchilada Fiesta, Las Cruces, NM 147

Wigwam Village, Cave City, KY 238

Wigwam Village Motel, Holbrook, AZ 75

Wildwood Inn Tropical Dome & Theme Suites, Florence, KY 238

Willie Nelson Museum, Nashville, TN 240

Winchester Mystery House, San Jose, CA 33

Windmill Museum & Park, Shattuck, OK 165

Wing Bowl, Philadelphia, PA 214

Wings Castle, Milbrook, NY 179

Wisconsin Concrete Park, Phillips, WI 83

Wisnieski, Bill 128

Witch's Dungeon Classic Horror Museum, Bristol, CT 208

Witch's House, Beverly Hills, CA 49

Wizard of Oz Fest, Chesterton, IN 114

Wolfsonian Museum, Miami, FL 268

Womenfest, Key West, FL 263

Wooldridge Monuments, Mayfield, KY 237

Woolly Worm Festival, Banner Elk, NC 246

World Championship Anvil Shooters Classic, Bay Springs, MS 252

World Championship Cardboard Boat Festival, Heber Springs, AR 171

World Chicken Festival, London, KY 236

World Cow Chip Throwing Contest, Beaver, OK 162

World Freefall Convention, IL 103

World Grits Festival, St George, SC 259

World Lumberjack Championship, Hayward, WI 82

World Peace Bell, Newport, KY 237

World Pillow Fighting Championship, Kenwood, CA 31

World Potato Exposition, Blackfoot, ID 11

World Snow Shovel Race, Angel Fire, NM 144

World's Biggest Ball of Twine, Darwin, MN 97

World's Largest Bagel Breakfast, Mattoon, IL 102

World's Largest Ball of Paint, Alexandria, IN 119

World's Largest Bureau, High Point, NC 249

World's Largest Ham Biscuit, Smithfield, VA 232

World's Largest Lava Lamp, Soap Lake, WA 8

World's Longest Breakfast Table, Battle Creek, MI 111

World's longest diary, Pullman, WA 11

World's Longest Outdoor Yard Sale, AL 254

World's Longest Outdoor Yard Sale, KY 235

World's Longest Outdoor Yard Sale, TN 239

World's Richest Tombstone Race (aka Billy the Kid's Tombstone Race), Fort Sumner, NM 147

World's Smallest Museum, Superior, AZ 71

Yagoda, Marvin 112

Yates, John & Nancy 74

Ye Olde Curiosity Shop, Seattle, WA 9

Yokoyama, John 9

York Bar's Go-Nuts Testicle Festival, York, MT 18

Yo-yo Convention, Burlington, WI 88

Zaccagnino, Bruce 212

Zimmerman, Richard ('Dugout Dick') XII, 12

Zucchini Fest, Ludlow, VT 194

Zukowski, Paul 190

Zweifel, John 268

NOTES

REVIEWS OF *ECCENTRIC AMERICA*

'If you ever suspected America was wacky, Eccentric America provides the proof. This blissfully weird travel guide contains 354 uniquely entertaining pages jam-packed with everything that's oddball, eerie, crazed and madcap about the great US of A. Some travel guides are such fun they are worth reading in their own right; this is, quite definitely, one of them.' Amazon.com

'Author Jan Friedman brings a wicked sense of the absurd to listings for places as strange as the Future Birthplace of Capt. Kirk in Iowa, the office building shaped like a giant picnic basket in Ohio, and the B&B in a cave in New Mexico.' *Chicago Tribune*, IL

'Instead of attending the Indianapolis 500, maybe we should consider the World's Richest Tombstone Race...the Ice Tee Golf tournament...the World Grits Festival...and Alhgrim Acres, a miniature-golf course in a mortuary basement.' *The Chronicle*, Houston, TX

'You could take all the strange things In Eccentric America and conduct your own poll on which one is most outlandish...' *San Diego Union Tribune*, CA

'Jan Friedman takes a romp on the wacky side of America and discovers events ranging from the mildly mad ... to the positively deranged!' *Daily Express*, UK

'Read the first couple of pages of this book and you'll realise just how much of the great US of A you've been missing...Friedman has tirelessly plumbed the depths of American eccentricity...' *The Sunday Times*, UK

'Americans revel in the weird and wonderful...Celebrate Spam? Only in America...' *Independent on Sunday*, UK

'If you think the drive across the center of the country is dull, you haven't stopped at the right places...Friedman writes in an entertaining, tongue-in-cheek style. You can't help but laugh...' *Road Trip*, 2002

'One very strange trip...Jan Friedman's new book is a guided tour to the weirdest and wackiest America has to offer...You'll love *Eccentric America*...' *Marin Independent Journal*

'The English may have a reputation for being eccentric, but our cousins across the pond are infinitely more bonkers.' *Footloose*, UK

'Recommended for public libraries' *Library Journal*, NY

'Where else but in America could you find a jail where the cells rotate around the jailer? Or a contest to find the stinkiest sneaker? Find these and lots more...' *New York Post*, NY

'What's with Colorado, anyway?...it has some of the weirdest festivals – Mike the Headless Chicken Days and the Emma Crawford Coffin Races' *The Enquirer*, Cincinnati, OH